Using Excel: Macintosh® Version

Christopher Van Buren

CORPORATION

LEADING COMPUTER KNOWLEDGE

Using Excel: Macintosh® Version
Copyright © 1990 by Que® Corporation.

Library of Congress Catalog No.: 89-61811

ISBN: 0-88022-494-0

93 92 91 90   9 8 7 6 5 4 3 2 1

Interpretation of the printing code: the rightmost double-digit number is the year of the book's printing; the rightmost single-digit number, the number of the book's printing. For example, a printing code of   90-1 shows that the first printing of the book occurred in 1990.

Using Excel: Macintosh® Version is based on Version 2.2 of Microsoft® Excel.

Microsoft® Excel icons ©1985-1989 Microsoft Corporation. Reprinted with permission from Microsoft Corporation.

Trademark Acknowledgments

DEDICATION ▼

For my father, Robert Van Buren.

—C.V.B.

Many thanks are due to Terrie Solomon of Que Corporation for offering me this project, and to my agent Bill Gladstone at Waterside Productions for constant support and representation. Thanks also to my brother, Alexander, for always reminding me of the truth, and for always being true. I would also like to thank my friends John and Heather for encouragement during slow times and for just being friends. Most of all, thanks to my wife Trudy for helping me make decisions throughout the book, and for everything.

▼ *ABOUT THE AUTHOR*

Christopher Van Buren

Christopher Van Buren has been in the computer industry for almost 10 years—first in education, teaching computer basics of educational technology, and then as a writer and editor for a computer book publisher. He has also worked as a contract writer on projects involving computer hardware and software in such industries as banking and semiconductor testing and was instrumental in writing the first Epson FX-80 user's manual for Epson America, Inc. Van Buren was also editor and publisher of several computer newsletters involving desktop publishing, Microsoft Works, and AppleWorks. He has written or co-written several computer books and has publishsed articles for major computer magazines, including *A+*, *Compute*, *The Computer Buyer's Guide*, and *Call A.P.P.L.E*. He has a B.A. in English from San Diego State University and has won awards from computer groups and technical societies for his user manuals.

Publishing Director

David P. Ewing

Acquisitions Editor

Terrie Lynn Solomon

Production Editor

Lisa Hunt

Editors

Kathy Simpson
Alice Martina Smith

Technical Editor

Daniel Zoller

Technical Support

Jerry Ellis
Timothy Stanley

Indexed by

Joelynn Gifford

Production

William Hartman
Tami Hughes
Charles Hutchinson
Jodi Jensen
Lori Lyons
Jennifer Matthews
Dennis Sheehan
Nora Westlake

Composed in Garamond by

William Hartman, Hartman Publishing

CONTENTS AT A GLANCE

TABLE OF CONTENTS ▼

▼

Part I Excel Worksheets

Part II Excel Charts

13   Using Presentation Graphics with Excel 443

Part III Excel Databases

14   Database Quick Start 467

15   Getting Started with Databases 481

Appendixes

Introduction

There certainly are a lot of spreadsheets on the market today, but none rivals Microsoft® Excel in its attention to detail, its flawless operation, and its combination of features. And because Excel has become the standard on the Macintosh, it comes with a vast network of support systems, such as ready-made Excel worksheets (templates), instructional videos, and user groups. Some companies have published ready-made macros for Excel that will make your applications easier to manage. Another plus is that Excel is a Microsoft product: Microsoft offers some of the best technical support in the industry, as well as excellent upgrade policies.

Spreadsheets and Excel

A spreadsheet program is an electronic version of the familiar columnar pad used for accounting, bookkeeping, and business analysis. When VisiCalc introduced the world to electronic spreadsheets back in 1978, it created a reason to buy a computer. With VisiCalc a computer could be used to speed up common business accounting and number crunching. Moreover, you could use an electronic spreadsheet to perform "what if" tests instantly—merely by changing variable information. The electronic spreadsheet used custom-made formulas to total columns, calculate averages, perform cost analysis, and more. And the results could be stored on disk for later use. Watching totals recalculate instantly after basic data was changed turned people on to computing.

Of course, there has been a host of spreadsheet products since VisiCalc, most significantly Lotus 1-2-3, which appeared in 1983. Lotus 1-2-3 took the electronic spreadsheet to the next level by adding not only larger capacities than VisiCalc offered but also built-in graphing and tools for sorting and extracting spreadsheet information—much like the tools used in a database. Thus the three components of 1-2-3 are worksheet, database, and graphing capabilities. The Lotus 1-2-3 macro language, a set of commands that could be combined to perform tasks automatically, quickly became the most popular programming language of all time. Because of the complexity that could be programmed into a spreadsheet, an entire industry of "template" products emerged. A spreadsheet template is a predesigned and preprogrammed spreadsheet file—a file that already contains the formulas, functions, and macros and that has been created by a spreadsheet expert. Without knowing much about spreadsheets, a computer user can buy a template, enter his own data, and get the results desired.

When the Macintosh had gained some popularity in business, Microsoft introduced Excel. The original version of Excel, first available in September 1985, was the most powerful spreadsheet available for a microcomputer. It included the same spreadsheet, database, and graphics found in Lotus 1-2-3 but improved dramatically on the user interface, offering the best the Macintosh had to offer. In addition, Excel included a significant number of spreadsheet functions not found in Lotus 1-2-3. The Excel macro language was equally impressive and easy to use.

Now Excel 2.2 takes the spreadsheet to new levels of sophistication. Its graphing (or charting) capabilities make it easy to illustrate numeric data in graph form. Excel gives you total control over the formatting of graphs: you can select from several graph types, add titles and legends, change colors and patterns, and much more. Excel's macro language has been updated and improved and now offers some of the most sophisticated commands available in spreadsheets. Using Excel's macros, you can create custom menus and dialog boxes that control various aspects of the spreadsheet, and you can program spreadsheet templates that offer the kinds of capabilities found in commercial programs.

With Excel you can design forms that practically fill themselves out. You can create custom applications that are self-documenting, password-protected, and self-modifying. You can perform financial analysis and chart the results, using presentation-quality graphs. Excel's possibilities are endless, including checkbook balancing, general ledger accounting, loan analysis, financial projections, break-even analysis, business statistics with charts, forms generation and printing, tax preparation, marketing and sales analysis, and payroll operations.

About This Book

You have certainly chosen the right spreadsheet for your computer. Now you're ready to get down to work, and that's what this book is all about. You should find it a valuable companion to your Excel program. Covering all of Excel's commands, options, and special features, the book is designed to get you using Excel quickly and with as few problems as possible. Although the book follows a natural progression, feel free to skip around. If you're eager to get a total picture of Excel, try the four Quick Start chapters (Chapters 2, 10, 14, and 17) at or near the beginning of each section. These will provide step-by-step instructions for each of the main parts of the program: worksheet, charts, databases, and macros. Although the Quick Start chapters give little explanation of commands and functions, they cover a slew of features in a short time; if you're able to pick up unfamiliar programs quickly, these chapters will involve you deeply in Excel. The following is a summary of the chapters in this book.

Part I: Excel Worksheets

This section of the book covers the Excel worksheet—the electronic version of a columnar accounting sheet. Using this electronic worksheet consists of entering numbers, formulas, and text onto the "page." All Excel worksheet features are covered in this section.

Chapter 1: Getting Started with Excel gives full details about the Excel worksheet tools, commands, and menu options. This chapter introduces you to Excel and what you can expect to see as you progress through the book.

Chapter 2: Worksheet Quick Start provides a step-by-step overview of the worksheet. It takes you through the process of building a basic worksheet, formatting the information, and entering formulas that calculate results. You'll use several features of the worksheet, but Chapter 3 provides a more complete explanation of features.

Chapter 3: Creating an Excel Worksheet shows you how to open an Excel worksheet, how to save your work, and how to enter three types of information into Excel: numbers, text, and formulas. The chapter also presents some details about formulas.

Chapter 4: Editing the Worksheet describes how to make changes to your worksheets. You can change the information in the worksheet, copy and move information, and remove parts of the worksheet.

Chapter 5: Formatting the Worksheet shows you how to enhance your worksheets by using numeric and text formatting. Such enhancements include the use of fonts, type styles, and color.

Chapter 6: Using Worksheet Functions provides descriptions and examples of each worksheet function. Worksheet functions offer special calculations for your applications and can save you a lot of time when you create a worksheet. This chapter is useful as a reference even after you have read the entire book and are familiar with Excel.

Chapter 7: Using Multiple Windows and Files shows you how to use more than one Excel worksheet at a time. As you get more advanced with Excel, you'll want to start using several applications at once. This chapter shows you how to link worksheets and use multiple windows.

Chapter 8: Building Advanced Worksheets contains information about some special worksheet features. You will find this information useful after you become familiar with Excel. Features include advanced copying, working with lookup tables, creating data tables, and performing date math.

Chapter 9: Printing Worksheets shows you how to create various reports from worksheet information and use the options available for formatting the reports. These options include page numbering, margin settings, font manipulation, headers, footers, and borders.

Part II: Excel Charts

This section covers Excel's special charting capabilities. Excel offers a host of tools for graphing your worksheet data, and version 2.2 offers some important new charting capabilities—all of which are explained in this section.

Chapter 10: Chart Quick Start provides step-by-step instructions on using Excel's charting features. You will create various types of charts and edit the information in those charts.

Chapter 11: Creating Charts provides complete instructions for creating and editing charts in Excel. The charting menus and commands are explained in a logical order as you progress through the chapter.

Chapter 12: Creating Advanced Charts covers the fine points of the charting process. These features give you more control over your charts. Here you will learn how to create combination charts, add and remove elements from existing charts, and more.

Chapter 13: Using Presentation Graphics with Excel offers techniques you can use to enhance your charts. The emphasis in this chapter is on effective presentations with charts. Using Excel's features in creative ways, you can produce attractive results.

Part III: Excel Databases

This part explains how to use Excel's database features to manage large amounts of data. Database management includes sorting, searching, extracting, and manipulating data. Although Excel is no match for a large, relational database, it is ideal for storing financial data and simple databases.

Chapter 14: Database Quick Start shows you how to set up a database in Excel. You'll create a database and extract information from it. These exercises will prepare you for the details covered in Chapter 15.

Chapter 15: Getting Started with the Database provides details about using Excel for database manipulation. You'll discover how to set up a database, enter information into it, and locate information in it—either manually or with the automatic data form.

Chapter 16: Using Advanced Database Techniques shows you how to build your own custom data forms for Excel databases. This process involves using the Dialog Editor program, which comes with Excel. By creating custom data forms, you can create database applications in Excel that store and retrieve information in a number of ways.

Part IV: Excel Macros

Macros let you perform complex or repetitive tasks with a single command or option. In addition to simplifying your work by performing lengthy tasks automatically, macros can be useful in worksheets that you create for others to use. This section provides complete details about macros, starting with the basics.

Chapter 17: Macros Quick Start provides a step-by-step guide to using macros in Excel. You'll create basic macros that automate commands and operations. This chapter also includes an exercise on using the macro recording feature.

Chapter 18: Getting Started with Macros provides details about the macro language and its uses in a worksheet. You will learn the way in which macros are created and the types of commands used in a macro. You will also learn how to enter and store macros for use in any worksheet.

Chapter 19: Using Macro Programming Techniques shows you how to use simple programming techniques in your macros to make them more powerful. Here you'll learn about variables, loops, and program logic. You'll also learn how to create custom menus for your worksheets, how to create custom options for those menus, and how to create custom dialog boxes for those options.

Appendixes

Appendix A: Installing Excel provides the essential information for installing Excel on your computer. Whether you use a hard disk or floppy disks, this appendix will get you started.

Appendix B: Using Excel's Macro Commands explains the dozens of macro commands available for use in your custom macros, and provides details about how to use the commands. Use this appendix as a reference while you are creating new macros.

Appendix C: Excel Command Guide groups the various menu commands by function, lists key combinations that are command equivalents, and lists shortcut keys for moving the pointer and selecting.

— Part I —

 # Excel Worksheets

Getting Started with Excel

Worksheet Quick Start

Creating an Excel Worksheet

Editing the Worksheet

Formatting the Worksheet

Using Worksheet Functions

Using Multiple Windows and Files

Building Advanced Worksheets

Printing Worksheets

1
Getting Started with Excel

Excel is an electronic version of a columnar pad. You will find this spreadsheet program a powerful tool for such financial functions as general accounting, projections, budgets, and tax planning. In addition, Excel provides tools for creating business charts and for storing database information.

This chapter offers an overview of Excel and its features. First is a brief discussion of the three basic keyboard styles, then an introduction to Excel worksheets, databases, charts, macros, and icons. Next the chapter describes the various parts of the Excel worksheet screen—such as the title bar, formula bar, and status line—and introduces the program's menus and Help feature. Even if you are familiar with other spreadsheets, you should find this chapter helpful because of its overall look at Excel particulars. The next chapter takes you through a step-by-step example of how to use Excel's basic worksheet tools.

Understanding Your Keyboard

Before using Excel, you should be aware of the type of keyboard you have. Three basic keyboard models are available for the Macintosh. (Actually, you can find many different styles made by third-party manufacturers, but Apple provides only three.) These three keyboards are the Macintosh Plus, the Macintosh SE, and the extended keyboard. Figure 1.1 shows all three keyboards (in that order).

Fig. 1.1.

The three standard Macintosh keyboards.

Macintosh Plus Keyboard

Macintosh SE Keyboard

Macintosh Extended Keyboard

A fourth type of keyboard is the one used with Macintosh 128 and 512 computers. This keyboard is the same as the Macintosh Plus keyboard, without the numeric keypad and arrow keys. Because this fourth type of keyboard is uncommon, it is not included in the discussion. If you have such a keyboard, treat it as a Macintosh Plus keyboard without the numeric keypad and arrow keys.

Special Keys

Whichever keyboard you have, a few keys common to all types should be noted. Besides the typical alphabetic and numeric keys (at the top of the keyboard), your keyboard includes the following keys, which perform special functions:

Return	Accepts an entry or command selection. When you type information into a cell and press Return, Excel moves the pointer down one cell.
Enter	Works like Return except that Enter leaves the pointer in place.
Shift	Creates uppercase letters when used with alphabetic keys. You also can use the Shift key in combination with special command keys to issue alternative commands. When this key is pressed while you access a menu, Excel presents alternative menu options.
⌘	Invokes Excel's special commands when pressed along with a character key. Pressing Command+Q, for example, invokes the Quit command.
Option	Used in conjunction with the alphabetic keys, the Option key accesses special characters within the active font. When used with the Command key and a character key, Option provides alternative command actions.
Tab	Moves the cell pointer or highlight bar.
← → ↑ ↓	Move the cell pointer in the direction of the arrow. These keys also perform other direction-oriented actions. Note that on the extended keyboard, the arrows appear between the alphabetic and numeric keypad.

Turns on capital (uppercase) letters until you press Caps Lock again.

 Erases the character to the left of the cursor. When the cursor is not present, you can use
(Delete) Backspace to "blank" a cell.

 Clears the information in a cell or selection. When used with the Shift key (that is, when you press Shift+Clear), Clear becomes the Num Lock key.

How To Use the Command, Shift, and Option Keys

By holding down Command or Option and pressing other keys, you can perform operations similar to those of the function keys. These combinations, such as Command+V, Command+Option+ PgUp, and Command+Shift+right arrow, are detailed later in this book. The plus signs are indications to press the designated keys at the same time.

Other keys vary among the different keyboards; one keyboard may have keys the others don't have. Such keys include the following:

 Works in combination with other keys to enable you to perform special actions.
(Ctrl)

 Cancels an action. Pressing Esc is identical to pressing Command+. (period). The Esc key is not present on the Macintosh Plus keyboard.

 Prints a copy of the screen. This key is present on the extended keyboard only. Use the
(PrtSc) equivalent version, Command+Shift+4, on the other keyboards.

Changes the way scrolling operates within a worksheet. When scroll lock is "active," the arrow keys scroll the screen without moving the cell pointer. The Scroll Lock key is present on the extended keyboard only. Press the key again to deactivate scroll lock.

Pauses macros.

The same as the Option key described earlier.

   Available on the extended keyboard, this key and the other function keys perform special functions that can be duplicated with Command-key combinations.

The Numeric Keypad

All three keyboards contain a numeric keypad—a set of numbers to the right of the main keys. The numeric keypad has two purposes: to serve as a 10-key pad for numeric entry, and to serve as directional keys for moving around inside Excel. The extended keyboard labels both these functions on the keys, but the other keyboards show only numerals on the keys. Nevertheless, all numeric keypads can serve as either numeral keys or directional keys. When you first start Excel, the directional keys are active on the keypad and perform these functions:

1 (End)	Moves the cell pointer to the last column that contains information. The pointer remains in the same row.
2 (↓)	Moves the cell pointer down one cell.
3 (PgDn)	Moves the worksheet down one screen.
4 (←)	Moves the cell pointer left one cell.
6 (→)	Moves the cell pointer right one cell.
7 (Home)	Moves the cell pointer to the first column in the same row.
8 (↑)	Moves the cell pointer up one cell.
9 (PgUp)	Moves the worksheet up one screen.
. (menus)	Activates the menu bar.

In other words, when you press the 4 key, you will get the left-arrow action, not the numeral 4. You can combine these numeric-keypad keys with Command and Shift to produce various effects. To make these keys represent their respective numbers, press Shift+Clear, which is called the Num Lock toggle (because that key combination "locks" the numbers into place). Press Shift+Clear again to switch back to the directional keys. As you will see later in this book, the directional keys 2, 4, 6, and 8 on the numeric keypad are not identical to the four arrow keys on the main part of the keyboard. Also, remember that you have a set of number keys in the usual "typewriter" position at the top of the main keys.

Function Keys

Function keys, available only on the extended keyboard, are labeled F1 through F15. These keys are assigned special purposes by the software package you are using. Excel uses function keys for single-key equivalents of the numerous Command-key combinations available throughout the program. For example, pressing either F4 or Command+V invokes the Paste command (which also is available from a menu). Used with the Shift key, the Command key, or the combination Shift+Command, the function keys provide more than 30 possible actions for a program. The effects of pressing these keys in Excel are described throughout this book.

Understanding the Excel Worksheet

The Excel worksheet (shown in fig. 1.2) is a grid of 256 columns and 16,384 rows into which you can enter numbers and labels. A *cell*—the basic unit in any worksheet—is the intersection of a row and a column. All worksheet information is entered into cells. You can create formulas that automatically add columns, add rows, calculate averages, perform statistical analysis, and do other functions. By moving to the various cells and entering text (such as headings and titles), numbers, or formulas, you build a worksheet. The worksheets you can design include those for budgets, income projections, expense projections, travel expenses, checkbook balancing, and loan analysis.

The power of a worksheet comes from the formulas you can enter into the cells. Formulas let you calculate information for a cell so that you don't have to enter the information directly. The formula can calculate its result by using information from other cells of the worksheet (and even from other worksheets). The benefit is that you can change the data at any time and have the formulas recalculate their totals to account for the changes.

Besides calculating data found elsewhere in the worksheet, formulas can access a host of special functions. One function, for example, computes the square root of any number. Worksheet functions are not much different from the functions on a hand-held calculator.

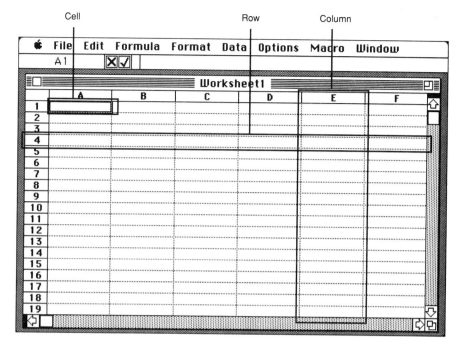

Fig. 1.2.

The Excel worksheet.

Understanding the Excel Database

A *database*—the electronic version of a file cabinet—stores data for reference and makes that data easily accessible. A database also makes it easy to rearrange the data and create reports based on information contained throughout the file. With Excel, you can set up a database within a worksheet. The Excel database is simply an area of the worksheet that contains data repeatedly accessed and extracted for reference. When a database section is established, it inherits numerous extra features that help you to retrieve information. Many commands in the Data menu, for example, become "active" when you establish a database section; these commands operate only on that section.

The database capabilities of the worksheet are useful when numeric or financial calculations—such as those for general ledger tasks, payroll tasks, and employee record-keeping—require data storage and retrieval.

Understanding Excel Charts

Chart is Excel's term for a graphic representation of a set of numbers (commonly called a *graph*). Types of charts include bar, line, pie, and scatter (also known as XY) charts. Excel gives you total control over each element of the chart. You can adjust the scale, add titles, change the type of chart, stack the chart (stacked charts are discussed in Chapter 11), change the fonts used for the labels, and so on. When the data on which a chart is based changes, the chart adjusts to reflect the change. Charts are the most powerful way to express numeric data, and with Excel, chart-building is easy.

Excel offers seven types of charts for your data, and each type comes in several different versions. In total, Excel offers 44 different charts from which to choose. You can start with one of these charts and customize it, expanding the possibilities for charts significantly. Furthermore, Excel offers a host of combination charts, which are like two different charts in one. Combination charts are explained in detail in Chapter 12.

Understanding Excel Macros

Macros are little programs that can control any aspect of Excel. Macros are useful for automating worksheet tasks—the same tasks that you may perform manually by using basic Excel commands and options. By building a macro, you can perform complex or repetitive tasks with a simple keystroke. This ability is especially valuable when you build a worksheet that will be used by others. Macros can control the information entered, check that the information is correct, and even control where the user can move within the worksheet.

Macros consist of a series of macro commands. Like the commands in any programming language, macro commands must be combined in specific ways, but macros are simple to create and use. This book shows you the basics of building macros in Excel and provides techniques that you can use to make macros more powerful. A macro commonly serves one of two purposes: it automates a lengthy or complex task, or it provides controls for making a worksheet easier to use by others.

The most common reason for building a macro is to automate a lengthy task. Using a macro, you can take a series of commands, options, and keystrokes and perform them with a single command. This command can take the form of a menu option, a keyboard command, a button, or one of many different action commands. Macros are commonly used to set up and print portions of the worksheet; alter data; format numbers and charts; change charts from one type to another, using the same data; and move information between worksheets.

Besides using macros to automate complex or repetitive tasks in Excel, you can use them to produce interactive screens and to control the actions available in a worksheet. For example, you can develop your own on-line help screens that are displayed at the touch of a button. You can create macros that check the accuracy of data entered into a worksheet. You can even develop macros that prompt for information to be entered into the worksheet and that then place the information into the correct cells so that the user never really manipulates the worksheet itself. Such macros make it easier for someone else to use a worksheet you have built; the worksheet becomes a kind of self-running program. These types of macros can become extremely involved.

Understanding Excel Icons

When you insert the Excel disks into your disk drive and examine their "desktop," you'll notice several types of icons. Excel has unique icons for worksheet files, macro files, charts, and the Excel program itself. Examples of these icons are shown in figure 1.3.

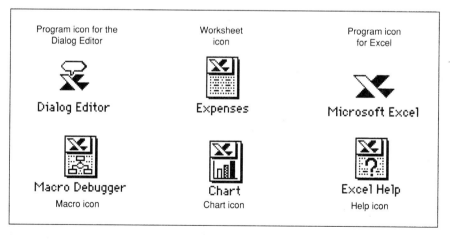

Fig. 1.3.

Sample Excel icons.

To start Excel and open a new, blank worksheet, double-click on the program icon for Excel. When you create worksheets with Excel, you can save them for future use. Saved worksheets are called data files, or *worksheet files.* Worksheet files are stored on disk and are assigned the worksheet icon. When you double-click on the icon for a particular worksheet, you will start Excel with that worksheet already open and in view.

Charts rely on the data in specific worksheets, but when you save a chart, Excel stores it in a special file on disk and assigns the chart a chart icon. You can double-click on a chart icon to start Excel with the chart in view on-screen. The worksheet to which it applies, however, will not be open. Macros created for Excel worksheets are stored in special files marked by a macro icon. Do not start Excel by double-clicking on a macro icon, unless the macro is specifically built for that purpose or unless you have a specific reason for doing so.

Another icon you will notice when using Excel is the Help icon, which represents the Excel on-line help information that you can access while you are using the program. When you click on this icon, Excel starts up with the Help dialog box in view.

Examining the Excel Screen

Excel has all the basic elements found in any worksheet, such as rows, columns, and menu options, and in addition contains special tools particular to Excel. Figure 1.4 shows the Excel screen, which includes a blank worksheet and the Excel worksheet menus.

Using figure 1.4 as a guide, the following sections describe each element on the screen.

The Menu Bar

A *menu bar* is a group of individual menus along the top of the screen. The bar displays only the name of each menu. From this bar, you can select one of the menus to view (so that you can choose one of a menu's options). In Excel, one of three menu bars (that is, one of three different groups of menus) may appear on-screen: one containing basic worksheet menus, one containing chart menus, and one containing the Info-screen menu. The reasons for these three groupings will become clear as you progress through this chapter.

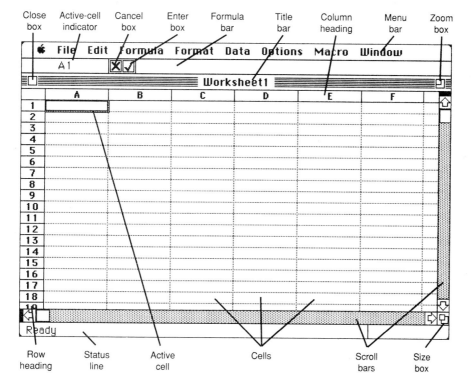

Fig. 1.4.

The Excel screen.

When you enter Excel but remove all worksheets from the screen, Excel presents a fourth menu bar, which is really just a subset of the worksheet menu bar. All the menus and options of this fourth menu bar are covered under the discussion of worksheet menus later in this chapter.

The Title Bar, Close Box, and Zoom Box

Each worksheet created with Excel has a title bar. The *title bar* displays the name of the worksheet and contains the *close box* and *zoom box*, which are common to most Macintosh windows. Clicking in the close box closes the worksheet (or removes it from the "desktop") and enables you to save any changes made. The zoom box toggles between a full-screen window and a modified window size. If the window has been shrunk through the use of the size box, the zoom box will return the window to its full size.

The Size Box

The *size box*, located in the bottom right corner of the window, lets you change the size and shape of the active window. Figure 1.5 shows an example of the effects of using the size box.

Fig. 1.5.

Shrinking or enlarging the window by using the size box.

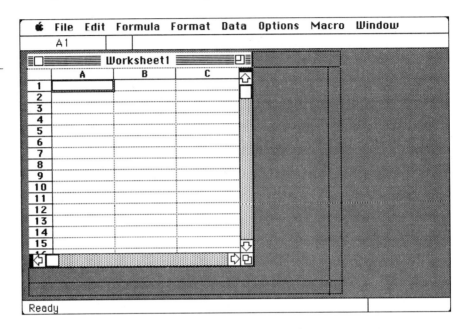

To shrink or enlarge the window, click on the size box and drag the mouse pointer to another location on the screen; then release the mouse button. Of course, when the window is already the size of the screen, you cannot enlarge it further.

Column and Row Headings

Column and row headings are simply the names of the various columns and rows in the worksheet. Rows are numbered, and columns can be either numbered or lettered. The column heading displays the style you have chosen through the Options Workspace command.

Normally, column headings are given letters, beginning with A. The column fifth from the left, for example, is column E. After labeling the columns A through Z, Excel begins with AA and continues through AZ, then begins with BA, and so on. The final column is IV. There are 256 columns.

Cells

As explained earlier, a worksheet cell is the intersection of a row and a column. All information in a worksheet is entered into cells. You can change the width of cells in a column or the height of cells in a row, and you can perform calculations by using cell references—that is, by having one cell refer to another. A *cell reference*, or *cell address*, is simply the name of a cell. Excel offers two types of addresses for each cell. One type—the R1C1 format—uses numbers for both rows and columns, in which case the cell at the intersection of row 4 and column 3, for example, is called R4C3. The second type of cell address—the A1 style—is the default; it uses numbers for rows and uses letters for columns, in which case the cell at the intersection of row 4 and column C is called C4. This book uses the second type of cell address.

To change the format in which the column and row headings appear, select the Workspace option from the Options menu. When the dialog box appears, check the R1C1 box in the set of Display options. Doing so switches the headings to the R1C1 format. Return to this dialog box and remove the check mark to change the format back to the A1-style headings. Figure 1.6 shows both styles.

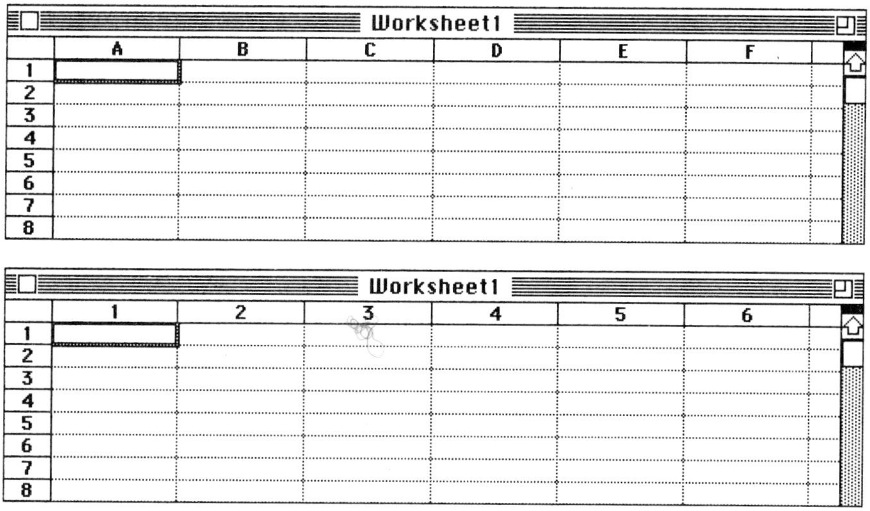

Fig. 1.6.

The A1- and R1C1-style cell addresses.

The Active Cell, Active-Cell Indicator, and Cell Pointer

The *active cell* is the cell in which the pointer is currently located. The *cell pointer* (or *pointer*) is a sort of highlighter that can rest on any worksheet cell. You can reposition the cell pointer by using the mouse, the arrow keys, the Tab key, the Return key, the Shift1Tab combination, the Shift+Return combination, and a host of automatic "find" options. The *active-cell indicator*, in the upper left corner of the screen, displays the address of the current cell. The contents of the active cell are displayed in the formula bar, discussed next.

The Formula Bar

As just mentioned, the *formula bar* displays the information contained in the active cell. The formula bar also is the place where you enter information into a cell; when you move to a cell and begin typing information, that information appears in the formula bar. The formula bar can contain more than one line of information, if necessary, and will automatically wrap your entry onto several lines as you type. Figure 1.7 shows what the screen looks like when the pointer is on a cell that already contains information.

Fig. 1.7.

The cell contents displayed in the formula bar.

É File Edit Formula Format Data Options Macro Window						
B4		Data				
		Worksheet1				
	A	B	C	D	E	F
1						
2						
3						
4		Data				
5						
6						

Scroll Bars

When you look at the worksheet screen, you see only a fraction of the entire "page" available for your work. Imagine that the worksheet rows and columns continue past the edge of the screen and that the screen is a window revealing about 20 rows and 8 columns at a time. The screen can move across and down the entire page area to reveal other sections of the worksheet. Figure 1.8 illustrates this concept.

Screen display   Worksheet

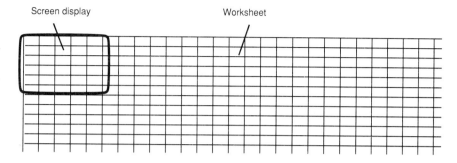

Fig. 1.8.

Your view of the worksheet is a portion of the entire worksheet.

The *vertical scroll bar* at the right side of the screen and the *horizontal scroll bar* at the bottom of the screen let you move the screen's view (which is your view also) around the entire page. As in all normal Macintosh applications, you can click on the scroll bar arrows to move slowly around the worksheet, and you can hold down the mouse button on the arrows to move quickly around the worksheet. You can also click on the scroll box and drag it to another location on the bar to jump to various locations on the worksheet. Moving the box up on the vertical bar advances you to the lower row numbers; moving the box down advances you to the higher rows. Moving the box to the left on the horizontal bar advances you to the lower column numbers (or letters); moving the box to the right advances you to the higher column numbers (or letters). You can also click in the gray portion of the scroll bar (that is, on the bar itself) to jump one screen at a time. You can click above, below, to the left of, or to the right of the scroll boxes to move the scroll box up, down, left, or right, respectively.

You can use the arrow keys, Tab key, and Return key to move around the worksheet. Details about moving through the worksheet are covered in the next chapter.

As you drag the scroll box to a new location on the bar, Excel displays in the active-cell-indicator box the column (if you are using the horizontal bar) or row (if you are using the vertical bar) to which you are moving. Before releasing the mouse button, you can determine the destination by glancing at this indicator, shown in figure 1.9. If the worksheet is empty or new, you will be able to scroll only to 20 by using this method.

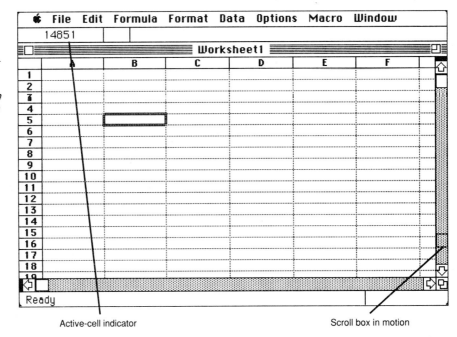

Fig. 1.9.

When you use the scroll bars, Excel displays the column or row to which you are moving.

Active-cell indicator   Scroll box in motion

The Enter Box and Cancel Box

When you enter information into a cell, you must either accept your entry or reject it. Clicking on the appropriate box informs Excel of your decision. These boxes appear in the formula-bar area when you begin typing into a cell. If you accept an entry, it will remain on the worksheet, becoming part of the worksheet. If you reject (or cancel) an entry, it will disappear, as if you never entered it. Excel offers keyboard equivalents for both the enter box and cancel box. Pressing Enter is the same as clicking on the enter box; pressing the Command key with the period (.) key is the same as clicking on the cancel box.

The Status Line

The status line displays information about menu options and Excel's modes. When you highlight, or *select*, a menu option, Excel displays a brief explanation of that option on the status line. Every menu option displays such a message when highlighted. Besides this information, the status line shows which mode Excel is in at any given time. The following is an explanation of the various modes you may see listed on the status line.

Mode Indicator	Indication
Calculate	Excel needs to be recalculated. Calculation has been set to manual, and changes have been made that affect worksheet formulas.
Circular:cell ref	Excel found a circular reference in the worksheet indicated by the cell address listed.
Copy	Excel expects you to complete the Copy operation that has been started.
Cut	Excel expects you to complete the Cut operation that has been started.
Edit	Excel is in Edit mode, and a cursor is active in the formula bar. Excel expects you to finish making changes to the cell's contents.
Enter	Excel is in Enter mode, in which you can enter information into the active cell.
Find	Excel is in the middle of the find operation.
Help	Excel is in the middle of the help operation.
Point	Excel expects you to enter a cell or range reference. You can point to the cell or range or just type the reference.
Ready	Excel is waiting for an action. You can select a command, move the pointer, or perform any number of operations at this point.
Recording	Excel is recording a macro.

The rightmost portion of the status line displays the keyboard indicator codes. These codes inform you of active keyboard settings, such as Num Lock. The following is a summary of these indicators.

Keyboard Indicator	Indication
EXT	The F8 key on the extended keyboard has been activated. The need to press Shift to extend a selection of cells is eliminated.
FIX	A fixed number of decimal places is active for the worksheet. This arrangement is accomplished through the Options Workspace command. All numbers entered into the worksheet will contain the fixed number of places.
NUM	The Num Lock option is active, which means that the numeric keypad can be used for numbers rather than as directional keys. This option is activated and deactivated through Shift+Clear.

Selecting Menu and Dialog-Box Options

Excel uses the standard Macintosh interface for menus and dialog-box options. (A *dialog box* contains a number of options or settings that you can choose from.) Thus learning Excel is easy if you already know how to use other Macintosh products. You can also use the keyboard to select options from menus and dialog boxes. The following two sections describe how to use the mouse and the keyboard interfaces in Excel.

Selecting Options with the Mouse

If you are familiar with the Macintosh, you probably know how to use the mouse to select menu options. Just click the mouse button on any of the menu titles and hold the button down. This action "pulls down" the appropriate menu, as shown in figure 1.10.

File

New...	⌘N
Open...	**⌘O**
Delete...	
Record Macro...	
Quit	⌘Q

Fig. 1.10.

A pull-down menu.

While still pressing the mouse button, drag down to the desired option in the menu list. When that option is highlighted, release the button. The option will be invoked. Often, menu options produce dialog boxes. In some cases, pressing the Tab key moves the highlight bar from option to option in the dialog box, but you can always click on any option name or button shown in the box. Figure 1.11 shows a typical dialog box.

File Format

- ● Normal   ○ SYLK/Excel 1.5   ○ DIF
- ○ Text   ○ WKS   ○ DBF 2
- ○ CSV   ○ WK1   ○ DBF 3

OK

Cancel

Password: [   ]

☐ Create Backup File

Fig. 1.11.

A dialog box.

Clicking on the OK button marks your acceptance of the changes made in the dialog box; clicking on Cancel returns the box to its prior state. Both buttons remove the box from view. One of the two buttons, OK or Cancel, will have a thick border around it. This border indicates that you can press the Return key to select the option instead of using the mouse. Press Command plus the period key to cancel the dialog box.

Selecting Options with the Keyboard

If you prefer to use the keyboard instead of the mouse, you can take advantage of the complete keyboard interface provided by Excel. To select a menu option by using the keyboard, follow these steps:

Selecting Options with the Keyboard

1. Press / (the slash key) to activate the menu bar. Key letters within each menu name will be underlined.

2. Press the letter associated with the desired option (the underlined letter); doing so "pulls down" the menu. Alternatively, use the right-arrow and left-arrow keys to move to the menu option you want; then press Return.

3. With the desired menu active, press the letter associated with the menu option (the underlined letter). Alternatively, use the down-arrow and up-arrow keys to move to the option you want; then press Return.

4. If at any time you want to cancel your selection, press Command plus the period key.

Viewing Alternative Menu Options

When you select a menu with the keyboard or mouse, you see various options within that menu. Excel also offers a set of alternative options throughout the menus. You can view these by holding down the Shift key before selecting the menu you want. (Using the keyboard, press the Shift key while you press the letter of the desired menu.) For details about each alternative option, see the listing of menu options later in this chapter.

Quickly Invoking a Menu

You can combine steps 1 and 2 into a single action for speedy menu selection. Just press the slash key along with the desired letter for the menu. (Essentially, use the slash key the way you use the Command key.) Excel will activate the menu bar and select the menu at once.

If you like, you can change the key used as the menu-activation key. Simply select the Workspace command from the Options menu. The dialog box shown in figure 1.12 appears.

```
┌─────────────────────────────────────────────┐
│  Workspace              ┌──────────────┐     │
│                         │      OK      │     │
│   ☐ Fixed Decimal       └──────────────┘     │
│                         ┌──────────────┐     │
│     Places: [2    ]     │    Cancel    │     │
│                         └──────────────┘     │
│  ┌─Display──────────────────────────────┐    │
│  │  ☐ R1C1          ☒ Scroll Bars       │    │
│  │  ☒ Status Bar    ☒ Formula Bar       │    │
│  └──────────────────────────────────────┘    │
│                                               │
│  Alternate Menu Key: [ / ]                    │
│                                               │
│  ☒ Move Selection after Return                │
│  ┌─Command Underline─────────────────────┐   │
│  │  ○ On    ○ Off    ● Automatic         │   │
│  └───────────────────────────────────────┘   │
└─────────────────────────────────────────────┘
```

Fig. 1.12.

The Options Workspace dialog box.

At the Alternate Menu Key space, press the key that you want as the menu-activation key. Press only one key (from the main keyboard). The Command Underline options control whether underlines appear on the command names. The On choice turns the underlines on for all situations; the Off choice turns the underlines off for all situations; the Automatic choice turns the underlines on when you invoke the menus with the menu-activation key but leaves them off otherwise. Click on the OK button to accept the changes you make in this dialog box. Note that these changes apply to Excel in general and will affect all your Excel worksheets.

Introducing Excel's Menus

Menus organize Excel's many worksheet features according to function. Menus appear together at the top of the screen, in sets. One of three sets of menus appears at the top of the screen at any given time: one for general worksheet needs, one for chart needs, or one for tasks involving Info windows. (Info windows are covered in Chapter 7.) Normally, you'll see the general worksheet menus at the top of the screen. These menus contain the majority of commands and options in Excel. When you create a chart, Excel replaces the worksheet menus with the chart menus. Likewise, the Info menus replace the general worksheet menus when you invoke an Info window. This section provides an overview of Excel's menus. Details about these options are found throughout the rest of the book.

 Actually, Excel presents a fourth set of menus when you have no worksheet open at all. This set, called the "null" menu, contains a subset of the general worksheet menus.

> ### Your Menus Don't Necessarily Show All the Options
>
> If your menus do not match those on the following pages, you probably have *short menus* active. Short menus do not show all the options available; they are designed to be easier to use for beginners. To activate *full menus*, select the Full Menus command from the Options menu.

The following is a description of the three main menu bars (sets) and each menu within a bar. Figure 1.13 shows these menu bars.

Fig. 1.13.

Excel's three main menus.

```
  File   Edit   Formula   Format   Data   Options   Macro   Window

  File   Edit   Gallery   Chart   Format   Macro   Window

  File   Info   Macro   Window
```

Worksheet Menus

The worksheet menus are the File, Edit, Formula, Format, Data, Options, Macro, and Window menus. These menus apply when a new or existing worksheet window is open and in view. When you close all worksheet windows, Excel removes most of these menus (see fig. 1.14).

	File	Edit	Formula	Format	Data	Options	Macro	Window

B5

≡□≡ ═══════════════ Worksheet1 ══════════════ □≡

	A	B	C	D	E	F
1						
2						
3						
4						

	File	Edit	Window

Fig. 1.14.

Worksheet menus with and without a worksheet in view.

Saving and Opening Files (File)

The File menu, shown in figure 1.15, contains options common to all Macintosh applications, such as options for opening new and existing files, saving files, setting up the printer, and printing. Each worksheet is an independent file and can be manipulated independently through the File menu options.

File

New...	⌘N
Open...	⌘O
Close	⌘W
Links...	
Save	⌘S
Save As...	
Save Workspace...	
Delete...	
Page Setup...	
Print...	⌘P
Quit	⌘Q

Fig. 1.15.

The File menu.

The following is a description of the menu options:

New	Opens a new, blank worksheet, chart, or macro sheet. You can choose the New command even if an existing worksheet, chart, or macro sheet is already open.
Open	Presents a selection box from which you can open a worksheet that has already been saved to disk.
Close	Removes the current worksheet from the screen. If changes have been made, you will be given the opportunity to save them. This option changes to Close All when you use the alternative options. Close All closes all open worksheets, charts, or macro sheets at once.
Links	Opens files that are linked to the current file.
Save	Saves the worksheet currently in view. If you have never saved the worksheet before, you will be given the opportunity to enter a name for the saved file.
Save As	Lets you save a worksheet under a name different from the worksheet's current name, as if you had never previously saved the worksheet. You can also save the file by using one of the nonstandard formats.
Save	Saves a set of files at once so that all the Workspace files can be opened together through the Open command. Using the Save Workspace command is helpful when several files are linked.
Delete	Permanently removes files that have been saved on disk. You can select from a list the files you want to delete.
Page Setup	Presents options for changing the page dimensions, the alignment of printed information, and other page-oriented matters.
Print	Presents printing options, such as the number of copies to print and the specific pages to print.
Quit	Enables you to leave Excel and return to the Macintosh system. If you have not saved changes to the open file, Excel gives you the opportunity to do so before you quit.

Changing the Worksheet (Edit)

Options in the Edit menu (see fig. 1.16), which are common to most Macintosh applications, let you cut and paste information within a worksheet or between worksheets. You also can insert and delete information by using these options.

Edit	
Undo	⌘Z
Repeat	⌘Y
Cut	⌘H
Copy	⌘C
Paste	⌘U
Clear...	⌘B
Paste Special...	
Paste Link	
Delete...	⌘K
Insert...	⌘I
Fill Right	⌘R
Fill Down	⌘D

Fig. 1.16.

The Edit menu.

The following is a description of the menu options:

Undo   Revokes your last action in Excel, leaving the worksheet as it was before the action. Some limits to this feature apply (not all actions can be undone).

Repeat   Repeats your last command or action. The Repeat option works only for commands or actions that are capable of being repeated.

Cut   Removes selected data and places a copy of it on the clipboard.

Copy

Copies the selected object or data to the clipboard. This option changes to Copy Picture when you use the alternative options. Copy Picture copies charts to the clipboard or copies the currently selected worksheet area to the clipboard as a picture.

Paste

Copies whatever is currently on the clipboard to the current location on the worksheet.

Clear

Clears selected cells of any information, leaving them blank.

Paste Special

Performs various paste functions that apply the contents of the clipboard to the currently selected cell(s).

Paste Link

Copies whatever is currently on the clipboard to the current location on the worksheet and establishes a link to the source of that data.

Delete

Deletes the currently selected cell, range, row, or column. This feature also can delete more than one row, column, or cell.

Insert

Inserts a cell, range, row, or column at the currently selected location. This feature also can insert more than one row, column, or cell.

Fill Right

Copies data from the leftmost column in a selected block of cells into the remaining portion of the block. If a single row is selected, only one cell will be copied to the right. If more than one row is selected, each cell in the first column will be copied to the right. If only one column is selected, nothing will happen. This option changes to Fill Left when you use the alternative options. Fill Left works like Fill Right but copies leftward.

Fill Down

Copies data from the top row in a selected block of cells into the remaining portion of the block. If a single column is selected, only one cell will be copied down. If more than one column is selected, each cell in the first row will be copied down. If only one row is selected, nothing will happen. This option changes to Fill Up when you use the alternative options. Fill Up works like Fill Down but copies upward.

Controlling Formulas (Formula)

The Formula menu, shown in figure 1.17, contains options that apply to constructing formulas. Such options include those for naming cells, ranges, and formulas; finding specific information in formulas; and selecting cells according to the information in them.

```
Formula
   Paste Name...
   Paste Function...
   Reference          ⌘T

   Define Name...     ⌘L
   Create Names...
   Apply Names...

   Note...

   Goto...            ⌘G
   Find...            ⌘H
   Replace...
   Select Special...
   Show Active Cell
```

Fig. 1.17.

The Formula menu.

The following is a description of the menu options:

Paste Name	Provides a list of currently defined names and lets you select one to paste into the current location.
Paste Function	Provides a list of Excel functions and lets you select one to paste into the current location.
Reference	Automatically changes selected cell references in formulas to absolute, relative, or mixed references. You choose the reference option you want.
Define Name	Enables you to define a name for the selected range of cells.

Create Names	Automatically creates a series of names, using information from a selected block of data. Labels in the top row, left column, or both are used for range names.
Apply Names	Automatically replaces range references throughout the worksheet with the corresponding range name (if defined). This command applies to selected cells or to the entire worksheet.
Note	Lets you attach a note to a cell. The note can contain any information you want it to.
Goto	Moves the cell pointer to any specified cell or range.
Find	Locates information in the worksheet by using specified criteria.
Replace	Locates information in the worksheet by using specified criteria; then replaces the information with your specified replacement text.
Select Special	Highlights worksheet data that has attributes specified in the dialog box. This command is useful for debugging worksheets.
Show Active Cell	Brings the active cell into view on-screen.

Dressing Up the Presentation (Format)

The Format menu options (see fig. 1.18) let you spruce up the information in a worksheet. You can select particular fonts, sizes, and styles to create more impact, and you can alter the color and texture of objects that are on-screen.

Format

Number...
Alignment...
Font...
Border...
Cell Protection...

Row Height...
Column Width...

Justify

Fig. 1.18.

The Format menu.

The following is a description of the menu options:

Number	Displays a set of options for changing the number formats. These options include adding dollar signs, displaying numbers as percentages, and so on. Options for date and time formats are included in this menu as well. In addition, you can create custom formats by using this command.
Alignment	Changes the alignment of selected data. The alignment of a piece of information is relative to the cell it occupies. Alignment options include those for centering, flush right, and flush left.
Font	Lists the fonts available in your system for formatting information in cells.
Border	Adds border lines to selected cells. The Border option is useful for creating boxes, lines, and other graphic elements on the worksheet. This option also can shade highlighted areas.
Cell Protection	Provides options for protecting information in the worksheet. This protection can consist of preventing changes to the data or hiding the contents of the cells. You must also use the Options Protect Document command to invoke the protection.

Row Height	Controls the height of the selected row (or rows). You can enter the height in points.
Width	Controls the width of the selected column (or columns). You can enter a column width in number of characters.
Justify	Reformats a block of text so that it fits into a defined column. This option is useful for creating uniform columns of text.

Using Databases (Data)

The commands in the Data menu, shown in figure 1.19, control the database features of Excel. You can set up a database, specify search criteria, and extract information from a database by using these options.

Fig. 1.19.

The Data menu.

```
┌─────────────────────┐
│ Data                │
├─────────────────────┤
│ Form...             │
├─────────────────────┤
│ Find           ⌘F   │
│ Extract...     ⌘E   │
│ Delete              │
│ Set Database        │
│ Set Criteria        │
├─────────────────────┤
│ Sort...             │
├─────────────────────┤
│ Series...           │
│ Table...            │
│ Parse...            │
└─────────────────────┘
```

The following is a description of the menu options:

Form
Presents options for creating a database entry form. This option is useful for making data entry easier.

Find
Locates and highlights database records that match the currently defined criteria.

Extract
Extracts database records that match the currently defined criteria. Extracted records are placed in the specified extract range.

Delete
Removes database records that match the currently defined criteria.

Set Database
Determines the active database, according to the selected range of cells. The active database can be used with other database commands.

Set Criteria
Determines the active criteria range. The criteria range contains the condition (or conditions) on which Excel finds information in the active database. The criteria range is essential for database extractions and statistical analysis.

Sort
Sorts a selected range of cells, using an ascending or descending key as a basis.

Series
Enters special information into a selected range. The fill information is determined by the first entry of the selected range and can include numbers or dates.

Table
Contains options for table calculations, including options for recalculating the table, selecting the table range, and determining the database range and extract range. Table calculations can be somewhat advanced.

Parse
Calculates frequency-distribution values, using selected ranges as a basis.

Using Other Worksheet Options (Options)

Miscellaneous options—such as those for printing and displaying worksheets—are found in the Options menu (see fig. 1.20).

Fig. 1.20.

The Options menu.

Options

Set Print Area
Set Print Titles
Set Page Break

Display...
Standard Font...
Freeze Panes

Protect Document...

Calculation...
Calculate Now   ⌘=
Workspace...
Short Menus

The following is a description of the menu options:

Set Print Area	Determines the exact worksheet area that will print when you use the Print option. You can change the print area at any time.
Set Print Titles	Determines the information that will be printed at the top of each page.
Set Page Break	Forces a new page at the position of the cell pointer. When printing, Excel will start a new page at the specified point.
Display	Offers options for changing the basic Excel display. These options include removing or changing the color of the cell grid and removing the column and row headings.
Standard Font	Sets the font used automatically throughout the worksheet. The standard font is used when you don't specify a different font.

Freeze Panes	This command applies when you have split the screen by using the split-screen markers. Normally, each half (pane) of a split screen can be scrolled independently. This command freezes the contents in one of the panes.
Protect Document	Determines whether a document's cell protection is active or inactive. This command acts like a master switch for cell protection.
Calculation	Offers various kinds of recalculation options for the worksheet. You can specify that manual recalculation be used so that the worksheet is calculated only when you choose the Calculate Now option. The option Iteration refers to the number of times Excel recalculates when you use the Calculate Now option.
Calculate Now	Recalculates the formulas in all open worksheets. This option is most useful when calculation has been set to manual through the Calculation option. This option changes to Calculate Document when you use the alternative options. Calculate Document calculates only the active worksheet, whereas Calculate Now calculates all open worksheets.
Workspace	Provides options for changing some attributes of Excel's worksheet. These options include those for handling decimal points and determining the style of cell addresses.
Short Menus	Removes many of the advanced menu options from Excel's menus. The option Short Menus appears on the Options menu when you are using full menus.
Full Menus	Makes all menus show all the available commands. The option Full Menus appears on the Options menu when you are using short menus.

Creating Macros (Macro)

Macro options, shown in figure 1.21, are used for creating and manipulating macros in Excel. You can create and edit macros, open specific macros, run macros, and more.

Fig. 1.21.

The Macro menu.

> **Macro**
> **Run...**
> **Record...**
> ....
> **Start Recorder**
> **Set Recorder**
> **Relative Record**

The following is a description of the menu options:

Run	Lists available macros from which you can choose. The macro you choose will be run on the current worksheet.
Record	Begins recording your keystrokes as a macro. Also, opens a macro sheet and lists the finished macro there.
Start Recorder	Begins recording your keystrokes and lists the macro in the range set with the Set Recorder command.
Set Recorder	Determines where a recorded macro will be listed.
Absolute Record	Records cell addresses in a macro as absolute references. This option appears on the full Macro menu if you have previously chosen the option Relative Record.
Relative Record	Records cell addresses in a macro as relative references. This option appears on the full Macro menu if you have previously chosen the option Absolute Record.

Arranging Windows (Window)

Most Macintosh applications present information in windows. A standard Macintosh window can be moved, resized, and reshaped. Also, you can view several windows on-screen at one time. In Excel the ability to see several windows at once means that you can look at several worksheets simultaneously or that you can look at one worksheet through several windows. The Window menu options (see fig. 1.22) let you create new windows for a worksheet, bring particular windows into view, and arrange windows on the screen.

Window
Help...
New Window
Show Clipboard
Show Info
Arrange All
Hide
Unhide...
✓1 Macro1

Fig. 1.22.

The Window menu.

The following is a description of the menu options:

Help	Presents Excel's Help window, which you can use to find help on many worksheet topics.
New Window	Opens a new window for the active worksheet. This window can display any of the information in the original worksheet.
Show Clipboard	Displays the contents of the clipboard in a separate window.
Show Info	Displays the Info window for the active document. This option and the Show Document option enable you to toggle between the Info window and the relevant document.

Show Document	Displays the document related to the active Info window. This option and the Show Info option enable you to toggle between the Info window and the relevant document.
Arrange All	Arranges windows on the screen when two or more are open. This command brings all windows into view.
Hide	Hides the active window from view but leaves it open for access by other sheets.
Unhide	Displays hidden windows.

Chart Menus

The chart menus—Gallery, Chart, and Format—appear when you create a new chart or activate an existing chart. Certain original worksheet menus are available as well: File, Edit, Macro, and Window. These four menus are the same as described in the section "Worksheet Menus," except that some unusable options have been removed.

Selecting a Chart (Gallery)

From the Gallery menu, shown in figure 1.23, you select one of the various chart types available in Excel. You can determine a chart type when you create a chart, or you can change the type of an existing chart.

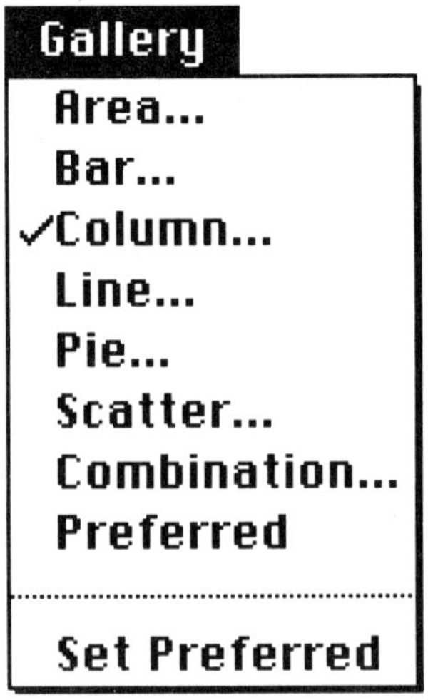

Fig. 1.23.

The Gallery menu.

```
Gallery
  Area...
  Bar...
✓Column...
  Line...
  Pie...
  Scatter...
  Combination...
  Preferred
..............................
  Set Preferred
```

The following is a description of the menu options:

Area	Specifies an area chart.
Bar	Specifies a bar chart (horizontal bar).
Column	Specifies a column chart (vertical bar).
Line	Specifies a line chart.
Pie	Specifies a pie chart.
Scatter	Specifies a scatter chart.
Combination	Specifies a combination chart. (A combination chart combines many of the previous types.)
Preferred	Specifies the chart type chosen with the Set Preferred command.
Set Preferred	Specifies any of the preceding chart types as the default for new charts.

Manipulating Charts (Chart)

The Chart menu (see fig. 1.24) provides options for creating and manipulating charts. You can control the legend, change the axes, and change the data being referenced by the chart. Other options in this menu include Protect Document, Calculate Now, and Short Menus, all of which are available in the standard worksheet menus.

Chart

Attach Text...
Add Arrow
Add Legend
Axes...
Gridlines...
Add Overlay

Select Chart   ⌘A
Select Plot Area

Protect Document...

Calculate Now   ⌘=
Short Menus

Fig. 1.24.

The Chart menu.

The following is a description of the menu options:

Attach Text	Adds titles to various elements of the chart, using selected information as a basis.
Add Arrow	Places an arrow on the chart in a specified location.
Add Legend	Creates a legend for the chart.
Axes	Determines whether either or both of the chart axes are visible.
Gridlines	Determines whether grid lines are visible on the chart.
Add Overlay	Creates an overlay chart, splitting the main chart into two separate charts superimposed on each other.
Select Chart	Activates the chart. This command is useful in conjunction with formatting commands.
Select Plot Area	Activates the current chart's plot area for formatting.
Protect Document	Determines whether a document's cell protection is active or inactive. This command acts like a master switch for cell protection.
Calculate Now	Recalculates the formulas in the worksheet. This command is most useful when calculation has been set to manual through the Calculation option.
Short Menus	Removes many of the advanced menu options from Excel's menus. The option Short Menus appears on the Options menu when you are using full menus.
Full Menus	Makes all menus show all the available commands. The option Full Menus appears on the Options menu when you are using short menus.

Formatting the Chart (Format)

The Format options accessed through the Chart menu let you change a chart's appearance. For example, you can change the patterns of bars and pie slices, change the font of the chart titles and legend entries, and change the chart legend and axis scale. Figure 1.25 shows the Chart Format menu.

```
┌─────────────────────┐
│ Format              │
│   Patterns...       │
│   Font...           │
│   Text...           │
│   Scale...          │
│   Legend...         │
│ ................... │
│   Main Chart...     │
│   Overlay...        │
│ ................... │
│   Move              │
│   Size              │
└─────────────────────┘
```

Fig. 1.25.

The Format menu for charts.

The following is a description of the menu options:

Patterns	Determines the patterns used for the various chart elements (bars, pie slices, and so on).
Font	Determines the font used for text labels on the chart.
Text	Controls the appearance of the chart's text labels, enabling you to, among other things, specify vertical text and one of six alignment options.
Scale	Determines the chart's axis scale.
Legend	Determines the position of the chart's legend.
Main Chart	Controls various elements of the main chart, including the spacing of bars, stacking, drop shadows, and the angle of a pie chart.
Overlay	Controls various elements of the overlay chart.
Move	Lets you move an element on the active chart.
Change	Changes the size of an element on the active chart.

The Info Menu (Info)

The Info menu (see fig. 1.26) gives you control over the Info window, a special window that contains information about the active worksheet cell. Every worksheet can have an Info window. The Info menu, which enables you to display various information in the Info window, is visible only after you have opened an Info window by using the command Window Show Info. (This command is available only from the worksheet menus, not the chart menus.) When an Info window is active, Excel adds the Info menu and removes many unusable options from the other menus.

Fig. 1.26.

The Info menu.

```
┌──────────────┐
│ Info         │
│ ✓Cell        │
│ ✓Formula     │
│  Value       │
│  Format      │
│  Protection  │
│  Names       │
│  Precedents... │
│  Dependents... │
│ ✓Note        │
└──────────────┘
```

The following is a description of the menu options:

Cell	Determines whether the address of the active cell appears in the Info window.
Formula	Determines whether the formula of the active cell appears in the Info window.
Value	Determines whether the value of the active cell appears in the Info window.
Format	Determines whether the format of the active cell appears in the Info window.
Protection	Determines whether the protection status of the active cell appears in the Info window.
Names	Determines whether any named ranges containing the active cell appear in the Info window.

Precedents Determines whether the addresses of cells on which the active cell depends appear in the Info window.

Dependents Determines whether the addresses of cells that depend on the active cell appear in the Info window.

Note Determines whether the cell note attached to the active cell (if any) appears in the Info window.

Getting Help

Excel includes an on-line help feature that contains information about each command and option in the program. The information is cursory but provides the necessary details to get you started with the command in question. You can search for the information you want by choosing a topic from the topics list.

Begin by calling up the Help window (see fig. 1.27), using the Help command from the Window menu. You can move this window to any location on the screen, change its size and shape, and move it behind other windows.

The six buttons on the window help you locate and review information. Moving the box in the scroll bar causes Excel to flip through the information currently in the window. Unlike the information in a user's manual, Help information is not continuous: each topic has a beginning and end. When you reach the end of one topic, you can, if you like, move on to the next topic in order. Or you can return to the list of topics and choose another.

When you first call up the Help window, the list of main topics appears. Simply click on a particular topic to see a list of related topics. Figure 1.28 shows the related topics that appear when you click on "Using Microsoft Excel Help." With the related topics in view, click on one of them to see the Help screen (the actual information) for that topic. To see the original list of topics at any time, click on the Topics button.

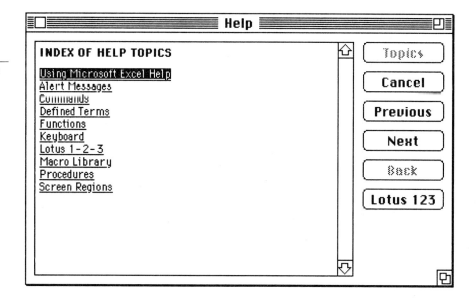

Fig. 1.27.

The Help window.

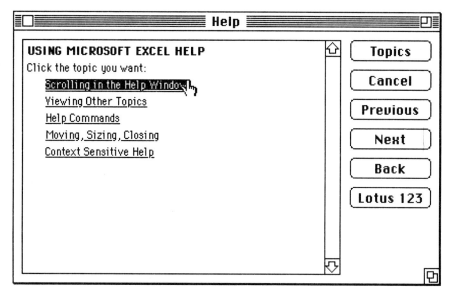

Fig. 1.28.

The topics related to the subject "Using Microsoft Excel Help."

When the Help information is visible, you can use the Next and Previous buttons. These buttons move you to the next and previous topics as they appear in the list. Within the screens that show the actual "Help" information is a list of related topics. Click on one of these topic names to jump right to that topic and circumvent the topics lists.

The Back button returns you to the previous topic selected. The button marked Lotus 123 presents the dialog box shown in figure 1.29. Enter any Lotus 1-2-3 command or function name in the space provided, and Excel will present a list of Excel commands that are related to that 1-2-3 command. Click on the desired item in the list for more information. For example, if you enter /WG to specify the 1-2-3 Worksheet Global command, Excel responds with the list shown in figure 1.30.

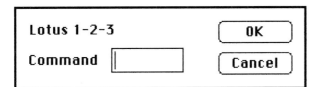

Fig. 1.29.

The dialog box that appears when you click on the Lotus 123 button.

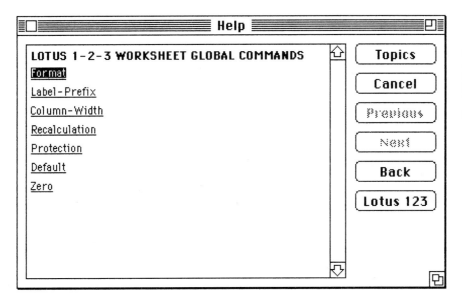

Fig. 1.30.

Excel equivalents to Lotus 1-2-3's Worksheet Global command.

Summary

This chapter covered some important Excel basics, including the differences among the various Macintosh keyboards, the parts of the Excel worksheet, and the available menu options. The following are key points to remember:

❑ The numeric keyboard toggles between number keys and directional keys. Pressing Shift+Clear changes back and forth between these two modes.

❑ The Command and Option keys work in conjunction with other keys on the keyboard to provide special actions.

❑ Each worksheet file you create and save in Excel is stored on disk and identified with the Excel worksheet icon.

❑ You can enter Excel by double-clicking on a worksheet icon or by double-clicking on the Excel program icon.

❑ The active cell is the cell on which the pointer is currently located.

❑ The worksheet has more rows and columns than will fit within one screen view. You can use the scroll bars to view other parts of the worksheet.

❑ All data is entered into cells of the worksheet.

❑ Excel categorizes data into three types: labels, numbers, and formulas.

❑ After entering data, you should accept the entry by pressing Tab, Shift+Tab, Enter, Return, Shift+Return, or one of the arrow keys. You can also click on the enter box to accept the entry.

❑ Although data appears in the cells of the worksheet, you access the data through the formula bar.

❑ You can move the pointer to any cell to access its data.

In the next chapter, "Worksheet Quick Start," you will learn to create an Excel worksheet that tracks expenses.

2

Worksheet
Quick Start

This chapter takes you step by step through the creation of a simple application: a worksheet that tracks expenses. You will start by opening a new Excel worksheet and entering the basic elements of a worksheet application, such as titles and column labels. Next you will enter numbers and formulas that calculate the proper results. As you build the worksheet, you will use several formatting commands to make it more readable. By the end of the chapter, you will have built, saved, and printed a simple worksheet for expense tracking. You will also be prepared for the next Quick Start lesson, in Part II of this book. This and all the other Quick Start chapters are designed for Excel users who have little or no familiarity with the Macintosh, worksheets, or Excel.

If you have not installed Excel on your system, be sure to read Appendix A before beginning this chapter. Also, be sure to read Chapter 1 for a look at spreadsheet technology in general and Excel in particular.

Opening a New Worksheet

The first step in creating the sample application is to start Excel with a new, blank worksheet in view. With your computer on and the Excel program icon in view, double-click on the Excel program icon to begin.

Performing this step starts Excel and presents a new, blank worksheet named "Worksheet 1." The cell pointer should be on cell A1 (see fig. 2.1).

Fig. 2.1.

When you open a new worksheet, the cell pointer is on cell A1.

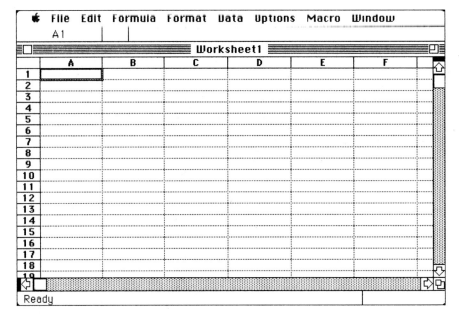

Notice that the worksheet "page" is made up of a series of rows and columns. The rows are numbered, and the columns contain letter names. The intersection of a row and a column is called a *cell*. The name of a cell (also called the *cell address*, or *cell reference*) is the combination of the column letter and row number, such as C5. The cell pointer can move from cell to cell throughout the worksheet as a result of a few movement keys you can press, the most basic of which are the four arrow keys. Notice also that Excel has a visible "grid" that shows the individual cells on the screen.

Saving a Worksheet

Although you have no work to save yet, saving your worksheet is an important step to learn up front. To save and name the new (blank) worksheet, complete the following steps:

1. Select the Save command from the File menu. The familiar Macintosh Save dialog box will appear (see fig. 2.2).
2. Enter the name **EXPENSES** and click on the Save button.

Fig. 2.2.

The Save dialog
box.

3. You can, if you like, specify a folder in which this file should be saved. Open any folder by double-clicking on its name in the list box. You can return to previously opened folders by clicking on the disk name above the Eject button.

The worksheet is now stored permanently on disk in the specified folder or, if you did not choose a folder, in the same folder that contains the Excel program icon.

Now that you have saved the file, a worksheet icon for that file will appear on-screen:

Be sure to save the sample worksheet when you reach the end of this chapter (or periodically throughout the chapter). The worksheet will be used in the next Quick Start chapter.

Quitting Excel

When you are ready to quit Excel, select the Quit command from the File menu. If you have not made any changes to the worksheet since you last saved, Excel will return to the Macintosh desktop (or startup screen). Otherwise, you will be given the opportunity to save your changes. Figure 2.3 shows the message you see when you quit.

Fig. 2.3.

When you quit, Excel asks whether you would like to save your changes.

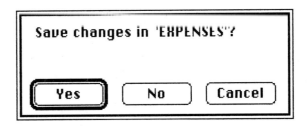

Simply click on Yes to save the changes, No to reject the changes, or Cancel to stop the Quit process. If you were to quit Excel now, the dialog box in figure 2.3 would not appear, because you just saved the worksheet.

Opening an Existing Worksheet

If you quit this Quick Start tutorial in the middle and want to pick up where you left off, simply open the existing EXPENSES worksheet and continue. To open this worksheet after it has been saved, double-click on the EXPENSES worksheet icon; you will automatically start Excel with that worksheet on-screen.

Entering Column Labels

The next step in designing the EXPENSES application is to enter the basic labels for the worksheet. These labels will appear in column A. Instead of starting in cell A1, however, you will leave some room at the top of the worksheet for other information. Complete these steps to enter the labels:

1. Press the down-arrow key three times to move the cell pointer to cell A4.
2. Type **Salaries** and press Return.
3. Type **Professional Svcs** and press Return.

4. Continue typing the following labels, pressing the Return key after each:

Advertising
Bank
Freight
Insurance
Office Supplies
Rent/Util/Phone
Depreciation
Taxes

When you are finished, the screen should look like figure 2.4.

	File	Edit	Formula	Format	Data	Options	Macro	Window

A14

EXPENSES

	A	B	C	D	E	F
1						
2						
3						
4	Salaries					
5	Professional Svcs					
6	Advertising					
7	Bank					
8	Freight					
9	Insurance					
10	Office Supplies					
11	Rent/Util/Phone					
12	Depreciation					
13	Taxes					
14						
15						
16						
17						
18						

Ready

Fig. 2.4.

The expense
worksheet, with
expense labels
entered.

If you make a mistake while typing the information, simply press the Backspace key to delete the characters to the left of the cursor. If you have already pressed Return to move to the next cell, press the up-arrow key to move back to the cell containing the error. When you get to the appropriate cell, simply retype the information. The new information will replace the old.

Changing the Column Width

Because some of the information in column A spilled into column B, the next step in designing the application is to widen column A. It's not always necessary to widen a column when information spills into the next column—only when you anticipate putting information into the adjacent column. If you enter information into an adjacent column to the right, Excel will display, in the first column, only the portion of the data that fits in the cell. For this exercise, complete the following steps to widen column A so that it displays all the data:

1. Using the mouse, move the cell pointer to the dividing line between columns A and B. When in place, the pointer should change shape, as shown in figure 2.5.

Fig. 2.5.

The cell pointer changes when you move it over the column dividers.

	A	B	C	D	E	F
1						
2						
3						
4						
5						
6						

File Edit Formula Format Data Options Macro Window A1 EXPENSES

2. Now click the mouse button, hold it down, and drag to the right to expand the width of column A. Release the mouse button when you have expanded the column to about two inches (see fig. 2.6).

Fig. 2.6.

Column A after the expansion.

File Edit Formula Format Data Options Macro Window A14 EXPENSES

	A	B	C	D	E	F
1						
2						
3						
4	Salaries					
5	Professional Svcs					
6	Advertising					
7	Bank					
8	Freight					
9	Insurance					
10	Office Supplies					
11	Rent/Util/Phone					
12	Depreciation					
13	Taxes					
14						
15						
16						

Notice that all the information fits into the new width of column A. You can change the width of any column in this way.

Entering Row Headings

The next step is to enter, across the top of the worksheet, headings that identify the four quarters of the year. To enter these headings, complete the following steps:

1. Click on cell B3 to position the cell pointer; type **First Q** and then press the Tab key to accept the entry and move to the next cell. The pointer should now be on cell C3.

2. Enter **Second Q** into cell C3; press the Tab key to move to cell D3.

3. Enter **Third Q**; press the Tab key to move to cell E3.

4. Enter **Fourth Q** and press Enter. Your worksheet should now look like figure 2.7.

	File	Edit	Formula	Format	Data	Options	Macro	Window
E3			Fourth Q					

EXPENSES

	A	B	C	D	E	F
1						
2						
3		First Q	Second Q	Third Q	Fourth Q	
4	Salaries					
5	Professional Svcs					
6	Advertising					
7	Bank					
8	Freight					
9	Insurance					
10	Office Supplies					
11	Rent/Util/Phone					
12	Depreciation					
13	Taxes					
14						
15						
16						
17						
18						

Ready

Fig. 2.7.

The expense worksheet, with all labels entered.

Entering Numbers

To enter numbers into the appropriate columns for each expense category, you must first highlight the block from cell B4 to cell E13 (this block is referred to as B4:E13). Doing so makes entering the data easier. Complete the following steps to highlight the block and enter the numbers:

1. Move the cell pointer to cell B4, click and drag down to cell E13, and then release the mouse button.

2. Type the following entries for row 4, pressing the Tab key after each entry (pressing Tab moves the cell pointer from left to right and then from top to bottom—that is, across the rows from top to bottom): **2300, 2300, 3500,** and **4500**.

3. For row 5 type the following entries, pressing the Tab key after each: **600, 600, 650,** and **650**.

4. For row 6 type the following entries, pressing the Tab key after each: **9000, 9000, 9000,** and **9000**.

5. For row 7 type the following entries, pressing the Tab key after each: **200, 200, 200,** and **245**.

6. For row 8 type the following entries, pressing the Tab key after each: **5000, 4500, 5690,** and **7500**.

7. For row 9 type the following entries, pressing the Tab key after each: **3500, 3500, 3500,** and **3500**.

8. For row 10 type the following entries, pressing the Tab key after each: **300, 300, 300,** and **300**.

9. For row 11 type the following entries, pressing the Tab key after each: **6500, 6500, 6200,** and **6900**.

10. For row 12 type the following entries, pressing the Tab key after each: **2200, 2000, 1800,** and **1600**.

11. For row 13 type the following entries, pressing the Tab key after each: **2500, 4500, 3500,** and **3500**.

The worksheet should look like figure 2.8.

If you make a mistake in entering the numbers, just press the Backspace key and retype the information. Because the block is highlighted (or *selected*), the cell pointer will automatically move from cell to cell within the block. As mentioned earlier, pressing Tab moves the cell pointer first from left to right and then from top to bottom (across the rows from top to bottom). When you press Return, the cell pointer moves first from top to bottom and then from left to right (down the columns from left to right). Pressing the arrow keys or clicking the mouse button removes the highlight. If you accidentally remove the block highlight, just highlight the block again and press Tab or Return until you reach the last cell you completed.

	File	Edit	Formula	Format	Data	Options	Macro	Window

| B4 | | 5000 | |

EXPENSES

	A	B	C	D	E	F
1						
2						
3		First Q	Second Q	Third Q	Fourth Q	
4	Salaries	5000	2300	3500	4500	
5	Professional Svcs	600	600	650	650	
6	Advertising	9000	9000	9000	9000	
7	Bank	200	200	200	245	
8	Freight	5000	4500	5690	7500	
9	Insurance	3500	3500	3500	3500	
10	Office Supplies	300	300	300	300	
11	Rent/Util/Phone	6500	6500	6200	6900	
12	Depreciation	2200	2000	1800	1600	
13	Taxes	2500	4500	3500	3500	
14						
15						
16						
17						
18						
19						

Ready

Fig. 2.8.

The expense worksheet, showing a highlighted block of cells into which data has been entered.

Performing Some Simple Formatting

Notice that the quarter headings you entered are not exactly aligned with the numbers in the columns. The reason is that numbers normally appear flush with the right side of the cell and that text appears flush with the left. The worksheet will look better if the numbers are aligned with the headings. To make the text flush right, follow these steps:

1. Place the cell pointer on the row heading *3* in row 3 and click the mouse button. The entire row should be highlighted, as shown in figure 2.9.

2. Select the Alignment command from the Format menu. When presented with the alignment options, choose Right.

3. Make the headings bold by pressing Command+Shift+B. (Alternatively, you can use the Font command in the Format menu and select the Bold style from the list provided.)

Fig. 2.9.

Highlighting row 3.

```
  File   Edit   Formula   Format   Data   Options   Macro   Window
        A3
═══════════════════════════ EXPENSES ═══════════════════════════
          A          B          C          D          E          F
 1
 2
 3           │    First Q     Second Q     Third Q     Fourth Q
 4  Salaries        5000        2300        3500        4500
 5  Professional Svcs 600         600         650         650
 6  Advertising      9000        9000        9000        9000
 7  Bank             200         200         200         245
 8  Freight         5000        4500        5690        7500
 9  Insurance       3500        3500        3500        3500
10  Office Supplies  300         300         300         300
11  Rent/Util/Phone 6500        6500        6200        6900
12  Depreciation    2200        2000        1800        1600
13  Taxes           2500        4500        3500        3500
14
15
16
17
18
19
Ready
```

Now that you're becoming familiar with formatting, try adding a main heading to the worksheet. This heading should be centered over the data and should be large and bold. Complete these steps to insert the heading:

1. First, move the pointer to cell C1 and type the heading **Expenses**. Press Enter or click on the enter box at the top of the worksheet when you have finished typing.

2. Select the Format Font command. Choose the Times font from the Font dialog box. (If your system does not have the Times font, use any font listed.)

3. With the Font dialog box still on-screen, select the 24-point type size. Press Return when finished. (If the font you selected does not have a 24-point size, type **24** in the size box and press Return.) The worksheet should look like figure 2.10.

After changing the font and size of the main title, Excel adjusts the height of row 1 to accommodate 24-point type.

Fig. 2.10.

The expense
worksheet after you
enter a main title.

```
 ✉  File  Edit  Formula  Format  Data  Options  Macro  Window
     C19
```

	A	B	C	D	E	F
			EXPENSES			
1			Expenses			
2						
3		First Q	Second Q	Third Q	Fourth Q	
4	Salaries	5000	2300	3500	4500	
5	Professional Svcs	600	600	650	650	
6	Advertising	9000	9000	9000	9000	
7	Bank	200	200	200	245	
8	Freight	5000	4500	5690	7500	
9	Insurance	3500	3500	3500	3500	
10	Office Supplies	300	300	300	300	
11	Rent/Util/Phone	6500	6500	6200	6900	
12	Depreciation	2200	2000	1800	1600	
13	Taxes	2500	4500	3500	3500	
14						
15						
16						
17						
18						

```
Ready
```

Entering a Formula

The next step is to enter formulas that total the numbers in each
column so that you can show the total expenses for each quarter. In
this section, you enter such a formula into cell B15. In the following
section, you will use the worksheet function Fill Right to copy the
formula into cells C15, D15, and E15. Complete the following steps to
enter the formula into cell B15:

1. Use the arrow keys to move the pointer to cell B15.
2. Type the following formula:

    =SUM(B4:B13)

   (Be sure to enter a colon character between the cell
   references.) Press Enter or click on the enter box to place
   the formula into the cell.

As soon as you press the Enter key or click on the enter box, the result
of the formula appears in the cell. The formula calculates the sum or
the range of cells between B4 and B13. You can now change any
number in column B, and the formula you entered will recalculate the
new result instantly. This capability plays an important role in what-if
analysis.

Copying the Formula

To get totals for each of the columns, you can enter the SUM formula three more times (for each of the three remaining columns), or you can copy the first formula into the remaining three cells all at once. To do the latter, complete the following steps:

1. Drag the mouse from cell B15 to cell E15 to highlight the four cells (including cell B15, which contains the original formula). Your screen should look like figure 2.11.

Fig. 2.11.

Selecting the formula and the cells that are to receive copies.

	☀ File Edit Formula Format Data Options Macro Window					
	B15	=SUM(B4:B13)				

EXPENSES

	A	B	C	D	E	F
1			Expenses			
2						
3		First Q	Second Q	Third Q	Fourth Q	
4	Salaries	5000	2300	3500	4500	
5	Professional Svcs	600	600	650	650	
6	Advertising	9000	9000	9000	9000	
7	Bank	200	200	200	245	
8	Freight	5000	4500	5690	7500	
9	Insurance	3500	3500	3500	3500	
10	Office Supplies	300	300	300	300	
11	Rent/Util/Phone	6500	6500	6200	6900	
12	Depreciation	2200	2000	1800	1600	
13	Taxes	2500	4500	3500	3500	
14						
15		34800				
16						
17						
18						

Ready

2. Select the Fill Right option from the Edit menu and watch the screen. The formula is instantly copied into the selected cells, with the correct result in each.

The new formulas calculate their respective values automatically. If you were to change some of the numbers in the columns, the formulas would instantly recalculate their values, accounting for the changes. In short, Excel copies the original formula, =SUM(B4:B13), to the new cells and changes the copies to =SUM(C4:C13), =SUM(D4:D13), and =SUM(E4:E13), respectively. The formulas automatically reflect their own columns.

More Formatting

As you become more familiar with Excel, you'll find that formatting constitutes much of the work in the construction of a worksheet. The worksheet's appearance plays an important part in organizing and displaying information clearly. In the following series of steps, you will remove the worksheet grid (the row and column guides), place a border around the column labels, and add a double line above the totals. Finally, you will format the numbers as dollar amounts.

Removing the worksheet grid is useful when your worksheet will be seen by others or when you simply find the grid annoying. To remove the grid, complete the following steps:

1. Select the Display option from the Options menu. Doing so brings up a dialog box.

2. With the dialog box in view, click on the Gridlines box to remove the check mark. Then press Return. Your screen should look like figure 2.12.

	File Edit Formula Format Data Options Macro Window

B19

EXPENSES

	A	B	C	D	E	F
1			Expenses			
2						
3		First Q	Second Q	Third Q	Fourth Q	
4	Salaries	5000	2300	3500	4500	
5	Professional Svcs	600	600	650	650	
6	Advertising	9000	9000	9000	9000	
7	Bank	200	200	200	245	
8	Freight	5000	4500	5690	7500	
9	Insurance	3500	3500	3500	3500	
10	Office Supplies	300	300	300	300	
11	Rent/Util/Phone	6500	6500	6200	6900	
12	Depreciation	2200	2000	1800	1600	
13	Taxes	2500	4500	3500	3500	
14						
15		34800	33400	34340	37695	
16						
17						
18						

Ready

Fig. 2.12.

Removing the grid lines.

The worksheet no longer displays the grid but is instead a clean slate showing the numbers. Now follow the next several steps to apply other formatting features to the data:

1. Highlight the block B3:E3 by clicking on cell B3 and dragging to cell F3

2. Select the Border command from the Format menu.

3. Click in the box beside the Outline option; doing so places a check mark in the box. Press Return. The highlighted block should now have a border around it, as shown in figure 2.13. (Press the down-arrow key to remove the highlight so that you can see the border more clearly.)

Fig. 2.13.

Applying a border to a block of cells.

| | File | Edit | Formula | Format | Data | Options | Macro | Window |

| B19 | | |

EXPENSES

	A	B	C	D	E	F
1			Expenses			
2						
3		First Q	Second Q	Third Q	Fourth Q	
4	Salaries	5000	2300	3500	4500	
5	Professional Svcs	600	600	650	650	
6	Advertising	9000	9000	9000	9000	
7	Bank	200	200	200	245	
8	Freight	5000	4500	5690	7500	
9	Insurance	3500	3500	3500	3500	
10	Office Supplies	300	300	300	300	
11	Rent/Util/Phone	6500	6500	6200	6900	
12	Depreciation	2200	2000	1800	1600	
13	Taxes	2500	4500	3500	3500	
14						
15		34800	33400	34340	37695	
16						
17						
18						

Ready

4. Highlight the range B14:E14, using the mouse.

5. Select the Border command from the Format menu.

6. Click on the boxes beside the Top and Bottom options; doing so places a check mark in both boxes. Press Return.

7. Select the Row Height command from the Format menu.

8. Type the number **6** to replace the number currently used for the row height. Press Return. The screen should look like figure 2.14.

File   Edit   Formula   Format   Data   Options   Macro   Window

| B21 | |

EXPENSES

	A	B	C	D	E	F
1			Expenses			
2						
3		First Q	Second Q	Third Q	Fourth Q	
4	Salaries	5000	2300	3500	4500	
5	Professional Svcs	600	600	650	650	
6	Advertising	9000	9000	9000	9000	
7	Bank	200	200	200	245	
8	Freight	5000	4500	5690	7500	
9	Insurance	3500	3500	3500	3500	
10	Office Supplies	300	300	300	300	
11	Rent/Util/Phone	6500	6500	6200	6900	
12	Depreciation	2200	2000	1800	1600	
13	Taxes	2500	4500	3500	3500	
15		34800	33400	34340	37695	
16						
17						
18						

Ready

Fig. 2.14.

The worksheet after more formatting.

You achieved the effect of a double line above the totals by adding top and bottom borders to the row above the totals and by then shrinking the height of that row. The row is merely an aesthetic addition to the worksheet. The final formatting procedure is to add dollar signs, two decimal places, and commas to the totals in row 15. Complete these steps:

1. Highlight the range B15:E15, using the mouse.
2. Select the Number option from the Format menu. The dialog box shown in figure 2.15 should appear.
3. Click on the sixth format option: $#,##0 ;($#,##0). Then press Return.

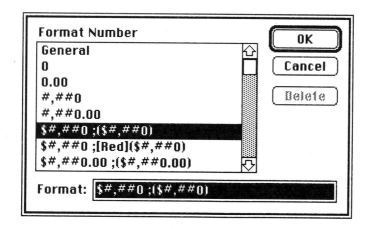

Format Number

OK
Cancel
Delete

General
0
0.00
#,##0
#,##0.00
$#,##0 ;($#,##0)
$#,##0 ;[Red]($#,##0)
$#,##0.00 ;($#,##0.00)

Format: $#,##0 ;($#,##0)

Fig. 2.15.

The Format Number dialog box.

The number format you chose displays the totals with dollar signs, two decimal places, and commas. The worksheet should now look like figure 2.16.

	File Edit Formula Format Data Options Macro Window					
B21						

☰☰☰ EXPENSES ☰☰☰

	A	B	C	D	E	F
1			**Expenses**			
2						
3		**First Q**	**Second Q**	**Third Q**	**Fourth Q**	
4	Salaries	5000	2300	3500	4500	
5	Professional Svcs	600	600	650	650	
6	Advertising	9000	9000	9000	9000	
7	Bank	200	200	200	245	
8	Freight	5000	4500	5690	7500	
9	Insurance	3500	3500	3500	3500	
10	Office Supplies	300	300	300	300	
11	Rent/Util/Phone	6500	6500	6200	6900	
12	Depreciation	2200	2000	1800	1600	
13	Taxes	2500	4500	3500	3500	
15		$34,800	$33,400	$34,340	$37,695	
16						
17						
18						
19						

Saving the Worksheet Again

Save your work by selecting the Save option from the File menu. Because you have saved the work before, Excel will save the new changes over the old version. (If you had not saved the work before, you would see a dialog box that you can use to name the worksheet.) It's a good idea to save your work periodically.

Printing the Worksheet

Because this Quick Start worksheet is small—taking up only one screen—printing it is easy. When you build large worksheets that take more than one page to print, you'll need to use some of the printing commands and techniques described in Chapter 9. To print the Quick Start worksheet, simply do the following:

Select the Print option from the File menu.

The Print Options dialog box appears. Make sure that it matches one of the examples in figures 2.17 and 2.18. Also, be sure that your printer is hooked up properly and that you have selected it with the Chooser.

ImageWriter	v2.7		OK
Quality:	◯ Best	◉ Faster ◯ Draft	
Page Range:	◉ All	◯ From: [ ] To: [ ]	Cancel
Copies:	1		
Paper Feed:	◉ Automatic ◯ Hand Feed		
☐ Page Preview	☐ Print Using Color		
┌Print───────────────────			
◉ Sheet	◯ Notes	◯ Both	

Fig. 2.17.

The Print Options dialog box for the ImageWriter.

LaserWriter "LaserWriter"	5.2		OK
Copies: [1]	Pages: ◉ All ◯ From: [ ] To: [ ]		Cancel
Cover Page:	◉ No ◯ First Page ◯ Last Page		Help
Paper Source: ◉ Paper Cassette ◯ Manual Feed			
☐ Page Preview	☐ Print Using Color		
┌Print───────────────────			
◉ Sheet	◯ Notes	◯ Both	

Fig. 2.18.

The Print Options dialog box for the LaserWriter.

To use the Chooser, select the Chooser accessory from the Apple menu (at the far left of the menu bar). In the dialog box that appears, click on the icon representing your printer. Then press Return. This is the standard way of selecting an output device for most Macintosh applications.

Depending on the printer you've selected, the File Print command will present a number of options. These print options are discussed in detail in Chapter 9. After making sure that your Print Options dialog box matches one of the corresponding boxes in figures 2.17 and 2.18, click on the OK button to begin printing. Note that you can preview the printout on-screen by checking the Page Preview box.

Summary

In this Quick Start, you set up a basic worksheet to total the quarterly expenses from several products. You learned the basics of entering information and formatting cells, as well as how to enter a formula and copy it to other cells. To become proficient in Excel, learn more about formulas and special functions by reading Chapters 3, "Creating an Excel Worksheet," and 5, "Formatting the Worksheet." And be sure to save this worksheet so that you can build on it in the next Quick Start chapter (Chapter 10).

3

Creating an
Excel Worksheet

In this chapter you learn the basics of creating and using an Excel worksheet. Although worksheets span a variety of tasks, most people use them for business analysis and management, developing worksheets for budgets, projections, inventory tracking, expense tracking, sales statistics, and so on. This chapter gets you off to a good start in creating and evaluating this type of numeric information.

The chapter begins with instructions for opening files and saving them for future use. You will then learn about the three types of information you can enter into worksheet cells: text, numbers, and formulas. Also in this chapter are details about such subjects as moving around inside the worksheet, selecting information, and applying names to groups (or ranges) of data. By the end of this chapter, you will be able to create a worksheet for almost any basic task, and you will be comfortable with many of Excel's menu commands and options. After covering these basics, you will be ready for Chapter 4's details about editing existing worksheets.

Opening and Saving Worksheets

If you have started Excel by clicking on the program icon, you have a new, blank worksheet in view. The rest of this chapter shows you how to turn that blank worksheet into a meaningful file. As you proceed through the chapter, you'll need to know how to save and retrieve your sample files. Commands for saving and opening files are located in the File menu and resemble file-saving and -opening commands in most other Macintosh programs.

To save a file, select the Save command from the File menu. You can save a file at any time. If your file does not already have a name, Excel will ask you to name the file before the program saves it to disk. You can enter any name and specify the folder in which Excel will store the document. If the file already has a name, Excel will save the file under the same name. This procedure consists of replacing an old copy on disk with the new copy.

To save a file under a different name, select the Save As command from the File menu. This command brings up the dialog box shown in figure 3.1. Excel's Save As dialog box is similar to that found in most Macintosh applications but, in addition, provides the Options button.

Fig. 3.1.

The Save As dialog box.

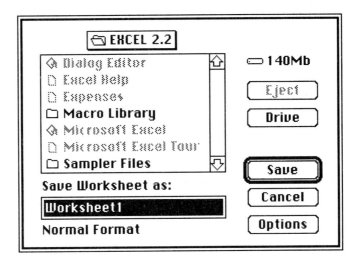

To open an existing file from within Excel, select the Open command from the File menu; then select the file from the list. If the file you choose is a text file, you can click on the Text button to open the file and to specify whether Excel is to use comma or tab delimiters in it. See the following section for details about this button and its options.

Other commands to note here include File New and File Close. The File New command opens a new, blank worksheet from within Excel. You can issue this command at any time, even when another worksheet is currently in view. The File Close command is equivalent to clicking in a window's close box, an action that removes the worksheet from view. If you issue the File Close command and have made changes since last saving the worksheet, Excel asks whether you would like to save the file before closing.

Using DIF, Text, and Other File Formats

Excel can save and retrieve files in a number of formats other than Excel worksheet files. As for reading other programs' files, there is little you can do in Excel to help the process; the trick is to save the file (using the original program) in a format that Excel will read. Similarly, if you plan to use an Excel file in some other program, use one of the formats that Excel makes available. Excel reads and writes to the following formats:

Normal	CSV
SYLK	Lotus 1-2-3
Text	dBASE
DIF	

With any of the program formats, the result will be accurate only to the degree that Excel is able to convert its data to the specified format. To read one of these files requires only that you open it by selecting the Open command from the File menu. To save an Excel worksheet in one of these formats, use the Save As command, specify the file name you want, and then click on the Options button. The dialog box in figure 3.2 appears.

File Format
- ◉ Normal ○ SYLK/Excel 1.5 ○ DIF
- ○ Text ○ WKS ○ DBF 2
- ○ CSU ○ WK1 ○ DBF 3

OK Cancel

Password: [ ]

☐ Create Backup File

Fig. 3.2.

The Save As Options dialog box.

Click on the button next to the file type you want to specify. The following are brief explanations of the file types supported by Excel for opening and saving files.

Normal

Normal is the standard Excel 2.2 file type. You do not have to select this option unless you have previously saved the file as a different type; this option is the default.

DIF

DIF (data-interchange format) is a longtime standard format for spreadsheet documents. DIF retains the row and column structure of data so that a file translated from DIF to another format will have data in the correct cells. Unfortunately, DIF files do not retain any worksheet formulas or formats. Thus bringing a DIF file into Excel will never create a calculation problem, because there are no formulas to translate. Use DIF files only if no better format in which to save the data is available.

Text

ASCII, or text, files are similar to DIF files but don't always contain the row and column structure. ASCII is most often used for word processor documents that do not contain rows and columns. However, Macintosh ASCII files commonly use a *tab-delimited* format. Tab-delimited ASCII files have tab characters between the columns of data, and carriage-return characters between the rows. The result is very much like DIF files. The advantage of using ASCII over DIF is that files other than worksheets can be saved this way. You can save a database file in tab-delimited ASCII format, for example, and read it into Excel. The result is an Excel worksheet in which rows of information equate to the records in the database and in which columns contain the fields. Likewise, an Excel file saved as text can be read by nonspreadsheet programs (for example, databases) with reasonable success.

The standard Macintosh Cut and Paste commands preserve the tab-delimited nature of data. For example, if you create a table in Microsoft® Word by using the Tab key between each column and by using the Return key between each row, you can copy the information and paste it directly into Excel. The word processor document might look like figure 3.3.

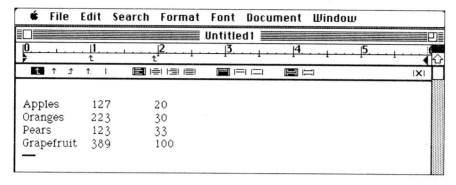

Fig. 3.3.

Tab-delimited columns in a word processor document.

Using the standard Copy command, you can temporarily store this information on the Macintosh clipboard in tab-delimited format. When you switch to Excel and use the Paste command, the information will retain its structure, as shown in figure 3.4.

Fig. 3.4.

Moving word processing data into Excel.

Similarly, you can move data from Excel to another program, retaining the tab-delimited nature of the data. See Chapter 4 for more information about the Copy and Paste commands.

CSV

CSV stands for comma-separated values. This format is identical to the text format except that in CSV, Excel uses commas to separate the columns of information. CSV (also called comma-delimited format) has been a standard data-translation format for years.

When you use this format, data coming from another program or computer should use commas to separate individual items or fields, and carriage returns to separate rows or records. When you open a file that uses this format, Excel removes the commas and places each piece of information into a separate cell.

SYLK

SYLK files are similar to DIF files in that both apply specifically to worksheets. SYLK files, however, include enough information for Excel to re-create the formulas from the original worksheet. The translated result is a fully operational worksheet. Different spreadsheet programs, however, contain different sets of commands. Excel 2.2 has introduced many commands that are not available in other spreadsheets (including earlier versions of Excel), and some spreadsheets have commands not supported in Excel. When Excel tries to translate an unsupported formula from an SYLK file, the program will turn the formula into a text string. Often, you can translate these formulas yourself. Use the SYLK format when your file will be used by an earlier version of Excel or by another spreadsheet.

1-2-3

Excel recognizes Lotus 1-2-3 files and translates formulas directly into Excel equivalents. The 1-2-3 formats WK1 and WKS are available. Some formulas do not have direct equivalents and will appear as text cells. 1-2-3 macros also will appear as text cells. To get a 1-2-3 file from a PC to a Macintosh disk requires a translation program, such as the Apple File Exchange, and a Macintosh disk drive capable of reading PC disks, such as the Apple Super Drive. (This drive comes standard with some Macintosh configurations.) After translating the file into a Macintosh file, Excel will read it and convert it to an Excel worksheet file. You also can save Excel files as 1-2-3 files and translate them into 1-2-3.

dBASE

Excel can write to a dBASE format by using either the DBF 2 or the DBF 3 option. DBF 2 can be read by dBASE II; DBF 3 can be read by dBASE III.

Protecting Your Files with Passwords

Another option available for Excel files is the use of a password. When you use the Save As command and click on the Options button, Excel gives you the opportunity to specify a password. If you enter a password into the space provided, Excel will require this password before the file can be opened. Using this feature is an excellent way to protect sensitive files from being viewed.

When you open a password-protected file, Excel presents the message shown in figure 3.5. Simply enter the password into the space provided and press Return. If the password is correct, the file will open, and all Excel commands and options will be available. If the password is incorrect, Excel will not open the file. Be sure to enter the password in its original capitalization. If the password is *Open Sesame*, for example, you cannot gain access by entering *open sesame*.

```
┌──────────────────────────────────────────────┐
│  'TEST FILE' is protected.      ╭────────────╮ │
│                                 │     OK     │ │
│  Password: ┌──────────────────┐ ╰────────────╯ │
│            └──────────────────┘ ┌────────────┐ │
│                                 │   Cancel   │ │
│                                 └────────────┘ │
└──────────────────────────────────────────────┘
```

Fig. 3.5.

The password-entry dialog box.

Caution: If you forget the password, there is no way to recover it. This problem can be serious if you need to change information that is protected. Be sure to write the password down and store it in a safe place or to keep a duplicate, unprotected copy of the file.

Making Backup Copies of Worksheets

You can make a backup of your worksheet files, using the File Save As command after using the File Save command. When you select File Save As, simply enter a new name for the file, and Excel will store the file on disk under the new name. Of course, the original file will still exist under the original name. Be sure to double-check which file you are using at any given time by looking in the title bar of the worksheet window.

Another way to back up your worksheet files is to use Excel's automatic backup feature. This feature creates a backup copy of the file each time you save it. Simply choose the File Save As command and then click on the Options button in the Save As dialog box. Finally, check the box marked Create Backup File and press Return.

Excel creates (or updates) the backup file each time you save the worksheet. The backup file is called "Backup of [*filename*]" and contains a copy of the most recently saved version of the file.

Entering Data

The first thing to know about creating worksheets is how to enter information. You can enter information into an Excel worksheet by simply moving the pointer to a cell and typing what you want the cell to contain. When you press Tab, Return, or Enter or use one of the arrow keys, the information will be "accepted" by the worksheet and will appear in the cell. Clicking on another cell is another method of accepting the entry.

Like all spreadsheets, Excel differentiates between two main types of information: labels (text) and values (numbers). If you type text into a cell, you are entering a label; if you type a number, you are entering a value. You also can get labels and values into cells, however, by calculating them with formulas. Thus you can enter three types of information into worksheet cells: text, numbers, and formulas.

 Remember that the numeric keypad toggles between directional keys and numeric keys. See Chapter 1 for a complete discussion of the Macintosh keyboard.

As you enter data into a cell (but before you accept the data), you can change the entry by using the Backspace key to erase characters to the left of the cursor. Using the Option key along with the arrow keys also moves the cursor within the text. Once data is accepted, however, you must either retype the entire contents of the cell or use the editing commands described in Chapter 4 to change the entry. If you return to a cell that contains information and begin typing new information, the new data will replace the old as soon as you accept it by using Tab, Return, Enter, or one of the arrow keys. You can also accept entries by using the enter box. If you use the cancel box, the new information will not replace the old but will be thrown out. Another way to reject the entry is to press Command and the period (.) key at the same time. The following is a summary:

To accept an entry, use...	*To reject an entry, use...*
Enter box	Cancel box
Tab	Command+.
Shift+Tab	
Arrows	
Return	
Enter	
Shift+Return	

Entering Text

Text consists of worksheet labels, such as column headings, titles, and descriptions. A text label can consist of up to 255 characters (the maximum allowed by the formula bar). Simply enter the text you want, and use one of the "accept entry" commands listed in the preceding section. A label too large to fit into one cell will spill into the next cell if that cell does not already contain information (see fig. 3.6). This effect is merely visual: the text is contained entirely by the original cell. If the adjacent cell contains information, the cell containing the label will show only what will fit in the current cell width (see fig. 3.7).

File	**Edit**	**Formula**	**Format**	**Data**	**Options**	**Macro**	**Window**

A13

=============== **Worksheet1** ===============

	A	B	C	D	E	F
1						
2						
3						
4	Salaries					
5	Professional Services					
6	Advertising					
7						

Fig. 3.6.

Text spilling over to the next cell.

File	**Edit**	**Formula**	**Format**	**Data**	**Options**	**Macro**	**Window**

B16

=============== **Worksheet1** ===============

	A	B	C	D	E	F
1						
2						
3						
4	Salaries	2300				
5	Professional Se	600				
6	Advertising	9000				
7						

Fig. 3.7.

Text cut off by the contents of the next cell.

Anything you type into a cell that does not begin with a number, minus sign, plus sign, decimal point (period), or equal sign is a label. Additionally, if you begin by typing a number and then include text, the information is recognized by Excel as a label. The following are examples of labels:

First Quarter

January 1989

45 Green

The quick brown fox jumps over the lazy dog

Occasionally you'll want to type numeric information but have it appear as a label. Code numbers or years commonly fall into this category. To enter a number as a label, be sure to type an equal sign and then surround the text with quotation marks. For example, to enter 1989 as a label instead of a number, type **="1989"**.

Labels are automatically aligned with the left side of the cell, numbers with the right. You'll know that a cell's contents are a label if they appear on the left side of the cell. (You can change the alignment of information by using the special formatting commands described in Chapter 5.)

Changing the Column Width

To increase or decrease the width of a column, position the pointer on any cell in the column whose width you want to change. Next, select the Column Width command from the Format menu. In the space marked Column Width, enter the number of characters you would like the column to display; then press Return. The actual width that corresponds to this number varies, depending on the active font. For more information on column width changes, see Chapter 5.

If the cell is too narrow to display the information in it, you can widen the column so that more information appears. How to change column widths is explained in detail in Chapter 5.

Entering Numbers

The second type of information you can enter into a cell is numbers. Numbers can begin with the characters - (hyphen), $ (dollar sign), + (plus), . (period), and ((left parenthesis) and can contain only numerals, the decimal point, and the characters) (right parenthesis), % (percent sign), $, (, +, and -. Including any other character turns the number into a label. The following are some acceptable number entries and their results:

Entry	Excel displays...
-349	-349
(349)	-349
35	35
23,200	23200
$40.23	$40.23
12%	12%*

*The actual value stored for percentages is the decimal equivalent—in this case, .12.

If entered properly, a number can be calculated with any other number in the worksheet. This capability is the primary value of a worksheet. See Chapter 5 for more information about adding special symbols (such as $ and %) to numbers and setting decimal places.

 Excel uses up to 14 digits when calculating numbers. The ROUND function, described in Chapter 6, enables you to control the number of digits used in calculations.

Entering Dates and Times

In Excel, dates are simply real numbers displayed in date formats. These real numbers represent the number of days elapsed since January 1, 1904. For example, the date January 2, 1904, is really just the number 1 shown as a date. Excel "thinks" that a cell containing the entry January 2, 1904, holds the value 1. Any number can be formatted as a date—even if it's not meant to be a date—because any number can represent days elapsed since 01/01/04. Of course, these date numbers (also called *serial numbers*) can be formatted as numbers instead of dates. In short, formatting a number as a date is for your benefit; Excel considers dates numbers no matter how they are formatted. If you intend to enter a date, however, it's best to choose one of the formats that Excel automatically recognizes (shown later). Because dates are just numbers, you can perform calculations with them (such as subtracting one date from another to determine the number of days elapsed).

Excel tries to act intelligently when you enter dates. If you enter what Excel considers a date, the program will interpret what you've typed and choose an appropriate format for the information. The format makes the date appear as a date rather than a label or a number. The following are examples of acceptable ways to enter dates in Excel:

Entry	*Excel displays...*
1/23/89	1/23/89
1-89	1/1/89
23-1-89	23-Jan-89
23 Jan 89	23-Jan-89
23 January 89	23-Jan-89
Jan-89	Jan-89
January-89	Jan-89

These are not the only date formats available; they are simply the ones that Excel recognizes as dates without your having to use the Format command to format the date manually. You could, for example, get the same result by entering the number 31069 into a cell and then formatting the cell with one of the date formats offered. (Date formats are discussed in Chapter 4.) But because it's unlikely that you will know a date by its serial number, the preceding list of entries is more useful.

Note that the cell containing one of these dates has an actual value of 31069—even though the entry appears to be a date. This value is the serial number for the date January 23, 1989.

One final way to enter a date into the worksheet is to use the special key combination Command+- (hyphen). Doing so enters the current date into the cell. The current date comes from the Macintosh internal clock.

Time entries, like dates, are recognized by Excel and formatted appropriately. You can enter time entries in any of the following ways:

Entry	Excel displays...
15:35	15:35
4:35*	4:35
4:35:15	4:35:15
15:35:15	15:35:15
4:35 pm	4:35 PM
4:35 am	4:35 AM

*If you enter a time value that is less than 12 but do not specify a.m. or p.m., Excel assumes a.m., according to the 24-hour format.

If you use the 12-hour format, it's best to include the a.m. or p.m. designation (which Excel displays in capital letters without periods). Notice that you can include seconds in the time entry. Like dates, times are numeric values. The actual time value is the number of milliseconds passed since 12 midnight. Thus the time 12:00:01 is the value 0.00001 formatted as a time entry. Any decimal number can be formatted as a time entry, but you're better off using the formats recognized by Excel as times. For example, if you enter the number .125414, then format it as a time, you'll get the result 3:00:36 AM.

Another way to enter a time into the worksheet is to press Command+; (semicolon). Doing so enters the current time into the cell. This time comes from the Macintosh internal clock.

Entering Formulas

The real power of a worksheet is its capability to use formulas that calculate values by using other information in the worksheet. When designing a worksheet, you will use a combination of labels, numbers, and formulas. Because formulas generally refer not to information in the worksheet but to cell locations where the information can be found, you can alter the information in the locations referenced, and the formulas will automatically recalculate the results, using your changes.

Formulas can be simple or complex, but their purpose is to allow changes to the information in the worksheet. The simplest kind of formula reference is a single cell location, as in the following:

=A5

This formula means, "Make the value of this cell equal to that of cell A5." The formula can appear in any cell other than A5, and that other cell will hold the exact value as cell A5, whether A5 contains a number, a label, or another formula. Note that the formula begins with an equal sign, which designates the information as a formula. All formulas must begin with an equal sign. If you entered the A5 without the sign, Excel would assume that you are typing a label.

 The value of a cell is the number or text that appears in the cell. If a cell contains a formula, the value is the result of the formula.

A variation on the formula =A5 is this:

=A5+10

This formula means, "Make the value of this cell equal to the sum of cell A5 and 10." If A5 contains the number 25, the result is 35. The cell reference A5 is called a *variable* because its value can vary, and the formula will adjust accordingly. The number 10 in this example is called a *constant* because it is part of the formula itself and remains constant. You can add constant numbers directly into a cell. For example, you can type the following formula into a cell:

=25+10

This formula provides the same result of 35 but is not based on variable information in cell A5. Such a formula defeats the purpose of the worksheet. With the reference to cell A5, you can enter any number into A5, and the result will change.

You cannot mix text and numbers in a formula (unless you use special functions discussed in Chapter 6); you would get the error message #Value if cell A5 in the formula =A5+10 contained text. However, as you saw earlier, you can refer to a cell that contains text, provided that you use a simple cell reference. For example, the formula =A5 returns whatever is in cell A5, even if it's text.

You can enter cell references within formulas in one of two ways: by typing the references or by using the pointer. To type the entire formula, including cell references, you simply enter every keystroke needed. For example, to enter the formula =A5, you can move to a cell; type an equal sign (=), **A**, and **5**; and then press Return to accept the entry. Another method is to type the equal sign and then "point" to cell A5 by using the mouse (that is, click on cell A5); finish by pressing Return. The value of using the pointing method is that if you don't know which cell you need to refer to, you can use the mouse to scroll to the cell you want and then point to it. To practice with the pointing method, try adding some cells in a column. Suppose that you want the formula in cell A5 of a sample worksheet to read =A1+A2+A3+A4, as in figure 3.8.

Fig. 3.8.

A formula that adds the numbers in a column.

🍎 File	Edit	Formula	Format	Data	Options	Macro	Window

| A5 | | =A1+A2+A3+A4 |

Worksheet1

	A	B	C	D	E	F	
1	34						
2	45						
3	25						
4	66						
5	170						
6							

Rather than type the formula directly into the cell, you can use the pointing method. Begin with the pointer on cell A5 and type the equal sign. Now use the mouse to click on each of the four cells A1, A2, A3, and A4 in sequence. Press Return. Notice that Excel automatically assumes that you are adding the cells and places the plus signs into the formula. You can control the use of operators by entering one from the keyboard before you select the cell that should follow it. (Operators, discussed in more detail in the following section, are instructions—such as a plus sign or minus sign—that appear in formulas.) For example, you can enter the equal sign to begin, click on cell A1, type the operator you want (a minus sign, perhaps), click on cell A2, and so on. Excel enters a plus sign only when you have not entered another operator.

Another way to point to cells is to use the arrow keys on the keyboard instead of using the mouse. When you use the arrow keys, the operator must be entered between each reference, even for addition. For example, you can enter the formula =A1+A2 by typing the equal sign and then using the arrow keys to move the pointer to cell A1 and then typing a plus sign. Finally, use arrows to move to cell A2 and press Enter.

Using Operators

Operators are symbols that represent mathematical processes. A plus sign stands for addition, a minus sign for subtraction, and so on. Formulas depend on operators in order to work, and Excel provides several types of operators: arithmetic, text, comparison, and relational.

Arithmetic Operators

Arithmetic operators perform basic mathematical tasks with numbers. The following is a list of Excel's arithmetic operators:

Operator		Example	Result
+	(addition)	=4+3	5
−	(subtraction)	=4-3	1
−	(negation)	-8	-8
/	(division)	9/3	3
*	(multiplication)	2*2	4
^	(exponentiation)	3^2	9
%	(percentage)	12%	.12

You can use these operators with constant numbers, special functions, or cell references, as in the following examples (the functions are explained in Chapter 6):

```
=-A1
=25+10
=25+A1
=A5+A1
=A5+SUM(A1:A4)
=SUM(A1:A4)+SUM(B1:B4)
```

The Text Operator

Excel provides only one text operator: the ampersand (&). This operator joins one piece of text (that is, a label) to another. The process of adding labels is known as *concatenation*.

Like most operators, the ampersand can work between specific pieces of text, cell references, or special functions, as in the following examples:

```
="Red"&"Wine"
="Red"&A5
=A5&B5
=A5&LEFT(B5,4)        (LEFT is explained in Chapter 6.)
```

Note that when entering text directly into a formula, you must surround the text with quotation marks. You can concatenate numbers along with text, or numbers with other numbers, as in the following examples:

="Rams"&17	produces *Rams17*
=19&A5	produces *1989* (where A5 contains 89)

When using concatenation, keep an eye on spacing requirements. To include a space between words, you must include that space either as part of the concatenated text or as a separate piece of text concatenated with the rest. Consider these examples:

="Red"&"Wine"	produces *RedWine*
="Red "&"Wine"	produces *Red Wine*
="Red"&" "&"Wine"	produces *Red Wine*
="Red"&" Wine"	produces *Red Wine*

Notice that the second example includes an extra space after the word *Red*. The third example includes an extra space within a set of parentheses between the two words *Red* and *Wine*. The fourth example includes a space in front of the word *Wine*.

Comparison Operators

Comparison operators test the relationship between two pieces of information (numbers, text, or formulas) and return an answer of TRUE or FALSE, using the results of the test as a basis. For example, the formula

   =A5>B5

uses the comparison operator > and means, "Is the value of cell A5 greater than the value of cell B5?" Depending on the values, the result will be either FALSE (or no) or TRUE (or yes). Excel provides the following relational operators:

Operator		Example	Result
=	(equal to)	=5=3	FALSE
>	(greater than)	=5>3	TRUE
<	(less than)	=5<3	FALSE
>=	(greater than or equal to)	=5>=3	TRUE
<=	(less than or equal to)	=5<=3	FALSE
<>	(not equal to)	=5<>3	TRUE

These operators can work between text, numbers, cell references, functions, or any combination thereof. When comparing text with something else, Excel uses the text's ASCII value, which is also the alphabetical value (in order from A to Z). ASCII always gives text a lower value than numbers, so a comparison of text to numbers always shows the text as "less than" the number. Few reasons come up for comparing text with numbers, however.

Reference Operators

Excel uses three other operators, which relate to the specification of ranges. These operators are used to combine references, creating a new reference from the combination. The exact uses for these operators will become clear as you progress through this book. The following is a list:

Operator	Example	References
: (range)	A1:A5	A1:A5
, (union)	A1:A5,B1:B5	A1:A5,B1:B5
Space (intersection)	A1:A5 A4:G4	A4

These operators are used when Excel expects a range reference. The union operator combines references into a single, multiple-area range. The intersection operator specifies only those cells that are common to the two (or more) referenced ranges.

Understanding the Order of Operations

When you combine various operators in worksheet formulas, you may need to specify the order of operations. An incorrectly specified order can result in incorrect values. First, keep in mind that operations have a natural order as prescribed by algebraic logic. That order is as follows (from highest to lowest priority):

1. Range (:)
2. Intersection (Space)
3. Union (,)
4. Negative and Positive (-,+)
5. Percentage (%)
6. Exponentiation (^)
7. Multiplication and division (*,/)
8. Addition and subtraction (+, -)
9. Concatenation (&)
10. Relations (=, >, <, <>, <=, >=)

When two operations of the same priority occur in the same formula, Excel evaluates them from left to right. Consider this formula:

=A5*2-B25/A5+3

If A5 contains 3 and B25 contains 6, the formula means the following:

3*2-6/3+3

Because multiplication and division are performed before subtraction and addition, the formula evaluates to this:

(3*2)-(6/3)+3   *or*   6-2+3

Performing the subtraction and addition operations from left to right, Excel provides this result:

(6-2)+3   *or*   4+3   *or*   7

You can use parentheses in the initial formula to change the natural order of operations. Suppose that you change the formula

A5*2-B25/A5+3

to the following (where A5 contains 3 and B25 contains 6):

A5*((2-B25)/A5)+3

The new formula evaluates to this:

3*((2-6)/3)+3   *or*   3*(-4/3)+3   *or*   3*-1.3333+3   *or*   -4+3   *or*   -1

Using Worksheet Functions

By combining various operators and cell references, you can design formulas for many tasks. For example, you can add the numbers in a column with a formula like this:

=A5+A6+A7+A8+A9

Creating such a formula can be tedious, however. Adding a dozen or more cells in a range requires a lot of typing or pointing. This is where Excel's worksheet functions come into action. A *worksheet function* is a special command that you can put into a formula to handle common mathematical operations, such as adding numbers in a column or getting the average of a series of numbers. The worksheet functions serve two purposes: they simplify the work involved in complex formulas, and they provide new types of logic that are not available through the basic arithmetic, comparison, or text operators. The formula that adds five cells in a column can be expressed with a function like this:

=SUM(A5:A9)

Besides offering a host of mathematical functions, such as SUM, Excel provides functions for business calculations, database functions, date-time functions, decision-making functions, and so on. There is no trick to using worksheet functions, and you probably don't need to learn all of them. But a good knowledge of functions will take you a long way in Excel. See Chapter 6 for a complete explanation and listing of the Excel worksheet functions.

Working with Complex Formulas

You have already seen how formulas can become rather complex through the inclusion of various operators and cell references. In addition to using operators and cell references, you can *nest* formulas inside one another, using parentheses to order the operations. You can increase the performance of your worksheets by learning the basics of nesting and combining formulas.

The simple cell reference gets information from another cell. Cell references are often used in formulas, as in this formula entered into cell C7:

=C5-C6

This formula means, "Subtract the value in cell C6 from the value in cell C5." If cell C5 contains the value 125, and cell C6 contains the value 100, the result is 25.

But what if C5 and C6 contain formulas that produce the values 125 and 100, respectively? Suppose that cells C5 and C6 contain these formulas:

C5: =A5*B5
C6: =A6*B6

In a certain way, cell C7 would be combining two formulas. You could enter either of these formulas into C7 and get the same result:

C7: =C5-C6
C7: =(A5*B5)-(A6*B6)

The second example combines the two formulas from C5 and C6 and makes the formulas in those cells unnecessary. The formula uses parentheses to specify the intended order of operations, although the natural order of operation produces the correct answer in this case. The following example is even more complex. Suppose that cells A5 and A6 have these contents:

A5: =G5<A6
A6: =(R5*S5)-(R6-S6)

Notice that the relational formula in A5 contains a reference to cell A6. You could substitute cell A5's reference to cell A6 with the formula actually in that cell, as in the following:

=G5<(R5*S5)-(R6-S6)

Why go to this trouble when both methods produce the same result? Generally, the fewer formulas in a worksheet, the easier it is to read and use. And there is no need to have cells that display various subcalculations within a larger calculation. However, if these complex formulas are confusing and undocumented, they can cause more problems than they solve. One way to document your formulas is to use cell notes that explain what is going on in the cell. Another way is to use named cells and named ranges in place of standard cell addresses and ranges. Naming cells and ranges is described later in this chapter. Cell notes are described in Chapter 8.

Understanding Error Messages

Occasionally Excel presents an error message when you attempt to accept information you've entered into a cell. Error messages are typically due to unacceptable syntax in formulas and functions or to typing errors.

Excel will not allow incorrect entries in cells and will not let you move on until the entry is corrected or erased. Often, the error message explains the problem and even positions the cursor at the location of the problem. Figure 3.9 shows an example of an Excel error message.

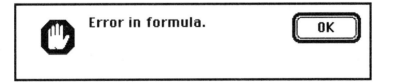

Fig. 3.9.

An error message.

Incomplete Formulas

Accurately designing large, complex formulas can take some time. Your initial attempts may produce errors instead of the result you want. If Excel does not accept your formula, but you want to keep it for future reference, try removing the equal sign that makes the entry a formula; save the entry as a label. Put the equal sign back when you make further attempts.

Understanding Circular Logic

Circular logic is a particular kind of error involving more than one formula. A formula that includes a cell reference depends on the referenced cell for its own value. When two or more cells reference each other in such a way that they all depend on one another for their calculation, you have a *circular reference*. Suppose, for example, that you have two cells with these values:

    A1: =C1
    C1: =A1

These two cells reference each other. It is impossible for either to calculate its value until the other calculates its value: hence a circular reference. Circular references can be hidden within a complex maze of formulas and can be difficult to detect. Fortunately, Excel detects errors of circular logic when you enter them and displays the message shown in figure 3.10.

Fig. 3.10.

A circular-reference error message.

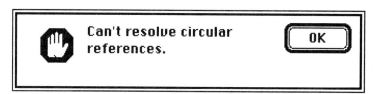

Take a closer look at the references in all cells involved. If you still have trouble finding the circular reference, try using the debugging tools described in Chapter 8.

 Circular logic is not always an error. Some advanced formulas can actually use circular references as part of their logic. Excel **NOTE** informs you of circular references, but you can use them anyway.

Moving around the Worksheet

Now that you know how to enter all kinds of information into the worksheet, you will need to move around to various parts of the worksheet. Because you have more than four million cells at your disposal, it's important to be able to locate any one of them at any time. There are four main tools for locating cells on the worksheet: scroll bars, keyboard commands, the Goto command, and the Find command. This section explains these tools and concludes with a discussion of wild cards, which you can use in specifying search criteria.

Scroll Bars

As in most Macintosh applications, Excel provides scroll bars that you can use to view various parts of the file. The vertical bar scrolls the worksheet up and down relative to the entire worksheet. The horizontal bar scrolls the worksheet left and right. By combining the two movements, you can view any segment of the entire worksheet page.

Scroll bars consist of three main parts, as shown in figure 3.11: the scroll arrows, the bar itself, and the scroll box. Clicking on an arrow scrolls the worksheet slowly in the direction of the arrow. When you click on the bar itself, the worksheet scrolls more quickly (about one screen at a time); the direction of the movement depends on the location of the scroll box relative to where you click on the bar. Click to the left of the box (on the horizontal bar), for example, and the screen moves to the left. Click above the box (on the vertical bar), and the screen moves up.

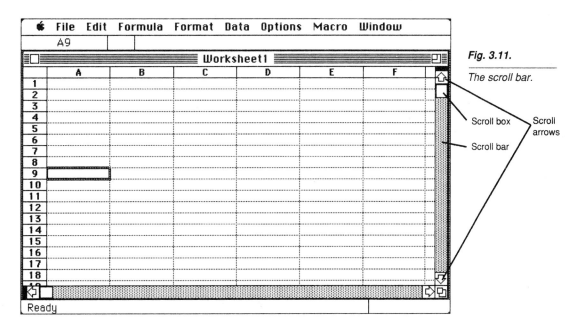

Fig. 3.11.

The scroll bar.

Scroll box

Scroll arrows

Scroll bar

You also can drag the scroll box to various locations on the bar; by doing so, you can move around the worksheet in large jumps. Just click on the box and drag to the new location on the bar; then release the mouse button. The length of the scroll bar represents the entire size of the worksheet, and the position of the scroll box represents the relative position of the screen on the worksheet. As you scroll across or down the worksheet, the screen shows other cells. The scroll bars control the position of the screen "view."

Keyboard Commands

Excel offers a number of keyboard commands for moving the pointer. The most common are the four arrow keys. Tapping an arrow key moves the pointer throughout the worksheet, one cell at a time, in the direction of the arrow. Of course, using arrow keys is not a recommended mode of travel if you need to cover a large distance. But those keys are ideal for moving across the screen when you are entering or editing information. Excel provides the following keys for movement:

Command	*Movement by Cell Pointer*
(Tab⇥)	Right one cell
(⇧Shift)(Tab⇥)	Left one cell
(Return)	Down one cell*
(⇧Shift)(Return)	Up one cell*
(↑)	Up one cell
(⌘)(↑)	To previous nonblank cell in current column
(↓)	Down one cell
(⌘)(↓)	To next nonblank cell in current column
(←)	Left one cell
(⌘)(←)	To previous nonblank cell in current row
(→)	Right one cell
(⌘)(→)	To next nonblank cell in current row
(Home)	To first nonblank cell in current row (first cell in row containing information)
(⌘)(Home)	To cell A1
(End)	To last nonblank cell in current row (last cell in row containing information)
(⌘)(End)	To high cell
(PgUp)	Up one screen

⊞ PgUp	Left one screen
PgDn	Down one screen
⊞ PgDn	Right one screen

*You can modify the Return key so that it does not move the pointer at all but simply accepts information. To do so, select the Options Workspace command and then click in the box marked "Move selection after Return" to remove the check mark. Click on OK when finished.

Remember, if you are not using the extended keyboard, you can press Shift+Clear to toggle between the number keys and the movement keys.

The current row or column is the row or column in which the cursor is currently located—that is, the row or column containing the active cell. When you combine the Command key with the four arrow keys, Excel jumps between blocks of data (a *block* is a group of cells containing data). The pointer will move to the end of the current block or the beginning of the next block, depending on the position of the pointer. Figure 3.12 illustrates this movement.

	A	B	C	D	E	F
1	45.35		35.34		56	34535
2	4.35				46.54	3.45
3	3.45				453	34.53
4	555.43				34.53	345
5	345.43				345345	34.53
6	5.65				4.53	3453
7	324.34					
8	4.53					
9	3.45					
10			34.53	3.45		
11			4.53	345.34		
12			34534.53	34.53		
13						
14						
15					45.45	3424.25
16					65.75	45
17						
18						

Fig. 3.12.

Using the Command key with the arrow keys. The arrows in the figure indicate possible pointer movements.

The *high cell* is the intersection of the last row and column containing information. The high cell does not necessarily contain information itself; it represents the bottom corner of the "used" portion of the worksheet (see fig. 3.13).

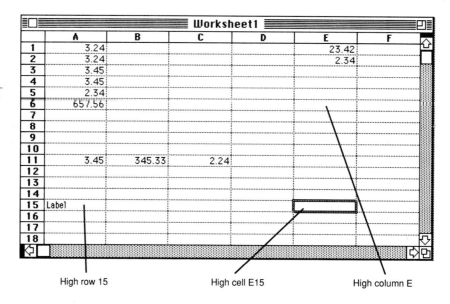

Fig. 3.13.

The high cell is the intersection of the high row and column.

The Goto Command

The Goto command is another way to travel over the worksheet. Issuing this command, which is available from the Formula menu, will move the cell pointer to any cell you specify. If you have the extended keyboard, just press F5 instead of selecting Formula Goto. The procedure is simple:

Issuing the Goto Command

1. Select the command Formula Goto, press F5 on the extended keyboard, or press Command+G for Goto. The dialog box shown in figure 3.14 appears.

2. Enter the cell address you want.

3. Press Return or click on the OK button.

Fig. 3.14.

The Goto dialog box, ready for your entry.

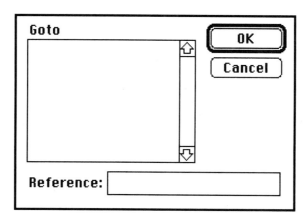

Excel selects the specified cell. Later you will learn how to name specific cells or groups of cells. When cells have names, you can use the Goto command to locate cells or groups of cells by name. See the section "Naming Cells and Ranges" later in this chapter for more details.

The Find Command

Another way to move around the worksheet is to use the Find command, available from the Formula menu. The Find command differs from the Goto command in that it finds specific information in the worksheet. That is, instead of locating cells, Find locates information you've entered into cells. When you select the Find command from the Formula menu, the options shown in figure 3.15 appear.

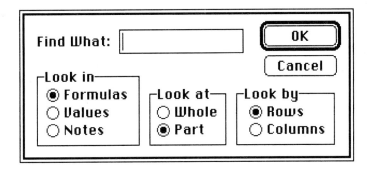

Fig. 3.15.

The Find options.

Enter the information you want to find into the space labeled Find What. This information is called the *criteria*. You can enter any text string, number, or combination thereof. You can also enter function names and cell addresses to be found within formulas. Besides entering this information, you can specify three options.

Look in

This option determines whether Excel will search for the specified information as part of a formula, value, or note. Normally, you'll want to search for a value—the information that appears in the cells of the worksheet, even if that information is the result of a formula. At times, however, you may need to find information that appears in formulas themselves. In such a case, specify the Formulas option.

Suppose that you want to find all references to cell B4 within formulas because, in some cases, you need to change this reference. Using the Find command, you can select the Look in Formulas option and enter B4 as the information to find. Excel will search only formulas for the specified information, not the values of cells or the results of formulas.

Look at

This option determines whether Excel will find the specified information *only* if it appears as a whole word or *even if* it's part of another word. For example, if you enter *Com* and select Look at Whole, Excel will find only the word *Com*, not *Computer*, *Communicate*, or any other word containing *Com*. On the other hand, selecting Look at Part locates all occurrences of *Com*, whether whole words or partial words.

Look by

This option simply determines the direction in which Excel searches: either by rows or by columns. If the information is close to the top of the worksheet, you may want to look by rows to speed up the search. But Excel will find the information in either direction.

When you specify the search information and select from the three special options, Excel begins searching from the current position of the pointer. Cells above and to the left of the pointer will be searched last. Excel thus finds the first occurrence of the specified text following the current row or column. For example, if the pointer is in column G and you search by columns, Excel will begin searching in column H and return to A when it reaches the end of the worksheet (that is, the last column). To search the entire worksheet, move the pointer to cell A1 before using the Find command. If Excel finds an occurrence of the specified information, the program will move the pointer to the cell containing the matching information. You also can search a specific block of information by highlighting the block before selecting the Find command. Excel will not search outside the highlighted block. The following steps summarize how to use the Find procedure:

Using the Find Procedure

1. Position the pointer on cell A1 or at the appropriate location in the worksheet. Alternatively, highlight the block of cells you want to search.

2. Select the command Formula Find.

3. In the space marked Find What, enter the information (or criteria) you want to find.

4. Select one of the three options: Look in, Look at, or Look by.

5. Press Return or click on the OK button to begin the search.

You can also use command keys to repeat the process and find more occurrences. After the first five steps, use the following:

⌘ H   Finds next occurrence

⌘ ⇧Shift H Finds previous occurrence

If you have an extended keyboard, you can use the following keys:

⇧Shift F5   Invokes the Find command (same as selecting Find from the Formula menu).

F7   Finds the next occurrence of the information specified in the Find command.

⇧Shift F7   Finds the previous occurrence of the information.

Wild Cards

The Find command can be quite powerful when you employ wild cards in your search criteria. A *wild card* is a special character that represents other information. You can use the following two wild cards in search criteria:

Wild Card	Purpose
*	Represents any number of characters appearing at the position of the * within the criterion.
	Example: Com*
	The criterion *Com** finds *Communicate*, *Computer*, and *Comm* but not *Com*.
?	Represents any single character appearing at the position of the ? within the criterion.
	Example: Th??
	The criterion *Th??* finds *Them*, *This*, and *That* but not *The*, *Therefore*, or *Th*.

If you use the * character at the end of a string, as shown in the first example, Excel will search for entries that begin with the specified string. If you place the * character at the beginning of a string, Excel will search for entries that end with the specified string.

Selecting Information

Selecting information (groups of cells) is an important part of worksheet manipulation because most commands apply to selected data. Often, you must select data before entering a command. Knowing how to select data efficiently can save you a great deal of time. The following sections discuss the various ways you can select information in Excel.

Selecting Ranges

A *range* is a group of cells in a row, column, or both. Highlighting ranges is a common task. At times, formulas and functions will require you to specify a range of cells. Almost all formatting commands (such as boldface) require that you select a range of cells. And sometimes, highlighting a range is useful when you enter information into the worksheet.

Using the Mouse

To select a range by using the mouse, first click the mouse button on the cell that marks one corner of the range; then drag until the entire range is highlighted. Release the mouse button when finished. You can highlight ranges of any size this way. If you move the mouse beyond the edge of the screen, Excel will scroll over to include more cells.

You can also highlight a range by clicking on the first cell (that is, one corner) and pressing the Shift key while you click on the opposite corner.

Using the Keyboard

If you have an extended keyboard, you can select a range by using a keyboard alternative to the mouse. Simply position the pointer on the first cell of the range, then hold the Shift key down and use any of the following movement keys to create the selection:

Movement Key	Extends selection...
← → ↑ ↓ (numeric keypad)	By one cell in the direction of the arrow
Home	To the beginning of the current row (the first information-containing cell in the current row)
End	To the end of the current row (the last information-containing cell in the current row)
⊞ Home	To the first cell in the worksheet
⊞ End	To the last cell in the worksheet (high cell)
PgUp	By one screen upward
PgDn	By one screen downward
⊞ PgUp	By one screen to the left
⊞ PgDn	By one screen to the right

As you may have noticed, these are the same key commands used for moving the pointer. When combined with the Shift key, these commands become range-selection keys. Here's another keyboard method:

Using F8 To Select a Range

1. Position the pointer on the first cell of the range you want (that is, in the upper left corner).
2. Press F8.
3. Move to the last cell in the range by using the mouse, the arrow keys, or any directional key listed earlier.

This technique has you substitute pressing the F8 key for holding down the Shift key. Pressing and releasing F8 once is like holding down the Shift key down while you select.

Using the Goto Command

A third way to select a range is to use the Goto command. The advantage of using this command is that you can cover a large area in a short time. The steps are these:

Using Goto To Select a Range

1. Position the pointer on the first cell of the range you want (that is, in the upper left corner).

2. Select the Goto command from the Formula menu.

3. Enter the reference of the last cell of the desired range.

4. Hold down the Shift key and press Return (or click on the OK button).

Another way to select a range of cells by using Goto is to choose, from any cell location, the Goto command from the Formula menu. Then, in the space provided, enter the name of the range you want to select. Unless you've named the range ahead of time, using the Range Name options, this name should be the references of the upper left corner and lower right corner, separated by a colon. For example, enter **A1:D10** into the dialog box, as shown in figure 3.16, to highlight the corresponding range. For more information about naming ranges, see "Naming Cells and Ranges" later in this chapter.

Fig. 3.16.

The range reference A1:D10.

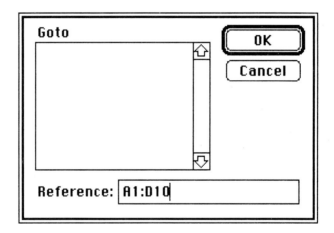

Be sure to include a colon between the cell references. After entering the range, press Return; Excel will highlight the block you specified.

Moving the Cell Pointer within a Selected Range

When you highlight a range of cells through one of these methods, the pointer will move from cell to cell within the range when you press any of the standard movement keys: arrows, Tab, Shift+Tab, Return, Enter, and so on. In other words, the pointer stays within the selected range. Try highlighting the block shown in figure 3.17; then experiment with pressing the various keys and watch the pointer.

🍎 File Edit Formula Format Data Options Macro Window						

| B5 | | January | | | | |

▤☐▤		Worksheet1				
	A	B	C	D	E	F
1						
2						
3						
4						
5		January	February	March		
6		3877	6765	6678		
7		6556	5565	678		
8		6546	566	865		
9		876	8766	6787		
10						
11						

Fig. 3.17.

Highlighting a block.

Selecting More than One Range

You can highlight more than one range at a time. This capability is useful when you need to format worksheet information or apply certain commands to noncontiguous blocks of information. There are several methods for highlighting multiple ranges. For example, after highlighting one range, you can add a second and subsequent ranges by holding down the Command key and selecting another range. To use this method, complete the following steps:

1. Highlight the first range, using any method described earlier.
2. Hold down the Command key.
3. Click on the first cell of the next range; then drag to the last cell in that range.
4. Release the mouse button and the Command key.

Highlighting Multiple Ranges, Using the Command Key

To highlight multiple ranges by using the keyboard, follow these steps:

1. Highlight the first range, using any method described earlier.
2. Press Shift+F8.
3. Highlight the second range, using any method described earlier.

Highlighting Multiple Ranges, Using Shift+F8

To highlight multiple ranges by using the Goto command, follow these steps:

1. Select the Goto command from the Formula menu.
2. Enter two or more ranges into the space provided. Separate each range with a comma. For example, to highlight the range A1:A10 and the range G5:H6 at the same time, enter the following into the Goto dialog box: **A1:A10,G5:H6**.
3. Press Return.

Highlighting Multiple Ranges, Using Goto

Finally, you can use the following shortcut method to highlight multiple ranges:

Highlighting Multiple Ranges, Using the Shortcut Method

1. Click on the first cell of the first range.

2. Hold the Shift key down while clicking on the last cell of the first range. This action highlights one range. Release the mouse button and the Shift key when finished.

3. Hold the Command key down while clicking on the first cell of the second range. Doing so moves the pointer without extending or removing the existing range.

4. Hold the Shift key down while clicking on the last cell of the second range. Doing so highlights another range while leaving the first intact. Release the mouse button and the Shift key when finished.

When more than one range is active, the movement keys (Tab, Shift+Tab, Return, Shift+Return, and so on) will move the pointer from cell to cell within a range, then from range to range. Figure 3.18 shows multiple active ranges.

Fig. 3.18.

Multiple active ranges.

	🍎	**File**	**Edit**	**Formula**	**Format**	**Data**	**Options**	**Macro**	**Window**	

B6		3877				

Worksheet1

	A	B	C	D	E	F	
1	Excel Spreadsheet						
2	XYZ Corporation						
3							
4							
5		January	February	March			
6		3877	6765	6678			
7		6556	5565	678			
8		6546	566	865			
9		876	8766	6787			
10							
11	Totals	17855	21662	15008			
12							
13							
14	Grand Total	54525					
15							
16							
17							
18							
19							

Ready

Selecting Rows and Columns

You can select entire rows and columns by clicking on the row or column heading at the left or top of the screen. To select a series of adjacent rows or columns, click on the first one and drag the mouse to highlight as many rows or columns as you like. Release the mouse button. Figure 3.19 illustrates this process.

	A	B	C	D	E	F
File Edit Formula Format Data Options Macro Window
A6						
Worksheet1
1	Excel Spreadsheet					
2	XYZ Corporation					
3						
4						
5		January	February	March		
6		3877	6765	6678		
7		6556	5565	678		
8		6546	566	865		
9		876	8766	6787		
10						
11	Totals	17855	21662	15008		
12						
13						
14	Grand Total	54525				
15						
16						
17						
18						

Ready

Fig. 3.19.

Selecting a series of rows.

To select multiple rows or columns that are not adjacent, hold the Command key down while clicking on the various row or column headings. Figure 3.20 shows multiple selected rows and columns.

You can use the keyboard to select rows or columns. The following is a list of keyboard commands that serve that purpose:

Command	*Purpose*
⇧Shift +space	Selects the current row
⌘ space	Selects the current column
F8	Extends the selection
⇧Shift +arrow (numeric keypad)	Extends the selection in the direction of the arrow
⌘ F8	Adds to the selection

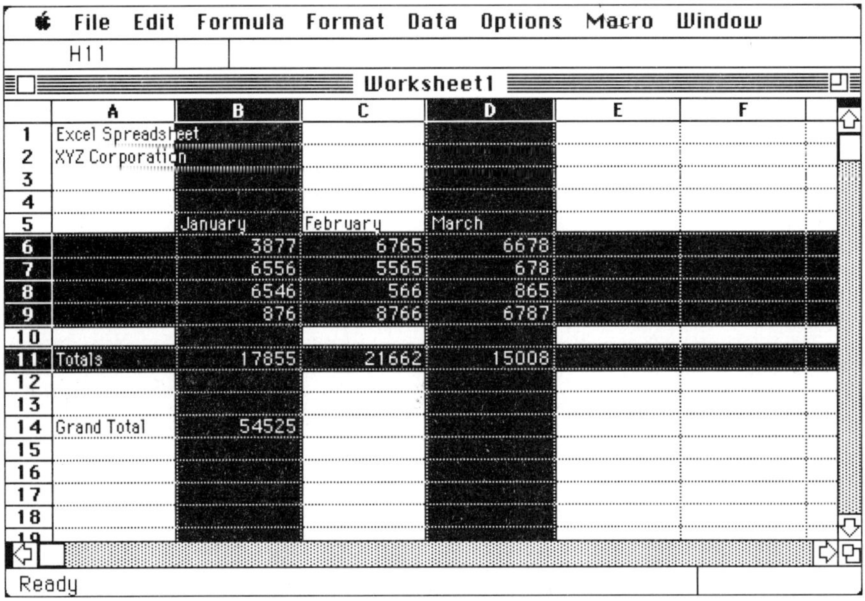

Fig. 3.20.

Multiple selected rows and columns.

Complete these steps to use the keyboard commands to select rows or columns:

Using Keyboard Commands To Select Rows or Columns

1. Position the pointer on the row or column you want to select.

2. Press Shift+space to highlight the current row, or press Command+space to highlight the current column.

3. To extend the selection, press F8; then use the arrow keys to highlight adjacent rows or columns. Alternatively, you can extend the selection by holding down the Shift key while tapping one of the arrow keys (the up or down arrow for rows; the left or right arrow for columns).

   If you like, you can complete the remaining steps to highlight a second (nonadjacent) row or column, leaving the first one highlighted.

4. To select a second row or column, press Command+F8.

5. Move the pointer to the row or column you want to select.

6. Press Shift+space or Command+space to select the current row or column.

7. Extend the selection as described in step 3.

Selecting the Entire Worksheet

Selecting the entire worksheet can be useful for making global changes to data. You can select the entire worksheet by clicking in the intersection of the row and column headings, at the upper left corner of the worksheet (see fig. 3.21).

	File	**Edit**	**Formula**	**Format**	**Data**	**Options**	**Macro**	**Window**

| A1 | | Excel Spreadsheet | | | | | |

Worksheet1

	A	B	C	D	E	F
1	Excel Spreadsheet					
2	XYZ Corporation					
3						
4						
5		January	February	March		
6		3877	6765	6678		
7		6556	5565	678		
8		6546	566	865		
9		876	8766	6787		
10						
11	Totals	17855	21662	15008		
12						
13						
14	Grand Total	54525				
15						
16						
17						
18						

Ready

Fig. 3.21.

Selecting the entire worksheet.

The keyboard alternative to this mouse command is Shift+Command+space.

Automatically Entering a Series

Excel provides a special feature that automatically enters a series of numbers, months, days, or years into a worksheet. Using a single entry that you type, Excel can finish a series of entries automatically. Suppose that you want to enter month names across the top of your worksheet. You can begin by entering only Jan-91 into the first cell, as shown in figure 3.22.

Fig. 3.22.

Beginning a series of months.

	File Edit Formula Format Data Options Macro Window					
	A4	1/1/1991				
			Worksheet1			
	A	**B**	**C**	**D**	**E**	**F**
1						
2						
3						
4	Jan-91					
5						
6						

Next, drag the mouse to highlight the range A4:D4 (the range that will contain the dates, including the first entry). Now select the Series option from the Data menu. Excel presents the dialog box shown in figure 3.23.

Fig. 3.23.

The Series dialog box.

┌─Series in─┐ ┌─Type─┐ ┌─Date Unit─┐   ┌───────┐
● **Rows**   ○ **Linear**   ● **Day**   │ **OK**   │
○ **Columns** ○ **Growth**   ○ **Weekday**   └───────┘
               ● **Date**   ○ **Month**   ┌───────┐
                              ○ **Year**   │ **Cancel** │
                                               └───────┘

Step Value: [1]   **Stop Value:** [   ]

Most likely, the options in this dialog box will already be set to your liking. You can, however, change these options as you like. In this case, you would select Rows, Date, and Month as the three options. This selection will increase each date by one month.

You can also use the Series command to enter numbers that increase or decrease uniformly. Just enter the starting number and choose the appropriate Series options. Figure 3.24 shows the starting values for three different entries, including the month example.

Fig. 3.24.

Examples of series entries.

	File Edit Formula Format Data Options Macro Window						
	A7						
				Worksheet1			
	A	**B**	**C**	**D**	**E**	**F**	**G**
1	Start Value					Type & Step	
2	1	3	9	27		Growth = 3	
3	0.01	1.01	2.01	3.01		Linear = 1	
4	Jan-91	Feb-91	Mar-91	Apr-91		Date /Month = 1	
5							
6							
7							

The following are descriptions of each series option.

Series in

Depending on your highlighted range, this option will display either the Rows or the Columns option as the selected option. All you really have to do is verify that the selection matches your highlighted range. It does little good to highlight a row and then select the Columns option.

Type

If you have entered a date that Excel recognizes as a date, this option will automatically show Date as the selection. The Type Date specification causes the day, week, month, or year portion to increase chronologically by the amount shown in the step value. The Linear and Growth selections apply to numeric entries. The selection Linear adds the step value to the first number in the series, to produce the second value. Then the step value is added to the second value to produce a third, and so on. The selection Growth multiplies the step value by each progressive number.

Date Unit

This option is available only when the Type option shows Date as its selection. Date Unit lets you select which portion of the date will increase by the amount of the step value. Select Day, Weekday, Month, or Year.

Step Value

The step value is the value used for the amount of increase over each cell in the range. Normally, Excel assumes a step value of 1. Enter any value you like. If you enter a negative number, Excel decreases the series accordingly. The stop value should then be less than the starting value.

Stop Value

The stop value sets the maximum value of the series. Even if more than enough cells are highlighted, Excel will end the series on this value.

Note that entering a date in any acceptable date format—including the custom date formats discussed in Chapter 5—causes the Date option to be selected. If you enter a number and then select the Date option in the Series dialog box, Excel will convert the number to a date. Most likely, however, you didn't want a date in the first place.

Automatically Filling a Range

The Series command is useful for sequential entries, but Excel also provides a useful command for filling a range with the same number, label, or formula automatically. These are the steps:

Filling a Range

1. Highlight the range (or ranges) you want, using any method described earlier in this chapter.
2. Type the label, number, or formula into one of the cells (while the range is still selected).
3. Press Option+Return.

When you press Option+Return after making the first entry, Excel copies the entry into all highlighted cells. If the information you entered is a number or label, each cell in the range will contain exactly the same number or label. This feature can be useful for entering information throughout a worksheet at one time. If the information you entered is a formula, Excel copies the formula into the remaining cells in the range—making them relative to their new locations. For more information about copying formulas, see Chapters 4 and 8.

Naming Cells and Ranges

To use Excel effectively, you will almost certainly have to make references to ranges of cells. A *range* is a group of cells (one or more cells) in a rectangular block. A single cell can be a range of one, but your ranges will most likely contain several cells. Often, a portion of a row or column is used as a range; sometimes a block of several rows and columns is needed.

Ranges are required by certain formulas and functions that process information over one or more cells. For example, the function SUM adds the values in a range. To specify a range within a function such as SUM, enter the cell addresses of two opposite corners, separated by a colon. For example, the range shown in figure 3.25 can be defined as any of the following:

A1:D5

D5:A1

A5:D1

D1:A5

★ File Edit Formula Format Data Options Macro Window						
A1						

	A	B	C	D	E	F
1		January	February	March		
2	Green	12	34	22		
3	Blue	30	14	28		
4	Red	22	21	40		
5	Orange	20	22	67		
6						

Worksheet1

Fig. 3.25.

A range of cells.

Rather than define a range by using two corner cells, you can name ranges and use the names instead. For example, instead of typing a function as =SUM(A1:D5), you can type =SUM(SALES). Using names for ranges makes them easier to identify—especially when they are frequently used in the worksheet. Range names also serve to document your worksheets if you use names that help identify the information in the ranges.

Range names can consist of several words but must begin with a letter. After the initial letter, you can include numbers, periods, or the underscore (_) character. Spaces and special symbols are not allowed. The following are some acceptable names (both upper- and lowercase letters are acceptable):

SALES

PRODUCT.TABLE

TABLE25

SINGLE_WEEKLY_STATE_TAX

Although you can specify range names that that look like cell addresses (such as B34), avoid doing so. Such names can cause problems in formulas. When using a range name in a formula, simply enter the name where the standard range reference would appear:

=SUM(SALES)

Using range names in formulas is explained in more detail later in this chapter. To create a range name, first highlight the range you want;

then select the Define Name command from the Formula menu. The range can include data or be blank. After you select Define Name, the dialog box in figure 3.26 appears.

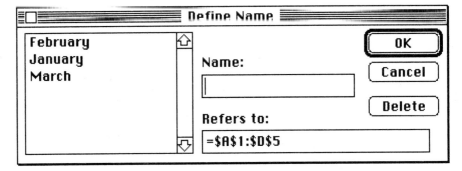

Fig. 3.26.

The Define Name dialog box.

Enter the name into the space provided, following the rules for range names. The name can consist of up to 255 characters, but a practical limit is about 21. The cell addresses defining the range are listed in the Refers To area of the dialog box. Excel uses absolute cell references in the range definition, as indicated by the dollar signs ($) in the cell addresses. (See Chapter 4 for more information about relative and absolute cell addresses.)

 If a label appears in the first cell of the range, Excel will suggest the label as the name for the range. If you don't want this label **NOTE** as the range name, simply type over the suggestion.

When you finish specifying the range name, press Return or click on the OK button. All previously defined range names appear in the left-hand portion of the dialog box so that you can avoid using the same name twice. If you enter a name that has already been used for a range, Excel will apply the name to the new range and remove the old range. In other words, the name will apply to the new range only. Although applying one name to two ranges is not acceptable, applying two names to one range is. Having two names for the same range can be useful, because different formulas can use the same range for different reasons. Each name can imply the purpose of the range. Not only can one range have two different names, but cells that are part of one range can appear in another.

Finally, you can highlight a range consisting of multiple blocks and give it a single name. As described earlier in this chapter, you highlight multiple-block ranges by highlighting the first range and then holding down the Command key while highlighting a second range (see fig. 3.27).

** ** **File** **Edit** **Formula** **Format** **Data** **Options** **Macro** **Window**						
B7		=SUM(B2:B5)				

	A	B	C	D	E	F
1		January	February	March		Total
2	Green	12	34	22		68
3	Blue	30	14	28		72
4	Red	22	21	40		83
5	Orange	20	22	67		109
6						
7	Total	84	91	157		
8						
9						

Fig. 3.27.

Highlighting a multiple-block range for a single range name.

If you use the Formula Define Name command while several ranges are highlighted, the name you specify will apply to all the highlighted cells, as if they were one range.

Automatically Defining Range Names

Because range names are so handy for worksheet references, you may want to use them wherever possible. A typical worksheet, showing a block of information in rows and columns, might use several names. Suppose that you created the worksheet shown in figure 3.28.

	A	B	C	D	E	F
1						
2						
3						
4		FIRST Q	SECOND Q	THIRD Q	FOURTH Q	
5	Salaries	9000.00	9000.00	9000.00	9000.00	
6	Utilities	200.00	200.00	200.00	250.00	
7	Professional Services	1000.00	1000.00	1000.00	1200.00	
8	Rent	1500.00	1500.00	1500.00	1500.00	
9	Advertising	3000.00	3000.00	3500.00	3000.00	
10	Bank	120.00	120.00	100.00	100.00	
11	Freight	2200.00	2200.00	2500.00	3000.00	
12	Insurance	3500.00	3500.00	3500.00	3500.00	
13	Office Supplies	300.00	300.00	300.00	300.00	
14	Depreciation	1000.00	1200.00	1000.00	1000.00	
15						
16	TOTAL	21820.00	22020.00	22600.00	22850.00	
17						
18						

Fig. 3.28.

A sample worksheet.

You may want range names for each of the four quarters of information (that is, the 4 columns) as well as for each of the expense lines (that is, the 10 rows), for a total of 14 named ranges. The best names for the ranges are probably the very titles contained in the worksheet. For example, the range B5:B14 may be called First Q, the range B5:E5 may be called Salaries, and so on.

Rather than use the Define Name command 14 times, you can use the Create Names option in the Formula menu to create all 14 names in one step. First, highlight the entire block A4:E14; then select the Create Names command. The dialog box shown in figure 3.29 appears.

Fig. 3.29.

The Create Names dialog box.

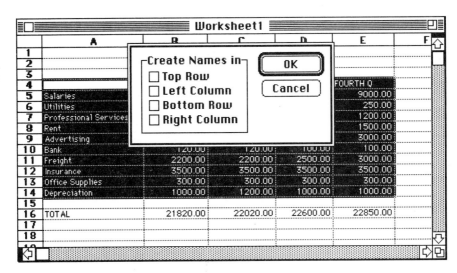

Selecting the Top Row option creates names for each of the *columns*; the labels contained in the top row (row 4 in the example) are used. Selecting the Left Column option creates names for each of the *rows*; the labels in column A are used. If you don't have labels in the specified row or column of the range, Excel will not name the ranges. For example, the block shown in figure 3.30 will not provide Left Column range names because there are no label cells highlighted on the left column of the block.

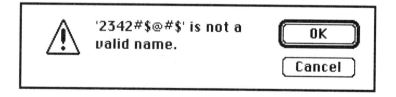

	A	B	C	D	E	F
1						
2						
3						
4		FIRST Q	SECOND Q	THIRD Q	FOURTH Q	
5	Salaries	9000.00	9000.00	9000.00	9000.00	
6	Utilities	200.00	200.00	200.00	250.00	
7	Professional Services	1000.00	1000.00	1000.00	1200.00	
8	Rent	1500.00	1500.00	1500.00	1500.00	
9	Advertising	3000.00	3000.00	3500.00	3000.00	
10	Bank	120.00	120.00	100.00	100.00	
11	Freight	2200.00	2200.00	2500.00	3000.00	
12	Insurance	3500.00	3500.00	3500.00	3500.00	
13	Office Supplies	300.00	300.00	300.00	300.00	
14	Depreciation	1000.00	1200.00	1000.00	1000.00	
15						
16	TOTAL	21820.00	22020.00	22600.00	22850.00	
17						
18						
19						

Fig. 3.30.

A block without left column range names.

If a label appears in the corner of a range when you select both Top Row and Left Column names, Excel will apply the name to the combination of columns and rows. In other words, the name will refer to the entire range (excluding other names).

A cell can be included in several named ranges. Likewise, an entire range, having its own name, can be included in a larger range. Keep in mind that restrictions apply to the characters you can use in range names and that Excel will not allow invalid names when you use the Create Names command. If you use invalid names, Excel will present the error message shown in figure 3.31.

⚠ '2342#$@#$' is not a valid name.

[OK]

[Cancel]

Fig. 3.31.

The error message indicating an invalid range name.

Although spaces are normally not allowed in range names, Excel will not display this error message if your names have spaces. Instead, Excel automatically converts spaces to underscore characters and then uses the name.

Creating a Multitude of Names

By using the Command key to highlight multiple blocks at the same time (as described in the section "Selecting Information" earlier in this chapter), you can name these multiple-block ranges by using the Create Name command. No matter how many blocks are highlighted, if labels exist in the top row of a block, they will constitute range names when you use the Top Row option; and if labels exist in the leftmost column of the range, they will constitute range names when you use the Left Column option.

Removing Names

Although there is no limit to the number of ranges you can name in a worksheet, you may need to remove a name. You don't have to highlight a range or even know where it is to remove its name. Simply use the Define Name command, click on the name you want to remove (shown in the window), and then click on the Delete button. The range name (not the information in the range) will be removed. If the range name is currently being used in a worksheet formula, Excel will enter the value #NAME? into the formula to indicate that a range name is needed. At this point, you can change the range name in the formula to the standard range reference or define a new range with the required name. Remember that you can have two names for the same range if necessary.

Changing Range Names and References

If you decide to make changes, you can edit any part of a range name specification, including the name itself and the range it references. One way to change a name or range reference is to delete the name, as described earlier, and then redefine the range by using the Define Name command. But Excel provides a shortcut. If you want to change the name of a range or change the range referenced by a name, simply follow these steps:

Changing a Range Name or a Referenced Range

1. Select the Define Name command from the Formula menu and click on the range name you want to change.

2. To change the name, click to place the cursor in the Name specification; then use standard editing commands to change the name.

To change the range reference, click to place the cursor in the Refers To specification; then use standard editing commands to change the range reference.* Be sure to include dollar signs to make the reference absolute.

3. Press Return.

*For a summary of the standard editing commands, see Chapter 4.

Finding Names

When you apply names throughout a worksheet, you can forget which range is which—even if you use descriptive names. Using the Goto command in the Formula menu, you can jump to any range by specifying its name. This feature is handy for moving quickly to specific locations throughout the worksheet. Simply choose the Goto command and then click on the name shown in the list. Alternatively, you can type the name in the space provided. Excel will highlight the specified name.

Using Names in Formulas and Functions

As mentioned earlier, range names can help make cell references easier to use and remember. Whenever Excel expects a range of cells, you can use a name. For example, rather than enter =SUM(A1:A5), you may enter =SUM(SALES), where SALES defines the range A1:A5. As you can see, range names are more descriptive than range references. Because ranges usually apply to a block of cells, they are most commonly used with the Excel functions that require a block designation. However, a name can represent a single cell, and Excel is smart enough to know whether a name is attached to a single cell or a block. Thus you can usually use range names when Excel expects a single cell reference. Table 3.1 shows the various types of formulas and how range names can be used.

CELL indicates a range name attached to a single cell. RANGE indicates a range name attached to a block.

The first column shows how you might use range names in formulas; the second column shows the same formula with cell or range references instead of range names. Notice that Excel understands the different uses of range names, even when the range is a single cell reference.

Table 3.1
Using Range Names in Formulas

Formula Example with Names	Formula Example with Cell References
=SUM(RANGE)	=SUM(A3:A9)
=SUM(CELL)	=SUM(A1)
=SUM(CELL:CELL)	=SUM(A2:A9)
=IF(CELL=0,1,2)	=IF(A2=0,1,2)
=CELL	=A2
=RANGE*	=A2:A5
=CELL+CELL	=A2+A6

*Returns first cell in range

Getting a List of Range Names

You can create, as part of the worksheet, a list of all defined range names. Such a list can be useful for reference. Simply position the pointer in a blank area and then select the Paste Name command from the Formula menu. When the dialog box appears, select the Paste List button. Each name will appear in a separate cell; the references, in adjacent cells.

Naming Formulas and Values

Besides being useful for naming cells and ranges, the Define Name command is useful for naming formulas and values that you use throughout a worksheet. Any formula or constant value can be assigned a name and then used, by name, in a cell or in another formula. This feature comes in handy with frequently used formulas and with values that have representative meaning. For example, you can define the formula =A4*(3/B4) with the name RATE. Whenever that formula is needed in a cell, simply type **=RATE**. As another example, suppose that the figure 75,565.59 is the amount of an investment and is used over and over throughout the worksheet. Rather than type this number each time it comes up, assign it a name and use the name. You might name the figure AMOUNT and then use that name in formulas or functions that require the number.

You can use cell addresses, or even other range names, in your formula. The only rule is to include an equal sign in front of the value or formula you are naming. Complete these steps to name a formula or value:

1. Select the Define Name command from the Formula menu.
2. Enter the name into the Name space.
3. Press the Tab key to highlight the Refers To information.
4. Type the formula or value into the Refers To space. Be sure to include the equal sign at the beginning. Also, make sure that your entry completely removes the existing information.
5. Press Return. The formula or value will not appear on the worksheet. Instead, it will be returned to any formula containing its name.

Naming a Formula or Value

Naming a formula or value is very much like naming a cell that contains the formula or value. The difference is that the formula or value does not have to appear on the worksheet. Instead, it can be defined with a name. Otherwise, this procedure is identical to naming a cell.

Changing Existing Formulas for New References

If you use a range reference in a formula and later name that same range, Excel does not replace the range reference with the range name. For example, suppose that your worksheet contains the formula =SUM(A1:A10). Now you highlight the range A1:A10 and name it SALES. Excel will not automatically replace the range reference in this formula with the name =SUM(SALES).

Use the Apply Names option in the Formula menu to replace all appropriate range references with a selected name. Using this option will save you some time.

If you forget a range name while entering a formula, select the Paste Name option from the Formula menu. A screen like that in figure 3.32 will appear, listing all available names for use in the formula. If you select a name from the list, Excel will automatically enter the name into the formula, at the position of the cursor.

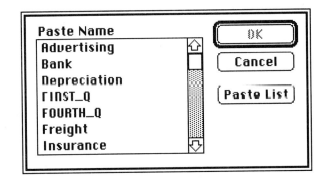

To select from the list the name you want, double-click on the name.
Or click on the name and then click OK.

Protecting Information

At the beginning of this chapter, you saw how Excel lets you assign
passwords to your worksheets to protect them from being viewed by
"unauthorized persons." But Excel offers another kind of protection,
called *cell protection*. Cell protection prevents a cell from being
changed. Thus cell protection can be used in addition to file protection
to prohibit unwanted changes to the worksheet. Cell protection is
often considered an unnecessary detail for applications. Its primary
value is for worksheets that are used by someone other than the
worksheet's designer. However, cell protection not only protects your
worksheets from being tampered with but also protects you from
unknowingly entering the wrong kind of information in the wrong
place.

When a cell is protected, it is "locked" from use. You cannot change
the information in it, and you cannot add information if the cell is
blank. If you try to enter anything into a protected cell, you will get the
message shown in figure 3.33.

To protect cells, first highlight the desired cells as discussed in
"Selecting Information" earlier in this chapter; then select the Cell
Protection option from the Format menu. The dialog box shown in
figure 3.34 appears.

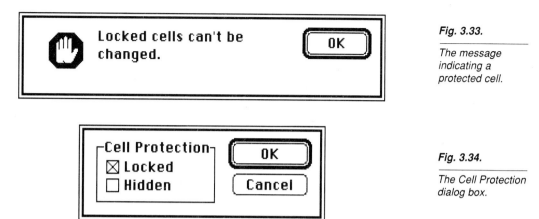

Fig. 3.33.

The message
indicating a
protected cell.

Fig. 3.34.

The Cell Protection
dialog box.

Excel offers two options for cell protection. Use the mouse to click in the check box next to the option you want. When the check mark is present, the option is on. To turn the option off, select the cells again and then click in the check box to remove the check. The following are explanations of each option.

Locked

The Locked option locks a cell from being tampered with. When you highlight a cell or range and then check this option, information in those cells cannot be changed, nor can you enter anything into the cells.

Hidden

The Hidden option hides from view the information in the formula bar. That is, the information in the cell will not appear in the formula bar when you move the pointer to it. This option is most useful for hiding involved formulas. The values of the hidden cells still appear in the cell itself. For information on completely hiding a cell from view, refer to the section "Using Number Formats" in Chapter 5.

When working on a worksheet that has many protected cells, you may find it inconvenient to continually unprotect cells so that you can edit the worksheet, only to have to protect them again. Excel thus provides a "master switch" that turns cell protection on and off for the entire worksheet. When the master switch is off, all cells that have been protected will be temporarily unprotected so that you can make changes. Turn the master switch back on, and the cells will be protected again. Turning protection on also deselects many of the Excel menu commands. Commands that can be used to change the worksheet are not available. Note that cell protection is normally off for all new worksheets.

This master switch is accessed through the Protect Document command in the Options menu. When you select this command, the dialog box shown in figure 3.35 appears.

```
┌────────────────────────────────────────────────┐
│  Protect Document            ╭──────────╮       │
│                              │    OK    │       │
│  Password: │                 ╰──────────╯       │
│                              ┌──────────┐       │
│  ⊠ Contents    □ Windows     │  Cancel  │       │
│                              └──────────┘       │
└────────────────────────────────────────────────┘
```

The following are descriptions of the options.

Password

This option prevents anyone who does not know the password from turning cell protection off. (If anyone could turn protection off with this master switch, the protection wouldn't be very useful.) If you enter a password into the space provided, Excel will require you to enter it whenever you use the Protect Document option. If the password is entered correctly, you will be able to turn cell protection on and off by using the next two options. If you do not enter a password into the space provided, Excel will not require one when you use this command.

Caution: If you forget the password you enter, there is no way to recover it. This problem can be a serious one if you need to change information that is protected. Be sure to write the password down and store it in a safe place.

Contents

If this option is checked, all cells that have been "locked" through the Cell Protection command in the Format menu will be protected. In other words, checking this option turns the master switch on. Click in the box again to uncheck the option, turning the master switch off. When the master switch is off, locked cells are temporarily unlocked.

Windows

This option freezes worksheet windows. When you use several windows for one worksheet, you may want to "freeze" them from being moved or resized. This command prevents all windows associated with the document from being changed. The windows will remain in place each time you open the document. See Chapter 7 for more information about using multiple windows in Excel.

Summary

This chapter discussed the basics of creating Excel worksheets. You should now know how to create, save, and reuse a worksheet. In addition, this chapter provided some details about entering text, numbers, and formulas into the worksheet. It also showed some basic ways to move around the worksheet and select various cells and ranges—important tasks that you will use in working with many worksheet features. The following is a list of key points covered:

- ❏ Save a worksheet by using the File Save command. To change a worksheet's name or to back up a worksheet while saving, use the File Save As command.
- ❏ Excel can store and retrieve worksheets stored in DIF, ASCII, SYLK, dBASE, and 1-2-3 formats.
- ❏ Number entries must begin with numerals or the characters -, +, $, ., and (. Although they cannot begin with them, number entries can also contain the characters % and).
- ❏ Text entries (or labels) can begin with numbers or letters but must contain letters somewhere in the entry.
- ❏ Dates and times are really just "serial numbers" formatted to look like dates and times.

❑ All formulas must begin with equal signs.

❑ Formulas use operators to perform calculations.

❑ Using cell references within a formula, one cell can calculate a value based on the values in other cells.

❑ You can move the pointer to various locations on the worksheet by using the arrow keys, the scroll bars, the keyboard commands, the Goto command, and the Find command.

❑ Besides moving the pointer to a specific cell, the Find command also locates information in the worksheet.

❑ You can select a row or column by clicking the mouse on the row or column heading.

❑ Using the Formula Define Name command, you can name cells and ranges to make them easier to reference.

❑ Excel stores all defined names and presents them to you on request. To see a list of defined names, select the Formula Define Name command.

❑ You can prevent a cell from being changed by protecting it.

The next chapter, "Editing the Worksheet," illustrates how you can change the contents of a worksheet by using the various editing features in Excel.

4

Editing the Worksheet

Now that you know how to successfully create a worksheet, you need to know how to edit one. Using the features described in this chapter, you can make changes to your worksheets. First you will learn how to edit information in cells, then how to erase information from the worksheet and insert and delete rows and columns. Finally, you'll discover how several commands can be used to duplicate information in the worksheet. Be sure that you have a sample worksheet on which you can practice some of these commands. If you use the Quick Start sample worksheet, be sure to keep one copy in its current state for the next Quick Start lesson.

Editing Cell Contents

In Chapter 3 you saw that typing information into a cell removes whatever information is already in that cell. However, one of the most common needs you'll encounter when creating worksheets is the need to edit cell contents without retyping the entire entry. Modifying cells in Excel is quite simple. To begin, place the pointer on the cell you want to edit. The contents of the cell will appear in the formula bar. By changing the information in the formula bar, you change the information in the cell.

Excel offers familiar Macintosh editing procedures for changing information in the formula bar. Simply position the cursor by clicking the mouse at the appropriate location in the formula bar. Alternatively, you can select a section of text by dragging the mouse or select a single word by double-clicking the mouse on the word. Another way to select text is to click at the beginning of the desired text, hold the Shift key down, and then click at the end of the desired text.

When this text is highlighted, press Backspace to remove it. Alternatively, you can begin typing to remove the text and replace it with new information.

Besides offering these standard Macintosh editing commands, Excel provides a host of special keyboard commands for editing text and formulas in the formula bar. First, click to place the cursor in the text shown in the formula bar. Then use the editing commands in the following list to make your changes:

Command/Action	Effect
Double-click	Selects a word.
Arrows*	Moves the cursor one character in the direction of the arrow. The left and right arrows are most commonly used; the up and down arrows are useful when the entry is very long.
⇧Shift+arrows†	Selects one character at a time in the direction of the arrow (left and right), or moves the cursor from its position to the same position on the next line (up and down).
⌘+arrows‡	Moves one word in the direction of the arrow (left and right).
⌘⇧Shift+arrows‡	Selects one word in the direction of the arrow (left and right).
Home*	Moves to the beginning of the current line (used for multiline entries).
⇧Shift Home*	Selects from the cursor position to the beginning of the current line.
⌘ Home*	Moves to the beginning of the entry.
⌘⇧Shift Home*	Selects from the cursor position to the beginning of the entry.
End*	Moves to the end of the current line (used for multiline entries).

⇧Shift End*	Selects from the cursor position to the end of the line.
⌘ End*	Moves to the end of the entry.
⌘ ⇧Shift End*	Selects from the cursor position to the end of the entry.

* Macintosh Plus keyboards require that you also press the Option key for this effect.

† You must use the numeric keypad arrows. On the Macintosh Plus keyboard, you must also press the Option key to get this effect.

‡ Command not available on Macintosh Plus keyboard.

On examining these commands, you'll notice that each of the three basic keys (Home, End, or any of the arrow keys) can be combined with the Command key for a different effect. Each of those six key commands can in turn be combined with the Shift key to switch from moving the cursor to highlighting data. In other words, adding the Shift key to any of the movement keys causes Excel to highlight as it moves.

Once the appropriate text is highlighted, pressing the Backspace key removes the text. You can also replace the text with new information by simply typing the new information when the old is highlighted.

Keep in mind that the cursor should be flashing somewhere in the text shown in the formula bar. If the cursor is not in the formula bar, these commands will perform other actions.

As an example of both methods of editing, suppose that you have the following label in cell A2 of the worksheet: *Net Salles for North Company Products.* You want to correct the word *Salles* and remove the word *Products.* Also, the word *Company* should be *Corp.* Follow these steps to make the corrections, using the mouse:

1. Using the mouse or the Goto command, select cell A2. The contents of the label appear in the formula bar, as shown in figure 4.1.

Making Corrections with the Mouse

2. Move the mouse pointer into the formula bar; notice that the pointer shape changes to the I-beam, which is used for entering and editing text.

3. Click between the 2 *l*'s in *Salles*.

4. Press the Backspace key.

Fig. 4.1.

To edit cell contents, select the appropriate cell, whose contents are then displayed in the formula bar.

| | File | Edit | Formula | Format | Data | Options | Macro | Window |

| A2 | | Net Salles for North Company Products |

Worksheet2

	A	B	C	D	E	F
1						
2	Net Salles for North Company Products					
3						
4						
5						
6						

5. Move the mouse pointer to the *C* in *Company*; then click and drag to the end of the entry.

6. Type **Corp.** and press Return.

The same edits can be made with keyboard commands. The steps are these:

Making Corrections with the Keyboard

1. Select cell A2.

2. Press Command+U to begin editing.

3. Press Command+Home to move the cursor to the beginning of the entry. (Remember, the Home key is the 9 on the numeric keypad, with Num Lock off.)

4. Press Command+right arrow to move one word to the right.

5. Press the right arrow until the cursor is between the two *l* characters in the word *Salles*, as shown in figure 4.2.

Fig. 4.2.

Use the movement commands to position the cursor in the formula bar.

| | File | Edit | Formula | Format | Data | Options | Macro | Window |

| A2 | | Net Salles for North Company Products |

Worksheet1

	A	B	C	D	E	F
1						
2	Net Salles for North Company Products					
3						
4						
5						
6						

6. Press the Backspace key once to remove the first *l*.

7. Press Command+right arrow three times to position the cursor at the beginning of the word *Company*. Select the word by pressing Command+Shift+right arrow.

8. Type **Corp.** As you begin typing, the new word replaces the one highlighted.

9. Finally, double-click on the word *Products* to highlight it; double-clicking on a word highlights the entire word. Since this word is to be completely removed, just press the Backspace key once to erase it. When finished, press Return.

Using these editing features, you can completely change the contents of a cell. By dragging the mouse, you can select larger portions of the information for editing. If you make changes to a cell's contents and decide that you don't want to keep the changes, click on the cancel box at the top of the screen. If you click on this box rather than press Return to accept your changes, Excel will replace the original information in the cell and throw out your changes.

Searching and Replacing

Another way to change information in a cell is to use Excel's search-and-replace feature, the Replace command. Similar to the Find command, Replace locates any information in your worksheet and then replaces it (or portions of it) with information that you specify. This command is most useful when you need to edit information that appears in more than one cell. For example, you might want to change a particular cell reference used in formulas throughout the worksheet. Rather than edit each formula individually, you can use the Replace command to change them all at once. The Replace command can be used to edit labels, numbers, or formulas. When you select the Replace command from the Formula menu, the dialog box shown in figure 4.3 appears.

```
┌──────────────────── Replace ────────────────────┐
│                                                  │
│  Replace: [                ]  ( Replace All )    │
│                                                  │
│  With:    [                ]  (  Cancel   )      │
│                                                  │
│  ┌Look at─┐ ┌Look by──┐                          │
│  │○ Whole │ │◉ Rows   │     ( Find Next )        │
│  │◉ Part  │ │○ Columns│     (  Replace  )        │
│  └────────┘ └─────────┘                          │
└──────────────────────────────────────────────────┘
```

Fig. 4.3.

The Replace options.

In the space marked Replace, enter the information you want to replace. This information can be any character, cell reference, word, or phrase.

Next, enter into the With space the information with which you want to replace the data. Perhaps a cell reference has changed from A1 to C5; enter A1 for the Replace information and C5 for the With information.

The Look At selection determines whether Excel finds your Replace entry only when it appears as a whole word or whether Excel finds occurrences that appear as parts of other words. When replacing parts of formulas, be sure to use the Part option. The Whole option can be useful when you replace portions of labels.

The Look By selection determines whether Excel searches by rows or by columns. This selection has no bearing on whether Excel finds matching information, only on whether Excel finds matching information as quickly as possible. Search by rows if you think that the majority of occurrences appears toward the top of the worksheet. Search by columns if you think that the occurrences appear toward the left side of the worksheet.

After you specify the Replace and With information and select the Look At and Look By options, you can replace all occurrences of the data at once by clicking on the Replace All button. Alternatively, you can make replacements one occurrence at a time so that you can review each occurrence and skip those you don't want to replace. Use the Replace button to replace the current occurrence and move to the next. Use the Find Next button to skip the current occurrence and move to the next.

Caution: Be careful when you use the Replace All option. If you use it mistakenly or inappropriately, restoring the original cell contents can be difficult.

If you highlight a range of cells before using the Replace command, Excel will search for matching information only in the highlighted range. Using this technique is a good way of limiting the search to a specific area to avoid mistakes. To use the entire worksheet, don't highlight any range (that is, highlight just one cell).

The following is the procedure for using the Replace command and its options:

Using the Replace Command

1. Select the range of cells you want (or select only one cell if you want to use the entire worksheet).
2. Select the Replace command from the Formula menu.
3. In the Replace box, enter the data you would like to find.
4. Enter the replacement data into the With box.
5. Select either Whole or Part from the Look At options.

6. Select either Rows or Columns from the Look By options.

7. Click on the Replace All button if you want to replace all matching occurrences (if you choose this option, steps 8 and 9 do not apply)

   Or

   Click on the Find Next button to begin searching.

8. Click on the Replace button to replace the current occurrence

   Or

   Click on the Find Next button to skip the current occurrence and find the next one.

9. Repeat the second part of step 7 and repeat step 8 until finished with all occurrences, or click on Cancel to exit from the Replace command.

Replacing Range References with Range Names

As you learned in the preceding chapter, you can apply names to ranges of cells (or even to individual cells) throughout the worksheet. The range A1:A5, for instance, might be named SALES. In formulas, you can use the name SALES instead of the typical range reference.

Most likely, you'll start naming ranges after you've begun the worksheet. You may even have used the standard range reference in many formulas before you name the range. It would be nice to automatically change all occurrences of the range reference to the appropriate name, but do not use the Replace command for this purpose. Using the Replace command to change range references to range names can be dangerous. Suppose that you want to change the range A1:A5 to the name SALES. Because you're changing a formula, you would have to use Replace's Part option in the Look At box. But doing so causes Excel to consider the following ranges as matches:

    A1:A5:
    A1:A5
    A1:A51
    A1:A55
    A1:A500

This would not do! And it would be tedious to examine each potential change by using the Find Next feature. Luckily, Excel provides a special command for replacing range references with their respective names. Just select the Apply Names command from the Formula menu. The dialog box shown in figure 4.4 appears.

Fig. 4.4.

The Apply Names dialog box.

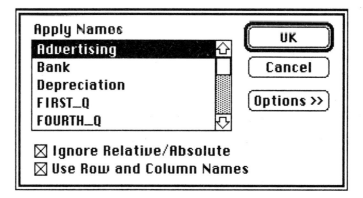

Select the appropriate name from the list provided and then press Return; alternatively, you can double-click on the name you want. Of course, you should take this step after you create the range name and when you are ready to apply it to formulas throughout the worksheet. The range name will be used instead of the range reference to which it applies. You can apply several range names at one time by holding down the Shift key while you select multiple names from the dialog-box list. Finally, you can apply range names in specific areas of the worksheet by highlighting the appropriate area before selecting the Apply Names command.

Deleting Information

You will probably want to delete information from a cell from time to time. Using the Delete key when the cursor is inside the formula bar is great for erasing portions of a cell's contents, but what if you want to remove everything from a cell? Of course, you could place the cursor in the formula bar and use the Delete key to remove all the information, accepting the changes when you're through. But Excel provides an easier way. First, select the cell containing the information you want to remove; then press the Backspace key. If you want to erase several cells at once, highlight the appropriate range and then press the Clear key. All information is removed, and the cell remains as if it had never been used.

As an alternative, you can highlight the cells you want and then select the Clear option from the Edit menu. Selecting this option brings up the dialog box shown in figure 4.5. The options include All, which removes everything in the cells; Formulas, which erases cells that contain formulas; and Formats, which erases special character formats (such as boldface) and returns the information to normal. See Chapter 5 for more information about character formats.

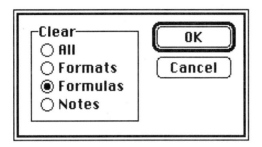

Fig. 4.5.

The Clear dialog box.

Another way to clear cells is to highlight them, then use the keyboard command Command+B. This procedure clears all information except formatting.

Besides being able to clear the contents of a cell or range, you can clear information in an entire row or column, multiple rows or columns, or the entire worksheet by selecting the appropriate ranges before using the Clear command. To select a row or column, click on the row or column title as described in the section "Selecting Information" in Chapter 3.

Caution: Because the act of clearing information does not store a copy of the removed information on the clipboard, you have only one opportunity to change your mind. To cancel the Clear command, you must issue the Undo command (or press F1) immediately after you clear the information. Otherwise, the information is permanently removed.

Deleting Cells

When you use the Clear option to delete information from a worksheet, the cells containing the information are emptied and remain in place on the worksheet. Another way to delete information is to remove the entire cell and its contents. This process causes cells to the right of the deleted cells to move left and assume the empty space. For example, if you were to delete cell C5, all cells from D5 to the end of the worksheet would move left one cell. Cell D5 would become the new C5, cell E5 would become D5, and so on. Actually, you can choose whether cells move to the left to fill the space or whether cells move up from below. These options appear in the dialog box shown in figure 4.6.

Fig. 4.6.

The Delete dialog box.

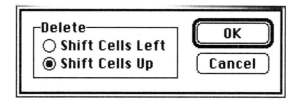

Cells are often deleted and inserted for aesthetic purposes, to reformat the layout of information. If a formula references a cell that has been relocated because of the Delete command, the reference will automatically adjust to show the new cell location. If, for example, cell C5 is removed, so that cell D5 becomes the new C5, any references to cell D5 will adjust to the new name of the cell: C5. However, references to the removed cell (C5) will not be able to adjust and will produce errors. The worksheet in figure 4.7 shows an example of this situation. Cell F6 contains the formula =C5; cell F7 contains the formula =D5. When cell C5 is deleted, cell F6 contains #REF!, and cell F7 contains =C5. Figure 4.8 shows the result of deleting cell C5.

Fig. 4.7.

Cell references before deleting.

🍎 File Edit Formula Format Data Options Macro Window						
F6		=C5				

Worksheet1

	B	C	D	E	F	G
1						
2						
3		Quantity	Description	Product No		
4		345	Oranges	100		
5		454	Apples	200		
6		256	Pears	300	454	
7		885	Lemons	400	Apples	
8		332	Grapes	500		
9						
10						

To delete a cell, first select it, then choose the Delete option from the Edit menu. You can delete a block of cells, an entire row, or an entire column by selecting it and using the Delete option.

	B	C	D	E	F	G	
1							
2							
3		Quantity	Description	Product No			
4		345	Oranges	100			
5		Apples	200				
6		256	Pears	300	#REF!		
7		885	Lemons	400	Apples		
8		332	Grapes	500			
9							
10							

Menu bar: File Edit Formula Format Data Options Macro Window
Cell reference: C5 — Apples
Worksheet1

Fig. 4.8.

The result of deleting cell C5.

Caution: If you change your mind about deleting information, you can use the Undo command immediately after deleting. Doing so replaces the information. Also, the Delete command places a copy onto the clipboard; you can paste information from the clipboard back into the worksheet to replace it. However, if you alter the contents of the clipboard by deleting or copying something else, you will be unable to retrieve the original data.

Inserting Cells

Suppose that you have entered information into your worksheet but would like to add information at the top left side of the page. Or perhaps you would like to move information to a location that already contains some information. One solution is to insert blank cells where you need them.

When you insert a blank cell, block, or column, existing information moves to the right or down, and cell addresses adjust accordingly. When you insert a blank row, existing information moves down. To insert a cell or block of cells, move to the area where you would like the new cells and then highlight the number of cells you want to insert. Next, choose the Insert command from the Edit menu. Existing information moves to accommodate the new cells. Figures 4.9 and 4.10 show how this procedure works.

In figure 4.9, the range C5:D6 is highlighted. After the Insert command is used, columns C and D from rows 5 and 6 become columns E and F from rows 5 and 6. Rows 7 and 8 are unaffected. You can insert an entire row or column at one time by selecting the row or column that will move down or to the right and by then selecting the Insert option from the Edit menu (see figs. 4.11 and 4.12).

Fig. 4.9.

Specify the size and location of the block to insert.

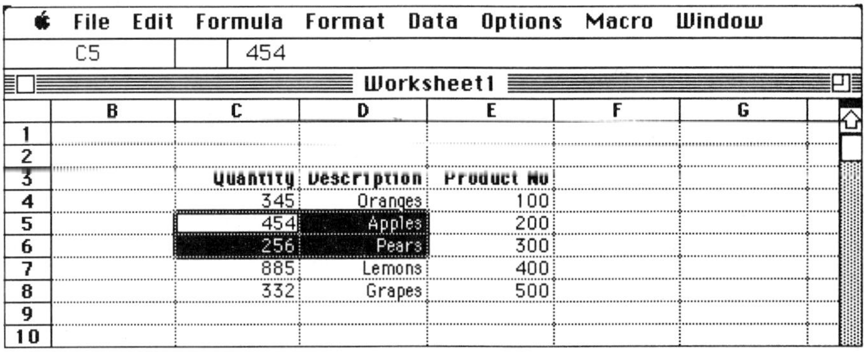

	B	C	D	E	F	G	
1							
2							
3		Quantity	Description	Product No			
4		345	Oranges	100			
5		454	Apples	200			
6		256	Pears	300			
7		885	Lemons	400			
8		332	Grapes	500			
9							
10							

C5 = 454

Fig. 4.10.

The worksheet after the insertion.

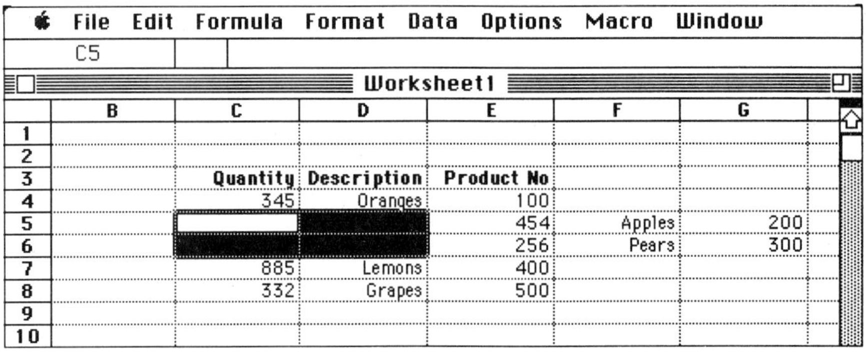

	B	C	D	E	F	G	
1							
2							
3		Quantity	Description	Product No			
4		345	Oranges	100			
5				454	Apples	200	
6				256	Pears	300	
7		885	Lemons	400			
8		332	Grapes	500			
9							
10							

C5

Fig. 4.11.

Selecting the location for the inserted row.

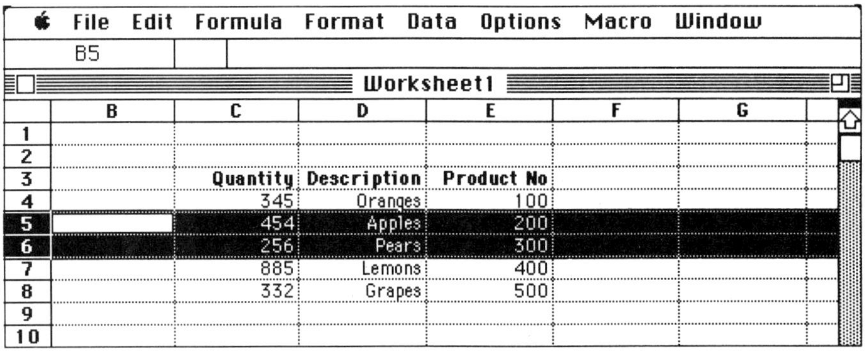

	B	C	D	E	F	G	
1							
2							
3		Quantity	Description	Product No			
4		345	Oranges	100			
5		454	Apples	200			
6		256	Pears	300			
7		885	Lemons	400			
8		332	Grapes	500			
9							
10							

B5

⌘	File	Edit	Formula	Format	Data	Options	Macro	Window

B5		

Worksheet1

	B	C	D	E	F	G	
1							
2							
3		Quantity	Description	Product No			
4		345	Oranges	100			
5							
6							
7		454	Apples	200			
8		256	Pears	300			
9		885	Lemons	400			
10		332	Grapes	500			

Fig. 4.12.

The worksheet after the insertion.

Moving Information

The process of moving information from one location to another is an extension of the Cut command. To move information, first use Cut to remove it from its original location. Next, select the new location for the information and select the Paste command from the Edit menu. The information will appear at the new location. You also can invoke Paste by pressing Command+V. If you cut a range of cells, you can paste the entire range into the new location. Simply position the pointer where you would like the upper left corner of the range to appear; then press Command+V to paste.

Before pasting, you can highlight a block of cells to designate the exact range for the pasted information. If the destination range is smaller or larger than the range that you cut, Excel will not fill the designated range.

NOTE To paste the information, it's easiest to simply not highlight a destination block at all; click on the cell that defines the upper left corner of the destination, then paste.

Note that if the information you move contains references to other cells, the references will remain the same when moved to the new location. For example, suppose that cell A5 contains the formula =A1+A2+A3 and that you want to move this information to cell C12. First, place the pointer on cell A5 and press Command+X to delete it. Next, move to cell C12 and press Command+V. Cell C12 will now contain the same formula: =A1+A2+A3. (If you want the formulas to adjust to their new location, so that they become relative references, use the Copy command instead of Cut.)

If information already exists at the location to which you are moving the data, it will be replaced with the data you paste in. If you do not want to replace this information, insert space for the new information before deleting it from its original location.

For more information about moving and copying information, see Chapter 8. For information about inserting cells, see "Inserting Cells" earlier in this chapter.

Copying Information

Copying worksheet information involves some special concerns. Besides simply duplicating data, copying involves the use of worksheet cell references. When formulas containing cell references are copied to other locations, this question comes up: Do the cell references remain exactly as the originals, or do they change to apply to the new position?

Earlier you saw how to use the Cut and Paste commands to move information. When you move information, cell references remain exactly as they were in the originals (that is, they reference the same cells). This arrangement is fine for labels and numbers, but formulas often need to be made relative to their new location. The Copy command keeps references relative when they are copied. (Of course, the Copy command also leaves the original intact, whereas the Cut command removes the original.)

Suppose that your worksheet has a column of numbers indicating the costs of store merchandise. In an adjacent column, your worksheet will calculate the price after incorporating a markup of 40 percent. You begin with the first formula, shown in the formula bar in figure 4.13.

Fig. 4.13.

A sample worksheet with a formula ready to be copied.

	File	**Edit**	**Formula**	**Format**	**Data**	**Options**	**Macro**	**Window**

C3		=B3*1.4				

Worksheet2

	A	B	C	D	E	F
1			140%			
2						
3	TTR-398	20.00	28.00			
4	TTR-3366	15.50				
5	BR-47	34.40				
6	GST-3389	29.95				
7	GST-2228	35.50				
8	GST-5505	33.50				
9	UMJR-100	54.00				
10	FRR-556	29.00				
11						
12						

The next step is to copy the formula into the remaining cells of column C. When the formula is copied, the cell references should adjust to be relative to the location of the formula. Cell C6 should reference cell B6, cell C7 should reference B7, and so on. To copy the formula, select cell C3 and select the Copy command from the Edit menu (you can also use the shortcut Command+C). Next, highlight the remaining cells C4:C10 and choose Paste from the Edit menu. The formula will be entered into the highlighted block with cell references relative to their new locations. Figure 4.14 shows the result.

	File	Edit	Formula	Format	Data	Options	Macro	Window
	C3		=B10*1.4					

	A	B	C	D	E	F
1			140%			
2						
3	TTR-398	20.00	28.00			
4	TTR-3366	15.50	21.70			
5	BR-47	34.40	48.16			
6	GST-3389	29.95	41.93			
7	GST-2228	35.50	49.70			
8	GST-5505	33.50	46.90			
9	UMJR-100	54.00	75.60			
10	FRR-556	29.00	40.60			
11						
12						

Fig. 4.14.

A formula copied into other cells makes references relative.

In this example, you could have, alternatively, used the Fill Down command to copy this information, since the targeted cells are adjacent to the original. Fill Down is exactly like the Copy command except that it's faster and easier to use in situations like this one—in which the destination cells are adjacent to (in this case, beneath) the original. Using Fill Down, you must highlight the entire range, with the original cell at the top of that range (in the example, the range C3:C10), and then select the Fill Down command from the Edit menu. The effect is identical to copying, but the Fill Down procedure takes fewer steps. Similarly, if you are copying data across several adjacent columns, you can use the Fill Right command instead of the Copy command. Just highlight the original cell plus all the adjacent cells to receive copies; then select Fill Right.

 When you press the Shift key while selecting the Edit menu, the Fill Down and Fill Right commands change to Fill Up and Fill Left. Use these commands when you are copying in the direction they indicate.

Unlike the Fill Down and Fill Right commands, the Copy command can copy into nonadjacent cells. Suppose that the sample worksheet contained an additional column of products next to the first. Now the goal is to copy the formula into both columns, as shown in figure 4.15.

Fig. 4.15.

Copying into nonadjacent cells.

| | ** File Edit Formula Format Data Options Macro Window** |

F3

Worksheet3

	A	B	C	D	E	F
1						
2						
3	TTR-398	20.00	28.00	LR-30	45.50	
4	TTR-3366	15.50		LR-1818	26.50	
5	BR-47	34.40		FRR-2398	22.25	
6	GST-3389	29.95		LRP-111	19.95	
7	GST-2228	35.50		M-389	22.35	
8	GST-5505	33.50		M-330	22.35	
9	UMJR-100	54.00		M-2323	12.50	
10	FRR-556	29.00		SSB-2	19.95	
11						
12						

The difference is that you must highlight all cells that will receive copies of the formula, as shown in the figure. When you use the Copy and Paste commands, all highlighted cells will receive copies relative to their locations.

Excel copies formulas in a relative fashion unless you specifically prevent it from doing so. Preventing this type of copying requires using absolute references in formulas—the topic of the next section.

Understanding Cell References

At times you may need to copy formulas without making some cell references relative. Perhaps a formula contains two cell references, and one should remain the same after copying. A reference that remains the same, no matter what its location, is called an *absolute* cell reference. As an example, take the price list from figure 4.14. In this case, however, the formula will be altered so that the markup amount can be entered into a worksheet cell (C1). This arrangement lets the operator experiment with different markup amounts to see how they affect the prices. Figure 4.16 shows the new example.

	File	**Edit**	**Formula**	**Format**	**Data**	**Options**	**Macro**	**Window**	

C3	=B3*C1					

Worksheet2

	A	B	C	D	E	F
1		MARKUP	140%			
2						
3	TTR-398	20.00	21.70			
4	TTR-3366	15.50				
5	BR-47	34.40				
6	GST-3389	29.95				
7	GST-2228	35.50				
8	GST-5505	33.50				
9	UMJR-100	54.00				
10	FRR-556	29.00				
11						
12						

Fig. 4.16.

An example requiring an absolute cell reference.

The formula in cell C3 now reads

=B3*C1

Cell C1 contains the markup amount. When this formula is copied into the remaining cells, the first cell reference (B3) should be adjusted for each copy, but the reference to cell C1 should remain the same for every copy. Here is what a few of the formulas should look like:

C4: =B4*C1
C5: =B5*C1
C6: =B6*C1

But if you copied the formula as shown, the resulting copies look like this:

C4: =B4*C2
C5: =B5*C3
C6: =B6*C4

Both cell references are adjusted. To make cell C1 an absolute reference in the formula in cell B3, add dollar signs in front of the column letter and row number, like this:

=B3*$C$1

Now try copying the formula; the reference to C1 will remain absolute. Figure 4.17 shows the formulas contained in the cell after the absolute reference is copied.

Fig. 4.17.

Copying absolute references.

	🍎 File Edit Formula Format Data Options Macro Window
	C14		

Worksheet2

	A	B	C	D	E	F
1		MARKUP	1.4			
2						
3	TTR-398	20	=B3*$C$1			
4	TTR-3366	15.5	=B4*$C$1			
5	BR-47	34.4	=B5*$C$1			
6	GST-3389	29.95	=B6*$C$1			
7	GST-2228	35.5	=B7*$C$1			
8	GST-5505	33.5	=B8*$C$1			
9	UMJR-100	54	=B9*$C$1			
10	FRR-556	29	=B10*$C$1			
11						
12						

As a final example, suppose that the worksheet uses two different cell references for the markups—each column with its own reference, as shown in figure 4.18.

Fig. 4.18.

A sample worksheet with two markup references, or one for each column. The resulting formulas are displayed in the cells.

	🍎 File Edit Formula Format Data Options Macro Window
	F3		=E3*F$1

Worksheet2

	A	B	C	D	E	F
1		MARKUP	1.4			1.35
2						
3	TTR-398	20	=B3*C$1	LR-30	45.5	=E3*F$1
4	TTR-3366	15.5	=B4*C$1	LR-1818	26.5	=E4*F$1
5	BR-47	34.4	=B5*C$1	FRR-2398	22.25	=E5*F$1
6	GST-3389	29.95	=B6*C$1	LRP-111	19.95	=E6*F$1
7	GST-2228	35.5	=B7*C$1	M-398	22.35	=E7*F$1
8	GST-5505	33.5	=B8*C$1	M-330	22.35	=E8*F$1
9	UMJR-100	54	=B9*C$1	M-2323	12.5	=E9*F$1
10	FRR-556	29	=B10*C$1	SSB-2	19.95	=E10*F$1
11						
12						

In this example, only the reference to row 1 was absolute in the original formula. The original formula in cell C3 was =E3*C$1. This setup causes the formulas to use the appropriate cell from row 1.

When this formula was copied, each column used the respective markup amount relative to the column, as shown by the formulas in figure 4.18. Notice that the dollar sign appears before the row reference only. Thus the row stays absolute, whereas the rest of the formula is relative.

You can also make a range reference absolute by including the dollar signs as part of the range. In the example, you might enter this formula into cell C12:

```
=SUM($C$3:$C$10)
```

The range C3:C10 is made completely absolute by the use of the dollar signs. When this formula is copied to another cell, the range remains constant: it does not adjust to the new location. Often, you'll want the range to adjust, such as when you duplicate formulas across a row or column. In the example, you might copy this formula from cell C12 to cell F12. In this case, you would want the range reference to be relative.

 Using dollar signs for absolute references affects the Fill Down and Fill Right commands also.

Using Absolute References with Range Names

When you define a range name, Excel assumes that you want the range reference to be absolute and includes the needed dollar signs in the Refers To information. For example, if you highlight the range A3:C3 and then select the Define Name command to give this range a name, Excel displays the dialog box shown in figure 4.19.

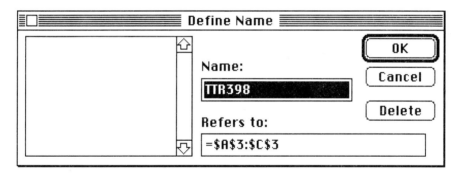

Fig. 4.19.

Range names assume absolute references in the Define Name dialog box.

As you can see, the range reference contains dollar signs to make it absolute. Thus when you copy a formula that contains this range name, the range will remain constant. Perhaps Excel makes these references absolute because named ranges are more likely to be unique blocks of data on the worksheet. In any event, you can remove the dollar signs from the reference if you want the range to be relative.

It's unlikely that you'll want to remove all dollar signs from range name references. More likely, you may remove only the row or column dollar signs. This way, the range can adjust when it needs to reference different rows or columns of data. Figure 4.20 shows an example.

Fig. 4.20.

Using relative range names.

	File Edit Formula Format Data Options Macro Window					
C12		=SUM(prices)				

	A	B	C	D	E	F
1		MARKUP	140%			135%
2						
3	TTR-398	20.00	28.00	LR-50	45.50	61.43
4	TTR-3366	15.50	21.70	LR-1818	26.50	35.78
5	BR-47	34.40	48.16	FRR-2398	22.25	30.04
6	GST-3389	29.95	41.93	LRP-111	19.95	26.93
7	GST-2228	35.50	49.70	M-398	22.35	30.17
8	GST-5505	33.50	46.90	M-330	22.35	30.17
9	UMJR-100	54.00	75.60	M-2323	12.50	16.88
10	FRR-556	29.00	40.60	SSB-2	19.95	26.93
11						
12			352.59			258.32
13						
14						

The range name PRICES refers to the range reference C$3:C$10—a result of selecting range C3:C10, choosing the Formula Define Name command, and removing the dollar signs from the column C references. The name PRICES was given to the resulting range reference. The formula =SUM(PRICES) was entered into cell C12 and copied to cell F12. Because of the relative nature of the range reference, the range PRICES refers to two different ranges in the two formulas—each one relative to its column.

Caution: Be careful when you use relative range names; you might later need to use the range in a different situation that requires an absolute reference. Forgetting that the range name is relative, you could end up with the wrong result. For this reason, you might consider naming the range a second time, with a reference that is completely absolute.

When you use the Formula Apply Names command to switch range references with their respective range names, Excel offers several options relating to the references. After selecting Formula Apply Names, you can choose the options at the bottom of the dialog box or choose the Options button to view more options. These options help save time when you must apply many names throughout the worksheet or when you are applying relative ranges throughout the worksheet. Use these options with care; they can be tricky!

The following sections discuss the options available from the Apply Names dialog box. You can access the last three options by clicking on the Options button in the initial Apply Names dialog box. Clicking on the Options button calls up the dialog box shown in figure 4.21.

```
┌──────────────────────────────────────────────┐
│  Apply Names                ┌──────────────┐   │
│ ┌──────────────────────┐┌─┐ │      OK       │  │
│ │ Advertising          ││⇧│ └──────────────┘   │
│ │ Bank                 │├─┤ ┌──────────────┐   │
│ │ Depreciation         ││▓│ │   Cancel      │  │
│ │ FIRST_Q              ││▓│ └──────────────┘   │
│ │ FOURTH_Q             ││⇩│ ┌──────────────┐   │
│ └──────────────────────┘└─┘ │  Options >>   │  │
│                             └──────────────┘   │
│  ☒ Ignore Relative/Absolute                    │
│  ☒ Use Row and Column Names                    │
│     ☒ Omit Column Name if Same Column          │
│     ☒ Omit Row Name if Same Row                │
│    ┌─Name Order──────────────────────────┐     │
│    │ ⦿ Row Column     ○ Column Row        │     │
│    └─────────────────────────────────────┘     │
└──────────────────────────────────────────────┘
```

Fig. 4.21.

The full set of Apply Names options.

Ignore Relative/Absolute

When this box is checked, Excel replaces all ranges that match the range name reference—regardless of relative and absolute status. For example, if the range name PRICES applies to the range $C$3:$C$10, applying the name PRICES with the Ignore Relative/Absolute box checked will replace, with the range name PRICES, the references

$C$3:$C$10
C3:C10
$C3:$C10
$C3:C10

and so on. Note that when the name PRICES appears in place of these references, it still applies to the range $C$3:$C$10. Therefore, you may be converting some references. Doing so will not change the results of those formulas, but it may affect the way those formulas can be copied for future needs. To replace only those references that match the range name exactly, remove the check mark from this box before applying the name.

Use Row and Column Names

Figure 4.20 showed why you might need a relative range reference in a formula. Basically, a relative range reference (or a name that applies to a relative reference) is desirable if you need to copy the formula and adjust the range reference to correspond to each copy.

That's great if you remember to create the range name before copying the formula, as was done in figure 4.20. But what if you have already copied a formula and then want to change the range references to range names? Figure 4.22 shows an example.

Fig. 4.22.

A worksheet with totals copied across the bottoms of columns. Formulas are displayed in this figure.

	File	**Edit**	**Formula**	**Format**	**Data**	**Options**	**Macro**	**Window**

A1			

Worksheet2

	A	B	C	D	E	F
1		MARKUP	1.4			1.35
2						
3	TTR-398	20	=B3*C$1	LR-30	45.5	=E3*F$1
4	TTR-3366	15.5	=B4*C$1	LR-1818	26.5	=E4*F$1
5	BR-47	34.4	=B5*C$1	FRR-2398	22.25	=E5*F$1
6	GST-3389	29.95	=B6*C$1	LRP-111	19.95	=E6*F$1
7	GST-2228	35.5	=B7*C$1	M-398	22.35	=E7*F$1
8	GST-5505	33.5	=B8*C$1	M-330	22.35	=E8*F$1
9	UMJR-100	54	=B9*C$1	M-2323	12.5	=E9*F$1
10	FRR-556	29	=B10*C$1	SSB-2	19.95	=E10*F$1
11						
12		=SUM(B3:B10)	=SUM(C3:C10)		=SUM(E3:E10)	=SUM(F3:F10)
13						
14						

This figure shows a typical row of totals created by copying one formula across the row, using the Fill Right command. Now suppose that you want to change the range reference in each of these cells to the name PRICES. How do you apply this name in one step when each range reference is different? First, define the range B$3:B$10 as the name PRICES, using the Formula Define Name command (note the removal of the columnar dollar signs). Next, use the Formula Apply Names command and select the name PRICES from the list. Before clicking on the Apply button, remove the check mark from the Use Row and Column Names box.

When you apply this column-relative range name to a series of column-relative formulas without the Use Row and Column Names box checked, Excel applies the name to each of the respective formulas—and keeps the range references column-relative. In short, although each formula simply refers to the range PRICES, that range is different for each of the formulas.

Omit Column Name If Same Column

When this box is checked (which is the normal setting), Excel ignores the row reference if the reference contains the same column but a different row as the name reference.

Omit Row Name If Same Row

When this box is checked (which is the normal setting), Excel ignores the column reference if the reference contains the same row but a different column as the name reference.

Name Order

This option determines whether the row or column name reference appears first in a range reference that matches both the row and column reference. The name order should make little difference.

Using the Ditto Commands

Another way to copy information into a worksheet is to use one of the ditto commands. The ditto commands, as the name suggests, duplicate information from above. Just as you might use a ditto mark on a piece of paper to indicate "same as above," you can use the ditto marks in a worksheet for the same reason.

Excel provides two ditto commands. The first is Command+' (single quotation mark), which inserts the formula contained in the cell that is above the active cell. This command is similar to Fill Down but is intended to speed up data entry. When the pointer is in a cell that is to contain the same information as the cell above, just press Command+'. This command duplicates formulas as though they are absolute references.

The second ditto command is Command+" (double quotation mark), which duplicates the value from the cell above. If the cell above contains a formula, only its value will be duplicated. For example, suppose that cell A1 contains the formula =B5+25 and that its result is 35. Using the command Command+" in cell A2 places the value 35 into cell A2.

Using Undo

When you make changes to a worksheet, such as copying and moving, you can use the Undo command if you change your mind about an action. If you select Undo from the Edit menu immediately after performing an action, Excel will "set the clock back" and pretend the action never happened. It's important that you use the command immediately after the action you want to undo. This command works only on the most recent action you perform. Thus you can always undo an undo operation.

Summary

This chapter covered everything you need to know about editing information in a worksheet. Basic editing involves changing information in cells, but you can also use Excel's special tools to make automatic changes to data, formulas, and references throughout the worksheet. The following is a list of points to remember:

❏ To edit information in a cell, select the cell and use the mouse to change information in the formula bar.

❏ You can accept your changes by pressing Return; you can reject them by clicking in the cancel box.

❏ Use the Formula Replace command to change formulas or text throughout the worksheet.

❏ Use the Edit Clear command to remove information from cells.

❏ Use the Edit Delete command to remove cells, rows, or columns from the worksheet.

❏ Use the Edit Insert command to add cells, rows, or columns to the worksheet.

❏ The Edit Cut command is useful for moving data from one location to another.

❏ You can make a cell reference absolute by adding dollar signs to its row and column specifications, as in $C$1.

Chapter 5, "Formatting the Worksheet," discusses how to format the worksheet.

5

Formatting the Worksheet

This chapter shows you how to use Excel's formatting commands to improve the appearance of a worksheet. After learning how to change the widths of columns, the heights of rows, and other display aspects of the worksheet, you learn how to use fonts, type styles, and color (the use of color applies only to color systems). Finally, the chapter explains the various numeric formats and attributes available in the Format menu. Format-menu options include those for setting the number of decimal places in numerals, showing dollar signs, and displaying negative numbers in parentheses.

With a few exceptions, formatting features apply to information that has been selected. In other words, to format information, you must first select the information and then select the formatting command. The data-selecting methods introduced in Chapter 3 will be useful in this chapter and throughout the book.

Aligning Information within a Cell

Whether a cell contains text, numbers, or dates, you can align the data horizontally within the cell's boundaries. Information can be left-aligned, right-aligned, or centered in the cell, as shown in figure 5.1.

Fig. 5.1.

The three types of alignment.

	A	B	C	D	E	F
1						
2		RIGHT				
3		LEFT				
4		CENTER				
5						
6						
7						
8						

Normally, numbers and dates are right-aligned; text, left-aligned. You can change the default alignment, however. To do so, first select the cell or cells you want to change; then select the Alignment option from the Format menu. The dialog box shown in figure 5.2 appears.

Fig. 5.2.

The Alignment options.

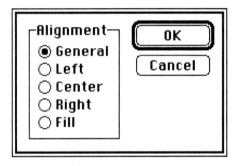

Choose the alignment option you want and then press Return. The option you choose affects any cells that are selected at the time. The General option, the default, causes numbers to align at the right and text to align at the left. The Fill option fills each cell with the information already in it. In other words, the information in the cell is repeated until the cell is full. This option can be useful for creating visual effects with special fonts and symbols. For example, if you enter the Option+Shift+~ character into a cell and then align the cell with the Fill option, the result will look like figure 5.3.

Fig. 5.3.

Using the Fill option with special characters.

	A	B	C	D	E	F
1						
2						
3		⌧⌧⌧⌧⌧⌧⌧				
4						
5						
6						

Creating Columns of Text

Although Excel is no word processor, it has a special feature for creating columns of text. You can use this feature to add explanatory information to a worksheet or chart. Using the font capabilities described later, you can make this column of information an attractive addition to the worksheet. Excel takes rows of text entered into the worksheet and merges them into a specified portion of the original area, making the width of each row uniform. This specified portion includes the leftmost column of the text plus any additional columns. To use this feature, move to the area of the worksheet where you want the column; then follow these steps:

1. Type each line of each paragraph in a separate row, using the down arrow or Return key between the lines. For now it's okay if the information spills into several columns. Just make sure that you begin each line in the column that will be used for the final information. Leave a blank row to separate paragraphs. The result will look something like figure 5.4.

Creating Columns

	A	B	C	D	E	F	
1							
2		This is a bunch of text that will be formatted in a column.					
3		Each row can extend as far as desired, but					
4		the rows should all start at the same column. That column					
5		must be the first column in which you want the final block of text to appear.					
6							
7		Just type each line of text, breaking with the Return key whenever you think					
8		have extended the line as far as you like.					
9		Remember that blank rows will remain blank-- forming paragraphs.					
10							
11							
12							

Worksheet6

Fig. 5.4.

Preparing a column of text.

2. Select a range of cells containing the first column of the text entered in step 1 plus as many rows or columns as you would like to fill with the text. If you're unsure how many rows to select, select as many as possible that do not interfere with other information. You can select more than one column to achieve the width you want; just make sure that the first column is selected. Figure 5.5 shows an example of a selected range.

Fig. 5.5.

The selected area
to be filled by
columnar text.

♠	File	Edit	Formula	Format	Data	Options	Macro	Window

| | B2 | | | This is a bunch of text that will be formatted in a column. |

	A	B	C	D	E	F
1						
2		This is a bunch	of text that will	be formatted in a column.		
3		Each row can extend as far as desired, but				
4		the rows should all start at the same column. That column				
5		must be the first column in which you want the final block of text to appear.				
6						
7		Just type each line of text, breaking with the Return key whenever you think				
8		have extended the line as far as you like.				
9		Remember that blank rows will remain blank-- forming paragraphs.				
10						
11						
12						
13						
14						
15						
16						

Notice that the selected area includes the first column of
the entered text plus one more column for extra width.

3. Select the Justify command from the Format menu. The
text will fit into the selected range, as shown in figure 5.6.

Fig. 5.6.

The finished
column of text.

	Worksheet6					
	A	B	C	D	E	F
1						
2		This is a bunch of text that				
3		will be formatted in a column.				
4		Each row can extend as far as				
5		desired, but the rows should				
6		all start at the same column.				
7		That column must be the first				
8		column in which you want the				
9		final block of text to appear.				
10						
11		Just type each line of text,				
12		breaking with the Return key				
13		whenever you think you have				
14		extended the line as far as you				
15		like. Remember that blank				
16		rows will remain blank--				
17		forming paragraphs.				
18						

Excel merges the lines of text together and fits them into the specified
range. Blank rows are used to separate paragraphs. If there is too much
text to fit into the selected range, Excel asks whether it can go beyond
the range you selected. Click on OK if you want Excel to proceed. Note,

however, that clicking on OK can cause information beyond the selected range to be overwritten. If you do not click on OK, Excel truncates the text at the bottom of the range.

Choosing Fonts, Sizes, and Styles

One of the most dramatic things you can do to control the appearance of information is to employ fonts, sizes, and styles. Like many Macintosh applications, Excel accesses fonts contained in your system file (or font files opened with the Suitcase desk accessory). The type and number of fonts available in your system depend on the way you have set up the system. Excel supports PostScript fonts as well as bit-mapped (or screen) fonts.

Changing the Standard Font

Excel automatically uses Geneva 10 as the default (or standard) font for worksheet information. Unless you specify a different font, Excel will enter all your information in Geneva 10. By using the Standard Font command in the Options menu, however, you can change this standard font. An example of available fonts and their sizes is shown in the Standard Font dialog box (see fig. 5.7). These fonts and sizes are not available on all systems; their availability depends on how the Macintosh has been set up.

Font	Size	Style	
Chicago	9	☐ Bold	OK
Courier	10	☐ Italic	Cancel
Geneva	12	☐ Underline	
Helvetica	14	☐ Strikeout	
Monaco	18	☐ Outline	
New York	20	☐ Shadow	

Geneva   10

Color

■ ☐ R G B Y M C ● Automatic

Fig. 5.7.

The Options Standard Font dialog box.

Select the font and size you want from the lists provided. Excel will use the selected font and size as the standard instead of Geneva 10. All cells that have not been formatted with a different font will change to this new standard. The standard-font change will not affect cells that have been formatted individually.

You can also set a character style for the standard font. Just check the box next to the style (or styles) you want to activate throughout the worksheet. You can combine styles if you like—just check all boxes that apply. The following are examples of all the styles available:

Bold	**Example**
Italic	*Example*
Underline	<u>Example</u>
Strikeout	~~Example~~
Outline	Example
Shadow	Example

In addition to changing the font, size, and style used throughout the worksheet, this procedure changes the widths and heights of cells throughout the worksheet. Even if you don't change the point size of a font, some fonts are naturally taller or wider than others. These differences may affect the way information fits into the cells. If changing the fonts or sizes (or both) makes the information too large to fit into the cell, Excel automatically adjusts the width and height of cells. This automatic change affects only those cells whose width and height have not been adjusted manually (as described later in this chapter).

Finally, you can choose a color for the standard font. Color selections appear at the bottom of the Font dialog box and include black, white, red, green, blue, yellow, magenta, and cyan. Of course, this selection applies only to color systems.

Standard Font Not Affecting All Cells?

If the standard-font change you make does not affect all the cells in the worksheet, the reason is that you have already formatted those cells manually. The standard-font procedure affects only cells that have not been assigned fonts, sizes, styles, or colors individually. Likewise, changes in height and width affect only columns and rows that have not been changed already. To reapply the standards to all cells in the worksheet, follow the steps on the next page.

1. Select the entire worksheet by pressing Command+Shift+space or Command+A.

2. Select the Font command from the Format menu.

3. Check the Standard Font button.

4. Click on OK.

Changing Individual Cells and Ranges

You can change the fonts used in individual cells throughout the worksheet by selecting the cells to be changed and then choosing the Font option from the Format menu. Available fonts and their sizes are shown in the dialog box (see fig. 5.8).

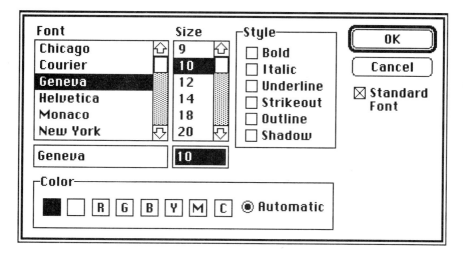

Fig. 5.8.

The Format Font dialog box.

From the lists, select the font and size you want. If you check the Standard Font box, Excel will apply the standard font to your selected cells. (This feature is useful for removing font changes from cells, returning them to normal.) The font selection will apply only to selected cells. You can specify a point size that is not listed: just enter the custom size (up to size 127) in the box directly under the list of available sizes, as shown in figure 5.9.

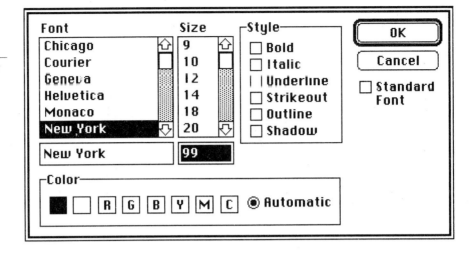

Fig. 5.9.

Defining a custom font size of 99 points.

Press the Tab key until you select the custom-size box; then type the size you want. If you do not change the information in this box, the box will reflect the size selected in the list. Besides changing fonts and sizes, you can select one or more of the character styles shown. You can also select one of the colors: black, white, red, green, blue, yellow, magenta, or cyan.

Excel will automatically adjust the heights and widths of cells to accommodate your font and size selection. However, this automatic adjustment applies only to rows and columns that have not been adjusted individually or that have been set to the standard width. If Excel does not adjust a column's width or a row's height to accommodate the selected font, the reason is that you have already set a width or height for the column or row. You can change the width and height as described later in this chapter.

Preformatting Blank Cells

You can select a range consisting of blank cells and then set the font, size, and style for that range. When you enter information into those cells, it will appear in the format specified. This arrangement can save you some time. The ability to preformat blank cells is especially useful for formatting a row or column that will contain headings and such.

Formatting before Copying

A useful technique is to format cells containing formulas before you copy the formulas to other cells. If the formula is formatted when you copy it, the formatting gets copied also. In other words, the Copy and Paste commands duplicate everything about a cell, including its format. Taking advantage of this feature can save you much time when you design worksheets.

Conversely, you may want to copy only a formula and not the formatting applied to it. Or maybe you want to copy only the formatting you've applied to a cell so that you don't have to repeat the formatting process. In these cases, copy the original cell normally (using the Copy command); then use the Paste Special command in the Edit menu. The dialog box shown in figure 5.10 appears.

```
┌─Paste──────┐  ┌─Operation──┐   ╭──────────╮
│ ⦿ All       │  │ ⦿ None      │   │    OK    │
│ ○ Formulas  │  │ ○ Add       │   ╰──────────╯
│ ○ Values    │  │ ○ Subtract  │   ┌──────────┐
│ ○ Formats   │  │ ○ Multiply  │   │  Cancel  │
│ ○ Notes     │  │ ○ Divide    │   └──────────┘
└─────────────┘  └─────────────┘

☐ Skip Blanks   ☐ Transpose
```

Fig. 5.10.

The Paste Special dialog box.

Normally, the dialog box is set to paste all information from the original cell. This information includes the formula (if any), its value, the cell's format, and any notes attached to the cell (cell notes are explained in Chapter 8). However, you can control what Excel pastes into the new cell by choosing one of the Paste options from this dialog box. Select the Formulas option to avoid getting the format of the original cell. Select the Formats option to paste only the format of the original, not the data itself. You can format existing data this way: simply copy a cell containing the format you want and then paste the cell to the range of cells that are unformatted. Use the Formats option in the Paste Special command when pasting.

Changing Column Widths

When a label or value does not fit into a cell, you'll most likely want to expand the width of the cell so that the information fits. To change the width of a cell, you must change the entire column in which the cell appears. First, place the pointer on the line between the column you are changing and the column to the right. Find this line within the column title area at the top of the worksheet. As you place the pointer onto the line, the pointer shape will change (see fig. 5.11).

Fig. 5.11.

Expanding column widths. The pointer shape changes when it passes over the column divider.

🍎 File Edit Formula Format Data Options Macro Window

| B3 | |

Worksheet1

	A	B	⊹ C	D	E	F
1						
2						
3						
4						
5						

Now click and drag the mouse to the right or left to increase or decrease the width of the column. You can expand a column's width almost indefinitely. Unfortunately, if you drag beyond the edge of the screen, Excel does not automatically scroll the page so that you can continue dragging. Also, you can sometimes lose the ability to click on the column border if the column is as wide as the screen (see fig. 5.12).

Fig. 5.12.

When a cell is as wide as the screen, you can lose contact with its right border.

Worksheet1

	A
1	
2	
3	
4	
5	
6	
7	

To expand the column further, you must specify a column width in characters. To manually specify a particular width for a column, position the pointer on any cell in the desired column. Next, choose the Column Width command from the Format menu. The dialog box in figure 5.13 appears.

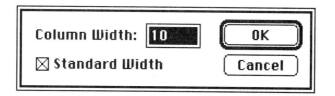

Fig. 5.13.

The Column Width
dialog box.

Enter the number of characters for the column; then press Return. The actual width of the column will vary depending on the active font. That is, 10 characters in Times may be smaller than 10 characters in Helvetica. Excel uses the width of the numeral 8 to measure columns. You can return a column to its original width by checking the Standard Width box and pressing Return. Column widths can be changed at any time.

Changing the Widths of Several Columns at Once

You can change the widths of several columns at one time by selecting all the columns before selecting the Column Width command. To change all the columns in a worksheet, select the entire worksheet. To select columns, see "Selecting Information" in Chapter 3.

Excel lets you enter a column width as small as zero characters. A column width of zero completely hides the column from view on the screen. Although the information in the column is still used in the worksheet (that is, formulas remain intact), the column will be invisible, and you may notice a skip in the sequence of column letters at the top of the screen.

Hidden columns can be useful in worksheets that contain sensitive data, such as payroll amounts, markup amounts, commission rates, and so on. However, Excel offers a more secure way of hiding information; for more information, see Chapter 3.

To expand a column that has been hidden with a zero width, select the column just left of the hidden column; then drag across to the column just right of the hidden column. For example, if column C is hidden, drag across columns B and D. Next, use the Column Width command in the Format menu to expand the width of all three columns.

Changing Row Heights

You can change the height of a row the same way that you alter the width of a column. Just select the rows you want and then use the command Format Row Height; the dialog box shown in figure 5.14 appears.

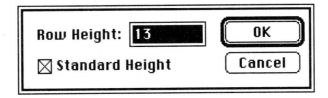

You can specify a row height by entering a specific point size. A point size of zero hides a row completely.

Adding Borders, Boxes, and Shading

The Border command in the Format menu lets you add borders and boxes to the worksheet and lets you shade areas of the worksheet for emphasis. Excel will draw lines around any cell or range, creating a box, or add single lines along the top, bottom, or sides of information. You can draw a line on any of the four sides of a cell. Drawing lines across many cells creates various effects. To draw a single line across the bottom of the worksheet, for example, just create line segments along the bottom of each cell in a row. You can create a grid pattern by adding lines to all four sides of several cells. Figure 5.15 shows various lines added to the sides of worksheet cells, as well as showing the shade pattern.

You don't have to draw these line segments one cell at a time. You can create lines for an entire range at once. Just select the range you want; then use the Border command. In addition, Excel provides an option for creating a box around a specified range, so you don't have to draw lines on the top, bottom, left, and right sides individually. The Border dialog box, shown in figure 5.16, shows the available options.

```
┌─────────────────────────────────────────────────┐
│ ▢▦▦▦▦▦▦▦▦▦▦ Worksheet1 ▦▦▦▦▦▦▦▦▦ ▢│
│    A    │   B   │   C   │   D   │   E   │   F   │ │
│ 1                                                │
│ 2            OUTLINE         SHADE    RIGHT SIDE  │
│ 3                                                │
│ 4                                                │
│ 5                                                │
│ 6                                                │
│ 7                                                │
│ 8         ALL SIDES                              │
│ 9                                                │
│10                                                │
│11                                                │
│12                                                │
│13                                                │
│14                                                │
│15         TOP                                    │
│16                                                │
│17              BOTTOM                            │
│18                                                │
│19                                                │
└─────────────────────────────────────────────────┘
```

Fig. 5.15.

Using the Border command to draw lines and boxes.

```
┌─────────────────────────────────────┐
│  ┌─Border─────┐  ┌──────────────┐    │
│  │ ☐ Outline  │  │      OK       │   │
│  │ ☐ Left     │  └──────────────┘    │
│  │ ☐ Right    │  ┌──────────────┐    │
│  │ ☐ Top      │  │    Cancel     │   │
│  │ ☐ Bottom   │  └──────────────┘    │
│  │ ☐ Shade    │                      │
│  └────────────┘                      │
└─────────────────────────────────────┘
```

Fig. 5.16.

The Border command options.

Check all the options that you would like to apply to the selected cell (or cells). Choosing the Outline option differs from selecting all four sides (left, right, top, and bottom). Selecting all four sides with a range of cells produces a grid pattern, in which all cells in the range contain borders. The Outline option produces an outline around the range without outlining each cell. The Shade option fills in the selected cells with a gray shade. You might want to combine shades with outlines for different effects. The following is the procedure for using the Border command.

1. Select the cell or range to which you want to add a line (or lines).

2. Choose the Border command from the Format menu.

Using the Border Command

3. Select Left, Right, Top, or Bottom to draw a line on the respective side of each selected cell. Select Outline to draw a box around the range. Select Shade to fill in the range with a gray pattern.

Because Outline is the most common of the border commands, Excel provides a keyboard shortcut to outlining a range. Just select the range and then press Command+Option+O to add the outline. You can change the dimensions of a box by manipulating row heights and column widths.

Line Thickness

To apply bold, thick lines to your worksheet, try using the Shade option in the Border command. First, shade an empty row or column (or portion thereof); then change the row height and column width to control the thickness of the "line."

Normally, placing a line on the bottom of one cell produces the same result as placing a line on the top of the cell below that first cell. For example, moving to cell A1 and using the Bottom option is the same as moving to cell A2 and using the Top option. Page breaks, however, may affect the appearance of these lines on the printed page. If a line appears on the bottom edge of a cell, and a page break occurs just after that cell, the first page will display the line and the second page will not. Alternatively, if a line appears on the top edge of a cell, and that cell marks the top of a new page, the new page will contain the line and the preceding page will not.

Changing the Display

One of the easiest ways to make a worksheet more readable is to change the way it is displayed on-screen. Besides enabling you to add your own display elements (such as borders), Excel lets you remove or alter some of the built-in display elements (such as the worksheet grid lines). By manipulating these built-in display features, you can make your worksheets more readable on-screen. Options to control the built-in display elements of a worksheet appear in two places: the Display command in the Options menu, and the Workspace command in the Options menu.

Changing Grid Lines and Headings

Excel provides commands for removing the grid lines (or cell grids) and the row and column headings. You also can change their color. Changes to the grid lines affect the entire worksheet and cannot be applied to portions of the grid. To change the grid lines or row and column headings, simply choose the Display option from the Options menu. The dialog box shown in figure 5.17 appears.

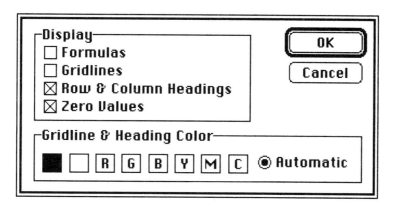

Fig. 5.17.

The Display dialog box.

To display the grid lines or the row and column headings, place a check in the appropriate boxes. To remove these elements, remove the check marks. Normally, these elements are displayed. Figure 5.18 shows a sample worksheet that doesn't display grid lines or row and column headings.

❤ File Edit Formula Format Data Options Macro Window

excel.mac

	FIRST Q	SECOND Q	THIRD Q	FOURTH Q
Salaries	9000.00	9000.00	9000.00	9000.00
Utilities	200.00	200.00	200.00	250.00
Professional Services	1000.00	1000.00	1000.00	1200.00
Rent	1500.00	1500.00	1500.00	1500.00
Advertising	3000.00	3000.00	3500.00	3000.00
Bank	120.00	120.00	100.00	100.00
Freight	2200.00	2200.00	2500.00	3000.00
Insurance	3500.00	3500.00	3500.00	3500.00
Office Supplies	300.00	300.00	300.00	300.00
Depreciation	1000.00	1200.00	1000.00	1000.00
TOTAL	21820.00	22020.00	22600.00	22850.00

Ready NUM

Fig. 5.18.

A worksheet with no grid lines or headings.

You can change the color of these elements by selecting one of the colors at the bottom of the dialog box. Colors apply only if the elements are displayed.

 The options Gridlines and Row & Column Headings affect the screen view only. Printouts may still display the grid lines and headings. To remove these elements from printouts, use the Page Setup options, discussed in Chapter 9.

Hiding Values of Zero

Worksheets can look neater when values of zero are displayed as blanks rather than as zeros. Eliminating zeros is especially useful in forms. To blank out values of zero, uncheck the Zero Values option in the Display dialog box of the Options menu. This option affects the entire worksheet and ignores your selected range. To hide zero values in specific cells or portions of the worksheet, use a custom number format as described later in this chapter. Actually, custom number formats give you even more control over values of zero, enabling you to display zeros in red, for instance. If you use a custom number format to control the display of zeros, the Zero Values option will not affect cells that use the custom format.

Displaying Formula Text

If your worksheet contains several complex formulas, you may find the Formulas option handy. This option, available through the Options Display command, controls whether cells display the results of formulas or the formulas themselves. Displaying the formulas can be useful when you create complex worksheets. If you display formulas by checking the Formula option, printouts from those worksheets will show formulas rather than results.

Removing Scroll Bars

Removing the scroll bars from the screen provides a little extra room for the worksheet. If you are familiar with the keyboard movement commands, you may find the scroll bars unnecessary. To remove the scroll bars, select the Workspace command from the Options menu; then click on the Scroll Bars option to remove the check mark.

Removing the Status and Formula Bars

Excel lets you remove two more screen elements: the status bar and the formula bar. Removing these bars can be useful in macros that control a worksheet used by someone else. Removing these elements also can come in handy when you use multiple windows to display a worksheet. Windows intended only as a means of viewing the worksheet and not as a means of entering or editing information may not need the status bar and formula bar. (Windows are discussed in Chapter 7.)

To remove either element, select the Workspace command from the Options menu; then click on the Status Bar option or the Formula Bar option to remove the check mark.

Hiding Multiple Elements at Once

You may find that you prefer working with several worksheet elements hidden. But constantly returning to the Options menu and selecting the appropriate commands can be tedious. This procedure is especially annoying when you hide the same elements for many worksheets. Try using a macro to show or hide a preset combination of elements. One macro can show the elements, and another can hide them. The following are examples of such macros:

```
Hide
=DISPLAY(,FALSE,FALSE)
=WORKSPACE(,,,,FALSE,,,,)
=RETURN
Show
=DISPLAY(,TRUE,TRUE,,)
=WORKSPACE(,,,,TRUE,,,,)
=RETURN
```

Using Number Formats

Number formats affect the way numbers appear on the worksheet. A number that normally appears as

3984.3

can be displayed in many ways, based on the particular format used.

Here are some of the ways the number can appear in Excel:

3984

3984.30

3,984.30

$3984.30

398400%

Number formats control special symbols that apply to numbers, the display of negatives, and the display of zeros. Excel provides several formats for numbers but also lets you design custom formats.

Built-In Number Formats

To select one of the predesigned formats, first select the cell or range you want to format; then choose the Number option from the Format menu. The dialog box shown in figure 5.19 appears.

Fig. 5.19.

The Format Number dialog box, showing 8 of 12 possible formats.

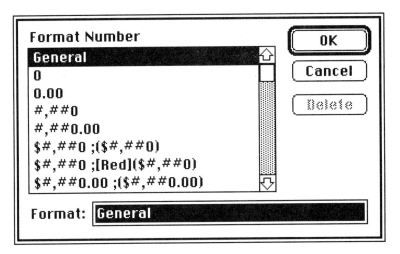

The dialog box lists all predesigned number formats, date formats, and time formats. Use the scroll bar to see more formats. Table 5.1 shows the effect of each built-in number format on a positive number, a negative number, and the number zero.

Table 5.1
Built-In Number Formats

Format	Positive	Negative	Zero
General	3595.5	-3595.5	0
0	3596	-3596	0
0.00	3595.50	-3595.50	0.00
#,##0	3,596	-3,596	0
#,##0.00	3,595.50	-3,595.50	0.00
$#,##0 ;($#,##0)	$3,596	($3,596)	$0
$#,##0 ;[RED]($#,##0)	$3,596	($3,596)*	$0
$#,##0.00 ;($#,##0.00)	$3,595.50	($3,595.50)	$0.00
$#,##0.00 ;[RED]($#,##0.00)	$3,595.50	($3,595.50)*	$0.00
0%	359550%	-359550%	0%
0.00%	359550.00%	-359550.00%	0.00%
0.00E+00	3.60E+03	-3.60E+03	0.00E+00

*Displays in red.

Excel provides keyboard shortcuts for some of these built-in formats. Just select the cell or range you want, and then use one of the following commands, pressing the Command key, the Option key, and the appropriate third key:

Command	Format
⌘ Option ~	General
⌘ Option !	0.00
⌘ Option $	$#,##0; ($#,##0)
⌘ Option %	0%
⌘ Option ^	0.00E+00

Formatting the Entire Worksheet

Remember that formatting applies to selected ranges. You can select rows, columns, or the entire worksheet if you like. The format you select applies to all selected cells. Formatting an entire worksheet can be useful when most cells use the format you specify.

Rounded Numbers

You may have noticed that some of the formats round numbers. This rounding effect is for display purposes only. Excel remembers the full value in the cell and uses the full value for all calculations. However, you can actually change the true number to the rounded version if you like. Such a change would affect all calculations based on the number. Use the ROUND function described in Chapter 6 for this purpose.

You can convert all numbers to their displayed format. Excel's Options Calculation Precision As Displayed command converts numbers from their true values (values entered) to their formatted values (displayed values). Be careful when using this command: values are permanently changed. Of course, because the values match the display, the number formats are no longer needed. Therefore, Excel applies the format 0.00 to all worksheet numbers after you convert.

Custom Number Formats

Although the built-in number formats are useful, you may need to create a custom format at times. Using a custom number format lets you deal with positive and negative numbers in a multitude of ways. In addition, you can add any text or symbol to a number format (such as *lbs* or *£*). Custom formats also give you control over colors used for positive numbers, negative numbers, zeros, and symbols. Finally, custom formats are stored with your worksheet, so they become a permanent part of your application.

To create a custom number format, select the cell or range that you would like to format. Then select the Number option from the Format menu and enter your custom format into the spaced marked Format. If this space already contains a format (that is, the one selected in the list), just erase the entry and begin a new format. When entering your format, follow these rules:

> *Rule 1. Use the number-formatting symbols discussed later in this section to specify the format.* Number formats use these symbols to indicate the various elements of a number. The symbols include # to represent a number, 0.00 to represent the treatment of zeros, and [RED] to indicate color. You've seen these and other symbols used in the built-in formats, but Excel provides many more symbols to use in custom formats.

> *Rule 2. Combine the symbols into three groups, separated by semicolons.* Each group represents a different element of a number. The first group controls positive numbers; the

second group controls negative numbers; the third group controls zeros. Using these three groups, you can format all types of numbers. For example, you can display positive numbers in blue; negative numbers in red, surrounded by the brackets < and >; and zeros in green. The custom format might appear as follows:

[BLUE]#;[RED]"<"#">";[GREEN]#

Notice that the three groups of symbols are separated by semicolons. If you leave any of the three groups blank, the appropriate type of number will appear blank. For example, to make values of zero blank (hidden) in the above example, you would use this variation:

[BLUE]#;[RED]"<"#">";

Notice that the third group (after the second semicolon) is empty. Be sure to specify three separate groups by including two semicolons—even if a group is blank. (If you're wondering why all the built-in formats do not use three groups, see rule 3.)

Rule 3. You can break rule 2 in some cases. To save time when creating certain formats, you can include only one or two groups of symbols. If you include only one group of symbols (no semicolons will be present), then the format applies to positive numbers, negative numbers, and zeros in the same way. If you use two groups (one semicolon), then the first group applies to positive numbers and zeros, and the second group applies to negative numbers. This practice is not the same as leaving groups blank by including the semicolon with no symbols after it. The following is an illustration of the various groupings:

format if positive; format if negative; format if zero
format if positive or zero; format if negative
format for all numbers

The following is a list of the symbols you can use in each group of your number format. You can combine any of these symbols for various effects.

0 (Zero)

Indicates any numeric digit. If 0 appears on the left side of a decimal point (or with no decimal point), you do not need to repeat the symbol to indicate the number of digits allowed. In other words, if the number entered is larger (more digits), Excel will display it anyway. However, if the number you enter has fewer digits than the number of repeated 0 symbols, Excel will display the extra zeros. Suppose that you enter the following as the number format:

00000

If you enter the number 1, Excel displays 00001. If you enter 8398727, Excel displays 8398727.

If the symbol 0 appears on the right side of a decimal point, then Excel will round the number if it exceeds the indicated length. But if the number you enter has fewer digits than the indicated length, Excel includes extra zeros to match the indicated length. Suppose that you enter the following as the number format:

.000

If you enter the number .55, Excel displays .550. If you enter .4568, Excel displays .457.

(Number Sign)

Indicates any numeric digit. This symbol is similar to the 0 symbol, but numbers that have fewer digits than specified with this symbol will appear as entered. Consider the following format:

##.##

If you enter 150.629, Excel displays 150.63 (as if you had used the 0 symbol). However, if you enter 3.5, Excel displays 3.5 (inserting no extra zeros to fill the places). Note that you should not use only # symbols to the left of a decimal point. Doing so causes all numbers smaller than 1 to be displayed with a decimal point. Instead, use at least one zero, as in the following:

#0.##

. (Period)

Indicates a decimal point. The placement of this symbol among the # and 0 symbols determines the number of digits displayed on either side of the decimal point. Be sure that at least one zero appears on the left side of the decimal point.

% (Percent Sign)

Indicates a percentage. Excel converts the entry to a percentage by multiplying by 100 and adding the % character. You should combine this symbol with the # and/or 0 symbol to specify digits, as in the following example:

0%

The format 0% is one of Excel's built-in formats. If you enter .016, Excel displays 2%.

, (Comma)

Indicates separation of thousands. Inserting a comma between # or 0 symbols causes Excel to include commas in all appropriate places of a number. The format

#,##0

is a standard comma format. If you enter 3892, Excel displays 3,892. If you enter 3892782, Excel displays 3,892,782.

$ - + ( ) [space]

These symbols appear as part of the number format. Their position in the number is relative to their position among the # and 0 characters. The format

$(#0.00)

displays numbers in parentheses and with a dollar sign preceding the number, as in $(123.00). You might use the format ###-#### for phone numbers or use (###)###-#### to handle area codes. Try ###-##-#### for Social Security numbers. Use a standard space character to insert a space in the format. To use other characters in your number formats, read the following discussion of the backslash and "Text" parameters.

\ (Backslash) and "Text"

These two parameters produce similar results. The backslash symbol enters any single character into a format at the location of the backslash.

The actual character to insert into the format should appear immediately after the backslash:

#0.00\¢

This format includes the ¢ character after all numbers. If you enter 12.45, for example, Excel displays 12.45¢. The backslash does not print.

The "Text" parameter enters any text into the format. Just enclose in quotation marks the text you want to insert:

#0.00 "units";(##0.00);0.00

This format prints the word *units* after all positive numbers but not after negatives or zeros. For example, if you enter 34, Excel displays

34.00 units

Notice the space that appears in front of the text "units" in the custom format. As you can see, this space appears in the final formatted number.

* (Asterisk)

This symbol causes the character that follows it to repeat until the cell is full. The repeated character will not replace other numbers or symbols used in the format. Consider this example:

#0.00*[space]

A space character appearing just after the asterisk causes the number to be left-justified in the cell. In this case, you can use an alignment option with better results. However, the asterisk is useful for many tasks. It is often used to align currency symbols with the left edge of the cell while leaving the numbers right-justified, as in this example:

$* #0.00

Notice the space character between the asterisk and the # symbol. If you enter 45.95 into a cell formatted this way, Excel displays this:

$ 45.95

Be sure to include an asterisk in each group if you use more than one group.

[BLACK], [BLUE], [CYAN], [GREEN], [YELLOW], [MAGENTA], [RED], [WHITE]

Indicates the respective color. Use one of these symbols to change the color of the number. You can use a different color in each group of the format if you like. To display negative numbers in red, enter something like this:

    #0.#;[RED]#0.#

The symbol [RED] does not have to be in uppercase letters.

Using Text Formats

A specialized feature of Excel, text formats let you display text in any color or add any character or phrase to the text you've entered. For example, you can make any text entry (label) appear in blue. Although they may not make sense now, text formats are really just an extension of number formats. The text format is added as a fourth group of symbols to a number format.

If you add a third semicolon to a number format and then use one or more of the symbols after the semicolon (that is, if you create a fourth group), Excel uses the fourth group as the format for the cell *if the entry is text*. The following illustrates this setup:

> *format if positive; format if negative; format if zero; format if text*

Most likely, if you expect a number to be entered into a particular cell, the text format is meaningless. However, the text-format group can be used to display a message in case someone enters text into a cell intended for numbers:

    #0.00;(#0.00);;[GREEN]"Please Enter a Number"

In this format, the third group (controlling the format of a zero value) is blank; zeros thus appear blank. The fourth section prints the message *Please Enter a Number* in green when a text entry is made. Since there is no text placeholder (discussed in the next section) in the format, the actual entry will not appear if it's text. This result is what you want for cells in which the user is to enter only a number.

At times, however, you may want to accept a text entry and format it with a color or other message. In this case, you need to use a text placeholder.

The text placeholder is the text equivalent to the # and 0 symbols. The following are descriptions of this symbol and other symbols available for the text-format group.

@ (At Sign)

Indicates text. You do not need to repeat this character to specify the length of the text entry. Whenever this character appears in the text-format group, any text entry is accepted. For example, the format

;;;[BLUE]@

displays all numbers as blank but displays text in blue. If you enter "Hello", Excel displays *Hello* in blue. Notice that the number-formatting groups are blank. This arrangement is common when you expect the entry to be text. You can, however, format all four groups at once if you like.

[BLACK], [BLUE], [CYAN], [GREEN], [YELLOW], [MAGENTA], [RED], [WHITE]

Indicates the respective color. Use one of these symbols to change the color of the text.

Using Date Formats

Date formats can be applied to any number. Usually, however, they are used to alter the format that Excel automatically applies to a date. You can enter the sample date January 23, 1990, in any of the following ways:

1/23/90
23 Jan 90
23 January 1990
January 90
23 January
23 Jan
1/23
1-23

According to the way you have entered the date, Excel formats your entry in one of four ways. These four date formats are the built-in formats shown when you select the Number command from the Format menu. Besides using these four built-in formats, you can design custom date formats.

Remember that these formats are simply displaying numbers as dates. The numbers represent the number of days elapsed since January 1, 1904. See Chapter 3 for details about dates and date serial numbers.

Built-In Date Formats

The four date formats appear directly under the number formats when you select the Number command from the Format menu. They are the following:

Format Listing	Example
m/d/yy	1/23/89
d-mmm-yy	23-Jan-89
d-mmm	23-Jan
mmm-yy	Jan-89

When you enter a date that Excel recognizes as a date, one of these formats is automatically applied. You can specify a particular format from this list. To select a format, choose the Number option from the Format menu and select one of the four date formats. You can also use the keyboard command Command+Option+$ to format a date in the *d-mmm-yy* style.

Custom Date Formats

Unlike number formats, date formats have no groupings. Just enter a single format for all dates, using the symbols listed below. After you custom-format a cell or range, if you enter a date that Excel recognizes as a date, the entry will be displayed in the specified format. The following are the symbols available for dates.

m

Indicates a single-digit numeral for the month name. If the month can be represented by a single digit (January through September), its number is displayed as a single digit. For example, January appears as month 1 as opposed to month 01.

mm

Indicates a two-digit numeral for the month name. A single-digit month is displayed with a leading zero. For example, January is displayed as month 01.

mmm

Indicates a three-letter abbreviation for the month name. For example, January is displayed as Jan.

mmmm

Indicates a full-name month. For example, January is displayed as January.

d

Indicates a single-digit numeral for the day. If the day can be represented by a single digit, it is displayed with only one digit.

dd

Indicates a two-digit numeral for the day. A single-digit day is displayed with a leading zero. For example, the fifth of August is displayed as day 05.

ddd

Indicates a three-letter abbreviation for the day name. For example, Sat is displayed for a day that falls on Saturday.

dddd

Indicates a full-name day. For example, Saturday is displayed for a day that falls on Saturday.

You can combine these symbols in the date format in any way you like. Feel free to use two different day symbols to include both the day name and the number. Consider the following example:

dddd,mmm d

If you enter 1/25/91, this format displays Friday, Jan 25. Notice that the format also includes a comma after the day-name symbol. Actually, you can include any of the formatting symbols listed for number formats, including color specifications.

Using Time Formats

Excel formats numbers to represent time in much the same way that it formats numbers into dates. Time values represent the amount of time elapsed since 12 midnight. Time math, like date math, can be applied to such values. To enter a valid time, you must enter the amount of time elapsed since midnight. For example, the number .2967 produces a valid time (7:07:14) when the number is formatted with one of the time formats. However, you will most likely want to enter a time in such a way that Excel recognizes it as a time. The following are various ways to enter the time 4:35:

15:35
4:35
4:35:15
15:35:15
4:35 pm
4:35 am

If you enter time values in one of these ways, Excel uses one of the built-in time formats to display your entry. However, you can specify a custom time format by using the special time-formatting symbols.

Built-In Time Formats

The built-in time formats, listed under the date formats in the Number command of the Format menu, are the following:

Format Listing	Example
h:mm AM/PM	9:35 PM
h:mm:ss AM/PM	9:35:15 PM
h:mm	21:35
h:mm:ss	21:35:15
m/d/yy h:mm	1/23/89 21:35

Just highlight the cell or range to be formatted and select the Number command from the Format menu. Then select one of the time formats listed. Notice that the last format includes the date and time. You also can use the command Command+Option+@ to format a time in the *h:mm* format.

Custom Time Formats

Custom time formats work much like custom date formats. You need only enter one group of symbols for all time values. The following are descriptions of the available symbols.

h

Displays the hour as a numeral. If the hour has only one digit to the left of the colon, Excel displays only one digit before the colon (as in 1:00). If you don't specify an AM or PM symbol, the symbol *h* uses the 24-hour format.

hh

Displays the hour as a numeral. If the hour has only one digit to the left of the colon (as in 1:00), Excel adds a leading zero (01:00). If you don't specify an AM or PM symbol, the symbol *hh* uses the 24-hour format.

m

> Displays the minutes as a numeral. If the minutes portion contains only one digit (as in 1:05), Excel displays only one digit (1:5).

mm

> Displays the minutes as a numeral. If the minutes portion has only one digit (as in 1:05), Excel adds a leading zero (1:05).

s

> Displays seconds as a numeral. If the seconds portion contains only one digit (as in 1:25:05), Excel displays only one digit (1:25:5).

ss

> Displays the minutes as a numeral. If the minutes portion has only one digit (as in 1:25:05), Excel adds a leading zero (1:25:05).

AM/PM or am/pm

> When added to the time symbols listed earlier, the AM or PM symbol (or its lowercase equivalent) specifies the 12-hour format for time values. Times are labeled *AM* or *am* if before 12 noon; they are labeled *PM* or *pm* if after 12 noon.

A/P or a/p

> These symbols are the same as the AM/PM and am/pm symbols listed in the preceding section, except that only *A, a, P,* or *p* is displayed.

Saving Formats

> Custom number, date, and time formats are saved with the worksheet. They appear in the dialog-box list along with all other formats (at the bottom of the list). To reuse a custom format, simply choose the Number command from the Format menu and select the custom format from the list.

To copy a custom number format to another worksheet, follow these steps:

*Copying a Custom
Number Format to
Another Worksheet*

1. In the original worksheet, select the Number command from the Format menu.
2. Click on the format you want. Its symbols should be highlighted in the Format box.
3. Press Command+C to copy the format.
4. Click on the Cancel button to close the dialog box.
5. Open the new or existing worksheet into which you want to copy this format.
6. Select the Number command from the Format menu.
7. Press Command+V to paste the format into the Format box.
8. Press Return.

Editing Formats

To save time when creating custom formats, try editing an existing format. Just use the standard editing command in the Format box after clicking on the desired format from the list. When you save the format, it will not replace the original, built-in format. In fact, there is no way to remove the built-in formats, not even by deleting them.

Deleting Formats

To delete a custom format, select it from the Format Number dialog box. Then click on the Delete button. If information in the worksheet is currently formatted under the deleted format, that information is returned to the General format.

Clearing Formats

When you use the Cut or Delete commands in the Edit menu to remove information, Excel also removes the format from the original cells. Using the Clear command, however, gives you the option of what you want to clear. By selecting the Formats option available through the Clear command, you can remove only the formatting applied to a range, not the information. If you select the Formulas option, Excel leaves the formats intact but removes the information.

Summary

Formatting your worksheets is an important step in processing data: it helps you organize the information and present it properly. This chapter discussed ways you can format data in Excel, including specifying alignment, number formats, and column widths. The following are some important points covered in this chapter.

- ❏ You can align information by using the Format Alignment command.
- ❏ Each cell in a worksheet can be formatted with a different font selected from the Format Font menu.
- ❏ You can change the standard font used on all new data by issuing the Options Standard Font command, which affects cells that have not been formatted already.
- ❏ To remove the formatting from a cell, use the command Edit Clear.
- ❏ Excel can add borders to cells or ranges with the Format Border command.
- ❏ Remove cell grid lines by using the command Options Display and clicking in the Gridlines box to remove the check mark.
- ❏ The Options Workspace command can be used to remove the scroll bars, status line, and formula bar from a worksheet.
- ❏ You can control the appearance of a number by using the Format Number command.
- ❏ Dates are really numbers formatted to appear as dates.

Turn to Chapter 6, "Using Worksheet Functions," for a discussion of how to use the worksheet functions available in Excel.

6

Using Excel Worksheet Functions

Functions are special, self-contained routines that calculate values or perform operations. By referencing a single command—the function's name—you can achieve a result as a series of calculations. Some functions can be duplicated through the use of formulas, but using the function will always be easier and faster. Other functions perform tasks that cannot be accomplished in any way.

Functions are the key to powerful worksheets. Since the early spreadsheet products appeared, developers have added function after function to provide more-powerful calculation capabilities. Excel has so many worksheet functions that they may be divided into 11 categories: mathematical, matrix, trigonometric, statistical, financial, text, lookup, special, logical, database, and date/time. Each category contains many functions that enable you to manipulate data.

This chapter is a guide to all worksheet functions available in Excel. Use it to learn basic functions; then use it as a reference on seldom-used functions. It's unlikely that you will need to know all the Excel functions. Most worksheets require only a few—and often the same few.

The following lists the functions in each category, in the order in which they are discussed:

Mathematical	ABS, INT, TRUNC, MOD, RAND, ROUND, SQRT, PI, EXP, FACT, PRODUCT, LN, LOG10, LOG, SIGN
Matrix	MDTERM, MINVERSE, MMULT, TRANSPOSE
Trigonometric	ACOS, ASIN, ATAN, ATAN2, SIN, COS, TAN
Statistical	AVERAGE, COUNT, COUNTA, GROWTH, LINEST, LOGEST, MAX, MIN, STDEV, STDEVP, SUM, TREND, VARP, VAR
Financial	DDB, SLN, SYD, FV, NPV, IRR, MIRR, NPER, PMT, PPMT, IPMT, PV, RATE
Text	CHAR, CODE, CLEAN, TRIM, DOLLAR, FIXED, TEXT, EXACT, FIND, SEARCH, LEFT, RIGHT, MID, REPLACE, SUBSTITUTE, LEN, UPPER, LOWER, PROPER, REPT, VALUE
Lookup	CHOOSE, MATCH, HLOOKUP, VLOOKUP, LOOKUP, INDEX
Special	CELL, COLUMN, ROW, AREAS, COLUMNS, ROWS, INDIRECT, NA, N, T, TYPE
Logical	TRUE, FALSE, IF, AND, OR, NOT, ISBLANK, ISERR, ISERROR, ISNA, ISNUMBER, ISTEXT, ISNONTEXT, ISREF, ISLOGICAL
Database	DAVERAGE, DCOUNT, DCOUNTA, DMAX, DMIN, DSTDEV, DSTDEVP, DSUM, DPRODUCT, DVAR, DVARP
Date/Time	DATE, DATEVALUE, DAY, MONTH, YEAR, WEEKDAY, TIME, TIMEVALUE, NOW, HOUR, MINUTE, SECOND

A Basic Guide to Functions

Because worksheets are often similar, requiring similar types of calculations, a handful of functions will prove to be the most useful. These include the following:

DATE	Calculates the current date, using the internal clock

IF	Tests a condition and then branches, based on the result
ROUND	Rounds a number
ISERR	Detects an error in the worksheet
HLOOKUP	Searches a table, based on input
VLOOKUP	Searches a table, based on input
ISNA	Detects an unavailable value
AVERAGE	Calculates the average of a series of values
SUM	Calculates the sum of a series of values
MAX	Finds the maximum value in a series
MIN	Finds the minimum value in a series
COUNT	Counts the number of entries in a series
CHOOSE	Finds a value in an established set, based on input

A working knowledge of these functions will take you a long way into worksheet construction. If you like, you can turn directly to the explanations of these functions and then examine some of the other functions available in Excel.

How Functions Work

To be used properly, all functions must be typed in a specific way. Each function has its own syntax and cell-entry requirements. Functions are composed of three basic parts: the function name, parentheses, and arguments, as in the function SUM(A1:A5,5).

All three parts of functions must be entered into cells or formulas. The parentheses are the same for all functions; they hold the *arguments*— the values on which the function operates—and come directly after the function name. Arguments differ greatly from function to function. Function names also differ and are designed to remind you of each function's purpose.

Some functions, such as SQRT, which calculates the square root of a number, operate on single values:

SQRT(value)   SQRT(9)   SQRT(A5)

Other functions, such as SUM, which calculates the sum of a range of cells, operate on a range of values:

SUM(range)   SUM(A1:A5)

Functions that operate on a range often operate on a list of values as well:

SUM(list)   SUM(4,5,1,6)   SUM(A1,A5,C5,G24)

Values, ranges, and lists are just a few of the many types of arguments used in functions. Some functions let you use more than one type; others require very specific syntax. Special requirements for any function will be noted along with the function description in this chapter.

The following are a few conventions for using arguments.

Using Range Arguments

A *range argument* can be any valid range of cells. This argument includes a range reference (such as A1:A5) or a range name (such as SALES). You also can specify a multiple range as a range reference (for example, A1:A5,B1:B5). Often, you can mix range references with values and range names. Any time you include more than one argument or mix arguments, you must separate them with commas, as shown in the following example:

SUM(A5:A9,B5:B9,SALES,G5)

Using Value Arguments

A *value argument* is any numeric value, numeric expression resulting in a value, or cell reference containing a numeric value. In other words, anything that results in a number can be used as a value argument. A numeric expression is any formula or calculation resulting in a number, as in the following:

SQRT(A5-40+(C5*3))

A value can also be a range name applied to a single cell, as described in Chapter 3.

Using List Arguments

A *list* is similar to a range argument, but it lists each cell reference or constant value, separated by commas. Lists can often be used when a range reference is needed, but range references usually cannot be substituted when a function requires a list. Actually, each item in a list is a value, subject to the rules described earlier. Therefore, a single item in a list can be an expression. The following is an example of a list:

SUM(A3,B3,B5,C24-10,45)

Notice that the fourth item is a numeric expression. You also can include a range as one of the items in a list. In a way, using a range by itself (as in SUM(A3:A10)) is really just specifying a list that has only one item.

Using Text Arguments

Text is any label, text string, text expression, or cell reference containing a label or text expression. If text is entered directly into a function, it must be surrounded by quotation marks:

LEN("Hello")

If you don't include the quotation marks, Excel thinks that you are entering a range name and looks for such a range. This situation usually results in an error.

The rule on using quotation marks applies even when text is part of a text expression:

LEN("Hello"&"there")

You can use a cell reference in a text argument, provided that the cell contains text or a text expression:

LEN(A5)

Using Functions in Formulas

You have just seen how some functions can use formulas (expressions) as arguments. But you also can use functions within other formulas, including other functions. The simplest of these is a function that is a formula by itself:

=SUM(A1:A5)

The only difference here is that the function includes an equal sign, making it a valid formula for a cell. But a function can be included in a more complex formula:

=A4*SUM(A1:A5)

Similarly, you can use functions whenever a value is expected in another function. Just be sure to use a function that returns an appropriate value. (Most functions return numeric values and can be used whenever a value is indicated.) The following is an example:

=SQRT(A4-SUM(A1:A5))

Displaying a List of Available Functions

You can display a list of Excel's functions at any time by using the Formula Paste Function command. In fact, if you select one of the functions from the list and then click on the OK button, the function will be entered at the position of the cursor. This method is useful for automatically entering functions into formulas as you need them. To include the names of the arguments, check the Paste Arguments box. While the list is in view, type the first letter of the function you want; Excel will go directly to the functions beginning with that letter.

Entering Ranges

Functions often apply to a range of cells. The SUM function, for example, adds the numbers in a range of cells. Cells must be adjacent in order to be considered a range.

You can enter a range reference into a function in two ways. One way is to type the entire function and its range argument by hand. The second way is to type

SUM(

Now use the mouse to click on the first cell in the range. Then, holding down the mouse button, drag the pointer to the last cell in the range. Or you can click on the first cell, type a colon, and then click on the last cell in the range and close the parentheses. You can also use the keyboard movement keys to specify the range.

You can indicate an entire column or row as a range reference by using the form A:A. (This form indicates the entire column A.) The designation for row 5 would look like this: 5:5. Multiple-range references should be entered with a comma between each range. For example, the reference for the ranges highlighted in figure 6.1 is A5:A15,8:8.

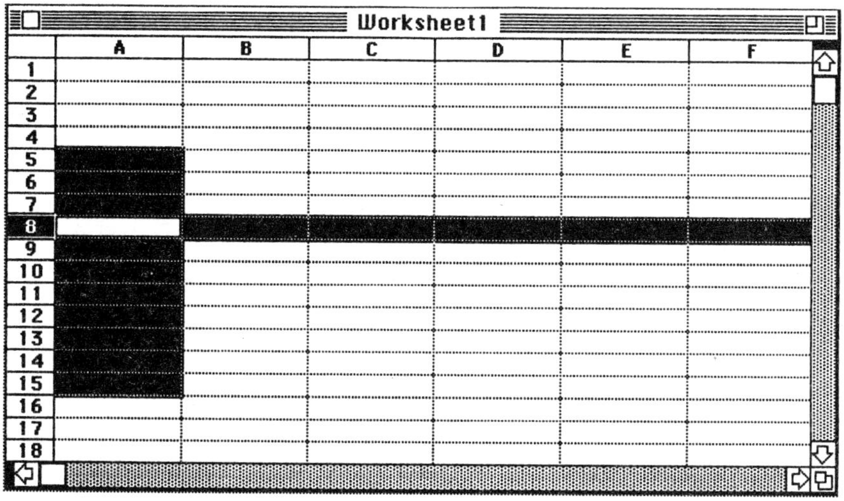

Fig. 6.1.

The range A5:A15,8:8.

Some functions do not allow multiple-range references. Details on each function appear later in this chapter.

Inserting and Deleting Information

One useful feature of range references is their capability to expand and contract so as to accommodate changes in the worksheet. Suppose that you use the function =SUM(A1:A8) in cell A10 to add the range A1:A8. Later you decide to insert a row above row 4; this insertion expands the range to A1:A9 so that the same data is covered. Excel automatically changes the range reference in the formula to read =SUM(A1:A9). Likewise, when you delete, copy, or move information, Excel automatically adjusts the cell or range references.

Keep in mind that the range adjusts only when the inserted or deleted cells are part of the range. If you use the same example, and insert a row at row 1, the function changes to =SUM(A2:A9), showing that the original range has moved down but has not grown or shrunk

Mathematical Functions

Mathematical functions apply to general mathematical needs, such as finding the absolute value of a number or rounding a number, and also include some logarithmic functions. The following are Excel's mathematical functions.

Calculating the Absolute Value (ABS)

The ABS function returns the absolute value of a number or cell reference. The *absolute value* of a number is that number without positive or negative status. (For example, the absolute value of -34 is 34.) The function's syntax is as follows:

ABS(value)

The argument *value* can be a number, formula, or cell reference. In other words, it can be any expression resulting in a value, as in these examples:

ABS(-354)
ABS(A5)
ABS(TOTAL)
ABS(TOTAL-(A5*4))

Calculating the Integer Value (INT)

The INT function rounds a number down to the nearest integer. The result will be a positive or negative number without decimal values. For example, the INT value of 829.98 is 829; the INT value of -829.98 is -830. This function, commonly used in financial worksheets, has the following syntax:

INT(value)

Insert a number, formula, or cell reference as the *value* argument, as follows:

    =INT(B5)

If cell B5 contains 45.55, the function returns 45.

Removing the Decimal Portion of a Value (TRUNC)

This function is similar to the INT function but does not round a number down to the nearest integer. Instead, TRUNC truncates the decimal value of a number, leaving the integer portion. The TRUNC value of -35.89 is -35. The function's syntax is as follows:

    TRUNC(value)

The TRUNC function is a natural way to calculate the decimal value associated with a number. (The decimal portion of 829.98, for example, is .98.) Suppose that you want to find the decimal portion of a number in cell C5. The formula is as follows:

    C10: =C5-(TRUNC(C5))

The formula in cell C10 takes the integer portion of the value in C5 and subtracts it from the original value in C5, resulting in the fractional portion.

Calculating the Modulus (MOD)

The MOD function returns the remainder, or modulus, of two numbers: a divisor and a dividend. For example, 3 goes into 10 three times, with 1 remaining. The modulus of 10 and 3 is, therefore, 1. The MOD function is useful in business worksheets for calculating overages or remaining inventory. It has the following syntax:

    MOD(dividend,divisor)

The dividend and divisor can be any number or expression resulting in a number. The divisor cannot be 0. Figure 6.2 shows a worksheet that uses the INT and MOD functions.

Fig. 6.2.

*The INT and
MOD functions*

	A	B	C	D	E
1					
2					
3		Formula text	Result		
4					
5	Total Pieces	2500	2500		
6	Pieces required per unit	16	16		
7	Able to make	INT(B5/B6)	156		
8	Pieces remaining	MOD(B5,B6)	4		
9					
10	Check	C6 * C7 + C8	2500		
11					

Notice that the formula at the bottom checks the results by multiplying the divisor by the dividend and adding the remainder. The result should match the original number.

Getting a Random Value (RAND)

The RAND function produces a random number between 0 and 1. Each time you calculate the worksheet, this function produces a new random number. Although the function requires no arguments, a set of parentheses must follow the function name in order for the function to work, as the syntax indicates:

RAND( )

To calculate a random number between any two numbers, use

=START+RAND( )*(END-START)

Substitute the starting number for START and the ending number for END. For example, to calculate random numbers between 4 and 24, enter =4+RAND( )*(24-4). Note that this formula produces the decimal values between two numbers. You might want to remove the decimals. Doing so, however, can distort the beginning and ending values. Often, you'll end up with numbers equal to or greater than the starting value but less than the ending value. To remove the decimal values, try this formula, which produces numbers from the START to the END values, inclusive:

=START+INT(RAND( )*(END-START)+.5)

To choose a random number from a list of numbers, try this:

=CHOOSE(1+RAND( )*5,33,35,39,45,60)

The 5 in the random-number calculation is equal to the number of items in the list.

Rounding a Number (ROUND)

This function rounds a value to a specified number of places. The difference between using this function and formatting the cell to display a specified number of places (using the Format Number command) is that the ROUND function permanently changes the number to the rounded version. Any subsequent calculations based on this number are made with the rounded number. A number rounded with the Format Number command merely displays a number in a certain format; it does not change the number. Calculations including the number use the original number, not the formatted version. The syntax of the ROUND function is this:

ROUND(value,precision)

Value is the number to be rounded; *precision* is the number of places to which it is rounded. If the number 5.2573 appears in cell A1, you can round it to two decimal places with this formula:

=ROUND(A1,2)

The result of this formula is 5.26.

The monetary standard for rounding is to two decimal places. This procedure can also be termed rounding to the nearest penny. You can round an amount to the nearest dime by entering 1 in place of 2 in the formula, as in the following:

=ROUND(A1,1)

When 0 is the *precision* argument, the formula rounds to the nearest dollar. When -1 is the argument, the formula rounds to the nearest 10 dollars, and when -2 is the argument, the formula rounds to the nearest 100 dollars.

Rounding to the Nickel

Although the ROUND function is useful for most rounding needs, it won't round to the nearest nickel. Rounding to the nearest nickel requires using this special formula:

```
=IF(C3*10-INT(C3*10)<0.25,INT(C3*10)/10,
   IF(C3*10-INT(C3*10)<0.75,(INT(C3*10)+0.5)/10,
   (INT(C3*10)+1)/10))
```

Enter any number into cell C3, and this formula will round the number to the nearest nickel.

Calculating the Square Root (SQRT)

This function calculates the square root of a number, using the following syntax:

SQRT(value)

Value is the number whose square root you want to find. This value can be any non-negative number, cell reference, or formula, provided that the formula does not calculate to a negative value. Consider this example:

SQRT(C5)

If C5 contains 9, this function returns 3.

Calculating the *n*th Root

It's easy to determine the square root of a number by using Excel's SQRT function. But how do you find, for example, the fifth root of a number? Try entering this formula into cell A3, with the desired root in cell A1 and the number in cell A2:

```
=A2^(1/A1)
```

For the fifth root of 259, enter 5 into cell A1 and 259 into cell A2. The formula will return 3.0385.

Calculating the Value of Pi (PI)

You can use this function wherever the value pi is required. Excel calculates pi to 14 decimal places and keeps track of all 14 places when you use the PI function. The syntax is the following:

PI( )

Be sure to include the empty parentheses even though there is no argument for the function. For example, to calculate the area of a circle, you can enter the following:

=PI( )*B5^2

Cell B5 contains the radius of the circle. If B5 contains 35, the resulting area is 3848.45.

Working with Exponentiation (EXP)

The EXP function has the syntax

EXP(value)

and computes the value of *e* raised to a specific power (*e* is the base of the natural logarithm). *Value* can be any number or cell reference. The constant *e* equals approximately 2.7182818.

Calculating the Factorial (FACT)

This function has the syntax

FACT(value)

and computes the factorial of a number. The factorial is equal to the following calculation:

(value) * (value – 1) * (value – 2) * (value – 3) *...
(value – (value – 1)) *[or 1]*

Value must be an integer and must be positive. The factorial of 4 is calculated as follows:

4 * 3 * 2 * 1   equals 24

Thus the function =FACT(4) returns 24.

Calculating the Product of a Series of Values (PRODUCT)

The PRODUCT function calculates the product of the specified values and has the syntax

PRODUCT(value, *value, value...*)

The product is based on the following calculation:

value * value * value *...

Excel ignores references to blank cells or cells containing text. You can list the values in the function or use a range reference to specify the values. The following are some examples:

=PRODUCT(5,3,7,8)	Returns 840.
=PRODUCT(A1:D1)	If the range contains 5, 3, 7, and 8, this function returns 840.
=PRODUCT(SALES)	If SALES is the name of the range A1:D1, this function returns 840.

Making Logarithmic Calculations (LN, LOG10, LOG)

The functions LN, LOG10, and LOG calculate the logarithm of a number and have the following syntax, respectively:

LN(value)

LOG10(value)

LOG(value, *base*)

LN calculates the logarithm at base *e*; LOG10 calculates the logarithm at base 10; LOG calculates the logarithm for a specified base. The value and base can be any number greater than 0. Consider this example:

=LOG(100,3)

This function calculates the value 100 at base 3.

Determining Positive or Negative Status (SIGN)

The SIGN function performs a query to test whether the sign of a number is positive or negative. If the sign of the value is positive, the function returns 1. If the sign is negative, the function returns -1. If the number is 0, the function returns 0. The syntax is as follows:

SIGN(value)

Consider this example:

=SIGN(C5)

If cell C5 contains -35, this function returns -1. If C5 contains the formula 24=4, the function returns 1.

Matrix Functions

Matrix functions perform calculations on matrixes of values. A *matrix* is simply a range of values in rows and columns. Often, the matrix must represent a perfectly square range, one consisting of the same number of rows and columns. These functions perform matrix calculations on these ranges. The following is a description of each.

Calculating the Determinant (MDTERM)

The MDTERM function calculates the determinant value of a matrix. This value is derived from a special calculation of the values in the matrix. Its syntax is as follows:

MDTERM(range)

Range can be any valid range reference, provided that the range has the same number of rows and columns (that is, the range must be perfectly square). However, none of the cells in the range can be blank or contain text, or the function will return an error. The function also returns an error if the range is not square. The example

=MDTERM(A1:C3)

performs the calculation

A1*(B2*C3-B3*C2)+A2*(B3*C1-B1*C3)+A3*(B1*C2-B2*C1)

which is the determinant of the range A1:C3.

Inverting a Matrix (MINVERSE)

This function calculates the inverse of a matrix of values. The matrix is any valid worksheet range that is perfectly square. That is, the range must have the same number of rows and columns. The syntax is as follows:

MINVERSE(range)

When *range* is any square range of cells, this function will calculate the inverse matrix of the specified range. To use this function, first highlight a range of cells the same proportions as the range specified in the argument. Then enter the function by using the syntax shown; press Command+Return to create an array range as the result. The range reference must not contain text or blank cells.

Multiplying Matrixes (MMULT)

This function multiplies the values in two ranges—returning the matrix product of the ranges. The syntax is as follows:

MMULT(range_1,range_2)

The number of columns in *range_1* must be equal to the number of rows in *range_2*. To enter the formula, highlight a perfectly square range of cells (a third range). The number of rows and columns in this highlighted range must match the number of columns in *range_1* and the number of rows in *range_2*. Next, enter the function, identifying the two ranges, and press Command+Return to enter the function as an array into the highlighted range.

Transposing a Matrix (TRANSPOSE)

This function transposes the values in a range of cells. For example, you can use this function to convert the range A1:A5 to the range A6:E6. The second range has the rows and columns from the first range transposed. A one-by-five range becomes a five-by-one range containing the same values. The syntax is

TRANSPOSE(range)

where *range* is any valid worksheet range. First, highlight a range of cells that is the transposition of the *range* reference. Then enter this function as an array calculation by pressing Command+Return. For example, if you have the values 1, 2, 3, 4, and 5 in cells A1:A5, highlight any range containing five columns and one row (the transposition of A1:A5). Next, enter the function **=TRANSPOSE(A1:A5)** into the first cell of the highlighted range and press Command+Return to complete the transposition. The result appears in figure 6.3.

	File	Edit	Formula	Format	Data	Options	Macro	Window	

A8   {=TRANSPOSE(A1:A5)}

Worksheet1

	A	B	C	D	E	F	
1	1						
2	2						
3	3						
4	4						
5	5						
6							
7							
8	1	2	3	4	5		
9							
10							
11							
12							

Fig. 6.3.

Transposing a range.

Trigonometric Functions

These functions perform various trigonometric calculations such as finding the degrees of an angle and figuring sine, cosine, and tangent values. Some of the following explanations give examples of how to use the functions; these explanations, however, do not offer complete lessons in trigonometry. The assumption in this book is that you know basically how to apply these functions.

The functions and their examples use a basic trigonometric model. The right triangle in figure 6.4 shows a quadrant in which the angle POX is identified as z.

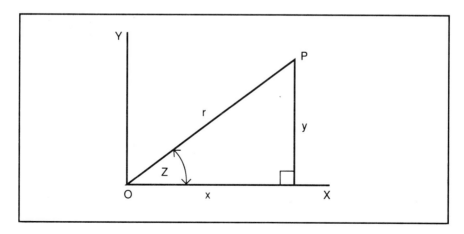

Fig. 6.4.

Basic trigonometric functions.

Given that the lines OP and OY increase in a positive direction, the following formulas apply:

$$\cos z° = x/r$$
$$\sin z° = y/r$$
$$\tan z° = y/z \text{ (where } x \text{ is not 0)}$$
$$\tan z° = \sin z°/\cos z°$$

Working with the values you know (that is, the given values in the problem), you can use the various functions in this section to calculate unknown values and angles. Remember that angles are always expressed in radians.

Calculating the Arccosine (ACOS)

This function calculates the arccosine of a value. The syntax is as follows:

ACOS(value)

Value must be in the range -1 to 1. The resulting value will be in the range from 0 to pi. If the value you supply is not acceptable, Excel returns an error.

Suppose that you are flying a plane at 140 miles per hour from point A to point B and that the wind is traveling at 5 miles per hour perpendicular to your direction (see fig. 6.5). You can use the angle ACB to calculate your flight. This example uses the ACOS function to calculate the angle, but you could use the ASIN function to get the angle CAB.

Fig. 6.5.

Calculating your flight.

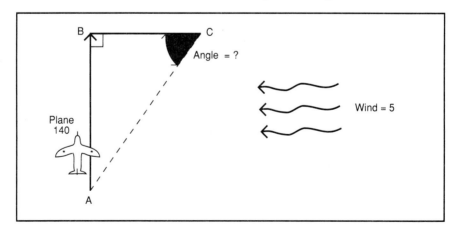

The formula for this calculation is =ACOS(5/140). Dividing 5 by 140 produces the cosine of the angle ACB. The result is 1.54—the radian value of the angle ACB. To display this value in degrees, use the following formula:

=ACOS(5/140)*180/PI( )

The result of this calculation is 87.95 degrees, which is the angle ACB.

Calculating the Arcsine (ASIN)

This function calculates the arcsine of a value and has the syntax

ASIN(value)

Value must be between -1 and 1; the value returned will be between the values -pi/2 and pi/2.

As an example of using the ASIN function, suppose that you are driving up a five-mile hill that is 1,000 feet above sea level, starting your drive 100 feet above sea level. The ASIN function will calculate the angle at which you are driving uphill, as shown in figure 6.6.

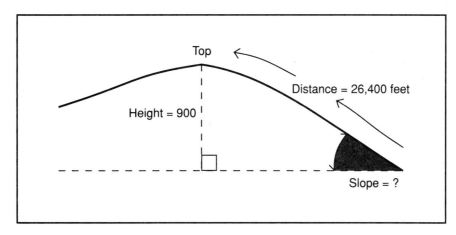

Fig. 6.6.

Using the ASIN function.

Note that the height of the hill is the difference between the two elevation levels, because the desired height is relative to the current elevation of the car. The ASIN function calculates the angle (in radians) by using the sine of the angle. You calculate the sine by dividing elevation by distance:

=ASIN(1000-100/(5280*5))*180/PI( )

The following is a breakdown of this function's calculations:

1000-100	Calculates the height of the hill relative to the current location of the car.
(5280*5)	Converts 5 miles to feet.
(1000-100/(5280*5))	Calculates the sine (in radians) of the desired angle. This expression is required as the argument for the ASIN function.
*180/PI( )	Converts the resulting angle (expressed in radians) to degrees.

This function displays the angle in degrees. The result is 1.95 degrees.

Calculating the Arctangent (ATAN)

The arctangent is calculated by the ATAN function, which uses the angle (in radians) of a tangent. The result is also expressed in radians. The syntax of the ATAN function is

ATAN(value)

where *value* is the tangent value. The result will be in the range -pi/2 to pi/2. This function is similar to ASIN, but instead of knowing the hypotenuse of the triangle, you know the two sides.

Using the example from the ASIN function, suppose that you don't know the distance of the road, but you know that the aeronautical distance between points A and B is 26,500 feet. Now the calculation is

=ATAN(900/26500)*180/PI( )

This function determines the slope of the hill in degrees, which is 1.945.

Calculating the Four-Quadrant Tangent (ATAN2)

The ATAN2 function has the syntax

ATAN2(x_value,y_value)

ATAN2 calculates the four-quadrant tangent of the tangent values *x_value* and *y_value*. The result is displayed in radians (unless converted to degrees). The two values cannot both be 0; if they are, Excel returns an error. The function

=ATAN2(140,25)

returns the value 0.18.

Note that the ATAN2 function acts on the two tangent values used to produce the tangent angle for the ATAN function. In other words, using the function ATAN2(x,y) is identical to using ATAN(y/x), as shown under the ATAN function earlier.

Calculating the Sine, Cosine, and Tangent (SIN, COS, TAN)

The SIN, COS, and TAN functions calculate the sine, cosine, and tangent of angles expressed in radians. The result is a value between -1 and 1. The syntax for these functions is the following:

SIN(radians)

COS(radians)

TAN(radians)

As an example, you can use the SIN function to figure out the height of a triangle for which you know the hypotenuse and an angle in degrees. This function is illustrated in figure 6.7.

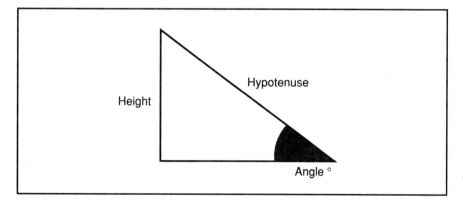

Fig. 6.7.

Calculating the sine.

The formula used to calculate the height of the triangle is

=hypotenuse * SIN(angle * 2 * PI( )/360)

Statistical Functions

Statistical functions work on groups of numbers. Common statistical tasks include calculating the average of a group, finding the minimum and maximum value of a group, and adding the numbers in a group. Statistical functions can get much more advanced than this, including standard deviation and sample statistics calculations.

Finding the Average (AVERAGE)

The AVERAGE function calculates the average of a group of numbers. Typically, the numbers being averaged fall in a row or a column, but you can use AVERAGE to average randomly plotted values. The syntax is as follows:

AVERAGE(range)

or

AVERAGE(value,*value,value*)

The first syntax line accommodates a range of cells in a row, column, or block; the second accommodates a group of cells placed at various spots in the worksheet. As with most formulas, you can substitute constant values, cell references, or other functions as the arguments.

Keep in mind that unwanted values of 0 will destroy the accuracy of an average when the values being averaged are derived from IF statements or contain text. When used with a range reference, the AVERAGE function interprets text as having a value of 0, and it skips blank cells. When used with individual cell references, the function interprets both text and blank cells as values of 0. This interpretation can cause inaccuracies in AVERAGE calculations.

One way to avoid including unwanted values of 0 in your AVERAGE functions is to use formulas that "manually" calculate the average. Suppose that you have these values in the range A1:A8:

36
66
18
99
Text
33
0
0

The task is to avoid any cell containing 0 and text. Add these formulas to the range B1:B8:

=IF(AND(A1<>0,ISTEXT(A1)<>TRUE),1,0)
=IF(AND(A2<>0,ISTEXT(A2)<>TRUE),1,0)
=IF(AND(A3<>0,ISTEXT(A3)<>TRUE),1,0)
=IF(AND(A4<>0,ISTEXT(A4)<>TRUE),1,0)
=IF(AND(A5<>0,ISTEXT(A5)<>TRUE),1,0)
=IF(AND(A6<>0,ISTEXT(A6)<>TRUE),1,0)
=IF(AND(A7<>0,ISTEXT(A7)<>TRUE),1,0)
=IF(AND(A8<>0,ISTEXT(A8)<>TRUE),1,0)

This basic formula means, "If the value in column A is not 0 and is not text, place 1 here; otherwise, place 0 here." This function will produce a column of 1's and 0's. Now add column B in cell B10; in the example, column B produces a sum of 5. Next, add column A in cell A10; in the example, column A produces a sum of 252. Finally, divide cell A10 by cell B10 (using the formula =A10/B10) to get the average, which is 50.4.

Counting Entries (COUNT, COUNTA)

These functions count the number of cells in a range or list of references. The COUNT function counts only numeric values; the COUNTA function counts all cells that are not blank. The syntax is as follows:

COUNT(range)
COUNTA(range)

or

COUNT(cell,*cell,cell,cell*)
COUNTA(cell,*cell,cell,cell*)

Suppose that the range A1:A7 contains these values:

A1: 1
A2: 0
A3: Text
A4: 983
A5:
A6: 298
A7: 2

The COUNT and COUNTA functions would produce the following results when you use this range:

COUNT(A1:A7)   produces 5

COUNTA(A1:A7)   produces 6

Calculating Growth (GROWTH)

This function calculates the exponential growth associated with known values, expressed as *known_x's* and *known_y's*. The resulting growth curve is expressed as *y* values along the exponential curve of the regression $y=b*m\hat{}x$. The syntax is as follows:

GROWTH(known_x's,*known_y's,new_x's*)

The *known_x's* and *known_y's* values can be any valid range reference or array range. The size and shape of these two ranges should be identical. The growth curve corresponds to the *new_x's* range. If this range is omitted, the function uses the *known_x's* range. The function returns an error if any *known_y's* values are negative.

This function should be entered into an array range that corresponds to the size and shape of the other ranges. To enter the function as an array, first highlight the range; then enter the formula by pressing Command+Return.

Calculating a Linear Trend (LINEST)

This function calculates the slope and y-intercept that defines the linear trend of a series of values expressed as *known_y's*. The linear trend is a line that best fits the data supplied and is calculated based on the regression $y=mx+b$. The syntax for the function is as follows:

LINEST(known_y's,*known_x's*)

The *known_y's* argument can be any valid range or array range. If *known_x's* is omitted, the function assumes the values 1, 2, 3, 4... to match, one for one, the *known_y's*. If you enter a range for *known_x's*, it should be the same size and shape as *known_y's*. The result will be returned as an array range of two elements. Therefore, you should highlight a one-by-two range, enter the function, and press Command+Return to calculate the *x* and *y* values that fit the sample data. These values can then be plotted to produce a line.

Calculating the Trend as a Curve (LOGEST)

This function is similar to LINEST but calculates the values m and b for an exponential curve, using $y=b*m\char`^x$. The result is a curve that best fits the sample data expressed as *known_y's*. The syntax is

LOGEST(known_y's,*known_x's*)

If *known_x's* is omitted, the function assumes the values 1, 2, 3, 4... to match, one for one, the *known_y's*. If you enter a range for *known_x's*, it should be the same size and shape as *known_y's*. The result will be returned as an array range of two elements. Therefore, you should highlight a one-by-two range, enter the function, and press Command+Return to calculate the x and y values that fit the sample data. These values can then be plotted to produce a line.

Finding the Maximum Value (MAX)

The MAX function returns the maximum value in a group of cells. The syntax is

MAX(range)

Range can be a range of cells, random cell references, a formula, direct entries, or some combination of these, as in the following examples:

MAX(A1:A5)
MAX(A1,25,C23*3,"green")

If the range A1:A5 contains the values 1, 25, 3, 6, and 13, the first function returns 25. If cell C23 contains 100, the second function returns 300.

Text cells or references to blank cells are ignored. If a maximum value cannot be found, the function returns 0.

Finding the Minimum Value (MIN)

The MIN function returns the minimum value in a group of cells. The syntax is

MIN(range)

Range can be a range of cells, random cell references, a formula, direct entries, or some combination of these, as in the following examples:

MIN(A1:A5)

MIN(A1,25,C23*3,"green")

Text cells or references to blank cells are ignored.

Calculating the Span of Numbers

When evaluating a column of numbers, you might need to determine the span between the smallest and largest numbers. For example, suppose that you have the list 25, 49, 33, 120, 101, and 40. The span is 95 because the difference between the smallest number (25) and largest number (120) is 95. The following is a formula that calculates this value:

=MAX(range)-MIN(range)

In both the MAX and MIN functions, enter the range containing the numbers.

Finding the Standard Deviation of a Sample Population (STDEV)

The STDEV function uses sample statistics to calculate its value. The syntax is as follows:

STDEV(range)

or

STDEV(value,value,value)

The standard deviation of a population is different from the standard deviation of a partial (or sample) population. Use either a range or list with this function. References to blank cells or text cause errors.

Finding the Standard Deviation of a Population (STDEVP)

The STDEVP function returns the standard deviation of a group of numbers (population), using the entire population as a basis. (Because standard deviation is an advanced statistical function, the assumption in this chapter is that you know why you want to use it.) The syntax is as follows:

STDEVP(list)

or

STDEVP(range)

List can be any combination of two or more cell references, values, or expressions resulting in values. Up to 14 arguments can be included in the list. References to blank cells or text cause errors. Figure 6.8 shows an example of the STDEVP function.

⌘ File Edit Formula Format Data Options Macro Window						
D4		=STDEVP(B4:B14)				

Worksheet1

	A	B	C	D	E	F
1						
2						
3		Population		STDEVP		
4		34		17.29		
5		34				
6		56				
7		46				
8		80				
9		68				
10		56				
11		84				
12		55				
13		30				
14		63				
15						
16						
17						
18						
19						

Fig. 6.8.

A worksheet that uses the STDEVP function.

The formula used in this worksheet is shown in the formula bar of the figure. Experiment with entering different numbers into the range. The more the numbers vary from one another, the higher the STDEVP value.

Finding the Sum of a Group of Cells (SUM)

SUM, the simplest of functions, is an easy way to add values. Its syntax is the following:

SUM(range)

or

SUM(list)

Range can be a row or column (or portions thereof) or a block of cells. If you want to add values that are not in a row or a column, use the *list* argument. Suppose that you have these values in your worksheet:

C1: 5
C2: 25
C3: 14
C4: 102
C5: 68

You can enter this formula into cell C6 to add the column:

=SUM(C1:C5)

The sum of the five cells, 214, will appear in cell C6.

You can also sum the numbers in a block of cells by entering the entire range as the argument for the SUM function. The formula =SUM(C1:D5) adds the numbers in a two-by-five block of cells. Any valid range can be used in this function.

Performing Trend Analysis (TREND)

This function is similar to the GROWTH function but calculates the trend as a line that best fits the sample data. The line is calculated as a series of *y* values that match the sample data, expressed as *known_x's*. The *y* values are based on the regression $x = mx + b$. The syntax is as follows:

TREND(known_y's, *known_x's, new_x's*)

The *known_x's* and *known_y's* values can be any valid range reference or array range. The size and shape of these two ranges should be identical. If this range is omitted, the function uses the *known_x's* range. If both *known_x's* and *new_x's* are omitted, the function assumes the values 1, 2, 3, 4... to match the *known_y's* values. The function returns an error if any *known_y's* values are negative.

This function should be entered into an array range that corresponds to the size and shape of the other ranges. To enter the function as an array, first highlight the range; then enter the formula by pressing Command+Return.

Finding the Variance of a Population (VARP, VAR)

Variance, which is similar to standard deviation, shows the amount of variance from an average that occurs over a population. The VAR function computes variance for a sample population, and the VARP function computes it for an entire population. Because these are advanced statistical functions, the assumption in this chapter is that you know why you want to use them. The syntax is

VARP(list)

VAR(list)

or

VARP(range)

VAR(range)

References to blank cells or 0 cause errors in the VAR function.

Financial Functions

Financial functions are used for such calculations as interest rates, loan terms, present values, and future values. Financial functions are essential for performing in-depth financial analysis for purchases, investments, and cash flows.

Working with Double-Declining-Balance Depreciation (DDB)

The DDB function calculates depreciation by using the double-declining-balance method, which allows for an accelerated rate of depreciation for the initial period. You also can use the function to accelerate depreciation by a specified rate. When the book value depreciates to the salvage value, depreciation stops. The syntax for the DDB function is

DDB(cost,salvage,life,period,*factor*)

You provide the initial cost, the salvage value (value after the life), the life of the asset, and the period for which depreciation is calculated. The *life* and *period* arguments should be given in the same terms; that is, they should both indicate years, months, days, or whatever period you choose. Optionally, you can enter a factor for the rate of depreciation. If you do not enter a factor, the function assumes a standard DDB factor of 2 (double-declining). *Period* should be equal to or smaller than *life*, and both variables must be integers. *Cost* and *salvage* can be any numbers. Figure 6.9 shows a worksheet in which the three depreciation methods are used.

Fig. 6.9.

A worksheet showing the results of three depreciation methods.

◆ File Edit Formula Format Data Options Macro Window				
B7		=DDB($B$1,$B$2,$B$3,B$4)		
		Worksheet3		
	A	**B**	**C**	**D**	**E**
1	Cost	$5,000			
2	Salvage Value	$350			
3	Life in Years	10			
4	Depreciation in Year #	1	2	3	
5					
6	Depreciation	Year 1	Year 2	Year 3	
7	DDB	1000.00	800.00	640.00	
8	SYD	845.45	760.91	676.36	
9	SLN	465.00	465.00	465.00	
10					

The variables for each method are taken from the appropriate values entered into the worksheet. The formula for the DDB depreciation in cell B7 looks like this:

=DDB($B$1,$B$2,$B$3,B$4)

Notice that the formula contains no factor value. The function thus calculates depreciation at a factor of 2. You can enter a different factor by changing the function in cell B7 as follows:

=DDB($B$1,$B$2,$B$3,B$4,3)

This variation calculates depreciation at a factor of 3.

Determining the best method to use for a particular asset and company can be a challenge, because so many variables should be analyzed together. A CPA or financial analyst can use these functions for in-depth study of a company's finances.

Working with Straight-Line Depreciation (SLN)

The SLN function calculates depreciation by the straight-line method, using the syntax

    SLN(cost,salvage,life)

For this function, you enter the initial cost, the salvage value, and the life of the asset (usually in years). Refer to figure 6.9 (shown earlier) to see how SLN depreciation compares with the DDB and SYD methods. The formula in cell B8 for the first year of depreciation looks like this:

    =SLN($B$1,$B$2,$B$3)

Working with Sum-of-the-Years'-Digits Depreciation (SYD)

The SYD function calculates depreciation by using the sum-of-the-years'-digits method. The syntax is as follows:

    SYD(cost,salvage,life,period)

For this function, you enter the initial cost, the salvage value, the life of the asset, and the period for which depreciation is calculated. *Period* should be equal to or smaller than *life*, and both variables must be integers. *Cost* and *salvage* values can be any numbers.

Refer to figure 6.9 (shown earlier) for a comparison of SYD depreciation with the DDB and SYD methods. The formula in cell B9 for the first year of SYD depreciation looks like this:

    =SYD($B$1,$B$2,$B$3,B$4)

Calculating the Future Value of an Investment (FV)

The FV function calculates the future value of an investment, which is the value after payments have been made at a particular rate and over a particular amount of time. You can use these functions to determine the amount of money you will have after the term of an investment is over. FV uses a regular payment amount over a period of time, the interest rate, and the number of payment periods. The syntax is as follows:

FV(interest_rate,periods,payment_amount,*present_value*,*type*)

Interest rate is the rate per period and can be any numeric value. *Periods*, which is the number of periods, should be given in the units used for *interest rate* (months, years, and so on), because FV figures interest earned per period. Both arguments should be integers. *Payment amount* is the income from the loan or outflow from the investment. *Present value* is the starting value of the investment.

Remember that cash paid out must be shown as a negative number, and interest or cash received as a positive number. Thus if you are calculating the future value of an investment such as a savings account, the present value (amount deposited) and the payment amount (monthly deposits) will be negative numbers because they are "paid out" to the investment. If there is no starting value, you can enter 0 as the *present value* argument or omit the argument.

Type can be either 1 or 0. If you enter 1, Excel assumes that payments occur at the beginning of the period; if you enter 0, Excel assumes that they occur at the end of the period. If you omit this argument, Excel assumes that 0 is correct. Figure 6.10 shows a worksheet in which the FV function is used.

Fig. 6.10.

An example of the FV function.

🍎 File Edit Formula Format Data Options Macro Window

B7	=FV(B1,B2,B3,B4,0)

	Worksheet3			
	A	**B**	**C**	**D**
1	Interest Rate	9.80%		
2	Number of Periods	10		
3	Payment Amount	($500)		
4	Investment (Present Value)	($5,000)		
5				
6				
7	**Future Value**	$20,628		
8				

This example calculates the future value of a standard loan. The formula in cell B7 is =FV(B1,B2,B3,B4,0). Each of the values except *type* is contained in the worksheet. Notice that the payment and investment amounts are negative, calculating the future value in terms of the investor, not the lender. The example shows that with an investment of $5,000 and deposits of $500, you will have $20,000 in 10 years. Notice that the *periods* and *rate* arguments are both given in terms of years.

You can use this worksheet to calculate the future value of a lump-sum investment (that is, an investment with no payments). Just enter the total lump-sum investment into cell B4 and enter **0** into cell B3.

Calculating the Net Present Value of an Investment (NPV)

The NPV function returns the net present value of an investment and has the syntax

NPV(rate,range)

The net present value, or NPV, is the present value of an investment's cash flows less the initial cash outlay. The interest rate used to compute the NPV is called the discount rate, which is the return that could be earned on investments of equivalent risk.

The argument *rate* is the interest rate of the loan and can be any value or expression. *Range* is the range of cells containing the monthly payments and can be any valid worksheet range.

The concept of present value is based on the premise that $1 today is worth more than $1 a year from now, because you can invest it. (For example, if you invested $1 today at 10 percent annual interest, you would have $1.10 a year from now.) The present value of a dollar that will be paid to you in a year can be determined to be worth approximately 90 cents at a prevailing 10 percent interest rate.

NPV tells you whether an investment is worthwhile, using the future value of your money as a basis. To calculate the NPV of an investment, you need a list of the payments that will be made to you for the use of your investment, as well as the current interest rate that you could be making on investments of equivalent risk.

Suppose that a friend wants to borrow $1,000 from you and agrees to pay you $100 a month for 12 months, for a total of $1,200 in one year. Suppose also that your bank would pay you 12 percent interest, compounded monthly, for the same $1,000. You can use the NPV function to determine whether it would be more profitable to loan the $1,000 to your friend or to deposit it in the bank.

To use the NPV function, first enter the 12 loan payments of $100 into the worksheet. Next, enter the NPV function into another cell. In this case, you would enter .01 as the interest rate (the monthly equivalent to a yearly rate of 12 percent) and A1:A12 as the range. The function returns the present value of the money you will receive back (see fig. 6.11).

Fig. 6.11.

Using the NPV function.

	File	**Edit**	**Formula**	**Format**	**Data**	**Options**	**Macro**	**Window**	

| D3 | | | =NPV(0.01,A1:A12) | | |

Worksheet4

	A	B	C	D	E
1	100				
2	100		Formula Text	Result	
3	100	Present Value	NPV(0.01,A1:A12)	$1,125.51	
4	100	Net Present Value	D3-1000	$125.51	
5	100				
6	100				
7	100				
8	100				
9	100				
10	100				
11	100				
12	100				
13					

Generally, if the result of the NPV function is a positive value, the investment is a good one. In this case, it would be better to loan the money to your friend—since that act results in a $125 difference in your favor (over the bank).

Because the function returns the present value, you have to calculate the net present value by using the formula shown in the figure. This function simply subtracts the original investment from the present value. Note that the values of the payments do not have to be the same. Remember that cash out is represented as negative and cash in as positive.

Calculating the Internal Rate of Return (IRR)

The IRR function calculates the internal rate of return on an investment, using the initial cash outlay and the expected payments as a basis. This function tells you the rate earned on your investment when the payments (income) equal the cash outlay. To begin, you can estimate that rate; Excel will then make 20 different calculations to find the IRR, based on the estimate. The syntax for IRR is the following:

IRR(range,*guess*)

Guess should represent your expected interest rate; *range* is the range of values representing payments out (on the investment) and in (return from the investment)—also known as the range of cash flows.

Suppose that you buy a video arcade game for the lobby of your hotel. You buy the equipment for $2,000 and estimate that it will earn you $200 a month. Beginning with your initial cash outlay, the cash-flow worksheet might look like figure 6.12.

	File	Edit	Formula	Format	Data	Options	Macro	Window	

B8	=IRR(B7:E7,0.05)

Worksheet4

	A	B	C	D	E
1					
2					
3		First Q	Second Q	Third Q	Fourth Q
4	COST	-2000.00	0.00	0.00	0.00
5	INCOME	300.00	450.00	600.00	450.00
6					
7	TOTAL	-1700.00	450.00	600.00	450.00
8	IRR	-6.01%			
9					

Fig. 6.12.

Cash flows for IRR investment function.

The IRR function is entered into cell B8 as follows:

    IRR(B7:E7,0.05)

The resulting rate of return for the first four quarters is -6.01 percent, which indicates that your investment will not pay off this year. If you spread the cost of the equipment over four quarters, however, the rate of return increases dramatically.

The rate of return is influenced by relative inflow and outflow over time. In this case, it would be worthwhile to pay more for the equipment in order to spread the payments out.

Calculating the Modified Rate of Return (MIRR)

MIRR provides a modified form of the internal rate of return on an investment and accounts for the reinvestment rate of the positive cash flows—rather like combining two IRR functions in one. The syntax for MIRR is as follows:

    MIRR(range,finance_rate,reinvest_rate)

Range is the worksheet range containing the investment's positive and negative cash flows. *Finance_rate* is the rate paid on those investment payments. *Reinvest_rate* is the rate at which you can reinvest the return on this investment. This formula is primarily used to provide more information for an investor; thus payments made to the investment should be negative, and income received from the investment should be positive. That income can then be invested at the *reinvest_rate*, making your total rate of return higher.

Figure 6.13 shows the worksheet that uses the IRR function, with the MIRR function added.

Fig. 6.13.

Comparing IRR with MIRR.

	★ File Edit Formula Format Data Options Macro Window				
	B9	=MIRR(B7:E7,B8,12%)			
			Worksheet4		
	A	B	C	D	E
1					
2					
3		First Q	Second Q	Third Q	Fourth Q
4	COST	-2000.00	0.00	0.00	0.00
5	INCOME	300.00	450.00	600.00	450.00
6					
7	TOTAL	-1700.00	450.00	600.00	450.00
8	IRR	-6.01%			
9	MIRR	-0.27%			
10					

Notice that the rate is much better for the MIRR function, although the investment is still not a good one.

Calculating the Number of Payments Required (NPER)

The NPER function determines the amount of time (number of payment periods) required in order for a payment amount to equal an investment, given a specific interest rate. Alternatively, you can use this function to calculate the number of periods required in order for a payment amount to build to a specific future value, based on a present value and an interest rate. This function is useful for playing "what if" with interest rates to see how they affect the term of an investment. The syntax for NPER is the following:

NPER(rate,payment,present_value,*future_value,type*)

Rate is the periodic rate of interest; you can calculate the rate from an annual amount by dividing the annual amount by the number of periods (for example, dividing the annual amount of 12 percent by 12 calculates monthly interest). This value should be consistent with *payment*, which is the periodic payment amount. (For example, if you enter a monthly payment amount for the *payment* variable, *rate* should be the monthly interest rate.) *Present_value* is the original investment without interest, otherwise known as the principal amount. *Future_value* is the amount of the investment after interest; if you omit this argument, Excel calculates the number of payments required for the payment to equal the principal. *Type* can be either 1, indicating that payments occur at the beginning of the period, or 0, indicating that payments occur at the end of the period. If you omit this argument, Excel assumes that 0 is correct.

Figure 6.14 shows a worksheet in which this function is used in two ways.

✿ File Edit Formula Format Data Options Macro Window

B7	=NPER(B1,B2,B3,B4)

Worksheet2

	A	B	C	D	E
1	Interest Rate	0.46%			
2	Payment Amount	-250			
3	Capital (Present Value)	$6,000			
4	Future Value	$20,000			
5					
6		To Equal $20,000	No FV		
7	Number of Payments	93.77	25.49		
8					
9					
10					

Fig. 6.14.

The NPER function.

The two formulas are NPER(B1,B2,B3,B4) in B7 and NPER(B1,B2,B3,0) in B8. Notice the difference when the future value is 0.

Calculating the Payment Amount Required (PMT)

The PMT function calculates the payment amount required to pay off an investment, given a specific term and interest rate. This function is useful for playing "what if" with the term or interest rate of an investment to see how a change affects the amount of the payment. The syntax is as follows:

PMT(rate,periods,present_value,*future_value,type*)

Rate should be entered as the periodic interest rate and should match the period desired for the payment result. For example, if you want to calculate a weekly payment amount, the rate should be a weekly rate (the annual rate divided by 52). *Periods* is the number of periods desired for the term of the investment. *Present_value* is the principal amount of the investment. If you want to determine how much the payment would be in order for the investment to equal a specific future value (after interest), enter that value as the *future_value* argument. If you omit this argument, Excel calculates the payment amount, based on its equaling the present value. *Type* can be either 1, indicating that payments occur at the beginning of the period, or 0, indicating that payments occur at the end of the period. If you omit this argument, Excel assumes that 0 is correct.

Figure 6.15 shows a worksheet in which the PMT function is used. When you enter the principal amount of the investment, the term, and the interest rate, the PMT function will use these entries to calculate the payment amount.

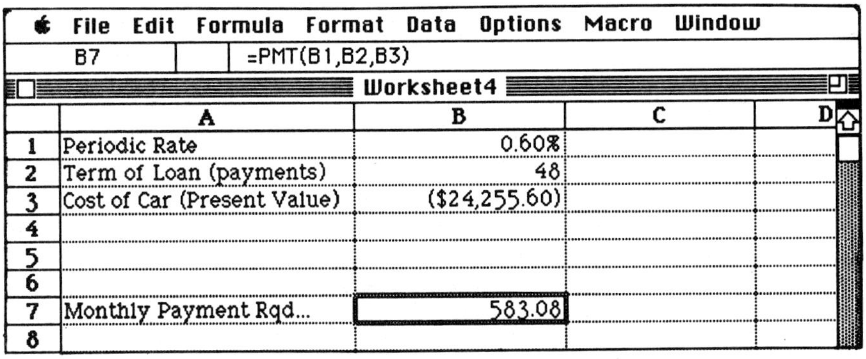

Fig. 6.15.

Using the PMT function.

	File Edit Formula Format Data Options Macro Window			
B7	=PMT(B1,B2,B3)			
	Worksheet4			
	A	**B**	**C**	**D**
1	Periodic Rate	0.60%		
2	Term of Loan (payments)	48		
3	Cost of Car (Present Value)	($24,255.60)		
4				
5				
6				
7	Monthly Payment Rqd...	583.08		
8				

In this example, the argument *future_value* is not required because of the type of investment involved.

Calculating the Principal Payment Amount (PPMT)

The PPMT function is similar to the PMT function. But whereas PMT returns the payment amount required for a given investment over a given time, at a given rate, PPMT returns the amount of principal being paid in any given period under the same conditions. The syntax is the following:

PPMT(rate,period,periods,present_value,*future_value,type*)

Figure 6.16 shows the worksheet used to illustrate the PMT function, with the PPMT amount shown for payment 20. The formula is =PPMT(B1,20,B2,B3). If the normal payment amount is $583.08, the principal being paid in month 20 is $490.22.

🍎 File Edit Formula Format Data Options Macro Window			
B8	=PPMT(B1,20,B2,B3)		
☐	Worksheet4		
	A	B	C	D
1	Periodic Rate	0.60%		
2	Term of Loan (payments)	48		
3	Cost of Car (Present Value)	($24,255.60)		
4				
5				
6				
7	Monthly Payment Rqd...	$583.08		
8	Principal Payment	$490.22		
9				

Fig. 6.16.

Comparing the PMT and PPMT functions.

Calculating the Interest Amount Required (IPMT)

The IPMT function calculates the interest paid for a particular payment, given the interest rate, the number of periods in the term, and the present value. The syntax is as follows:

IPMT(rate,period,periods,present_value,*future_value,type*)

Specify the period for which you want to determine the interest being paid by entering the period value as the *period* argument. *Type* determines whether payments are made at the beginning of the period or at the end. If you omit the *type* argument, Excel assumes that 0 is correct. A type of 1 indicates the beginning; a type of 0 indicates the end. Figure 6.17 shows the preceding example with the IPMT function added. This function determines the interest being paid in month 20.

Fig. 6.17.

Calculating the interest paid in a given period.

	File Edit Formula Format Data Options Macro Window
	B9 =IPMT(B1,20,B2,B3)

Worksheet4

	A	B	C	D
1	Periodic Rate	0.60%		
2	Term of Loan (payments)	48		
3	Cost of Car (Present Value)	($24,255.60)		
4				
5				
6				
7	Monthly Payment Rqd...	$583.08		
8	Principal Payment	$490.22		
9	Interest Payment	$92.87		
10				

Calculating the Present Value of an Investment (PV)

This function calculates the present value (principal) of an investment, given the payment amount, interest rate, and number of payment periods. You can supply the argument *future_value* to base the present value on a specific future value. The syntax is as follows:

PV(rate,periods,payment,*future_value,type*)

These arguments can be any valid numbers or expressions. *Periods* should be an integer value; *rate* is the periodic interest rate. *Type* can be either 1, indicating that payments occur at the beginning of the period, or 0, indicating that payments occur at the end of the period. If you omit this argument, Excel assumes that 0 is correct.

Calculating the Interest Rate Required (RATE)

The RATE function calculates the interest rate required in order for a present value to become a future value, given a particular number of periods. The syntax is

RATE(periods,payment,present_value,*future_value,type,guess*)

The variables can be any numbers or expressions. *Periods* should be an integer.

This function is useful for determining the interest rate you are paying on a loan. When you are quoted a price and a monthly payment amount, you can figure the periodic interest rate by using the RATE function. Knowing the interest rate, you can then calculate the total interest you are paying, using the IPMT function.

Excel calculates the interest rate by using an estimate entered into the formula. Start by leaving the *guess* argument blank; a blank here tells Excel to try the calculation on its own. If Excel fails to calculate a correct interest rate (indicated by the #NUM statement in the cell), enter an estimate of the interest rate as the *guess* argument. Enter the payment amount as a negative number if you are the investor; enter the present and future values as negative if you are the lender. Figure 6.18 shows an example of the RATE function.

🍎 File Edit Formula Format Data Options Macro Window			
B7	=RATE(B1,B2,B3,B4)		

Worksheet4

	A	B	C	D
1	Term (in Months)	48		
2	Monthly Payment	-250		
3	Present Value	($10,000.00)		
4	Future Value	$30,000		
5				
6				
7	Interest Rate	0.87%		
8				

Fig. 6.18.

Using the RATE function.

Auto dealers often play with the payment amount so that the payments will "fit your budget." Using this formula, you can determine what you're really paying in interest for that low monthly payment. In the example, multiply the result by 12 for the annual interest rate.

Text Functions

Text functions let you manipulate text strings. Besides simple concatenation, text manipulation involves dividing strings, extracting text from strings, determining the length of a string, changing upper- and lowercase status, and converting strings to values and back. Text functions are useful when you create forms or manipulate database information.

Determining the ANSI Value of a Character (CHAR)

You can use the CHAR function to send a character to the worksheet (and consequently to the printer) by entering the character's decimal value. The function is most useful for sending control codes to printers and for achieving special results such as color print on special characters. The syntax is as follows:

CHAR(decimal_value)

ANSI code charts, which you will find in your printer manual or computer manual, show the character value (ASCII or ANSI) and decimal value of all keyboard characters. The CHAR function accommodates decimal values ranging from 1 to 255. Sending a printer control code by this method may require you to stack CHAR functions, as in the following:

CHAR(27) CHAR(88)

This combination, when sent to the ImageWriter printer, sets the line spacing at 8 lines per inch by sending the ANSI characters Escape and X. Remember that this function does not send the decimal value to the worksheet but converts the value to the character equivalent and sends the ANSI character.

Determining the Decimal Value of a Character (CODE)

This function complements the CHAR function. Rather than return a character based on a decimal value, the function returns the decimal value based on a character. Using this function, you could produce your own ASCII chart by converting every keyboard character. The syntax for CHAR is this:

CODE(character)

Character can be any single character or reference to a cell containing a character, or it can be a full text string or reference to a string. If a string is used, only the first character in the string is converted to the decimal value.

Removing Nonprintable Characters (CLEAN)

This seldom used function removes nonprintable characters from a text string. The primary use for CLEAN is for converting data from another system that uses Excel. Characters that cannot be printed on the screen will be removed. The syntax is

CLEAN(text)

Cleaning Up a Text String (TRIM)

The TRIM function removes unnecessary spaces from a string—spaces in front of the string, spaces after the string, and extra spaces between words. This function can be useful when you are splitting text strings or searching strings for specific information. Unwanted spaces may confuse the process; the TRIM command can remove them. The syntax is the following:

TRIM(text)

Consider this example:

=TRIM(B4)

If cell B4 contains " Now is the time   for all   ", the function returns *Now is the time for all*.

Displaying Numbers as Text in Currency Format (DOLLAR)

The DOLLAR function converts a number to a text string (label). After converting the number to a label, the function adds a dollar sign and two decimal places. The syntax is as follows:

DOLLAR(value,*decimal_places*)

Value can be any number or numeric expression. *Decimal_places* is the number of places you want to apply to the converted number. If you omit this argument, Excel assumes 2 places. The following is an example:

=DOLLAR(B5)

If cell B5 contains the numeric value 54.5, TRIM returns the text value $54.50. This function is useful when you are using various text functions and must convert a number to text before a function will accept the value.

Displaying Numbers as Text with Fixed Decimal Places (FIXED)

The FIXED function converts any number to a text string with a fixed number of decimal places. The syntax is the following:

FIXED(value,*decimal_places*)

Value is the number being converted; *decimal_places* is the number of places to which the number will be rounded—very much like the DOLLAR format without the dollar signs. Note that the value is rounded to the number of places specified. Consider this example:

=FIXED(23.558,2)

This function returns the text string 23.56. If you omit the *decimal_places* argument, Excel assumes 2.

Displaying Numbers as Text in Any Format (TEXT)

The TEXT function is the same as the DOLLAR function except that it lets you choose any number format for the resulting text string. The syntax is

TEXT(value,format)

Value can be any number or reference to a cell containing a number. *Format* is any format specification, as described in Chapter 5. If you reference other cells, Excel will ignore the original format of the number.

TEXT functions are most useful in macros when you want to place numeric information where text is more appropriate, such as in the text column of a custom-dialog-box control. The following is an example:

=TEXT(B5,$#,##0 ;($#.##0))

If cell B5 contains -5445.5, this function returns the text string ($5,445.50). For more information on numeric formats, see "Using Number Formats" in Chapter 5. You also can use date and time formats in this function.

Determining Whether Two Strings Match (EXACT)

The EXACT function compares two text strings to determine whether they match. The syntax is

EXACT(text1,text2)

If *text1* and *text2* match, upper- and lowercase included, the function returns the value TRUE; otherwise, it returns FALSE. Consider this example:

=EXACT(A1,A2)

If A1 contains *Elaine Smith* and A2 contains *Elaine smith*, this function returns FALSE. To circumvent Excel's consideration of upper- and lowercase status, use EXACT with the LOWER function, as in this example:

    =EXACT(LOWER(A1),LOWER(A2))

This variation converts both strings to lowercase letters before comparing them. The conversion does not appear on the worksheet; it is used only within this formula. The EXACT function is often combined with the IF function to act on the result of the test:

    =IF(EXACT(LOWER(A1),LOWER(A2))=TRUE,"Match","No
    Match")

This formula returns *Match* if the two cells match and *No Match* if they don't. For more details, see the descriptions of the IF and LOWER functions later in this chapter.

Finding a Text String in Another Text String (FIND)

The FIND function searches for a text string within another text string and enables you to begin looking at a specified position. The function then returns a number representing the character position of the matched string. The syntax is as follows:

    FIND(text1,text2,*position*)

If you omit the *position* argument, the function returns the first position of the matching text, relative to the leftmost character. The following is an example:

    =FIND("a","Atlas")

This function returns 4, the position of the matching character relative to the left of the string. Notice that the function considers the case of the characters you specify. In this example, the formula did not return the position of the uppercase *A*. If you include a starting position for the FIND function, the result is the same, except that Excel begins searching at the specified character:

    =FIND("a","atlas",3)

This function returns 4, showing that the first *a* was skipped because of the starting position. To ignore the case of the characters, use this function with the LOWER function to convert the text to lowercase letters before searching:

    =FIND("a",LOWER(B5))

If B5 contains "Atlas", this function returns 1, indicating that the first *A* was found. If Excel cannot find the specified string, it returns #VALUE! to the cell—a message that can be interpreted as an error.

Use Quotation Marks in Constant Text Values

Remember to use quotation marks when you enter a text string directly into a function or formula. Otherwise, Excel will think that you have entered a range name.

Searching for Text in Another Text String (SEARCH)

The SEARCH function is identical to the FIND function, except that the former ignores the case of the characters in the text and allows wild cards as part of the *text1* variable. The syntax is

SEARCH(text1,text2,*position*)

Excel searches for *text1* within *text2*, beginning its search at the location specified by *position*. You can include either of the following wild cards in the search string:

Wild Card	Purpose
*	Represents any number of characters appearing at the position of the * within the criteria
?	Represents any single character appearing at the position of the ? within the criteria

Dissecting a Text String (LEFT, RIGHT, MID)

These three functions return a specified portion of a text string. They have the following syntax:

LEFT(text,*position*)

RIGHT(text,*position*)

MID(text,position,length)

The function LEFT returns the leftmost portion of a text string, beginning at the first character and ending at the specified position. RIGHT returns the rightmost portion, beginning at the specified location and ending at the last character in the string. MID returns a specified portion from the middle of the string, beginning at the specified character and ending at the specified length.

The *text* argument is any text string in quotation marks, a reference to a cell containing a text string, or any text expression resulting in a text string. *Position* is the character position for the function and can be any integer value less than the total number of characters in the string; the position entered here would be the starting character for the MID and RIGHT functions and the ending character for the LEFT function. The *length* variable is the number of characters to return from the middle of the string.

These functions are useful for concatenating or separating text. Suppose that you are converting an address database from another computer system. When you read the information into Excel, you notice that the city, state, and ZIP-code fields are merged into one field. Your preference is to separate the ZIP code from the city and state so that you can use the ZIP-code field independently. The RIGHT function will help you separate the ZIP field. Figure 6.19 shows what this database might look like.

🍎 File	Edit	Formula	Format	Data	Options	Macro	Window

E2			=RIGHT(D2,5)		

Worksheet1

	A	B	C	D	E
1					
2	Mary	Hilborne	98 First St	Los Angeles, CA 91001	91001
3	Betty	Smart	398 Euclid Ave #30	San Francisco, CA 94011	94011
4	Terri	Sachs	71 Green St	San Francisco, CA 94123	94123
5	Larry	MacEntire	100 Golden Hills Lane	San Diego, CA 92011	92011
6	Judy	Probini	2298 President's Way	New York, NY 10023	10023
7	Robert	Siliman	2388 Sunset	Miami, FL 33033	33033
8					

Fig. 6.19.

A database with the city, state, and ZIP-code data combined in one field.

The formulas in column E use the RIGHT function to extract the last five characters in the address. If the address contains a ZIP+4 code, however, you must use a more complex formula—one that extracts the ZIP+4 code when one exists but that extracts a standard ZIP code when that is the existing form. The formula in cell E2 looks like this:

=IF(ISERR(FIND("—",D2))<>TRUE,MID(D2,FIND("—",D2)
-5,10), RIGHT(D2,5))

Copy this formula down column E to get all the ZIP codes. The result looks like figure 6.20.

Fig. 6.20.

Using the MID and RIGHT functions to extract ZIP+4 codes from a database.

🍎	File	Edit	Formula	Format	Data	Options	Macro	Window	
	E2			=IF(ISERR(FIND("-",D2))<>TRUE,MID(D2,FIND("-",D2)-5, 10),RIGHT(D2,5))					

	B	C	D		
1					
2	Hilborne	983 First St	Los Angeles, CA 91001-3002	91001-3002	
3	Smart	124 Euclid Ave #30	San Francisco, CA 94019	94019	
4	Sachs	78 Green Street	San Francisco, CA 94010-2309	94010-2309	
5	MacEntire	100 Golden Hills Lane	San Diego, CA 92011-1234	92011-1234	
6	Probini	45719 Presidents Way	New York, NY 10011	10011	
7	Sandolucci	330 Diamond	Pittsburgh, PA 66002	66002	
8					
9					
10					
11					
12					

For more information about this formula, see the descriptions of the IF, ISERROR, and FIND functions elsewhere in this chapter.

Replacing a Portion of a Text String (REPLACE)

The REPLACE function works very much like the MID function. Instead of extracting a particular portion of a text string, however, REPLACE replaces it with a specified replacement string. As with the MID function, you specify the text string to use for the function, the starting character within the string, and the number of characters to use (that is, to replace). Then you can specify the replacement text. The syntax for REPLACE is the following:

REPLACE(text,position,length,replacement_text)

Position is the starting position in *text*. The first character is at position 1, the second is at 2, and so on. *Length* determines how many characters after the starting position will be replaced. *Replacement_text* can be any text, text expression, or cell reference containing text. The replacement string does not have to have the same number of characters as the text being replaced. You can, for example, replace the word *white* with *very bright and shiny*, as shown in this formula:

    =REPLACE(B5,16,5,"very bright and shiny")

If cell B5 contains *The object was white*, the new string will read, *The object was very bright and shiny*.

Substituting a Portion of a Text String (SUBSTITUTE)

The SUBSTITUTE function, which is similar to REPLACE, searches for a specified text string within another string, then replaces that text with new text. Unlike REPLACE, which begins replacing at a specified location, SUBSTITUTE searches for specified text within the specified string, then replaces it. The syntax is the following:

    SUBSTITUTE(text,search_text,replace_text,*occurrence*)

Text is the string in which you are replacing information. *Search_text* is the information in *text* that you want to replace. *Replace_text* is the new information replacing *search_text*; the replacement text does not have to be the same length as the original text. Finally, *occurrence* determines which occurrence of the search text is replaced (assuming that there is more than one occurrence). If you omit this argument, Excel assumes that you want to replace the text only at the first occurrence. The following are examples of using SUBSTITUTE:

    =SUBSTITUTE("Adam","a","o")   returns "Adom"
    =SUBSTITUTE("one on one",   returns "one on two"
    "one","two",2)

Determining the Length of a Text String (LEN)

The LEN function, which returns the number of characters in a text string, can be useful in conjunction with the LEFT, RIGHT, and MID functions. The syntax is as follows:

    LEN(text)

You can use any text string, text expression, or cell reference as the *text* argument. All spaces and special characters are counted. For example, the function

    =LEN("This is the string")

yields the result 18.

Converting Uppercase and Lowercase Characters (UPPER, LOWER)

The UPPER function converts text from lowercase to uppercase; LOWER converts text from uppercase to lowercase. The syntax is the following:

UPPER(text)

LOWER(text)

The functions convert the entire string specified. You can change only certain parts of the string by combining these functions with the MID, LEFT, and RIGHT functions. For example, you can make the first character of a string an uppercase character with a formula like this:

=UPPER(LEFT(B4,1))&MID(B4,2,100)

This formula uses the UPPER function with the LEFT function to make the first character of the string in cell B4 uppercase. Then the formula uses the MID function to concatenate this uppercase character with the rest of the string. Notice that the MID function uses the value 100, meaning that the function can return up to 100 characters in case the string is long.

Using Proper-Name Format (PROPER)

The PROPER function converts the first character of a text string to uppercase, exactly like the example in the UPPER function. But PROPER does everything for you, so you don't need the LEFT and MID functions. The syntax is as follows:

PROPER(text)

The function

=PROPER(john doe)

returns *John Doe*. Notice that the first character in both words is capitalized. If the first character in any word is already capitalized, no harm has been done.

Repeating a Text String (REPT)

The REPT function repeats a text string across a cell or cells. You determine the character or string you want to repeat and the number of times you want to repeat it, using the syntax

REPT(text,value)

Text is the character or string that you want to repeat; *value* is the number of times you want it repeated. REPT is useful for creating borders and divisions in a worksheet; its primary purpose is to enhance the appearance of a worksheet. The most common use of this command—creating a line across the page—is demonstrated in the formula bar of figure 6.21.

 The example in cell B7 uses Option+Shift+~ in the New York typeface to produce the line. Cell B10 uses the same character in Monaco type. Since the formula bar uses Geneva 12, this character appears there as the "little bunny."

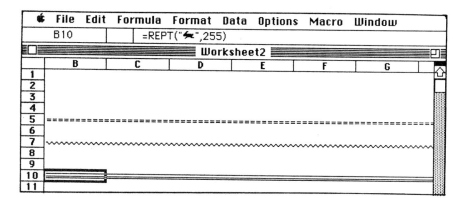

Fig. 6.21.

Using REPT to create a line across the page.

Converting Text to a Numeric Value (VALUE)

The VALUE function converts text strings into numeric values, as long as the string contains only characters that can be interpreted as values. The function recognizes numeric symbols as parts of numeric values, including the symbols

$, . ( ) %

The syntax is the following:

VALUE(text)

For example, the function

=VALUE(A1)

returns 2 if cell A1 contains the text ="2". If cell A1 contains the text string ="$(2,443.00)," the function returns the numeric value -2443.

Lookup Functions

Lookup functions search for values within tables or lists. Each lookup function uses a different method for searching and returning values. You will find that each method is suited for a particular task. Any time your worksheet uses tables (such as tax tables or price tables) to hold values, you can employ a lookup function for added power in the application.

Choosing a Value from a List (CHOOSE)

The CHOOSE function uses a value to look up another value in a set that you have determined. The syntax is as follows:

CHOOSE(value,list)

Value can be any number, formula, or cell reference that results in a value. The argument designates which number from the *list* is to be returned. *List* is a series of values to be returned. If the value is 1, the first item in the list is returned; if the value is 2, the second value is returned, and so on. Suppose that the formula is entered as follows:

=CHOOSE(A1,"primero","second","trio")

If the value of cell A1 is 3, the formula returns *trio*, because it is the third item in the list. In this example, the list contains text references, but numbers, cell references, formulas, or mixtures thereof are also acceptable. The values must be supplied as a list, however; a range reference is not acceptable. If *value* is a blank cell or text, that argument is assumed to be 0.

You probably can already see some limitations to this function. What if the first value is 141? Would you have to have 142 values in the list? The answer is yes. Keep in mind, however, that the CHOOSE function is meant to be used when the first value is sequential, not variable. An example would be 141, 142, 143, 144, and so on. Because the possible values are sequential, not variable, you could convert them to 0, 1, 2, 3, 4, and so on, using this formula:

=CHOOSE(A1-140,"primero","second","trio")

Notice that the first value consists of the formula A1-140, which converts the values to a more manageable range for the function (that is, the values 1, 2, 3, and 4).

The CHOOSE function is very much like the HLOOKUP and VLOOKUP functions, described later. One major advantage of the CHOOSE function is that you can use it to randomly choose its parameters, whereas HLOOKUP and VLOOKUP require parameters to be in a range of cells. For example, CHOOSE might look like this:

CHOOSE(A5,C4,G25,H2,B33,F2)

The listed items are not adjacent cell references. If the value in the CHOOSE function is larger than the greatest item in the list, the function returns #VALUE!

Finding the Offset of Two Matching Items (MATCH)

The MATCH function is the opposite of the CHOOSE function. Whereas CHOOSE uses a sequential value to select items from a list, MATCH finds a value in a list and returns its sequential value (that is, its placement in the list). The syntax for MATCH is

MATCH(value,range,*type*)

Value is the number or text that you want to find in the table. *Range* is the row or column range containing the table; the items in this table should be in ascending order and can be numbers or text. If *value* matches the first item in *range*, the function returns 1; if *value* matches the second item in *range*, this function returns 2; and so on.

Type is a value that determines the type of search made on the range. The following are the type entries you can make:

1 Excel finds the value closest to, but smaller than, *value* if a match cannot be made. If a smaller value cannot be found, Excel returns an error. If *value* is larger than all values in the table, Excel returns the last value in the table (that is, the largest).

-1 Excel finds the value closest to, but larger than, *value* if a match cannot be made. If a larger value cannot be found, Excel returns an error. If *value* is smaller than all values in the table, Excel returns the first value in the table (that is, the smallest). When using this type, make sure that the values appear in descending order, not ascending order.

0 Excel finds only the value that matches *value*. If a match cannot be found, Excel returns an error.

If you use 0 as the type and if *value* is a text string, then you can include wild cards in the string. As mentioned earlier, the ? wild card represents any single character; the * wild card represents any number of characters. (For more information about wild cards, see Chapter 3.) Figure 6.22 shows an example of this function.

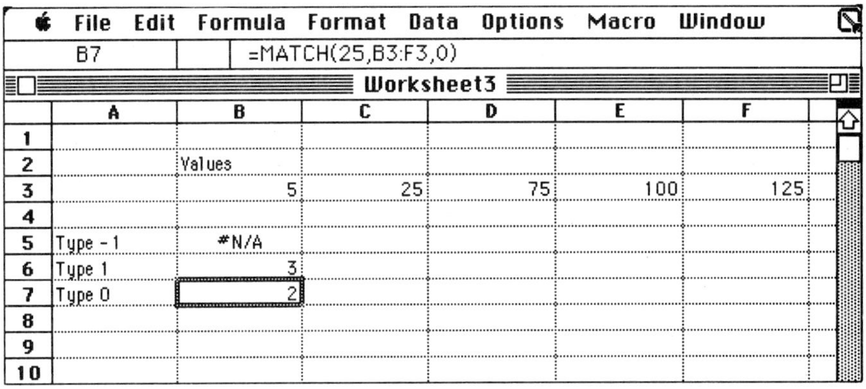

Fig. 6.22.

Using the MATCH function.

	File	**Edit**	**Formula**	**Format**	**Data**	**Options**	**Macro**	**Window**	
	B7			=MATCH(25,B3:F3,0)					

Worksheet3

	A	B	C	D	E	F	
1							
2		Values					
3		5	25	75	100	125	
4							
5	Type – 1	#N/A					
6	Type 1	3					
7	Type 0	2					
8							
9							
10							

The range B3:F3 contains the table of values. The functions in cells B5, B6, and B7 are as follows:

=MATCH(24,B3:F3,-1)

=MATCH(80,B3:F3,1)

=MATCH(25,B3:F3,0)

The three types of MATCH values produce different results. The first formula returns #N/A because the values are listed in ascending order.

Finding Values in a Simple Table (HLOOKUP, VLOOKUP)

These lookup functions search for values in tables, using a lookup value as a basis. A lookup value is the value you are trying to match in the table. For example, a tax table contains tax rates based on income; income is the lookup value. VLOOKUP searches vertically in a column of values, then returns a corresponding value from the table. HLOOKUP searches horizontally in a row of values, then returns a corresponding value from the table. The syntax of the two functions is as follows:

HLOOKUP(value,range,row_offset)

VLOOKUP(value,range,column_offset)

Value is any valid number, text string, or expression resulting in a valid number or string, including formulas and cell references. *Range* is the worksheet range containing the table. *Row_offset* and *column_offset* determine the value to be returned.

The VLOOKUP function takes the search variable and looks down the first column of the table for a match. When a match is found, the function maintains the row position of the matched value but moves across the table to return one of the columns. The column used is determined by the offset value specified.

Suppose that your worksheet contains the table of values shown in figure 6.23.

&	**File**	**Edit**	**Formula**	**Format**	**Data**	**Options**	**Macro**	**Window**		

B16	=VLOOKUP(A1,A6:D13,2)

LOOKUP

	A	B	C	D	E	F	G	H
1	Fiddle-Leaf Fig							
2			Tree-Green Nursery Price List					
3			Size in Inches					
4								
5			1	2	3			
6	Baby Tears	5.00	9.95	16.00				
7	Creeping Charlie	4.00	7.00	10.50				
8	Ficus	4.00	7.00	10.50				
9	Fiddle-Leaf Fig	5.50	9.95	12.00				
10	Geranium	7.00	11.00	16.50				
11	Philodendron	9.95	14.95	21.00				
12	String of Pearls	3.00	5.50	8.00				
13	Variegated Ivy	4.00	7.00	10.60				
14								
15								
16	Size 1	5.50						
17	Size 2	9.95						
18	Size 3	12.00						
19								

Fig. 6.23.

An example of a table lookup worksheet.

In the figure, cell B16 contains the formula

=VLOOKUP(A1,A6:D13,2)

and cell B17 contains the formula

=VLOOKUP(A1,A6:D13,3)

The first formula (in cell B16) takes the value in cell A1 and tries to match it in the first column of the range A6:D13, which is the column A6:A13. This column is called the *lookup column*, and in a VLOOKUP statement, it is always the first column in the specified range. (In an HLOOKUP statement, it is always the first row.) When a match is found, the function returns the corresponding value from a column of the table, where the lookup column itself is 1. Because the offset value in the formula is 2, the first column to the right (that is, column 2 of the table) is used; the corresponding value in that column is 5.50. The second formula (cell B17) performs the same operation but returns the value from the third column of the table.

 You cannot use negative values for the offset.

NOTE

Figure 6.24 shows an example of an HLOOKUP function. HLOOKUP follows the same rules as VLOOKUP but searches horizontally across the first row of the specified range and returns the corresponding value from rows below the lookup row.

Fig. 6.24.

An example of the HLOOKUP function.

	File	Edit	Formula	Format	Data	Options	Macro	Window	
	C14			=HLOOKUP(B12,B5:E9,2)					

	A	B	C	D	E	F
				LOOKUP.2		
	A	B	C	D	E	F
2						
3				LENSES		
4				Size in mm		
5		50	125	150	200	
6	Vivitar	135.00	255.00	305.00	500.00	
7	Minolta	240.00	300.00	389.00	515.00	
8	Cannon	245.00	308.00	410.00	500.00	
9	Olympus	300.00	450.00	600.00	700.00	
10						
11						
12	Size Desired	125				
13						
14		Vivitar	$255.00			
15		Cannon	$308.00			
16		Olympus	$450.00			
17		Minolta	$300.00			
18						
19						
20						
21						

In this example, the HLOOKUP function in cell C14 searches across row 5 for the size entered into cell B12. Row 5 is the lookup row for the table in the range B5:E9. Remember that this row is also the first offset row; an offset value of 1 returns a value from row 5. Hence the formula in cell C14 uses an offset of 2 to return the row corresponding to Vivitar.

Making the Offset Variable

The preceding VLOOKUP example uses a separate lookup function for each possible column in the table. Because there are only three columns, this arrangement is not prohibitive. Each of the functions (cells B15, B16, and B17) returns a value from one of the three columns in the table, using the search value as a basis. But what if you want to make the offset selectable instead of using a different formula for each possible offset? In the preceding example, the three formulas can be narrowed to one, and the offset can be selected according to another input. Figure 6.25 shows what the new worksheet would look like. The formula in cell B16 is as follows:

=VLOOKUP(A1,A5:D12,A2-8)

	File	Edit	Formula	Format	Data	Options	Macro	Window	
	B16			=VLOOKUP(A1,A5:D12,A2-8)					

LOOKUP

	A	B	C	D	E	F	G	H
1	Fiddle-Leaf Fig							
2		12	Tree-Green Nursery Price List					
3			Size in Inches					
4								
5			10	11	12			
6	Baby Tears	5.00	9.95	16.00				
7	Creeping Charlie	4.00	7.00	10.50				
8	Ficus	4.00	7.00	10.50				
9	Fiddle-Leaf Fig	5.50	9.95	12.00				
10	Geranium	7.00	11.00	16.50				
11	Philodendron	9.95	14.95	21.00				
12	String of Pearls	3.00	5.50	8.00				
13	Variegated Ivy	4.00	7.00	10.60				
14								
15								
16	Price	12.00						
17								
18								
19								

Fig. 6.25.

Making the VLOOKUP offset variable.

The value in cell A2 is now used to calculate the appropriate offset value. Because the offset value must be a number ranging from 1 to the number of columns in the lookup table, the calculation A2-8 is used to convert the value to a usable form. This formula works only when the values are sequential and an equal amount apart; otherwise, a double-variable table is required. (Double-variable tables are explained in detail in Chapter 8.)

Noting Lookup Table Rules

Several rules apply to performing lookups with HLOOKUP and VLOOKUP. First, if the search variable is numeric, the values in the lookup column (or row) should be numeric. Moreover, these values should be in ascending order, as in figure 6.25. If the lookup column is not in ascending order, the functions may return incorrect values. Excel searches the lookup column until it finds a match; if a match cannot be found, Excel uses the value closest to, but smaller than, the search variable. Therefore, if a lookup value is greater than all values in the table, the last value in the table is used because it is the largest. If the lookup value is smaller than all values in the table, the function returns the error #VALUE! Remember that if a match is not made, Excel will use the first value smaller than the search variable.

If the lookup range within the specified table range contains text strings, the search variable must also be a text string. In such cases, the lookup function must be able to find a match for the specified information, including uppercase and lowercase letters. If no match is found, the function will return the error #VALUE! The data in the table (that is, the value to be returned) can be numeric or text.

Looking Up Values in Nonstandard Tables (LOOKUP)

This LOOKUP function uses the same basic principle as HLOOKUP and VLOOKUP: it searches a horizontal or vertical range (that is, a row or column) for a specified value and returns a corresponding value. With HLOOKUP and VLOOKUP, Excel assumes the position of the resulting value by using the position of the lookup range as a basis. But with the LOOKUP function, both ranges are specified as arguments, as the syntax indicates:

LOOKUP(value,lookup_range,result_range)

Thus the result range can be anywhere on the worksheet. In fact, it can be vertical (a row) when the lookup range is horizontal (a column) and vice versa. The only restriction is that the number of cells in the lookup range and result range must match. Figure 6.26 shows an example.

In this example, the lookup range is C3:F3, and the result range is B5:B8. Notice that the two ranges have the same number of cells. Enter the

	B	C	D	E	F	G	
1	50						
2	Fifty						
3		25	50	68	89		
4							
5	Twenty-five						
6	Fifty						
7	Sixty-eight						
8	Eighty-nine						
9							
10							
11							

 File   Edit   Formula   Format   Data   Options   Macro   Window

B2   =LOOKUP(B1,C3:F3,B5:B8)

Worksheet7

Fig. 6.26.

Using the LOOKUP function.

search value into cell B1. Cell B2 will display the result of the lookup, using this function:

=LOOKUP(B1,C3:F3,B5:B8)

Another form of the LOOKUP function is as follows:

LOOKUP(value,lookup_range)

Using this syntax, the function searches for the *value* in the specified *lookup range* and returns a corresponding value. However, the corresponding value will always be taken from the last column in the lookup range—as if you had used an offset value pointing to the last column. The uses for this function are obscure.

Looking Up Cell References (INDEX)

The INDEX function returns a value from a table, using the row offset and column offset as a basis. Rather than match a value in the table, INDEX goes directly to the row and column offset values you specify and returns the contents of the intersection. The syntax is the following:

INDEX(range,row_offset,column_offset)

Row_offset must be equal to or less than the number of rows in *range*. *Column offset* must be equal to or less than the number of columns in *range*. If either argument is too large, the function returns the error #REF! If either is 0, the function returns the error #VALUE!

Figure 6.27 shows an example of the INDEX function as used in a previous worksheet table.

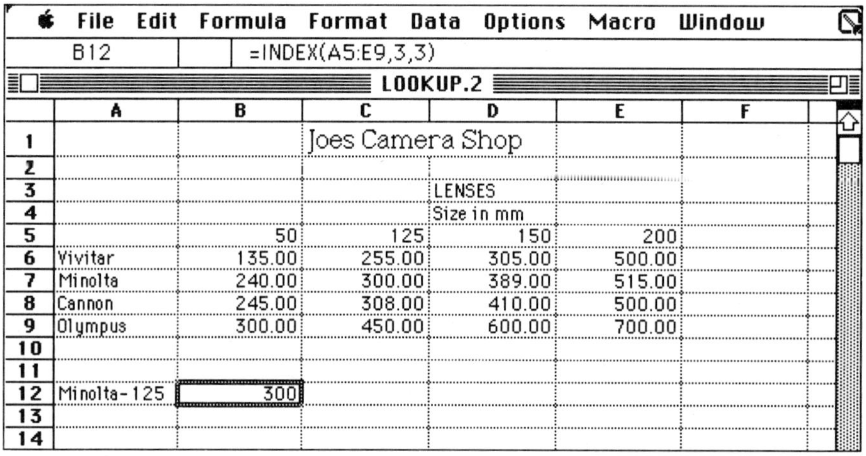

Fig. 6.27.

Using the INDEX
function.

```
 ¤   File   Edit   Formula   Format   Data   Options   Macro   Window         ▨
        B12              =INDEX(A5:E9,3,3)
 ▤▢                          LOOKUP.2                                     ▨▤
         A          B          C          D          E          F          ⇧
  1                        Joes Camera Shop
  2
  3                                    LENSES
  4                                    Size in mm
  5                  50         125        150        200
  6   Vivitar      135.00     255.00     305.00     500.00
  7   Minolta      240.00     300.00     389.00     515.00
  8   Cannon       245.00     308.00     410.00     500.00
  9   Olympus      300.00     450.00     600.00     700.00
 10
 11
 12   Minolta-125      300
 13
 14
```

The function in cell B12 is =INDEX(A5:E9,3,3). The result is 300, the value at the intersection of row 3 and column 3 of the range.

If a range entry includes two or more ranges, the INDEX function requires an additional argument. This argument, placed after the others, indicates which range to use in a multiple-range reference. The ranges are numbered sequentially from top to bottom and from left to right.

The function

=INDEX(A5:D12,H24:K30,3,3,2)

returns the value in cell J26, the intersection address of row 3 and column 3 of the second range in the reference.

Special Functions

These functions serve various purposes that do not fit into the other categories. Many of these functions are designed primarily for macros. Uses for many of these functions appear in the sample macros provided later in this book.

Determining the Attributes of a Cell (CELL)

This multipurpose function can tell you virtually everything about a cell—its format, location, contents, alignment, and so on. The syntax for CELL is

CELL(type,*cell*)

The *type* argument, which must be enclosed in quotation marks, specifies which type of information you want for *cell*. You can get only one type of information. If *cell* is a range, Excel uses the first cell in the range. If you omit *cell*, Excel uses the currently highlighted cell or range. The CELL function can be useful in macros when you want the reference to be variable or selectable. Table 6.1 lists the *type* arguments allowed.

Table 6.1
Types for the CELL Function

Type	Information Returned
"width"	The cell's width. Excel estimates the width of a font by using the width of a numeral character.
"row"	The cell's row number. Similar to ROW.
"col"	The cell's column number. Similar to COLUMN.
"lock"	The cell's protection status. If the cell is protected, Excel returns 1. If the cell is not protected, Excel returns 0.
"address"	The cell's address. The address is returned as a text string but can be used where any cell address is expected in a formula.
"contents"	The cell's contents.
"prefix"	The cell's alignment. One of the following characters may be returned: " If the cell is right-aligned ' If the cell is left-aligned ^ If the cell is centered (this type returns no value if any other alignment is used)
"type"	The type of data in the cell. One of the following characters may be returned as a text string: b If the cell is blank l If the cell contains a label v If the cell contains a numeric value
"format"	The number format of the data (if the data is numeric). This value is returned as a text string. See table 6.2 for a list of the symbols returned for each format.

Table 6.2
Formats Returned When Type Is "format"

Symbol	Description	Format
G	General	General
F0	Fixed—0 decimal places	0 or #,###0
F2	Fixed—2 decimal places	0.00 or #,###0.00
C0	Currency—0 decimal places	$#,##0 ;($#,##0) or $#,##0 ;[RED]($#,##0)
C2	Currency—2 decimal places	$#,##0.00 ;($#,##0.00) or $#,##0.00 ;[RED]($#, ##0.00)
P0	Percent—0 decimal places	0%
P2	Percent—2 decimal places	0.00%
S2	Scientific—2 decimal places	0.00E+00
D1	Date format 1	d-mmm-yy
D2	Date format 2	d-mmm
D3	Date format 3	mmm-yy
D4	Date format 4	m/d/yy or m/d/yy h:mm
D6	Date format 6	h:mm:ss AM/PM
D7	Date format 7	h:mm AM/PM
D8	Date format 8	h:mm:ss
D9	Date format 9	h:mm

Remember that the symbol is returned as a text string indicating the format.

If the *reference* is to a cell that has a custom format, Excel may not accurately reflect this fact with the CELL function. Custom number formats are supposed to return a value of F1, but Excel often interprets your custom format as one of its built-in formats and returns one of the values in the table. For example, if you use the custom format ;;; to make a cell's value invisible, Excel will return the value G when you get the cell's format code with the CELL function.

NOTE When you change the format of a cell, you might need to recalculate the worksheet before the CELL function reflects the change. Use Command+= to recalculate.

Make It Easy on Yourself

The CELL function, when combined with the logic of the IF function, can duplicate the effects of certain other functions. For example, you can test for a blank cell by using either of these functions:

=IF(CELL("type",B5) = "b",TRUE( ),FALSE( ))

=ISBLANK(B5)

The ISBLANK function is, obviously, easier to use. The CELL function also duplicates the ISNUM, ISNONTEXT, and ISTEXT functions, but you will probably find CELL more difficult to use.

Converting Columns and Rows to Numbers (COLUMN, ROW)

The COLUMN function returns the column number of the *cell* reference; ROW returns the row number. The syntax is the following:

COLUMN(*cell*)

ROW(*cell*)

Simply enter any cell address as the argument; the functions will return the corresponding column or row number. Consider this example:

=COLUMN(G5)

This function returns 7 because column G is also column 7. If you omit the argument, the function assumes the address of the cell containing the formula. Because it is unlikely that you will need to know the column or row number of a range that you have already specified, the command is intended for use with range names, as in

=COLUMNS(SALES)

If SALES is the name of a cell, the function returns the column number of that cell. If SALES is the name of a range, the function returns the column numbers of the leftmost cell in the range.

The COLUMN and ROW functions are also useful in macros for finding the position of the pointer. Omitting the arguments (that is, COLUMN( ) and ROW( )) serves this purpose.

Finding the Number of Ranges within a Range (AREAS)

The AREAS function, which tells you how many individual ranges make up the specified range reference, is most helpful when used with range names or in macros when a range reference is variable and selectable. The syntax is

AREAS(range)

The following is a simple example:

=AREAS(A1:A5,B5)

This function returns 2, indicating that the reference contains two range areas.

Determining Areas in the Currently Selected Range

You can determine the number of areas that are currently selected by using a macro. After you select a range, the macro can use the Formula Define Name command to assign a temporary name to the currently selected range. You might use the name CURRENT. Then the AREAS function can return the number of areas in this range, using the formula =AREAS(CURRENT). When the macro is run, the cell containing this AREAS function will return the number of areas in the current selection. The macro appears as follows:

```
macro
=DEFINE.NAME("current")
=AREAS(!current)
=ALERT("You've selected "&A3&" areas.",1)
=RETURN
```

Finding the Number of Columns and Rows in a Range (COLUMNS, ROWS)

These functions return the number of columns or rows in a specified range of cells. The syntax is the following:

COLUMNS(range)

ROWS(range)

The range can be any valid worksheet range. For example, entering =COLUMNS(A1:D1) returns the value 4, indicating that the range has 4 columns.

Referencing Cells Indirectly (INDIRECT)

The INDIRECT function returns the value of any cell specified with a text string. This function is useful when you need the value of a variable cell reference. INDIRECT converts the text string into a cell reference, then returns the value of that cell reference. The text must contain characters that can be interpreted as a cell reference in either the R1C1 style or the A1 style. The syntax is as follows:

INDIRECT(text)

Consider this example:

=INDIRECT(B5)

If cell B5 contains the text string "A24" and cell A24 contains 100, the function returns 100. This function is intended for use as the parameter of other functions or formulas. For example:

=SQRT(INDIRECT(B5))

If cell B5 contains "A24" and cell A24 contains 9, this function returns 3 (the square root of 9). If the text reference is in the R1C1 style, add the parameter FALSE to the end of the function:

=INDIRECT(B5,FALSE)

If B5 contains "R5C6" and cell E5 contains 100, the function returns 100. Omitting the second argument or making it TRUE indicates the A1 reference style.

Indicating an Unavailable Value (NA)

The NA function has the syntax

NA( )

and returns #N/A to a cell, indicating that the information needed to produce a result is not yet available. Excel does not know when information is not available; you must program that logic into your worksheets with the NA function.

As you can see, this function has no arguments. If a cell produces the value #N/A, all calculations that use that cell produce the value #N/A. Then, using an IF statement, you can convert the #N/A value to some meaningful message. For example, suppose that the formula in cell B2 calculates its value based on the number you enter into cell B1. In cell B2 you might want to use the #N/A function in a formula to test whether anything has been entered into B1, as in the following:

=IF(ISBLANK(B1)=TRUE,NA( ),B1*2)

This formula means, "If cell B1 is blank, return #N/A; otherwise, calculate B1*2." (See the ISBLANK function for more information about its syntax.)

Now suppose that a formula in cell B3 calculates its value based on the value of cell B2. That formula, shown here, might test whether the value of B2 is #N/A before making its calculation:

=IF(ISNA(B2)=TRUE,"Amount not entered in cell B1",B2+100)

This formula means, "If the value of B2 is #N/A, print the message *Amount not entered in cell B1*; otherwise, calculate B2+100." The formula converts the #N/A value into something more useful to the operator. (See ISNA for more information about testing for the #N/A value.)

Figure 6.28 shows the result before a value is entered into cell B1.

	File	Edit	Formula	Format	Data	Options	Macro	Window	
B2			=IF(ISBLANK(B1)=TRUE,NA(),B1*2)						

Worksheet1

	A	B	C	D	E	
1	Enter Amount					
2	Double the Amount	#N/A				
3	Double Amount + 100	Amount not entered in B1				
4						
5						
6						
7						

Fig. 6.28.

Testing for a blank cell in B1, then testing for #N/A in B2.

Determining the Value of a Cell (N)

The N function returns the value of a cell if the cell contains a numeric value, numeric expression, or cell reference resulting in a numeric value. The syntax is

N(value)

If the reference is formatted as a date or time, this function returns the numeric value (serial number) of the date or time. If the reference contains the logical value TRUE, Excel returns 1. If the reference contains the logical value FALSE, Excel returns 0. If the reference contains text, Excel returns 0. Figure 6.29 shows several N functions in column B and the cells they reference in column A.

	File	Edit	Formula	Format	Data	Options	Macro	Window	
B5			=N(A5)						

Worksheet1

	A	B	C	D	E	F	
1	TRUE	1					
2	1/1/91	31777					
3	2982	2982					
4	FALSE	0					
5	Text	0					
6							
7							
8							
9							

Fig. 6.29.

Using the N function.

Determining the Text of a Cell (T)

The T function returns the value of a cell if the cell contains text, a text expression, or a cell reference containing text. The syntax is as follows:

T(value)

If *value* is text, this function returns the value as a text string. If *value* is not text, this function returns a null string (""). This function can be useful in translating worksheets created by other programs.

Determining the Type of Information in a Cell (TYPE)

The TYPE function tells you the type of information a cell contains. The syntax is

TYPE(cell)

Cell can be a range or a constant value. If *cell* is a range, the function returns the type of information contained in the first cell of the range. The following is a list of values that this function returns; the values correspond with the type of information in the cell.

Values Returned	Cell Contents
1	A numeric value
2	Text
4	A logical value (TRUE or FALSE)
16	An error
64	An array

The formula =TYPE(B5) returns 2 if cell B5 contains "January". This formula returns 16 if B5 contains the error #VALUE!

Logical Functions

Logical functions are used to create logical tests. A test enables a formula to account for more data. A test may determine, for example, whether a particular value is greater than 25. The formula making the test can perform one function if the value is true and another if the value is false. In short, logical functions enable formulas to branch according to particular values. The most common and useful logical function is IF, with which you can develop several kinds of tests based on the operators used in the test statement. IF is often combined with other logical functions for more variety.

Returning a Logical Value (TRUE, FALSE)

The TRUE and FALSE functions are used primarily with logical tests to return the value TRUE or FALSE, depending on the result of the test. Although you can achieve the same result by using the text strings "TRUE" and "FALSE," the TRUE and FALSE functions can be useful when text strings are not accepted. The syntax is the following:

TRUE( )
FALSE( )

As you can see, the functions have no arguments.

The following functions serve the same purpose. One uses the TRUE and FALSE functions; the other uses the "TRUE" and "FALSE" text strings.

=IF(A1=25,TRUE( ),FALSE( ))
=IF(A1=25,"TRUE","FALSE")

Making a Decision (IF)

The IF function is probably the most powerful and useful of all worksheet functions, providing most of the logic you will need for evaluating information. The IF function tests whether a condition is true or false. If the condition is true, one value is returned; if the condition is false, another value is returned. The syntax for IF is the following:

IF(condition,value_if_true,value_if_false)

Proving a condition true or false requires a comparison operator. Excel offers several:

>	is greater than
<	is less than
=	is equal to
>=	is greater than or equal to
<=	is less than or equal to
<>	is not equal to

In the following examples, you can substitute any of these operators for the ones given. Consider this example:

IF(A1=A2,"Right","Wrong")

This formula means, "If the value of A1 is equal to that of A2, then return *Right*; otherwise, return *Wrong*." *Value_if_true* and *value_if_false* can be any constant value, cell reference, or formula resulting in either a numeric value or text.

Suppose that you are creating a worksheet for signups on a group vacation. Two packages are being offered, and you have numbered them 1 and 2. Package 1 costs $1,500, and package 2 costs $2,000. The worksheet is designed to hold the names and addresses of the participants in columns A through C. Column D holds the number of the trip package—1 or 2—that a participant wants. Finally, column E automatically enters the cost of each package entered in column D. Figure 6.30 shows the worksheet.

Fig. 6.30.

Using the IF function.

♦ File	Edit	Formula	Format	Data	Options	Macro	Window

E8		=IF(D8=1,1500,2000)				

Worksheet9

	A	B	C	D	E	F
1	FIRST	LAST	ADDRESS	PACKAGE	PRICE	
2						
3	John	Doe	23 First St	1	1500	
4	Patty	Rowly	298 May Ave	1	1500	
5	Larry	Smith	2399 Ash St	2	2000	
6	Fran	Brown	4 Maybury	2	2000	
7	Art	Shawley	440 C St	1	1500	
8	Terri	Shroeder	2388 Lay St	2	2000	
9						

The formulas in column E use the IF function to calculate the price of the package. For example, cell E3 contains

=IF(D3=1,1500,2000)

This formula means, "If cell D3 contains 1, enter 1500; otherwise, enter 2000." Because you know that only two options are available, this formula does not need to test for a 2 in cell D3; if cell D3 does not contain a 1, it should contain a 2. What happens if you enter a 3 into cell D3? You get 2500 by default. The 2500 is returned because cell D3 does not contain a 1.

Many people like to be sure of a correct answer by adding another level to the formula. The following formula will test for two conditions and will enter 0 if neither of them is met (the preceding example tested for only one condition and entered 2500 if it was not met):

    =IF(D1=1,1500,IF(D1=2,2500,0))

This formula contains two nested IF statements. The second IF statement is entered as the "else" of the first statement. Now, if D3 contains neither 1 nor 2, you end up with 0 in cell E1.

Creating a "Not To Exceed" Formula

A simple IF formula will provide "not to exceed" protection for your worksheet. If the value in question exceeds your limit, the formula will return *Too Large* in place of the value. The formula is this:

    =IF(A1<100,A1,"Too Large")

This formula ensures that the number in cell A1 does not exceed 100. If the number is smaller than 100, the formula returns the number in A1; if the number is 100 or larger, the formula returns *Too Large*. The "not less than" formula works in reverse:

    =IF(A1<100,"Too Small",A1)

This formula ensures that the number in cell A1 is no smaller than 100. If the number is smaller than 100, *Too Small* is returned.

Using Multiple Conditions for IF Tests (AND, OR)

You have learned that you can *nest* IF functions to make multiple tests in one formula. Excel also provides two important logical functions for this purpose. You can add more power to the IF function by adding the logical functions AND and OR. The AND function, when added to an IF function, adds a second test to the condition, using the syntax

    AND(condition1,condition2)

If *both* conditions are true, the IF statement proves true. If either or both are false, the IF statement proves false. An example might look like this:

    =IF(AND(A1=A2,A1=A6),"Right","Wrong")

This function adds a second test to the condition and means, "If cell A1 equals the value of A2 *and* if cell A1 equals the value of A6, print *Right*; otherwise, print *Wrong*." Notice that two conditional tests appear before the first comma in the IF function. Both tests fall in the parentheses of the AND function, such that the AND function and its two tests replace the single test used before.

The OR function also adds a second test to the IF function. If either or both conditions are true, the IF statement proves true. If both conditions are false, the IF statement proves false. The syntax for OR is the following:

OR(condition1,condition2)

Consider this example:

=IF(OR(A1=5,B1=25),"Right","Wrong")

This function is similar to the preceding example, but it means, "If the value of A1 equals 5 *and/or* if the value of B1 equals 25, print *Right*; otherwise, print *Wrong*." Note that the OR function serves as an AND/OR condition, meaning that both conditions can be true in order for the statement to prove TRUE. You can stack several tests into one AND or OR statement, as in the following:

=IF(AND(A1=5,B1=25,G5=G6),"Right","Wrong")

This statement is true if all three conditions are true.

Exclusive OR

When you use the OR logical operator, remember that it means "and/or." That is, either or both of the operands must be true for the statement to be true. Some applications call for an exclusive OR statement, in which only one of the operands can be true if the statement is true; if both operands are true, the statement is false.

Excel does not provide an exclusive OR logical operator (often listed as XOR), but you can achieve the same results by using nested IF functions. The statement can apply to any information in the worksheet and looks like this:

=IF(A1=5,(IF(B1=5,FALSE( ),TRUE( )),IF(B1=5,TRUE( ),FALSE( )))

In this example, if cell A1 equals 5 and B1 does not, or if B1 equals 5 and A1 does not, Excel returns TRUE. Otherwise, Excel returns FALSE.

Proving a Statement Not True (NOT)

The NOT function causes the function to return TRUE if a condition does not match your criterion. The syntax is

NOT(condition)

The example

=NOT(A5>B5)

asks, "Is A5 not greater than B5?" The answer is TRUE if A5 is *not* greater than B5 (rather like saying "yes, it is not true"). You can use the NOT function with any of the comparison operators listed earlier, as in this example:

=IF(OR(C5=25,NOT(A5=B5)),TRUE( ),FALSE( ))

Testing for a Blank Cell (ISBLANK)

The ISBLANK function tests for a blank cell and has the syntax

ISBLANK(cell)

If the specified cell is blank, the function returns TRUE; otherwise, the function returns FALSE. The referenced cell can be any valid cell in the worksheet. The function is commonly used along with the IF function to test for a blank cell, then to perform some action based on the outcome. For example, you can use ISBLANK along with IF to print a message next to cells that need to be filled in; you can remove the message once the data is entered. Consider this example:

=IF(ISBLANK(B5)=FALSE,"","Enter your ID number in cell B5")

The IF function tests whether the result of the ISBLANK test is 0. If so, the blank string is returned. Otherwise, the message appears.

Another use for the ISBLANK function is to determine whether a value has been entered before you use it in a formula. For example, the formula

=IF(ISBLANK(B5) = FALSE, NA( ), B5*B6)

means, "If B5 is blank, return #N/A; otherwise, multiply it by B6 and return the result." The formula suspends calculation until the number is entered.

Testing for Errors (ISERR, ISERROR)

These functions test whether a specified cell contains an error. If so, the function returns TRUE; otherwise, the function returns FALSE. The syntax is the following:

ISERR(cell)

ISERROR(cell)

The ISERR function ignores the #N/A error, but the ISERROR function picks it up. These functions are commonly used along with the IF function to "trap" errors in the worksheet and enable the operator to control the errors. Normally, any calculation that references a cell containing an error will calculate to #VALUE! or some other error. But when you use the ISERR function, you can pinpoint the error. Consider this example:

=IF(ISERR(B5)=TRUE,"Invalid entry in cell B5",B5*B6)

This formula tests whether the value of B5 is an error. If so, the function returns *Invalid entry in cell B5*. Otherwise, the calculation is performed.

Testing for #N/A (ISNA)

The ISNA function tests whether a cell contains #N/A. The syntax is

ISNA(cell)

The value #N/A may appear because a function is unable to find data or because a formula has specifically returned it. #N/A implies that information the function needs in order to continue is not available. You can use ISNA to convert #N/A into something more meaningful through a formula like this:

=IF(ISNA(B5)=TRUE,B5*B6,"Unable to complete this calculation")

This formula returns the phrase *Unable to complete this calculation* if #N/A is discovered in cell B5.

Testing for Numbers and Text (ISNUMBER, ISTEXT, ISNONTEXT)

The functions ISNUMBER, ISTEST, and ISNONTEXT have the syntax

ISNUMBER(cell)
ISTEXT(cell)
ISNONTEXT(cell)

and test whether a cell's value is a number or a text string. Such a test is useful if you want to determine whether a cell contains a number before you use it in a formula. Blank cells are considered text. You really don't need all the functions; if you use ISNUMBER to determine that a cell does not contain a number, you already know that the cell must contain a text string. The only reason for using ISNONTEXT is to distinguish between text and blank cells.

The functions are often used with the IF statement to act on the result of the test. You can differentiate among text, numbers, and blank cells by using a formula like this:

=IF(ISBLANK(B1)=TRUE,"BLANK",IF(ISNUMBER(B1)=TRUE,
"NUMBER","TEXT"))

Because the function tests for a blank cell first, the ISTEXT function is not needed and therefore will not evaluate a blank cell as text. To determine whether a cell is text but not blank, use the ISNONTEXT function:

=IF(ISNONTEXT(B1)=TRUE,FALSE( ),TRUE( ))

This formula returns TRUE if the cell B1 contains text and FALSE if the cell does not contain text. You can blank a cell by using the Clear command in the Edit menu.

Testing for Cell References (ISREF)

This function, which tests whether a cell contains a cell reference, has the syntax

ISREF(cell)

If a cell contains a cell reference, Excel returns TRUE; otherwise, Excel returns FALSE. Use this function with IF to act on the result of the test:

=IF(ISREF(B5)=TRUE,"Reference","Not a Reference")

This function returns the message *Reference* if cell B5 contains a reference to another cell. Otherwise, the function returns *Not a Reference*.

Testing for TRUE and FALSE (ISLOGICAL)

The ISLOGICAL function tests whether a cell contains the logical value TRUE or FALSE. The syntax is as follows:

ISLOGICAL(cell)

If *cell* contains either TRUE or FALSE, as produced by a logical test, the function returns TRUE. Otherwise, it returns FALSE. The uses for this function are rather esoteric because it does not distinguish between TRUE and FALSE.

Database Functions

Database functions apply to information found in a database. A *database* is a table of information in which the rows equate to records and the columns equate to fields. The structure of an Excel database is discussed in Part III (Chapters 14 through 16) of this book. The following pages will not provide details about how to set up an Excel database or the rules that apply to databases. Before you can use these functions, you should have a general idea about how to use Excel databases.

The primary reason for setting up a database is to find or extract information, using specific criteria as a basis. When you establish search criteria for a database, the matching records become a subset of the entire database, having the criteria in common. The database functions let you perform statistical analyses of these database subsets. You can establish search criteria to find the subset, then make calculations on the results of the search. When dealing with a large block of information, using a database function is the only way to perform statistical analysis on particular groups.

Normally, you set up a database by selecting the database block and designating it the database range. Another range, called the criteria range, contains the criteria used to search the database range. When a search is performed, matching records are either highlighted or extracted into an extract range. That's the function of an Excel database, in a nutshell.

Surprisingly, you don't need to set up a database range or criteria range in order to use these database functions. The arguments within the functions themselves specify the database range, criteria range, and information to return for the calculation. Because database functions are mirror images of statistical functions, this section will not include examples for each database function. Rather, it will explain how to use these database functions properly. The first function, DAVERAGE, includes a full explanation and example that applies to all the functions. For more information about the calculations being performed, see the statistical functions described earlier in this chapter.

Finding the Average of a Database Group (DAVERAGE)

The DAVERAGE function calculates the average of particular fields over a database subset, which is determined by search criteria. The particular field used for the average is determined by an offset value. The database itself is determined by the database range. The syntax for DAVERAGE is this:

DAVERAGE(range,field_offset,criteria)

Range is the range of cells containing the database information and should adhere to the guidelines for databases described in Chapter 14. Namely, the database range should include field names (column labels) over each column. You do not, however, have to have previously established this range as the database range by using the Data Set Database command. In other words, the range can be any block of data that represents a database. If you use a database that has been set with the Data Set Database command, you can simply enter the range name *database* as this argument. Excel interprets that as the name of the currently set database range.

Field_offset is the field that will be used as the operand for this function; in this case, it is the field to be averaged across the database subset. This variable should be any number from 1 to the number of fields in the database, where 1 represents the first field, 2 represents the second, and so on.

Criteria is the range of cells containing the search criteria for the database. This reference should adhere to the rules for criteria ranges described in Chapter 14. Namely, the criteria range should contain required field names and search formulas beneath those names. This range does not have to be the criteria range currently set with the Data Set Criteria command. However, if you plan to use the current criteria range, you can enter the range name *criteria* as the *criteria* argument; Excel will assume the currently set criteria range.

Figure 6.31 shows an example of a database and the DAVERAGE function used to calculate the average of a subset of data.

Fig. 6.31.

Using the DAVERAGE function.

	File Edit Formula Format Data Options Macro Window					
	E4		=DAVERAGE(A2:C7,3,A10:A11)			
			Worksheet9			
	A	**B**	**C**	**D**	**E**	**F**
1						
2	Name	Age	Amount		Statistics	
3	John Doe	32	5500			
4	Fred Smith	35	3500	DAVERAGE	4650	
5	Lois Fry	30	3800			
6	Jenny Smart	40	4000			
7	Larry Aimes	52	6000			
8						
9						
10	Age					
11	<35					
12						

In the example, the database contains the names, ages, and salary amounts of a small group of workers. The database is contained in the range A2:C7. The criteria range, A10:A11, contains the formula <35. This formula will establish a subset of all workers under the age of 35. The DAVERAGE function is set up to calculate the average income of all workers under 35 when you specify the database range, the criteria range, and the offset value. The offset value should point to the third column in the database, because the third database column contains the income figures. The third column's offset is 3. Therefore, the formula for the DAVERAGE function is as follows:

DAVERAGE(A2:C7,3,A10:A11)

Unless the database range or criteria range changes, you need not alter this formula to calculate other salary averages; simply enter new criteria for the search. You can, for example, find the average income of all workers 35 and over by changing the criteria formula to >=35. The DAVERAGE formula will recalculate its value, using the new criteria as a basis.

> ### Naming Criteria Formulas
>
> If you commonly switch among several criteria formulas in the database criteria range, try naming each criteria formula by using the Formula Define Name command. Then you can enter the appropriate criteria by typing the formula name in the correct cell of the criteria range (with an equal sign). The name might be easier to remember and enter than the criteria formula. In the example in figure 6.31, you might name one formula "Income_Over_34" and another formula "Income_Under_35".

Counting Items in a Database Group (DCOUNT, DCOUNTA)

The DCOUNT function counts the number of records that match the criteria established for a database search. Only records containing numbers are counted. The DCOUNTA function counts both database records and all matching records that are not blank. The syntax is the following:

DCOUNT(range,*field_offset*,criteria)

DCOUNTA(range,*field_offset*,criteria)

Range is the range of cells containing the database information and should adhere to the rules for databases described in Chapter 14. *Range* can be any block of data that represents a database. *Field_offset* is the field that will be used as the operand for this function; in this case, the offset is insignificant because the function is counting the number of *records* that match the criteria, with no regard to any particular field. In fact, you can leave this argument out of the function. If you use a field offset, and some records do not have information in that field, those records will not be counted.

Criteria is the range of cells containing the search criteria for the database. This reference should adhere to the rules for criteria ranges described in Chapter 14.

Figure 6.32 shows the same sample worksheet for the previous function, with the DCOUNT function added.

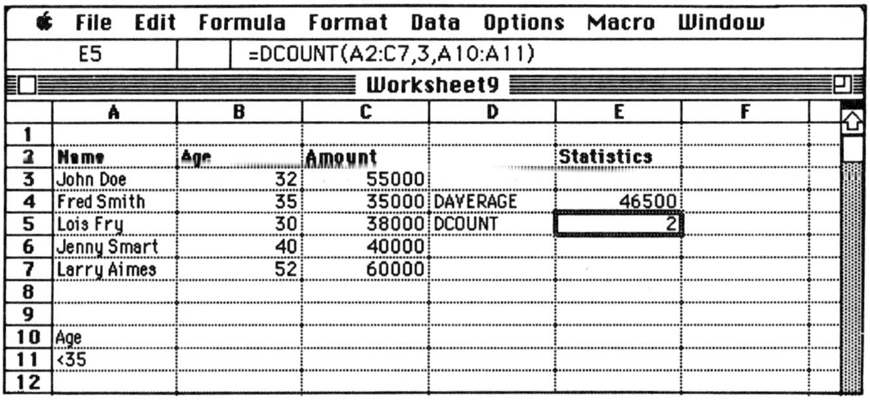

Fig. 6.32.

Using the DCOUNT function.

			File Edit Formula Format Data Options Macro Window			

E5		=DCOUNT(A2:C7,3,A10:A11)				

Worksheet9

	A	B	C	D	E	F
1						
2	Name	Age	Amount		Statistics	
3	John Doe	32	55000			
4	Fred Smith	35	35000	DAVERAGE	46500	
5	Lois Fry	30	38000	DCOUNT	2	
6	Jenny Smart	40	40000			
7	Larry Aimes	52	60000			
8						
9						
10	Age					
11	<35					
12						

The formula used for the DCOUNT function appears in the formula bar of the figure. This function uses the same database range and criteria range as the DAVERAGE function. Database functions, when used together like this, perform *different* calculations based on the *same* data. Note that you can substitute *database* as the argument for the database range and *criteria* as the argument for the criteria range. When you make these substitutions, Excel uses the database and criteria ranges currently set.

Finding the Maximum and Minimum Values in a Database Group (DMAX, DMIN)

The DMAX and DMIN functions find the maximum and minimum values in a database subset. The functions require offset values to determine the particular field used for the search. The syntax is as follows:

DMAX(range,field_offset,criteria)

DMIN(range,field_offset,criteria)

Range is the range of cells containing the database information. *Field_offset* is the field that will be used as the operand for this function; in this case, the offset is the field through which the function will search for the maximum value. *Criteria* is the range of cells containing the search criteria for the database.

Figure 6.33 shows the worksheet for the previous function, with the DMAX function added.

File	Edit	Formula	Format	Data	Options	Macro	Window

E6	=DMAX(A2:C7,3,A10:A11)

Worksheet9

Fig. 6.33.

	A	B	C	D	E	F
1						
2	Name	Age	Amount		Statistics	
3	John Doe	32	55000			
4	Fred Smith	35	35000	DAVERAGE	46500	
5	Lois Fry	30	38000	DCOUNT	2	
6	Jenny Smart	40	40000	DMAX	55000	
7	Larry Aimes	52	60000			
8						
9						
10	Age					
11	<35					
12						

The formula used for the DMAX function appears in the formula bar in the figure. This function uses the same database and criteria range as the previous functions and establishes the offset of 2 to return the maximum salary within the selected subgroup. An offset of 1 would return the maximum age.

Finding the Standard Deviation of a Database Group (DSTDEV, DSTDEVP)

These functions find the standard deviation among the subset of records selected with the criteria range. DSTDEVP assumes that the subset is an entire population, which is almost never the case because a subset is defined as a sample of the whole. Therefore, the DSTDEV function is more likely to be used in database statistics. The DSTDEV function uses sample statistics to determine the standard deviation. The syntax for the two functions is as follows:

DSTDEV(range,field_offset,criteria)

DSTDEVP(range,field_offset,criteria)

Range is the range of cells containing the database information. *Field_offset* is the field that will be used as the operand for this function; in this case the offset is the field for which the deviation will be determined. *Criteria* is the range of cells containing the search criteria for the database.

Finding the Sum of a Database Group (DSUM)

The DSUM function is commonly used to calculate the total of a particular field in a database subset. The syntax is the following:

DSUM(range,field_offset,criteria)

Range is the range of cells containing the database information. *Field_offset* is the field that will be used as the operand for this function; in this case the offset is the field for which the sum is calculated, and it should be a numeric field. *Criteria* is the range of cells containing the search criteria for the database.

Figure 6.34 shows the sample database with the DSUM function added.

Fig. 6.34.

Using the DSUM function.

	File Edit Formula Format Data Options Macro Window						
	E7		=DSUM(A2:C7,3,A10:A11)				
			Worksheet9				
	A	B	C	D	E	F	
1							
2	Name	Age	Amount		Statistics		
3	John Doe	32	55000				
4	Fred Smith	35	35000	DAVERAGE	46500		
5	Lois Fry	30	38000	DCOUNT	2		
6	Jenny Smart	40	40000	DMAX	55000		
7	Larry Aimes	52	60000	DSUM	93000		
8							
9							
10	Age						
11	<35						
12							

The formula for the DSUM function appears in the formula bar of the figure. The arguments for this function are the same as for the other database functions. Hence this function returns the total salaries earned by the workers under 35.

Finding the Product of a Database Group (DPRODUCT)

The DPRODUCT function works like its counterpart PRODUCT, multiplying each value in the database group by each preceding value in a running total. The syntax for DPRODUCT is

DPRODUCT(range,field_offset,criteria)

Range is the database range. *Field_offset* is the field for which the product is being calculated (on every record that matches the criteria).

Criteria is the range containing the lookup criteria for the database group.

Figure 6.35 shows the sample worksheet with the DPRODUCT function added.

🍎 File Edit Formula Format Data Options Macro Window

E3		=DPRODUCT(A2:C7,3,A10:A11)

▤ ▤ Worksheet9 ▤ ▤

	A	B	C	D	E	F	
1							
2	Name	Age	Amount		Statistics		
3	John Doe	32	55000	DPRODUCT	2090000000		
4	Fred Smith	35	35000	DAVERAGE	46500		
5	Lois Fry	30	38000	DCOUNT	2		
6	Jenny Smart	40	40000	DMAX	55000		
7	Larry Aimes	52	60000	DSUM	93000		
8							
9							
10	Age						
11	<35						
12							

Fig. 6.35.

Using the DPRODUCT function.

Finding the Variance of a Database Group (DVAR, DVARP)

Similar to DSTDEV and DSTDEVP, the functions DVAR and DVARP show the amount of variance over a database group. In this case the group is the subset of data that matches the criteria. DVAR uses sample statistics to calculate the variance. DVARP calculates the variance by using the entire population as a basis. The syntax for these functions is the following:

DVAR(range,field_offset,criteria)

DVARP(range,field_offset,criteria)

Range is the range of cells containing the database information. *Field_offset* is the field that will be used as the operand for this function; in this case the offset is the field for which the variance is calculated. *Criteria* is the range of cells containing the search criteria for the database.

Date/Time Functions

Date and time functions are used specifically for date and time math calculations and conversions. Using date and time math means calculating elapsed time, adding time to a given date or time, or calculating the difference between two dates or times. This type of math is useful for creating payment schedules or for determining payment delinquency. The following functions are used for these purposes. (For more information about date math, see Chapter 8.)

Creating a Valid Date from Variables (DATE)

The DATE function is useful for creating a date out of individual values for the day, month, and year. This function is primarily used in macros when a date specification must be variable; it lets you use variables as the arguments for the date. The syntax is the following:

DATE(year,month,day)

The *year* variable can be any value from 1904 to 2040. The *month* variable can be any value from 1 to 12. The *day* variable can be any value from 1 to 31. If any of the variables is invalid, the function returns an error. Otherwise, the function returns a number corresponding to the number of days elapsed since January 1, 1904. You can format this number into a date by using the Format Number option.

Converting Text into a Valid Date (DATEVALUE)

This function converts a text string into a valid date and has the syntax

DATEVALUE(text)

The text string must contain data that is recognizable as a date. The function recognizes text entered in any of the date formats available through the Format Number command. You can specify any date from January 1, 1904, to February 6, 2040. Consider this example:

=DATEVALUE(B5)

If cell B5 contains the text string "1/25/91", this function returns 31801— the number of days between 1/1/04 and 1/25/91. You can format this date value by using any of the date formats available through the Format Number command.

Dissecting a Date (DAY, MONTH, YEAR)

These functions return the day, month, or year corresponding to a specified date. The syntax is the following:

DAY(date)

MONTH(date)

YEAR(date)

The *date* variable can be any valid date entered as the number of days elapsed since January 1, 1904. The variable can also be a reference to a cell containing a valid date or any date expression resulting in a valid date. These functions break a date into its various portions. Consider these examples, in which cell B2 contains the date 2/24/90:

DAY(B2)   returns 24

MONTH(B2)   returns 2

YEAR(B2)   returns 1990

You can use this feature with the IF function to test the value of a date. For instance, you can determine whether a person is within a certain age limit by checking whether the birth date entered falls before a minimum date:

=IF(YEAR(B2)<=1970,"OK","Must be 21 or older")

This formula tests whether the year portion of the date in cell B2 falls before 1970.

Displaying the Day of the Week (WEEKDAY)

The WEEKDAY function returns the "day" name of any valid date as a value from 1 to 7. The value 1 equals Sunday, 2 equals Monday, and so on. The syntax is as follows:

WEEKDAY(date)

To format the returned value as the appropriate day name, use the Format Number command and specify the custom date format *dddd*. For example, the function

=WEEKDAY(1/1/91)

returns 6, which you can format as the name *Thursday* by using the *dddd* format.

Creating a Valid Time from Variables (TIME)

The TIME function converts individual numeric values for hours, minutes, and seconds into a valid date. The syntax is the following:

TIME(hour,minute,second)

This function is most useful in macros when a time must be variable. The three arguments represent the elements of the time and can range from 0 to 59. Excel will create a valid time from these specifications and will return that time in "time-elapsed" format. You can then format this value by using the Format Number command. Be sure to enter the time in 24-hour format. For example:

=TIME(23,30,05)

This function returns the time 0.97922454, which can be formatted as 11:30:05 PM.

Converting Text to a Valid Time (TIMEVALUE)

The TIMEVALUE function converts a text string to a valid time. The text string must be recognizable as a time entry. This requirement should be no problem if the text string resembles any of the time formats in the Format Number command. The result will be displayed in "time-elapsed" format, but you can format it by using the Format Number command. The syntax for TIMEVALUE is the following:

TIMEVALUE(text)

Enter times as text strings by typing them in two or three parts (for example, 12:30 or 12:30:15) or by including the AM or PM (for example, 12:30:00 AM). Here is an example:

=TIMEVALUE(B4)

If cell B4 contains the text string "11:35:15 PM", this function returns 0.9828125, which can be formatted as the valid time 11:35:15 PM.

Displaying the Current Time (NOW)

The NOW function pulls the current date and time from the Macintosh internal clock, returning the value as a number with a decimal, as in 2245.2025. The integer part of this number represents the date (in "days-elapsed" format), and the fractional part represents the time (in "time-elapsed" format).

The syntax for NOW is

    NOW( )

As you can see, the function has no argument. You can format the value into a date by using any of the date formats in the Format Number menu, or you can format the value into a time by using the time formats in the Format Number menu. You can also use the TRUNC function to separate the two portions, as in the following line:

    =TRUNC(NOW( ))

This formula strips off the decimal portion of the date/time serial number, turning it into a date only. You can then format this date or use the DAY, MONTH, and YEAR functions to split the value even further.

 Excel gets the time from the internal clock so fast that even if you have hundreds of NOW functions throughout the worksheet, the variance in time among them will be less than one-millionth of a second.

Entering the Current Date and Time

A quick way to enter the current date into a worksheet cell is to press Command+- (Command and the hyphen key). To enter the current time, use Command+; (Command and the semicolon).

Stopping the NOW Calculation

Each time the worksheet recalculates its values, the NOW function updates the current date and time. If you want to stop the date and time or archive the date and time with a worksheet, convert the NOW function to its value. First, move the pointer to the cell containing the NOW function. Copy the contents of the cell by pressing Command+C. Now move to a blank cell and choose the Edit Paste Special command. Select the Values option from those provided, then press Return. The value of the NOW function will be pasted into the cell, but it will not be recalculated. Alternatively, you can highlight the =NOW( ) function in the formula bar and press Command+= to convert it. Either of these methods should be done immediately after you enter the =NOW( ) function.

> **Formatting Dates and Times Together**
>
> If you use the NOW function to retrieve the current date and time, and you want to format the entire value (without splitting off the date or time), use a custom number format that includes both date- and time-format symbols, as in *dddd, mmm dd, yyyy hh. mm. ss AM.* This format will convert the value into the format *Sunday, May 25, 1991 5:35:15 PM.*

Dissecting a Time (HOUR, MINUTE, SECOND)

These functions return the hour, minute, or second corresponding to a specified time. The syntax is the following:

HOUR(time)

MINUTE(time)

SECOND(time)

The *time* variable can be any valid time or cell reference containing a valid time. Suppose that cell B2 contains the time 3:30:25 AM. These functions would return the following values:

HOURS(B2)   returns 03

MINUTES(B2)   returns 30

SECONDS(B2)   returns 25

For details about time math, see Chapter 8.

Summary

This chapter provided details about each Excel worksheet function. Worksheet functions perform special calculations that you can use in your formulas. Many of them are useful for financial calculations. When entering a function, remember that Excel expects you to follow the specific syntax for that function. Each function has its own syntax, although all functions have three basic parts: the function name, the parentheses, and the arguments. The following are some additional points to remember:

❏ Arguments come in many different types, including ranges, values, text, and cell references.

❏ Usually, any argument requiring a numeric value can be entered as a number, a numeric expression, or a reference to a cell containing a number or numeric expression.

❏ Usually, any argument requiring a text value can be entered as a text string in quotation marks, a text expression, or a reference to a cell containing text or a text expression.

❏ Use the ROUND function to round a number up or down. Doing so changes the value of the number for subsequent calculations.

❏ The trigonometric functions return values representing angles. These angles are usually expressed in radians, not in degrees. You can convert the values to degrees if you like.

❏ Many financial functions let you assume "either side" of a transaction—such as the lender's side or the borrower's. Negative values (cash out) for the lender would be positive values (cash in) for the borrower. The use of negative and positive values determines which "side" of the transaction you are on.

❏ The VLOOKUP and HLOOKUP functions are useful for finding a value in a table.

❏ The IF function is one of the most powerful functions available. It lets your worksheet formulas make decisions based on values throughout the sheet.

❏ Date and time functions are useful for performing date and time math calculations.

Chapter 7, "Using Multiple Windows and Files," discusses using more than one Excel worksheet and window at a time.

7

Using Multiple Windows and Files

As your worksheets grow larger and more complex, you may need to view more than one part of the worksheet, or more than one worksheet, at one time. Suppose that you have a worksheet that contains a complex table of values used in a lookup procedure and an area for data input. Since both of these areas cannot fit in a single screen, how do you view both areas at once?

Or suppose that you want to view a single worksheet in two ways at the same time—one screen showing the formulas used throughout the worksheet, and another screen showing the results of those formulas. (This procedure can be useful in editing and debugging worksheets.) You can do so in several ways, all of which will be explained in this chapter.

Sometimes, you may need to break up tasks into individual worksheets. But because the data in each worksheet is related, you may want to link them so that worksheets reference one another's information. When you change the information in a worksheet, all other worksheets that reference the information change accordingly.

This chapter will teach you how to link worksheets. First, you will learn how to split a single worksheet into multiple areas, or *panes*—a method that is especially useful for creating permanent worksheet titles. Next, you will learn how you can view several worksheet windows at one time, and even how to display one worksheet in several windows. Finally, you will learn the powerful technique of linking worksheets by using external references.

Displaying Titles and Splitting the Screen

Often, worksheets are designed to display permanent titles, such as month names, in the first few rows at the top. The first column or two on the left side may also be used for displaying permanent titles. As you scroll down and across the worksheet, you may want to keep these titles from scrolling out of view.

Suppose that you have a 12-month-projection worksheet in which all month names appear across the top and expense categories appear in the first column. This worksheet may look something like figure 7.1.

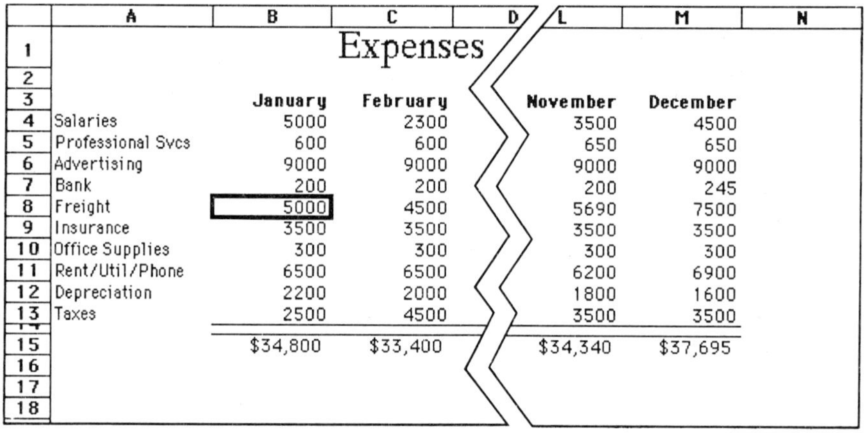

Fig. 7.1.

A large worksheet.

	A	B	C	D	L	M	N
1			Expenses				
2							
3		January	February		November	December	
4	Salaries	5000	2300		3500	4500	
5	Professional Svcs	600	600		650	650	
6	Advertising	9000	9000		9000	9000	
7	Bank	200	200		200	245	
8	Freight	5000	4500		5690	7500	
9	Insurance	3500	3500		3500	3500	
10	Office Supplies	300	300		300	300	
11	Rent/Util/Phone	6500	6500		6200	6900	
12	Depreciation	2200	2000		1800	1600	
13	Taxes	2500	4500		3500	3500	
15		$34,800	$33,400		$34,340	$37,695	
16							
17							
18							

Because all 12 months do not fit into one screen view, you have to scroll left and right in order to see the various months. When you do this, however, the expense categories in the left column scroll out of view, making it difficult to determine which categories are which. Likewise, when you scroll up and down past the bottom of the screen, the month names disappear from the top.

Excel's split-screen feature can solve this problem. You can designate a portion of the worksheet (at the top and/or side) a title area by splitting the screen at the appropriate location. Each section, or *pane*, operates independently, which enables you to keep one pane in view as you scroll through another. This feature is especially useful for keeping headings in a fixed position above or to the side of your data.

To split the screen at the top of the worksheet, click on the vertical split-screen marker, as shown in figure 7.2. The cursor changes shape as it passes over this marker.

 File Edit Formula Format Data Options Macro Window					
B5		600			

EHPENSES

	A	B	C	D	E	F
1				Expenses		
2						
3		First Q	Second Q	Third Q	Fourth Q	
4	Salaries	5000	2300	3500	4500	
5	Professional Svcs	600	600	650	650	

Fig. 7.2.

The split-screen marker (notice the cursor shape).

Click and hold the mouse button, and drag the pointer downward to move the marker to the desired position; then release the mouse button. Figure 7.3 shows the marker in a new position.

 File Edit Formula Format Data Options Macro Window					
B8		5000			

EHPENSES1

	A	B	C	D	E	F
1				Expenses		
2						
3		January	February	March	April	Ma
4	Salaries	5000	2300	3500	4500	500
5	Professional Svcs	600	600	650	650	60
6	Advertising	9000	9000	9000	9000	900
7	Bank	200	200	200	245	20
8	Freight	5000	4500	5690	7500	500
9	Insurance	3500	3500	3500	3500	350
10	Office Supplies	300	300	300	300	30
11	Rent/Util/Phone	6500	6500	6200	6900	650
12	Depreciation	2200	2000	1800	1600	220
13	Taxes	2500	4500	3500	3500	330
15		$34,800	$33,400	$34,340	$37,695	$35,60
16						
17						
18						

Ready

Fig. 7.3.

The split-screen marker in a new position.

When you move the marker into place, the screen is effectively split into two panes. Each pane acts independently of the other with respect to vertical movement, such as vertical scrolling. In fact, each pane has its own vertical scroll bar, as shown in figure 7.3. Because both panes reflect the same worksheet, you can display the same information in both areas by moving both vertical scroll bars to their topmost positions, as shown in figure 7.4.

Fig. 7.4.

Both panes of the split screen, showing the same information.

⚫	File	Edit	Formula	Format	Data	Options	Macro	Window	
	B8			5000					

EXPENSES1

	A	B	C	D	E	F
1			Expenses			
2						
3		January	February	March	April	Ma

	A	B	C	D	E	F
1			Expenses			
2						
3		January	February	March	April	Ma
4	Salaries	5000	2300	3500	4500	500
5	Professional Svcs	600	600	650	650	60
6	Advertising	9000	9000	9000	9000	900
7	Bank	200	200	200	245	20
8	Freight	5000	4500	5690	7500	500
9	Insurance	3500	3500	3500	3500	350
10	Office Supplies	300	300	300	300	30
11	Rent/Util/Phone	6500	6500	6200	6900	650
12	Depreciation	2200	2000	1800	1600	220
13	Taxes	2500	4500	3500	3500	330

Ready

When you split the screen horizontally, as shown in figure 7.4, vertical movement is independent; but horizontal movement—that is, horizontal scrolling—is synchronized. In other words, when you scroll left and right, both panes move simultaneously.

The worksheet can also be split vertically. When you split the screen vertically, using the horizontal split-screen marker, the two panes of the worksheet appear side by side, as shown in figure 7.5. In this case, each pane has its own horizontal scroll bar and moves independently of the other horizontally; when you use the vertical scroll bar, both sides move simultaneously.

```
  é   File   Edit   Formula   Format   Data   Options   Macro   Window
     E11                6900
```

	A	B	C	D	E	F
1			Expenses			
2						
3		January	February	March	April	Ma
4	Salaries	5000	2300	3500	4500	500
5	Professional Svcs	600	600	650	650	60
6	Advertising	9000	9000	9000	9000	900
7	Bank	200	200	200	245	20
8	Freight	5000	4500	5690	7500	500
9	Insurance	3500	3500	3500	3500	350
10	Office Supplies	300	300	300	300	30
11	Rent/Util/Phone	6500	6500	6200	6900	650
12	Depreciation	2200	2000	1800	1600	220
13	Taxes	2500	4500	3500	3500	330
15		$34,800	$33,400	$34,340	$37,695	$35,600
16						
17						
18						

Ready

Fig. 7.5.

Setting the vertical split-screen display.

As you may have guessed, you can set both the vertical and horizontal split-screen markers to create four panes, as shown in figure 7.6.

```
  é   File   Edit   Formula   Format   Data   Options   Macro   Window
     E11                6900
```

EHPENSES1

	A	B	C	D	E	F
2						
3		January	February	March	April	Ma
4	Salaries	5000	2300	3500	4500	500
5	Professional Svcs	600	600	650	650	60
6	Advertising	9000	9000	9000	9000	900
7	Bank	200	200	200	245	20
8	Freight	5000	4500	5690	7500	500
9	Insurance	3500	3500	3500	3500	350
10	Office Supplies	300	300	300	300	30
11	Rent/Util/Phone	6500	6500	6200	6900	650
12	Depreciation	2200	2000	1800	1600	220
13	Taxes	2500	4500	3500	3500	330
15		$34,800	$33,400	$34,340	$37,695	$35,600
16						
17						
18						
19						
20						

Ready

Fig. 7.6.

Setting both vertical and horizontal split-screen markers.

To move among the various panes of the split-screen display, click on any cell in the pane you want to move to, or use the following keys on the extended keyboard:

Key Combination	Effect
F6	Moves the pointer to the next pane of the split-screen display
⇧Shift F6	Moves the pointer to the previous pane of the split-screen display

Because you are looking at one worksheet, changes made in one part will appear in all other parts. To return to the normal display, move the split-screen markers to their original positions.

If you do not see a separate scroll bar on each side of the split screen, you have not allowed enough room for a scroll bar on each side. But if the information you want to see is showing, you may not need to make adjustments.

Freezing Split-Screen Panes

Although you can use the split-screen feature to show any two parts of a worksheet at any time, you can also split the screen to display titles at the top or side. Each pane need not have its own scroll bar for independent movement; in fact, you might want to freeze the information in place at the top or side of the screen.

Suppose that you split the screen to display month names at the top. When you scroll the bottom pane vertically, the month names will remain in place. You do not care about scrolling the top pane at all. You can prevent vertical scrolling in the top pane and horizontal scrolling in the left pane, thus keeping the title information in place.

To freeze the panes, move the split-screen markers into place and then use the Freeze Panes command in the Options menu. When you have frozen the panes, the individual scroll bars will disappear, as shown in figure 7.7.

You can move the pointer to any area of the screen, including the frozen panes. To prevent the titles from being changed, combine the split-screen features with the cell-protection features described in Chapter 3.

		EXPENSES1				
	A	**B**	**C**	**D**	**E**	**F**
2						
3		January	February	March	April	Ma
4	Salaries	5000	2300	3500	4500	500
5	Professional Svcs	600	600	650	650	60
6	Advertising	9000	9000	9000	9000	900
7	Bank	200	200	200	245	20
8	Freight	5000	4500	5690	7500	500
9	Insurance	3500	3500	3500	3500	350
10	Office Supplies	300	300	300	300	30
11	Rent/Util/Phone	6500	6500	6200	6900	650
12	Depreciation	2200	2000	1800	1600	220
13	Taxes	2500	4500	3500	3500	330
15		$34,800	$33,400	$34,340	$37,695	$35,600
16						
17						
18						
19						
20						

B8 — 5000

🍎 File Edit Formula Format Data Options Macro Window

Ready

Fig. 7.7.

Freezing the panes removes the individual scroll bars.

When you have frozen the panes in a worksheet, the Options Freeze Panes command changes to Options Unfreeze Panes. Use this command to return the worksheet to normal. You cannot use the Freeze Panes command to freeze one pane and not the other; the command applies to the top and left panes at the same time.

Using Two or More Windows

The split-screen feature is handy for keeping some information in view as you scroll through other parts of the worksheet. This feature can help extend your limited view of the worksheet imposed by the screen. You might, however, find the split-screen technique insufficient for displaying exactly what you want, because not all information will fit neatly into rows at the top of the screen or into columns on the left side. The split screen is really meant for headings.

But what if you have a large block of information, such as a table or chart, that you want to keep in view? The best solution is to open a new window in the worksheet and display various parts of the worksheet in the various windows. Windows are similar to split screens, but you can adjust their dimensions.

To create a new window in a worksheet, use the New Window command in the Window menu. This command will duplicate the current window, providing two identical views. The next time you pull down the Window menu, Excel will display the names of the two windows at the bottom of the menu. The new window has the same name as the original, but Excel adds ":1" to the original name and ":2" to the new name, indicating that there are two versions of the same worksheet. Figure 7.8 shows an example.

Fig. 7.8.

The Window menu, showing the names of original window and the new window.

When you create a new window, its dimensions will be the same as those of the original, and the two windows will probably overlap. For convenience's sake, you may want to change the sizes of the two windows.

To close a window, click in its close box. As long as other windows to the same worksheet are open, Excel will not close the worksheet.

Sizing and Arranging Windows

The best aspect of the window feature is that you can use the size box to shrink the windows so that you can see all of them simultaneously. Then you can use each window's various scroll bars to display the information you want. Figure 7.9 shows an example of resized windows.

Using standard Macintosh techniques, you can move the windows to any location on the screen, shape them, overlap them, expand them, and so on. In addition, Excel provides a special command that enables you to arrange multiple windows quickly. When more than one window is open, select the Arrange Windows command in the Window menu; Excel will arrange all open windows side by side in an orderly fashion. Figure 7.10 shows an example.

Fig. 7.9.

Two windows, resized so that both are in view at one time.

	File Edit Formula Format Data Options Macro Window				

EXPENSES:1

	A	B	C	D	E
1		Expenses			EXPENSES:2
2					A
3		First Q	Second Q	Third Q	1
4	Salaries	5000	2300	3500	2
5	Professional Svcs	600	600	650	3
6	Advertising	9000	9000	9000	4 Salaries
7	Bank	200	200	200	5 Professional Svcs
8	Freight	5000	4500	5690	6 Advertising
9	Insurance	3500	3500	3500	7 Bank
10	Office Supplies	300	300	300	8 Freight
11	Rent/Util/Phone	6500	6500	6200	9 Insurance
12	Depreciation	2200	2000	1800	10 Office Supplies
13	Taxes	2500	4500	3500	11 Rent/Util/Phone
15		$34,800	$33,400	$34,340	12 Depreciation
16					13 Taxes
17					15
					16

Ready

Fig. 7.10.

Windows after the Arrange Windows command is used.

	File Edit Formula Format Data Options Macro Window		

A1

EXPENSES:2

	A	B		
1			Ex	
2				
3		First Q	S	
4	Salaries	5000		
5	Professional Svcs	600		
6	Advertising	9000		
7	Bank	200		
8	Freight	5000		
9	Insurance	3500		
10	Office Supplies	300		
11	Rent/Util/Phone	6500		
12	Depreciation	2200		
13	Taxes	2500		
15		$34,800	$	
16				
17				
18				
19				
20				

EXPENSES:1

	A	B	C
2			
3		First Q	Seco
4	Salaries	5000	2
5	Professional Svcs	600	
6	Advertising	9000	9
7	Bank	200	
8	Freight	5000	4
9	Insurance	3500	3
10	Office Supplies	300	

Worksheet1

	A	B	C
1			
2			
3			
4			
5			
6			
7			
8			
9			

Activating a Window

When you click on the Window menu, the bottom of the menu will display the names of all open windows. Notice that one of the names has a check mark beside it, indicating that the window is currently selected and in view; the other windows are beneath it. The current window (the one on top) is the one that you can work in. To work in another window, bring it to the top. One way to do this is to select its name from the Window menu. (You can always tell which window is selected by comparing title bars. The active window displays its entire title bar.)

If you have used the Arrange Windows command or shrunk the windows, using the size box, you may be able to see more than one window at a time. In this case, the active (or current) window will not necessarily be on top of the others; it may be beside the others. You can still select a window name from the Windows menu; but if several windows are in view, you might find it easier to click on the window you want.

Besides using the Window menu or mouse to activate a window, you can use any of the following combinations on the extended keyboard:

Key Combination	Effect
⌘ F6	Moves the pointer to and activates the next window
⇧Shift ⌘ F6	Moves the pointer to and activates the previous window

The extended keyboard also provides keys for closing and maximizing windows (also called "zooming out"). To close the current window, press Command+F4. To maximize the current window, press Command+F10.

You can add as many windows as you like, within the limit of available memory, by using the New Window command. Remember that each window displays the same worksheet; when you make changes in one window, those changes appear in all other windows. Likewise, when you save the worksheet, only one file appears on the disk.

Some Uses for Multiple Windows

Creating several windows in a worksheet can be useful in many ways. For one thing, you can enter tables, lists, and other reference data in a remote area of the worksheet and use a separate window to display that area for data-entry reference. (This procedure is also a good way to display notes or help screens designed for your worksheet.) For another, you can display formulas in one window and the results of those formulas in another. To display formulas, select the Options Display command, then check Formulas in the dialog box. (This procedure is useful for debugging worksheets.) Finally, you can use multiple windows instead of using the scroll bar or Goto command. When you want to enter information in a certain area of the worksheet, activate the appropriate window and enter the information there.

Freezing Windows

Suppose that you add a second window to your worksheet in order to view two areas at once. It might take some time to scroll into view the information you want, and you do not want the window to be changed. Because you do not plan to use the scroll bars to display different data, you might decide to protect, or *freeze*, the arrangement of the worksheet windows so that they cannot be changed. When you freeze windows, you prevent them from being moved or sized and prevent them from being closed independently of the others.

To freeze your window arrangement, select the Options Protect Document command, then check the Windows box. When the check mark is present, all open windows in the active worksheet will be frozen.

Frozen windows contain no close boxes. You can still activate any window by clicking on it or by selecting its name from the Window menu. You can remove scroll bars by using the Options Workspace command with the Scroll Bars option.

To close the worksheet, select the Close command in the File menu. This command closes all windows associated with the worksheet. See Chapter 3 for more information about the Options Protect command, such as the use of passwords.

Saving a Worksheet with Multiple Windows

When you save a worksheet that has more than one window, Excel will save one copy of the worksheet, but it "remembers" how many windows were open, as well as their positions. When you open the worksheet again, all windows will be intact. If you used the Options Protect command to freeze the windows, Excel will remember that also. The windows will appear just as they were when you saved the worksheet.

To save a file without its various windows, first close the windows by clicking in their close boxes; then save the worksheet in the usual way. Remember that this procedure applies to multiple windows in the same worksheet created through the Windows New Window command, and not to different worksheets.

Using Multiple Windows in Multiple Worksheets

Although you can create multiple windows in one worksheet, you can also create multiple windows in multiple worksheets. Excel enables you to open several worksheets simultaneously, each in a separate window. To do this, select the Open option in the File menu, even though another worksheet is already open and in view. Because each worksheet also creates a new window, the worksheets' names are displayed in the Window menu.

Opening multiple worksheets at one time is an important part of linking worksheets. This procedure is explained in more detail later in this chapter.

Because all new windows look roughly the same, it can be confusing to open multiple windows in a worksheet *and* multiple worksheets at the same time. Some windows will apply to different worksheets; others will apply to the same worksheet.

If you open several windows at one time, the Window menu might not be able to display all the names at once. In this case, the More Windows option appears in the menu, as shown in figure 7.11.

When you select the More Windows command, Excel will present a dialog box containing the names of the other open windows. Be careful when you open many windows at one time, however; you can easily run out of memory this way.

Window

New Window
Show Clipboard
Show Info
Arrange All

Hide
Unhide...

1 DATABASE
2 EXPENSES
3 LOAN1
4 LOOKUP:1
5 LOOKUP:2
6 MENUS:1
7 MENUS:2
8 SALES:1
✓9 SALES:2

More Windows...

Fig. 7.11.

The Window More Windows option.

Linking Worksheets

Linking is the procedure by which a worksheet accesses information in a different worksheet through special formulas called *external references*. Very much like standard cell references, external references draw information from other cells by using the cell's address. Unlike standard references, external references also include the name of the worksheet in which the information appears. The worksheet containing the formula (in which the linked information will appear) is called the *dependent worksheet* because it depends on the other for its values. The worksheet containing the original data is called the *supporting worksheet*.

You are not limited to linking one worksheet to only one other; you can link a worksheet with many others or design complex links among several independent worksheets. This procedure can take the form of an interoffice accounting or job-tracking system.

Linking enables you to design large worksheets by using separate worksheets, or *modules*, each of which interacts with the others, making it easier to create and update the application. Because linking enables you to open only those modules that you need at any given time, the application takes less memory and therefore runs faster. Another advantage of using several linked worksheets instead of one large worksheet is that you may be able to use some of the modules over again in different systems. When several people in an organization need to use different parts of a system, linking may be the only efficient way to handle the task.

Using Simple Linking Formulas

To link worksheets, you enter a linking formula into the dependent worksheet. The formula must contain the names of the supporting worksheets and the cell that you want to extract. Consider this example:

=Payroll!B5

This simple external-reference formula begins with the equal sign and includes the name of a worksheet (Payroll), followed by an exclamation point. The worksheet name and exclamation point tell Excel that this formula is an external reference. The particular cell being referenced in the Payroll worksheet is B5. The two worksheets involved in this link might look like those in figure 7.12.

Use this type of external reference when the supporting and dependent worksheets are open. If the supporting worksheet is closed when you enter the formula, you must include the disk name and any folder names in which the supporting worksheet is located. More on this in a moment.

 If the name of the supporting worksheet contains spaces—as in Payroll 1991—the external reference must include the name in single quotation marks, as in ='Payroll 1991'!B5. Notice that the exclamation point falls outside the quotation marks. To avoid this requirement, use a period or underscore instead of a space.

⚫ File Edit Formula Format Data Options Macro Window					
B5	=Payroll!$B$5				

Worksheet4

	A	B	C	D	E	F
4						
5	Total from Payroll	6183.29				
6	Adjusted Total	6461.29				
7						

Payroll

	A	B	C	D	E	F
1						
2	Date	7/31/92				
3	This Period	35				
4	Year To Date	278189.12				
5	This Period Total	6183.29				
6						
7						
8	**Employees:**					
9	**Name**	**SS#**	**Reg Hrs**	**Overtime**		
10	Smith, Mary	227-27-2892	40	5		
11	Trout, Frank	555-28-2882	40	0		

Ready

Fig. 7.12.

A dependent and supporting worksheet.

Whenever you change the information in the Payroll worksheet, the dependent worksheet will update its own information upon the next recalculation. As long as you use a simple external reference, the supporting worksheet does not have to be open before the dependent worksheet can reference its information; Excel remembers where the worksheet is located on disk and accesses the information. (Of course, the supporting worksheet can be open if you like.) If the supporting worksheet is not open, the external reference in the dependent sheet should use an absolute cell address, as in

=Payroll!$B$5

This type of cell address prevents reference errors when the supporting worksheet is closed. When you open a dependent worksheet and its supporting worksheet is closed, Excel will ask whether you want to update nonresident worksheets. Excel will use the most current information in external references to recalculate all worksheets.

If Excel cannot find the supporting worksheet because it was moved, erased, or renamed, the program will ask you to locate the file on disk. Once the file is located, Excel will store the location for the next time.

If the supporting worksheet is not open, Excel will display the external-reference formula differently: the reference will include the entire path name of the supporting worksheet, rather than just the file name. For example, if you use the reference =Payroll!B5 in a dependent worksheet and then close the Payroll worksheet, Excel will display this reference as the following:

    ='Disk_name:Folder:Payroll'!:B5

The Folder name represents the folder in which the Payroll worksheet is located. If more than one is required, Excel will simply stack up the references with colons between. Excel produces these names automatically; you should not alter them. When you open the supporting worksheet, Excel will return the reference to its original state without the folder names. When you enter the linking formula, the supporting worksheet does not have to be open. However, you must then enter the entire path name of the worksheet and use an absolute cell address for the reference:

    'Disk_name:Folder:Worksheet'!$B$5

Notice that the name is entered in single quotation marks.

You can reference an external cell by using a defined name instead of a cell address. For example, if the supporting worksheet contains the name SALES_TOTAL for cell B5, the external-reference formula can be entered as follows (assuming that the supporting worksheet is open):

    =Payroll!SALES_TOTAL

Using names instead of cell references is good practice when you link worksheets. This procedure eliminates many problems when a supporting worksheet is changed, because Excel does not automatically update external references when a supporting worksheet is altered. In the example in figure 7.12, the dependent worksheet refers to cell B5 in the Payroll worksheet.

If you inserted a row above row 5, cell B5 would become B6. Excel adjusts references when you insert or delete information such as this, but it will not update external references and will continue to reference cell B5, causing an error. But if you apply a name to cell B5 and then use the name in the external-reference formula, this problem will not occur.

Creating Simple Linking Formulas

The following list summarizes the guidelines for creating simple external references and includes information about saving linked worksheets:

- *If the supporting and dependent worksheets are open together, create a link by typing the name of the supporting worksheet, followed by an exclamation point and the external cell reference.* This formula constitutes the external-reference formula. Be sure to include an equal sign at the beginning of the formula.

- *Use absolute references in your linking formulas.* This guideline is especially necessary if the dependent worksheet will ever be opened without the supporting worksheet. If the two worksheets will always be open at the same time, then you can avoid the absolute references.

- *If the supporting worksheet is closed when you create a linking formula, include the entire path name to the worksheet in the form ='Disk_name:Folder:Worksheet'!$B$5, where $B$5 can be any absolute cell reference.* Note the use of the single quotation marks.

- *Use names instead of cell addresses whenever possible.* The cell reference in the external-reference formula can be a name applied to a single cell of the supporting worksheet. Simply name the cell first, then use the name in the external reference. This practice eliminates problems in linked worksheets.

- *If the name of the supporting worksheet contains spaces or special characters, enter its name in single quotation marks.* This rule does not apply to names that contain periods or underscore characters. Remember that the exclamation point should go outside the quotation marks.

- *If the external references are entered properly, you do not have to open the supporting worksheet in order for the dependent worksheet to update its link.* Excel remembers where the supporting worksheet exists.

- *Whenever possible, save linked worksheets in the same folder.* Saving linked worksheets together is not necessary, but it is good practice. If linked worksheets must be in different folders, you must save the supporting worksheets by using the File Save As command, not the File Save command. Open the appropriate folders and enter the worksheet name in the Save As dialog box; then click on the OK button to save the worksheet. Do this step before you save the dependent worksheet.

- *Do not use the same name for two supporting worksheets referred to in the same dependent worksheet.* Excel cannot access information from two different worksheets that have the same name. (Although this rule may seem obvious, worksheets saved in different folders may have the same name; you may make this error inadvertently.)

Entering Linking Formulas

Entering the linking formula is like entering any other formula. First, open the supporting and dependent worksheets. Next, move to the appropriate cell in the dependent worksheet and type the entire formula. When you press the Return key, Excel finds the appropriate reference in the supporting worksheet and enters it into the cell.

You can also use the pointing method to enter an external reference. First, open the supporting and dependent worksheets. Next, move to the appropriate cell in the dependent worksheet and type the equal sign. Then activate the supporting worksheet by clicking on it or selecting its name from the Windows menu. Click on the cell that will be linked to the dependent worksheet (or use the keyboard movement commands to highlight the cell you want). To complete the formula, press Enter or Return. The dependent worksheet will move back to the top of the screen, and the external-reference formula will be complete.

Repairing Damaged Links

When an external link is damaged, an error message will appear in the dependent worksheet when it attempts to calculate its values. The following are a number of actions that can damage links:

- Changing the name of a supporting worksheet on the desktop.
- Moving a supporting worksheet into a different folder.
- Changing the name of a supporting worksheet from within Excel when the dependent worksheet is not open.
- Inserting or deleting cells, rows, or columns in a supporting worksheet, causing the referenced cell to change position. (This change occurs when the dependent worksheet uses the cell address in the external reference.)
- Changing the name of a cell that is being referenced by its name.

- Entering the linking formula without absolute references (possible when both worksheets are open) and then opening the dependent worksheet without its supporting worksheet.

When an error occurs, you can fix the damaged links by using the File Links command. Follow these steps:

1. Open the dependent worksheet.

2. Select the Links option from the File menu.

3. Choose the name of the supporting file that contains the damaged links. You can select more than one file by holding down the Shift key as you click on the names. Excel will produce the dialog box shown in figure 7.13.

Using the File Links Command

Fig. 7.13.

Updating external references with the File Links command.

4. In the dialog box provided, enter the name of the supporting worksheet. Type the entire path name, including any folders in which the file is located. Use colons between folder references, as follows:

Disk_name:Folder:Filename

Do not type the exclamation point or cell reference; this procedure only updates the location of the supporting file. Press the Return key when you are finished.

5. If you selected more than one supporting file in step 3, repeat step 4 for each file you selected.

If this procedure does not solve the problem, you will have to remove the old external-reference formulas and link the documents again. Be sure to open all supporting files before linking them.

Linking Ranges

Often, a dependent worksheet contains a range of cells that comes from a similar range in a supporting worksheet. In other words, the entire range is extracted from the supporting worksheet. In such a case, you might find it tedious to enter all the external-reference formulas independently. Instead, you can enter the first external-reference formula containing the appropriate relative and absolute references to the supporting worksheet, then use the Copy or Fill command to copy the formula to the rest of the range. If you use the pointer method of creating an external reference, Excel will assume that you want the absolute cell reference and will enter the dollar signs accordingly, as in the following:

=Payroll!$B$5

To remove the dollar signs, use the editing techniques described in Chapter 4. Then use the Formula Copy, Formula Fill Down, or Formula Fill Right command to copy this formula into the remaining cells.

Another way to reference a range of cells in an external worksheet is to use the Edit Paste Link command. To do so, follow these steps:

Using the Edit Paste Link Command

1. Open the dependent and supporting worksheets.
2. Copy the desired range of cells from the supporting worksheet by using the Edit Copy command.
3. Return to the dependent worksheet and position the pointer on the first cell in the range that will contain the external references (the upper left corner).
4. Select the Paste Link command from the Edit menu.

The result of these steps is a range of cells in the dependent worksheet that contains external references to the range you copied from the supporting worksheet. It is important to note, however, that these references are array references, as indicated by the braces surrounding the formulas:

{=Payroll!$B$5}

Array references have special qualities and must be treated differently from standard references; most important, they cannot be edited individually. (For details on array references, see Chapter 8.)

Using Complex Linking Formulas

So far, only simple external references have been discussed. A simple external reference is one that contains no calculations, only a reference to a cell in an external worksheet. You can enter an external reference as part of a formula, as in the following example:

=Payroll!B5*A6

This formula, a complex external reference, takes the value of cell B5 in the supporting worksheet, Payroll, and multiplies it by the value in cell A6 of the current worksheet. Any calculation added to an external reference, no matter how simple the calculation, constitutes a complex reference. Whenever you use a complex reference, the supporting worksheet must be open whenever the dependent worksheet is open; otherwise, Excel will not be able to locate the external worksheet. (In other words, Excel cannot read the contents of a supporting worksheet from the disk when the external reference is complex.) For this reason, it is better not to use complex references unless they are necessary.

There is no reason why you would have to use a complex external reference. Just use simple external references to bring the information to the dependent worksheet, then make calculations in other cells of the dependent worksheet. These calculations would reference the linked values after they are brought in from the supporting worksheet.

One reason to use a complex reference is that in large, complex calculations, you may want to avoid using too many cells to perform the operation. Using complex references cuts down on the number of cells required when linked values are used in calculations in the dependent worksheet.

If you use complex references, keep two special features in mind. One feature enables you to hide the open window of the supporting worksheet so that you cannot tell that it is open. The other feature enables you to save the window arrangements of all open worksheets so that you can automatically return to the same arrangement each time you open the dependent worksheet. The following two sections describe these features.

Hiding Windows

When you have multiple files open, such as those linked with complex external references, you may want to hide one or more of the open windows, thus cleaning up the desktop and protecting the hidden worksheets from tampering. The hidden worksheets are still open and available to other worksheets. To hide a window, first activate it by clicking on it or selecting its name from the Window menu. Next, choose the Window Hide command. The window will disappear, and its name will no longer appear in the Window menu. The worksheet will appear to be closed, but in fact the worksheet will still be open, and any complex external references will function normally.

When you hide a window, the Window Unhide command appears. Use this command to return hidden windows to normal. If you hide all the windows on the desktop, however, Excel will place the Unhide command in the File menu.

Saving Multiple Worksheets at Once

If you spend a lot of time arranging windows, hiding them, and generally setting up the workspace, you might decide to save the arrangement for future use. Suppose that you have several linked worksheets open and in view. In order to clean up the desktop, you decide to hide one of the windows. You arrange the other two for maximum efficiency and even protect one of them by using the Options Protect command. Normally, if you quit Excel or close the worksheets, the worksheets will return to normal, and to view all the worksheets at the same time again, you would have to open each one individually.

Fortunately, you can save a particular arrangement of windows by using the File Save Workspace command. This command saves the arrangement of windows, including hidden and protected windows, in a special file. The file, called a *workspace file*, appears on disk as this icon:

When you enter Excel by double-clicking on this icon, all files will be opened in the arrangements that you saved. (You also can use the File Open command to open a workspace file.) To use this command, first open the files you want, and arrange their windows; then use the File Save Workspace command to save the arrangement. The dialog box shown in figure 7.14 will appear.

Enter a name for this workspace. *Do not use the name of an existing worksheet.* Remember that a workspace is not a worksheet; do not replace a worksheet file with a workspace file by giving them the same name. Likewise, do not delete worksheet files because you have saved them in a workspace file. The workspace file contains only the window arrangement of the worksheets, not the worksheets themselves. Saving the workspace also saves the worksheets, each in its original file under its original name. You can open the files individually by using the File Open command and choosing the worksheet name—not the workspace name.

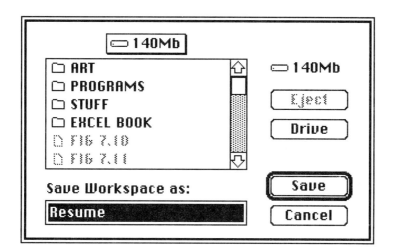

Fig. 7.14.

The Save Workspace dialog box.

Avoid moving the individual worksheets to different folders when they are part of a workspace. Also, if you rename the worksheets, you will have to recreate the workspace.

Summary

Using multiple worksheets and windows is a natural part of using Excel. Excel makes it easy to view your worksheets in different ways by adding more windows to the worksheet. You can also link two different worksheets together so that one worksheet references data contained in the other. The key to this arrangement is the external-reference formula. The following are other points to remember:

❑ You can split a worksheet into as many as four panes. This feature is useful for keeping titles in place along the top and left side of the worksheet.

❑ To move between panes, simply click on a cell in the pane you want to move to.

❏ Use the Window New Window command to create a second window for the active worksheet. This step lets you view two different parts of the worksheet at one time.

❏ Excel remembers how many windows were open for a particular worksheet when you save it. The next time you open the worksheet, the same windows will appear.

❏ Although you can have several windows to the same worksheet, Excel stores only one copy of the worksheet itself.

❏ To activate a window, click on it (if possible) or select its name from the Window menu.

❏ You can prevent a window from being closed or moved by using the Options Protect Document command.

❏ To reference data contained in an external worksheet (that is, a different worksheet), use an external-reference formula, which consists of the worksheet name and the cell name.

❏ The easiest way to create an external reference is to open both worksheets and use the pointing method to create the formula.

❏ The File Save Workspace command saves the arrangement of all open windows (including hidden ones) so that you can return to the arrangement later. The arrangement is stored as a worksheet file on disk.

Chapter 8, "Building Advanced Worksheets," covers such worksheet operations as advanced copying and pasting, working with tables, using arrays, and trapping errors.

8

Building Advanced Worksheets

Once you have a general understanding of the worksheet and how to enter text, numbers, and formulas, you are ready for information that is more advanced. This chapter goes into some special techniques that you can use in your worksheets, beginning with details on using tables (including double-variable tables) and table lookup functions. Other advanced topics include date math and array-calculation formulas. Finally, this chapter explains how to locate and trap errors in worksheets so that you can make applications more self-sufficient. (Error trapping occurs when the worksheet locates and reacts to an error before the operator is aware of it. Worksheet errors are not the same as worksheet bugs; errors are often inevitable, whereas bugs should always be eliminated.) The chapter concludes by discussing some tools you can use to debug your worksheets.

Advanced Copying and Pasting

Excel provides a special set of options for copying and pasting information. These options are available through the Edit Paste Special command, which enables you to paste various types of information into the worksheet while performing mathematical operations on that information. After you copy or cut information, you can paste it into a worksheet by using either the Paste command or the Paste Special command. If you choose the Paste Special command, the dialog box in figure 8.1 appears, displaying your options.

Fig. 8.1.

The Paste Special dialog box.

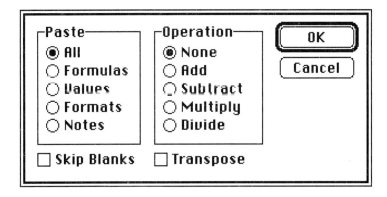

The Paste options on the left side of the box paste one of four parts of the copied cell or cells: the formula or data entered into the cell; the value produced by any formula (that is, the displayed result in the cell); the format of the cell (such as boldface type or special fonts); or the note attached to the cell. (Cell notes are described later in this chapter.) The Operation options perform calculations when you are pasting information on top of existing information. The following sections discuss the benefits of each Paste Special option.

 If you choose the Paste option All and the Operation option None, the Paste Special command will act exactly like the standard Paste command.

Converting Formulas to Values

You may need to copy information without using the formulas that produce the values. In other words, you may want to copy only the numbers produced by the formulas, not the formulas themselves. You can copy information, stripping away the formulas, by pasting with the Edit Paste Special command and choosing the Values option from the dialog box. The result will be the value of the original cell, not the formula that produced it.

 You also can access the Paste Special command by pressing Command+Shift+V.

You can convert a formula to its value without using the Paste Special command: simply position the pointer on the cell containing the formula and then highlight the entire formula in the formula bar, as shown in figure 8.2.

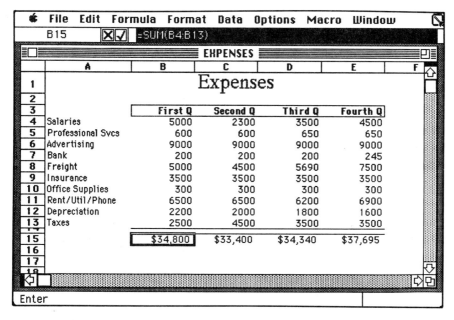

Fig. 8.2.

Highlighting the formula in a cell.

You can use the mouse or keyboard commands to highlight the formula. Now select the Formula Calculate command or press Command+= to calculate the formula. Excel will calculate the highlighted formula and replace it with its value. Press the Return key to enter this value into the cell.

An advantage of using this technique is that you can convert any portion of a formula to its value by highlighting the portion that you want to convert. Figure 8.3 shows an example of converting a segment of a formula. To convert the segment A1+100 to its value, highlight it and press Command+=.

Fig. 8.3.

Converting a segment of a formula.

The advantage of using the Edit Paste Special command to convert values is that it can convert several cells at one time. Also, you can paste the values to cells other than those containing the formulas themselves.

Copying Cell Formats

When you apply several formatting options to worksheet data, you might want to copy those formats to other areas of the worksheet, rather than reselect each option over and over. You can apply all Format options to unformatted data by copying them from other cells. First, copy the cell containing the formats you want, using the Copy command. Next, move to the destination cell (or cells) and paste the information, using the Edit Paste Special command. Select the Formats option from the dialog box. Only the format of the copied information will apply to the destination cell. If the destination cell already contains information, that information will be formatted accordingly.

You can copy the information from one cell to another and ignore all formatting by selecting the Formulas option from the Edit Paste Special dialog box. This option copies only the formula of a cell (or the value of a cell, if no formula exists).

 If you copy a range of cells containing one or more formatted blank cells, Excel normally pastes the blank cell along with the rest. You can tell Excel to eliminate the formats used in the blank cells, however, by checking the Skip Blanks option in the Edit Paste Special dialog box.

Copying Notes

You can attach a note or message to any cell in the worksheet by using the Formula Note command. To copy that note from one cell to another, use the Edit Paste Special command with the Notes option. Only the note attached to the cell will be copied to the destination cell. If the destination already contains a note, it will be replaced by the copied note.

For more information about creating notes, see "Working with Error Trapping and Cell Notes" later in this chapter.

Combining Values When Pasting

On occasion, you may want to copy information from one location and paste it into an area that already contains data. Instead of replacing the information in the destination range, you might want to add the two values. Suppose that your worksheet contains a list of merchandise costs that you have entered as constant values. This worksheet might look like figure 8.4.

	A	B	C	D	E	F	
1							
2		DESCRIPTION	COST				
3		Model 15	345.98				
4		Model 25	220.98				
5		Model 115	1012.49				
6		Scope 112	58.99				
7		Scope 15	120.99				
8		DC 2378	120.99				
9		DC 220	149.98				
10							

Worksheet6

Fig. 8.4.

A worksheet showing merchandise costs.

Now suppose that you want to adjust the cost of each item to reflect the added 3 percent cost of acquiring the merchandise, thus raising the cost of each item by 3 percent. Because the values are simply typed into the worksheet, you would normally have to retype each item with the extra 3 percent added. If you have a lot of items, however, that procedure can be time-consuming. Instead, you can enter 1.03 into an empty cell on the worksheet, as shown in figure 8.5.

 File Edit Formula Format Data Options Macro Window

E1   1.03

	A	B	C	D	E	F	
1					1.03		
2		DESCRIPTION	COST				
3		Model 15	345.98				
4		Model 25	220.98				
5		Model 115	1012.49				
6		Scope 112	58.99				
7		Scope 15	120.99				
8		DC 2378	120.99				
9		DC 220	149.98				
10							
11							

Worksheet1

Fig. 8.5.

Typing 1.03 into an empty cell.

In this figure, the value 1.03 is entered in the anticipation that that figure will be multiplied by the cost figures—resulting in a 3 percent increase. You could enter 103% (including the percent symbol) to get the same value in the cell.

Next, copy cell E1, using the Edit Copy command. Highlight the destination cells (the column of cost figures) and paste the information, using the Edit Paste Special command. Then highlight the Multiply option and press the Return key. This procedure multiplies the existing value of the cells by 1.03. Figure 8.6 shows the result.

Fig. 8.6.

The result after using the Edit Paste Special command and the Multiply option.

	A	B	C	D	E	F	
1					1.03		
2		DESCRIPTION	COST				
3		Model 15	356.36				
4		Model 25	227.61				
5		Model 115	1042.86				
6		Scope 112	60.76				
7		Scope 15	124.62				
8		DC 2378	124.62				
9		DC 220	154.48				
10							
11							
12							

Of course, you can add, subtract, multiply, or divide information when pasting. This feature is especially useful for consolidating several similar worksheets into one master worksheet. Suppose that each of five salespeople in an organization uses a specially designed worksheet for tracking sales figures. At the end of each month, the sales manager can copy totals from each of the five worksheets and paste them into the master worksheet, then find the grand total of the five worksheets by using the Edit Paste Special Add command. Often, consolidating worksheets in this fashion eliminates the need for worksheet linking.

Transposing Ranges

The final option in the Edit Paste Special command is Transpose, which changes the row and column order of the original data. Suppose that you copy a range of cells four columns wide by two rows high. If you paste the range, using the Transpose option, the result will be two columns wide by four rows high; the rows and columns will have been transposed. Figure 8.7 shows an example of a transposed range.

	A	B	C	D	E	F
		C9		45		
1		BEFORE				
2		45	45	78	983	
3		78763	87	76	56	
4						
5						
6						
7						
8		AFTER				
9			45	78763		
10			45	87		
11			78	76		
12			983	56		
13						

Fig. 8.7.

Copying by using the Edit Paste Special Transpose option.

Notice that this option works along with any of the other options in the dialog box. For example, you can transpose the cells while pasting only the format of cells.

Working with Tables

Table lookups are an important part of many worksheet applications. To find a value in a table, you must search horizontally, vertically, or both ways to match values. For example, to find a value in a tax table, you must match the salary range vertically, then find the number of withholdings horizontally. The cross section of the salary and withholdings ranges is the value that will be returned. A sample tax table is shown in figure 8.8.

Notice that the values across the top (horizontal lookup values) are sequential; therefore, this table is actually a single-variable table, because the horizontal variable is the same as the column number. The lookup function for this table searches vertically for the salary range, then returns the column corresponding to the number of withholdings. The actual formula is shown in the formula bar of the figure:

    =VLOOKUP(B1,A6:I12,B2+1)

The formula looks up the value from cell B1 in the table range A6:I12, then returns the amount corresponding to the value in cell B2, plus 1 (to account for the first column). For more information about single-variable tables, see the VLOOKUP and HLOOKUP functions in Chapter 6. This chapter will discuss the more complex double-variable tables.

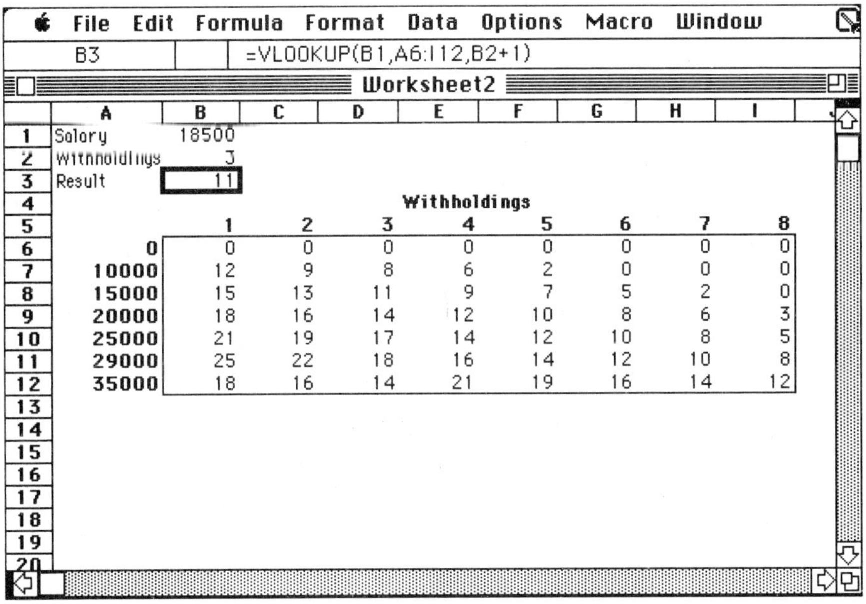

Fig. 8.8.

A sample tax table.

	File	Edit	Formula	Format	Data	Options	Macro	Window	
B3			=VLOOKUP(B1,A6:I12,B2+1)						

Worksheet2

	A	B	C	D	E	F	G	H	I	
1	Salary	18500								
2	Withholdings	3								
3	Result	11								
4						Withholdings				
5			1	2	3	4	5	6	7	8
6	0		0	0	0	0	0	0	0	0
7	10000		12	9	8	6	2	0	0	0
8	15000		15	13	11	9	7	5	2	0
9	20000		18	16	14	12	10	8	6	3
10	25000		21	19	17	14	12	10	8	5
11	29000		25	22	18	16	14	12	10	8
12	35000		18	16	14	21	19	16	14	12
13										
14										
15										
16										
17										
18										
19										
20										

Working with Double-Variable Tables

A *double-variable table* is required when the vertical and horizontal lookup values are variable and nonsequential. The tax table shown in figure 8.8 would require a double-variable table if the withholding amounts were random. Figure 8.9 shows an example of a double-variable table.

Notice that the text labels in the column are arranged in alphabetical order, which is important in performing text lookups.

The top row and the left column are variable. Ideally, you want to look up the price of a plant by using its name and size as input. The column offset used in the VLOOKUP function must be a number ranging from 1 to the number of columns in the table. What do you use if the column values do not correspond to the offset value? You can perform table lookups for double-variable tables in several ways. The following sections discuss three techniques, each of which has advantages and disadvantages. Choose the method that works best for your applications.

	File	Edit	Formula	Format	Data	Options	Macro	Window	

B18

======================= LOOKUP =======================

Fig. 8.9.

A sample double-variable table.

	A	B	C	D	E	F	G	H
2		Tree-Green Nursery Price List						
3		Size in Inches						
4								
5		4	8	12	18	24	36	
6	Baby Tears	5.00	9.95	16.00	20.00	24.50	30.00	
7	Creeping Charlie	4.00	7.00	10.50	14.99	21.00	24.95	
8	Ficus	4.00	7.00	10.50	14.99	21.00	24.95	
9	Fiddle-Leaf Fig	5.50	9.95	12.00	16.00	24.00	28.00	
10	Geranium	7.00	11.00	16.50	20.00	24.50	30.00	
11	Philodendron	9.95	14.95	21.00	25.00	32.50	39.95	
12	String of Pearls	3.00	5.50	8.00	11.95	15.00	21.00	
13	Variegated Ivy	4.00	7.00	10.60	14.99	21.00	24.95	
14								
15								
16	Desired Type	Baby Tears						
17	Desired Size	12						
18	Price							
19								
20								

Method 1: Numbering Columns

One way to find a value in a double-variable table is to number the columns in the table. The lookup function uses the column number as the offset for the vertical lookup. Figure 8.10 shows a worksheet in which this technique is used.

The lookup function is entered into cell B18 and looks like this:

```
=VLOOKUP(B16,A4:G13,HLOOKUP(B17,B4:G13,2))
```

Notice that a row of sequential values is inserted—as column numbers—below the horizontal lookup values. The HLOOKUP function returns the number corresponding to the column of the table by means of the following portion of the function:

```
HLOOKUP(B17,B4:G13,2)
```

The result is used as the offset value of the VLOOKUP function. The VLOOKUP function thus knows where to find the correct value, horizontally, in the table. You can use this same technique with numbered rows instead of numbered columns.

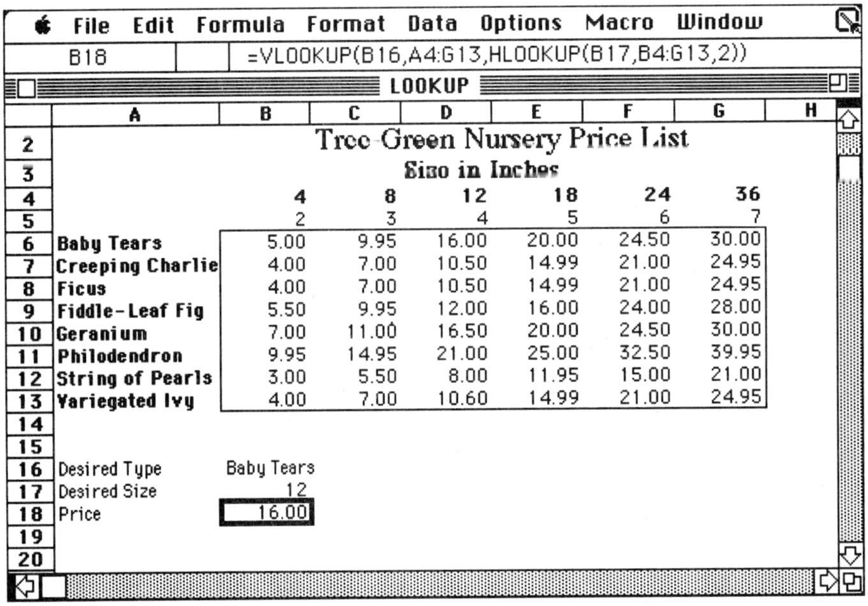

Fig. 8.10.

A double-variable table with the lookup function in place.

	A	**B**	**C**	**D**	**E**	**F**	**G**

	A	B	C	D	E	F	G	H
2		\multicolumn{6}{c}{Tree Green Nursery Price List}					
3				Size in Inches				
4		4	8	12	18	24	36	
5		2	3	4	5	6	7	
6	Baby Tears	5.00	9.95	16.00	20.00	24.50	30.00	
7	Creeping Charlie	4.00	7.00	10.50	14.99	21.00	24.95	
8	Ficus	4.00	7.00	10.50	14.99	21.00	24.95	
9	Fiddle-Leaf Fig	5.50	9.95	12.00	16.00	24.00	28.00	
10	Geranium	7.00	11.00	16.50	20.00	24.50	30.00	
11	Philodendron	9.95	14.95	21.00	25.00	32.50	39.95	
12	String of Pearls	3.00	5.50	8.00	11.95	15.00	21.00	
13	Variegated Ivy	4.00	7.00	10.60	14.99	21.00	24.95	
14								
15								
16	Desired Type	Baby Tears						
17	Desired Size	12						
18	Price	16.00						
19								
20								

B18: =VLOOKUP(B16,A4:G13,HLOOKUP(B17,B4:G13,2))

Hiding the Extra Row of Numbers

If you don't like the extra row of numbers required for this technique, try hiding those cells with the number format ;;; in the Format Number command.

Method 2: Extracting a Row

Another way to perform this lookup function is a two-step method. Rather than number the columns, use a lookup function to return a particular value from each column. To do this, add a row at the bottom of the table. In each cell of this new row, use a VLOOKUP function that returns a value from the column based on the vertical match. This extra row, in other words, will contain one full row extracted from the table. Figure 8.11 shows what this type of lookup might look like.

The formulas in this row (row 14) are the following:

A14:   VLOOKUP(B16,A5:G12,1)

B14:   VLOOKUP(B16,A5:G12,2)

C14:   VLOOKUP(B16,A5:G12,3)

D14:   VLOOKUP(B16,A5:G12,4)

E14:   VLOOKUP(B16,A5:G12,5)

F14:   VLOOKUP(B16,A5:G12,6)

G14:   VLOOKUP(B16,A5:G12,7)

⚹ File Edit Formula Format Data Options Macro Window								🔲
B18		=HLOOKUP(B17,A4:G14,11)						

LOOKUP

	A	B	C	D	E	F	G	H
2			Tree-Green Nursery Price List					
3				Size in Inches				
4		4	8	12	18	24	36	
5	Baby Tears	5.00	9.95	16.00	20.00	24.50	30.00	
6	Creeping Charlie	4.00	7.00	10.50	14.99	21.00	24.95	
7	Ficus	4.00	7.00	10.50	14.99	21.00	24.95	
8	Fiddle-Leaf Fig	5.50	9.95	12.00	16.00	24.00	28.00	
9	Geranium	7.00	11.00	16.50	20.00	24.50	30.00	
10	Philodendron	9.95	14.95	21.00	25.00	32.50	39.95	
11	String of Pearls	3.00	5.50	8.00	11.95	15.00	21.00	
12	Variegated Ivy	4.00	7.00	10.60	14.99	21.00	24.95	
13								
14	Ficus	4.00	7.00	10.50	14.99	21.00	24.95	
15								
16	Desired Type	Ficus						
17	Desired Size	18						
18	Price	14.99						
19								
20								

Fig. 8.11.

A double-variable table lookup, using an extracted row for the horizontal lookup.

Together, these formulas serve to extract one of the rows from the table, based on the matching VLOOKUP. When the VLOOKUP function finds its match, the entire row is placed at the bottom of the table. The next step is to perform a simple HLOOKUP function within this extracted row. Because one of the values on the row is the desired value, the HLOOKUP function will match its value with the top row, then return the corresponding column from the extracted row. In the example, the offset value for this HLOOKUP function is 11:

=HLOOKUP(B17,B4:G14,11)

Method 3: Reducing the Table

The final technique for performing a double-variable lookup is to make the table itself change its values, using one of the two variables as a basis. By using IF statements in the table itself, you can condense the data down to a single row or column; the IF statements will alternate among the various amounts, based on one of the input variables. The example worksheet would look like figure 8.12.

Fig. 8.12.

Condensing a double-variable table down to a single column of data.

```
 ✿  File  Edit  Formula  Format  Data  Options  Macro  Window
     B15              =VLOOKUP(B13,A4:B11,2)
▓▓▓▓▓▓▓▓▓▓▓▓▓▓▓▓▓▓▓▓▓ LOOKUP ▓▓▓▓▓▓▓▓▓▓▓▓▓▓▓▓▓▓
           A          B       C     D     E     F     G     H
  1
  2   Tree Green Nursery Price List
  3
  4   Baby Tears        5.00
  5   Creeping Charlie  4.00
  6   Ficus             4.00
  7   Fiddle-Leaf Fig   5.50
  8   Geranium          7.00
  9   Philodendron      9.95
 10   String of Pearls  3.00
 11   Variegated Ivy    4.00
 12
 13   Desired Type    Geranium
 14   Desired Size           4
 15   Price               7.00
 16
 17
 18
 19
```

On the surface, it looks as though all the columns from the table were removed but one. Actually, the one column contains all the values from the extended table but shows only one column (that is, one set of values) at a time. Based on the size entered into cell B14, the column changes its values. The formulas used in this column are as follows:

B4:   =IF($B$14=4,5,IF($B$14=8,9.95,IF($B$14=12,16,
      IF($B$14=18,20,IF($B$14=24,24.5,IF($B$14=36,30,
      "Invalid Size"))))))

B5:   =IF($B$14=4,7,IF($B$14=8,10.5,IF($B$14=12,14.99,
      IF($B$14=18,14.99,IF($B$14=24,21,IF($B$14=36,24.95,
      "Invalid Size"))))))

B6:   =IF($B$14=4,7,IF($B$14=8,10.5,IF($B$14=12,14.99,
      IF($B$14=18,14.99,IF($B$14=24,21,IF($B$14=36,24.95,
      "Invalid Size"))))))

B7:   =IF($B$14=4,5,IF($B$14=8,9.95,IF($B$14=12,16,
      IF($B$14=18,20,IF($B$14=24,24.5,IF($B$14=36,30,
      "Invalid Size"))))))

B8:   =IF($B$14=4,5,IF($B$14=8,11,IF($B$14=12,16.5,
      IF($B$14=18,20,IF($B$14=24,24.5,IF($B$14=36,30,
      "Invalid Size"))))))

B9:   =IF($B$14=4,12,IF($B$14=8,14.95,IF($B$14=12,21,
      IF($B$14=18,25,IF($B$14=24,32.5,IF($B$14=36,39.95,
      "Invalid Size"))))))

B10:   =IF($B$14=4,3,IF($B$14=8,5.5,IF($B$14=12,8,
        IF($B$14=18,11.95,IF($B$14=24,15,IF($B$14=36,21,
        "Invalid Size"))))))

B11:   =IF($B$14=4,7,IF($B$14=8,10.5,IF($B$14=12,14.99,
        IF($B$14=18,14.99,IF($B$14=24,21,IF($B$14=36,24.95,
        "Invalid Size"))))))

These formulas contain the values found in each column of the original table. The IF statements test for the input value in cell B14 and return the appropriate values from the table. The only thing remaining is the simple VLOOKUP function for the final variable. This function is entered into cell B15 as shown in the figure:

    =VLOOKUP(B13,A4:B11,2)

As you might guess, this method requires more work than the others. Another disadvantage is that the amounts in the formulas are difficult to change because they are constant values in the formulas. Making values constant like this is not recommended for large tables, because changes are difficult to make. The advantages to this technique are that it takes less room for the table and that the VLOOKUP function is very simple.

Performing a What-If Analysis

One of the most useful features of a worksheet is that it enables you to perform what-if tests based on variable information. By changing the values referenced in formulas, you can view different results. You might, for example, use a formula to calculate the future value of a series of deposits over time. Then, by substituting various monthly deposit amounts, you can determine how your savings will add up as you deposit more or less of your monthly income.

At times, you may want to compare several what-if tests, but it can be tiresome to substitute values for those tests over and over. Besides, you might want to view the resulting values side by side. This type of what-if testing calls for a *data table*—a table of values that Excel automatically creates from a series of variables.

Suppose that you want to examine the result of saving part of your income each month for five years, at 9.6 percent interest. You want to see how much you would have saved after five years, specifying different monthly deposit amounts. The FV function performs the basic calculation, as shown in figure 8.13.

Fig. 8.13.

Using what-if tests to examine different monthly savings amounts.

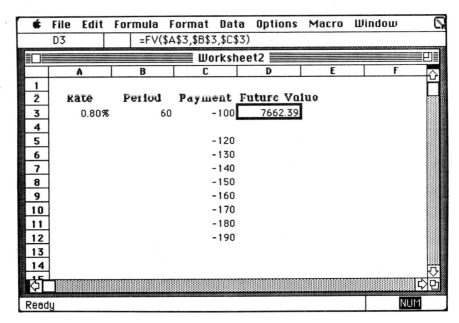

In the figure, the FV formula in cell D3 calculates the future value of the deposits, using the rate, period, and payment information from row 3. (Note that the rate is entered as the monthly interest rate: =9.6/12.) Notice also that rows 5 through 12 contain additional tests for the payment amount. The plan is to show the future value, using each of the payment amounts in the column (substituted for -100). The original payment amount, in cell C3, is the variable for the data table and is called the *input cell.*

The first step in creating this automatic data table is identifying the *table range*—the area that contains the test variables plus an extra column for the results. This range should include an extra row above these two columns. In the example, the table range is C4:D12. In cell D4, enter the formula that calculates the future value for the first set of variables. Because this formula already exists in cell D3, the formula in cell D4 would be =D3. Now highlight the entire table range, as in figure 8.14.

Next, select the Data Table command. The dialog box in figure 8.15 appears. Excel will ask for either the row or column input cell. Cell C3 is already identified as the input cell. But is it row or column input? Because the data table will appear in a column, it is the column input cell, so enter **$C$3** into the space provided and press the Return key.

Excel will automatically calculate the formula, using each of the variables listed, and then place the result beside each variable, as shown in figure 8.16.

☀	File	Edit	Formula	Format	Data	Options	Macro	Window	
C4									

Worksheet2

	A	B	C	D	E	F	
1							
2	Rate	Period	Payment	Future Value			
3	0.80%	60	-100.00	7662.39			
4				7662.39			
5			-120.00				
6			-130.00				
7			-140.00				
8			-150.00				
9			-160.00				
10			-170.00				
11			-180.00				
12			-190.00				
13							
14							
15							

Ready NUM

Fig. 8.14.

Highlighting the table range, including the first formula (in cell D4).

Table

Row Input Cell:		OK
Column Input Cell:		Cancel

Fig. 8.15.

The Data Table dialog box.

The input cell can appear anywhere in the worksheet; it does not have to appear on top of the other input variables. The formula that uses the variable information, however (the FV formula in the example), must appear at the top of the second column in the table range (the column that will contain the results). Correct placement of this formula is very important, because Excel uses the formula to calculate the values of the table. In the example, the formula in cell D3 could be removed and placed in cell D4. You need not duplicate this formula; it can appear only in the second column of the data table.

Fig. 8.16.

The result of a data table calculation.

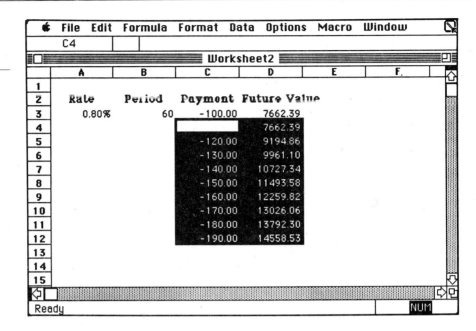

 File Edit Formula Format Data Options Macro Window

C4

≡≡≡≡≡≡≡≡≡≡≡≡≡≡≡≡≡ **Worksheet2** ≡≡≡≡≡≡≡≡≡≡≡≡≡≡≡≡≡

	A	B	C	D	E	F.
1						
2	**Rate**	**Period**	**Payment**	**Future Value**		
3	0.80%	60	-100.00	7662.39		
4				7662.39		
5			-120.00	9194.86		
6			-130.00	9961.10		
7			-140.00	10727.34		
8			-150.00	11493.58		
9			-160.00	12259.82		
10			-170.00	13026.06		
11			-180.00	13792.30		
12			-190.00	14558.53		
13						
14						
15						

Ready   NUM

The following summarizes how to perform a data-table calculation:

Performing a Data-Table Calculation

1. Create a single example of the calculation that you want to use in the table. Make sure that the variables used in the calculation appear in the worksheet. One of these variables will be the input cell (the cell containing the value that will be tested over and over).

2. List the variables that you want to use for the what-if tests. List these variables in a column, leaving a blank column at the right for the answers. You can use as many variables as you like, and these columns can appear anywhere in the worksheet.

3. Enter the formula that uses the variables specified in step 1 into the cell above the empty column of the table range. You might think of this as a heading for the column that will contain the results. Be sure that this formula references the input cell specified in step 1. This cell should calculate the first resulting value.

4. Highlight the column of test variables and the adjacent column. Be sure to include the row containing the formula that you entered in step 3. In other words, the first cell in the first column will be blank; the first cell in the second column will contain the first formula.

5. Select the Data Table command and enter the input cell into the dialog box. If the table is columnar, as described in these steps, enter the input cell in the space marked Column Input Cell.

You can set up the input table with rows instead of columns. In this case, the input cell must be entered into the space marked Row Input Cell. The first row should contain the input variables, and the second row should be blank.

Working with Complex Data Tables

The data table described earlier is not the most complicated table you can use; you also can perform what-if tests on a second variable. The result will be a matrix of values that corresponds to combinations of the two variables. In order to add a second variable to the data table, you must enter test values across the top of the table range and down the first column. The table range must have an equal number of columns and rows.

Using the preceding example, suppose that you want to test the future value of your savings, based on various monthly deposits and various periods of time (terms). You want to find out what a deposit of $100 per month will earn over 60 months, over 72 months, and so on. You want to find out the same thing for deposits of $120 per month, $130 per month, and so on. Figure 8.17 shows how this table is set up.

★ File Edit Formula Format Data Options Macro Window							
A6	=FV(B2,B3,B4)						

Worksheet2							
	A	B	C	D	E	F	G
1							
2	Periodic Rate	0.80%					
3	Period	60					
4	Payment	-100.00					
5							
6	7662.39	72	84	96	108	120	
7		-120.00					
8		-130.00					
9		-140.00					
10		-150.00					
11		-160.00					
12		-170.00					
13		-180.00					
14		-190.00					
15		-200.00					

Ready   NUM

Fig. 8.17.

A data table in which two variables are used.

The worksheet has been rearranged slightly so that the values appear in column B rather than row 3, as in the preceding example. This change helps keep the entire table and all related values in view at one time.

As in the preceding example, the values for the first test variable are listed in a column. An equal number of values are used for the second test variable. These values are listed in a row across the top of the table. The column shows the various monthly payment amounts, and the row shows the various terms. In the example, the table range is A6:F15.

Next, enter a formula to calculate one iteration of the test. Enter this formula into the corner cell of the table range. The variables used in this formula should not be in the table. In the example, the formula is entered into cell A6 and uses the values in cells B2, B3, and B4:

   =FV(B2,B3,B4)

Notice that the example uses three variables. The interest rate in B2 will remain constant for the entire table. Also note that this formula uses variables outside the table range, and the table continues the tests.

The final step is to highlight the entire table and select the Data Table command. Enter the row and column input cells into the dialog box, then press the Return key. In the example, the row input is cell $B$3 because the row of variables in the table will be used instead of cell B3. The column input cell is $B$4. Figure 8.18 shows the result of this data table calculation.

The formula in the upper left corner of the table does not have to be the original calculation of the variables; you can simply reference a formula from another cell in the worksheet if you like. In the example, cell A6 might contain the formula =B5 if cell B5 contains the formula =FV(B2,B3,B4).

The following summarizes how to create a data table with two test variables:

Creating a Data Table with Two Test Variables

1. Enter the series of values for the first test variable into a column.
2. Enter the series of values for the second test variable into a row. The first cell in this row should be one cell above and to the right of the first cell in the column created in step 1. This procedure will form an empty table with entries at the top and along the left side.

```
 File  Edit  Formula  Format  Data  Options  Macro  Window
      A6              =FV(B2,B3,B4)
                        Worksheet2
          A          B        C        D        E        F        G
2  Periodic Rate    0.80%
3  Period             60
4  Payment        -100.00
5
6           7662.39      72       84       96      108      120
7          -120.00  11622.55 14293.82 17233.12 20467.35 24026.10
8          -130.00  12591.09 15484.97 18669.21 22172.96 26028.27
9          -140.00  13559.64 16676.12 20105.31 23878.57 28030.45
10         -150.00  14528.18 17867.27 21541.40 25584.19 30032.62
11         -160.00  15496.73 19058.42 22977.49 27289.80 32034.80
12         -170.00  16465.27 20249.57 24413.59 28995.41 34036.97
13         -180.00  17433.82 21440.72 25849.68 30701.02 36039.14
14         -190.00  18402.36 22631.88 27285.77 32406.64 38041.32
15         -200.00  19370.91 23823.03 28721.87 34112.25 40043.49
16
Ready                                                     NUM
```

Fig. 8.18.

The result of a data table in which two test variables are used.

3. Enter another test value for each of the two variables outside the table range. These values can duplicate two of the values in the table.

4. Enter the desired formula that uses the two variables. Be sure that this formula includes references to the input cells outside the table range, not to cells inside the range. Enter this formula into the cell, marking the upper left corner of the table range (the intersection of the row and column). This formula can use more variables than the two used in the table, but it must include at least those two.

5. Highlight the entire table, then select the Data Table command.

6. Find the cell outside the table range that corresponds to the values in the column of the table. Enter this cell address as the column input cell. Find the cell outside the table range that corresponds to the values in the row of the table. Enter this cell address as the row input cell.

7. Press the Return key to complete the calculation.

NOTE

You can produce the values in the row and column of the data table by using formulas.

Recalculating and Editing a Data Table

You can change any of the row or column input values in a data table, and the table will recalculate, using the new values as a basis. In the preceding example, you can change the values in row 6 and column A to calculate a new table. You can also change other values used in the formula in cell A6. For example, changing the value of cell B2 changes the calculation for the entire table.

Remember that you cannot change any of the values inside the table itself; these values were produced by array formulas, and you cannot edit individual values in arrays. For more information about handling arrays, see "Working with Arrays and Array Calculations" later in this chapter.

Using Date Math

Date math is the process by which you can make calculations based on dates—for example, finding the number of days elapsed between two dates; adding a number of days or months to a date; and determining what a particular date will be, using a given number of days and a starting date as a basis. Date math has many uses in business-worksheet applications, such as determining the delinquency of payments and calculating due dates based on worksheet variables. The following sections discuss the various date-math operations that you can perform, using many of the date and time functions discussed in Chapter 6. Be sure to read about those functions before you continue with this section.

Calculating the Difference between Two Dates

Calculating the difference between two dates is fairly easy, especially if you want the result to be displayed in days or weeks. The task is simply a matter of subtracting the earlier date from the later one. Suppose that you have the two dates Jan-1-89 and Mar-4-91 in cells A2 and A3, as shown in figure 8.19.

The formula =A3-A2 will produce the number of days between the two dates. Because Excel tracks dates by the number of days elapsed since 1-1-1904, a result showing the difference in days will always be accurate. To calculate weeks, you can use the formula =(A3-A2)/7, which divides the number of days between the dates by 7. Because there are always seven days in a week, this figure will always be accurate, no matter what the year is. This calculation, however, will often produce fractional values for the number of weeks. You may want to display the number of weeks as whole weeks and the remainder as days. Figure 8.20 shows such a calculation.

	A	**B**	**C**	**D**	**E**	**F**
1						
2	1-Jan-89					
3	4-Mar-91					
4						
5						
6						
7						

Worksheet1 — A5

Fig. 8.19.

Two dates ready for date calculation.

	A	**B**	**C**	**D**	**E**	**F**
1						
2	1-Jan-89					
3	4-Mar-91					
4	Total Days					
5	792					
6	Weeks	Days				
7	113	1				
8						
9						

Worksheet1 — A5 =A3-A2

Fig. 8.20.

Calculating weeks and days between dates.

The formulas look like this:

    A5: =A3-A2
    A7: =INT(A5/7)
    B7: =MOD(A5,7)

The formula in A5 calculates the number of days elapsed between the dates. The formula in A7 calculates the number of elapsed weeks and displays only the integer portion, showing only whole weeks. The formula in B7 shows the days left after the number of days is divided by 7.

Showing the number of months and years between two dates is more complicated because the number of days in a month and a year varies. You can approximate this number by finding the difference between two dates and dividing by 365 (for years) or 30 (for months). Because different months have different days, and because leap years add a day to February, the result of this division will be approximate. For a more accurate count of months, you can use 30.4 as the divisor, but that practice still will not account for leap years.

A more accurate display would account for leap years by adding an extra day. You know that a date is a leap year if it is evenly divisible by 4. This function will tell you whether a year is a leap year:

    =IF(MOD(YEAR(B4),4)=0,"LEAP","NO LEAP")

If cell B4 contains a date, this formula will determine whether the date falls in a leap year. You must also determine whether the month portion of the date is before or after February. If the month is before February, the leap has not yet occurred for that year. Here is an extended formula:

    =IF(MOD(YEAR(B4),4)=0,IF(OR(AND(DAY(B4)=29,Month
    (B4)=2, MONTH(B4)>2),"Leap", "No Leap Yet."),"Sorry, Not
    a Leap Year.")

Using date math to account for leap years is very complex. If at all possible, use days as a unit of measurement for elapsed time.

Adding Days and Weeks to a Date

Because Excel dates are represented in units of days, adding a number of days to a date is a simple calculation. To add 30 days to the date in cell B5, use the formula =B5+30. The result is the serial number of the date 30 days after the original. Because Excel knows how many days occur in each month of each year, the resulting serial number represents the correct date. To add a number of weeks to a date, first convert the weeks to days by multiplying them by 7. Adding months is more complicated because the number of days differs in each month. Try using the Data Series command to add months to a given month.

Working with Arrays and Array Calculations

An *array* is a special type of range. Although an array resembles a normal range of cells, Excel treats an array (also called an *array range*) as a single unit. You cannot alter information in individual cells of an array range. Array ranges are useful only in *array calculations*, which are calculations that use or produce arrays.

The purpose of an array calculation is to save time and memory in your worksheets. Although arrays and array calculations may seem complicated now, they actually make worksheets simpler and can save you time in entering formulas.

Making Basic Array Calculations

A basic array calculation takes the place of a series of individual calculations spread over a range. In the example in figure 8.21, the formulas in column C add the corresponding values in columns A and B.

É	File	Edit	Formula	Format	Data	Options	Macro	Window	
C3			=A3+B3						

Worksheet2

	A	B	C	D	E	F
1						
2						
3	45	289	334			
4	24	999	1023			
5	4	451	455			
6	2	334	336			
7	34	112	146			
8	88	445	533			
9	344	737	1081			
10	99	288	387			
11						
12						

Fig. 8.21.

A sample range of formulas.

Each cell in column C contains an individual formula, such as =A3+B3. An array formula can take the place of these formulas by calculating the range A3:A10 plus the range B3:B10. The result is a range of answers in cells C3:C10. The formula used for this calculation is entered as an array into column C; Excel treats the other two ranges as arrays. Enter the formula in this way:

1. Highlight the range C3:C10.
2. Type the formula **=A3:A10+B3:B10**.
3. Press Command+Enter to accept the formula.

The result is a range of cells (an array range) containing the answers to the set of calculations. You cannot alter individual cells in this range; you must treat them as a single unit. Excel uses special array math to calculate these values, all of which are dependent on one another. Each cell in the array contains the formula surrounded by brackets, as the formula bar in figure 8.22 indicates.

Fig. 8.22.

Each cell in the array contains this formula.

	A	B	C	D	E	F
	File	**Edit**	**Formula**	**Format**	**Data**	**Options**	**Macro**	**Window**
C3		{=A3:A10+B3:B10}				

Worksheet2

	A	B	C	D	E	F
1						
2						
3	45	289	334			
4	24	999	1023			
5	4	451	455			
6	2	334	336			
7	34	112	146			
8	88	445	533			
9	344	737	1081			
10	99	288	387			
11						
12						

You can use constant values as part of the array formula, and the array ranges used in the formula do not have to be adjacent. Also, you do not have to use two arrays in the formula. Figure 8.23 shows an array produced with the formula =A3:A10+$B$3.

Fig. 8.23.

An array formula that adds one range to a single cell.

	File	**Edit**	**Formula**	**Format**	**Data**	**Options**	**Macro**	**Window**
C3		{=A3:A10+$B$3}						

Worksheet2

	A	B	C	D	E	F
1						
2						
3	45	2	47			
4	24		26			
5	4		6			
6	2		4			
7	34		36			
8	88		90			
9	344		346			
10	99		101			
11						
12						

When you use this formula, Excel will add each cell in the range A3:A10 to the cell B3, producing eight values. You can replace the reference to B3 with a constant value, as in =A3:A10+5. You can even enter an array formula that contains no ranges, as in the formula =A3+B3. The result is a range of cells containing the same value. (Remember that in order to enter the array formula, you must highlight the range that will contain the results, then enter the formula by pressing Command+Enter.) Normally, the resulting array (the array containing the results) must be the same size as the largest range referenced in the formula. In the previous examples, the resulting array contains eight cells because the ranges in the formula contain eight cells. If you highlight fewer cells, Excel will complete the array calculation for as many cells as you highlight. If you highlight a range that is larger than the largest referenced range, Excel will enter an error into the extra cells.

Figure 8.24 shows the effect of highlighting a resulting range that is smaller or larger than the referenced ranges. (The range C3:C7 is smaller than the ranges referenced in the formula bar; the range D3:D16 is larger.)

File	Edit	Formula	Format	Data	Options	Macro	Window	
D3		{=A3:A10+B3:B10}						

Worksheet2

	A	B	C	D	E	F	
1							
2							
3	45	4	49	49			
4	24	4	28	28			
5	4	5	9	9			
6	2	2	4	4			
7	34	3	37	37			
8	88	8		96			
9	344	1		345			
10	99	6		105			
11				#N/A			
12				#N/A			
13				#N/A			
14				#N/A			
15				#N/A			
16				#N/A			
17							
18							

Fig. 8.24.

A resulting array range that is smaller or larger than the referenced ranges.

You cannot insert new cells, rows, or columns into an array range. Excel will present an error message if you try. To change the size of an array range, reenter the array formula into the desired range. To remove an array range, highlight the range and press Command+B to clear it.

Using Functions in Array Calculations

When you use a function in an array calculation, keep in mind that there are three types of functions: those that have no arguments, those that have values or expressions as arguments, and those that have ranges as arguments. The following are examples of each:

PI( )   no arguments
SQRT(value)   numeric expression or value argument
SUM(range)   range argument

Each type of function is handled differently in an array calculation. The simplest function is the one that has no arguments. You can use this function in an array calculation just as you would use any value or single cell reference. For example, you might highlight the range C3:C10 and enter the formula =B3:B10*PI( ), pressing Command+Return to create the array. The function is part of the array calculation. The result would be a series of values in cells C3:C10, which are the values of B3:B10 times pi.

When you use a function that requires values as arguments, you must enter the value as a range, thus causing the function to work on an array range rather than a single value. Of course, you should highlight an equal-size range for the results. To calculate the square root of each cell in the range B3:B10, first highlight a blank range for the result, then enter the formula **=SQRT(B3:B10)** and press Command+Return.

You also can use this expression in a larger array calculation, such as the following:

=A3:A10+SQRT(B3:B10)

This formula takes the square root of each cell in the range B3:B10 and adds it to the corresponding cell in the range A3:A10.

The final type of function includes those with ranges as arguments, such as SUM, AVG, and COUNT. These functions are used very much like those with no arguments and can be used in array calculations just as you would use any numeric expression. Because these functions produce a single value from a standard range, they act like single values in an array calculation. But because they use standard ranges for their arguments, the formulas can be confusing. The array formula =SUM(A3:A10)*B3:B10 multiplies the sum of the range A3:A10 to each cell in the range B3:B10 and places the eight results in the result array (see fig. 8.25).

Fig. 8.25.

Using a range function in an array formula.

	⌘ File Edit Formula Format Data Options Macro Window					
	C3	{=SUM(A3:A10)*B3:B10}				
			Worksheet2			
	A	B	C	D	E	F
1						
2			Result			
3	45	4	2560			
4	24	4	2560			
5	4	5	3200			
6	2	2	1280			
7	34	3	1920			
8	88	8	5120			
9	344	1	640			
10	99	6	3840			
11						
12						

Another way to use a range function in an array calculation is to make a calculation in the argument of the function. Suppose that you have values in the ranges A3:A10 and B3:B10. You can enter an array formula such as =SUM(A3:A10*B3:B10). In this case, the result is a single value, and you should highlight only one cell as the result array. Why? Because the SUM function calculates a single value from a range—even an array range. When one cell is used as the only expression in an array calculation, Excel calculates only one result. The resulting range (one cell) will still be an array range. In this example, the formula multiplies each cell in the range A3:A10 by its corresponding cell in the range B3:B10, then totals the values. You might express the formula like this:

(A3*B3)+(A4*B4)+(A5*B5)...(A10*B10)

Calculating the Worksheet

Excel calculates the results of formulas each time you make a change in the worksheet. When you start to create large, complex worksheets, this feature might get in your way. By performing a manual calculation, you can calculate the worksheet whenever you like. To perform a manual calculation, select the Options Calculation command. The dialog box shown in figure 8.26 appears.

```
┌─Calculation──────────┐        ┌─────────────┐
│ ● Automatic          │        │     OK      │
│ ○ Automatic Except Tables │    └─────────────┘
│ ○ Manual             │        ┌─────────────┐
└──────────────────────┘        │   Cancel    │
                                └─────────────┘
  ┌─────────────────────────┐
  │ ☐ Iteration             │
  │ Maximum Iterations: 100 │
  │ Maximum Change:  0.001  │
  └─────────────────────────┘
  ┌─Sheet Options───────────┐
  │ ☐ Precision as Displayed│
  │ ☒ 1904 Date System      │
  └─────────────────────────┘
```

Fig. 8.26.

The Options Calculation dialog box.

The following are explanations of these options:

Automatic	Sets the normal mode of calculation. Excel calculates the worksheet after every change.
Automatic Except Tables	Calculates the entire worksheet (except data tables) at each change.
Manual	Calculates the worksheet only when you select the Options Calculate Now command.
Iteration	Enables or disables the iteration feature, causing the worksheet to calculate a certain number of times, based on changes in worksheet data.
Maximum Iterations	Sets the maximum number of calculations performed during each calculation (for example, repeated calculations).
Maximum Change	Sets the amount of change that is unacceptable to Excel. If data does not change this much, Excel will stop the repeated calculations.
Precision as Displayed	Sets the number of decimal places used in calculations to the number displayed in the cells. Unless the number is rounded off by the ROUND function, Excel normally uses the maximum number of decimal places (15) for each value, even if the decimal places are not displayed. When this box is checked, Excel will use only the digits displayed in the cells. Thus you will not have to use the ROUND function throughout the worksheet.
1904 Date System	Sets the starting date for all date calculations to 1904 when checked. When this option is not checked, the starting date is 1900. This option is useful for making Excel compatible with PC-based worksheets that use the 1900 date system.

When you perform a manual calculation, the Options Calculate Now command is the only way to calculate the worksheet. (You can also use the keyboard equivalent Command+=.) This command enables you to calculate whenever you wish.

Working with Error Trapping and Cell Notes

Error trapping is, essentially, anticipating errors in worksheets and accounting for them with user-friendly messages or with specific actions. Errors can occur when Excel does not accept an entry. The functions VLOOKUP and HLOOKUP, for example, return an error when the lookup data cannot be found in the table. Trapping such an error is just a matter of anticipating the problem.

Suppose that a value is being calculated in cell B15. The result might be an error if the operator enters an incorrect value somewhere else in the worksheet. But rather than print the error message in the cell, you can trap the error and print a more useful message. The formula goes into a unique cell and looks like this:

=IF(ISERR(B15)=1,"Please check your entry and try again","")

Wherever an operator can possibly enter an unacceptable value, you should include an error-trapping formula to anticipate it. Using IF logic, the formulas can respond to specific problems with messages such as *Value must be under 100* or *Please enter first name only.*

Another way to provide this type of information about a cell is to attach a note to the desired cells. When there is a problem with the cell or related cell, the operator can find specific information about that cell in the note. To enter a cell note, follow these steps:

1. Select the cell you want.
2. Select the Formula Note command.
3. Enter the note into the space provided.

Entering a Cell Note

Excel uses the first line of the cell note as a title for the note. Therefore, you might enter a descriptive word or phrase on the first line, then begin the text of the note on the next line. Use Option+Return to move the cursor to the next line before you reach the end of the current line. Pressing Return accepts the note and returns you to the worksheet. Figure 8.27 shows a sample cell note.

Fig. 8.27.

An example of a cell note.

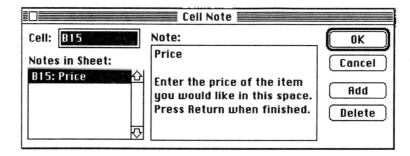

The following are descriptions of the various options in the Notes dialog box:

Cell	Displays the highlighted cell or the cell corresponding to the note selected in the Notes in Sheet list. You can enter a cell note for any cell, even if it is not currently highlighted, by entering its address in this box before entering the note. When you are finished, click on the Add button. This option is useful for entering several notes without having to return to the sheet.
Note	Displays the text of the note. You can type beyond the bottom of this box; Excel will scroll down to display the text. To view text beyond the edge of this box, click on the box and drag the pointer down.
Notes in Sheet	Lists all notes in the worksheet, using the first line of each. When you click on one of these listings, the note will appear in the Note box, and the associated cell address will appear in the Cell box. You can then edit the note without having to return to the worksheet and highlight the cell.
Add	Adds the note to the cell listed in the Cell box. Clicking on Add is not necessary if the cell listed in the Cell box is also the highlighted cell.
Delete	Removes the note from the cell listed in the Cell box.

To view a note, move the pointer to the appropriate cell and select the Formula Note command, or select the command from any cell; then choose the note you want from the Notes in Sheet list.

You also can view a cell note by moving the pointer to the cell and selecting the Window Show Info command. The Info window is explained in the next section.

Debugging Worksheets

Because worksheets can contain a tangled network of formulas that refer to one another, finding problems in formulas can be difficult. Excel provides some tools for locating incorrect values and problematic calculations. Although these tools will not help you correct the problems, they can help you find them.

Finding Dependents and Precedents

A cell that contains a reference to another cell is dependent on that value for its own value. Thus all cells containing references are *dependent cells*. The precise cells they depend on, however, can be difficult to determine.

Suppose that cell A2 contains a reference to cell A1 and that cell A3 contains a reference to A2. Cells A2 and A3 are dependent on cell A1. Cell A2 is a direct dependent; cell A3 is an indirect dependent. Cell A3 is a direct dependent of A2.

Knowing which cells depend on a value can be helpful in tracking down worksheet bugs. To find all dependents of a particular cell, move the pointer to the desired cell and select the Formula Select Special command, then choose either the All Levels or Direct Only option. Excel will highlight the cells on which this cell depends (either all dependents or just the direct dependents). By examining the formulas in these cells, you can find potential problems. You can follow a worksheet's logic by moving to cells in succession and using this command with the Direct Only option.

Excel also enables you to find *precedent cells*—cells that are used to produce the value of other cells (the opposite of dependent cells). By highlighting a formula and selecting the Precedents option available through the Formula Select Special command, you can locate all cells used to produce that value.

Displaying Cell Information (Info Worksheet)

Another useful debugging tool is the *Info worksheet*—a special pane that displays information about the highlighted worksheet cell. To view this sheet, move the pointer to a cell and select the Window Show Info command.

At first, the Info worksheet will display the cell address, the formula (if any), and any notes attached to the cell. You can add to this information by selecting items from the Info menu. This menu appears whenever an Info worksheet is activated. Figure 8.28 shows an example of an Info window.

Fig. 8.28.

The Info window.

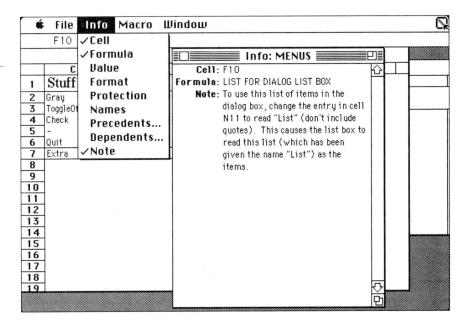

Summary

Excel contains many advanced features that your worksheet applications may require. These include ways of using complex tables, using multiple windows, linking worksheets, using arrays, and debugging worksheets. This chapter discussed these features and provided some examples of their use. Some important points to remember are these:

❑ You can convert formulas to their values by using the Edit Paste Special command or by highlighting the formula in the formula bar and pressing Command+=.

❏ The Edit Paste Special command also lets you copy particular aspects of data, such as the data's formatting. In addition, you can perform mathematical operations when pasting data into a worksheet.

❏ The HLOOKUP and VLOOKUP functions work well by themselves when the lookup tables require only a single variable. When the table requires two lookup variables, you need to employ one of the double-variable table techniques described in this chapter.

❏ A data table helps you create what-if scenarios by using one or two variables for a formula.

❏ An array calculation takes the place of a series of normal calculations and saves computer memory.

❏ Create an array formula by highlighting the destination range, entering the formula, and pressing Command+Return to accept it.

❏ Array ranges cannot be split, expanded, or edited. Instead, you must reenter the array.

❏ Turn automatic worksheet calculations off by using the command Options Calculation.

❏ You can attach a note to any cell on the worksheet by highlighting the cell and entering the Formula Note command. You can also view an existing note this way.

❏ Cell notes also appear in the Info window. Display this window by entering the Windows Show Info command.

Chapter 9, "Printing Worksheets," discusses techniques for formatting and printing reports.

9

Printing Worksheets

This chapter describes how to print a worksheet. Although Excel makes printing an easy task, some special features and complexities may be involved. This chapter will begin with the basics of printing and move on to features such as margin settings, page breaks, headers, and page numbers. Before continuing, make sure that your printer is properly installed and running with your Macintosh system.

Printer support is not so much a feature of Excel as of the Macintosh itself. Excel supports PostScript printers as well as Macintosh-compatible dot-matrix printers. You can also get printer drivers for Apple's Quick Draw printer. These are available from Microsoft. For information about printer support and installation, refer to your Apple dealer or to a basic book about the Macintosh. In this book the assumption is that your printer is installed and is selectable from the Chooser in the Apple menu.

Performing Basic Printing

You can get a no-frills printout by using the automatic setup in Excel. In the automatic setup, Excel gives you standard letter-size pages printed vertically. Excel begins printing at the top left side of the worksheet and continues page by page down the sheet until there are no more active cells. It then moves one page to the right and begins at the top again, continuing until there are no more active cells in the worksheet.

You can change the automatic setup and add special effects to the printout if you like; such changes are discussed later in this chapter. To begin printing without making changes, choose the Print command from the File menu, then click on the OK button. Provided that you have chosen the correct printer with the Chooser, Excel will begin printing your file.

The Chooser is an Apple-menu desk accessory that lets you select from various printers and output devices. When you installed the 6.02 (or later) System file, you were instructed to copy the printer devices to the System Folder. This step made the printer drivers available for Apple-brand printers. You can buy other printer drivers for your system from various manufacturers.

Using the Page Setup and Print Options

Excel provides several options for controlling printouts. Like many Macintosh applications, these options appear in the File Page Setup and File Print dialog boxes. When you select the File Page Setup command, the dialog box in either figure 9.1 or figure 9.2 appears, depending on whether you use a laser printer or a dot-matrix printer. You can add effects to the printout by using the options in either dialog box. Note that some printers (non-Apple printers) will provide slightly different options.

Fig. 9.1.

The Page Setup dialog box for laser printers.

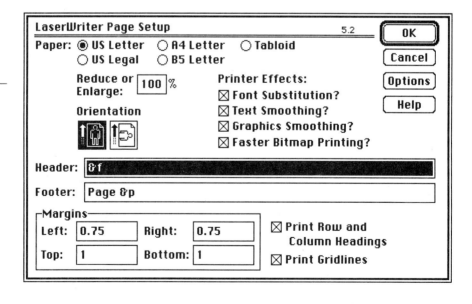

The options in these dialog boxes are common to many Macintosh programs. The following section briefly describes these options.

```
ImageWriter                                    v2.7    [  OK  ]

Paper:     ● US Letter          ○ A4 Letter
           ○ US Legal           ○ International Fanfold    [ Cancel ]
           ○ Computer Paper

Orientation      Special Effects:   □ Tall Adjusted
                                    □ 50 % Reduction
                                    □ No Gaps Between Pages


Header: [ &f                                              ]

Footer: [ Page &p                                         ]

─Margins──────────────────────────
 Left: [ 0.75 ]    Right:  [ 0.75 ]    ⊠ Print Row and
                                          Column Headings
 Top:  [ 1    ]    Bottom: [ 1    ]    ⊠ Print Gridlines
```

Fig. 9.2.

The Page Setup dialog box for dot-matrix printers.

The Page Setup Options

The following are the Page Setup options. Note that printer options vary, depending on the particular version of the Macintosh System you are using.

Paper   For both the LaserWriter and ImageWriter printers, several paper sizes are available for printing. Select the size you want by clicking on the appropriate button. Your choices include US Letter, US Legal, A4 Letter, B5 Letter, and Tabloid.

Printer Effects   The LaserWriter Page Setup dialog box includes various printer options that alter the printout. The option Font Substitution provides laser fonts when nonlaser fonts are used in a document. Text Smoothing takes some of the jagged edges off curved lines in large fonts. Graphics Smoothing takes the jagged edges off curved lines in graphics. Faster Bitmap Printing speeds the printing of bit-mapped graphics. It is common to leave all these special options on.

Special Effects	The ImageWriter dialog box offers the options 50% Reduction, which reduces the image to 50 percent of its normal size; Tall Adjusted, which makes the dot-matrix printout match the proportions of the screen; and No Gaps Between Pages, which prints continuously on tractor-fed paper (useful for printing large worksheets sideways).
Orientation	Pages can be printed horizontally or vertically. Because the paper feeds through the printer in only one direction, producing horizontal pages is up to the Macintosh. This feature is useful for printing worksheets sideways across many sheets of paper.
Reduce or Enlarge	This option, available for laser printers and some other types, enables you to control the size of the final printout. Normally, the size is 100 percent of the original size. To change the size, enter a percentage into this box. To enlarge the printout, enter a figure larger than 100 percent.
Page Header	This option adds a header to the top of each page in the printout. You can include any text, as well as special commands, to control the appearance of the header. (See "Working with Report Headers and Footers" later in this chapter for more details.)
Page Footer	This option adds a footer to the bottom of each page.
Margins	These four measurements control the top, bottom, left, and right margins of the printout. Excel will cause information to break to the next page if it does not fit within the specified margins.
Print Row & Column Headings	This option prints your specified row and column headings along with the data. The option is useful when you print a worksheet with formula text showing.
Print Gridlines	This option, which prints the cell grid lines on the page along with the data, can be useful for debugging worksheets.

Besides the options in the initial Page Setup dialog box, Excel offers another set of print options for LaserWriter printouts. If you click on the Options button, another dialog box, shown in figure 9.3, will appear.

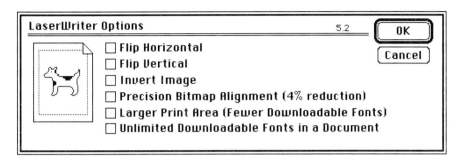

Fig. 9.3.

The LaserWriter Options dialog box, accessed through the LaserWriter Page Setup dialog box.

The following section describes the options available in this dialog box.

More Page Setup Options

The choices in the Page Setup Options dialog box are these:

Flip Horizontal	This option creates a mirror image of the print area. When used with text, the option makes the text unreadable. This option can be useful when you are printing graphics or printing onto film to create a reversed image.
Flip Vertical	This option creates a vertical mirror image of the print area. In other words, the printout will appear to be upside down.
Invert Image	This option changes everything that is white to black and everything that is black to white. Invert Image can be useful when you are printing to film to create negatives.
Precision Bitmap Alignment	This option makes bit-mapped graphics appear to be more true to scale, producing a 4 percent reduction.
Larger Print Area	This option expands the print area available for the page by reducing the margins to a minimum. Because this option uses part of the LaserWriter's memory, you cannot download as many fonts when this option is selected.

Unlimited	This option frees memory from the printer by
Downloadable	reducing the printable area of the page. As a
Fonts in a	result, you can get more downloaded fonts in
Document	each document. (Most users prefer the larger
	image area.)

Once the special LaserWriter options are set, click on the OK button to return to the Page Setup options. When the Page Setup options are established, click on OK to continue with the printout.

Print Options

After clicking on OK in the Page Setup dialog box, you can establish the print options by selecting the File Print command. The File Print dialog box in either figure 9.4 or 9.5 will appear, depending on which type of printer you have.

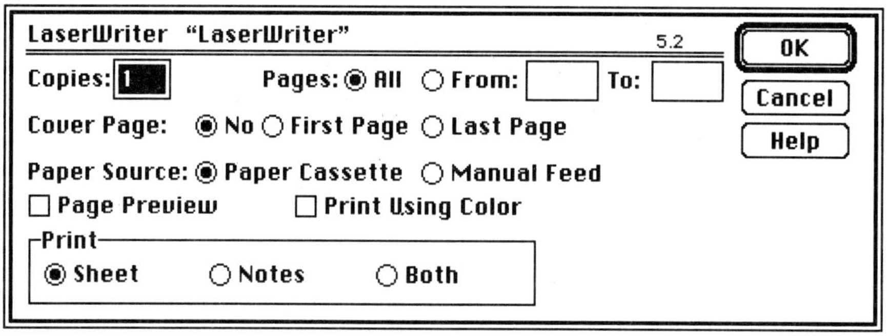

Fig. 9.4.

The File Print dialog box for laser printers.

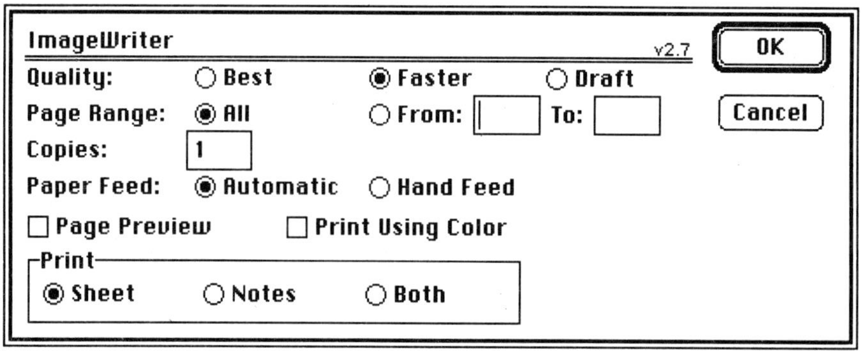

Fig. 9.5.

The File Print dialog box for dot-matrix printers.

The options available are the following:

Print Quality	This dot-matrix-printer option enables you to select any of three print qualities. The Best option causes the print head to strike the paper twice on each pass across the page. The Faster option prints in full graphics mode but causes the print head to strike the page only once. The Draft option prints the data by using the printer's built-in font.
Pages	This option enables you to select the page or pages you want to print. You can specify the range or indicate that you want to print all pages.
Copies	This option enables you to print multiple copies of each page.
Cover Page	This LaserWriter option enables you to use the first or last page as a cover sheet for the printout. The cover sheet will not contain a header or footer and will not be numbered.
Paper Source	You can use tractor-feed paper (Automatic) or individual sheets (Hand Feed) with your ImageWriter by selecting the appropriate option. LaserWriters enable you to select the Paper Cassette (automatic feed) or the Manual Feed option, which causes the printer to wait for you to insert a page.
Page Preview	This option, which causes the printout to appear on the screen, enables you to examine the printout before printing.
Print Using Color	This option prints the worksheet along with all colors you've established for color output devices.
Print	Select Sheet to print the worksheet, Notes to print the notes attached to the worksheet cells, or Both to print both.

When you finally print the worksheet, Excel will adhere to the specified page-setup and printer options. If you are not satisfied with the printout at this point, you can use many other features to enhance the final printout.

Previewing the Printout

Excel offers a print-preview feature that enables you to view each page before printing it. To preview the printout, select the Page Preview option from the File Print dialog box. You will see the first page of the worksheet (in reduced form) on the screen, as shown in figure 9.6.

If the printout consists of multiple pages, you can click on the Next and Previous buttons to flip back and forth among them. The Cancel button returns you to the worksheet. The Print button tells the printer to print directly from the preview screen. The Zoom button enlarges the preview to actual size so that you can examine the printout more closely. Instead of using the Zoom button, you can click on the area of the preview that you would like to view more closely. (The pointer changes to a magnifying glass when you do this.)

Fig. 9.6.

The print-preview feature.

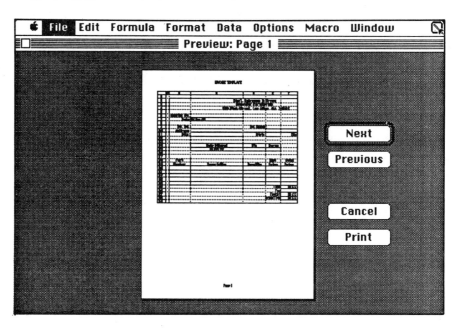

Printing Sideways

When you have large worksheets, you may need to print them without breaks between pages, so that you get one long printout of the worksheet.

Excel makes it easy to print worksheets sideways. To do so, specify horizontal orientation in the Page Setup dialog box, then check the No Gaps Between Pages box (for dot-matrix printers), thus eliminating the margin between pages. If you are using a laser printer, you might also select the additional Options button and the Larger Print Area option to help reduce the margins.

Setting Custom Page Breaks

If the automatic page breaks are not adequate for your worksheet, try setting your own custom page breaks, which will give you control of the information on each printed page. As long as the page you specify fits into the prescribed page size and setup, you can set a page break anywhere on the worksheet.

You can set page breaks in three ways:

1. You can establish the rightmost side of each page and let Excel break the pages at the bottom. To do this, move the pointer in row 1 to the column designating the right side of the first page; then select the Options Set Page Break command. The page break will occur to the left of the column in which the cursor is located. Unless you specify another column for the next set of pages, Excel will automatically break the pages.

   Figure 9.7 shows an example of a page break at column H. This break affects the right side of all pages in columns A through G. Excel determines the right edge of the pages in columns to the right of H. You could, however, establish breaks for those pages too.

   Notice that Excel marks the page break with a thick dotted line, indicating a manual page-break setting.

2. You can also set the bottom of a page by moving the pointer to the row below the last row on the page. (Be sure to remain in column A.) Then select the Options Set Page Break command. The page break will affect all pages above the selected row.

3. You can set both the bottom and right side of a page by selecting the cell below and to the right of the bottom right corner of the page, then selecting the Options Set Page Break command. The cell you select will establish bottom and right-edge breaks for the page. If you use cell G25, for example, the right margin will appear at column F, and the bottom will be at row 24. This option will affect only pages

Setting Page Breaks

appearing to the left of column G and above row 25 (see fig. 9.8). All other pages require their own settings or will use the default setting.

Fig. 9.7.

Adding page breaks.

Fig. 9.8.

Setting right-side and bottom page breaks.

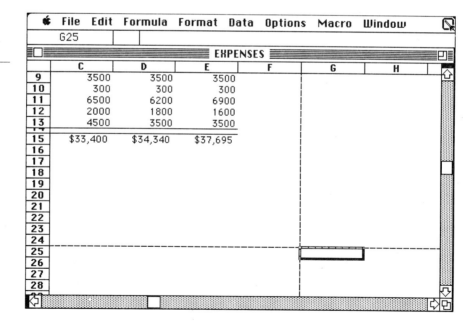

Removing Page Breaks

Page breaks remain active until you remove them. Establishing new page breaks does not alter existing breaks. To remove a page break, reselect the column, row, or cell that was used to create the break, and select the Options Remove Page Break command. This command appears only when the pointer is in the correct cell, row, or column.

Removing Manual Page Breaks

Remember that manual page breaks show up as darker dotted lines than automatic page breaks do. Trying to remove an automatic page break is useless. Try turning the worksheet grid lines off to view the page breaks more easily. This procedure will help you distinguish between manual and automatic breaks.

Printing Specific Areas

You may need to print specific sections of a worksheet, such as a range of cells or a graph. Although you can set the right and bottom margins to include the area you want, you will probably find it easier to single out the area as a separate page, then print that page. Do so by highlighting the range you want to print, then selecting the Options Set Print Area option. When you select the File Print command, Excel will print only the established print area. If the area is too large to fit on one page, Excel will break it into multiple pages. If the print area is larger than one page, use manual page breaks to establish the desired area; then print the appropriate pages.

 If your selected print area does not fit on one page, try reducing the printout by using the Enlarge option in the File Print dialog box to shrink the printout.

If you highlight multiple ranges as the print area, Excel will print all the ranges at one time, each range on a separate page. To highlight multiple ranges, press the Command key when you select the second and subsequent ranges. When all the ranges are highlighted, choose the Options Set Print Area command. Figure 9.9 shows a worksheet with two print areas established.

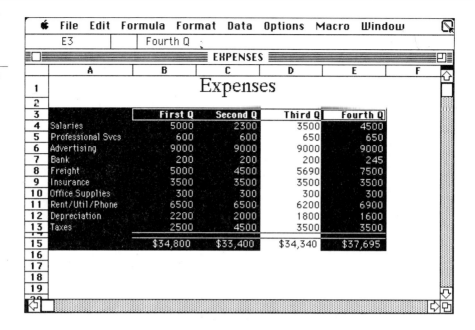

Fig. 9.9.

Selecting multiple print areas.

The print areas will print in the order in which they were selected. If you include page numbers in the printout, this feature can be an important aspect of printing multiple ranges. Remember that print areas remain set until you remove them or establish new print areas. You can reprint the same area over and over without reselecting it as long as you have not removed or changed the area.

Using the Goto Command to Select Print Areas

You may find that you switch among a few frequently used print areas, which might require you to set and reset the same areas over and over. To save time, try defining a range name for each area, using the Formula Define Name command. (You might use names such as *Report_1* and *Report_2*.) To print one of the areas, select the Formula Goto command and select the desired print area from the list provided. Then select the Options Set Print Area command and print.

Using a Macro To Automate Printing

Perhaps the easiest way to switch among multiple print areas is to use a macro to select and print the desired range. You can, for instance, create a custom menu that presents a list of named ranges on the worksheet, then prints the one that you select. The macro would use the Goto command to select the range, the Set Print Area command to make the range the current print area, and the Print command to print it. All these steps would take place automatically.

Erasing the Print Area

To remove the established print area, first use the Formula Define Name command to view all established names. If a print area is set, you will see the name *Print_Area* in the name list. Excel will automatically apply this name to the currently selected print area. Select this name and click on the Delete button; Excel will remove the print area setting. You can now establish manual page breaks or set a new print area.

Working with Report Headers and Footers

Excel includes options for adding headers and footers to your printouts. A *header* is a line of text repeated at the top of each page (except the title page). A *footer* is a line of text repeated at the bottom of each page. Headers and footers can contain any text you like, plus commands for automatically entering the date, time, and page number. Other commands placed inside the header or footer control the placement and style of text in the header or footer.

Excel automatically prints the header one-half inch from the top of the page. If you define a header, make sure that your top margin is greater than one-half inch so that it does not interfere with the header. Likewise, Excel prints the footer one-half inch from the bottom of the page, and your bottom margin should accommodate this.

To define a header or footer, select the File Page Setup command, enter the header text and any special codes into the Header space, and then enter the footer text and any special codes into the Footer space. Table 9.1 explains the special codes.

Table 9.1
Special Printer Codes

Code	Effect
Alignment	
&L	Aligns with the left margin the characters that follow
&R	Aligns with the right margin the characters that follow
&C	Centers the characters that follow
Inserting Values	
&P	Prints the page number at the location of this command
&D	Prints the current date in the format 2/24/91 at the location of this command
&T	Prints the current time in the format 1:30:00 PM at the location of this command
&F	Prints the current file name at the location of this command
Character Attributes	
&B	Prints in boldface the information that follows
&I	Prints in italics the information that follows
&U	Prints in underscore the information that follows
&O	Prints in outline the information that follows
&S	Prints in strikeout the information that follows
&H	Prints in shadow the information that follows
Fonts and Sizes	
&"fontname"	Prints in the specified font the information that follows
&"size"	Prints in the specified font size the information that follows
&&	Prints the & character

Aligning Headers and Footers

The commands &L, &R, and &C align information in the header and footer. You can use these codes individually—to align the entire header or footer—or together, to break the header or footer text into sections. The following are some examples:

Header entry: &RSales Report
Result:

                                                    Sales Report

Header entry: &LSales Report&RJohn Smith
Result:

Sales Report   John Smith

Header entry: &LSales Report&CJanuary&RJohn Smith
Result:

Sales Report   January   John Smith

Header entry: &CSales Report&RJohn Smith
Result:

                    Sales Report   John Smith

By using more than one alignment code, you can break the header or footer into three areas. Just be sure that the text in any area does not overlap into other areas. Also, enter the text for each area in order from left to right, as shown in the examples.

Working with Automatic Page Numbering, Dating, and Time Stamping

Excel offers codes for entering the current date, time, and file name into the header or footer. Another code prints page numbers on each page. Enter these commands at the place in the header or footer where you want the information to appear; align the commands with the alignment codes. You cannot change the format of the date and time entries, nor can you change the type of numbering system used for page numbering. You can, however, begin numbering the pages at any number you choose. To start numbering at page 15, for example, enter the page-numbering code like this:

&P+15

To start numbering at a page number that is less than the natural page number, use the minus sign (which is the hyphen on your keyboard):

&P-15

This procedure can be useful when you are printing some pages from the middle of a worksheet as a separate report.

Printing Report Titles

At times, you will need to print column headings at the top of each page in the report. These headings should match with the columns printed in the report. The headings might be the first row of a table that provides the titles for the numbers below. You might be tempted to use the header as a way of printing column headings on each page, but Excel offers a better way. Highlight the rows in the worksheet that contain the title information (often, the top few rows). Be sure to highlight the entire row by clicking in the row heading area. Next, select the Options Set Print Titles command to establish the selected rows as the titles.

Excel uses an intelligent titling system, printing only the column headings (titles) that correspond to the columns selected for the report. See the column titles shown in figure 9.10.

Fig. 9.10.

Column titles.

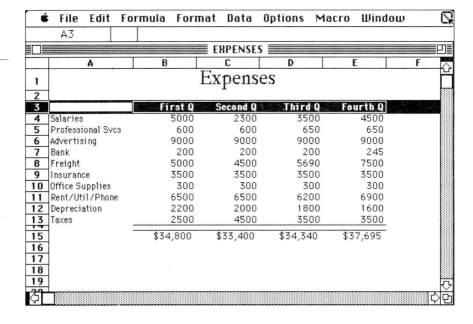

If you print any of the columns A through C, the titles in cells A3 through C3 will be used for each page of the table in columns A through C. If you then print from columns D through E, the titles in cells D3 through E3 will print. Thus the titles apply only when information from the respective columns is printed.

To remove the print titles you've established, choose the Formula Define Name command and delete the name *Print_Titles* from the list of names. Press Return when finished.

In the printout, the titles appear below the header and top margin, taking up part of the space used by the printout.

Summary

When it comes to printing your worksheets, Excel offers several options for setting up the printout—as well as the standard printer options that reflect the particular printer you are using. The commands File Print Setup and File Print provide most of the options. The following are points to remember:

❏ Use the File Page Setup options to control the printout before printing.

❏ Print Setup options will be different for different printers. For example, the ImageWriter and LaserWriter produce different options.

❏ You can add a header and footer to your printouts by using the Print Setup options.

❏ Entering &P in the header or footer prints the page number on each page.

❏ You can print the worksheet sideways, without gaps between the pages, by changing the print orientation and by selecting the No Gaps Between Pages options. These are located in the Print Setup dialog box.

❏ To print a specific area of the worksheet, highlight the area and select the Options Set Print Area command.

Chapter 10, "Chart Quick Start," begins the section "Excel Charts" and offers a brief lesson in building a chart.

— Part II —

 Excel Charts

Chart Quick Start

Creating Charts

Creating Advanced Charts

*Using Presentation Graphics
with Excel*

10

Chart
Quick Start

This second Quick Start chapter is designed to get you up and running with Excel's charting features. If you have not completed and saved the worksheet from Chapter 2, please do so before starting this chapter; the step-by-step guide provided here builds on that worksheet. First, you will select the data range and create a new chart representing the data. Next, you will customize the chart by changing its typeface and by adding titles and other elements. By the end of this chapter, you will be ready for more details about Excel's charting options.

Opening the Worksheet

To open the worksheet that you saved from Chapter 2, click on the worksheet icon (which should be named EXPENSES) from the Macintosh desktop view. If you are already in Excel, use the File Open command and select the EXPENSES file from the list provided. Soon the worksheet will appear on the screen, as shown in figure 10.1.

The goal is to create a chart that best displays the change in total expenses from quarter to quarter. In other words, you want to compare expenses for each of the four quarters.

Fig. 10.1.

The sample worksheet created in Chapter 2.

 File Edit Formula Format Data Options Macro Window

	C21					

EXPENSES

	A	B	C	D	E	F
			Expenses			
1						
2						
3		First Q	Second Q	Third Q	Fourth Q	
4	Salaries	5000	2300	3500	4500	
5	Professional Svcs	600	600	650	650	
6	Advertising	9000	9000	9000	9000	
7	Bank	200	200	200	245	
8	Freight	5000	4500	5690	7500	
9	Insurance	3500	3500	3500	3500	
10	Office Supplies	300	300	300	300	
11	Rent/Util/Phone	6500	6500	6200	6900	
12	Depreciation	2200	2000	1800	1600	
13	Taxes	2500	4500	3500	3500	
15		$34,800	$33,400	$34,340	$37,695	
16						
17						
18						

Ready   NUM

Selecting Data

The chart will represent all expense items and will make it easy to compare changes over the four quarters. The first step is to select the data that will be represented in the chart—the entire data range from cell A3 to cell E13. Do the following:

Click on cell A3 and, holding down the mouse button, drag the pointer to cell E13 to select the entire block of data (without the heading or totals).

The worksheet should look like figure 10.2 when all the information is selected.

Drawing the Chart

When the chart data (or data range) is selected, the next step is to create the chart as a new chart window. To do so, complete the following steps:

1. Select the File New command. Excel will present a dialog box with three options.
2. Click on the Chart option in the dialog box; then click on the OK button. Depending on the size of your monitor, the screen should look like figure 10.3.

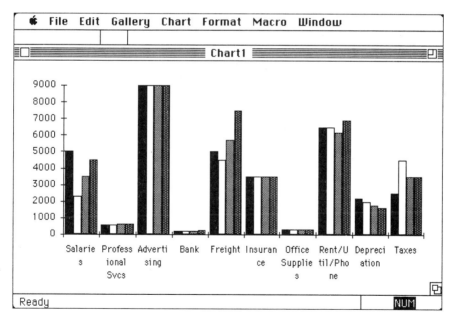

Fig. 10.2.

Selected
information for the
chart.

Fig. 10.3.

The basic chart.

The basic chart displays the selected data in columns. Unless you specify otherwise, the column chart will be the default (or preferred) format for all new charts. You may change this format to meet your needs; Excel provides many commands for this purpose.

Enlarging the Chart

Because the chart appears in its own window, you can manipulate the chart's size and dimensions by changing the window's size and dimensions. As with all windows, you do this by clicking on the size box in the lower right corner and, holding down the mouse button, dragging the pointer outward (see fig. 10.4). Experiment with various dimensions to see how this works. When you are finished, click on the zoom box in the upper right corner.

Fig. 10.4.

Changing the dimensions of the chart.

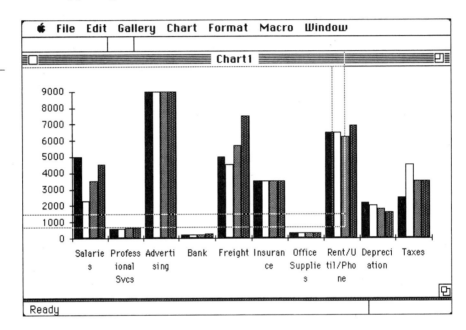

Changing the Chart's Orientation

Currently, the chart displays the expense items as categories along the horizontal axis (or *category axis*). The four bars in these categories represent the four quarters. When the data is presented in this way, you can easily compare the quarterly changes, but you cannot get a clear picture of how the expense items compare with one another. The idea for the chart is to compare expense items and totals quarter by quarter; this chart, however, compares the quarters item by item.

In this case, you should flip the orientation of the data so that the categories become quarters and the bars become items. Because Excel determines the orientation of all new charts, you must make any changes to the orientation after you create the basic chart. Follow these steps to change the orientation:

1. Select the EXPENSES window from the Windows menu to activate the original worksheet. The chart's data range should still be selected.

2. Press Command+C to copy the chart data.

3. Select the File New command and click the Chart options. Press Return when finished. This step begins a new chart with no data in it.

4. Select the Edit Paste Special command. Excel presents the dialog box shown in figure 10.5.

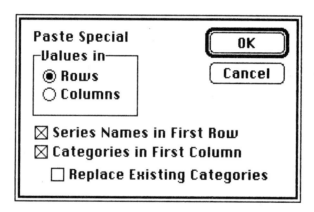

Fig. 10.5.

The Edit Paste Special dialog box for charts.

5. Select the Rows option; then press the Return key. Excel will flip the orientation and paste the chart range back into the chart window. The result is the chart shown in figure 10.6.

6. Select Chart 1 from the Windows menu to activate the original chart. Then select File Close to remove it.

Now the chart displays the quarters as categories and the expense items as bars (or *data points*). This revision makes it easier for you to compare quarters and prepares the chart for the next step.

Fig. 10.6.

The new chart with tho proper orientation of data.

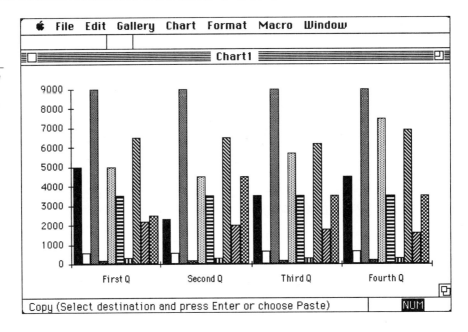

Changing the Chart Type

Excel can produce many kinds of charts—including bar, column, line, scatter, pie, and area—and several variations on each kind. If none of the variations meets your needs, you can customize the one that comes closest.

To change the chart type, select the appropriate main type from the Gallery menu. Excel will present a dialog box with the available variations. Click on one of the variations and press the Return key. The chart will change to the selected format.

As you experiment with chart formats, you will find that some data is not represented well in certain formats. When you are finished experimenting, follow these simple steps to change the column chart to a stacked-column chart:

1. Select the Column option from the Gallery menu.
2. Select chart 3, click on the OK button, and then press the Return key. The chart should now look like the one in figure 10.7.

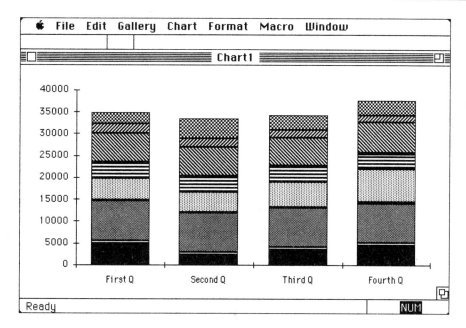

Fig. 10.7.

Changing the chart to a stacked-column format.

Now the chart displays the data according to the original plan. You can easily compare expenses for each quarter by comparing the heights of the bars, and you can determine the proportion that each expense item represents within each bar.

Adding and Formatting a Legend

Because this chart has so many plot points, supplying a legend would be helpful. Excel already knows the titles for the plot points (the titles are part of the data range), so all you have to do is activate the legend. The following is the procedure:

1. Select the Add Legend command from the Chart menu.

   The legend will appear along the right side of the chart. Notice that the chart adjusts to fit the legend in the window. Notice also that the legend does not display all the items in the chart. The reason is that they do not all fit in the chart window. If you cannot enlarge the window any more, try formatting the legend by using the Format Legend command after you select the legend box. See Chapter 11 for more details.

   The next goal is to format the legend. Excel offers several formatting options; you will use one of them here.

2. Click on the legend box to select it; then click on or near one of the border lines. The legend is selected when the squares appear around it.

3. Select the Format Patterns command.

4. Select the Invisible option (at the top of the dialog box) as the border option; then press the Return key. The legend box will now be invisible, as shown in figure 10.8.

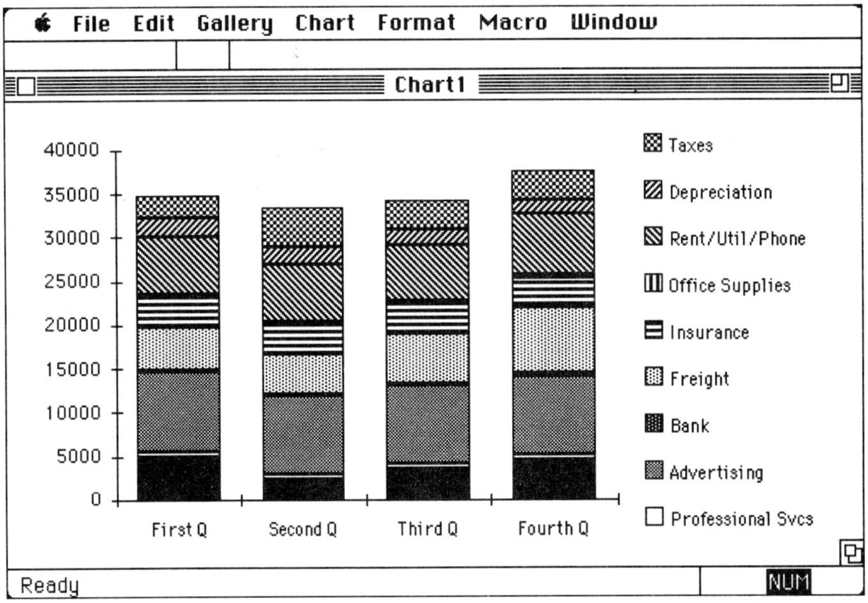

Fig. 10.8.

Removing the legend border.

Adding a Chart Title

When you create a chart title, Excel centers it above the chart. After creating a title, you can select its font, size, and style, as described in the following steps:

1. Select the Chart Attach Text command. Excel will present a dialog box showing the various chart elements to which you can attach text.

2. Confirm that Chart Title is selected; then press the Return key. A title "placeholder" will appear in position above the chart (see fig. 10.9).

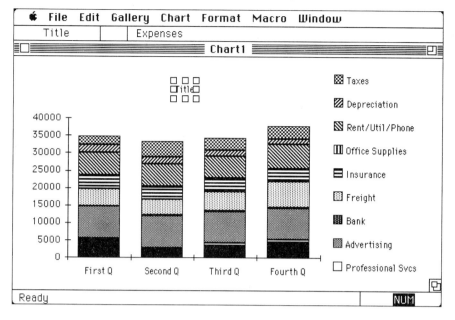

Fig. 10.9.

The chart, showing a title placeholder.

3. Type **Expenses** as the title; then press the Return key. The word *Title* is now replaced by *Expenses*.

4. Select the Format Font command to choose a font, size, and style for the title. (You may want to use a large typeface, such as 18-point Times.) To add an underline, press Command+Shift+U. Figure 10.10 shows the result.

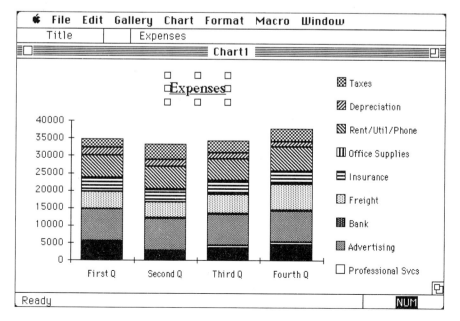

Fig. 10.10.

Adding a title.

Notice that when the title is selected, a formula bar will appear at the top of the screen, as shown in figure 10.10. You can edit the information in this formula bar and change the title information. One way to edit is to link the title text with information in the original worksheet. If you have read Chapter 7, this procedure will be familiar.

5. When the chart title is selected, place the cursor in the formula bar.

6. Select the entire title by double-clicking on the word. Now type an equal sign to replace the existing text with the beginning of a new formula. If your title has more than one word, be sure to highlight the entire title before pressing the equal sign.

7. Activate the EXPENSES worksheet from the Window menu.

8. Click on cell C1; then press the Return key.

When you press the Return key, Excel activates the chart and completes the linking formula. The chart title is now linked to cell C1 of the EXPENSES worksheet. Whenever this cell changes, the chart title changes. Experiment with entering various titles in this cell.

Adding Other Descriptive Text

Text or labels also can be added to the chart as *descriptive text*. This text is not attached to any particular element of the chart and can be moved around the chart window at will. The trick to adding this text is to make sure that nothing is selected on the chart. If an axis or the plot area is selected, the added text will attach itself to this element. If another text box is selected, the added text will replace the text in that box. You can cancel all selections by moving the pointer to a corner or edge of the chart window and clicking the mouse button. Try the following procedure to add descriptive text to your chart:

1. With no chart element selected, type **Exceeds Last Year** and then press the Return key. The text will appear in a box on the chart. You can deselect all elements by clicking the mouse on the outside edge of the chart window as close to the edge of the window as possible.

2. Click on this text box and drag it into position, as shown in figure 10.11.

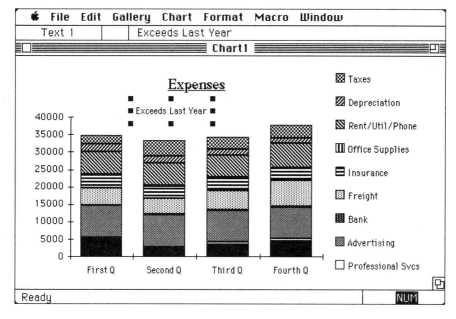

Fig. 10.11.

Moving the descriptive text into position.

Notice that the descriptive text, when selected, has a border of black squares; the chart title and other elements will have borders of white squares. The black borders indicate that the text is not attached to any element and can be freely moved around the chart. You can also change the size and shape of an unattached text box.

You can use descriptive (or unattached) text in place of attached text and position the text as you wish. Remember that descriptive text does not necessarily adjust to various chart types. Attached text will remain in place at all times.

Adding and Deleting Data Points

After you select a data range and create a new chart, you can still add or remove data. Suppose that you decide that the sample chart shows too many expense items. Instead of creating a new chart with fewer items, remove some from the existing chart as follows:

1. Change the chart back into a standard column chart by selecting the Gallery Column command and choosing chart type 1. You need not do so to remove data points, but for this example, following this step will be helpful.

2. Click on the first column in the chart, selecting the four matching bars.

3. Press the Backspace key. The information in the formula bar will disappear. (Excel uses this information to create the corresponding data points.)

4. Press the Return key. The chart now reflects fewer expense items.

5. Repeat steps 1 through 4 so that the chart contains only four expense items. The result should look like figure 10.12.

Fig. 10.12.

Removing several data points from the sample chart.

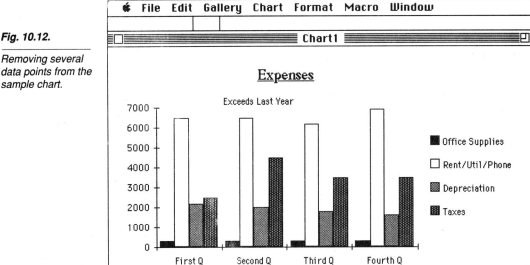

Notice that the proportions of the remaining chart elements change to fill the available space. Likewise, the legend changes, and the patterns adjust to the new set of bars.

You can add data points just as easily as you can remove them. You do this by simply copying the data from the worksheet and pasting it into the chart window. Try adding the "Insurance" item back into the chart. These are the steps:

1. Activate the original worksheet window—the EXPENSES worksheet.

2. Select the range A9:E9, which contains the data for the "Insurance" item.

3. Press Command+C to copy this data.

4. Activate the chart window.

5. Press Command+V to paste the data into this chart. Excel automatically creates a new bar for this item and places it at the end of each series.

Notice that Excel adds the new data point after the existing ones, so that it appears last in the legend and last in each series. Although you cannot use this feature to control the placement of the added data, you can use it to rearrange the columns. Cutting and pasting is not the best way to rearrange columns, however; a better way will be described later.

Making a Combination Chart

A combination chart splits the data points between two different kinds of charts and overlaps them in one chart. If a chart contains four items, two will be represented as one type of chart and the other two as a different type. The first two items compose the *main chart;* the second two items compose the *overlay chart.* One common combination uses columns for the main chart and lines for the overlay chart. If a chart contains an odd number of items, the main chart will receive the extra item.

If you add an overlay chart to an existing chart, Excel will automatically split the data items and make the overlay chart a line chart. Do the following to add an overlay to the sample chart:

Select the Chart Add Overlay command.

Excel now displays the items as two types of charts. Notice that the legend now shows the last two data items with their respective line markers. You can now format the main and overlay charts individually. In this case, you will do three things to the overlay chart. First, you will put one of the data items back into the main chart so that the overlay charts only one item. Next, you will make the line thicker for the line chart. Finally, you will rearrange the data items so that the line represents one of the other items.

Changing the Overlay Split

You can change the way Excel splits the items between the main chart and overlay chart. For example, rather than splitting the items evenly, you may want to have only one item in the overlay and the rest in the main chart. You can make this change by using a single setting in the overlay chart. Try this procedure on the sample chart:

1. Select the Format Overlay command. The dialog box shown in figure 10.13 will appear.

Fig. 10.13.

The Format Overlay dialog box.

Format Overlay Chart

| OK |
| Cancel |

┌─Type─────────────────────────────
  ○ Area   ○ Bar   ○ Column
  ● Line   ○ Pie   ○ Scatter

┌─Format───────────────────────────
  ☐ Stacked   ☐ 100%
  ☐ Vary by Categories   ☐ Overlapped
  ☐ Drop Lines   ☐ Hi-Lo Lines

  % Overlap: `0`   % Cluster Spacing: `50`

  Angle of First Pie Slice (degrees): `0`

First Series in Overlay Chart: `5`
☒ **Automatic Series Distribution**

2. Change the number displayed in the First Series in Overlay Chart option to 5; then press the Return key. This change tells Excel to begin the overlay chart with item 5 in the data, the last item in the sample chart. The result should look like figure 10.14.

Formatting the Overlay Chart

Excel enables you to format the overlay and main charts independently. The following is a simple procedure for formatting the line in the sample overlay chart:

1. Click on the line in the overlay chart to select it. (Actually, this step selects one segment of the line.)

2. Select the Format Patterns command.

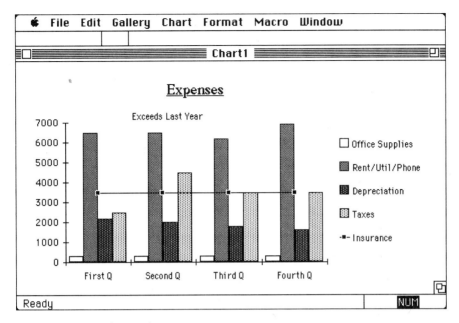

Fig. 10.14.

The combination
chart with a
customized overlay
chart.

3. Select the thickest weight for the line and click on the box;
then click on the Apply to All box to check it. Finally,
press the Return key.

Rearranging the Columns

The final step is to change the sequence of the columns in the chart.
Suppose that you want to show the largest data point first in each series.
In this case, the largest data item in the chart is "Rent/Util/Phone."
Complete these steps:

1. Click on one of the "Rent/Util/Phone" columns to select
the item.

2. Examine the formula displayed in the formula bar. Excel
uses this formula to create the selected column. The last
number in the formula indicates its position in the series.
In this case, the formula indicates that "Rent/Util/Phone" is
item 2.

3. Change the 2 to a 1 to move the item to the first position.
(Be careful not to change any other elements in this
formula.) The formula should look like the one in figure
10.15. Press the Return key when you are finished.

Fig. 10.15.

Changing the series formula.

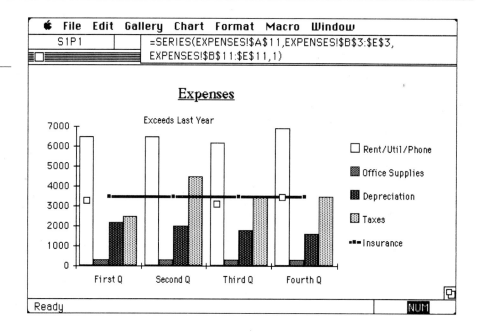

Upon changing the formula, Excel rearranges the columns in the chart. Because Excel renumbers the remaining items, begin with the first item if you plan to make several changes. This way, subsequent changes will not affect your progress.

Printing the Chart

Printing a chart is quite simple. With your printer hooked up and ready to print, use the File Page Setup command to select the size and orientation of the printout. Then use the File Print command to begin printing. (For more details on the Page Setup and Print options, see Chapter 9.)

Saving the Chart

Charts are saved apart from the worksheets that created them. You can store charts on disk as you would any other files; Excel uses the special chart icon to identify them. You can then reopen the chart by clicking on its icon. You can also open a chart by using Excel's File Open command.

The original worksheet does not have to be open when you open a chart. If you open a chart without the original worksheet, however, Excel will ask whether you want to update the chart with the most current worksheet information. Try these steps on the sample chart:

1. With the chart window active, select the File Save command.
2. Type the name **Expense Chart**; then press the Return key.

Charts do not have to be saved in the same folder as the original worksheet; Excel remembers where the original is located. Moving the worksheet may break the link between the chart and the worksheet, and Excel may ask you to reestablish this link.

Summary

The chapter continued with the worksheet you started in the first Quick Start lesson. Here, you used Excel's charting capabilities to represent the expense data in chart form. You saw how Excel automatically creates a chart with your selected data and how it assumes a particular row-column orientation. In this chapter, you also saw how you can change the orientation of Excel's default chart and how to customize many other aspects of the chart. Customizations include changing the chart type; adding titles, text, and legends; changing the size and shape of the chart; and displaying data by using two different chart types in one. From here, you are ready to proceed to the next Quick Start lesson—Chapter 14, "Database Quick Start"—or you can find out more details about Excel's charting commands in the following chapter, "Creating Charts."

11

Creating
Charts

In this chapter you will learn how to create and manipulate charts in Excel. Because Excel's charting capabilities are extensive, this chapter covers a lot of information, first defining the basic elements of a chart, describing the charting process, and outlining the chart menus. The chapter then describes how to get started making charts and continues with a discussion of the various kinds of charts you can produce. You also learn how to manipulate the chart window. The chapter then discusses several ways to customize a default chart by adding a legend, changing the axes, changing the fonts of chart text, and using other enhancement techniques.

Because Excel automates much of the charting process, all charts start out pretty much the same. The key to getting what you want is to edit what Excel provides. The bulk of this chapter is devoted to describing the power behind Excel's charting features and the methods for customizing charts.

Getting an Overview of Charting

The following sections provide some basic information about charting. Figure 11.1 shows a sample chart with the various elements labeled. Excel offers numerous charting features that can make the charting process seem complicated. Actually, you can create most charts with a minimum of effort; follow the basic procedure for creating charts, and you can start charting data right away. The various menu options offered by Excel are available whenever a chart window is active. By using the menu commands, you can customize a chart to your liking.

Fig. 11.1.

The elements of a chart.

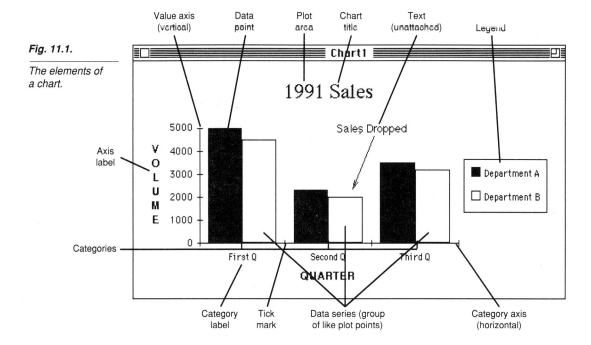

Understanding the Parts of a Chart

Look at figure 11.1 to review the names of a chart's elements. The following paragraphs describe each element in detail. The names of the elements are used throughout this chapter and the rest of the book.

Data points, or *series markers*, are the bars of a bar chart, the pie slices of a pie chart, the plot points of a line chart, and so on. Data points are the essential data elements that make up the chart; they represent the values being charted. Excel automatically assigns colors and patterns to these markers, but you can change their colors. There are six data points in figure 11.1.

Data series are groups of like data points. When you chart more than one value for a particular item, Excel creates more than one data point for that item; each data point gets the same color and pattern— indicating that they belong to the same data series. For example, if you chart the sales of apples over four quarters, you will probably get four similar bars: one data series consisting of four plot points. There are two data series in figure 11.1—one for department A and one for department B.

Categories consist of different plot points within a single grouping. When you chart more than one value for an item, you get a data series, which is divided into categories. Using an earlier example, if you chart sales of apples over four quarters, you have one data series and four categories; the quarters are the categories. In other words, the number of like markers within a data series is the number of categories for that series. When you chart several items (say, apples and oranges), the data series are grouped into categories—where each category contains a set of different data points. There are three categories in figure 11.1, labeled First Q, Second Q, and Third Q. Each category contains two plot points.

A *tick mark* appears on an axis and shows the increments by which a data series increases. You can choose to display or remove tick marks in Excel; you can also change the line thickness of the tick marks.

Charts contain two types of axes: value (vertical) and category (horizontal). The *value axis* usually shows the scale that measures the various series. The *category axis* displays the various categories.

Category labels appear on the category axis and relate to the category groupings. Category labels are not the same as labels appearing in the legend. Normally, worksheet column headings are used as category labels; row headings are used as the legend entries (series marker labels).

The *scale* is the numeric measurement of the chart data. This measurement compares one series to another. The scale usually appears on the value axis. Excel lets you specify the upper and lower values of the scale.

A chart *grid* is a formatting element that you can add if you like. Grids are useful for showing the height of bars or series relative to the scale. You can control the color, pattern, and thickness of the grid lines.

The *legend* is the key to the chart. It displays the names of the series markers and shows the pattern or color used for each. Normally, the entries in the legend come from the row headings used in the worksheet.

You can add various *chart titles* to a chart, including a main heading, horizontal- and vertical-axis titles, and footnotes. Although Excel uses standard default positions, you can position the titles where you want them.

The *axis label* describes the scale of the value axis. It appears vertically along the axis.

The *plot area* is the background for the chart itself. You can change the color and pattern of this area to give the series more emphasis.

You can add *text* to a chart and position it anywhere you like. Text you add is called *unattached text* because you are free to move it around the chart.

Understanding the Charting Process

Version 2.2 of Excel makes charting simple. You can create a chart in two simple steps and make some basic chart selections and changes in a few more steps. The entire process takes only a few moments. The following is the basic procedure:

Creating a Chart

1. Select the data you want to chart. You can use the mouse or keyboard to highlight a range consisting of a single row, a single column, or a block. You also can highlight multiple ranges.

2. Use the File New command to open a chart window. When the dialog box appears, press C or click on the Chart button and press Return. Be sure that the chart range is still highlighted when you choose this command.

3. Use the Gallery command to change the chart type from a standard column chart to any of the 44 built-in types.

The result is a standard chart representing the data you highlighted. You can go beyond these basic steps and customize the chart in some of the following ways:

- Change the orientation of the charted data. Doing so affects the number of data points within each category.
- Change the fonts used by the chart.
- Add labels to the axes and select the fonts for the labels.
- Move the text labels to any location on the chart.
- Add a legend and change the fonts used in it.
- Change the background color or pattern of the legend.
- Move the legend to another location on the chart.
- Change the vertical-axis scale.
- Change the color and pattern of the plot points.

- Change the background color and pattern of the chart itself.
- Add a main title to the chart and choose its font.
- Change the data being charted.

Using the Charting Menus

When you create a chart and activate the chart window, Excel provides a set of charting menus: the Gallery, Chart, and Format menus. The File, Edit, Macros, and Window menus are still available.

The Gallery Menu

The Gallery menu contains options for selecting a chart type. You can change the chart type at any time. Experimenting with various types can present some interesting possibilities. The following list describes the options on the Gallery menu:

Option	*Description*
Area Bar Column Line Pie Scatter Combination	The first seven menu options present various chart types from which to choose. Each option contains a selection of formats that can save you time in creating charts.
Preferred	Selects the chart type currently established as the preferred (or default) type.
Set Preferred	Sets the preferred chart type to that of the currently active chart.

The Chart Menu

The Chart menu contains commands for formatting and customizing charts. You begin with a basic chart provided by Excel, then add features to it by using various commands. In doing so, you can turn a basic chart into a sophisticated tool for communication. The following list describes the options on the Chart menu:

Option	Description
Attach Text	Creates a box in which you can enter text. You can place this text anywhere on a chart.
Add Arrow	Creates an arrow you can position anywhere on the chart. Arrows are useful for emphasizing particular parts of a chart.
Add Legend	Displays the chart legend.
Axes	Displays or hides the chart axes.
Gridlines	Contains options for adding and removing the chart grid lines.
Add Overlay	Creates a chart on top of a chart so that you can make your own combination charts.
Select Chart	Activates the chart.
Select Plot Area	Activates the chart's *plot area* (the area containing the actual plotted values).
Protect Document	Contains options for protecting the chart, including password protection and freezing the chart window.
Calculate Now	Calculates the chart, using the most current values from the corresponding worksheet.
Short Menus	Removes some options from the menus to make Excel less complicated. When Short Menus is active, the command changes to Long Menus.

You might recognize some of these commands—such as Calculate Now—from the previous worksheet chapters. In fact, these are not specifically charting commands; they are carried over, unchanged, from the worksheet menu. They have the same function as always.

The Format Menu

Format options control the appearance of various chart elements, such as the titles, the axis labels, and the legend. You can change the patterns used in the background of a chart or in the chart's data points. The Format menu also provides options for manipulating the fonts used in a chart. The following list describes the options on the Format menu:

Option	Description
Patterns	Controls the appearance of various chart elements. With this option, you can change the thickness and pattern of chart borders, axis lines, and so on.
Font	Controls the font, size, and style of selected text.
Text	Contains options for aligning text in a chart and other text-oriented functions.
Scale	Controls the appearance of the chart's axes, including their values and divisions.
Legend	Controls the position of the legend.
Main Chart	Contains options for making major changes to the chart itself, such as stacking the chart's bars or columns, changing the chart type, and changing the spacing of data points. Most of these options are available in the built-in chart formats.
Overlay	Contains the same options as Main Chart but applies to the overlay chart.
Move	Activates movement commands for the selected chart element.
Size	Activates commands for changing the size of a chart element.

Selecting Information for Charting

To create a chart, you must first have data that can be displayed in chart form. Chart data can be any range of cells: a single row or column or a block of rows and columns. The most important feature of chart data is that it is contiguous; that is, data fills each cell in the range, with no blank cells, rows, or columns. Blank cells appear to the chart as values of zero and are charted.

Once you highlight the chart data you want to use, you can create the chart by opening a new chart window. You open a chart window with the File New command. Suppose that you want to chart the range A3:E13 in figure 11.2. The first step is to highlight the entire range, as shown in the figure. Then select the File New command and choose Chart when the dialog box appears. When you press Return, Excel creates a column chart out of the selected data. Figure 11.3 shows the chart created from the data in figure 11.2.

Fig. 11.2.

Selecting a chart range.

	A	B	C	D	E	F
				Expenses		
1						
2						
3		First Q	Second Q	Third Q	Fourth Q	
4	Salaries	5000	2300	3500	4500	
5	Professional Svcs	600	600	650	650	
6	Advertising	9000	9000	9000	9000	
7	Bank	200	200	200	245	
8	Freight	5000	4500	5690	7500	
9	Insurance	3500	3500	3500	3500	
10	Office Supplies	300	300	300	300	
11	Rent/Util/Phone	6500	6500	6200	6900	
12	Depreciation	2200	2000	1800	1600	
13	Taxes	2500	4500	3500	3500	
15		$34,800	$33,400	$34,340	$37,695	

 File   Edit   Formula   Format   Data   Options   Macro   Window

A3

EXPENSES

Ready   NUM

Fig. 11.3.

The resulting chart.

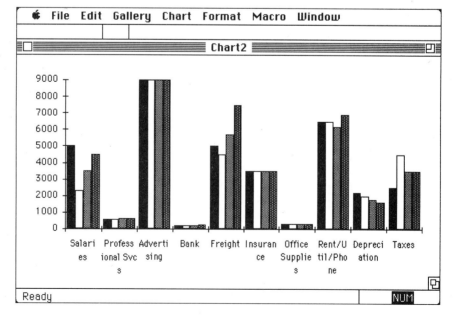

 File   Edit   Gallery   Chart   Format   Macro   Window

Chart2

Ready   NUM

Notice that the category labels come from the rows of the worksheet and that they do not fit well into the chart. This problem will be remedied later in the chapter.

If the chart data does not appear in an orderly block, you can highlight multiple ranges. Just be sure that each range contains the same number of data points and that no blank cells appear within the highlighted ranges. Figure 11.4 shows an example of highlighted multiple ranges.

⚫ File Edit Formula Format Data Options Macro Window						
A13		Taxes				

EXPENSES

	A	B	C	D	E	F
1			Expenses			
2						
3		First Q	Second Q	Third Q	Fourth Q	
4	Salaries	5000	2300	3500	4500	
5	Professional Svcs	600	600	650	650	
6	Advertising	9000	9000	9000	9000	
7	Bank	200	200	200	245	
8	Freight	5000	4500	5690	7500	
9	Insurance	3500	3500	3500	3500	
10	Office Supplies	300	300	300	300	
11	Rent/Util/Phone	6500	6500	6200	6900	
12	Depreciation	2200	2000	1800	1600	
13	Taxes	2500	4500	3500	3500	
15		$34,800	$33,400	$34,340	$37,695	
16						
17						
18						

Ready   NUM

Fig. 11.4 .

Selecting multiple ranges for the chart.

Changing the Orientation

When the data range for a chart contains more than one row or column, Excel assumes that you are plotting more than one category, where each category contains a similar set of data points. Excel must decide whether the columns represent the categories or whether the rows represent the categories. The difference is significant. Figures 11.5 and 11.6 show the same data range plotted according to two different orientations.

In both figures, the chart represents two expense items plotted for four quarters. In figure 11.5, the emphasis is on the difference between the two expense items during each quarter. In figure 11.6, the emphasis is on the comparison of quarters.

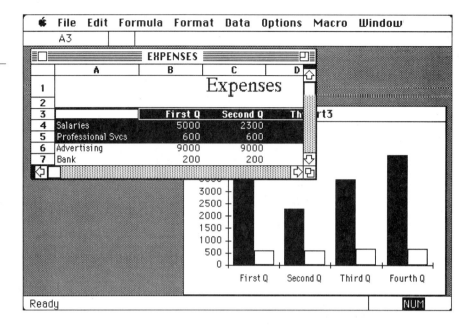

Fig. 11.5.

A chart using columns as the categories.

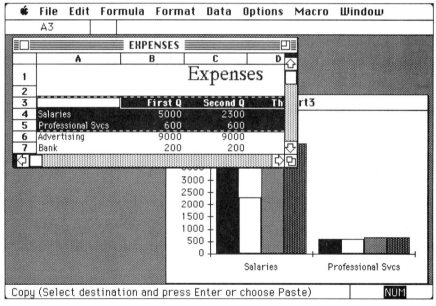

Fig. 11.6.

A chart using rows as the categories.

Because Excel cannot know how you intend to display the data, it makes an assumption: that the larger proportion represents the categories. For example, a block of five columns and two rows produces a chart with five categories, each containing two data series. A block of five rows and two columns produces the same chart. Excel's default orientation may be confusing because the categories do not consistently correspond to rows or columns.

The default orientation anticipates the most likely organization of the data. However, if you want to "flip" the orientation, follow these steps:

Changing the Orientation of a Chart

1. With the incorrect chart active and in view, select the Edit Clear command to erase the entire chart.

2. Return to the worksheet containing the data range by selecting its name from the Window menu.

3. Rehighlight the appropriate chart data range, making sure that you include the labels for the series and plot points.

4. Select the Edit Copy command.

5. Return to the chart window by selecting its name from the Window menu.

6. Select the Edit Paste Special command.

7. Select Rows to use the rows as the categories; select Columns to use the columns as the categories. Because you are changing Excel's default order, the option you want is probably the one not currently selected.

8. Specify the location of the series and category labels and press Return. Depending on the orientation you want, series labels will be either in the first row or first column of the copied block. If they are in the first row, check the box marked Series Labels in First Row. Similarly, category labels will be in the first row or column. The chart should now reflect the orientation you want.

Be sure to change the orientation of your chart before adding any custom formats to the chart. Custom formats are removed during the orientation-swapping process. Also note that charts made from noncontiguous blocks of data cannot be reoriented, because you cannot copy noncontiguous data. Thus these charts are stuck in Excel's default orientation.

Using the Chart Window

Charts are not part of the worksheets used to create them. A chart exists in its own window, which acts like any other window. You can change the window's size and shape, arrange it with other windows, activate it through the Windows menu, and so on. When you change the size and shape of the chart window, the chart adjusts proportionally. To make a chart larger, enlarge the window; to make a chart taller, make the window taller. You can perform these window changes by clicking on the window's grow box and dragging. Figure 11.7 shows two versions of the same chart.

Fig. 11.7.

Chart proportions affected by the window proportions.

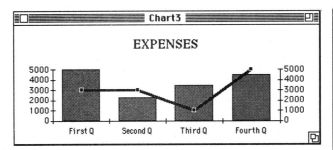
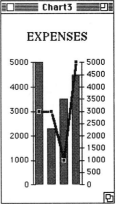

The disadvantage to having the chart in its own window is that you cannot merge the chart with the worksheet data. You also cannot easily print a chart along with its corresponding worksheet data. Another disadvantage is that the chart window can be enlarged only as much as the Macintosh screen allows; this situation can limit the size of your chart.

Although charts are separate from their corresponding worksheets, they are linked to them. Therefore, when the worksheet and the chart windows are open, you can make changes to the worksheet, and the chart immediately reflects those changes. This feature is excellent for experimenting with values for what-if analysis. Just enter various amounts into the worksheet and watch the effect on the chart. If you don't save the changes to either the chart or the worksheet, everything returns to its original state.

Saving and Opening Charts

To save a chart, activate the chart window by selecting its name from the Window menu and using the File Save command as you do with any worksheet file. Charts are stored on the disk in individual files marked with the chart icon. You can return to a chart in one of two ways: double-click on the chart icon from the desktop or open the chart from Excel by using the File Open command. The worksheet used to create the chart does not have to be open when you open a chart. If the original worksheet is not open, the dialog box shown in figure 11.8 appears when you open the chart.

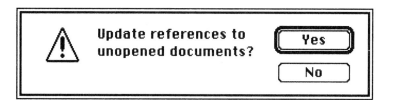

Fig. 11.8.

The dialog box that appears when you open a chart without opening the original worksheet.

Excel remembers which charts are linked to which worksheets and offers to update the chart, using the current worksheet data. If you choose Yes, Excel locates the original worksheet on disk and updates the chart accordingly. The worksheet, however, is not opened. If Excel cannot find the original worksheet (for example, if it has been moved, renamed, or deleted), Excel presents a dialog box so that you can select the file from disk. When you choose the file, Excel updates the chart's link so that it can find the worksheet file the next time you open the chart.

If you forget which worksheet is attached to a chart, open the chart and select No from the Update References dialog box. Then select the File Links command. Excel presents the linked file in a dialog box. Select the file's name and choose Open to open the worksheet. If you have moved, renamed, or deleted the worksheet, Excel is unable to find it when you select File Links. Instead, you must find the file manually by using the file-selection dialog box. As soon as you open the worksheet, Excel updates the chart if necessary.

Changing the Chart Type

Once you create a basic chart (and, if necessary, change its orientation), you can make all kinds of changes to it. One of the most basic changes is to select a different type of chart. Excel offers several types of charts: area, bar, column, line, pie, scatter, and combination. Within each of these main categories, Excel offers several variations, which are really just shortcuts to formatting a chart from scratch. Because many formatting combinations are used commonly, Excel offers them as predesigned chart formats. You have a total of 44 built-in chart formats from which to choose. If one of these formats isn't to your liking, you can customize your chart—beginning with one of the built-in charts and changing it as you like.

To change the chart type, activate the chart window and select one of the seven chart types from the Gallery menu. Excel displays the built-in chart formats, in picture form, for the selected type. (The following sections show the formats available for each chart type.)

Click on the picture representing the format you want. If you want to view other chart types, just click on the Next button to view the next Gallery menu item. Click on the Previous button to view the previous Gallery menu item. The following sections describe the seven main chart types and the various built-in chart formats. For more information on the uses of each chart type and for techniques that will make your charts more attractive, refer to Chapter 13.

 You can change any existing chart to any of the formats listed here. However, if the chart has custom formatting, that formatting disappears when you change chart types.

Area Charts

Area charts, such as the one in figure 11.9, are commonly used to track changes in volume or intensity over time. Instead of comparing one bar to another, these charts compare changes over one or two series. Area charts show continuous divisions of data but stack several series together to show how they relate to the whole. Such charts are useful when you have too many divisions for your stacked bar chart. They can also be effective for plotting a single item over time but showing how that item represents volume. Figure 11.10 shows the area-chart formats available through the Gallery Area option.

The following list describes the format options shown in figure 11.8:

Option	Description
1	This format is the basic area chart. Each data series represents a new "layer" of the area chart.
2	This format displays the area chart in percentages, where the combination of the data series is 100 percent and the individual data series represent percentages of the whole.
3	This format adds drop lines to the data points in each series and is best used for charting a single data series. Drop lines emphasize the exact

Option	Description
	placement of plot points on the chart by connecting the plot point to the base of the chart.
4	This format adds grid lines to the basic area chart. Grid lines emphasize the values of the plot points by providing a visual scale for reference.
5	This format adds series labels to the basic area chart. Series labels help identify the various "areas" in the chart.

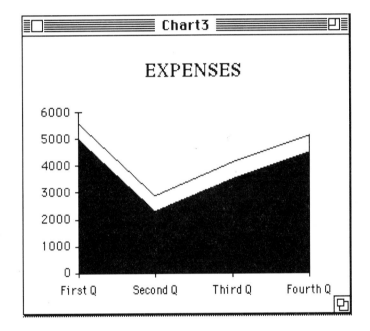

Fig. 11.9.

A sample area chart.

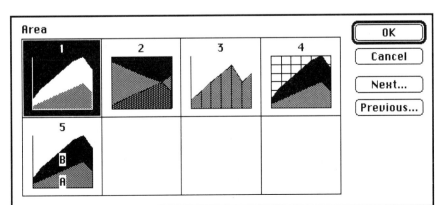

Fig. 11.10.

The area formats available through Gallery Area.

Bar Charts

Bar charts, also known as *histograms*, consist of horizontal bars and are primarily used to indicate a distance or goal achieved. The primary purpose of bar charts is to show the quantity or quality of items in comparison. They are not as effective as column charts for comparing one item over time; rather, their purpose is to establish the "rank" of several different items. The eye is more easily drawn to the length of the bars when the bars are turned sideways. Often, the bars in a bar chart are not shown in different colors or patterns because labels frequently accompany the bars. Use bar charts instead of column charts when the comparison has no connection with changes over time. Figure 11.11 shows a sample bar chart; figure 11.12 shows the bar-chart formats available through the Gallery Bar option.

Fig. 11.11.

A sample bar chart.

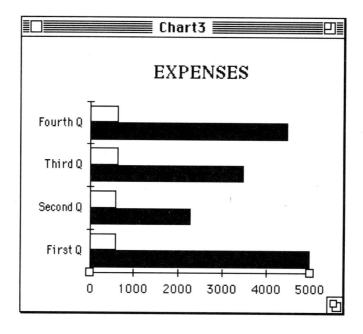

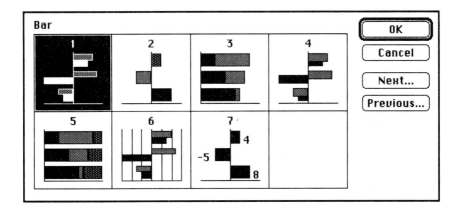

Fig. 11.12.

The bar formats available through Gallery Bar.

The following list describes the format options shown in figure 11.12:

Option	Description
1	This format displays data points as bars in a horizontal chart. Negative values appear as bars at the left of the vertical axis.
2	This format applies a different pattern to each bar in the series when you plot only one data series. (Normally, each bar has the same pattern.)
3	This format stacks the data points within the various series. The chart shows the same number of series, but with only one bar in each series. The bar can contain various patterns. This format is usually used when you have more than one series and is a good alternative to pie charts.
4	This format overlaps the bars in a bar chart; otherwise, this format is the same as format 1.
5	This stacked-bar-chart format displays each data point as a percentage value. The total of each series is 100 percent.
6	This format adds vertical grid lines to the basic bar chart.
7	This format adds value labels to the bars of a basic bar chart to help emphasize the values of the bars.

Column Charts

Column charts, such as the one shown in figure 11.13, are used for standard business applications. Column charts are ideal for directly comparing items over time or over a series of changes. The immediate ability to compare the heights of the columns helps bring the message home. The periods of time are the series of the chart. You can contrast two or more data items in one column chart if you like. This capability is useful for comparing the performance of two related items, such as two products or two expense categories. As with bar charts, you can stack a column chart, overlap the data points, and include various formatting elements. Figure 11.14 shows the column-chart formats available through the Gallery Column option.

Fig. 11.13.

A sample column chart.

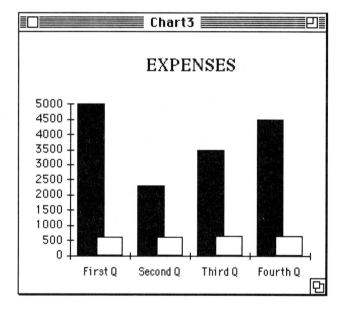

Fig. 11.14.

The formats available through Gallery Column.

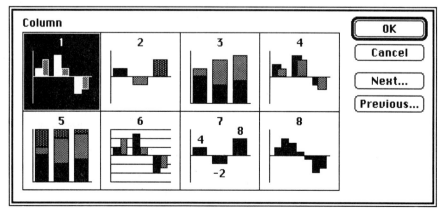

The following list describes the format options shown in figure 11.14:

Option	Description
1	This format—the default format for all new charts—displays data points as columns (bars) in a vertical chart.
2	This format applies a different pattern to each column in the series when you plot only one data series. (Normally, each column has the same pattern.)
3	This format stacks the data points within the various series. The chart shows the same number of series, but with only one column in each series. The column can contain various patterns. This format is usually used when you have more than one series and is a good alternative to pie charts.
4	This format overlaps the columns in a column chart; otherwise, this format is the same as format 1.
5	This stacked-column-chart format displays each data point as a percentage value. The total of each series is 100 percent.
6	This format adds horizontal grid lines to the basic column chart.
7	This format adds value labels to the columns of a basic column chart.
8	This format displays columns without space between columns and uses the same pattern for each data point. This format is usually used to plot only one series; it is similar to an area chart but does not smooth the tops of the plot points.

Stacked column charts can often be used in place of several pie charts. Such column charts present information in much the same way as pie charts, showing how several series of data represent a whole column. The height of one column can be compared to the height of another. Use stacked column charts when several series and divisions are required at the same time.

Line and High-Low Charts

Line and high-low charts are used for showing trends and charting numerous plotted points, as in stock analysis. Line charts are similar in purpose to column charts. However, line charts represent the time factor more dramatically than column charts because the divisions are connected on a continuous line. Line charts can display more divisions than column charts without losing effectiveness. Often, the distinct time intervals (plot points) are not important—only the change over time (that is, the line's path). Figure 11.15 shows a sample line chart; figure 11.16 shows the line-chart formats available through the Gallery Line option.

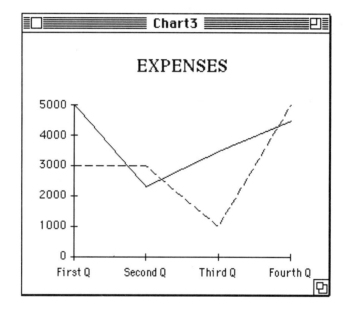

Fig. 11.15.

A sample line chart.

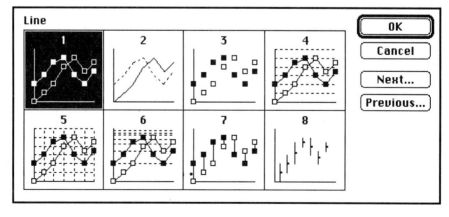

Fig. 11.16.

The formats available through Gallery Line.

A high-low chart is simply a line chart (any type of line chart) with high-low lines added. High-low lines are vertical lines that connect the plot points of two or more data series. Often only these high-low lines are shown; the series lines are removed, as in gallery format 7. Note that the two (or more) series used in a high-low chart are usually two values for the same item, rather than two different items. A high-low-close chart (gallery format 8) requires three values to be charted. These values are equivalent to three data series, but they will relate to the same item, not three different items.

The following list describes the format options shown in figure 11.16:

Option	Description
1	This format draws a line for each data series and plots the data points, using a square marker.
2	This format is identical to format 1 but does not show the markers.
3	This format is identical to format 1 but does not show the lines.
4	This format adds a horizontal grid to the basic line chart.
5	This format adds grid lines to the basic line chart.
6	This format is a basic line chart that uses a logarithmic scale for the vertical axis.
7	This format is a high-low chart; it uses markers for the plotted points and lines to connect the markers.
8	This format is a high-low-close chart showing three amounts for each data series. The correlation to the stock market is obvious, providing a daily high, low, and closing stock value. High-low charts also can be used for purposes such as comparing bids turned in for a contract—the high bid, the low bid, and the winning bid.

Pie Charts

Pie charts, such as the one in figure 11.17, are the most graphic representation of parts that make up a whole—where the whole is

100 percent and the slices are proportional values of the whole. A single pie chart shows only one series of data, which is its primary disadvantage to other types of charts. Figure 11.18 shows the pie-chart formats available through the Gallery Pie option.

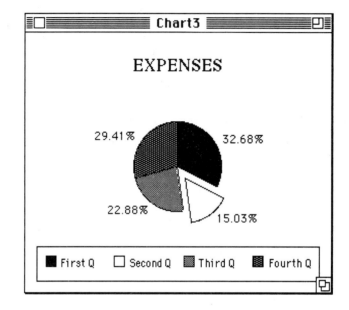

Fig. 11.17.

A sample pie chart.

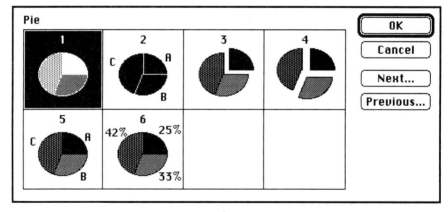

Fig. 11.18.

The formats available through Gallery Pie.

The following list describes the format options shown in figure 11.18:

Option	Description
1	This format is a basic pie chart with each data point shaded differently.
2	This format is a basic pie chart with each data point shaded the same. This format includes labels for the wedges.
3	This format is the same as format 1, but with one wedge exploded.
4	This format is the same as format 1, but with all wedges exploded.
5	This format is the same as format 1, but with labels for the wedges.
6	This format is the basic pie chart with wedges labeled as percentages of the whole.

You do not need to use an exploded format (formats 3 and 4) to explode a pie wedge. To determine which wedge of a pie chart is removed from the others, simply click on the wedge you want to move and drag it to the new location. Pie wedges are independent objects and can be moved at any time.

Scatter Charts

Scatter charts compare pairs of numbers that are treated as coordinates for plotting graph points. Each data series in a scatter chart consists of exactly two plot points: the first plots the horizontal point, and the second plots the vertical. Figure 11.19 shows a sample scatter chart; figure 11.20 shows the scatter-chart formats available through the Gallery Scatter option.

Fig. 11.19.

A sample scatter chart.

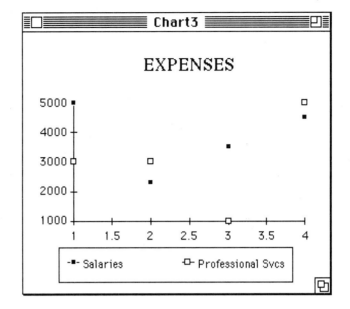

Fig. 11.20.

The formats available through Gallery Scatter.

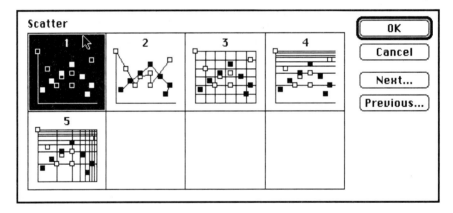

The following list describes the format options shown in figure 11.20:

Option	Description
1	This format is a basic scatter chart with markers representing the data points.
2	This format is a basic scatter chart with markers representing the data points and lines connecting like markers.

Option	Description
3	This format is a scatter chart with vertical and horizontal grid lines.
4	This format is a scatter chart with a logarithmic vertical axis.
5	This format is a scatter chart with logarithmic vertical and horizontal axes.

Combination Charts

Combination charts, such as the one in figure 11.21, are charts that combine two to four different types into one. These charts are useful for showing different data series in different chart types. The emphasis is not so much on the comparison of the data but on the way the two data series fit together. Figure 11.22 shows the combination-chart formats available through the Gallery Combination option.

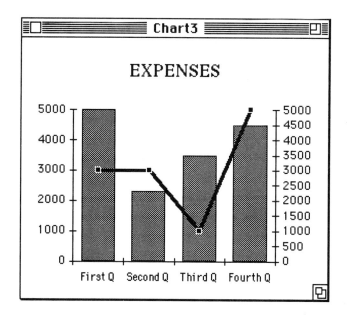

Fig. 11.21.

A sample combination chart.

Fig. 11.22.

The formats available through Gallery Combination.

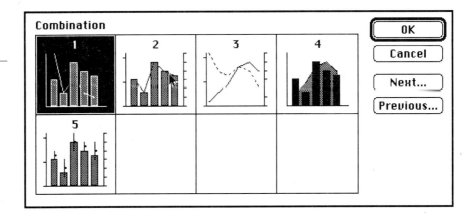

The following list describes the format options available through Gallery Combination:

Option	Description
1	This format is a column chart with a line chart overlay.
2	This format is a column chart with a line chart overlay. The line chart contains its own vertical scale. Thus this chart contains two vertical axes.
3	This format is a line chart with another line chart overlay. The second line chart has its own vertical scale.
4	This format is an area chart with a column chart overlay.
5	This format is a column chart with a high-low-close chart overlay. The high-low-close chart has its own vertical scale.

Because combination charts involve complex options, this chart type is discussed in a separate chapter. See Chapter 12 for details on using combination charts.

Changing the Default (Preferred) Chart

When you first create a chart by using a new chart window, Excel automatically draws a standard column chart. The chart Excel first draws is known as the default, or *preferred,* chart. You can make the preferred chart any one of the built-in chart formats; you can even change it to a custom-designed format. Being able to specify the default chart is handy when you use the same chart format over and over. Just create a chart that uses the format you want. With this chart active, select the Gallery Set Preferred command. The preferred chart is now the same format as the active chart. The next time you create a chart in this worksheet, the chart will appear in the preferred format.

You can change any existing chart to the preferred setting by choosing the Gallery Preferred command. Making such a change is most useful when the preferred chart is a custom format; if the preferred chart is a built-in format, you can change a chart by selecting the appropriate built-in format or by selecting the Gallery Preferred command.

Customizing Charts

It's unlikely that Excel's built-in chart formats will provide everything you want in a chart. So the next step in charting is learning some basic customization commands. Even making basic changes, like adding a legend, requires that you customize one of the built-in charts. The following sections discuss various tasks you can accomplish with the customization commands.

Highlighting Chart Elements

Many of Excel's customization features apply to specific chart elements. Often, you must select, or highlight, the element you want before you can make a change to it. You might find it easiest to simply click on the element you want in order to select it. However, you have other options, as described in this section.

You can highlight a chart element by clicking on it with the mouse. If you click in the correct area, the element is surrounded with the familiar highlight squares. You can also use the Chart Select Chart and Chart Select Plot Area commands to select chart elements. If you use the keyboard to highlight chart elements, remember that Excel groups chart elements into the following classes:

Chart
Plot area
Legend
Axes
Chart text
Chart arrows
Grid lines
Data series
Drop lines (area charts only)
High-low lines (high-low charts only)

Use the following keys to select chart elements within the classes:

Key	Selection
Up arrow	First item in next class
Down arrow	First item in previous class
Left arrow	Next item in current class
Right arrow	Preceding item in current class

As an example, suppose that a chart arrow is highlighted. Pressing the up-arrow key would highlight the first grid line in the chart (if any exist). Once the grid line is highlighted, pressing the right-arrow key would select the next grid line; pressing the up-arrow key would highlight the first data series.

Changing Chart Legends

The chart legend is the key to the plot points in the chart. If you have more than one plot point, Excel automatically uses a unique pattern or color for each. These patterns and colors appear in the legend next to the name of the item. Remember that Excel considers the larger number of items (that is, the larger proportion in the data range) to be the categories; Excel considers the smaller number of items to be the data series. The category labels appear on the horizontal axis, and the series labels appear in the legend. For example, if you chart two rows from the EXPENSES worksheet (shown in fig. 11.5) over all four quarters, you get the chart shown in figure 11.23. The row labels become the legend items because they refer to the data series. In other words, you have two bars appearing in four groups.

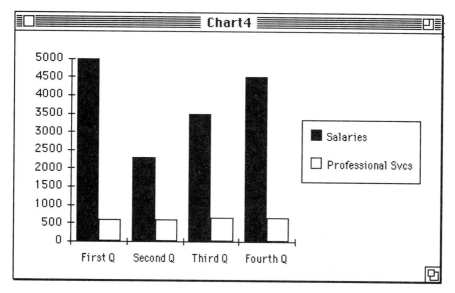

Fig. 11.23.

Columns as categories, rows as data series.

If you chart four rows over two quarters from the same worksheet, you might expect to have four bars appear in two groups with the legend showing the four row labels. Because the proportions of the data range have changed, Excel replots the chart, using the columns as the plot points and rows as data series. Figure 11.24 shows how the chart appears.

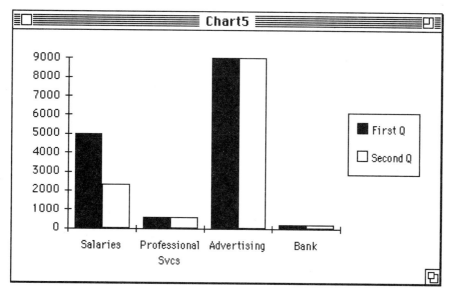

Fig. 11.24.

Rows as categories, columns as plot points.

You still have two bars appearing in four groups, but the bars now represent the quarters instead of the expense items. In both cases, the legend displays the data series labels, the labels associated with the bars. When a chart contains only one data series, however, the legend does not display the names of the series but duplicates the names of the categories. For example, if you chart one row from the EXPENSES worksheet over four quarters, the resulting chart and legend appear as shown in figure 11.25.

Fig. 11.25.

The legend duplicating the category labels in a chart with only one data series.

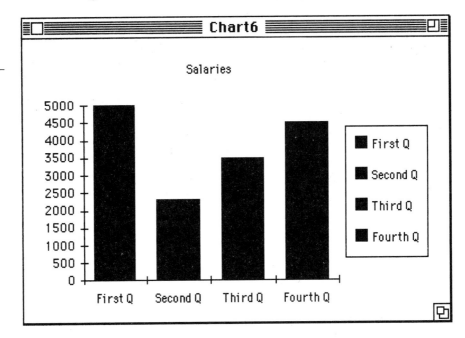

In figure 11.25, the legend contains not the series label but the same labels as the category axis. Excel deviates from the basic rule (of using series labels in the legend) by assuming that you would not want only one label in the legend.

Adding and Removing a Legend

To display the chart legend, activate the chart and select the Chart Add Legend command. The legend appears vertically on the chart. Excel redraws the chart so that it fits into the window along with the legend. If the chart is now too small, enlarge the window.

The legend items should match the labels in either the first row or first column of the data range (whichever is not used as the category labels). If the legend does not use these labels, you may not have included the labels when you highlighted the data range. Be sure that no extra blank space appears between the labels and the chart values. To remove a legend, simply select Delete Legend from the Chart menu.

Moving the Legend

After adding a legend to the chart, you may decide to change its position. You can do this by clicking on the legend box in the chart, an action that highlights the legend and displays small squares around the legend box (see fig. 11.26). With the legend highlighted, select the Format Legend command. Excel presents the dialog box shown in figure 11.27.

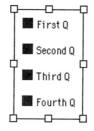

Fig. 11.26.

Highlighting a legend by clicking on the legend box.

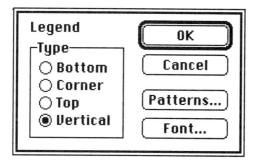

Fig. 11.27.

Positions for the legend.

Select the position you want for the legend. Experiment with the various options for best results. Excel changes the proportions of the chart to accommodate the position of the legend. Unfortunately, you cannot move the legend to areas other than those provided in the Format Legend dialog box.

The Top and Bottom options are self-explanatory: they place the legend at the top or bottom of the chart, respectively. The Corner option places the legend in the upper right corner of the chart, and the Vertical option places the legend along the right side of the chart. The Patterns and Font buttons shown in the dialog box take you directly to the Format Patterns and Format Font dialog boxes. These are explained in the next section.

Formatting the Legend

Using the legend-formatting features, you can change the fonts used for the legend items, change the pattern in the legend box, add a shadow to the box, and much more. As you might guess, formatting changes are *not* made with the Format Legend command. (Format Legend is not used to format the legend but to move it.) Two other commands in the Format menu are used to format the legend: Patterns and Font. Figure 11.28 shows some of the ways you can format the legend.

Fig. 11.28.

Various formatted legends.

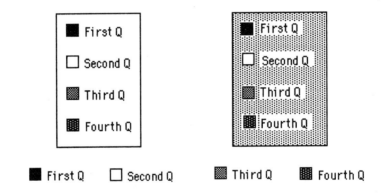

To format the legend, first click on the legend box to highlight it. Select the Format Patterns option to change the border and interior of the legend box; select the Format Font option to change the fonts of the labels inside the legend box.

The Format Patterns command contains options for changing the border and the interior (or *area*) of the legend. Figure 11.29 shows the Format Patterns dialog box for legends.

Table 11.1 lists the options available in the Format Patterns dialog box and offers a short description of each.

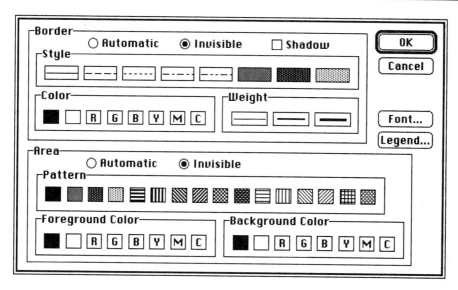

Fig. 11.29.

The Format Patterns options for legends.

Table 11.1
The Format Patterns Options for Legends

Option	Description
Border Options	
Automatic	Tells Excel to select the style, color, and weight for the border of the legend box itself.
Invisible	Makes the border of the legend box invisible.
Shadow	Adds a drop shadow to the legend box. The drop shadow appears below and to the right of the box.
Style	Sets the pattern of the border line. The three shaded options are useful only when the line weight is thick enough to support the pattern.
Color	Sets the color of the border line. Colors include black, white, red, green, blue, yellow, magenta, and cyan.
Weight	Sets the thickness of the border line.

Table 11.1—(continued)

Option	Description
Area Options	
Automatic	Tells Excel to select the colors and pattern for the interior of the legend box itself.
Invisible	Makes the interior invisible. An invisible area often looks white but is actually transparent. Making the area invisible is useful when you transfer charts into other programs for added graphic effects.
Pattern	Sets the interior pattern.
Foreground Color	Sets the foreground color of the selected pattern. The foreground color is the color of the pattern itself. The foreground color you select controls the color of the solid (black) pattern.
Background Color	Sets the background color of the selected pattern. The background color is the color behind the pattern. The background color you select controls the color of the solid (white) pattern. In black-and-white systems, you can use the foreground and background options to reverse the patterns (that is, specify white on black or black on white).

The Format Font command contains options for changing the font, size, and style of the text inside the legend box. The options in this dialog box (see fig. 11.30) are similar to those for formatting worksheet fonts.

Table 11.2 lists the options available in the Format Font dialog box and offers a short description of each.

Customizing the Legend Text

You may decide to change the legend labels themselves so that they are no longer linked to the labels in the worksheet. You can change the legend labels by editing the series formulas Excel produces to create the chart. This procedure is described in Chapter 12.

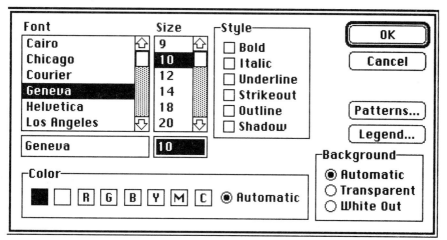

Fig. 11.30.

The Format Fonts dialog box.

Table 11.2
The Format Font Options for Legends

Option	Description
Font	Determines the font. Font selections appear for fonts installed in your system or contained in the open suitcase file.
Size	Determines the size of the text. You can specify a size that is not offered by typing it into the box under the Size listing.
Style	Sets the style of the text. Choose as many of these options as you like.
Color	Sets the color of the text for color systems.
Background	Determines the status of the area behind the text. This is not the background of the legend box, but the area directly behind the text. Select Automatic if you want Excel to select the background; select Transparent if you want the background of the legend box to show through the text; select White Out to create a white box surrounding the text.

Changing the Series Patterns

Excel automatically chooses the patterns and colors of the data series when you create a chart. You can change these settings: you can change the border of the data series, their patterns, and their colors. Figure 11.31 shows an example of several different settings in a data series.

Fig. 11.31.

Changing the patterns and borders of the data series.

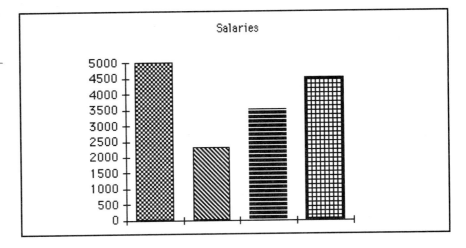

You can change each data series individually. First, highlight the series you want by clicking on it or by using the up-arrow or down-arrow key. In a bar or column chart, just click on one of the bars; in a pie chart, click on a pie wedge; in a scatter chart, click on a plot-point marker. Then choose the Format Patterns command. Figure 11.32 shows the dialog box that appears.

Fig. 11.32.

The Format Patterns dialog box for changing series patterns.

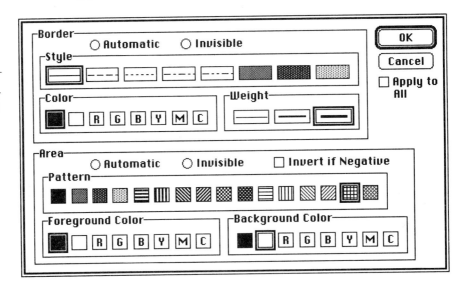

This dialog box is very similar to the dialog box used to format legends. Choose the options you want for the border and area (interior) of the series markers. For details about the options in this dialog box, see "Formatting the Legend" earlier in this chapter. If you check the box marked Apply to All, Excel applies your pattern selections to all data series on the chart—not just the one you highlighted. Note that you cannot change each plot point individually, only entire series at a time. The exception is when the chart contains only one series.

Changing Chart Titles and Labels

Excel automatically applies labels to the category axis and legend, using the worksheet data range as a basis. But what about axis labels or a main chart title? You can add these chart labels yourself. You can simply type information for the labels onto the chart, or you can refer to a cell in the original worksheet—a cell that contains the text you want used as a chart label. Figure 11.33 shows a chart with the various types of labels you can add.

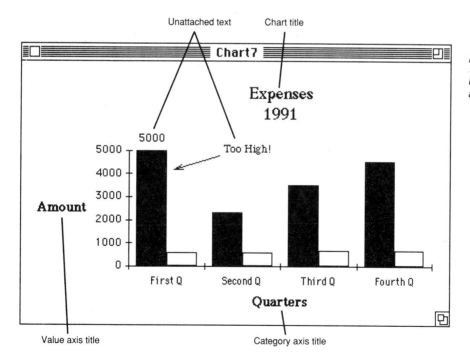

Fig. 11.33.

Labels you can add to a chart.

Adding Chart Titles, Axis Labels, and Data Labels

With the exception of descriptive, or "unattached," text, all chart labels are "attached" to specific elements of the chart. A value-axis label is attached to the value axis. If the value axis moves or changes, the label moves or changes with it. Changes can include proportional as well as placement changes. To attach a label to an element, first click on the element to highlight it. A highlighted element should have small squares around its edges.

After selecting the element, choose the Chart Attach Text command. Excel presents a dialog box listing the various chart elements to which you can attach text. Confirm that the element you want is selected, or select the element to which you want to attach text; press Return. If you like, you can select the Chart Attach Text command without highlighting a chart element. Excel places a small text box on the chart in the appropriate area. Figure 11.34 shows a text box attached to the category axis.

Fig. 11.34.

Adding text to the category axis.

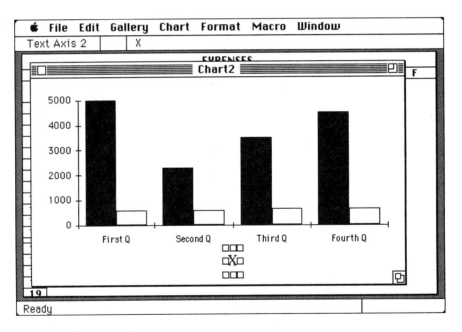

Notice that when the text box is highlighted, the formula bar appears, enabling you to type information. Enter the label for this box and press Return. The label appears in the text box.

> ### Creating Subtitles
>
> Subtitles are really just part of the main title. To create a second line of a title, press Command+Return when entering the title text.

By using the worksheet-linking techniques discussed in Chapter 7, you can link the text in the text box to a cell in the original worksheet—or to any other worksheet. Linking labels to worksheets is especially useful for creating data-point labels, because they often represent the values of the data in the worksheet. Just enter a simple linking formula such as =EXPENSES!$G$5 into the text box. You can even point to the appropriate cell by using the following steps:

1. Attach a text box to the element you want, as described earlier in this section. Click on the text box to make sure that it is selected.

2. Type an equal sign.

3. Activate the worksheet containing the cell you want to reference.

4. Click on the cell you want to reference.

5. Press Return.

Linking Chart Labels to Worksheets

Note that you cannot use subtitles or have more than one cell referenced. Also, this procedure does not bring the format of the text to the chart.

Adding Descriptive Text

Descriptive text is not attached to any element of the chart. Because it's not attached, the text can be moved around the chart. To add descriptive text to a chart, first make sure that none of the chart elements is highlighted. To "unhighlight" everything, click the mouse in one of the corners of the chart until all highlighting disappears. With nothing highlighted, just begin typing the text. When you press Return, the text appears on the chart. You can now move the text into place by dragging it with the mouse. As with attached text, you can reference external worksheet cells for descriptive text.

Moving Descriptive Text

Descriptive text can be moved at any time. Just click on the text box and drag the mouse to the new location. The entire text box moves with the mouse. When you highlight descriptive text, the usual white highlight squares appear as black, indicating that the text is unattached.

You can enlarge the text box of unattached text by dragging one of the highlight squares. By enlarging the text box, you can make room for practically any amount of descriptive information for the chart. You can also use keyboard commands to move and resize an unattached text box.

To move unattached text by using the keyboard, follow these steps:

Using the Keyboard To Move Unattached Text

1. Highlight the text box, using the mouse or arrow keys.
2. Select Format Move.
3. Use the arrow keys to move the text box.
4. Press Enter when finished.

To resize unattached text by using the keyboard, follow these steps:

Using the Keyboard To Resize Unattached Text

1. Highlight the text box, using the mouse or keyboard.
2. Select Format Size.
3. Use the arrow keys to change the size of the box.
4. Press Enter when finished.

Editing and Deleting Existing Chart Labels

After creating various chart labels, you may have to edit or add to the information in a label. To do so, use the mouse or keyboard to highlight the appropriate text box and insert the cursor in the formula bar containing the text. Click in the formula bar to insert the cursor, or press Command+U to place the cursor in the formula bar of the highlighted text box. With the pointer in the formula bar, use the editing commands listed in Chapter 4 to change or add to the data. Press Return when finished. Although you cannot change the information used for the horizontal-axis labels, you can change the values of the vertical axis. See "Changing the Axes" later in this chapter for details.

To remove a chart label, highlight it and press Backspace, then Return.

Formatting Chart Labels

Formatting a chart label is identical to formatting a chart legend. After highlighting the appropriate label, choose either the Format Font or the Format Patterns command. The Format Font command controls the text used in the text box; Format Patterns controls the interior and border of the text box itself. In addition, you can use the Format Text command to change the alignment of the label text. Using Format Text, you can rotate the text so that it appears vertically down the axis. Excel automatically formats text boxes with invisible borders and invisible interior patterns. For details about these two commands, see "Formatting the Legend" earlier in this chapter.

To change the font used for the horizontal- and vertical-axis labels, highlight the axis you want, select the Format Font command, and change the font. The Format Font dialog box also contains three options for the background of the labels; select from Invisible, White, or Automatic. You cannot use the Format Patterns command with axis labels.

Using Descriptive Text for Emphasis

Don't be afraid to enlarge the text box to any size you want. You can use unattached text for all kinds of interesting purposes. Drag the text box to a different area of the chart worksheet to create a page of instructions or descriptive information. See Chapter 13 for interesting uses for text boxes.

Changing the Chart Background and Plot Area

The chart background and plot area are two important elements of a chart. The *background* contains all the other elements and can be formatted with a unique interior pattern and border. The background also controls the fonts used in the labels automatically applied by Excel. Likewise, the *plot area*, which is the area containing the plot points, can be formatted with a unique pattern and border. Figure 11.35 shows a chart with the background and plot area formatted.

To change one of these two chart elements, first select it by using the mouse or the arrow keys. Then choose the Format Patterns command. This command controls the border and interior of the highlighted element. Refer to table 11.1 for a list of the options available in the Format Patterns dialog box.

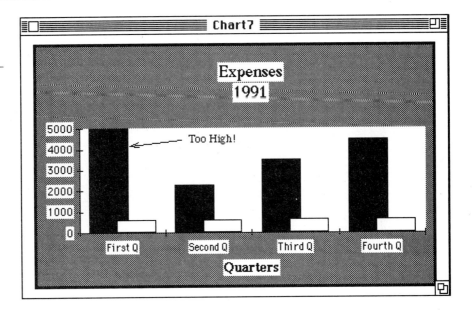

Fig. 11.35.

Formatting the background and plot area.

Remember that the background also controls the fonts used for the vertical-axis scale numbers and the horizontal-axis labels. To change the font of these labels, highlight the background and choose the Format Font command. Select the font, size, style, and color for the label text from the dialog box presented. You can also change these fonts independently by highlighting the axis and selecting the Format Font command.

Changing the Axes

Excel provides two important ways to customize the chart axes. You can change the appearance of an axis line, making it a different color or thickness; and you can change the axis values, making them fall within the range you specify. The following four commands affect the axes:

Chart Axes	Specifies the axes displayed on the chart
Format Scale	Changes the scale and tick marks on the axes
Format Patterns	Changes the line type used for the axes
Format Font	Changes the font of the axes labels

The following sections provide details about each of these commands.

Hiding and Displaying Axes

The Chart Axes command hides or displays the axes. Simply choose the Chart Axes command; the dialog box shown in figure 11.36 appears. Now you can check the boxes corresponding to the axes you want to display.

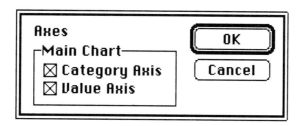

Fig. 11.36.

The Chart Axes dialog box.

Changing the Axis Scale

The Format Scale command controls many aspects of the chart axes and offers a different set of options for vertical (value) and horizontal (category) axes. To use this command, first use the keyboard or mouse to highlight the value or category axis you want to change. Then select the Format Scale command. If you highlight the value axis, the dialog box shown in figure 11.37 appears.

```
┌─────────────────────────────────────────────┐
│ Value Axis Scale            ╭──────────╮     │
│ Auto                        │    OK    │     │
│   ⊠  Minimum:    [0      ]   ╰──────────╯     │
│                             ( Cancel  )      │
│   ⊠  Maximum:    [5000   ]                   │
│                             ( Patterns... )  │
│   ⊠  Major Unit: [1000   ]                   │
│                             ( Font...  )     │
│   ⊠  Minor Unit: [200    ]                   │
│   Category Axis                              │
│   ⊠    Crosses at: [0     ]                  │
│   ☐ Logarithmic Scale                        │
│   ☐ Values in Reverse Order                  │
│   ☐ Category Axis Crosses at Maximum Value   │
└─────────────────────────────────────────────┘
```

Fig. 11.37.

The Format Scale dialog box for vertical axes.

On bar charts, the value axis is horizontal and the category axis is vertical—the opposite of most other charts.

Notice that most of the boxes under Auto are checked. This means that Excel controls these values. To customize the axis, enter your own minimum and maximum values into the spaces provided. In the Major Unit field, enter the number of divisions you want along the axis; in the Minor Unit field, enter the number of tick marks between these divisions. Figure 11.38 shows some examples of scale-option settings.

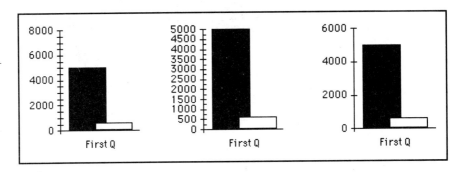

Fig. 11.38.

Some examples of charts with axis scales changed.

 The Format Scale command controls the upper and lower limits of the axis values and the number of divisions along the axis. However, it does not control the format of the tick marks, nor does it control whether the tick marks appear at all. Use the Format Patterns command to make these formatting determinations for the axis tick marks. See "Formatting the Axis Line" later in this chapter.

Table 11.3 lists the Format Scale options for value axes.

Table 11.3
The Format Scale Options for Value Axes

Option	Description
Minimum	Sets the minimum value of the axis scale. Values less than this minimum are not visible on the chart.
Maximum	Sets the maximum value of the axis scale. Values greater than this maximum are not visible on the chart.

Table 11.3—(continued)

Option	Description
Major Unit	Sets the number of "steps," or divisions, along the axis. Each division is labeled numerically. Enter a number corresponding to the step value you want. Using a value into which the maximum divides evenly is a good idea.
Minor Unit	Sets the number of tick marks between the major units. This number corresponds to the step value of the major-unit entry. Using a number into which the major-unit value divides evenly is best. The tick marks are not labeled.
Crosses at	Determines the horizontal position of the vertical axis; that is, where along the category axis this axis starts. Positioning the vertical axis is useful for emphasizing a particular value on the chart. When you use this feature on bar charts, the category and value axes are reversed.
	Normally, the category axis crosses the value axis at the bottom—which is usually zero. In this arrangement, negative plot points are drawn as columns extending below the category axis line. By moving the category axis, you can change the way the chart draws negative values. For example, making the category axis cross at 10 instead of 0 places below the line all plot points that are less than 10. Figure 11.39 shows an example of this change.
Logarithmic Scale	Changes the axis to a logarithmic scale.
Values in Reverse Order	Charts the values in reverse order (that is, with the highest value at the bottom and the lowest at the top).
Category Axis Crosses at Maximum Value	This option appears for scatter charts only. It makes the value axis cross the category axis at the last (maximum) value on the chart.

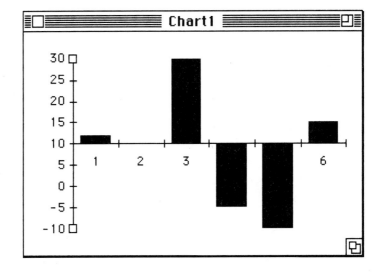

Fig. 11.39.

Making the category axis cross at a different value.

If you highlight the category axis before choosing the Format Scale command, the dialog box shown in figure 11.40 appears.

Fig. 11.40.

The Format Scale dialog box for category axes.

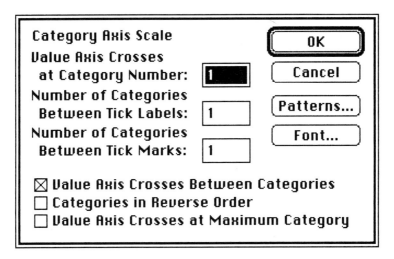

These options control the display of category-axis labels and the position of the axis. Table 11.4 lists the Format Scale options for category axes.

Table 11.4
The Format Scale Options for Category Axes

Option	Description
Value Axis Crosses at Category Number	Determines where on the value axis the category axis begins. Changing the position of the value axis can be useful for showing the current point in time on a graph. Consider the graph in figure 11.41, which places the vertical axis at the beginning of the second category to show that the current quarter is the second—the first quarter being "behind us." Note that the value axis labels have been removed in this example.
Number of Categories Between Tick Labels	Determines the number of category-axis labels that appear along the axis. By increasing the number of categories plotted between these labels, you effectively decrease the number of labels that can fit onto the axis. For example, increasing this number from 1 to 2 causes every other label to appear along the axis.
Number of Categories Between Tick Marks	Determines the number of tick marks that appear along the axis. This option is the same as Number of Categories Between Tick Labels but affects the tick *marks* instead of the *labels*. Being able to control the tick marks independently from the labels can be useful.
	You can use this option along with the preceding option to group categories into sets and label the sets as a unit. Using the example in figure 11.41, figure 11.42 shows how you can arrange the four quarters (categories) into two groups and label them each as half-year categories. Although you still have four categories in the graph, it appears that you have only two, because there is only one tick mark between sets. Note that the number of categories between tick labels is set to 2 on this graph and that the number of categories between tick marks is set to 2. The first and third category labels on the worksheet were changed from First Q and Third Q to First Half and Second Half.

Table 11.4—(continued)

Option	Description
Value Axis Crosses Between Categories	This option works with the Value Axis Crosses at Category Number option. When this box is checked, the value axis crosses the category axis *between* the category specified in the first option and the next category. When this box is not checked, the value axis crosses the category axis *in the middle of* the category. This option can be useful for area and scatter charts.
Categories in Reverse Order	Plots the axis labels and their respective data series in reverse order.
Value Axis Crosses at Maximum Category	This option appears for scatter charts and causes the value axis to cross the category axis at the maximum category.

Fig. 11.41.

Changing the position of the value axis.

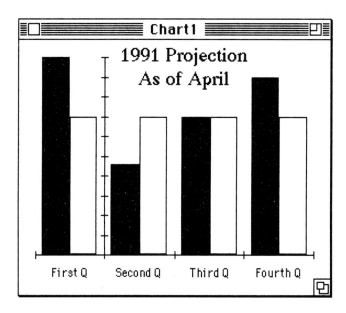

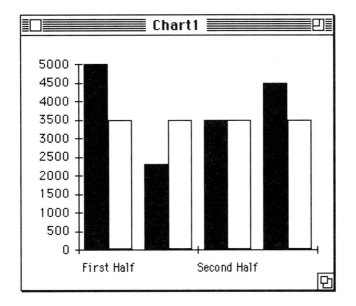

Fig. 11.42.

Changing the number of tick marks to arrange categories into groups.

Formatting the Axis Line

Using the Format Patterns command, you can change the pattern and thickness of the axis lines. To do so, highlight the horizontal or vertical axis and select Format Patterns. A dialog box appears, containing various patterns and line thicknesses (see fig. 11.43). Choose the appropriate options from this box.

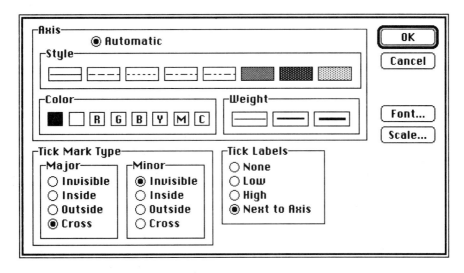

Fig. 11.43.

The Format Patterns dialog box for axis lines.

In addition to the standard pattern and line-thickness options, this dialog box contains options for formatting the tick marks and tick labels. You can place the major tick marks, minor tick marks, or both inside, outside, or on the axis line. You can also specify that the tick marks be invisible. Options for the labels determine where they appear relative to the axis line.

Formatting the Axis Labels

You can change the font, size, style, and color of the axis labels by using the Format Font command. (First, highlight the axis.) The familiar font dialog box appears for your selections. See table 11.2 for details about this dialog box. Note that the vertical axis labels cannot be changed— they are calculated according to the Format Scale settings. You can change the category axis labels by editing the series formula, as described in Chapter 12.

Adding and Moving Chart Arrows

To emphasize a specific message in a chart, or to direct a chart label to a specific element, use chart arrows. Adding and manipulating chart arrows is very much like adding and manipulating descriptive text. You can add as many arrows as you want and place them anywhere on the chart. You also can format chart arrows for various effects.

To add an arrow, activate the chart window and select the Chart Add Arrow command. An arrow appears in the chart. Use the mouse or keyboard to move the arrow into the proper position. Using the mouse, simply click on the arrow and drag it to a new location. If you use the keyboard, highlight the arrow, select the Format Move command, and use the arrow keys to move the arrow around the chart. Press Enter when finished.

You can enlarge an arrow by dragging the highlight squares that surround the arrow object. Alternatively, you can use the keyboard to enlarge the arrow: highlight the arrow, select the Format Size command, use the cursor-arrow keys to change the size of the arrow object, and press Enter when finished.

You can format the arrow itself with the Format Patterns command. When you highlight an arrow and select Format Patterns, the dialog box shown in figure 11.44 appears.

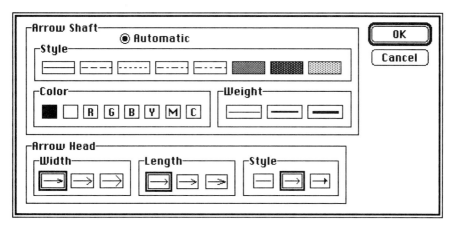

Fig. 11.44.

The Format
Patterns dialog box
for arrows.

Table 11.5 lists the options available for formatting the arrows used in a chart.

Table 11.5
The Format Patterns Options for Arrows

Option	Description
Arrow Shaft	
Style	Sets the style of the arrow line. Patterns are effective only when the line thickness can support the pattern.
Color	Sets the color of the arrow line.
Weight	Sets the thickness of the arrow line.
Arrow Head	
Width	Determines the width of the arrow head (that is, the distance between the edges).
Length	Determines the length of the arrow head (that is, the distance from the tip to the edges).
Style	Sets the arrow-head style.

Figure 11.45 shows some examples of arrows. Notice that these arrows have different shafts and heads (or no head at all).

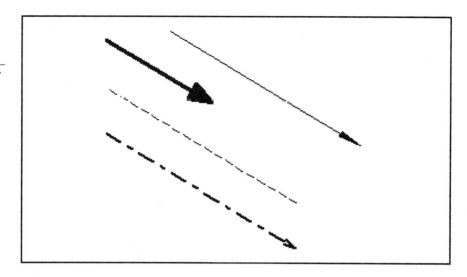

Fig. 11.45.

Examples of arrow formats.

Adding and Modifying Grid Lines

Adding grid lines to a chart is another simple enhancement you can make. Excel lets you add vertical and horizontal grid lines to any chart. In fact, Excel offers two types of vertical and two types of horizontal grid lines. *Major grid lines* extend from the major axis divisions; *minor grid lines* extend from the minor axis divisions. Figure 11.46 shows an example.

Fig. 11.46.

A chart with major and minor grid lines.

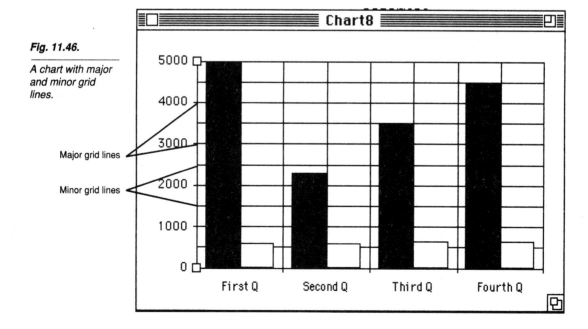

To add grid lines, select the Chart Gridlines command. The dialog box that appears presents major and minor grid lines for both axes. Check the appropriate boxes and press Return to add the lines.

After you add grid lines, you may want to change their color or pattern. You can format the category-axis grid lines independently of the value-axis grid lines. First, highlight the desired grid lines (either category or value). Using the mouse to highlight grid lines can be tricky. To avoid problems, click on one of the lines in the middle of the grid—as opposed to the lines at the edges of the chart—to ensure that you select the grid and not the plot area. A single vertical or horizontal grid line should be highlighted, as shown in figure 11.47.

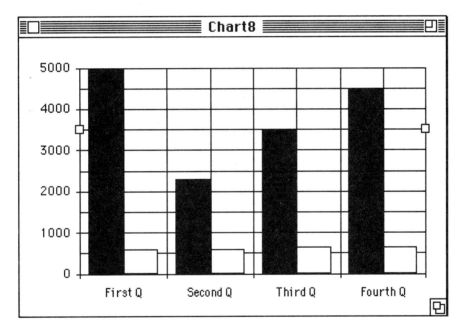

Fig. 11.47.

Highlighting a grid line.

When a grid line is highlighted, select the Format Patterns command. The dialog box shown in figure 11.48 appears. Select the desired options from this dialog box to change the pattern, color, and thickness of the lines. When you press Return, Excel applies the format to all the horizontal or vertical lines—depending on your selection. Major and minor grid lines are changed separately. Select a minor grid line to change all minor grid line patterns; select a major grid line to change all major grid line patterns.

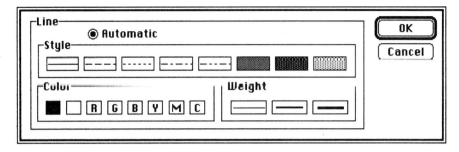

Fig. 11.48.

*The Format
Patterns dialog box
for grid lines.*

 Grid lines extend throughout the entire plot area but not beyond it.

Don't Start with a Plain Chart

Remember that you can select many predesigned, or built-in, charts from the Gallery menu. Customizing a chart does not mean just adding to one of these formats. You may want to start with one of the built-in charts and remove elements from or add elements to it. Working with a built-in chart may be faster than starting with a basic chart and adding the formats.

Changing Overall Chart Formats

The Format Main Chart command has the most dramatic effect on a chart because it affects the overall chart format, including stacking, overlapping plot points, changing the type of chart, and setting the angle denoting pie wedges. The built-in charts apply many of these options to the basic charts, but you may want to add these formats to a chart without selecting one of the built-in formats.

If you change an existing chart to a built-in format, all custom formatting is erased. However, if you add formats by using the Format Main Chart command, existing custom formats remain intact. When you select the Format Main Chart command, the dialog box shown in figure 11.49 appears.

Table 11.6 lists the options available from the Main Chart dialog box.

Format Main Chart

┌─Type─────────────────────────┐
│ ○ Area   ○ Bar   ◉ Column   │
│ ○ Line   ○ Pie   ○ Scatter │
└──────────────────────────────┘

[OK]

[Cancel]

┌─Format───────────────────────────────────┐
│ ☐ Stacked   ☐ 100%   │
│ ☐ Vary by Categories   ☐ Overlapped   │
│ ☐ Drop Lines   ☐ Hi-Lo Lines   │
│ % Overlap: [0]   % Cluster Spacing: [50] │
│ Angle of First Pie Slice (degrees): [0]   │
└──┘

Fig. 11.49.

The Main Chart
dialog box.

Table 11.6
The Main Chart Options

Option	*Description*
Type	Changes the type of chart without changing any custom formatting already applied. You may have to move unattached text after changing the chart type.
Stacked	Stacks the plot points on top of one another within each data series. Stacking is most useful for bar and column charts. Use this option in conjunction with the Overlapped and % Overlap options to make sure that the stacking is correct. (For example, to get normal stacking, you must check Stacked, check Overlapped, and enter 100 in the % Overlap field.)
Vary by Categories	Assigns a different pattern to each plot point when the chart includes only one data series. Normally, similar plot points have the same patterns and colors. When you use this option, you can change the pattern of each plot point individually by selecting it and using the Format Patterns command.
Drop Lines	Adds a vertical separator line between plot points of area and line charts. This option is useful when the points merge together, as in an area chart.

Table 11.6—(continued)

Option	Description
100%	Displays each data series as 100% and the plot points within the series as percentages of the total. This option should be used with the Stacked, Overlapped, and % Overlap options. In other words, first stack the chart as desired, then add this option and the other two options.
Overlapped	Overlaps the plot points within each series. Use this option with the % Overlap option to control the amount of overlap. When using this option in conjunction with the Stacked option, you probably will want to enter 100 as the % Overlap value.
Hi-Lo Lines	Adds lines that extend from the highest value to the lowest value in each series. To get vertical lines, you must also enter 100 in the % Overlap option and select Overlapped. This option is available for line charts only.
% Overlap	Determines the amount of overlap when the Overlapped option is selected.
% Cluster Spacing	Determines the amount of space between data series. The value you enter represents a percentage of the width of a column or bar.
Angle of First Pie Slice	Sets the angle of the first slice in a pie. An angle of 0% places the first slice vertically at the top of the pie. Angles are measured clockwise from the top of the pie.

Figures 11.50 through 11.53 show examples of some Main Chart options applied to a basic column chart. Figure 11.50 shows the basic chart. Figure 11.51 adds the stacking option with no overlap. Figure 11.52 adds 100% overlap to the chart in 11.51. Finally, figure 11.53 takes the normal chart and changes the cluster spacing to 350.

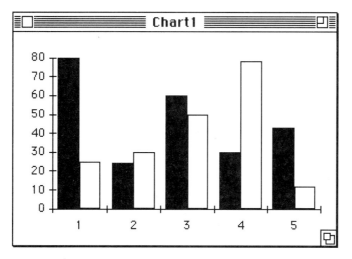

Fig. 11.50.

A standard
column chart.

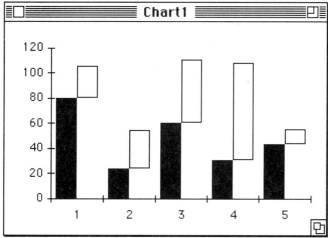

Fig. 11.51.

Adding the
stacked option.

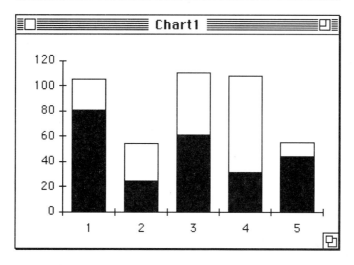

Fig. 11.52.

Adding 100%
overlap.

Fig. 11.53.

*Using cluster
opaoing.*

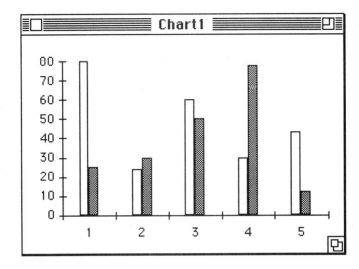

If you use any of these options to customize a chart and want to use the chart format again, set this chart as the preferred format by using the Format Set Preferred command. You also can move chart formats into other chart worksheets if you like. This procedure is described in the next chapter.

Printing Charts

Printing a chart is simple. Use the File Page Setup options to establish the page size, margins, and orientation. Then use the File Print command to print. For details about using the Page Setup and Print options, see Chapter 9.

One set of options is unique to printing charts: When you select the File Page Setup command with a chart window active, the three options Screen Size, Fit to Page, and Full Page appear at the bottom of the Page Setup dialog box.

The Screen Size option prints the chart to its exact screen size. Thus changes to the chart's window size and proportions will be reflected in the printout. The Fit to Page option prints the chart in a standard size that fits the page size you have set. The Full Page option fills the printed page with the chart—printing it as large as possible.

Summary

Charting is an important feature of Excel. In this chapter you discovered all the necessary steps for creating and customizing charts. You saw how Excel offers several preformatted charts that you can use or customize. In addition, the Chart and Format menus provide many commands for altering chart elements. The following are points to remember:

❑ The Gallery menu contains many preformatted charts that you can customize if you like.

❑ When you select a data range for charting, Excel uses rows as data series and columns as categories—unless there are more rows than columns. If there are more rows than columns, Excel uses columns as data series and rows as categories.

❑ You can change a chart's orientation by using the Paste Special command.

❑ If a chart window is opened without the associated worksheet, Excel offers to update the chart's references. This updating makes the chart current with the worksheet but does not automatically open the associated worksheet.

❑ If a chart and its worksheet are open at the same time, changes to the worksheet are reflected in the chart immediately.

❑ Chart legends contain the series labels—which are often contained in the first column of the data range. Use the Chart Add Legend command to create a legend.

❑ You can customize the patterns and colors used for the chart's series markers by selecting a marker and issuing the Format Patterns command.

❑ Chart text can be either attached or unattached. Unattached text can be moved around the chart freely.

For more details on charts, see Chapter 12, "Creating Advanced Charts."

12

Creating Advanced Charts

If you use Excel's charting capabilities often, you will eventually discover some problems that you will want to overcome. (This discovery might happen right away if you use combination charts.) This chapter discusses some advanced charting features and presents ways to overcome common problems. First, the chapter explains how to use combination charts and how to control the way those charts display data. Next, the chapter explains how to add and remove data from an existing chart without creating a new data range. (Another common need is to rearrange the data points in a chart.) Finally, the chapter shows you how to control the data referenced by a chart; this method lets you specify different data for the data items, category labels, and legend labels.

When you are finished with this chapter, you will be ready to try some special charting techniques described in the next chapter.

Using Combination Charts

A *combination chart* splits data items into two different types of charts. One combination chart may show quarterly sales totals as four columns and use a line to show last year's totals. Another combination chart might show data points in a scatter chart, with a line representing the trend or regression among the points. You can combine charts in several ways; Excel provides many formats for doing this. These formats appear in the Gallery Combination menu.

You can also create combination charts "manually" by using a series of commands and options. Building a combination chart manually gives you more control of the chart's format. This chapter will discuss the commands and options available for building custom combination charts.

Creating a Combination Chart

You can create a combination chart in two ways. One way is to choose one of the preformatted combination charts available through the Gallery Combination command. (Of course, you can then customize one of these charts however you like.) The other way is to start with any chart type and use the Chart Add Overlay command to turn it into a combination chart that splits the data items into two groups, one group for each type of chart.

When you use the Chart Add Overlay command, Excel automatically creates a line chart as the second chart type. You can, however, change the types of charts used in the combination. You can also format both types of charts by using the formatting options discussed in Chapter 11.

Creating a Combination Split

Although the name *combination* suggests two charts combined into one, combination charts are just one chart split into two charts. Some of the data items are represented by one type and the rest by another, but all items relate to the same categories. The chart in figure 12.1, for example, shows columns representing actual sales and a line representing projected sales. But all the data relates to the same four quarters. Thus the data comes from the same data range. As discussed later in this chapter, this distinction affects some types of combinations.

When you turn a regular chart into a combination chart (by using either the Gallery Combination command or the Chart Add Overlay command), Excel automatically splits the data items into two groups. For example, if you start with a standard column chart and turn it into a column-line combination, Excel displays half the original columns as lines. The original chart type (showing the first half of the items) is called the *main chart*, and the new type (showing the second half of the items) is called the *overlay chart*, which is on top of the main chart. If the chart has an odd number of items, the main chart gets the extra one.

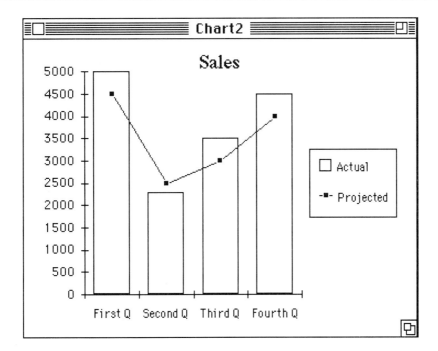

Fig. 12.1.

A combination chart is a single chart split into two types of charts.

By using the Format Overlay command after splitting the data, you can control the split of data, determining how many series are displayed in the main chart and how many in the overlay. This command produces the dialog box shown in figure 12.2. The option First Series in Overlay Chart controls where the split occurs. If a chart has 10 items (that is, 10 different series), entering 6 splits the chart in half (series 6 being the first one in the overlay chart); entering 10 specifies only the last item in the overlay chart; entering 9 specifies the last two; and so on.

You might wonder how to split the chart randomly. Perhaps you want one item from the middle of the chart used in the overlay. Although you cannot change the way in which Excel splits the chart, you can rearrange the items to get the desired ones in the overlay chart, and you do not have to rearrange the data in the worksheet data range to do this. See "Rearranging Chart Data" later in this chapter for complete details.

Changing Combination Chart Types

Excel uses a line chart as the default type for an overlay chart, but you can change the types used for both the main chart and the overlay chart. To change the overlay chart, select the Format Overlay command.

Fig. 12.2.

*The Format
Overlay dialog box.*

Format Overlay Chart

OK

Cancel

Type

○ Area   ○ Bar   ○ Column
◉ Line   ○ Pie   ○ Scatter

Format

☐ Stacked   ☐ 100%
☐ Vary by Categories ☐ Overlapped
☐ Drop Lines   ☐ Hi-Lo Lines

% Overlap: `0`   % Cluster Spacing: `50`

Angle of First Pie Slice (degrees): `0`

First Series in Overlay Chart: `2`
☒ **Automatic Series Distribution**

Next, select type and format options for the chart. These options are
explained in detail in Chapter 11. You can make the same changes to
the main chart by selecting the Format Main command. These options
(which are the same as the Format Overlay) affect only the main chart.

Using Stacked Charts in Combination Charts

Be careful in using stacked or 100 percent charts in combination charts,
because the resulting plot points may not represent the data accurately.
For example, the height of a stacked column chart would represent the
total value of items, but if some of those items were split into an overlay
chart, their values would still be figured into the stacked chart. This
situation would distort the height of the stacked columns and may not
be accurate.

Suppose that you want to display quarterly expense items in stacked
columns, with the expense totals for each quarter represented by the
height of each column. Now suppose that you want to display last year's
totals as a line in an overlay chart. Unfortunately, adding a data item with
last year's totals changes the heights of the stacked columns and the
distribution of data within each stack. The heights of the bars no longer

reflect "this year's totals" but "this year's plus last year's," even though last year's data is displayed in the overlay chart.

Remember that the overlay chart is always on top of the main chart. Thus if you use overlapping chart types, such as an area with a column, format the main chart as the area chart and the overlay chart as the column. Figures 12.3 and 12.4 show the difference.

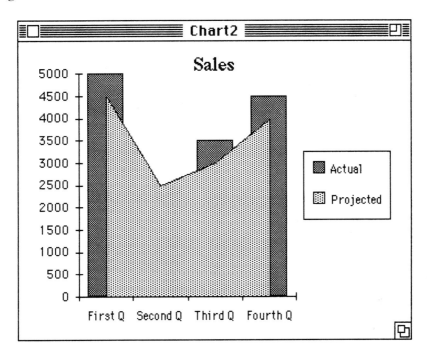

Fig. 12.3.

A combination chart in which the area chart is the overlay chart.

Make sure that the overlay chart uses a type that looks appropriate over the main chart.

Notice that in figure 12.4 the area chart begins and ends between the columns of the overlay chart. In other words, the area chart does not extend to the edges of the plot area. This is Excel's way of combining area charts with columns. Similarly, the lines in a line chart begin and end between columns in a combination chart. You might think that the chart would look better if the area or line started at the left edge of the plot area and ended at the right edge; unfortunately, there is no way to control this arrangement.

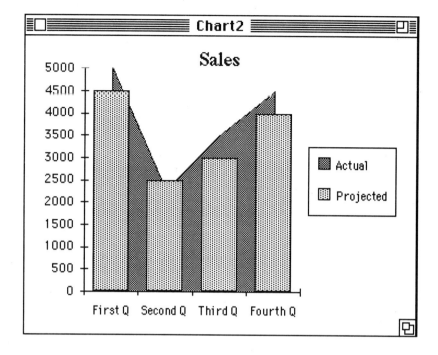

Fig. 12.4.

A combination chart in which the column chart is the overlay chart.

You can create some interesting combinations by using only column charts. The chart in figure 12.5 combines two column charts; the overlay chart contains all the data series but one. Because the main chart has only one data series, the four columns representing that series (that is, the first data series) are expanded to fit comfortably in the chart. The overlay chart was overlapped by 50 percent through the Format Overlay command, which provided the interesting overlapped approach, using the Jones and Smith data series.

Chapter 13 describes more techniques you can use to enhance your charts.

Deleting and Adding Chart Data

Although a chart is linked to its respective data range in a worksheet file, you can remove or add data without having to specify a new data range. If you decide to remove an item from the chart, simply delete it. If you want to add a new item, simply copy it. The next two sections provide details.

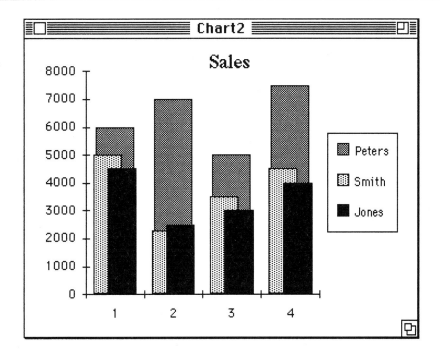

Fig. 12.5.

Using two column charts in a combination.

Deleting Chart Data

Deleting data from a chart is simple. Just remember that data points are grouped in series. One item may be represented by several columns or plot points, depending on the number of categories in the chart. When you remove a data item, you will be removing the entire series. The steps are these:

1. Click on the data series to select it. (You can click on any data point in the series you want.)

2. Press the Backspace key to remove the formula in the formula bar.

3. Press the Return key.

Deleting Data from a Chart

When you select a data item, its formula appears in the formula bar. Excel uses this formula to create the data item in the chart. By removing this formula, you essentially remove the item. See "Changing a Chart's Data Range" later in this chapter for more information about these formulas.

You can also delete all the data associated with a chart by selecting the chart, then selecting the Edit Clear command. Excel enables you to clear everything (All), just the format of the chart (Formats), or just the formulas creating the chart (Formulas). Clearing a chart's data can be useful for changing the orientation of the data and for creating blank formatted charts into which you can "copy" any data. Blank formatted charts are useful as templates for new data.

Adding Chart Data

Adding data to a chart is just as easy as deleting it; simply copy the data from the original worksheet, using the Edit Copy command. Although this data range does not have to be adjacent to the original data range, it should contain the same number of categories. After copying the information, activate the chart and use the Edit Paste command to paste the data into the chart. Excel will automatically create a new data series from the pasted data, adding a column, bar, or other appropriate point to the chart.

If the copied data range contains fewer categories than the others, Excel will add the extra series to the first few categories only. For example, if you copy a block of three data points to a chart that has four categories, Excel adds the extra series (column or bar) to the first three categories. The last category will thus have fewer bars than the others.

Figure 12.6 shows an example of copying a fourth data series into an existing chart. The fourth series is in the range A7:E7.

Fig. 12.6.

Copying data into an existing chart.

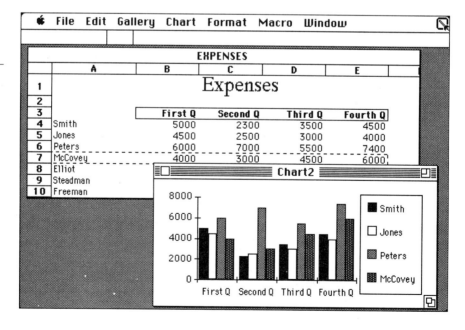

When you copy a new series into an existing chart, Excel places the series after the others. Thus if the chart is a combination type, the new item will appear in the overlay chart. Use the procedure described in the section "Rearranging Chart Data" to move the series to another position in the chart.

When you paste data into an existing chart, Excel assumes a particular order for the information. Often, the columns will be considered categories, and the rows will be new data series; this arrangement may fit properly with your existing chart. You can control the orientation of Excel's paste command by using the Edit Paste Special command in place of Edit Paste. When you use Edit Paste Special, the options shown in figure 12.7 appear.

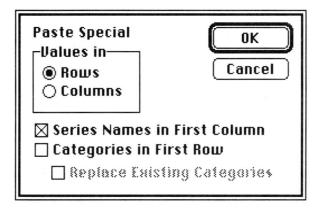

Fig. 12.7.

The Edit Paste Special dialog box.

Figure 12.7 shows the Edit Paste Special dialog box with the Rows button selected; figure 12.8 shows the dialog box with the Columns button selected. Selecting rows turns the columns of the data range into categories on the chart—rows become data series. Selecting the Columns button does the opposite.

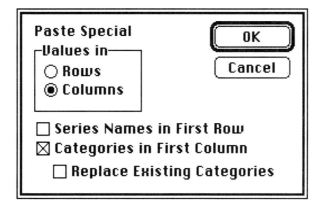

Fig. 12.8.

The dialog box with Columns selected.

Using the Paste Special command is probably necessary only when Excel is not pasting the new data properly. Perhaps you are expecting to add some new data series to the chart, and Excel is adding the data as new categories. This situation would result when the proportions of the copied data force a different orientation than expected. For more information on data proportions and chart orientation, see Chapter 11.

If Excel is pasting the data improperly, chances are that by choosing the opposite option in the Paste Special dialog box, you will correct the problem. In any case, these options let you control the arrangement of pasted information. The following is an explanation of the options:

Rows	Uses the rows of the pasted data as a new data series. Each column will produce a category.
Columns	Uses the columns of the pasted data as a new data series. Each row will produce a new category.
Series Names in First Column	This option appears when you select the Rows option. If your copied data includes labels in the first cell of each row, check this option. Excel will use the first cell of each row in the copied data (that is, the first column) as item labels for the legend. If your data selection does not include labels, do not check this box.
Categories in First Row	This option appears when you select the Rows option. If your copied data includes column headings to be used as new category labels, check this box. Otherwise, do not check this box; Excel will use the existing categories for the new data.
Series Names in First Row	This option appears when you select the Columns option, indicating that each column represents a new data item. Checking this box tells Excel to use the first cell in each column (that is, the first row of the selection) as the item labels for the legend. If the selection contains no labels, do not check this box.
Categories in First Column	This option appears when you select the Columns option, indicating that each column represents a new data item. If your selection includes labels in the first column, checking this box tells Excel to use those labels as category labels. If your data selection contains

no labels in the first column, do not check this box; Excel will leave the existing category labels intact.

Replace Existing Categories — Checking this option replaces the existing category labels with the new labels in your current selection. This option is available only when you have indicated that the data selection contains category labels.

Orienting chart data can be tricky. Experiment with these options to get comfortable with their effects.

Rearranging Chart Data

Rearranging chart data can be useful for several reasons. Most commonly, you may rearrange combination charts in order to display the desired data series in the overlay chart. You might want to change the order of wedges in a pie chart or the columns in a column chart as well. You do not have to change the order of data in the worksheet data range to accomplish this task; instead, make a simple change in the series formulas.

When you select a data series, such as a column or pie wedge, Excel displays the formula used to create that series in the formula bar. This formula may look confusing, but it consists of four simple arguments in a SERIES function:

    =SERIES(series_name,category_label_range,data_item_range,
      placement_in_chart)

The last argument in the function represents the placement of the data item in the chart and will be a number ranging from 1 to the number of data items in the chart. You can change the order of items by changing their *placement_in_chart* arguments. Simply edit the formula as you would any worksheet formula, placing the appropriate order number as the final argument. (Editing procedures are discussed in Chapter 4.)

When you change the placement of a data item, Excel rearranges the remaining items so that they assume the other positions. Therefore, it is a good idea to begin rearranging with the first item; that way, subsequent changes will not change the order you have already established.

Figure 12.9 shows a chart before the order of the items has been changed; figure 12.10 shows the same chart after the order of the items has been changed. Notice the change in the formula and in the columns.

Fig. 12.9.

A chart in which the order of the items will be changed.

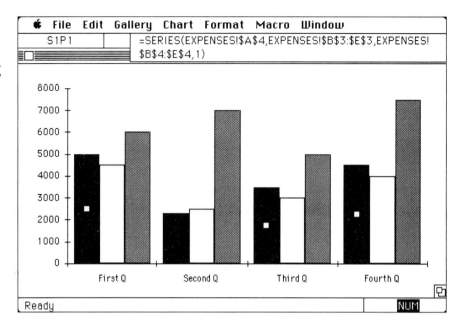

Fig. 12.10.

The same chart, with the items rearranged.

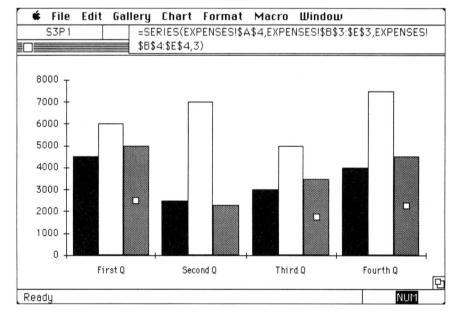

Notice that the series do not keep the same patterns after they are moved. You can change the patterns by using the Format Patterns command, described in Chapter 11.

Changing a Chart's Data Range

Series formulas enable you to control the data used in a chart. With a little knowledge of the arguments used in the formula, you can make all sorts of changes. For example, you can make a chart reference data from two worksheets, or you can change the category-axis titles used in the chart. You can also change the labels used for the chart's legend. Remember that the series formula uses the following format:

    =SERIES(series_name,category_label_range,data_item_range,
        placement_in_chart)

An example might look like this:

    =SERIES(EXPENSES!$A$2,EXPENSES!$B$1:$E$1,
        EXPENSES!$B$2:$E$2,1)

This formula indicates the following:

- The name of this data item (used in the legend) is located on the EXPENSES worksheet in cell A2.
- The range containing the category labels (used for the category axis) is B1:E1 on the EXPENSES worksheet.
- The range containing the values of this series is B2:E2 on the EXPENSES worksheet.
- This particular data series is the first in each category.

By changing various elements, you can control the data the chart uses. For example, you might want to use different labels for the category axis. Enter the new category labels into cells G1:G5 of the original worksheet and change the formula as follows:

    =SERIES(EXPENSES!$A$2,EXPENSES!$G$1:$G$5,
        EXPENSES!$B$2:$E$2,1)

Notice that the new range specified for the category labels contains the same number of cells as the old range. Unlike the old range, however, the new range is in a column rather than a row.

Another consideration for changing series formulas is changing the external cell and range references to range names. Thus the formula might read as follows:

    =SERIES(EXPENSES!Salaries_Title,EXPENSES!Headings,
        EXPENSES!Salaries,1)

The titles *Salaries_Title*, *Headings*, and *Salaries* represent the appropriate ranges in the worksheet. (Of course, you must apply these range names in the original worksheet before you use them in the chart's formulas.) The advantage to using names instead of cell and range references is that changes in the original worksheet will not affect the chart. You can add or remove cells, and the range names will not change.

Finally, you can use a constant value in the formula if you like. The most likely use for a constant value is as the *series_name* argument. This argument controls the label used in the legend:

=SERIES("Constant",EXPENSES!$G$1:$G$5,EXPENSES!$B$2:$E$2,1)

Be sure to place the constant value in quotation marks, as shown here.

Summary

Creating and manipulating combination charts can be tricky. The first part of this chapter discusses combination charts and how to customize them. The keys to combination charts are the command Format Main and Format Overlay, which control the appearance of the two "combined" charts. This chapter also shows how you can add data elements from a chart by using the copy and paste commands. The following are some points to remember:

❏ Combination charts are created out of standard charts. Use the Chart Add Overlay command to turn a normal chart into a combination chart. Alternatively, select one of the combination charts from the Gallery menu.

❏ Excel automatically splits the data series evenly between the overlay and main charts in the combination chart. You can change this split by using the First Series in Overlay option in the Format Overlay command. Excel always creates the main chart beginning with the first series.

❏ You can reposition the series in the chart by editing the series formula.

❏ Add data series to a chart by copying the data from the worksheet and pasting it into the chart. You can control the orientation of the new data by using the Edit Paste Special command instead of Edit Paste.

❏ By editing the series formula, you can customize the chart's category labels and series labels. You can also make the chart reference data from two or more worksheets.

See Chapter 13, "Using Presentation Graphics with Excel," for details on creating more-effective charts.

13

Using Presentation Graphics with Excel

Studies have found that values shown graphically are remembered over 60 percent longer than values shown as numbers. In business, charts do more than show information effectively: they make a statement about the presenter. With Excel, you have a powerful tool for creating presentation-quality charts.

This chapter discusses how to manipulate charts to produce creative, effective presentations. First the chapter offers three guidelines for creating effective charts, then it shows you several charts of varying complexity, all of which present information by using standard Excel charting features in bold and interesting ways. As the charts are explained, they will exemplify important principles for presentation graphics—principles you can apply to all charts—and you will learn techniques for getting more control over your charts. Because this chapter contains advanced information about Excel charts, the assumption is that you have completed the previous chapters in this part of the book.

Constructing Effective Business Charts

The next three sections discuss ways in which you can make your charts more attractive and therefore more effective. Each topic discusses one of the three basic rules for charting: First, keep the chart simple. Second, emphasize the message. Third, choose the right type of chart for your purpose.

Keeping Charts Simple

You can completely defeat the purpose of a chart by crowding it with too much information. Make sure that you have included only essential data. If you have more than three data series, consider whether using two or more charts would be better. Often, multiseries charts are best displayed as line or scatter charts. Try to limit charts to three or four series. If more series are required, consider the best chart type for the purpose. And use only as many labels as are necessary. Consider placing descriptive information outside the chart itself. Doing so will help free the chart from clutter. Figures 13.1 and 13.2 show two charts that present the same data. The less complex of the two, figure 13.2, is the more effective chart.

Fig. 13.1.

A sample chart.

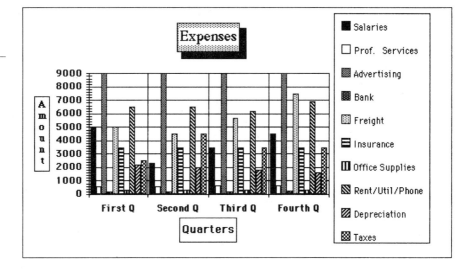

Fig. 13.2.

A less cluttered chart showing the same data.

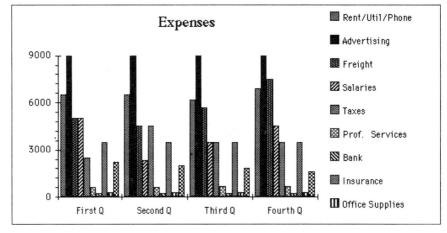

Another difference evident in figure 13.2 is the arrangement of the data series; the extremely tall columns are grouped together, which makes it easier on the eye to see the various columns. Unless a specific order is required, consider such a change in your complex column charts.

Avoid using too many series in a column chart. Comparing more than four can make the chart difficult to read. Consider, instead, creating pie charts to compare the series to one another, each category getting a separate pie. Then, to compare the performance of one category to the next, create a column chart that uses only the totals. This chart will have only one column (bar) and will effectively compare the category.

Categories also should be kept to a minimum. Seven or eight categories in one column chart, however, can still be effective (see fig. 13.3).

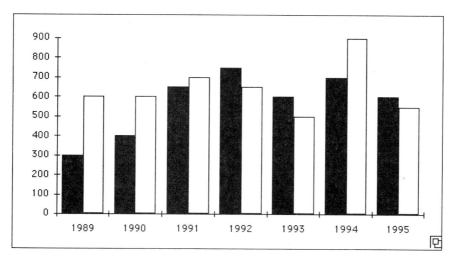

Fig. 13.3.

Column charts are best when showing changes in a few series over time.

When stacking a column chart, keep in mind that too many series confuse the stacking message. The point of a stacked column chart is to show how many parts make up the whole. Too many parts can make the chart difficult to look at. Figures 13.4 and 13.5 show stacked column charts.

Line charts look best with only a few lines. Bold lines against an understated background will present the data more effectively than a maze of grid lines and labels (see figs. 13.6 and 13.7).

Fig. 13.4.

A stacked column chart showing several series.

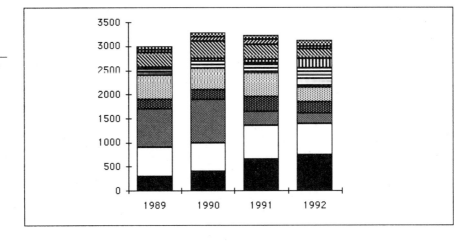

Fig. 13.5.

A stacked column chart showing only a few series.

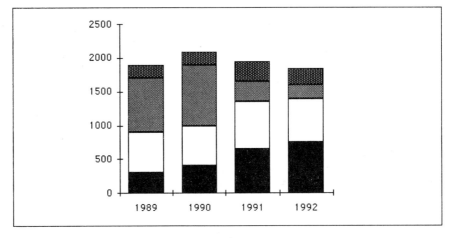

Fig. 13.6.

A sample line chart.

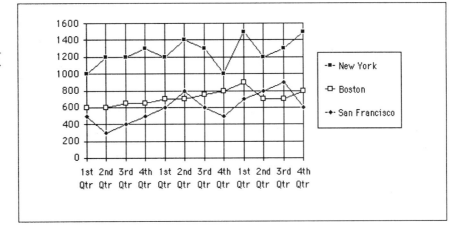

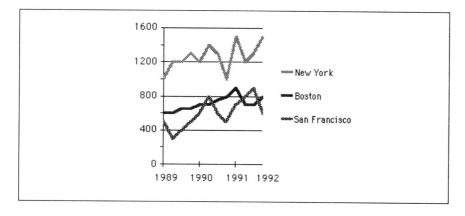

Fig. 13.7.

A less cluttered line chart showing the same data.

Emphasizing the Point

The second rule of creating effective charts is to emphasize the point. Charts are naturally more meaningful than numbers, but even the simplest charts can be ambiguous. The exact point you're making may not be clear from the chart. Consider the chart shown in figure 13.8.

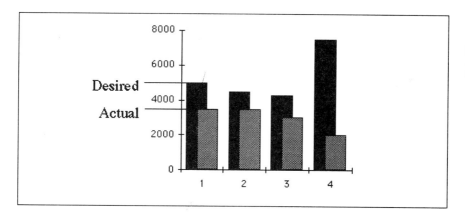

Fig. 13.8.

A simple bar chart.

The possible messages from this chart include the following:

- The actual amounts are significantly lower than the desired amounts.
- The fourth quarter reflects an unexpected market situation.
- Budgets and sales projections for next year must be revised.

Now consider the chart shown in figure.13.9. This chart uses the same data but emphasizes the intended message: that the fourth quarter reflects an unexpected market situation.

Fig. 13.9.

A bar chart that emphasizes the intended message.

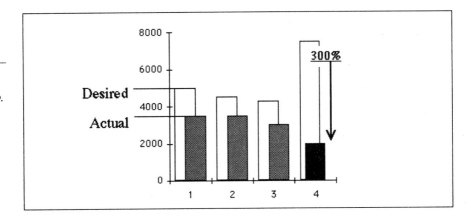

The bar chart in figure 13.9 emphasizes the difference in the fourth category of plot points in two ways: First, the text and arrow were added to explicitly explain the point of the chart. Second, the pattern of the Actual plot point in the fourth category was changed to solid black so that the fourth Actual plot point is different from the first three.

But you're not supposed to be able to change the patterns of plot points independently when you have more than one series in the chart. In other words, all plot points within the same series must have the same pattern. The only exception is when the chart contains only one series; the chart in figure 13.9 contains more than one.

The trick used to accomplish this feat was the addition of a third series to the chart. This series contained no values in the first three categories and the value 2000 in the fourth category. Next, the value in the fourth category of the second series (the Actual series) was erased (that is, erased from the worksheet data range). Finally, the third and fourth series were split onto an overlay chart and overlapped by 50 percent. If you look closely, you will notice that the solid black plot point is overlapped differently from the gray plot points—revealing that it's actually a different series made to look like part of the Actual series.

Emphasizing information on a pie chart can be as simple as exploding a wedge. One technique you might find useful is to match the patterns of all pie wedges except for the wedge you're emphasizing. Figure 13.10 shows an example.

You can emphasize certain trends in a line chart by changing the patterns and line thicknesses used for certain segments of the line. Do this by clicking on the appropriate segment and using the Format Patterns options. Figure 13.11 shows an example.

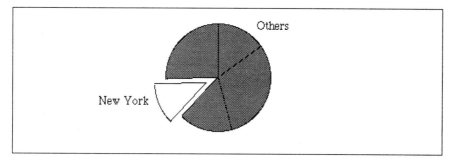

Fig. 13.10.

Emphasizing a particular wedge with shading.

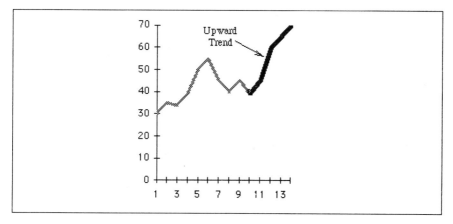

Fig. 13.11.

Emphasizing segments of a line chart.

Another technique used in this chart was the inclusion of more category labels than plot points. This technique shows how the chart reflects a trend that is continuing beyond the charted range of data.

Choosing the Right Chart

The third rule for constructing effective business charts is this: Choose the right chart for the data. Bar charts emphasize different aspects of the data than do area charts. Sometimes stacking a chart is the best thing to do. Other times, it's best to use several simple charts instead. The following sections explain which type of chart to use, as a general rule, for particular types of data.

Using Several Pie Charts To Compare Categories

Pie charts show only one category of data; they are used to compare series to one another and in relationship to the total. However, if you have to chart more than one category, you might find it useful to construct several pie charts—one for each category. Figure 13.12 shows an example that uses the same series over three categories (that is, three pies).

Fig. 13.12.

Showing several categories by using several pie charts.

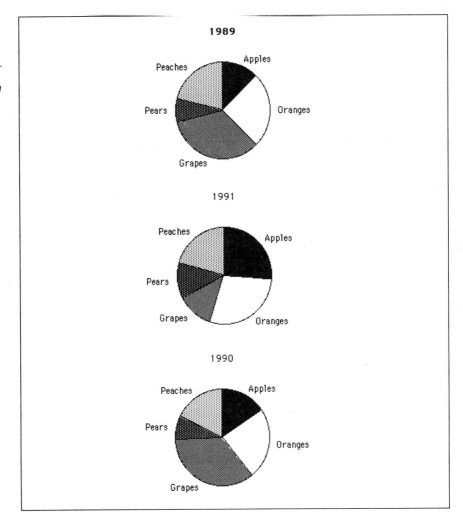

Although using several pie charts may serve the purpose, it can also confuse the message. The three pie charts in figure 13.12, for example, are all the same size, but the total volume represented by each pie is different. So these pies offer no information on how one pie compares to the next. You could fake a volume comparison by adjusting the overall size of each pie to reflect its volume compared to the others, as in figure 13.13.

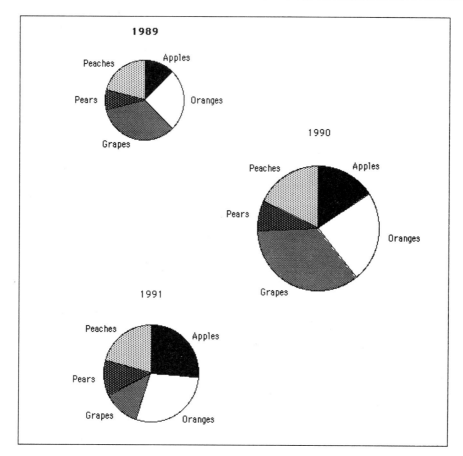

Fig. 13.13.

Pie charts adjusted for volume comparison.

If an approximation is good enough, this technique can be effective. You simply adjust the window size of each pie before printing, then use the Screen Size option in the Print Setup dialog box to retain the relative sizes. If you need a more accurate representation, consider a stacked column chart or stacked bar chart. Figure 13.14 shows the data charted as a stacked bar.

Using an Area Chart in Place of a Stacked Column

Stacked column charts can be effective for some situations, but when you begin to accumulate too many categories, consider using an area chart instead. Area charts are better at showing numerous categories. If you want to distinguish one category from another, add drop lines to the area chart.

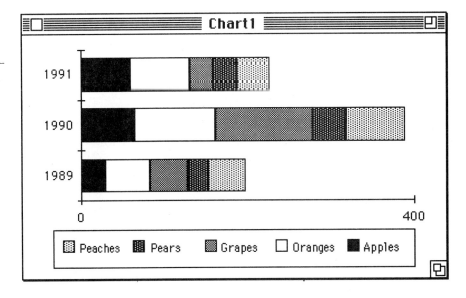

Fig. 13.14.

A stacked bar can be used instead of several pies.

Figures 13.15 and 13.16 show data charted with a stacked bar chart and an area chart. As you can see, stacked bar charts can often be clearer as area charts.

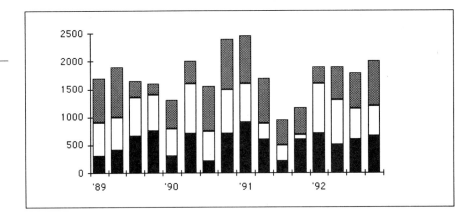

Fig. 13.15.

A stacked bar chart.

Looking at Sample Charts

The rest of this chapter shows a few sample charts that demonstrate specific Excel charting techniques. These charts are designed to show how you can stretch the limits of Excel's charting capabilities to create more effective charts.

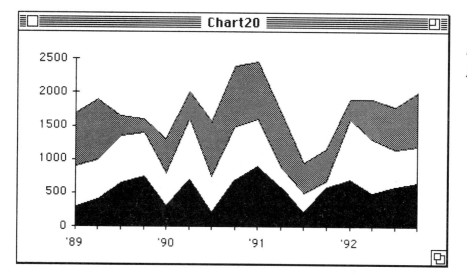

Fig. 13.16.

An area chart.

Customizing a Pie Chart

The standard format for legends and titles is not always the most interesting. The pie chart in figure 13.17 shows how these elements can be customized for more effective presentations.

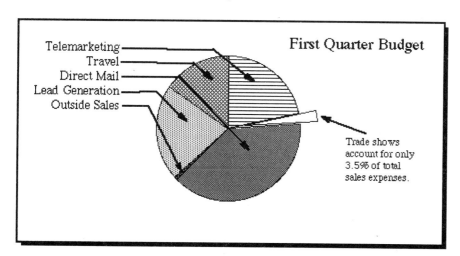

Fig. 13.17.

A pie chart with custom legend, title, and descriptive text.

Notice that the chart title is not centered above the chart in the usual position. The reason is that this title was created from a descriptive text box. Because pie charts automatically include titles, the standard title had to be removed. Rather than use the standard legend, this chart uses another box of descriptive text to duplicate the legend items. Lines connecting each item to the appropriate pie wedge are arrows with no points (two arrows for each line). These are the steps for creating this chart:

1. Create the worksheet shown in figure 13.18. Highlight the data range A3:B9 and create a new chart by using the File New command.

Fig. 13.18.

A worksheet for a
pie chart.

	A	B	C	D	E	F
			EXPENSES			
1			Sales			
2						
3		**First Q**	**Second Q**			
4	Telemarketing	1500	2000			
5	Travel	1000	1200			
6	Direct Mail	2800	3200			
7	Lead Generation	1500	1800			
8	Outside Sales	200	400			
9	Tradeshows	500	600			
11		$7,500	$9,200			
12						
13						

2. Select the Gallery Pie command and choose the first pie format.

3. Highlight the chart title and press Backspace to remove the text. Then press Return to remove the text box. The chart expands into the empty title area.

4. Click on the Trade Shows series—the wedge containing the white pattern (refer to fig. 13.17); then drag it away from the pie. This step creates the "exploded" pie.

5. Select the first wedge (shown in fig. 13.17 as Telemarketing) and change its pattern, using the Format Patterns command.

6. Select the last wedge (shown in fig. 13.17 as Travel) and change its pattern, using the Format Pattern command.

7. Click on the edge of the chart window to deselect the chart. Now type the title **First Quarter Budget** and press Return.

8. Use the Format Font command to change the font of this title (the font used in the figure is Times 18).

9. Drag the title into position at the right side of the chart, as shown in figure 13.17.

10. Create another descriptive text box containing the five budget items. Use Command+Return after each one to move to a new line.

11. With this text box highlighted, choose the Format Font command and set the font to Times 14. Next, click on the Text button in the Format Font dialog box to move to the Format Text dialog box.

12. Set the text alignment to Right. Press Return.

13. Select the Chart Add Arrow command to create the first arrow, then use Command+Y nine times to add nine more arrows. Since the arrows appear on top of one another, separate them, using the mouse. Figure 13.19 shows what the chart should look like at this point.

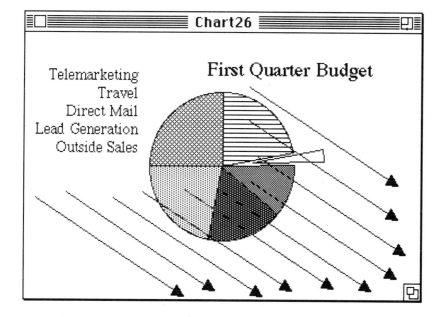

Fig. 13.19.

The pie chart so far.

14. Remove the arrow head from five of the arrows, using the Format Patterns command. Use this command to change the line thickness of all 10 arrows.

15. Place the five headless arrows horizontally at each of the five legend items. Then connect the five diagonal arrows to these.

16. Add the final text box and arrow at the right side of the chart.

17. Choose the Chart Select Chart command.

18. Select Format Patterns and check the shadow box to create the drop shadow. Select the thick border weight along with the first Style option. Press Return when finished.

The most difficult part of this process is to align the 10 arrows properly. Print the chart and make adjustments to the lines as needed.

Combining Chart Types Effectively

Combination charts can be direct and powerful graphic statements. But making the right combinations can be crucial. The chart shown in figure 13.20 is simple and effective, combining a column chart with a single line.

Fig. 13.20.

A simple combination chart.

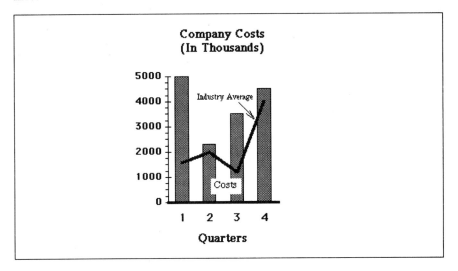

The chart is effective partly because it uses only two series. The line has been made extra thick through the use of the Format Patterns command, so that the line has as much importance as the bars. Because there are so few series to identify, callouts were used instead of a legend.

Notice that the series containing smaller values was used for the line. The line is more effective when it intersects the bars. The line uses the data in the second series of the chart range, as seen in the figure (this order can be changed, however). The following steps demonstrate how to apply some of the techniques used in this chart:

1. To scale the vertical axis, use the Format Scale command. The values of the axis are the following:

    Minimum = 0

    Maximum = 5000

    Major Divisions = 1000

    Minor Divisions = 250

    Use the Format Patterns command with the Tick Mark Type options to customize the tick marks of this axis. The Major tick marks use the Cross option; the Minor tick marks use the Outside option (see fig. 13.21).

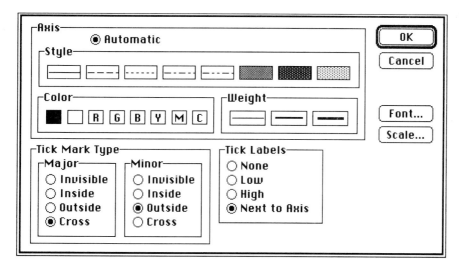

Fig. 13.21.

The tick mark options.

    To make the tick labels bold, highlight the vertical axis and press Command+Shift+B.

2. Remove the Major and Minor tick marks of the horizontal axis by using the Invisible options available through the Format Patterns command. Also, use Format Patterns to set the line thickness to "medium." Make the labels bold by highlighting the axis and pressing Command+Shift+B.

3. To set the patterns of the columns, highlight one of them and select the Format Patterns command. Then set the pattern and check the Apply to All box. Doing so applies the pattern to all the columns. Similarly, you set the line thickness by highlighting one segment of the line and

selecting the Format Patterns command with the Apply to All option. The thickness is set to "maximum."

4. Much of the effect of this chart comes from the dimensions of the chart window. This "tall and narrow" effect emphasizes the heights of the bars and the changes in the line. To add still more emphasis, use the Format Main Chart command with the % Cluster Spacing option set to 100. This step makes the bars narrower, so that they appear even taller.

Using Text in a Chart

At first you may think that Excel's charting capabilities are limited as far as text is concerned. Although you can create any text you like, you can position the text only within the chart area—which cannot be extended. In addition, attached text, such as titles and legends, can be moved only to Excel's established locations. The chart in figure 13.22, however, displays text outside the chart area, and the legend appears in a custom location.

Fig. 13.22.

A line chart with customized labels and text.

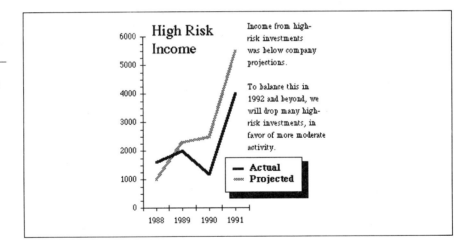

The following steps demonstrate how to apply some of the special techniques used in this chart:

1. Create the space on the right side of the chart by adding a legend with the Chart Add Legend command, then covering up the legend with a blank *unattached* text box. Create a blank text box by adding some unattached text in the usual way. Then format the interior (or area) of the

text box with the solid white pattern available from the Format Patterns dialog box. To get a solid white pattern, you might have to make the foreground white and the background black in the Format Patterns dialog box.

Enlarge the text box and position it to cover the entire legend. Remove any text in this box by highlighting it and pressing Backspace and then Return. (You must do this after formatting the pattern of the text box; otherwise, the box will disappear. In other words, an empty text box will remain on the chart if its pattern or border is not invisible.)

2. The large text block is simply another unattached text box moved into position. Manipulating text boxes containing this much text can be difficult, because every time you click on the box to move it, Excel displays the entire contents of the box in the formula bar (see fig. 13.23).

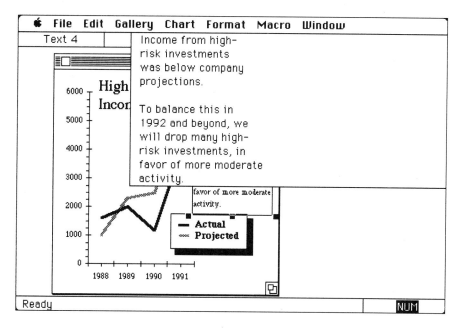

Fig. 13.23.

Manipulating large text boxes can be difficult.

Try moving the chart window down to avoid the large formula bar.

3. The legend is entirely custom-made and consists of four pieces:

- An empty text box formatted with a white interior and a shadow.

- A text box containing the two legend labels. This box has an invisible interior and border.

- A short arrow formatted with no head and a thickness and pattern that match those of one of the chart lines.
- Another short arrow with no head, formatted to match the other chart line.

These four elements should be created in the order listed above so that the elements are "on top of" the others in correct order. Of course, the background box (the first element) is sized and positioned as shown in the figure.

Faking legends like this can be a good way around limitations in legend formats. You might want to link the text in the custom legend box to the worksheet so that the legend accurately reflects the information in the sheet.

Using Text Boxes Creatively

The preceding example shows how you can format a blank text box to cover other elements in a chart or to create a custom background for other text. The uses for blank, formatted text boxes are numerous. Since you can control the size, border, and background of text boxes, you might try using them for legend items, as shown in figure 13.24.

Fig. 13.24.

Using blank, formatted text boxes as legend items.

As shown in the figure, this technique makes it possible to control the spacing of the legend items. Another blank text box is used as the background. However, if you eliminate the background, you can position legend items in creative ways (see fig. 13.25).

You can also use text boxes to create custom borders and shadows. Combine two or more text boxes for various effects. Figure 13.26 shows a few examples.

Consider some special uses for arrows. One idea is to use arrows (without heads) to thicken the lines in a line chart (see fig. 13.27). You can also attach arrows to the ends of the lines to extend the chart beyond the borders of the plot area (see 13.28).

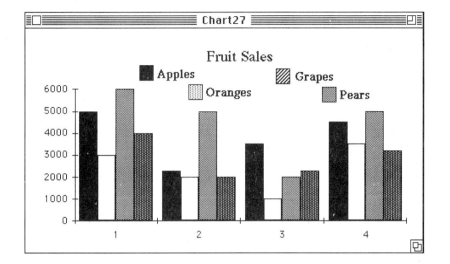

Fig. 13.25.

One idea for
custom legend
items.

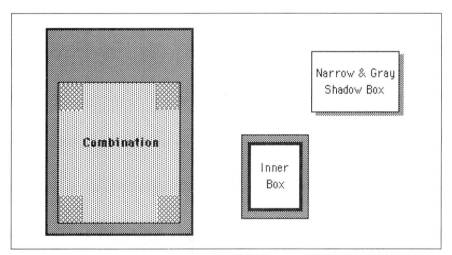

Fig. 13.26.

Some custom
boxes and borders.

Fig. 13.27.

Using arrows to thicken the lines in a line chart.

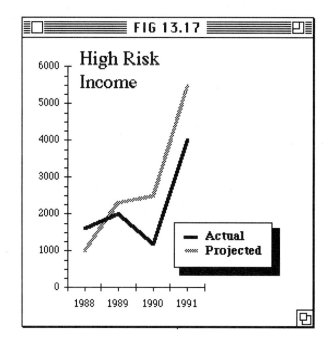

Fig. 13.28.

Using arrows to extend the chart.

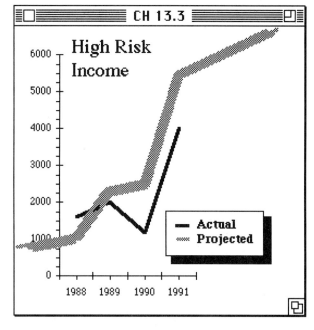

Summary

Excel's charting capabilities let you get creative with presentations. By using some of the special techniques described in this chapter, you can improve the effectiveness of your Excel charts. These techniques revolve around three main ideas: Keep your charts simple, emphasize the message, and use the right chart for the data. Other points to remember include these:

❑ Line charts look best with only a few lines (data series). Too many series can clutter the message.

❑ Use unattached text to "spell out" the messages of a chart. Use arrows to point to the key elements.

❑ You can adjust the sizes of several pie charts to show how their totals relate to one another.

❑ Area charts often serve the same purpose as stacked bar charts—and they can be more effective.

❑ You can use text boxes and arrows to create custom legends for your charts and thus overcome some of the limitations of built-in legends.

❑ Use attached text and the automatic legend features to create space around the chart. You can then "cover up" these elements with information of your own. Without the extra space these elements create, however, you are limited to creating text within the chart's borders.

Chapter 14, "Database Quick Start," begins the three-chapter section "Excel Databases."

Part III

Excel Databases

Database Quick Start

Getting Started with Databases

Using Advanced Database Techniques

14

Database
Quick Start

This chapter takes you on a brief but complete tour of Excel's database features. (A *database* is simply a collection of records, each of which may contain several pieces of information.) Using Excel as a database is really just an extension of using the worksheet. Any worksheet data can be treated as database data; the difference is that database information has been designated as such. This designation increases the number of features you can use on that data: besides being able to use all the standard worksheet commands and options on database data, you can use Excel's database options. These options are generally useful for routinely adding, changing, and locating data within the database.

In this chapter you will set up a simple database for an imaginary video rental store. You will then discover how to add new records to the database and find records by specifying criteria. Finally, you'll learn how to extract a list of records from the database. After reading this chapter, you will be ready for the details of database management, presented in the next chapter.

Entering Labels and Data

The first step in creating a database is to plan and enter the data. In Excel, databases must be set up so that records appear in worksheet rows. The data going across the row (that is, in the cells) makes up the record. A collection of rows full of data is a database. To create the Quick Start sample database, enter the heading for each piece of data that the records will contain (see fig. 14.1) and then enter the data. Complete the following steps:

1. Start Excel with a new worksheet, either by double-clicking on the Excel program icon or by using the File New command.

2. Move the pointer to cell A6 and type **Description**; then press the Tab key.

3. With the pointer in cell B6, type **Inv. No.** and press Tab again. Continue in this manner with the headings **Units Avail**, **Cost/ Unit**, **Total Value**, and **Purchased**. The resulting worksheet should look like figure 14.1.

Fig. 14.1.

A sample database with the column headings entered.

🍎	File	Edit	Formula	Format	Data	Options	Macro	Window

	F6			Purchased				

Worksheet1

	A	B	C	D	E	F	
1							
2							
3							
4							
5							
6	Description	Inv. No.	Units Avail	Cost/Unit	Total Value	Purchased	
7							
8							

4. Highlight the range A7:F11.

5. With the pointer in cell A7, enter the following data for row 7, pressing the Tab key after each entry:

> **Casablanca**
> **13378**
> **2**
> **35.5**
> **C7*D7**
> **1/15/85**

NOTE

After completing step 5, you may try skipping the values for column E in steps 6 through 9. If you do, use the Edit Copy Down command to copy the formula in cell E7 into the remaining cells of column E. See Chapter 3 for details about Copy Down.

6. Enter the following data for row 8, pressing the Tab key after each entry:

> **Batman**
> **22442**
> **15**
> **19.95**
> **C8*D8**
> **11/15/89**

7. Enter the following data for row 9, pressing the Tab key after each entry:

> **Wall Street**
> **14554**
> **5**
> **19.95**
> **C9*D9**
> **5/1/88**

8. Enter the following data for row 10, pressing the Tab key after each entry:

> **African Queen**
> **17459**
> **1**
> **45.95**
> **C10*D10**
> **1/15/88**

9. Enter the following data for row 11, pressing the Tab key after each entry:

> **Star Trek VI**
> **27789**
> **9**
> **24.95**
> **C11*D11**
> **3/1/91**

The worksheet should look like that in figure 14.2. Notice that each row represents a different video record.

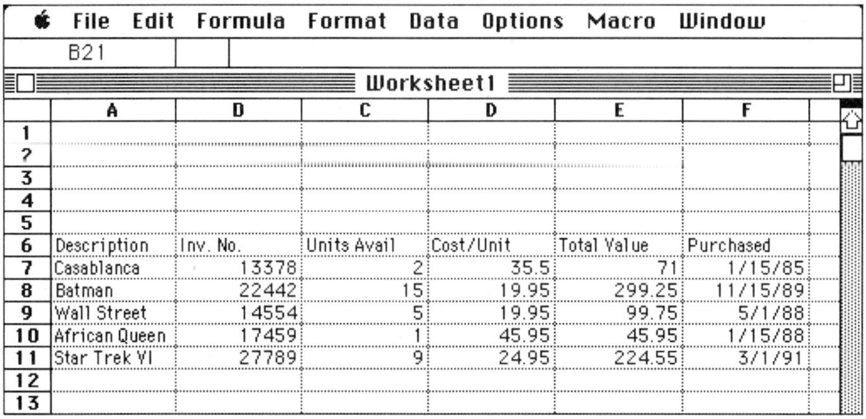

Fig. 14.2.

A sample database with data entered.

	A	B	C	D	E	F
1						
2						
3						
4						
5						
6	Description	Inv. No.	Units Avail	Cost/Unit	Total Value	Purchased
7	Casablanca	13378	2	35.5	71	1/15/85
8	Batman	22442	15	19.95	299.25	11/15/89
9	Wall Street	14554	5	19.95	99.75	5/1/88
10	African Queen	17459	1	45.95	45.95	1/15/88
11	Star Trek VI	27789	9	24.95	224.55	3/1/91
12						
13						

Defining the Database Range

Now that the data is in place in the appropriate range, the next step is to define that range as the *database range*. Defining the database range lets Excel know where the database exists on the worksheet. Once aware of the database range, Excel provides several special features that you can use on that data. Defining the database range in the sample database requires only two simple steps:

1. Highlight the range A6:F11, as shown in figure 14.3.
2. Choose the Data Set Database command. Doing so tells Excel that the selected range is a database.

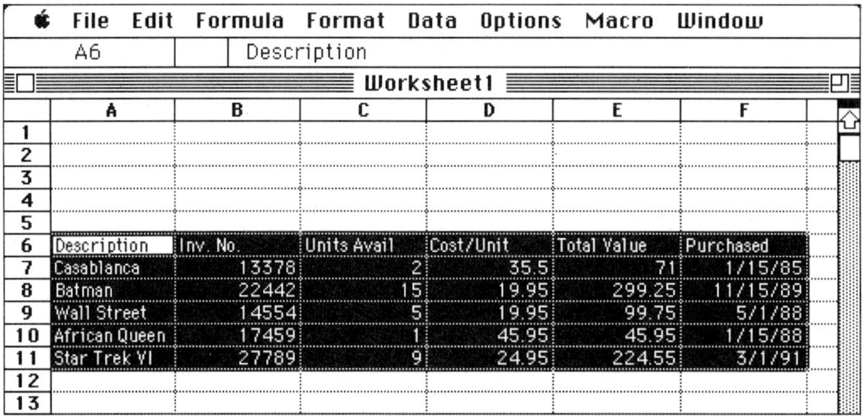

Fig. 14.3.

The selected database range, containing the records and headings.

	A	B	C	D	E	F
1						
2						
3						
4						
5						
6	Description	Inv. No.	Units Avail	Cost/Unit	Total Value	Purchased
7	Casablanca	13378	2	35.5	71	1/15/85
8	Batman	22442	15	19.95	299.25	11/15/89
9	Wall Street	14554	5	19.95	99.75	5/1/88
10	African Queen	17459	1	45.95	45.95	1/15/88
11	Star Trek VI	27789	9	24.95	224.55	3/1/91
12						
13						

> ### Adding a Blank Row to the Bottom of the Database Range
>
> Including an extra, blank row at the bottom of the database range is good practice. Doing so lets you add new records at the bottom of the others, rather than in the middle. This procedure will become more clear as you complete the next few sections.

Once you set the database range, Excel applies the name *Database* to the range. This name appears with all other defined range names when you use the Formula Define Name command. Because only one range can have the name Database at any given time, you can have only one active database per worksheet. However, you can always apply the name to some other range and switch from one active database to another. Simply use the Data Set Database command on the new range.

Adding Records

You can add records to the database any time after your database is established and the range is set. Excel provides two ways to add records to a database. The first method is to insert rows into the middle of the data and to then insert new information into the rows. The second method is to use the automatic data form. When you add records through either of these methods, Excel expands the database range to include the new information.

Inserting Rows

If you choose to insert rows into the database range, you can insert them anywhere but at the bottom of the database (that is, anywhere but below the last record). This area may seem the most likely place to insert new records, but inserting at the bottom will not expand the database range to include the new rows (unless you add a blank row as described in the preceding tip). The following is the proper procedure for adding records by inserting rows:

1. Highlight a row within the database range. The row can be any database row containing a record. Be sure to highlight the entire row by clicking the mouse on the row number on the left side of the screen. To insert more than one new record, highlight more than one row (that is, highlight as many rows

as you would like to insert). Figure 14.4 shows an example of inserting two rows; try matching this example.

2. Select the Edit Insert command. The familiar Insert dialog box appears. Select the Shift Cells Down option from this box; then press Return. Figure 14.5 shows the result of inserting two rows into the sample database.

3. Fill in the new rows with the appropriate information. (For the sample database, fill in any sample information—for instance, the titles *Raiders* and *Rocky 22* with accompanying data.)

Fig. 14.4.

Highlighting rows before inserting new ones.

	File	Edit	Formula	Format	Data	Options	Macro	Window

A8   Batman

Worksheet1

	A	B	C	D	E	F
1						
2						
3						
4						
5						
6	Description	Inv. No.	Units Avail	Cost/Unit	Total Value	Purchased
7	Casablanca	13378	2	35.5	71	1/15/85
8	Batman	22442	15	19.95	299.25	11/15/89
9	Wall Street	14554	5	19.95	99.75	5/1/88
10	African Queen	17459	1	45.95	45.95	1/15/88
11	Star Trek VI	27789	9	24.95	224.55	3/1/91
12						
13						

Fig. 14.5.

The inserted rows.

	File	Edit	Formula	Format	Data	Options	Macro	Window

A8

Worksheet1

	A	B	C	D	E	F
1						
2						
3						
4						
5						
6	Description	Inv. No.	Units Avail	Cost/Unit	Total Value	Purchased
7	Casablanca	13378	2	35.5	71	1/15/85
8						
9						
10	Batman	22442	15	19.95	299.25	11/15/89
11	Wall Street	14554	5	19.95	99.75	5/1/88
12	African Queen	17459	1	45.95	45.95	1/15/88
13	Star Trek VI	27789	9	24.95	224.55	3/1/91
14						
15						

Using the Data Form

The second way to insert records into the database is to use the *data form*, a special window containing the names of all the fields in the database and spaces for your new information. When you insert a record this way, Excel takes care of inserting it into the database and expanding the database range. The following is the procedure:

1. Select the command Data Form. Excel presents the data form, as shown in figure 14.6.

2. Click on the New button.

3. Enter the new information for each field of the new record. Press the Tab key after making each entry on the form. (For the sample database, enter any sample information.)

4. When the form is completely filled out, click on the New button again to insert another record.

5. When you finish entering the last new record, don't click on New to get another new screen. Instead, just click on the Exit button or click in the close box of the data form window. Doing so returns you to the worksheet and enters the last record.

```
┌─────────────────────────────────────────────┐
│ ▤□▤▤▤▤▤ Worksheet1 ▤▤▤▤▤▤                   │
├─────────────────────────────────────────────┤
│                                    1 of 5    │
│ Description: Casablanca  ⇧                   │
│                             ┌─ New ─┐        │
│ Inv. No.:   13378           └───────┘        │
│                             ┌ Delete ┐       │
│ Units Avail: 2              └────────┘       │
│                             ┌ Restore ┐      │
│ Cost/Unit:  35.5            └────────┘       │
│                             ┌ Find Prev ┐    │
│ Total Value: 71             └──────────┘     │
│                             ┌ Find Next ┐    │
│ Purchased: 1/15/1985        └──────────┘     │
│                             ┌ Criteria ┐     │
│                        ⇩    └─────────┘      │
│                             ┌─ Exit ─┐       │
│                             └───────┘        │
└─────────────────────────────────────────────┘
```

Fig. 14.6.

The data form.

Notice that the data form inserts new records at the end of the database. Nevertheless, the database range has been expanded to account for these new records.

Finding Information in the Database

One of the features of a database is that you can use complex searches to find records. The more records you accumulate, the more useful this feature becomes. Using search criteria, you can find all records matching specific information, such as all records for Jane Doe. You can use comparison operators to find particular records such as those with a total less than 125. The more specific the criteria, the fewer records will match. Thus you can find a specific record more quickly by entering as much information as possible about it.

There are two ways to find information in a database. The first is to establish a *criteria range*, which contains the search criteria used to locate records in the database. The second method is to use the data form. Because this chapter provides only an overview of database operations, it offers an identical example for each method. In Chapter 15, however, you'll discover some advantages and disadvantages to each method.

Using a Criteria Range

The criteria range contains a copy of each database heading and contains criteria specifications beneath those headings. To establish a criteria range for the sample database, first copy the database headings by completing the following steps:

1. Highlight the range A6:F6.
2. Select the Edit Copy command.
3. Move the pointer to cell A1.
4. Select the Edit Paste command.

A duplicate of the headings should appear in the range A1:F1, as shown in figure 14.7. In this example, the criteria range is placed above the database range, with a few extra rows to spare. This is a good practice for setting up the two ranges, because it keeps them together. In addition, if the criteria range is below the database range, the criteria range will move down each time you add a record to the database. The criteria range headings can appear anywhere on the worksheet, however.

	File	**Edit**	**Formula**	**Format**	**Data**	**Options**	**Macro**	**Window**

A1 | Description

Worksheet1

	A	B	C	D	E	F
1	Description	Inv. No.	Units Avail	Cost/Unit	Total Value	Purchased
2						
3						
4						
5						
6	Description	Inv. No.	Units Avail	Cost/Unit	Total Value	Purchased
7	Casablanca	13378	2	35.5	71	1/15/85
8	Batman	22442	15	19.95	299.25	11/15/89
9	Wall Street	14554	5	19.95	99.75	5/1/88
10	African Queen	17459	1	45.95	45.95	1/15/88
11	Star Trek VI	27789	9	24.95	224.55	3/1/91
12	Rocky 22	56778	20	19.95	399	11/1/93
13	Raiders	11235	10	19.95	199.5	2/5/87
14						
15						

Fig. 14.7.

To establish the criteria range, first copy the headings.

The next step is to tell Excel where the criteria range is located. Do so by highlighting the range that consists of the headings, plus the row below them. Complete the following steps:

1. Highlight the range A1:F2.
2. Select the Data Set Criteria command.

Now that the database range and criteria range are defined, you can perform database searches by entering criteria formulas into the bottom row of the criteria range. A database search will locate all records that match the criteria. For example, you can locate all video tapes that cost $19.95 or all titles for which you have fewer than 10 copies and that also cost less than $20. Complete these steps to search for all tapes that cost $19.95:

1. Move the pointer to cell D2, which is directly under the Cost/Unit heading in the criteria range.
2. Type the search formula **19.95** and press Return or Enter when finished.
3. Select the Data Find command to find the first matching record, which is shown in figure 14.8.
4. Press the down-arrow key to view the next matching record or the up-arrow key to find the preceding matching record.
5. When you have finished viewing the matching records, select the Data Exit Find command.

Fig. 14.8.

The first matching record: Batman.

	A	**B**	**C**	**D**	**E**	**F**
6	Description	Inv. No.	Units Avail	Cost/Unit	Total Value	Purchased
7	Casablanca	13378	2	35.5	71	1/15/85
8	Batman	22442	15	19.95	299.25	11/15/00
9	Wall Street	14554	5	19.95	99.75	5/1/88
10	African Queen	17459	1	45.95	45.95	1/15/88
11	Star Trek VI	27789	9	24.95	224.55	3/1/91
12	Rocky 22	56778	20	19.95	399	11/1/93
13	Raiders	11235	10	19.95	199.5	2/5/87
14						
15						

Be sure to remove the criteria formula before you establish the next criteria formula. Remove the formula by moving the pointer to cell D2 and pressing Command+B; then press Enter to clear the data.

Complete the following steps to search for tapes that cost less than $20 and for which there are fewer than 10 copies:

1. Move the pointer to cell C2, which is directly under the heading Units Avail in the criteria range.
2. Type the search formula **<10**. Press Return or Enter.
3. Move the pointer to cell D2.
4. Type the search formula **<20**. Press Return or Enter.
5. Select the Data Find command to find a matching record, shown in figure 14.9.

Fig. 14.9.

The matching record: Wall Street.

	A	**B**	**C**	**D**	**E**	**F**
6	Description	Inv. No.	Units Avail	Cost/Unit	Total Value	Purchased
7	Casablanca	13378	2	35.5	71	1/15/85
8	Batman	22442	15	19.95	299.25	11/15/89
9	Wall Street	14554	5	19.95	99.75	5/1/88
10	African Queen	17459	1	45.95	45.95	1/15/88
11	Star Trek VI	27789	9	24.95	224.55	3/1/91
12	Rocky 22	56778	20	19.95	399	11/1/93
13	Raiders	11235	10	19.95	199.5	2/5/87
14						
15						

6. Press the down-arrow key to view the next matching record or the up-arrow key to find the preceding matching record. (Only one record matches in this example.)
7. When you have finished viewing the matching records, select the Data Exit Find command.

You can continue to enter criteria formulas in this manner. Be sure to clear the old formulas before entering new ones. Also, make sure that you enter the formula in the related column of the criteria range.

Using the Data Form

The data form provides a simple way to find records in the database. If you use the data form, you do not need to establish a criteria range as described earlier. If you have already defined a criteria range, however, it will not interfere with the data form search: the two methods are independent of each other. Complete the following steps to use the data form to search for tapes that cost less than $20 and for which there are fewer than 10 copies:

1. Select the Data Form command.
2. Press Tab until you reach the Units Avail field.
3. Enter the criterion **<10**.
4. Press Tab until you reach the Cost/Unit field.
5. Enter the criterion **<20**.
6. Click on the Find Next button. Doing so locates the first record. Click on Find Next again to find the next matching record, or click on Find Prev to find the preceding matching record.
7. Click on the Exit button.

Extracting Records

If you removed the search criteria specified in the last set of steps in the section "Using a Criteria Range," go back through the procedure to enter the criteria again. In this section you will use the same criteria for extracting data. Data extraction is very much like searching, but in the former process, matching records are duplicated in an established area of the worksheet. You can use data extraction to print lists of matching records.

Using the sample database, suppose that you want to circulate a list of all tapes that cost less than $20 and for which you have fewer than 10 copies. Complete these steps:

1. Move to cell A16 below the database range and enter **Description**. Then move to cell B16 and enter **Units Avail**. These two fields represent the data that will appear in the

extracted list. As you can see, the extracted list does not have to include all the headings.

2. Highlight the extract headings (cells A16 and B16) and then select the Data Extract command; press Return at the dialog box. All matching records will appear beneath the extract headings. Remember, these records match the criteria you entered into the criteria range. Figure 14.10 shows the results.

Fig. 14.10.

Extracted data from the database range.

	File	**Edit**	**Formula**	**Format**	**Data**	**Options**	**Macro**	**Window**
A16			Description					

Worksheet1

	A	B	C	D	E	F
1	Description	Inv. No.	Units Avail	Cost/Unit	Total Value	Purchased
2			<10	<20		
3						
4						
5						
6	Description	Inv. No.	Units Avail	Cost/Unit	Total Value	Purchased
7	Casablanca	13378	2	35.5	71	1/15/85
8	Batman	22442	15	19.95	299.25	11/15/89
9	Wall Street	14554	5	19.95	99.75	5/1/88
10	African Queen	17459	1	45.95	45.95	1/15/88
11	Star Trek VI	27789	9	24.95	224.55	3/1/91
12	Rocky 22	56778	20	19.95	399	11/1/93
13	Raiders	11235	10	19.95	199.5	2/5/87
14						
15						
16	Description	Units Avail				
17	Wall Street	5				
18						
19						

Ready

Place the Extract Range in the Proper Place

The extract procedure erases all information below the extracted records. In other words, after the data is extracted and placed in the extract range, all data below the range is removed. Be sure to place the extract range at the bottom of the worksheet.

Sorting the Database

You may find it useful to sort the database from time to time. Not only will sorting the database make the data easier to examine, but extracted data will appear sorted. Complete the following steps to sort the sample database alphabetically by movie title:

1. Highlight the entire database range, excluding the column headings (that is, highlight the range A7:F13).

2. If the pointer is not already in the first column (column A), press the Tab key until the pointer *is* in column A. The range should still be highlighted.

3. Select the Data Sort command. The dialog box shown in figure 14.11 appears.

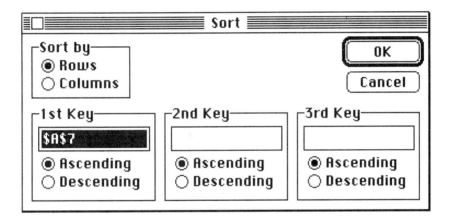

Fig. 14.11.

The Sort dialog box.

Notice that the active cell is automatically entered into the first-key (1st Key) box. The first key determines which column will be sorted. You can specify the column by entering the address of any cell contained in the desired column. If you enter C10, for example, Excel will sort the database by Units Avail. In this case, the cell address is already entered for the Description column.

4. After specifying the sort column you want, press Return. The data will be sorted as shown in figure 14.12.

You can re-sort the data by using other headings. Just use the preceding steps as a guideline.

Fig. 14.12.

The database after being sorted by description.

```
 🍎  File  Edit  Formula  Format  Data  Options  Macro  Window
        D18
╔══════════════════════ Worksheet1 ══════════════════════╗
        A              B           C           D           E           F
1   Description     Inv. No.    Units Avail  Cost/Unit   Total Value  Purchased
2                               <10          <20
3
4
5
6   Description     Inv. No.    Units Avail  Cost/Unit   Total Value  Purchased
7   African Queen      17459          1         45.95       45.95      1/15/88
8   Batman             22442         15         19.95      299.25     11/15/89
9   Casablanca         13378          2         35.5        71         1/15/85
10  Raiders            11235         10         19.95      199.5       2/5/87
11  Rocky 22           56778         20         19.95      399        11/1/93
12  Star Trek VI       27789          9         24.95      224.55      3/1/91
13  Wall Street        14554          5         19.95       99.75      5/1/88
14
15
16  Description     Units Avail
17  Wall Street         5
18
19
Ready
```

Saving the Database

Although this database will not be used in the next Quick Start lesson (Chapter 17, "Macro Quick Start"), you may want to save it so that you can experiment with database manipulation. As you read through the next chapter, you can use this database to try out the commands and options presented.

Summary

This chapter introduced the database features of Excel by providing a step-by-step application. You saw how to set up a worksheet database, including the database range, criteria range, and extract range. The chapter also discussed how to insert and remove records from the database and explained how to enter search criteria for record location and extraction. Finally, you saw the basic steps for sorting worksheet information, using up to three key fields. For more details on databases, see Chapter 15, "Getting Started with Databases."

15

Getting Started with Databases

You can use the Excel worksheet as a database for such data management tasks as searching, sorting, and reporting information. Database management in Excel is useful in accounting applications and custom business applications, but you also can use database features to create simple address lists and inventory lists. The Excel database is fast and easy to use, and the fact that it provides powerful worksheet math capabilities gives it an advantage over traditional database products.

An Excel database is really just part of the worksheet; database information is entered into worksheet rows and columns. These rows and columns, however, are specifically dedicated to holding database information. In designating rows and columns as a database, you gain access to features not available to other worksheet data. This chapter explains those features, first discussing database structure and then describing how to set up an Excel database, enter data, sort the database, and find information in the database.

Understanding Database Structure

A *database* is a place where information is stored in some regular order. The order in which the information is stored makes finding particular pieces of information easy. Consider a filing cabinet that contains information in alphabetical order. To find a particular file or record, you simply search under the appropriate letter in the alphabet.

481

Some databases, including most computerized databases, are even more structured, including data entry "forms" that ensure that every item of data can be found in the same place within each record. The card catalog in a library, for example, contains thousands of cards (records) within the file (database). Each card is organized the same way: the data items (fields) appear in the same spot on each card. When you flip through the catalog for an author's name, your eyes do not have to roam the cards to find the line containing the name (see fig. 15.1).

Fig. 15.1.

A typical card catalog record.

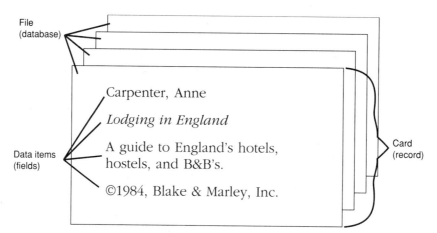

The card catalog in a library is not very flexible. The author index is sorted by authors' names. If you want to search for a book's title, you need to search the title index, which is a completely different database even though it contains the same data. In a computerized version of the author index, you could re-sort the records by title, subject, page count, or anything else contained on the cards. You would not need more than one copy of the data.

Finding information in a database is a matter of determining what information you already know and then sorting the data by that piece of information. It's easy to find a known piece of information when the records are sorted by that piece. Thus the card catalog is sorted by author, title, and subject—the three pieces of information you are most likely to know about a book. A computerized database lets you re-sort the data at any time, by any piece of information within the database.

The Excel database stores information in rows and columns. Each row contains a *record* (the equivalent of a card in a card catalog). In each cell of the row, or record, is a piece of information (the equivalent of data on the card). The cells are called *fields*. The column headings, or *field names*, indicate what every piece of information is (see fig. 15.2).

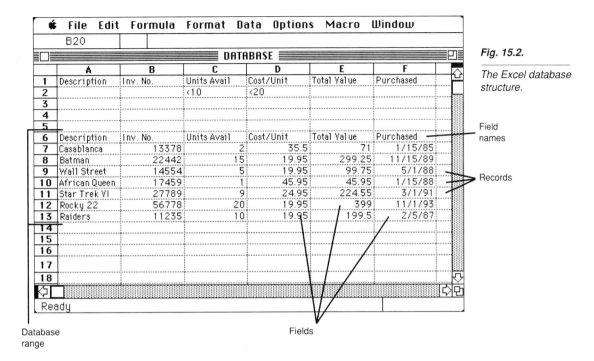

Fig. 15.2.

The Excel database structure.

The following is a summary of the terms used for databases:

| Field | An individual piece of information within a record. Each record within a database must have the same field setup, but the number and type of fields are up to you. |

Record — A database unit containing a set of fields that pertains to a single source. All records within a database have the same fields, but each field contains information unique to that record. Thus all records are different. Records are the units that can be sorted within a database.

Database range — The range of cells in the worksheet that contains database information.

Field name — The title given to a field within the database. Field names remind you which information goes into each field, but Excel also uses them to perform database functions. For example, to find a record containing the name *Smith*, you must indicate the field in which you want to search for that name. Most likely, this field will be called something like *Last* or *Last Name*.

Determining When You Need a Database

So far, you may be wondering what makes a database so different from a worksheet. Worksheet information can be sorted even if it's not in a database range, and the Formula Find command provides some searching capabilities. The row-and-column format is a commonly used structure for data. So what do you gain by establishing a block of cells as a database?

What you gain is an extended range of search criteria for finding information, the ability to make statistical calculations on subsets of the database, the ability to use the automatic *data form* for manipulating data (adding records, deleting records, finding records, and so on), and the ability to extract a subset of data from the database by using custom criteria. These capabilities are most significant when you consider that databases are constantly changing. Usually, records are regularly added and changed in a database, which makes the searches and extracted subsets change as well.

If your data does not change much, you don't need a database. Nor do you need a database if the Formula Find command provides enough power for your searching needs or if you don't need to extract particular information from a range.

A good application for a database would be an order-processing system. Specific worksheet calculations might be required for the order itself. Then, after being generated and sent, a purchase order should be stored. Reports can be built that analyze purchases over time—or you might want to search for orders that have common information, such as all orders to the same manufacturer.

Setting Up a Database

Setting up a database is simply a matter of entering data according to the guidelines of database structure. Make sure that each row contains a separate record and that the column headings represent the fields in the database. The column headings (or field names) must be text labels and may be created from text calculations.

Since the nature of a database is to grow, leave enough room at the bottom of the database for added records. In fact, give the database its own area of the worksheet, below everything else, to allow unlimited growth. Also, avoid placing a database to the right or left of other worksheet data. When you add or remove database records, the change can affect adjacent areas of the worksheet. The only absolute requirements are that you include field names (column headings) for the data and that no blank rows appear below the column headings.

Once the database area and field names are established, you can begin entering data. This process is no different from entering any other data into the worksheet; just begin typing the information under each column heading. You may want to highlight the database range before entering data; doing so causes the pointer to remain in the range as you move from cell to cell by pressing the Tab and Return keys.

You can insert and delete records by simply inserting rows into or deleting rows from the database range, a process described later in this chapter, or by using the data form, also described later in this chapter. The following are guidelines for creating databases:

- Start the database below and to the right of existing worksheet data so that the database does not interfere with existing data. (This guideline is not mandatory but is nevertheless helpful.)

- Enter column headings in the first row and leave no blank rows below this row. In other words, the first records should begin immediately below the headings, and there should be no blank records.

- Records do not have to be be filled out completely. Although you should avoid having blank records, you don't have to fill out each column of each record. Sometimes data is not available or pertinent for all records.

- When entering data, highlight a block of cells containing the fields. Doing so helps control the movement of the pointer. When you reach the end of a record, simply press Tab to move to the beginning of the next record.

- Enter data in the form of text, numbers, or formulas. Any type of worksheet information is acceptable for database data. Any worksheet function or formula technique can be used in a database field.

- Field names should be unique. Duplicate field names can make data searching unpredictable.

Formatting the Database

Besides the standard font, size, style, color, and alignment options available for all worksheet data, there are a few formatting considerations to make for a database. First, expand the column widths to match the largest piece of information in the column. If a column of numbers comes before a column of text, the information will run together, as shown in figure 15.3.

Fig. 15.3.

Number columns run into adjacent text columns, making the data difficult to read.

	⚫ File Edit Formula Format Data Options Macro Window					
B21						

	A	B	C	D	E	F
1						
2		389	Bob Smith			
3		2333	Susan Loredo			
4		43	Larry Carnelli			
5		63	Josh Hardy			
6		234	Luke Hardy			
7		2398	Erin Lee			
8						
9						

Second, you may want to add small blank columns as separators for columns containing data. A separator column can remain blank, as in figure 15.4, or can contain a separation line.

Fig. 15.4.

A blank column acting as a separator in a database.

	⚫ File Edit Formula Format Data Options Macro Window					
E21						

	A	B	C	D	E	F
1						
2		389		Bob Smith		
3		2333		Susan Loredo		
4		43		Larry Carnelli		
5		63		Josh Hardy		
6		234		Luke Hardy		
7		2398		Erin Lee		
8						
9						

Activating the Database

Once you have entered the field names and one row of data (a record), you can activate the database. Activating the database means telling Excel where your database range is located on the worksheet. When

Excel is aware of the database, a number of database features become available. To activate a database, follow these two steps:

1. Highlight the field names and all records beneath them, as in figure 15.5.

Activating a Database

2. Select the Data Set Database command.

🍎 File Edit Formula Format Data Options Macro Window					
A7	Author				

Worksheet3

	A	B	C	D	E	F
1						
2						
3						
4						
5						
6	Database Range					
7	Author	Title	Pages	Pub Number	Date Published	Locatic
8	M.Smith	Integrated Systems	324	100389	1987	LIB4
9	L. Duchamp	Pre-Stressed Concrete	300	138998	1989	LIB2
10	L. Duchamp	Low Intensity Micro	295	100390	1990	LIB2
11	R. Freberger	Depth Measurement	455	100391	1988	LIB3
12	S. Yandewick	High Speed Transfer	290	138999	1987	LIB4
13	S. Lokler	Stress Testing Since 1930	194	139000	1986	LIB5
14	J. Bingham	Heat Resistance Treatment	563	139001	1986	LIB3
15	M. Smith	Cooling Systems	550	100392	1991	LIB4
16	M. Smith	Safety Factors in Test Labs	399	100393	1991	LIB4
17	R. Freberger	Networking	380	100394	1987	LIB5
18						

Ready / NUM

Fig. 15.5.

Highlighting the database range before using the Data Set Database command.

You won't notice any change when you complete these steps; Excel has simply recorded the database range and named it *Database*. This range name will appear with all the other range names when you use the Formula Define Name command (see fig. 15.6). However, because the range is named *Database*, it has special properties found only in databases.

Like any other range name, the name *Database* can apply to only one range at a time. Thus a worksheet can have only one database active at a time. However, you can set up several database ranges on the same worksheet and then activate the one you want at any given time by using the Data Set Database command.

Fig. 15.6.

The database
range, named
Database, is listed
as any other named
range.

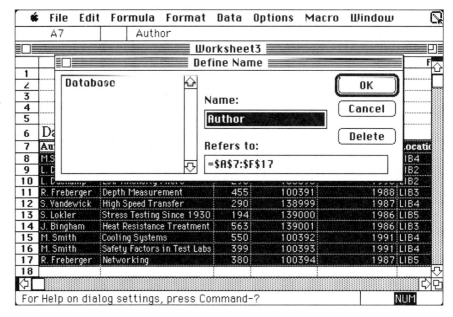

Naming a Database Range Manually

You may be wondering whether you can highlight a range of cells, use the Formula Define Name command (instead of the Data Set Database command) to apply the name *Database* to that range, and thus create a valid database range. The answer is yes. In fact, this technique is a way to establish databases from ranges in external worksheets. Simply enter an external range reference in the Refers To space of the Formula Define Name command and then name the range *Database*.

Because the database range name is like any other, you can use the various range name commands on the database. For example, to quickly highlight the database range, use the Formula Goto command and select the name *Database* from the list provided. To remove the database range specification, use the Formula Define Name command, select the name *Database*, and click on the Delete button. See Chapter 3 for more information about using range names.

> **Naming the Database Range**
>
> You may consider using the Formula Define Name command to name the database range something other than *Database*. If your worksheet has more than one database, give them each a unique name. Then, to select one of the ranges as the database range, just use the Formula Goto command. Finally, use the Data Set Database command.
>
> Basically, any range that is ever used as a database can be named through the Formula Define Name command. Then, when you activate that range by using the Data Set Database command, the range will have two names; one of them is *Database*, and the other is the unique name. The reason for adding a second name is that you can quickly jump to any range that contains a name. Thus you can quickly move between databases to activate whichever you like.

Using the Data Form

One of the most notable features that Excel provides for the established database is the data form. The *data form* is a special window that makes it easy to insert records into the database, delete records from the database, and find records in the database. As soon as you establish the database range, using the Data Set Database command, the data form is ready to be used. View the data form by using the Data Form command. Figure 15.7 shows an example of a database and its form.

The data form contains each of the fields from the database range, as well as a set of buttons. Excel makes the form large enough to hold all the fields in the database. Therefore, your database can contain more fields than the data form can display on-screen at one time. For example, if you have a standard Macintosh Plus or Macintosh SE screen, creating more than 10 fields will expand the data form beyond the edge of the window (see fig. 15.8). One way to overcome this limitation is to customize the data form, using the advanced procedure described in Chapter 17.

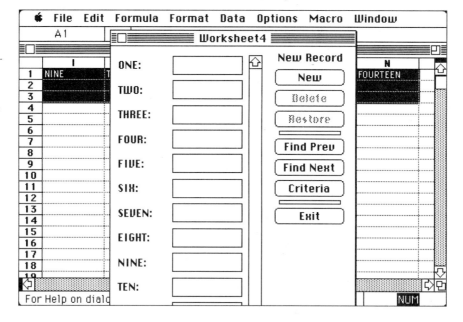

Fig. 15.7.

A database range and data form.

Fig. 15.8.

A data form that contains more fields than the screen can display.

The following is a description of each part of the data form (excluding the command buttons):

Form   The area in which you can enter or edit information. The form represents a single record (or row) from the database range.

Field name   The name describing the field data. Each field name in the database range appears in the data form. Excel includes the colon marks and places the field data next to the appropriate name.

Field data   The data associated with a field name. This data is displayed one record at a time. You can edit the information in these field boxes (unless the information is calculated).

Calculated field data   Data that is determined by a formula. The contents of formula-containing cells in the database are presented in the data form as "uneditable" data. Other data can be changed in this form.

Record number   The number indicating the particular record in view.

Scroll bar   A feature that enables you to move through the various records in the database range.

The following describes the data form's command buttons:

New   Adds a new record to the database. After clicking on the New button, you see a blank form into which you can enter any information you like. When you move to another record or exit from the form, the new record will be added to the end of the database.

Delete   Deletes from the database the record currently displayed in the form.

Restore   When you edit or add records, clicking on this button "throws out" your changes and restores the record to its previous state.

Find Prev   Locates the preceding record in the database.

Find Next   Locates the next record in the database.

Criteria   Enables you to specify criteria so that you can search for a particular record. Click on this button and enter the criteria into the form. Then click on the Find Next button to start the search.

Exit   Returns you to the worksheet.

With this general overview of the data form, you're ready for information about performing specific tasks. The following sections describe the tasks you can accomplish with the data form.

Editing a Record

Although you can edit database information in the worksheet by using standard editing commands (see Chapter 4), you may find the data form a handy way to change database records. When you correct the information displayed in the form, Excel updates the database immediately, as if you had edited the cells themselves. Follow these steps to edit a record with the data form:

*Editing a Record
with the Data Form*

1. Locate the record you want by using the Find Next button or by establishing search criteria.
2. Click on the field you want and use standard editing techniques to make changes.
3. Repeat step 2 for all the fields you want to change.
4. Apply the changes to the database either by exiting from the form (using the Exit button) or by moving to another record (using the scroll bar, the Find Next button, or the Find Prev button).

Excel updates the worksheet as soon as you accept the changes. Fields containing calculations (that is, cells in the database that contain formulas) cannot be edited. Similarly, cells protected with the Format Cell Protection command cannot be changed.

Adding a Record

Adding a record with the data form is easy. Just click on the New button to get a blank form. Then enter the information you want and accept the new record by exiting from the form or moving to a different record. The only way to cancel the new record before adding it is to use the Restore button.

When you add a new record through the data form, Excel places that record at the end of the database. If blank records are at the end of the database, the first one will be filled with the new information. If there are no blank records, Excel adds a new record at the end and expands the database range accordingly. However, if there is no room to expand the database (without interfering with existing information), Excel will not add the new record and will display a message to that effect.

Remember that calculated fields in the database cannot be added or edited. In other words, if the cells in a database column contain formulas, you cannot type information into the corresponding field in the data form. Instead, Excel duplicates the formula for the new record. Likewise, protected fields cannot be edited or added.

Removing a Record

To remove a database record, locate the record you want by using the data form (click on the Find Next and Find Prev buttons). When the record you want appears in the form, click on the Delete button to remove the record from the database. Excel asks you to confirm your decision and then removes the record. If you change your mind, click on Restore before moving to another record. Otherwise, the record is removed from the database, and the database range is adjusted accordingly.

Finding a Record

Although you can find any record in the database by using the data form's Find Next and Find Prev buttons, this process is too slow for most purposes. These buttons are handy for "flipping through" the database records. To speed up the search, use the Criteria button first. Using this button, you can establish a set of *search criteria* for locating a specific record or group of records. These are the basic steps:

1. With the data form in view, click on the Criteria button. Doing so produces a blank data form into which you can enter criteria.
2. Enter the criteria into the fields of the blank data form. Use the Clear or Restore button to make changes to your criteria entries.
3. Click on Find Next to find the first matching record in the database.
4. Click on Find Next again to find the next matching record. Click on Find Prev to find the preceding matching record.
5. Click on Form to return to the normal data form.

Specifying Criteria To Find Records

Entering Criteria

To find a record that contains a specific piece of information, just type that information into the criteria form. For example, to find a record containing the name *Smith* in the Last (name) field, type **Smith** into the appropriate field in the criteria form; then click on Find Next. You can fill as many of the fields as you like with criteria. The more fields you specify, the fewer records are likely to match the criteria. Suppose that five records contain the last name *Smith*, but only one of those contains the ZIP code 91006. To find this record without finding the other four, type **Smith** into the Last (name) field and **91006** into the Zip (ZIP code) field, as shown in figure 15.9.

Fig. 15.9.

Entering multiple criteria to narrow the search.

```
┌───────────────────── Worksheet5 ─────────────────────┐
│                                        Criteria        │
│  First: ┌──────────────┐                               │
│         └──────────────┘              (    New    )    │
│  Last:  ┌──────────────┐                               │
│         │ Smith        │              (   Clear   )    │
│         └──────────────┘                               │
│  Street:┌──────────────┐              (  Restore  )    │
│         └──────────────┘                               │
│  City:  ┌──────────────┐              ( Find Prev )    │
│         └──────────────┘                               │
│  State: ┌──────────────┐              ( Find Next )    │
│         └──────────────┘                               │
│  Zip:   ┌──────────────┐              (   Form    )    │
│         │ 91006        │                               │
│         └──────────────┘              (   Exit    )    │
└────────────────────────────────────────────────────────┘
```

Excel looks for direct matches and for matches that are parts of a larger word or phrase. For example, if you enter *Rob* as a first-name criterion, Excel will match it with *Rob, Robert, ROBERTA,* and *Rob and Susan.* Whether letters are upper- or lowercase is ignored. In addition, you can include the two standard wild cards in your search criteria. For details about wild cards, see "Wild Cards" in Chapter 3.

Entering a criteria string into the criteria form starts a search for a matching record—that is, a record that is "equal to" the specified criteria. The operator implied is an equal sign. You can, however, specify comparison operators. For example, you can find all records containing an amount of less than 1,500. To specify the comparison, just type one of the following operators in front of the comparison information:

Operator	Meaning
>	Greater than
<	Less than
<=	Less than or equal to
>=	Greater than or equal to
<>	Does not equal
=	Equals (implied when no operator is present)

For example, to specify all amounts less than 1,500, enter the criterion **<1500** into the amount field.

Using the Criteria Form Buttons

As you may have already noticed, the buttons change when you enter the criteria form. The buttons Clear and Form replace Delete and Criteria, respectively. Also, the Restore button becomes active, as you can see in figure 15.10.

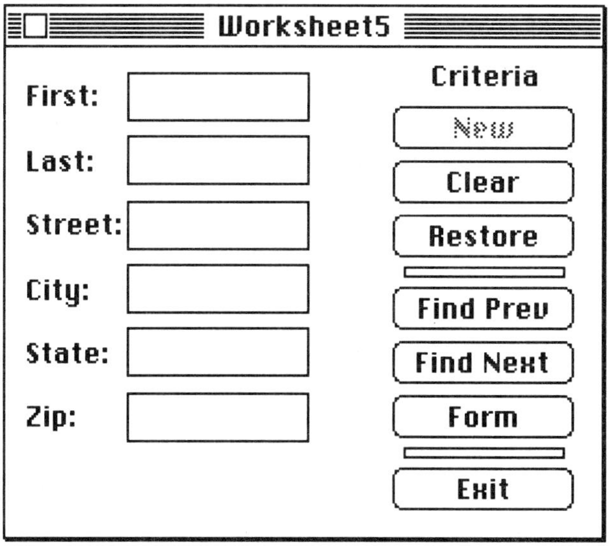

Fig. 15.10.

The criteria form's buttons are different from those on the normal data form.

Use these buttons to make changes to your criteria entries. The Clear button erases existing criteria entries; the Restore button restores entries that have been erased. When you find an entry, click on the Form button to return to the normal data form. The same record will remain in view.

Alternatively, if you find an entry by using criteria and then make changes to the entry, Excel automatically returns to the normal data form. In this case, you must use the Criteria button again to remove or change the criteria.

Inserting and Deleting Records without the Data Form

You can insert and delete records from the database without using the data form. To insert a record, just insert a new row into the middle of the database range and fill the row with new information. To insert a new row, highlight a row in the middle of the range and then use the Edit Insert command as described in Chapter 4. When prompted, make sure that you shift cells down to make room for the new information. The highlighted row is then bumped down to allow room for the new row. Excel expands the database range to include the extra row.

When you insert a new record, be sure to insert it into the middle of the database range and not at the end (that is, not after the last row). If you insert a new record at the end of the existing range, Excel will not expand the database range to include the new data. Thus the record does not become part of the existing database, and you may be forced to respecify the database range. For this reason, it's a good practice to include an extra blank row at the end of the database range. Then, if you insert a new record below the existing records, you are actually still within the database range. Excel thinks you are one record from the end of the database and expands the range to include your new row.

To delete a record, simply delete the row containing the unwanted information. Use the Edit Delete command as described in Chapter 4, making sure to delete the entire row.

Changing Recalculation to Manual

When inserting database records, you may find that automatic recalculation slows data entry. Try changing recalculation to manual until you are finished inserting new data. Then you can recalculate the entire worksheet with the Options Calculate Now command. For more information about automatic and manual recalculation, see Chapter 8.

Sorting the Database

You can sort the information in a database by using any of the fields as the key. A Rolodex, for example, is sorted by last name; that is, all the cards are arranged in alphabetical order by last name. In this example, the last-name field is the *key field*. Excel lets you sort in ascending or descending order and makes a distinction among numbers, text, and dates. Numbers are sorted numerically, text is sorted alphabetically, and dates are sorted chronologically. If a column contains a mixture of these types of values, the following order is used:

1. Numbers (negative to positive—includes date values)
2. Text (in order of ASCII values)
3. Logical values (FALSE, then TRUE)
4. Error values
5. Blank cells

Start by highlighting the entire database range, excluding the column headings. Next, use the Tab key to move the pointer into the column by which you want to sort the data. Finally, choose the Data Sort command. The dialog box in figure 15.11 appears.

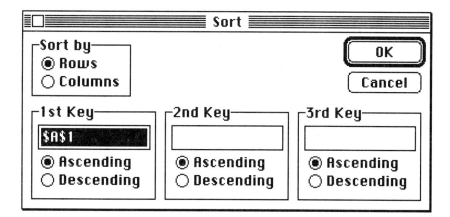

Fig. 15.11.

The Data Sort dialog box.

The assumption is that you are sorting the rows of the database range— that the rows will be rearranged in order, based on the first-key field. The first-key field is the one in which the pointer is located. Its address appears automatically in the 1st Key box. Of course, you can change this entry manually if you like. Press Return to accept these specifications. Excel proceeds to sort the highlighted range by the active column.

Often, sorting by one key field is not enough. Some databases contain duplicate information in the first-key field. For example, if you are sorting an address database by the field Last Name, you may find some duplicate last names; perhaps your database contains six people with the last name *Smith*. In this case, you'll need a "tie breaker" to sort the database effectively. So after sorting by the Last Name field, you sort the database by the First Name field. Doing so places *John Smith* before *Mary Smith*.

Adding a second-key field is simple: After highlighting the database and placing the pointer in the first-key field (that is, anywhere in the column), select the Data Sort command. The first-key field should be entered for you in the dialog box. Next, press the Tab key to position the pointer in the space marked 2nd Key. Now click on the worksheet cell that marks the second-key field; you might have to move the Data Sort dialog box out of the way to do this. When you click on the worksheet cell, Excel enters its address at the cursor location. You now have two key fields for the sort. You can add a third in the same manner.

As an alternative to "pointing" to the second-key field, you can simply type its address into the space provided. Likewise, you can change the address of the first key by using standard editing commands. Note that you can sort each key field in either ascending or descending order, independently of the other keys. For example, you can sort last names in ascending order and first names in descending order. The uses for such arrangements are obscure, however.

Use Names To Specify Sort Keys

You can use range names to specify the sort keys in the Data Sort dialog box. First, highlight the entire database range (including field names), issue the Formula Create Names command, and choose the Top option. Doing so creates a name for each of the database columns, using the field names. Then use these field names in place of cell addresses for the 1st Key, 2nd Key, and 3rd Key specifications when you sort the data. Just enter the field name by which you would like to sort the database.

Sorting Columns

Besides sorting the records of a database, you can rearrange the columns in ascending or descending order. To arrange the columns, highlight the entire database range, including the field names. (You can use the Formula Goto command and specify the range named *Database*.) With the database range highlighted, issue the Data Sort command. Next, click on the Columns button. Finally, enter the address of the first key into the space marked 1st Key; this address should be any cell in the first row of the database (that is, the row containing the field names). Press Return to sort the data.

If you want the columns in an order other than alphabetical, try this technique: number the columns as you would like them to appear, and enter these numbers above each column label, as shown in figure 15.12.

	É File Edit Formula Format Data Options Macro Window					
	A19					

DATABASE

	A	B	C	D	E	F
1	Description	Inv. No.	Units Avail	Cost/Unit	Total Value	Purchased
2			<10	<20		
3						
4						
5	2	3	6	4	5	1
6	Description	Inv. No.	Units Avail	Cost/Unit	Total Value	Purchased
7	African Queen	17459	1	45.95	45.95	1/15/88
8	Batman	22442	15	19.95	299.25	11/15/89
9	Casablanca	13378	2	35.5	67	1/15/85
10	Raiders	11235	10	19.95	199.5	2/5/87
11	Rocky 22	56778	20	19.95	399	11/1/93
12	Star Trek VI	27789	9	24.95	224.55	3/1/91
13	Wall Street	14554	5	19.95	99.75	5/1/88
14						
15						
16	Description	Units Avail				
17	Wall Street	5				
18						
19						

Ready   NUM

Fig. 15.12.

Numbering columns for a custom sort.

Include this extra row when you highlight the database range for the sort. Specify any cell in this row as the first key in the Sort dialog box. When you press Return, the columns will be sorted in numeric order (see fig. 15.13).

Fig. 15.13.

Sorting by
numbers.

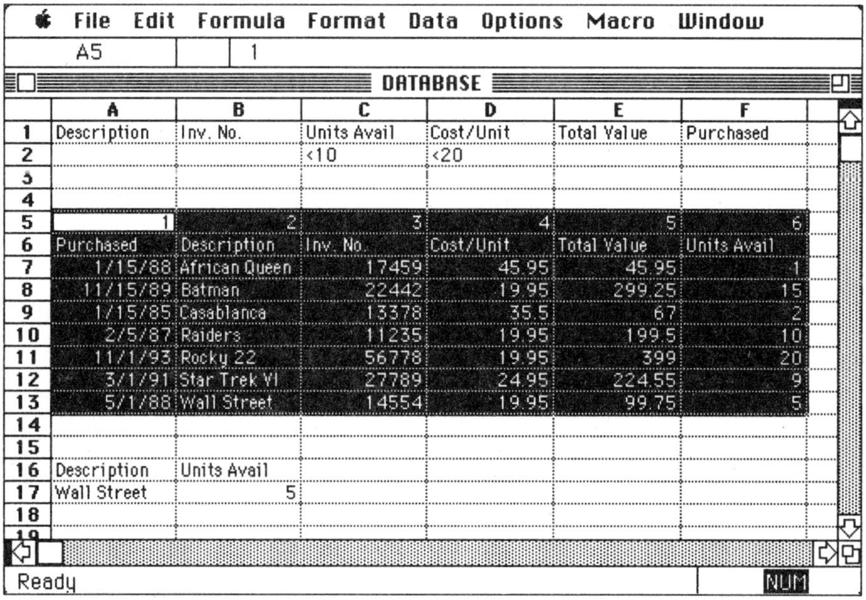

		File	Edit	Formula	Format	Data	Options	Macro	Window	

	A5		1				

DATABASE

	A	B	C	D	E	F
1	Description	Inv. No.	Units Avail	Cost/Unit	Total Value	Purchased
2			<10	<20		
3						
4						
5	1	2	3	4	5	6
6	Purchased	Description	Inv. No.	Cost/Unit	Total Value	Units Avail
7	1/15/88	African Queen	17459	45.95	45.95	1
8	11/15/89	Batman	22442	19.95	299.25	15
9	1/15/85	Casablanca	13378	35.5	67	2
10	2/5/87	Raiders	11235	19.95	199.5	10
11	11/1/93	Rocky 22	56778	19.95	399	20
12	3/1/91	Star Trek VI	27789	24.95	224.55	9
13	5/1/88	Wall Street	14554	19.95	99.75	5
14						
15						
16	Description	Units Avail				
17	Wall Street	5				
18						
19						

Ready   NUM

Solving Data-Sorting Problems

If records are entered randomly into the database, you will not be able
to restore the original order of the data after you sort it. Because there
was no order to the data to begin with, there is no way to restore that
order—unless you include a column of sequential numbers as part of the
database. By numbering the entries, you can return the data to its original
order by sorting the column of numbers. Simply enter the number of
the worksheet row into the first column of the database, as shown in
figure 15.14. As a shortcut, use the Data Fill command to create
sequential numbers down the column. Or try entering the number 1 into
any blank cell of the worksheet; let's use cell B1 as an example. Next,
enter the formula **=IF($B$1=1,ROW( ),A1)** into cell A1. If cell A1 does
not correspond to the first record in the database, use the appropriate
cell instead. Perhaps cell A7 matches the first record in the database. In
this case, change the reference from A1 to A7 in the IF statement so that
it reads =IF($B$1=1,ROW( ),A7).

```
 ╭─────────────────────────────────────────────────────────────╮
 │  ●  File  Edit  Formula  Format  Data  Options  Macro  Window │
 │     ┌─A19──────┬─────┬──────────────────────────────────────┐ │
 ╞═══════════════════════════ DATABASE 2 ════════════════════════╡
 │     A │    B    │        C         │  D  │    E    │    F     │
 │  1  │          │                  │     │         │          │
 │  2  │          │                  │     │         │          │
 │  3  │          │                  │     │         │          │
 │  4  │          │                  │     │         │          │
 │  5  │          │                  │     │         │          │
 │  6  │   Database Range                                        │
 │  7  │    Author   Title        Pages  Pub Number  Date Published  Lo│
 │  8  │ 8 M.Smith   Integrated Systems       324   100389      1987 LIE│
 │  9  │ 9 L. Duchamp Pre-Stressed Concrete    300   138998      1989 LIE│
 │ 10  │10 L. Duchamp Low Intensity Micro      295   100390      1990 LIE│
 │ 11  │11 R. Freberger Depth Measurement      455   100391      1988 LIE│
 │ 12  │12 S. Vandewick High Speed Transfer    290   138999      1987 LIE│
 │ 13  │13 S. Lokler  Stress Testing Since 1930 194  139000      1986 LIE│
 │ 14  │14 J. Bingham Heat Resistance Treatment 563  139001      1986 LIE│
 │ 15  │15 M.Smith    Cooling Systems          550   100392      1991 LIE│
 │ 16  │16 M.Smith    Safety Factors in Test Labs 399 100393     1991 LIE│
 │ 17  │17 R. Freberger Networking             380   100394      1987 LIE│
 │ Ready                                                         │
 ╰─────────────────────────────────────────────────────────────╯
```

Fig. 15.14.

Copying the row number into the database ensures that you can return the data to its original order.

Notice that this formula creates a circular reference by relating back to the cell in which the formula actually appears. This is part of the technique. As long as cell B1 contains the value 1, then copying this formula down column A produces a sequential list of numbers (use the Edit Fill Down command to copy this formula down the column). After copying the formula, erase the value in cell B1, using the Clear command. Excel then informs you of the circular reference; just press Return at the error dialog box to accept the "mistake." As long as cell B1 does not contain the value 1, the formulas have "frozen" their values into place in the column, and they can be used to sort the database. In other words, the formulas will not recalculate their values after you sort them with the database records.

When you add records to the database, replace the 1 in cell B1 and recopy the formula down the column. Make sure that the database is sorted in numerical order (that is, sort the database by using these numbers as the key) before repeating the process.

Another potential problem with data sorting is that you may accidentally miss a few of the columns when you sort a range of data. Such an omission causes records to be mixed with one another. Unless you have numbered the records as described earlier, the problem could be disastrous, because all records will be ruined. To avoid this problem, define a name for the sortable portion of the database (that is, the entire database minus the field names). Use a name like SORT_RANGE. Next, to highlight the sort range, use the Formula Goto command and specify the appropriate range. Then sort the database.

Finding Records without the Data Form

Although the data form offers adequate searching capabilities for databases, the most powerful searching is accomplished without the form. For one thing, you cannot use OR logic within a data form. When you enter criteria into more than one field, the criteria constitute an implied AND statement. In other words, if you enter *Smith* into the Last (name) field and *91006* into the Zip (ZIP code) field, as shown in figure 15.9, Excel locates only those records that match both criteria— *Smith* and *91006*. To find records whose Last field contains *Smith* or whose Zip field contains *91006*, you must use a special *criteria range*. The basic steps for searching without the data form are these:

Searching with a Criteria Range

1. Create the criteria range, which consists of the desired field names and, below them, the criteria entries. Make sure that this range appears in an unused portion of the worksheet.

2. Highlight the criteria range (the field names plus the criteria entries) and activate it with the Data Set Criteria command.

3. Begin the search by selecting the Data Find command.

4. Use the search options to "flip through" the various matching records.

Specifying Criteria in the Criteria Range

A criteria range is a special range of cells in the worksheet that contains search criteria for the database. The criteria range can contain complex and specialized search criteria for finding, deleting, and extracting records. To create a criteria range, start by copying the database column headings (field names) to another area of the worksheet. A few rows above the originals is a good place to copy to; just be sure that you leave a few rows under the copied headings in which you can enter specific criteria. It's not really necessary to duplicate every field name—only the ones you intend to use in the search. However, duplicating them all adds flexibility because you can then search in any or all of the fields. Figure 15.15 shows a sample database of company documents. Notice that the field names are repeated at the top of the worksheet and that a few extra rows separate the two ranges.

```
  ¤   File   Edit   Formula   Format   Data   Options   Macro   Window
        D19      │         │
 ▤▭▭▭▭▭▭▭▭▭▭▭▭▭▭▭▭ Worksheet3 ▭▭▭▭▭▭▭▭▭▭▭▭▭▭▭▭▭▭▭▭▭
 │         A      │        B       │   C    │    D     │      E       │   F  ⬆
  1 │Criteria Range
  2 │Author      Title              Pages   Pub Number  Date Published  Locatic
  3 │
  4 │
  5 │
  6 │Database Range
  7 │Author      Title              Pages   Pub Number  Date Published  Locatic
  8 │M.Smith     Integrated Systems    324     100389          1987 LIB4
  9 │L. Duchamp  Pre-Stressed Concrete 300     138998          1989 LIB2
 10 │L. Duchamp  Low Intensity Micro   295     100390          1990 LIB2
 11 │R. Freberger Depth Measurement    455     100391          1988 LIB3
 12 │S. Yandewick High Speed Transfer  290     138999          1987 LIB4
 13 │S. Lokler   Stress Testing Since 1930  194  139000        1986 LIB5
 14 │J. Bingham  Heat Resistance Treatment  563  139001        1986 LIB3
 15 │M. Smith    Cooling Systems       550     100392          1991 LIB4
 16 │M. Smith    Safety Factors in Test Labs  399  100393      1991 LIB4
 17 │R. Freberger Networking           380     100394          1987 LIB5
 │
 Ready                                                            NUM
```

Fig. 15.15.

A sample database whose field labels are copied to the criteria range.

Under each of the duplicate heading names, you can enter a criteria formula. If, for example, you want to find all records containing *1989* in the Date Published field, enter **1989** below the Date Published heading in the criteria range (see fig. 15.16).

```
  ¤   File   Edit   Formula   Format   Data   Options   Macro   Window
        E3       │    1989   │
 ▤▭▭▭▭▭▭▭▭▭▭▭▭▭▭▭▭ DATABASE 2 ▭▭▭▭▭▭▭▭▭▭▭▭▭▭▭▭▭▭▭▭▭
 │         A      │        B       │   C    │    D     │      E       │   F  ⬆
  1 │Criteria Range
  2 │Author      Title              Pages   Pub Number  Date Published  Locati
  3 │                                                   │    1989   │
  4 │
  5 │
  6 │Database Range
  7 │Author      Title              Pages   Pub Number  Date Published  Locati
  8 │M.Smith     Integrated Systems    324     100389          1987 LIB4
  9 │L. Duchamp  Pre-Stressed Concrete 300     138998          1989 LIB2
 10 │L. Duchamp  Low Intensity Micro   295     100390          1990 LIB2
 11 │R. Freberger Depth Measurement    455     100391          1988 LIB3
 12 │S. Yandewick High Speed Transfer  290     138999          1987 LIB4
 13 │S. Lokler   Stress Testing Since 1930  194  139000        1986 LIB5
 14 │J. Bingham  Heat Resistance Treatment  563  139001        1986 LIB3
 15 │M. Smith    Cooling Systems       550     100392          1991 LIB4
 16 │M. Smith    Safety Factors in Test Labs  399  100393      1991 LIB4
 17 │R. Freberger Networking           380     100394          1987 LIB5
 │
 Ready
```

Fig. 15.16.

Specifying criteria by using a criteria range.

Entering the criteria is much like using criteria in the data form. You can use any of the comparison operators (>, >=, <, <=, <>, and =) within the cells. Note that the equals operation is implied when no operator is present. Figures 15.17 and 15.18 show more examples of search criteria in a database range.

Fig. 15.17.

Finds all records with a publication date earlier than 1989.

	File Edit Formula Format Data Options Macro Window
E3	<1989

DATABASE 2

	A	B	C	D	E	F
1	Criteria Range					
2	Author	Title	Comp	Pub Number	Date Published	Locatio
3					<1989	
4						
5						
6	Database Range					
7	Author	Title	Pages	Pub Number	Date Published	Locatio
8	M.Smith	Integrated Systems	324	100389	1987	LIB4
9	L. Duchamp	Pre-Stressed Concrete	300	138998	1989	LIB2
10	L. Duchamp	Low Intensity Micro	295	100390	1990	LIB2
11	R. Freberger	Depth Measurement	455	100391	1988	LIB3
12	S. Vandewick	High Speed Transfer	290	138999	1987	LIB4
13	S. Lokler	Stress Testing Since 1930	194	139000	1986	LIB5
14	J. Bingham	Heat Resistance Treatment	563	139001	1986	LIB3
15	M. Smith	Cooling Systems	550	100392	1991	LIB4
16	M. Smith	Safety Factors in Test Labs	399	100393	1991	LIB4
17	R. Freberger	Networking	380	100394	1987	LIB5

Ready

Fig. 15.18.

Finds all records for M. Smith with a publication date earlier than 1989.

	File Edit Formula Format Data Options Macro Window
A3	M. Smith

DATABASE 2

	A	B	C	D	E	F
1	Criteria Range					
2	Author	Title	Comp	Pub Number	Date Published	Locatio
3	M. Smith				<1989	
4						
5						
6	Database Range					
7	Author	Title	Pages	Pub Number	Date Published	Locatio
8	M.Smith	Integrated Systems	324	100389	1987	LIB4
9	L. Duchamp	Pre-Stressed Concrete	300	138998	1989	LIB2
10	L. Duchamp	Low Intensity Micro	295	100390	1990	LIB2
11	R. Freberger	Depth Measurement	455	100391	1988	LIB3
12	S. Vandewick	High Speed Transfer	290	138999	1987	LIB4
13	S. Lokler	Stress Testing Since 1930	194	139000	1986	LIB5
14	J. Bingham	Heat Resistance Treatment	563	139001	1986	LIB3
15	M. Smith	Cooling Systems	550	100392	1991	LIB4
16	M. Smith	Safety Factors in Test Labs	399	100393	1991	LIB4
17	R. Freberger	Networking	380	100394	1987	LIB5

Ready

Activating the Criteria Range

When the criteria have been entered, highlight the duplicate field names and the criteria; then select the Data Set Criteria command. Figure 15.19 shows the highlighted range. Issuing the Data Set Criteria command tells Excel where the criteria range is located—and activates the range. You need not select this range again unless it moves or expands, even if you change the criteria entries.

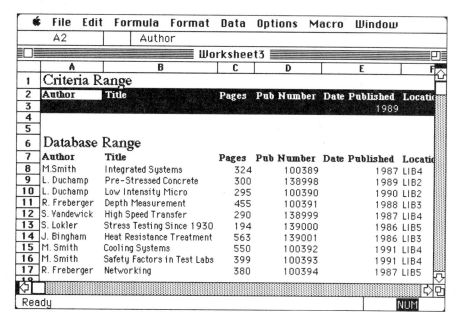

Fig. 15.19.

Highlighting the criteria range.

Excel stores the criteria range under the name *Criteria*. Like the database range name, *Criteria* is a standard range name and can be used as such. For instance, you can highlight the criteria range by using the Formula Goto command, and you can edit the range reference by using the Formula Define Name command.

Searching with the Criteria Range

After you create and activate the criteria range, the final step is to select the Data Find command to locate the first record that matches the established criteria. When you use this command, Excel locates the first matching record that appears below the current pointer location. In other words, you can position the pointer in the database and search from that point forward. If the pointer is outside the database range, Excel starts at the top of the database range. Figure 15.20 shows an example of finding a record.

Fig. 15.20.

Finding records that match the criteria.

```
 ⬛ File  Edit  Formula  Format  Data  Options  Macro  Window
         2                 L. Duchamp
═══════════════════════════ Worksheet3 ═══════════════════════════
           A              B              C       D           E          F
  7  Author        Title                 Pages  Pub Number  Date Published  Locatio
  8  M.Smith       Integrated Systems    524    100389            1907 LID4
  9  L. Duchamp    Pre-Stressed Concrete 300    138998            1989 LIB2
 10  L. Duchamp    Low Intensity Micro   295    100390            1990 LIB2
 11  R. Freberger  Depth Measurement     455    100391            1988 LIB3
 12  S. Vandewick  High Speed Transfer   290    138999            1987 LIB4
 13  S. Lokler     Stress Testing Since 1930  194  139000         1986 LIB5
 14  J. Bingham    Heat Resistance Treatment  563  139001         1986 LIB3
 15  M. Smith      Cooling Systems       550    100392            1991 LIB4
 16  M. Smith      Safety Factors in Test Labs  399  100393        1991 LIB4
 17  R. Freberger  Networking            380    100394            1987 LIB5
 18
 19
 20
 21
 22
 23
 24
 25
Find (Use direction keys to view records)                          NUM
```

Notice the number 2 in the upper left corner of the screen. This number indicates that the highlighted record is the second from the top (that is, record number 2). This number will be updated as you "flip through" the records.

After the first matching record is found, you can use any of the following options to find matching records. Until you halt the search, all these options apply to matching records:

Option	Moves highlight and pointer...
⬇ or ⌘F	To the next matching record.
⬆ or ⌘⇧Shift F	To the preceding matching record.
Scroll arrows	Forward or backward through the matching records, one record at a time.
Scroll box	To a matching record elsewhere in the database. By dragging the scroll box, you can make large jumps within the database and highlight the first matching record at the new position.
PgDn	To the nearest record one screen down from the current record.
PgUp	To the nearest record one screen up from the current record.

When Excel is in "find" mode, the scroll boxes change patterns to indicate their changed function. To exit from the database search and return the scroll boxes to normal, select any cell outside the database range. Alternatively, you can select the Data Exist Find command or press Command+. (period).

Using Complex Search Criteria

Establishing criteria for searches is what a database is all about. The Excel database and criteria structure allows many different types of searches. The following sections describe some special techniques and features you can apply to conduct more powerful searches. These techniques include combining criteria with AND and OR operators and building advanced formulas for criteria.

Using AND and OR Logic

When you use more than one formula to establish criteria for the search, you can assume an AND operator between them. For example, entering **>1989** under Date Published and **M. Smith** under Author finds all records with a Date Published value greater than 1989 *and* an Author value of M. Smith. Although the AND operator does not appear between the two criteria entries, the AND is automatically assumed because the formulas are on the same row. Each entry is under its appropriate heading. Using multiple criteria entries in this way narrows the possible matching records, because fewer records are likely to meet both criteria.

You can use OR logic between criteria entries by placing the different entries on different rows. The OR operator extends the possible matching records, because more records are likely to meet one or another criterion; records that meet any of the criteria qualify as matching records. Suppose that you want to search the sample database for all records with a Date Published greater than 1989 *or* an Author value of M. Smith. The example worksheet would look like figure 15.21.

Notice that the formulas appear on different rows below their corresponding field names. This is why it's a good idea to leave plenty of space between the duplicate field names and the originals. When highlighting the criteria range for the search, be sure to include all rows containing formulas. Formulas on the same row assume the AND operator; formulas on different rows assume the OR operator. This setup allows for some intricate search criteria.

Fig. 15.21.

Using the implied OR operator between formulas that appear on different rows.

	File	Edit	Formula	Format	Data	Options	Macro	Window

A4		M. Smith				

Worksheet3

	A	B	C	D	E	F
1	Criteria Range					
2	Author	Title	Pages	Pub Number	Date Published	Locatio
3					>1989	
4	M. Smith					
5						
6	Database Range					
7	Author	Title	Pages	Pub Number	Date Published	Locatio
8	M.Smith	Integrated Systems	324	100389	1987	LIB4
9	L. Duchamp	Pre-Stressed Concrete	300	138998	1989	LIB2
10	L. Duchamp	Low Intensity Micro	295	100390	1990	LIB2
11	R. Freberger	Depth Measurement	455	100391	1988	LIB3
12	S. Vandewick	High Speed Transfer	290	138999	1987	LIB4
13	S. Lokler	Stress Testing Since 1930	194	139000	1986	LIB5
14	J. Bingham	Heat Resistance Treatment	563	139001	1986	LIB3
15	M. Smith	Cooling Systems	550	100392	1991	LIB4
16	M. Smith	Safety Factors in Test Labs	399	100393	1991	LIB4
17	R. Freberger	Networking	380	100394	1987	LIB5

Ready   NUM

As an example, suppose that you want to find all records in the publication log that have a Date Published of 1989 or that have a Date Published greater than 1987 and a Location of LIB4. The statement may be expressed like this:

Date Published = 1989 OR (Date Published > 1987 AND Location = LIB4)

Notice that the parentheses around the second set make it a single criterion. This statement has two separate conditions separated by the OR operator. Translating this statement to the criteria range would result in something like figure 15.22.

Be sure to reset the criteria range so that it includes all three rows.

Using Computed Criteria

You can use formulas in the criteria range to search for records that match specific calculations or statements. For example, you might search for records containing a particular amount that, when added to 100, produces a result of less than 150. The formula bar in figure 15.23 shows a formula (criterion) that specifies such a condition.

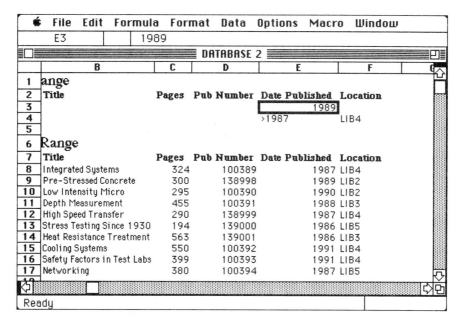

Fig. 15.22.

Specifying more complex criteria.

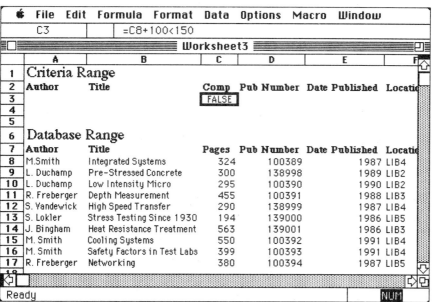

Fig. 15.23.

A computed criterion (notice the formula in the formula bar).

Notice that the formula refers to the first cell in the column you are searching (not counting the cell containing the field name). In this case the reference is to C8, the first cell in the Pages column. (This part of the formula searches for all records with fewer than 50 pages.) This reference causes Excel to repeat the same formula for each record, beginning with the first. The sample criterion in figure 15.23 is the computation of a database field plus a constant value. However, any formula can be used as a search criterion. You can calculate two fields from the database or use references to cells outside the database range. If you use external references, be sure to make them absolute by adding the dollar signs. Figures 15.24 and 15.25 show more examples of computed criteria.

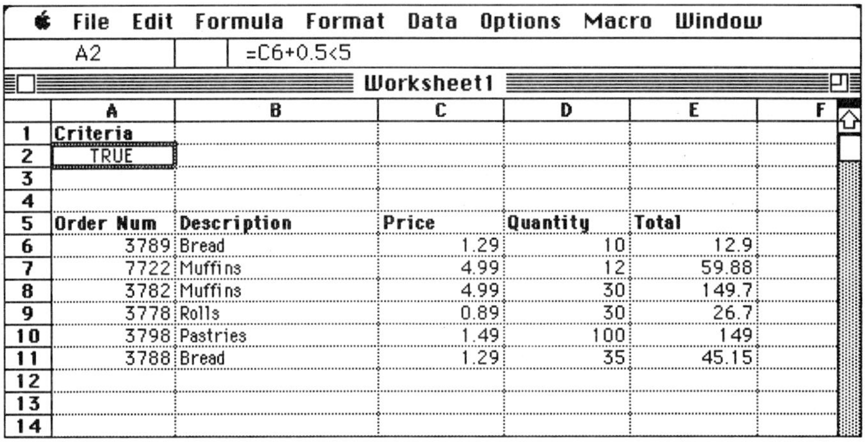

Fig. 15.24.

A formula that finds records in which Price plus 50 percent is less than $5.

	File Edit Formula Format Data Options Macro Window					
A2	=C6+0.5<5					

Worksheet1

	A	B	C	D	E	F
1	Criteria					
2	TRUE					
3						
4						
5	Order Num	Description	Price	Quantity	Total	
6	3789	Bread	1.29	10	12.9	
7	7722	Muffins	4.99	12	59.88	
8	3782	Muffins	4.99	30	149.7	
9	3778	Rolls	0.89	30	26.7	
10	3798	Pastries	1.49	100	149	
11	3788	Bread	1.29	35	45.15	
12						
13						
14						

Notice that you can use logical functions within the computed criteria. The functions ISBLANK, ISERR, ISNUMBER, and ISTEXT are handy for finding various values within a database. The final point to note about computed criteria is that you must change the headings used in the criteria range so that they no longer match the field names exactly. This step tells Excel that the criteria are computed, not constant. The following is a summary of guidelines for using computed criteria:

- Change the headings in the criteria range so that they do not match the field names. This step is necessary when you use computed criteria, but when you use standard criteria, the labels must match the field names.

- Enter computed criteria as formulas. Be sure to include the equal sign and any cell references for the calculation. This formula will produce an initial result, which should relate to the first record in the database but is meaningless for the search operation.

	A	B	C	D	E	F
1	Criteria					
2	FALSE					
3						
4						
5	Order Num	Description	Price	Quantity	Total	
6	3789	Bread	1.29	10	12.9	
7	7722	Muffins	4.99	12	59.88	
8	3782	Muffins	4.99	30	149.7	
9	3778		0.89	30	26.7	
10	3798	Pastries	1.49	100	149	
11	3788	Bread	1.29	35	45.15	
12						
13						

A2 =ISBLANK(B6)

File   Edit   Formula   Format   Data   Options   Macro   Window

Worksheet1

Fig. 15.25.

A formula that finds records whose Description field is blank.

- When entering a computed criterion, refer to the appropriate cell in the first record of the database. Using the first record tells Excel to repeat the formula for each record in the database. Excel will then find all records that match your computed criteria.

- You can use any valid formula in the computed criteria, including special functions, constant values, cell addresses, and linked cells from external worksheets.

(Almost) Eliminating the Criteria Range

If you like, you can narrow the criteria range to two cells, a label, and a criteria entry and eliminate the need to duplicate the field names for the criteria range. In other words, you can design a single formula that accomplishes all the matching requirements of several formulas. That single formula will be sufficient for an Excel criteria range.

An earlier example used several cells in the criteria range to find all records in the publication log that have a Date Published of 1989 or that have a Date Published greater than 1987 and a Location of LIB4 (see fig. 15.22). Rather than enter several formulas, you can enter this one formula and use it as the criteria range:

=OR(E8=1989,(AND(E8>1987,F8=LIB4)))

Enter this formula into cell B3 and specify B2:B3 as the criteria range. Since this entry is a computed criteria entry, be sure that cell B2 contains a label different from those in the database. The resulting search or extraction will be the same as in the earlier example.

This technique also lets you specify a range of values for a single field. For example, if you want to find all records whose Date Published value is *between* 1987 and 1989, you can enter the formula as follows:

=AND(E8>1987,E8<1989)

Summarizing the Find Process

In summary, these are the steps for setting up a database search from scratch:

Setting Up a Database Search

1. Highlight the entire database range, including field names (column headings), and issue the Data Set Database command.
2. Copy the field names to another part of the worksheet.
3. Enter criteria formulas into any of the criteria fields; enter this data into the row directly under the field names.
4. Highlight the duplicate field names and the criteria formulas below them; then select the Data Set Criteria command.
5. Select the Data Find command.
6. Use any of the search options to flip through the matching records.

Remember that you do not need to rehighlight the database and criteria ranges once they are set. You can update any information in those ranges and search again and again. To remove criteria specifications from the range, be sure to use the Clear command in the Edit menu. You can also use the Backspace key to clear the old data. If you don't clear old data, Excel may still contain information in seemingly empty cells. This information, which may include empty spaces, formatting designations, or other "invisible" codes, can cause your search to fail.

Extracting Records

Extracting records from a database can be useful for calculating subtotals or printing reports based on a subset of the data. If you already know how to find records, learning to extract them will be easy, because extracting is an extension of searching.

To extract records from a database, first set up the database range and criteria range as described for the database search (without using the data form). Next, determine the area, or *extract range*, where you want the extracted records to appear. (Extracted records are not removed from the database; copies of them are placed in the extract range.) The extract range should be at the bottom of the worksheet, because Excel clears all data below this range when extracting. Every record that matches your criteria will be placed into this extract area.

You don't need to extract entire records; you can pull out only the information you want from the records that match the criteria. Suppose that you want to extract records from the publication log database used in an earlier example. The criteria are already set up to find all publications with a Date Published value greater than 1987. But suppose that you don't want the extracted list to contain all the fields in the records; you need only the Author, Title, and Date Published information. Enter these three fields at the top of the extract range, which appears in the lower portion of figure 15.26.

	File Edit Formula Format Data Options Macro Window					
	A5					
			Worksheet3			
	A	B	C	D	E	F
6	Database Range					
7	Author	Title	Pages	Pub Number	Date Published	Locatic
8	M.Smith	Integrated Systems	324	100389	1987	LIB4
9	L. Duchamp	Pre-Stressed Concrete	300	138998	1989	LIB2
10	L. Duchamp	Low Intensity Micro	295	100390	1990	LIB2
11	R. Freberger	Depth Measurement	455	100391	1988	LIB3
12	S. Vandewick	High Speed Transfer	290	138999	1987	LIB4
13	S. Lokler	Stress Testing Since 1930	194	139000	1986	LIB5
14	J. Bingham	Heat Resistance Treatment	563	139001	1986	LIB3
15	M. Smith	Cooling Systems	550	100392	1991	LIB4
16	M. Smith	Safety Factors in Test Labs	399	100393	1991	LIB4
17	R. Freberger	Networking	380	100394	1987	LIB5
18						
19	Extract Range					
20	Date Publish	Title	Author			
21						
22						

Ready   NUM

Fig. 15.26.

Preparing to extract records.

Notice that the three extract fields are not in the same order as they are in the database. You do not need to use all the fields for the extract, nor do you need to maintain their order. Also, the extract fields do not have to include the fields used in the search criteria. You can base your search on the Date Published field and extract only the Author information from the matching records. Or you can extract the entire record.

The next step is to highlight the extract fields you specified, as shown in figure 15.27. Finally, choose the Data Extract command. Excel will copy the information from matching records in the database and fill in the cells below the extract fields, as shown in figure 15.28.

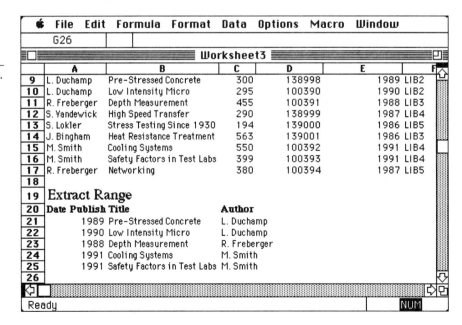

Fig. 15.27.

Highlighting the extract fields before extracting.

Fig. 15.28.

The extracted data.

Highlighting the single row containing the extract fields causes Excel to extract all matching records and fill in the cells below the extract fields. However, you can limit the number of records that will be displayed by highlighting a block of two or more rows, where the top row contains the extract fields. Excel will stop extracting when it fills the highlighted range (see fig. 15.29).

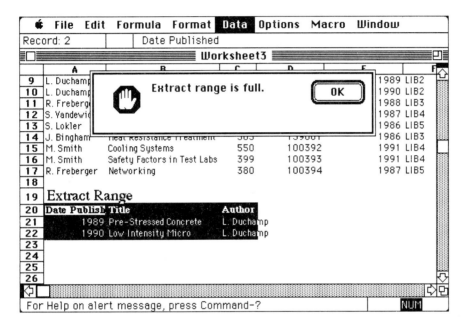

Fig. 15.29.

The message displayed when the extract range is full.

Caution: Remember to place the extract range below all other worksheet information. When extracting, Excel erases all information below the extracted data. If data appears below the extract range, that data will be deleted from the worksheet.

When you use the Data Extract command, Excel presents a dialog box that asks whether you want to extract unique records only (see fig. 15.30). Normally, the box is unchecked; Excel thus extracts all matching records from the database. If two records are identical, Excel extracts both. You may, however, have an application requiring that only one of each matching record be extracted. This requirement is common for databases that keep a historical record of activity—in which the same activity might occur several times, creating several identical records. Customer purchases, shipping logs, purchase order records, and other such databases fall into this category.

Suppose that you have a database of customer purchases. You want to extract a list of all customers who have purchased a particular item so that you can send them a letter. Now suppose that one customer has purchased this item several times and has several records in the database to match. But because you want to send only one letter to this customer, you want to extract only one record noting her purchase. By checking the Unique Records Only box, you limit the matching records to one for each client. Thus your resulting extracted list contains no more records than you want.

 When extracting, Excel considers two records identical when the extracted fields are identical—not when all fields are identical. **NOTE** Therefore, customer records that have different dates (but are otherwise identical) might still be considered identical if the Date field is not one of the extracted fields. Thus you may be more likely to have duplicates in your database.

Deleting Records

Deleting database records is the same as finding records, except that after the criteria are established, you choose the Data Delete command instead of the Data Find command. These are the steps for deleting records:

1. Set up the database and criteria ranges as specified throughout this chapter.
2. Enter the criteria that will locate the records you want to delete.
3. Choose the command Data Delete.

Deleted records cannot be replaced once this operation is complete. They are permanently removed from the database.

Summary

This chapter explained all the commands used for basic database operations in Excel. These operations include setting up a database, inserting and deleting records, searching for records, and extracting records based on criteria. Whereas the previous chapter gave you a brief tour of these procedures, this chapter provided all the details. The following are some important points to remember:

❏ In an Excel database, each row equates to a record, and cells within the rows (that is, the columns) equate to fields.

❏ Activate a database by highlighting the entire database range (the range including the column headings and any records beneath them) and using the Data Set Database command.

❏ You can have only one database active at a time in Excel.

❏ Once a database has been activated, you can use the automatic data form to browse through the records, add records, remove records, and find records. Use the command Data Form to view this form.

❏ You can conduct powerful searches without the data form by using a criteria range in the worksheet.

❏ You can use calculations as criteria entries.

❏ You can sort the database data by highlighting the records (do not include the column titles) and using the Data Sort command.

❏ Use the Data Extract command to extract records.

The following chapter, "Using Advanced Database Techniques," discusses other techniques you can use in Excel.

16

Using Advanced Database Techniques

This chapter introduces some advanced techniques that you can use for data management. Primarily, the chapter explains how you can build a custom data form by using Excel's Dialog Editor program. Custom data forms let you organize information any way you want—and help you to overcome the screen's limitation on the size of the data form. In addition, because you cannot use a data form for printing records, this chapter provides a technique for creating custom print forms for individual database records. Also in this chapter is a technique for removing duplicate records from the database.

Customizing the Data Form

The automatic data form provided by Excel is a useful tool for speeding up the data entry process and the search process. Because the data form presents records in a neat and uniform way, it makes database management easy to understand. The data form has its shortcomings, however. As mentioned in Chapter 15, the data form cannot display more than 10 fields on a standard monitor (larger monitors may allow more fields). By customizing the data form, however, you can overcome this limit and control the size and shape of the form, as well as the fields used in the form.

Customizing the data form is really a matter of rearranging the fields displayed on the form. By changing their positions, you can gain more working space. Also, you can remove fields and change the titles and text used in the form. You cannot change the buttons or the scroll bar, however; these are added and controlled by Excel.

Excel provides a tool that makes creating a custom data form simple: the Dialog Editor program, which comes with Excel and is found on the Excel program disk. Although you don't have to use the Dialog Editor to customize a data form, you must do tedious extra work if you create a custom data form without using the program.

Using the Dialog Editor

The Dialog Editor is a program that helps you design dialog boxes. Technically, the data form is a dialog box. As you'll see in the next section of this book, you can use the Dialog Editor for other types of custom dialog boxes—specifically, those controlled by macros. For now, this book will concentrate only on those features of the Dialog Editor that apply to data forms.

 As you read the next section of this book, you'll discover how you can employ more-advanced Dialog Editor features, along with macros, to customize a data form beyond the stage described in this chapter. These more-advanced features include the addition of custom buttons, check boxes, and other *controls* to the data form. The controls can perform any action you like. But before you can add and use custom controls, you must know something about creating macros.

To learn the basics of the Dialog Editor, start the program from the desktop by double-clicking on the Dialog Editor program icon. When you enter the program, the screen should look like figure 16.1. Notice that you begin with a blank dialog box (data form) and a series of menu options.

Changing the Size of the Data Form

The first thing you may want to do is specify the size and position of the data form itself. The Dialog Editor starts with a default size in the middle of the screen. To change the position of the form, click the mouse button anywhere inside the form, drag the box to the screen location you want, and release the button. The data form will appear in the same relative screen position when you use it in Excel with the Data Form command. You also can use the keyboard to move the form. Just click on the form to highlight it; then use the four arrow keys to change its position.

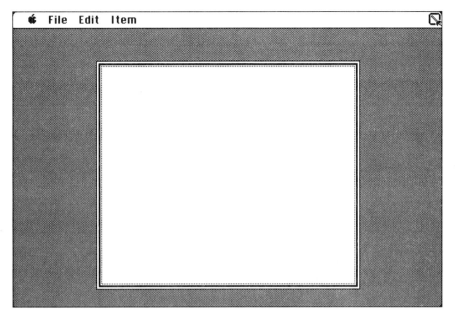

Fig. 16.1.

The Dialog Editor screen.

To change the size and shape of the form, click on the bottom or right edge of the box. The pointer will change shape to indicate that you can click and drag the mouse to change the box. You can also click in the lower right corner of the box and drag diagonally to change the position of that corner. Clicking in that manner changes the overall dimensions of the box. In addition, you can use the keyboard to change the size of the dialog box. Just highlight the box by clicking the mouse button (or using the Edit Select Dialog command); then press the Shift key along with one of the four arrow keys. Figure 16.2 shows a data form whose initial size and shape have been changed.

Adding Text to the Data Form

Another important part of building a data form is adding text. You can add any text to the data form by using the Item Text command. Initially, this command adds a text box containing the word *Text*. When the box is highlighted, however, you can type any information for the text box. The new information will replace the old. To highlight a text box, click on the box or use the Tab key. A text box is highlighted when a dotted border surrounds it (see fig. 16.3).

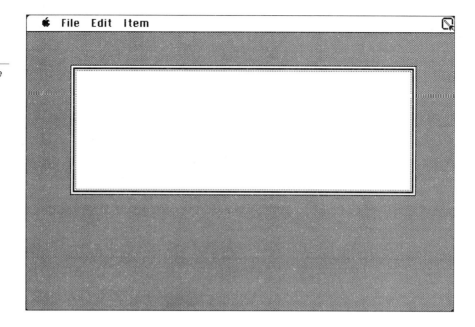

Fig. 16.2.

Changing the size
and shape of the
data form.

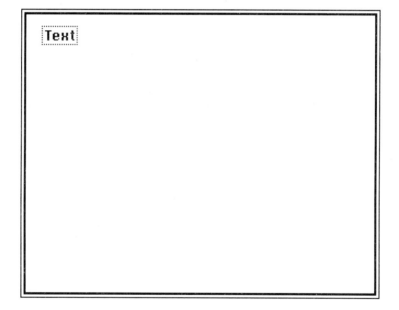

Fig. 16.3.

A highlighted text
box.

Add a different text box for each field in the database range (or, at least, for each field that is to appear in the form). The field names in the data form do not have to match those in the database; they can, in fact, be completely different. Add another text box for a main title and other descriptive titles. To move the text boxes into position, simply click on them and drag them to the new position. Alternatively, you can use the keyboard to move a text box; just highlight the box and use the arrow keys to change its position.

The Dialog Editor automatically makes the text box just large enough to hold all the text. Therefore, you should not need to change the size of a text box. You might consider using text boxes to display fancy characters created with Option-key combinations (see fig. 16.4).

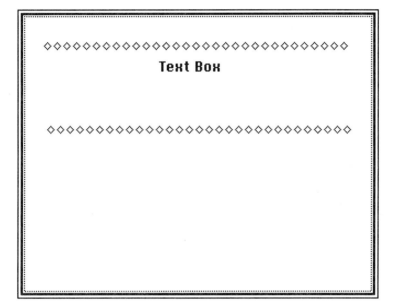

Fig. 16.4.

Using special characters in a text box.

Adding Fields to the Data Form

The next step is to add fields to the data form. These are the boxes that will display the data from the database range. Because they relate to the field names, you should line them up with the labels you entered in the preceding section. To create a field box, use the Item Edit Box command. Add as many field boxes as you like. Usually, these field boxes will match up with the text labels you create. However, you do not have to have a text field to describe each field box. Text and field boxes are completely independent. Note that Excel places the words *Edit Text* in the boxes to indicate that they are edit boxes. This phrase will not appear when you use the form.

> **Inserting Multiple Field Boxes**
>
> After inserting the first field box, press Return to enter a second. Keep pressing Return to enter as many as you like.

So how does Excel know what database data to place into the various field boxes? It knows because you tell it which database fields are linked to which field boxes. This process is described in the next section.

You can move field boxes as you do other objects in the data form. Just click on the box and drag the mouse. Alternatively, use the keyboard commands to move the boxes. Figure 16.5 shows a completed set of text boxes and field boxes for a custom data form.

Fig. 16.5.

Field boxes for the data form.

◇◇◇◇◇◇◇◇◇◇◇◇◇◇◇◇◇◇◇◇◇◇◇◇◇◇◇◇◇◇◇◇

Name

| Edit Text |

Company

| Edit Text |

Street

| Edit Text |

City, St ZIP

| Edit Text | | Edit | | Edit Text |

Noting Special Information about the Data Form

The size and position of the various data form elements are measured and stored by the Dialog Editor. Although you position the elements by using the mouse or keyboard, you can view the coordinates for each data form element—and for the data form itself. Just highlight the item you want to view, and select the Edit Info command. The Dialog Editor presents a screen like the one in figure 16.6.

```
┌─────────────────────────────────────────────┐
│  Edit Text Info           ☐ Resettable       │
│                                               │
│          H: [20      ]  ☐ Auto    ╭────────╮  │
│                                   │   OK   │  │
│          Y: [53      ]  ☐ Auto    ╰────────╯  │
│                                   ╭────────╮  │
│      Width: [171     ]  ☐ Auto    │ Cancel │  │
│                                   ╰────────╯  │
│     Height: [        ]  ☒ Auto                │
│                                               │
│       Text: [                              ]  │
│                                               │
│ Init/Result:[                              ]  │
│                                               │
│    Comment: [                              ]  │
└─────────────────────────────────────────────┘
```

Fig. 16.6.

The Info screen.

This screen contains the coordinates for the upper left corner of the highlighted element. These coordinates are the X and Y values in the Info screen. In the case of the data form itself, these values indicate the distance (in picas) from the upper left corner of the screen. The X coordinate indicates the horizontal position; the Y coordinate indicates the vertical position. In the case of text boxes or field boxes, the X and Y coordinates are relative to the upper left corner of the dialog box. Thus X and Y coordinates of 1,1 for a text box place the box in the upper left corner of the data form, regardless of its position on the screen.

The height and width also are measured in picas. These measurements are relative to the upper left corner of the item itself; they are thus constant values. A width of 100 is a specific width, regardless of the item's X and Y values.

The Init/Result value is important only for the field boxes. In fact, you should not enter anything into this space for items other than field boxes. This value specifies the database field that is linked to this field box. In other words, a field box is linked to the database field you specify. Enter the desired database field (by name) in the Init/Result space for each field box. Be sure to enter the field name as it appears in the first row of the database. If you forget the names of the fields or make mistakes when entering them, you can make corrections later.

The Text box will contain information only for text box items; it will indicate the text displayed in the text box. You should not enter anything into this space for items other than text boxes.

In the Comment box, you can enter comments about the item. This information will not appear in the data form.

Saving and Using the Data Form

Because the Dialog Editor is a special tool for customizing the data form, the assumption is that you will be returning to Excel as soon as you finish creating the form. The program thus contains no Save command for permanently storing the form. Instead, you must store the form on the clipboard and then pass the form into Excel.

To store the data form on the clipboard, select the Edit Select Dialog command. Next, use the Edit Copy command to copy the form. The specifications for the form are now on the clipboard. Another method is to use the File Quit command and answer Yes when asked whether you want to save the form to the clipboard. Once you quit the program, go immediately into Excel with the desired database worksheet active.

The exact procedure for activating the data form once you return to Excel is described in the next section.

Activating the Custom Data Form in Excel

When you finish creating the data form and storing it on the clipboard, return to Excel with the desired worksheet in view (the worksheet containing the database that relates to the form you created). Next, click the mouse button in an empty area of the worksheet. This area should be a block of at least 8 cells by 20 cells (actually, the number of rows needed corresponds to the number of items contained in the data form). Finally, choose the Edit Paste command.

When you paste the data form into the empty area of the worksheet, Excel stores the coordinates and other values relating to the data items. In other words, the data form does not appear in the worksheet; what appears are a number of values that "describe" the data form for Excel. Figure 16.7 shows a data form after being pasted into a worksheet.

In this example, the column headings were added to indicate what data is in each column. Also, the border was added to help separate this data from the rest of the worksheet. Each row of data represents (or defines) one of the items in the form. Notice that the data in these rows was contained in the Edit Info screens back in the Dialog Editor program. Now that the information is part of the worksheet, the information can be used for the database data form.

Fig. 16.7.

Pasting the data form into a worksheet.

The last step is to highlight the range of cells containing this new data (the range should already be highlighted when you paste it into the worksheet). Do not include the headings in this range (assuming that you add them as shown in the figure). Using the Define Name command, name this range *Data_Form* (include the underscore character). Once you name this range, Excel uses it to define the data form for the currently defined database. Therefore, be sure that the correct database has been defined with the Data Set Database command. The field names in this database should match the field specifications in the Init/Result column of the data form. Unless you delete the name *Data_Form* from the Define Name dialog box, Excel will use this information as the data form whenever you use the Data Form command.

NOTE You can create a data form without the Dialog Editor by setting up a range containing the columns shown in figure 16.7 and by then entering the coordinates and other values into the appropriate cells under each column. Each item gets a new row in this range. Note that the specifications for the form itself are contained in the first row (directly under the headings). The following is a description of each column:

Type   The type of each item. In a data form, you should have only two types: 5 indicates a text box, and 6 indicates a field box.

X Position	The horizontal position of the upper left corner of the item.
Y Position	The vertical position of the upper left corner of the item.
Item Width	The width of the item.
Item Height	The height of the item.
Text	The text (if any) used for the item. Field boxes will not have anything in this column.
Field (Initial Result)	The name of the field to which the field box is linked. This name should exactly match one of the database field names. Text boxes should not have anything in this column.
Comment	Any comments regarding the item.

Be sure to highlight the data and define its name as *Data_Form*. You also can edit an existing data form by changing the information in this box.

Summarizing How To Build Custom Data Forms

The following is a summary of the steps used to create a custom data form:

Creating a Custom Data Form

1. Enter the Dialog Editor program.

2. Use the Item Text command to add text to the data form.

3. Use the Item Edit Box command with the Edit Text option to add field boxes to the data form. If you want to change the length of these boxes, use the mouse or keyboard commands (Shift+right arrow and Shift+left arrow).

4. Move the elements created in steps 2 and 3 into place on the form, using the mouse or keyboard commands.

5. If you want to change the size, shape, and position of the data form itself, select the Form outline and then use the mouse or keyboard commands.

6. Highlight one of the field boxes and choose the Edit Info command.

7. Link this field box with one of the fields in the database by entering the desired field name into the space marked Init/Result. Be sure to enter the names exactly as they appear in the database.

8. Repeat step 7 for each of the field box items.

9. Quit the Dialog Editor program and save the dialog information to the clipboard when prompted.

10. Go immediately into Excel and open the appropriate worksheet file.

11. Move the cell pointer to an empty area of the worksheet.

12. Use the Edit Paste command to paste the data form specifications into the worksheet.

13. With the data still highlighted after pasting, use the Formula Define Name command and enter the name **Data_Form.**

14. Save the changes to the worksheet. The custom data form will now appear every time you use the Data Form command (assuming that the database has been activated with the Data Set Database command).

Purging Duplicate Records from a Database

The need to remove duplicates is common in database management. Often, record-keeping tasks involve accumulating multiple copies of the same information. In these cases, you may decide to remove duplicates. Here's how: Determine which field you want to use as the "determining field" for duplicates. In other words, choose a field in the database that contains information unique to each record, so that if two records contain the same information in this field, they can be considered duplicates. In address lists, the Street field often serves this purpose. At times, you may need two or three determining fields for this procedure. In an address list, for example, it's possible to have two different people living at the same address. Thus you might use both the Name and Address fields.

After settling on the determining field or fields, sort the database by the field (or fields) you have chosen. Enter the first field into the 1st Key location. If you use two or three fields, use the 2nd Key to specify the second field and the 3rd Key to specify the third field. Doing so places all like records together.

Enter a criteria formula (calculated criteria) for each of the fields used in the sort. Each formula should compare the appropriate field in the first record of the database with the same field in the record above it. Figure 16.8 shows an example based on a simple address list.

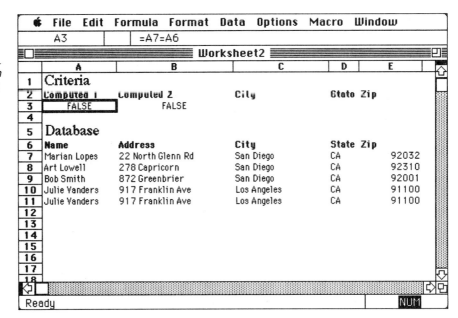

Fig. 16.8.

Entering duplication criteria after sorting the database.

Notice that the formula in cell A3 reads =A7=A6. This formula finds all records whose name field matches the name above it. It's all right that the first cell (A7) refers to a cell that is not really a record (A6) in this case. The formula performs its function regardless. The formula in cell B3 reads =B7=B6 and adds the address field to the name field for matching records. In short, these formulas find records whose address fields and name fields match the record above.

Finally, use the command Data Delete to remove the records that match the criteria. As long as the database is sorted properly, this step removes duplicates.

Displaying Database Records

One disadvantage of Excel's database structure is that records are displayed in row-and-column order. This arrangement is great for viewing many records at one time, but it's not always suitable when you need to examine or print a single record. The data form provides a single-record view of the data, but you cannot use the form to format a record for printing. Besides, you cannot control the fonts or other graphic elements used in the data form. That limitation can be a problem if, for instance, you want to display records in a report that contains various type formats.

Consider the database discussed in Chapter 14 (see fig. 16.9). This database contains information about video tapes for a rental store. Suppose that you want to display information about a title, using a form layout as in figure 16.10.

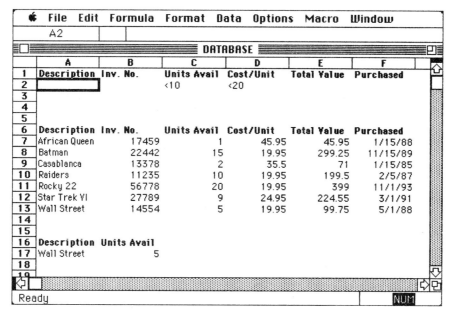

Fig. 16.9.

The video store sample database.

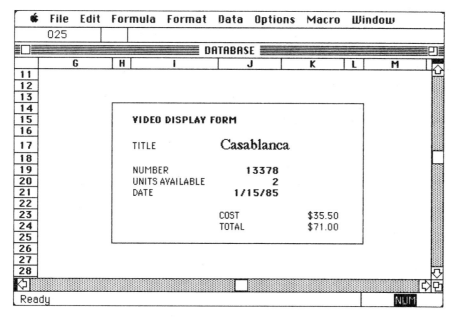

Fig. 16.10.

Displaying single records in a form layout for printing.

Using the database extract commands, you can automatically display records in forms for viewing or printing. By indicating which record you want (using the criteria range), Excel can extract the desired record and display it in the form. Because only one record will be displayed in the form at a time, the task is relatively easy.

Start by setting up the data range, criteria range, and extract range of the worksheet. In this case, reproduce all field names at the top of the extract area; doing so causes complete records to be extracted. Use the criteria range to find the record you want displayed in the form. Then highlight the extract headings and extract the record. The record should appear below the extract headings, as shown in figure 16.11.

Fig. 16.11.

Use standard extract methods to extract the desired record from the data range.

♠	File	Edit	Formula	Format	Data	Options	Macro	Window

A16		Description

DATABASE

	A	B	C	D	E	F
1	Description	Inv. No.	Units Avail	Cost/Unit	Total Value	Purchased
2		13378				
3						
4						
5						
6	Description	Inv. No.	Units Avail	Cost/Unit	Total Value	Purchased
7	African Queen	17459	1	45.95	45.95	1/15/88
8	Batman	22442	15	19.95	299.25	11/15/89
9	Casablanca	13378	2	35.5	71	1/15/85
10	Raiders	11235	10	19.95	199.5	2/5/87
11	Rocky 22	56778	20	19.95	399	11/1/93
12	Star Trek VI	27789	9	24.95	224.55	3/1/91
13	Wall Street	14554	5	19.95	99.75	5/1/88
14						
15						
16	Description	Inv. No.	Units Avail	Cost/Unit	Total Value	Purchased
17	Casablanca	13378	2	35.5	71	1/15/85
18						

Ready — NUM

So far, this is a standard extract procedure. The next step is to create the form. Choose an area of the worksheet where changes to the column widths and row heights will not affect other data. Most likely, this area will be below and to the right of the data range but above the extract range. Using simple cell references to the extracted fields (range A19:F19 in this example), indicate where each piece of information is to appear in the form. As you build the form with cell references to the extracted row, the record in that row will appear in the form. Adjust the cell widths and heights as desired for the data. Use whatever formatting options you like. Figure 16.12 shows the cell references used for the sample form.

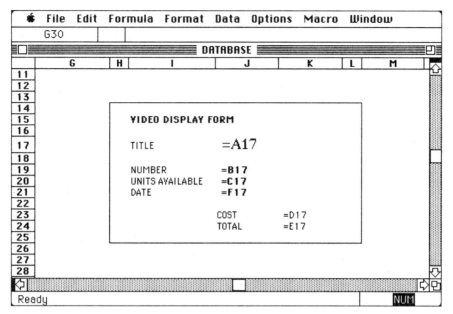

Fig. 16.12.

Use cell references to build the form.

Note that this form is created by the manipulation of the column widths and row heights of the worksheet area. Also, special fonts were used for certain fields in the form. The border was added through the use of the Format Border command. In this figure, the formulas are displayed rather than the values they produce. Normally, the form will display whichever record has been extracted from the database.

Now, every time you extract a record from the database, that record automatically appears in the form. The reason is that the extract range does not change, and the references to it remain intact for the form. When a new record is extracted into this extract range, the cells in the form use its information. Extract any record by specifying criteria unique to that record—criteria that will extract only that record from the database.

Summary

This chapter discussed some of the more-advanced database tools available for your worksheet databases. In particular, you learned how to create a custom data form. Creating a custom data form lets you overcome basic limitations of the default form. In the custom form, you can include any fields you want, arrange them in any order, and change the basic size and shape of the form itself. This chapter also included a technique for removing duplicate records from a database and a way to print database records in a free-form style. The following are points to remember:

❏ Use the Dialog Editor to create a custom data form.

❏ The size, shape, and position of the data form in the Dialog Editor determine the size, shape, and position of the form when used in Excel.

❏ Add text to a data form by using the Item Text command.

❏ Add field boxes to the data form by using the Item Edit Box command.

❏ After you add one field box or text box to the form, pressing Return adds another.

❏ Use the mouse to move the boxes into position in the form.

❏ Use the Edit Info command to link each field box to a field in the database. Enter the field name into the space marked Init Result.

❏ To use the custom data form in the Excel worksheet, copy the form within the Dialog Editor program, then enter the Excel worksheet and use the Edit Paste command to insert the form into a blank area. Finally, name the highlighted data *Data_Form*, using the Formula Define Name command.

Chapter 17, "Macro Quick Start," begins the book's last section, "Excel Macros." Turn to that chapter for a lesson on creating macros.

Part IV

Excel Macros

Macro Quick Start

Getting Started with Macros

Using Macro Programming Techniques

17

Macro
Quick Start

Macros, a popular feature of sophisticated programs, make your work easier by automating complex or repetitive tasks. But perhaps you've been avoiding macros because you think that they are advanced and complicated. That may have been true once, but today macros are quite easy to use. You don't have to become an advanced macro programmer to benefit from them.

To get you started with macros, this chapter provides a step-by-step lesson in the basics of creating and running macros. From here, you'll be ready to design your own macros for specific needs.

Recording a Macro

A macro is a sort of invisible user in the computer that enters commands while you sit back and watch. Whatever you can do from the keyboard or mouse, the macro can do too. All you have to do is show it one time, and the macro can repeat the actions over and over.

You may be wondering why macros are so great if they simply repeat your commands—commands that you could enter yourself by using the keyboard or mouse. The benefit is that macros don't just repeat your commands: they repeat them instantly. A macro can perform dozens of commands in a second. And the macro never makes mistakes. It's like a tape recorder that plays back your commands as you entered them, but much faster. As a matter of fact, you can teach a macro its commands by recording them with other, special commands. These are the basic steps:

- Turn the recorder on with the command Macro Record.
- Perform any commands or actions that you want to record.
- Turn the recorder off with the command Macro Stop Recorder.
- Run the macro.

Each of these steps is described in this chapter.

Starting the Macro

To create a macro, you must open a new worksheet, turn on the recorder, and choose a name for the macro. Complete these steps to start a sample macro:

1. Start a new worksheet by entering Excel from the desktop or by using the File New command.
2. Start the recorder by selecting the command Macro Record. The dialog box shown in figure 17.1 appears.

Fig. 17.1.

The Macro Record dialog box.

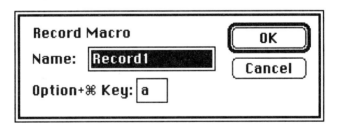

This dialog box asks you to name the macro and select a "shortcut" key for it. The dialog box already contains the name *Record1* and the shortcut key *a*. You can replace these entries with your own. You should choose a name that reminds you of the macro's purpose. When you are ready to run the macro later, you can choose it, by name, from a list of available macros, or you can press Command+Option along with the key you specified.

3. Enter the name **MONTHS** into the space provided. If there is already a name in that space, replace it with the new name. Press Tab.

4. Press the M key to specify a lowercase *m* as the shortcut key for this macro. Press Return. (Actually, this step is optional, because macros do not have to have shortcut keys. To avoid specifying the shortcut key, remove the entry and press Return.)

You are now ready to record the macro named MONTHS. Everything you do from this point on will become part of the macro until you stop the recorder. The next section continues with this example and lists the steps that are to be recorded in this macro.

Making the Recording

Now you're ready to begin recording the macro. Follow these steps:

1. Move the pointer to cell A3.

2. Enter **1/1/90** and press Tab to move to cell B3.

3. Type the formula **=DATE("90",MONTH(A3)+1,"1")** and press Enter.

4. Highlight the range B3:L3.

5. Choose the command Edit Fill Right.

6. Click the mouse in the horizontal scroll bar to return to the left side of the worksheet. Alternatively, you can drag the scroll box all the way to the left. Now highlight the range A3:L3.

7. Choose the Format Number command and, at the space provided, type **mmmm** in the Format dialog box to specify a custom format. Press Return.

8. With the range still highlighted, press Command+B to "blank" it (that is, to erase the information). Now select the Edit Undo command to undo that erasure. These two actions simulate making a mistake and correcting it while you record. You will read more about this step later in the chapter.

9. Turn the recorder off by issuing the command Macro Stop Recorder.

You have now completed recording the macro called MONTHS. Steps 1 through 8 enter the month names into a row of the worksheet, a task that is frequently required on new worksheets. Now you can accomplish that task at any time by running the macro. The following section shows two ways to run it.

Running the Macro

Remember that the macro you just created operates on a new worksheet and enters information into the range A3:L3. To see how this macro works, you'll need to blank out the current worksheet first. Follow these steps to run the macro:

1. Highlight the entire worksheet by clicking in the upper left corner of the sheet (in the intersection of the row and column headings); then press Command+B.

2. Click to place the pointer in any cell.

3. Press Command+Option+m (lowercase *m*).

Instantly the macro fills in the month names for the new worksheet. The result should look like figure 17.2.

Fig. 17.2.

Running the macro.

	File	**Edit**	**Formula**	**Format**	**Data**	**Options**	**Macro**	**Window**

A3		1/1/1990			

Worksheet1

	A	**B**	**C**	**D**	**E**	**F**	
1							
2							
3	January	February	March	April	May	June	
4							
5							
6							

Another way to run the macro is to use the Macro Run command. This command is useful if you forget the shortcut key or if you don't assign one for the macro. You also can use this command to view all available macros (by name) at one time. To run a macro with this command, just select Macro Run and then double-click on the appropriate macro name that appears in the dialog box.

Viewing and Saving the Macro

When recording your actions as a macro, Excel translates everything you do into codes and places those codes in a macro worksheet. The codes represent the keys you pressed, the mouse movements you made, and the commands you selected. And the codes appear in the order in which you took those actions. These codes, called *macro commands*, are part of a group of codes called the *macro command language*. As you've already seen, it's not necessary to know what each of these codes means in order to create a macro—but when you take a look at them, you'll see how easy they are to understand. Here's how to look at the macro codes for the macro you just created:

From the Window menu, select the sheet named Macro1.

Performing this step activates the macro sheet, which was added and placed behind the current worksheet. The screen should look like figure 17.3.

	File	**Edit**	**Formula**	**Format**	**Data**	**Options**	**Macro**	**Window**

A1		MONTHS

Macro1

	A	B	C
1	MONTHS		
2	=SELECT("R3C1")		
3	=FORMULA("1/1/1990")		
4	=SELECT("R3C2")		
5	=FORMULA("=DATE(""90"",M		
6	=SELECT("R3C2:R3C12")		
7	=FILL.RIGHT()		
8	=HPAGE(-1)		
9	=SELECT("R3C1:R3C12")		
10	=FORMAT.NUMBER("mmmm"		
11	=CLEAR(3)		
12	=UNDO()		
13	=RETURN()		
14			

Fig. 17.3.

The macro sheet.

The macro sheet was created when you selected the Macro Record command in step 2 of the section "Starting the Macro." The sheet was automatically placed behind the active worksheet, and the macro commands were entered on the sheet "behind the scenes." Notice that the macro sheet contains a column of commands that represent your actions. At the top of the column is the macro name as you entered it in step 3 of the section "Starting the Macro." Looking over these commands, you can get a pretty good impression of what each does. For complete details about macro commands, however, see Chapter 18 and Appendix B.

Any time this macro sheet is open, you can run the macro in it; if a sheet contains several macros, you can run any of them. (Chapter 18 explains how to place more macros on the same sheet. See also "Creating a Second Macro" later in this chapter.) Remember, however, that you must open the macro sheet in order to run a macro contained on it. Although the sheet must be open, it does not have to be active (that is, in view); it can be behind the active worksheet, for example.

To save the sample macro for future use, use the File Save command, as you would for a typical worksheet. Because the macro sheet is saved independently of a worksheet, you can use the macro with any worksheet you like. The sample macro is useful on new worksheets.

Editing the Macro

You can change a macro by editing the codes that appear on the macro sheet. Editing a macro requires a minor amount of knowledge about macro commands. Sometimes, you'll make mistakes while recording a macro. For example, you might select the wrong command and then undo the action with the Undo command (as simulated in step 8 in the section "Making the Recording"). The macro will record the error and the Undo command and repeat them faithfully each time you run the macro. Of course, the result will be what you intended, but the mistake and its correction are unnecessary in the macro.

You can edit mistakes out of a macro or simply change a macro to suit your needs better. To remove the mistake and the Undo operation from the sample macro, do the following:

1. Highlight cells A11 and A12.
2. Select the command Edit Delete.
3. Choose the Shift Cells Up option.

Now the macro will not repeat the error each time the macro runs. The next thing to notice is the entry in cell A8. This command shows that you scrolled the window to the left by one screen. (Your cell may contain a slightly different entry.) That action was included as a step so that you could highlight the range A3:L3 for the next procedure. However, the macro does not need to scroll the page in order to highlight a range. Do the following to remove cell A8 from the macro:

1. Move the pointer to cell A8 and select the Edit Delete command.
2. Choose the Shift Cells Up option.

Now that you have edited the macro, save it again by using the File Save command.

Changing Cell References

Notice in figure 17.3 that all cell references in the macro were recorded in the R1C1 style. This style is simply the format in which Excel records references. More important is the fact that the cell references are "literal." Cell A6, for example, contains the range reference R3C2:R3C12, indicating the range B3:L3. This range was designated in preparation for the Fill Right command. Every time you run this macro, the range B3:L3 will be highlighted for the Fill Right command that occurs in the next cell of the macro. In other words, this macro does its work on the same range every time you use it.

Suppose that you want this macro to be able to add the month names to any range in the worksheet. You want, for instance, to be able to position the pointer in a cell and then have the macro add the month names, beginning in the active cell. Depending on where you begin, the area to be filled with month names could be any 1-by-12 range of cells. Tailoring the macro to meet this requirement does not really change the macro much; you must simply make the range references relative to the active cell.

You can make a macro's cell references relative by selecting the command Macro Relative Record before starting to record your actions as a macro. For the sample macro, you should select this command after performing step 4 in the section "Starting the Macro." Then finish the recording process. Remember that Excel now records the current location of the pointer and records your movements relative to this position. When you reexamine the macro, the cell addresses will look different. For more details, see Chapter 18.

Creating a Second Macro

Creating another macro on the same macro sheet is different from creating the first macro. Because the sheet already exists and contains a macro in cell A1, you must begin the macro in a different cell. In this case, start the macro in cell B1. Complete the following steps to create a second sample macro:

1. Move the pointer to cell B1 of the macro sheet. You may need to activate the sheet first. Enter the macro name **GRIDOFF** into cell B1 and press Return. The pointer should be in cell B2.

2. Select the command Macro Set Recorder. This action tells Excel that the active cell (B2) is the starting cell for this macro.

3. Activate the worksheet. If you don't have a worksheet open, create a new one with the command File New. Make sure that you use the Spreadsheet option when you issue this command, or you could end up with another macro sheet.

4. Use the command Window Arrange All to arrange the two windows on the screen. This step is not necessary, but it lets you see the macro record your actions as you perform them.

5. Select the command Macro Start Recorder.

6. Select the command Options Display and then remove the check mark from the Gridlines option. Click on the OK button. This step removes the grid lines from the active worksheet. Notice that your actions are being recorded in the macro sheet, beginning at cell B2.

7. Select the command Macro Stop Recorder.

   You have now recorded a new macro that turns the grid lines off in the current worksheet. But unlike the first macro created with the Macro Record command, this macro is not ready to run yet. You must first perform the remaining steps.

8. Activate the macro sheet and move the pointer to cell B1.

9. Select the command Formula Define Name. The dialog box should look like figure 17.4.

10. Confirm that the name in the dialog box corresponds to the macro name and that its cell reference is B1. Now click on the Command Key button to designate this a command macro.

11. In the space provided for a shortcut key, press the G key (lowercase). Press Return.

Now the macro is ready to run. Steps 8 through 11 activate the macro by giving it a name and a shortcut key. These steps are necessary when you do not use the Macro Record command to create the macro (the Macro Record command performs these steps for you). You can now run the macro by pressing Command+Option+g. Try it on a new worksheet. (Remember to leave the macro sheet open.)

Define Name

MONTHS

Name:

GRIDOFF

Refers to:

=$B$1

Macro

○ Function ○ Command Option+⌘ Key: [ ] ◉ None

OK

Cancel

Delete

Fig. 17.4.

The Formula Define Name dialog box.

Summary

This chapter provided a brief step-by-step lesson on creating macros. You learned how to record a macro by using the Macro Record command, which opens a macro sheet, asks you to name the macro, and begins recording your actions. You also saw how the Macro Stop Recorder command concludes the recording. Running a macro consists of opening the appropriate macro sheet and entering the Command+Option+key combination that you specified for the macro. Finally, you saw how to create a second macro on an existing macro sheet. With this information, you're ready to discover the details about creating and running macros—which is covered in the next chapter, "Getting Started with Macros."

18

Getting Started with Macros

This chapter presents the basics of Excel's macro capabilities. If you have read Chapter 1, you are probably familiar with the purpose of macros. The Macro Quick Start (Chapter 17) provides step-by-step instructions for building a basic macro. You are now ready to discover how to put macros to powerful uses in your worksheets. Excel's macro language includes dozens of special commands to control the worksheet. It is unlikely that you will need or want to learn all the available commands and functions; it is more important that you fully understand how to create, edit, and run macros. This chapter will show you how.

First you will learn how macros operate, as well as what they are used for. Then you will learn the guidelines for creating basic macros. You will learn how to create two types of macros: command and function. By the end of the chapter, you will be ready to progress in many directions. If you want to begin some macros of your own, you might first glance through the macro commands listed in Appendix B. If you want to learn more about creating menus and dialog boxes, read Chapter 19, where you will also find more details about programming, such as using variables, loops, and special routines.

Understanding How Macros Work

A *macro* is a special program that controls various operations of Excel. A macro is like an invisible operator that is using Excel from within the computer; it can issue commands just as you would. Besides entering commands and options, macros offer special features. For example, macros enable you to create your own menus that contain options designed for special purposes.

Like programs, macros have a specific language—not unlike programming languages such as Pascal, C, and BASIC. But the macro language can be much easier to use than programming languages are, and Excel can do much of the programming work for you. Nevertheless, knowing the macro language and its specific commands is helpful. And if you are also familiar with programming concepts such as loops and variables, you are ahead of the game.

Because macros use special commands, these commands must be entered somewhere for Excel to read. Thus commands are entered on a *macro sheet.* A macro sheet is similar to a worksheet, but it is a separate window designed to hold macro commands. When commands are typed into this window, the macro sheet can be saved as a separate file. Therefore, macros are independent of the worksheets to which they apply. In fact, a single macro can be used with several worksheets, although many macros are designed to be used with only one worksheet.

Figure 18.1 shows a macro sheet and a standard worksheet next to it.

You may be thinking that the macro sheet looks very much like a worksheet. A macro sheet *is* a worksheet, one formatted with wide columns and with cells that display formulas rather than the results of formulas. You will also notice that all the standard worksheet menus and options are available for your macro sheet.

Why does the macro sheet display formula text rather than the values produced by formulas? Excel perceives macro commands as being formulas. As you will see, these commands are entered with equal signs, and they all produce values. (Many macro commands produce values of TRUE or FALSE, indicating whether the command has been used. Some macro commands, however, produce values just as standard worksheet formulas do.) Generally, the values produced by macro commands are not as important to view as are the macro commands themselves, but you can always display the values instead of the formulas by using the Options Display command on the macro sheet.

	File	Edit	Formula	Format	Data	Options	Macro	Window	

A1		MACRO				

Worksheet2

	A	B	C	D	E	F
1						
2	Amounts					
3	1289.35	238.3	2332	2198.99	1200	
4						
5						
6						

Macro1

	A	B
1	MACRO	
2	=SELECT("R3C1:R3C5")	
3	=FORMAT.NUMBER("#,##0.[	
4	=FORMAT.FONT("Times",18,F	
5	=RETURN()	
6		
7		
8		

Fig. 18.1.

A typical macro sheet.

Notice that the macro in figure 18.1 consists of a series of individual commands, each command in a separate cell in column A (the standard arrangement of a macro). The first cell contains a name; the following cells contain the commands that constitute the actions of the macro. These commands appear in a single column with no blanks. The end of the macro is the special command =RETURN( ). Most macros end with this command.

Notice that each command in figure 18.1 (not including the macro name) is entered with an equal sign, like a worksheet formula. All macro commands must include an equal sign, because Excel ignores any entry that does not have the equal sign. (Ignored entries can be useful, however, as you will see later.)

Because each macro has a definite beginning (the name) and ending (the =RETURN( ) command), you can store several different macros on the same macro sheet, each with a unique name. Storing macros in this manner can be useful when the macros are related to one another or to the same worksheet. When you are ready to use one of the macros, you can specify which one.

The final thing to note about macros is that you can run (or invoke) them at any time. You can run a macro in several ways. Remember, however, that you cannot run a macro unless the appropriate macro sheet is open. The sheet that you open should not be the active sheet; instead, you should place the desired worksheet in front of the macro sheet. Macros will generally apply to the currently active worksheet.

Macros are fairly simple, but as you can see by now, you must follow certain steps in order to make a macro work properly. The following is a summary of these steps:

Creating a Macro

1. Open the worksheet to which the macro applies. If you are designing a macro that applies to several worksheets, open any of them.

2. Open a new worksheet with the File New command. Make the worksheet a macro sheet by selecting the Macro Sheet option.

   or

   Select the Macro Record command; then enter a macro name and shortcut key. Next, perform the actions that you want to record. Excel will record everything you do. When you are finished, select the Macro Stop Recorder command. If you use this version of step 2, you can eliminate steps 3 through 6 and proceed directly to step 7.

3. Enter a name for the macro in any cell of the macro sheet.

4. Enter the macro commands under the name you typed. You can do so by simply typing the commands (each command preceded by an equal sign) or by using the automatic macro recorder. Both methods are described in full later in this chapter.

5. Conclude the macro with the =RETURN( ) command.

6. Activate the macro by moving the pointer to the cell containing the macro name; then use the Formula Define Name command. Click on the Command+Option+⌘ button (hereafter called the Command Key button, for simplicity's sake) and then enter any character into the corresponding space. Click on OK when you are finished.

7. Save the macro sheet if you want to keep the macro.

8. Activate the worksheet in which the macro will be used.

9. Run the macro. You can do so by using the Macro Run command and selecting the appropriate macro name from the list provided, or by pressing the Command key along with the Option key and the "shortcut" key specified in step 6.

Each of these steps is explained in detail in this chapter. After you are familiar with these steps, browse through the macro commands and experiment with macros on sample worksheets. For more-advanced information about creating macros, see Chapter 19.

Noting Typical Uses for Macros

Macros are useful for many reasons. Most commonly, they perform repetitive or lengthy tasks when you press a single Command+Option+key combination. Anything that you can do by using Excel's menu commands, you can do by using a macro. For this reason, macros are often used to combine sets of menu commands into one simple key command.

Suppose that you prefer to work on worksheets without the grid lines and formula bar showing—and that you frequently use the Options Display command to remove the grid lines and the Options Workspace command to remove the formula bar. Because you have to hide the grid lines and formula bar separately (that is, you have to use two different menu commands), the process can become tedious. However, you can easily create a macro that hides both in one step. This macro may look like the one in figure 18.2.

⚫ File Edit Formula Format Data Options Macro Window		
A6		

	A	B	C
	≡ Macro1 ≡		
1	FORMAT		
2	=DISPLAY(,FALSE,,,)		
3	=WORKSPACE(,,,,FALSE,,,)		
4	=RETURN()		
5			
6			
7			
8			

Fig. 18.2.

A simple macro.

Uppercase and Lowercase

It is not necessary to enter macro commands in uppercase letters. This book uses the convention of placing command and function names in uppercase and variable information in lowercase.

Any task that you would perform by using the standard Excel menus, you can assign to a macro that you run with a Command+Option+key combination. Possible tasks for macros include formatting blocks of data, changing charts from one type to another, copying information over and over, printing certain areas of a worksheet, and even just moving the pointer to specific locations of a worksheet. Every menu command in Excel has a macro-command equivalent; and every nonmenu command, such as the one for moving the pointer, has a macro-command equivalent. Other nonmenu commands include those for typing data, highlighting cells, scrolling windows, splitting windows, and changing the sizes and shapes of windows.

By using macros that mimic nonmenu commands, you can add new information to a worksheet. The key to adding information is the macro function FORMULA. When used in a macro, this command performs the equivalent of typing a formula (or text) into the currently selected cell. (More information on the FORMULA function appears later in this chapter.)

You can also use macros to provide user interface and worksheet support. Many businesspeople create worksheets that will ultimately be used by other people, so the more documentation and support you can build into a worksheet, the more effectively it will be used.

Macros are an excellent way to add support; they are commonly used to control the user's actions in a fashion that prevents errors. Macros can also be used to display messages as responses to certain actions. By creating custom menu commands, you can almost eliminate the user's need to know Excel. Although you would be limiting the user's capabilities and possible actions, this very limitation would control errors.

Preparing To Enter Macro Commands

Macros are created in a macro sheet. Before you can begin a macro, you must open a new sheet into which the macro will be entered. To open a macro sheet, select the File New command; then click on the Macro Sheet button. A new macro sheet will come into view. This worksheet is very much like a typical worksheet, except that it is specifically designed to store macros. Nevertheless, most worksheet features apply to a macro sheet just as they apply to a normal worksheet.

Once the macro sheet is open, you may begin entering macro commands or using the macro recorder. (Both of these procedures will be explained later.) When you finish, save the macro by using the Save or Save As option in the File menu, or close the macro window; Excel will prompt you to save any changes. Excel will store the file on disk as a macro file with the name you specified. If the macro contains errors, it will not run properly or at all. But you can save the macro anyway by using the File Save or File Save As command.

When a macro has been saved, you can reopen it by using the File Open command. Remember that a macro must be open (that is, its file must be open) before you can run it. If you would like to open the macro file every time you open a particular worksheet file, use the File Save Workspace command to save both files as a workspace file. When you open the workspace file, the worksheet and the macro files will be open. (See Chapter 7 for more information about this command.)

Once you open a macro and run it, you may decide to make changes. Because a macro window is like any other worksheet window, you can use standard worksheet commands to insert cells, delete cells, edit the contents of cells, and so on. These worksheet commands are explained in Chapter 4.

Creating Macros

You can create macros in two ways, each of which has advantages and disadvantages. You might find it useful to combine these methods for more control of macros. The first method is to enter the macro commands by hand. The second method is to use the macro recorder to enter macro commands as you perform them. The latter method is especially useful for beginners because it does much of the work for you.

Entering Macros Directly

One way to create a macro is to type the commands and functions directly into the macro window. By typing commands and functions in the proper order, you can create powerful macros. One disadvantage to this method is that you must know the proper macro command for each action you want to take. Another disadvantage is that these macros are subject to typing errors and improper usage, which can cause the macro to run improperly or not at all. Many commands and functions are not available through menus, however, and are therefore not available to the macro recorder. For this reason, the direct-entry method offers the most control of macros and is usually preferred for advanced macro programming.

When you enter a macro by hand, be sure to begin with a name, followed by the macro commands (entered as formulas) and ending with the =RETURN( ) command. When finished, you must name the macro by selecting the first cell (the cell containing the name) and issuing the Formula Define Name command. The name and address of the macro should already be showing in the Define Name dialog box. Just click on the Command Key button and press Return. (If you like, you can enter a shortcut key into the space provided. This key will run the macro when the sheet is open.) The macro is now ready to run.

Using the Macro Recorder

The second (and easier) way to create a macro is to let Excel create it for you by recording actions that you can play back later. The macro recorder is most useful when several simple menu commands are combined into one macro command. You can create a macro by simply turning the recorder on, issuing the commands, and then turning the recorder off.

To turn the recorder on, use the Macro Record command. This command not only starts the recording process but also opens a new macro sheet and begins the macro in cell A1 of that sheet. (Make sure that you are ready to begin recording before you select this command.) You then may name the macro and specify a shortcut key for it. (When you have finished recording the macro, you can run it by pressing the Command key, the Option key, and the specified shortcut key.) After you specify a name and a shortcut key, press Return and begin performing the commands and options you want to record. At this point, everything you do will be recorded.

When you finish, select the Macro Stop Recorder command. You can see the finished macro by activating the new Macro1 window that Excel has opened for you. This window will be behind the worksheet window; you can activate it by selecting its name from the Window menu. After saving the new macro sheet, you can use the macro at any time.

The following is a summary of the basic steps for using the macro recorder:

Using the Macro Recorder

1. Open the worksheet in which you want to use the macro.

2. Select the Macro Record command. The dialog box shown in figure 18.3 will appear.

3. Enter a name for the macro, replacing the default name that appears.

```
┌─────────────────────────────────────────────────────┐
│  Record Macro          ╭───────────────╮            │
│                        │      OK        │            │
│  Name:  Record1        ╰───────────────╯            │
│                        ┌───────────────┐            │
│  Option+⌘ Key: a       │    Cancel     │            │
│                        └───────────────┘            │
└─────────────────────────────────────────────────────┘
```

Fig. 18.3.

The Macro Record dialog box.

4. Specify a character to be used with the Command and Option keys as a shortcut key for the macro. Any alphabet character except *e, i, n,* or *u* is acceptable. Excel distinguishes between uppercase and lowercase letters.

5. Press Return to continue.

6. Perform the actions that you want to record. Remember that every move you make is being recorded.

7. When you finish, select the Macro Stop Recorder command.

8. Save the new macro sheet (you might decide to change its name before saving). Do this by activating the sheet, using the Window menu, and then selecting File Save As.

These steps complete the macro and make it available for future worksheets. To use the macro, just open the saved macro sheet, activate the desired worksheet, and use the appropriate Command+Option+key combination to run the macro. You can also use other methods, which are explained later in this chapter.

The Macro Record command takes care of many steps for you, such as opening a new macro sheet and naming the macro for future use. The disadvantage of this command is that you cannot use it to place a second or subsequent macro on an existing macro sheet.

You may find it convenient to store related macros on the same sheet. You can always type second and subsequent macros by hand as described earlier—or you can use a variation of the macro recorder. This second method requires that after recording the macro, you name it by using the Define Name command. The steps are these:

*Using Macro Set
Recorder*

1. Open the appropriate worksheet and a new macro sheet. (If you are adding a macro to an existing sheet, open the existing macro sheet.)

2. Arrange the two windows, using the Window Arrange All command.

3. Enter the macro name into cell A1 (or any other cell) of the macro sheet; then move the pointer down one cell.

4. Select the Macro Set Recorder command, which tells Excel to start entering macro commands at the active cell (the cell below the macro name).

5. Activate the worksheet window by clicking on it or by selecting its name from the Window menu.

6. Position the pointer at the appropriate location; then select the Macro Start Recorder command.

7. Perform the actions that you want to record. Remember that every move you make is being recorded.

8. When you finish, select the Macro Stop Recorder command.

Excel will translate the recorded actions into macro commands and enter them into the open macro sheet at the location you specified with the Macro Set Recorder command. You can repeat this procedure to enter more macros on the same worksheet; remember to set the recorder on a different cell each time, and be sure that Excel has plenty of space under this cell to list the macro commands. Notice that choosing the Macro Stop Recorder command automatically concludes the macro by entering the =RETURN( ) command. Figure 18.4 shows a completed recording of the following actions (that is, these actions were performed after the recorder was turned on):

Select cells A3:E3.

Select the command Format Number.

Choose the number format #,##0.00 and press Return.

Choose the command Format Font.

Select the font Times 18 and press Return.

Select the command Macro Stop Recording.

Notice that the macro commands in the figure match the actions listed. You can often decipher a macro without really knowing the macro commands in detail.

	A	B	C
	A20		
	Macro1		
1	MACRO		
2	=SELECT("R3C1:R3C5")		
3	=FORMAT.NUMBER("#,##0.(		
4	=FORMAT.FONT("Times",18,F		
5	=RETURN()		
6			
7			

🍎 File Edit Formula Format Data Options Macro Window

Fig. 18.4.

A sample recording of a few simple menu commands.

The last step is to name the macro. All macros must be named before they can be used. To name a macro, position the pointer on the cell containing the macro's name and then select the Formula Define Name command. The dialog box shown in figure 18.5 will appear. In this figure, the macro FORMAT begins in cell A1, which is referenced as $A$1. If you position the pointer correctly before choosing the Define Name command, the correct name and reference will already be in place for the macro, saving you some time. (The name used to define the macro does not have to match the name used in the first cell of the macro, but keeping these names the same is good practice; Excel automatically uses the name in the first cell unless you specify otherwise.) The only thing you have to do at this point is click on the Command Key button, which tells Excel that the name in the box relates to a command macro. This step distinguishes the name from standard named ranges.

Define Name

Recorder

Name:
FORMAT

Refers to:
=$A$1

[OK]
[Cancel]
[Delete]

—Macro—
○ Function   ◉ Command   Option+⌘ Key: [ ]   ○ None

Fig. 18.5.

Defining the name of your macro and selecting the Command Key button.

If you like, you can enter a keyboard character into the space provided, thus assigning the macro a shortcut key. When you press the Command and Option keys along with the specified character, Excel runs the macro. Notice that Excel distinguishes between uppercase and lowercase letters for shortcut keys, giving you twice as many keys for macros. For example, pressing Command+Option+x can run one macro, and pressing Command+Option+X can run a different macro.

Even if you do not assign a shortcut key to the macro, you must still click on the Command Key button, name the macro, and enter the cell address of the first cell in the macro. Be sure to save the macro sheet after you define the macro name (or names). Saving the sheet will ensure that the macros will be active the next time you open the macro sheet.

Editing the Macro Name

You can edit the macro name and its cell reference the same way that you would edit a range name in a worksheet. Simply activate the appropriate macro sheet and select the Formula Define Name command. Next, select the macro you want from the list provided. Now you can change the name, cell reference, and shortcut key assigned to this macro.

Duplicate Macro Names and Command Keys

You may use the same macro name for two different macros as long as they appear in two different macro sheets. Excel associates the macro name with the sheet name. If two macros (regardless of their names) have the same shortcut key, however, pressing Command+Option and that key will run only the macro that was defined first. If you define two macros with the same name and they appear in the same macro sheet, the name will apply only to the macro you defined last. The first macro will be undefined and, therefore, unavailable.

Remember that before you can use a macro, you must open its macro sheet by using the File Open command.

Understanding Cell and Range References in Macros

In figure 18.4, the command =SELECT("R3C1:R3C5") represents highlighting the range A3:E3 by using the mouse or keyboard commands. Notice that the range reference is entered into the parentheses in R1C1 format. You cannot change this format, which is simply the way Excel records range or cell references. Several macro commands use range references in this way. If you need to examine a macro, you might find it handy to convert the worksheet to the R1C1 format by using the Options Workspace command, which makes the worksheet references match the macro references.

A1 versus R1C1

Excel will accept either the A1- or R1C1-style reference in a macro command. When you program a macro by hand, you can make the choice yourself. In this case, you might use whichever style corresponds to the worksheets that are being referenced. When you record a macro, however, Excel uses the R1C1 style.

If you use A1-style references, be sure to enter them as external references, or Excel will not accept them. The form !A1 refers to any worksheet that is currently active. The form *sheet*!A1 refers to cell A1 on the sheet worksheet.

Another thing you should notice about the range reference is that it is entered as a text string (in quotation marks). The macro command SELECT requires that references be entered in this fashion. In fact, most macro commands use these text-style cell references; the commands convert the text to a meaningful address when you run the macro. If you use the A1-style references as suggested in the preceding tip, do not enter them as text. Only the R1C1-style references are required as text.

Perhaps the most important thing to notice about the range reference is that it reflects an exact range, regardless of the pointer position. The macro in figure 18.4 applies its formatting commands to the range A3:E3 and only the range A3:E3. Excel calls such a reference an *absolute range reference*.

Updating Macro Sheet References

Remember that inserting and deleting cells from a worksheet updates affected references in that worksheet. Excel does not, however, update external references in other worksheets or in the macro sheet. Thus making changes in a worksheet does not update the macro sheet. When you are programming a macro by hand, it is a good idea to use range names whenever possible.

The opposite of an absolute range is a *relative range*. In a macro command, a relative range reference represents a range that is created relative to the current position of the pointer. Rather than highlighting the range A3:E3, you might want to highlight a range starting with the current position of the pointer and including the next four cells. If the pointer happens to be on cell A3 when you issue this macro command, you would get the range A3:E3. However, if the pointer were on cell C4, you would get the range C4:G4. This relative reference is very useful for creating macros that work in any worksheet, especially those that apply formatting commands to cells.

You can use relative references to record a macro by selecting the Macro Relative Record command before you select the Macro Start Recorder command. The first command causes all cell references to be recorded relative to the position of the pointer. The range reference in the preceding example would read =SELECT("RC:RC[4]") if it were created with the relative record active. The reference RC is the active cell, because it has no row or column positions; the [4] means "add four." This command thus means, "Highlight the range starting with the current row and column and ending with the current row and the current column plus four columns." Consider these other examples:

RC:R[2]C[2]	Add two rows and two columns to the current position.
RC:R[-1]C[-4]	Subtract one row and four columns from the current position. In other words, move up one row and to the left four columns.
R[4]C[-2]:R[1]C[1]	Move the pointer four rows down and two columns to the left; then highlight from that position to the current position plus one row and column. If the current position were C5, this action would produce the range A9:D6.

"RC"&X

Add *x* columns to the current address. This command is useful when you use variables to determine the desired reference. Because variables cannot be entered into the brackets (for example, "R10C[X]"), you must use concatenation to create the reference. If X is 5, the result is "RC[5]." For more information on using variables, see Chapter 19.

"Sales!R1C10"

Use the reference J1 on the worksheet named Sales. Normally, external references are unnecessary in macros that use the R1C1-style reference. However, by including a sheet name, you can limit the macro's use to only that sheet. If the specified sheet is not active when the macro is run, an error is returned.

Using Variable References in Standard Worksheet Functions

As described in this section, the R1C1-style reference used in macro commands is useful for creating variable and relative references. For this reason, it is preferred over the !A1-style external reference for macros. But can you use the R1C1-style reference in nonmacro functions, such as SUM or SQRT?

These functions do not let you enter cell references as text, which is required for the variable R1C1 references. (If you switch the worksheet to R1C1-style headings, these formulas will display their references in R1C1 format, but it's not the same as the text format used in macro commands.) When using one of these functions in a macro, you might need to make the cell reference variable. You can do so by entering the following expression in place of the cell reference in the function:

    GET.CELL(5,OFFSET(ACTIVE.CELL( ),x,y))

In this expression, the *x* and *y* values represent the row and column variables you want to use. These will add or subtract rows and/or columns to or from the active cell, and they can be variable names as well as numeric values.

Using the Run Command

If you assign a shortcut key to a macro when you define its name, you can run the macro whenever the macro sheet is open by pressing Command+Option and the specified character. When you run a macro, be sure to activate the worksheet (not the macro sheet) in which the macro will operate. (If the macro sheet is still active when you run the macro, the commands will apply to the macro sheet.)

> **Hiding the Macro Sheet**
>
> If you do not like having the macro sheet open at the same time as the worksheet, try making the macro window invisible with the Window Hide command.

Besides using the shortcut key to run a macro, you can use the Macro Run command. When you choose this command, Excel displays the dialog box shown in figure 18.6. This dialog box displays the names of all macros that can be run at this time.

Fig. 18.6.

The Macro Run dialog box.

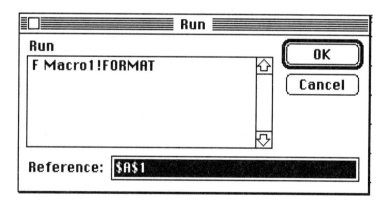

All named macros in all open macro sheets appear in this dialog box. If you have opened two or more macro sheets, all their names appear.

When a Macro Name Does Not Appear in the Dialog Box

If the macro name you want does not appear in the dialog box, follow the steps listed in the section "Working with Macro Names and Shortcut Keys." These steps will show you how to define a name for the macro. Normally when you use the Macro Record command, the name already exists and should appear in the Run dialog box.

Using Macros That Run Automatically

Another way to run a macro is to tell a worksheet to run it automatically. Any worksheet can have two macros defined as the *autoexec macros*, which can be run by the standard methods as well as automatically. Autoexec macros can be any valid macros on any macro sheets. One macro will run as soon as the worksheet is opened; the other will run as soon as the worksheet is closed. Your worksheets can include either or both autoexec macros. Before you can tell a worksheet which macros to use as the autoexec macros, they must be created and defined as described earlier. Usually, these macros are specifically designed for the worksheet that runs them.

On the other hand, you can use the same macros as the autoexec macros for several different worksheets. Autoexec macros are often used to create custom menus and to take control of a worksheet by limiting the actions available to an operator.

To designate which macros are to be autoexec macros, open the worksheet that will run the macros (the macro sheets do not have to be open). Next, use the Formula Define Name command. The familiar Define Name dialog box will appear. If a name and reference appear in the dialog box, erase them. Enter **Auto_Open** as the name. In the Refers To box, enter the name of the macro that you would like this worksheet to run whenever it is opened. Be sure to enter the macro name as an external reference—that is, include the macro-sheet name along with the macro name. For example, if you want to use the macro named

FORMAT, which is on the macro sheet named MACROS, the Define Name dialog box would look like figure 18.7.

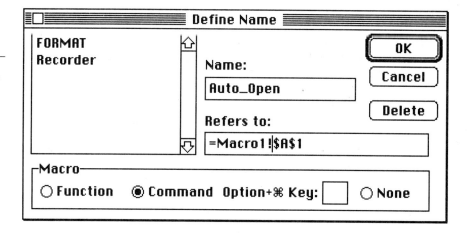

Use the name **Auto_Close** to define the macro that will be run when the worksheet is closed. Be sure to save the changes to the worksheet. When you open the worksheet containing the Auto_Open reference, the corresponding macro sheet does not have to be open. Along with running the macro automatically, Excel also opens the macro sheet.

Using Macros within Macros

The final way to run a macro is to let another macro run it. Because macros can do anything you can do manually, why not let them run other macros? The purposes for this setup may seem obscure at first, but as you create macros that are more complex, you will discover more and more uses for the feature. The main command used to run a macro within another macro is RUN.

The following is a simple macro that includes a RUN command. This command locates the specified macro and runs it; the macro then finishes its own commands.

```
=SELECT("R3C1:R3C5")
=FORMAT.NUMBER("#,##0")
=RUN("Macros1!Special")
=FORMAT.FONT("Times",18,FALSE,FALSE,FALSE,FALSE,0,FALSE,
    FALSE)
=RETURN( )
```

Notice that the RUN command (located in the middle of the macro) includes the name of the macro sheet and the macro within that sheet. The sheet name is needed only if the reference is external. If the reference is external, the specified sheet should be open and ready to be used. The commands in the referenced macro are executed after the FORMAT.NUMBER command. Then the macro continues with the FORMAT.FONT command. For more details on the RUN command, see Appendix B.

You can use two other commands to run macros from within other macros. The ON.TIME command runs a macro at a specific time, and the ON.KEY command runs a macro when a specified key is pressed. These commands also are explained in Appendix B.

Stopping Macros

You can interrupt a macro while it is running by pressing Command+. (period) or by pressing Escape on the extended keyboard. The dialog box shown in figure 18.8 will appear.

Fig. 18.8.

Stopping a macro.

Here, you can halt the macro, continue it, or "step through" it. The Step button lets you run the macro one step at a time; it presents a dialog box that shows each cell in the macro just before the macro is run. This feature is useful for debugging macros.

Documenting Macros

Documenting your macros as you create them is good practice; providing informative comments throughout the macro will help you correct errors later. Because macros are usually entered in a column of the worksheet, many people enter comments about the macro in an adjacent column. Figure 18.9 shows an example.

Fig. 18.9.

Comments about a macro.

	File **Edit** **Formula** **Format** **Data** **Options** **Macro** **Window**

	B6			

Macro1

	A	B	C
1	OPENING		
2	=DISPLAY(FALSE)	Remove Gridlines	
3	=WORKSPACE(FALSE)	Remove Formula Bar	
4	=RETURN()	End Macro	
5			
6			
7			
8			

Notice that the comments are placed in cells adjacent to the macro itself. Each important part of the macro has a comment. Also notice that the comment entries have no equal signs. Excel ignores cells that contain no equal signs.

Another handy practice is naming important cells in your macros. In particular, try naming cells that calculate results to be used in the macro. You can then refer to the cell's name whenever you need to make a calculation based on that result. Also, if you create large macros, you can easily select these result cells by using the Formula Goto command.

Understanding Function Macros

You probably are already familiar with worksheet functions; they were discussed in Chapter 6. A *function* is a special set of algorithms or other functions that provides a value based on a calculation. Often, a function is a shortcut to calculating the value another way. Most important, functions can be entered into cells as formulas, and they can be used in macros for special calculations. The values they return can be used in other calculations or simply displayed in a cell. One common function is SQRT(value). In this function, *value* represents any number for which you want the square root.

Besides providing these built-in functions, Excel enables you to use custom functions (called *function macros*) in macros and formulas. A function macro is a set of commands or calculations that produces a special result and that can be used as you would use a built-in worksheet function. Function macros, like worksheet functions, return values that are the results of complex mathematical calculations. You can run them by using a unique name that you have specified.

Function macros often require arguments (also specified by you) that are used to produce the value. In other words, they are like built-in functions in every way, except that you create them.

Suppose that you want to create a function macro that calculates the cube root of a number. You can calculate the result with a formula, but if you often calculate cube roots, creating a function is much more convenient. This function requires that you specify the number whose cube root you want to calculate (just like the SQRT function). The function might have the following syntax:

=CUBERT(value)

Value is any value or expression for which you want the cube root. The function must process this argument before Excel can calculate the cube root. When you design a function macro, this macro must take into consideration each argument and the calculation that produces the result. The calculation must operate on the argument and return its calculated result. The actual function macro that produces the result looks like figure 18.10.

	File **Edit** **Formula** **Format** **Data** **Options** **Macro** **Window**		
	A7		
	Macro1		
	A	**B**	**C**
1	CUBERT		
2	=RESULT(1)		
3	=ARGUMENT("value",1)		
4	=value^(1/3)		
5	=RETURN(A4)		
6			
7			
8			

Fig. 18.10.

A function macro designed to calculate the cube root of a number.

The variable *value* is part of the function using the command ARGUMENT("value",1). You enter this value into the function as its argument. The ARGUMENT command is needed to define the argument inside the function macro, thus making it available for calculations throughout the macro. In fact, the next line uses the *value* argument as the basis of the cube-root calculation. The ARGUMENT command uses the following syntax:

ARGUMENT(name_text,*data_type,ref*)

Name_text is the name of the argument entered as a text string (in quotation marks). This name helps you decipher your functions and can be used in subsequent calculations in this macro; use a name that describes the argument you are defining. *Data_type* determines what type of value is allowed as the argument. The following are the acceptable type values:

Value	Type
1	Number
2	Text
4	Logical
8	Reference
16	Error
64	Array

Entering any of these numbers restricts the argument to the corresponding type. You can specify a combination of types by adding the values and entering the total. For example, a data type of 3 enables you to use numbers and text as the argument. Of course, the function macro should be able to produce a result based on the types you specify. You can calculate the type as part of the command if you like. Consider this example:

ARGUMENT("value",1+2+4)

Because the reference and array types are cell references, they cannot be combined with other types; therefore, do not use the numbers 8 and 64 with other values. The *ref* variable can be added for special purposes. If this variable is present, it specifies that the argument does not come from the function itself but from a cell in the macro worksheet. This feature is useful for making calculations on arguments that are not to be entered by the user. (More details will be provided later in this chapter.)

The final thing you should notice about the function macro in figure 18.10 is that it begins with the RESULT command and ends with the RETURN command. The RESULT command specifies the type of result that is returned when the RETURN command is used. Often, this type will be the same as that used in the ARGUMENT commands, but not always. The list of data types, shown earlier, also applies to the RESULT command. The RETURN command is needed to conclude any macro. In a function macro, however, this command also returns the result of your calculation. Enter the address of the cell containing the final calculation as the parameter for the RETURN command. In the example, this address is entered as RETURN(A4). Cell A4 is the cell containing the final cube-root calculation.

Creating Function Macros

The following is a summary of the guidelines for creating function macros:

1. *Begin the macro with a name.* This name will be used as the function name, so use a name that reminds you of the function's purpose. Do not include spaces in the name or use an equal sign in front of the name. Excel does not distinguish between uppercase and lowercase letters.

2. *Start with a RESULT command.* This command defines the type of value that will be returned. Be sure that the function macro calculates the correct value indicated by this result. You can specify a combination of results by adding the types. RESULT should be the first command under the macro's name and should begin with an equal sign.

3. *Enter the ARGUMENT commands after the RESULT command.* Each argument required for the calculation must have its own ARGUMENT command, which defines its name and type. The argument types do not necessarily have to be the same as the RESULT type. You may want to create a function macro that converts values. The ARGUMENT commands must begin with equal signs.

4. *Enter the required calculations for the function.* Begin with an equal sign and enter the formula or formulas that calculate the results. These formulas should act on the arguments listed in the ARGUMENT commands.

5. *Conclude with a RETURN command.* This command should return the value produced by the formulas described in the preceding paragraph. Reference the appropriate cell (the cell that calculates the result) in the RETURN command.

6. *Use the Formula Define Name command to define the command macro.* The following section explains how to do so.

7. *Save the macro sheet for future use.* Many function macros can be used with all worksheets, so you might keep those macros on one macro sheet that can be used globally.

8. *Open the macro sheet before using a function macro.*

*Creating a
Function Macro*

Defining Function Macros

After you create a function macro, you will be ready to define the macro as a function macro, making it available for your worksheets. The procedure is similar to defining a command macro, as described earlier in this chapter. Follow these simple steps:

1. Highlight the cell containing the macro's name.
2. Select the Formula Define Name command.
3. Confirm the name and cell address listed in the dialog box, or enter a new name and address.
4. Click on the Function button.
5. Press the Return key.
6. Save the macro sheet.

Using Function Macros

To use a function macro, enter its name into a worksheet formula, along with the required arguments. The arguments used for the function are passed to the macro as the starting values of the corresponding variables. The order in which the ARGUMENT commands appear dictates the order in which you should enter the arguments in the function (if there are more than one). In the example, to find the cube root of 245, enter this formula into any worksheet cell:

=MACRO1!CUBERT(245)

The external-reference style is required because the function appears on a different sheet. To make your job easier, Excel lists your custom function at the bottom of the Formula Paste Function dialog box. You can use the function in a worksheet by selecting its name from this box. Of course, you can enter a cell reference or expression resulting in a number. The value 245 becomes the *value* variable in the function. Functions can be more complex than this. You might, for example, use two or three arguments in the function.

Suppose that you want to create a function that calculates any root of a number. In this example, the number is a variable and the desired root is a variable (see fig. 18.11).

```
 File   Edit   Formula   Format   Data   Options   Macro   Window
     A8
```

	A	B	C
1	ROOT		
2	=RESULT(1)		
3	=ARGUMENT("value",1)		
4	=ARGUMENT("root",1)		
5	=value^(1/root)		
6	=RETURN(A5)		
7			
8			
9			
10			

Fig. 18.11.

A function macro that uses two variables.

The syntax for using this function in a formula is as follows:

   =ROOT(value,root)

Value is any value or expression for which you want to calculate the root. *Root* is the root to be calculated. The formula =ROOT(25,5) would produce the fifth root of 25.

Suppose that your function calls for a range of cells. Because valid worksheet ranges can be passed as variables, this requirement presents no special problem; simply use a variable to represent the desired range. Now suppose that you want to create a function that calculates the span of numbers existing in a range. The span is the difference between the largest and the smallest numbers in the range. The syntax might look like this:

   =SPAN(range)

Range is any valid worksheet range. The function that makes this calculation uses the variable *range* to indicate the range entered. Its type is 8 (see fig. 18.12).

```
 File   Edit   Formula   Format   Data   Options   Macro   Window
     A7
```

	A	B	C
1	SPAN		
2	=RESULT(1)		
3	=ARGUMENT("range",8)		
4	=MAX(range)-MIN(range)		
5	=RETURN(A4)		
6			
7			
8			
9			

Fig. 18.12.

Using a range as an argument.

The calculation MAX(range)–MIN(range) subtracts the smallest number in the range from the largest, producing the span of numbers in the range. Excel returns this result to the worksheet.

Summary

This chapter has shown you that macros are not really difficult to use and that they can simplify the task of creating worksheets. Most likely, your first macros will be designed to simplify repetitive tasks. You have seen two types of macros for this purpose. A command macro duplicates any menu command or action (or combination thereof) and can be run with a single keystroke. A function macro mimics Excel's worksheet functions but performs custom mathematical procedures. This type of macro returns results to your worksheets and is useful when you use a calculation over and over in your work. The following are other points to remember:

❏ You can create a macro by hand or by using the macro recorder.

❏ A macro entered by hand must be named with the Formula Define Name command. A macro recorded with the Macro Record command is named automatically.

❏ A macro must begin with a label cell (the macro's name) and end with the =RETURN command.

❏ When you record a macro, Excel shows cell and range references as R1C1-style references entered as text strings (that is, in quotation marks). When you create a macro by hand, you can use this R1C1-style text reference, or you can use an A1-style reference entered as an external reference (not as text). If you do not want to specify a particular external worksheet for the reference, use the exclamation point without the sheet name, as in !A1.

❏ The text R1C1-style references are useful when you want to specify a cell or range that is relative to the active cell. The reference "RC" is the active cell; "R[1]C[1]" is one row and column greater than the active cell.

❏ You can use variables in relative cell references by concatenating them to the end of the text string, as in "R1C"&X.

❏ You must open a macro sheet before you can run any of its macros.

❑ To run a macro, use the Command+Option+key shortcut you specified when you named the macro. If you did not include a shortcut key, use the Macro Run command and choose the macro's name from the list provided.

❑ You can cause macros to run automatically whenever a worksheet is opened or closed. These are called autoexec macros.

❑ Function macros return values to the worksheet and can be used like any worksheet function.

❑ Function macros must begin with a name, followed by the =RESULT( ) command; each argument in the function must be defined by an =ARGUMENT( ) command following the =RESULT( ) command; and the function macro should end with the =RETURN( ) command.

You may not need any additional macro power, but Excel offers more. When you begin creating worksheets to be used by other people, you will be ready for more-advanced macros. These macros involve custom menus and custom dialog boxes. The next chapter, "Using Macro Programming Techniques," provides details.

19

Using Macro Programming Techniques

Creating macros for your worksheets can involve some programming concepts. Although programming in Excel's macro language is not unlike programming in Pascal, C, or other languages, the macro language is very simple and takes much less time to learn. Nevertheless, a few programming concepts will go a long way in your macros.

This chapter begins with a discussion of simple programming concepts, such as the use of variables and loops. Once you have grasped a few of these concepts, you will be ready to build custom menus and dialog boxes with your macros. The rest of the chapter is devoted to such tasks. You'll learn how to bring up a custom menu, program your own menu options, call up dialog boxes from those options, and act on the choices made in those dialog boxes. The whole process may sound complicated, but Excel makes it easy.

Using Variables

One reason why macros are so powerful is that they can use variable information. The variables can be determined by your input, from calculations, or by many other methods. Many macro commands require arguments, and any argument can be turned into a variable. For example, the ROW.HEIGHT command uses an argument as the height of the row (in points):

=ROW.HEIGHT(18)

You can substitute a variable as the height, letting the macro adjust the row height according to variable information. The simplest kind of variable is a cell reference to another cell in the macro sheet; the referenced cell might be created from a calculation. The command uses the address of the cell as its argument. Figure 19.1 shows an example.

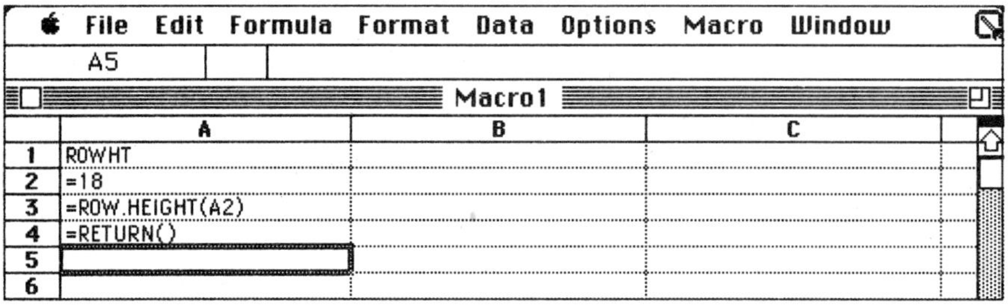

Fig. 19.1.

Using variables in a macro.

Fig. 19.1.

Using variables in a macro.

This command uses whatever value is in cell A2 (R2C1) as its argument. This cell contains the value 18. If you change the value in R2C1, the ROW.HEIGHT command adjusts to the specified height. This example is rather pointless, but it shows how you can refer to any cell in the macro sheet as a variable for any macro command. Sometimes, you may want to refer to a cell in the worksheet for variable information. In this case, you would use an external cell reference, such as the following:

    =ROW.HEIGHT(WORKSHEET!R2C1)

This command takes the value from cell A2 of the worksheet called WORKSHEET. You can enter different values each time you run the macro. Any macro command that requires an argument can use a variable as its argument. The syntax of each command determines whether it has an argument. (All commands and their syntaxes are listed in Appendix B.) Some commands require numbers as arguments; others require range references; still others require text strings. Consider these examples:

    FORMAT.FONT("New York")   (constant string)
    FORMAT.FONT(FONT)   (variable string)

In the first example, the FORMAT.FONT command uses the constant "New York" as the argument. The second example uses the range name FONT as a variable. You can enter any valid font as a text string into the cell named FONT, and the function would use that font as its argument. When a command requires a text string as an argument, the text string must be enclosed in quotation marks. However, cell references, numbers, expressions, and other variables require no quotation marks.

As another example, you can use expressions as arguments for macro commands:

ROW.HEIGHT(R2C1+50)

You can even use worksheet functions in the expression:

ROW.HEIGHT(INT(R2C1+50))

The calculation INT(R2C1+50) is used as the argument for the ROW.HEIGHT command. Notice that the INT function is a standard worksheet function. Almost any worksheet function can be used in this way. (These functions are listed in Chapter 6.) Also, you can use function macros as arguments in commands. These macros must be completed and defined according to the guidelines noted in Chapter 18. To use a function macro, open the macro sheet containing the function macro; then use it in any macro you want. Remember that both macro sheets must be open in order for the macro to run properly. On the other hand, you can define a function macro in a different portion of the same macro sheet and avoid using two sheets.

Another way to use variables in macros is to prompt the operator for the values as part of the macro itself. When you run the macro, it asks for a value and then uses that value for whatever calculation or function the macro performs. The macro asks for the value through one of the query commands. Consider this example (which starts at at cell A1):

VARIABLE
=INPUT("Enter the row height",1)
=ROW.HEIGHT(R2C1)
=RETURN

The INPUT function queries the operator for the value. This value is used by the ROW.HEIGHT command to change the row height of the current row. (See Appendix B or the section "Getting User Input" later in this chapter for more information about the INPUT command.)

As with any worksheet formula, you can combine macro commands into a single cell. The preceding example could combine commands as follows:

VARIABLE
=ROW.HEIGHT(INPUT("Enter the row height",1))
=RETURN

This formula eliminates the need for the cell reference and uses fewer cells for the macro.

Using Loops

A *loop* is piece of the macro that repeats. Commands contained in a loop are repeated a specified number of times. Excel has two types of loops: FOR-NEXT and WHILE-NEXT. The following sections describe them.

FOR-NEXT Loops

The FOR-NEXT loop repeats an action or series of actions a given number of times. Many types of macros can use the FOR-NEXT loop to handle repeated actions. Figure 19.2 shows an example of such a loop.

Fig. 19.2.

A FOR-NEXT loop.

	File	Edit	Formula	Format	Data	Options	Macro	Window	
	A6								

Macro1

	A	B	C
1	LOOP		
2	=FOR("Counter",1,10,1)		
3	=ALERT("counter is at "&counter,1)		
4	=NEXT()		
5	=RETURN()		
6			
7			

Notice first that the FOR-NEXT loop contains the FOR command and the NEXT command. The actions to be performed are contained between the FOR and NEXT commands. In this case, a message is printed; the message contains the current value of "counter." The value of "counter" changes (from 1 to 10) because of the FOR loop. The result of this macro is that a message comes to the screen 10 times, each time with a new value. Try this macro on a sample worksheet. You will end up with messages like the one in figure 19.3.

Fig. 19.3.

A message reflecting the loop counter.

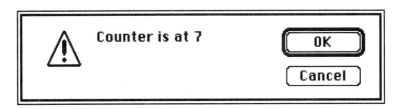

The syntax of the FOR command is as follows:

FOR(counter_name,start_value,end_value,*step_value*)

The *counter_name* variable is any text string. This text string is a variable that holds the value of the counter; the value increases each time the NEXT command is reached. It does not matter what name you use for the counter variable, but the name should not include spaces. Also, if you use more than one FOR loop in the same macro, the loops should have different counter names. *Start_value* and *end_value* determine the minimum and maximum values of the counter; *step_value* determines the increment of increase. If *step_value* is omitted, Excel assumes it to be 1.

Often, the counter variable is used only to track the repetitions of the loop; at other times, the variable becomes an important value to the macro. In figure 19.3's example, the counter variable is actually used as part of the ALERT message (ALERT is discussed in the section "Displaying Messages" later in this chapter). Notice that the message concatenates the string "Counter is at " with the counter variable. Here is another example:

FOR("counter",1,10,2)

This formula means, "FOR counter equals 1 to 10 with a step of 2," and it produces five repetitions, which have the values 1, 3, 5, 7, and 9, respectively. Try this variation:

FOR("counter",50,40,-2)

Notice that the step value is negative, creating a descending counter.

WHILE-NEXT Loops

The FOR-NEXT loop is useful when an action is repeated for a known number of times. The WHILE-NEXT loop is useful when an action is repeated as long as a condition is met, which may be an unknown number of times. For example, you might perform some action as long as a variable is less than 100. If the condition is not met, the macro branches to the NEXT statement and continues operating, skipping all the commands between.

WHILE-NEXT loops, which are not very common, are usually used in large macros for internal programming techniques. Often, you can use IF-THEN-ELSE logic instead of the WHILE-NEXT loop.

Using IF-THEN-ELSE Functions

Perhaps the most powerful programming construct is the decision-making IF function. This function lets you test for a condition and act on the results of the test. The function is described in Chapter 6 for worksheet formulas, but it can be used in macros as well. IF tests whether a condition is true or false. If the condition is true, the function returns one value; if the condition is false, the function returns a different value. The syntax is as follows:

IF(condition,value_if_true,value_if_false)

You can use the IF function in a macro in many ways. You can, for example, use it to select one of two values, based on a given condition. Figure 19.4 shows an example.

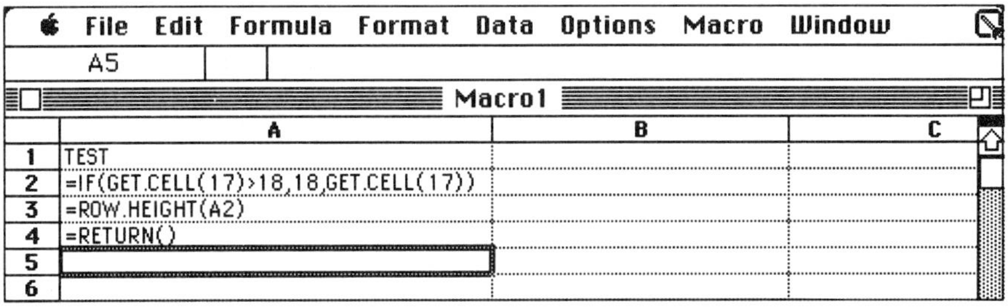

Fig. 19.4.

An example of the
IF function.

	A	B	C
1	TEST		
2	=IF(GET.CELL(17)>18,18,GET.CELL(17))		
3	=ROW.HEIGHT(A2)		
4	=RETURN()		
5			
6			

In this example, the IF function uses the expression GET.CELL(17)>18 to check whether the current cell's height is greater than 18. GET.CELL is described in Appendix B, but you should note here that the value 17 in this expression tells Excel to get the row height of the active cell. If the current cell's height is greater than 18, the function returns the value 18; if the height is less than 18, the function uses the command GET.CELL(17) to return the height of the cell. Basically, this arrangement results in a row height that is never greater than 18. To what cell is the row height returned? To the cell containing the IF function—in this case, cell A2 of the macro sheet. Although you cannot see them, each cell in a macro has a value. Cell A2 in the example has the value returned by the IF function—that is, a row height value of 18 or less. The ROW.HEIGHT command in cell A3 uses the result of the IF function to adjust the height of the current row through the reference to cell A2 of the macro sheet.

Although this example may seem pointless, its purpose is to show that the IF function chooses one of two values, which is in turn used by other commands in the macro.

Another way to use the IF function is as a branching command for the macro's logic. By using IF with GOTO, you can choose between two different sets of commands in the macro. The GOTO command causes the macro to jump to a specific cell and continue from there. Figure 19.5 shows an example.

⚫ File Edit Formula Format Data Options Macro Window		
A7		

	A	B	C
1	TEST		
2	=IF(Worksheet1!$A$1=1,GOTO(A5),GOTO(A3))		
3	=ALERT("Value is not 1",1)		
4	=GOTO(A6)		
5	=ALERT("Value is 1",1)		
6	=RETURN()		
7			
8			

Macro1

Fig. 19.5.

Using the IF function with GOTO.

The IF function branches to cell A5 if the value of A1 is 1, producing the message *Value is 1.* If the value of A1 is not 1, the macro branches to cell A3, producing the message *Value is not 1,* and then concludes by jumping to the RETURN command. By jumping to the RETURN command, the macro skips the command in cell A5.

Working with Branches and Subroutines

Excel processes each command in a macro from top to bottom, beginning with the first cell under the macro's name. A macro should have no blank cells. You can, however, change the normal flow of a macro by using the GOTO command. When a macro encounters this command, the macro flow branches to the specified location. The syntax is as follows:

=GOTO(reference)

Reference can be any cell or range name to which the macro should jump—a cell within the same macro, or a cell in a different macro. After the macro jumps to the specified cell, the flow continues with the next cell under the new branch. If you branch to a different macro (for example, a subroutine), a RETURN command in that macro returns the flow to the original macro at the previous location. Often, the HALT command is useful for stopping a macro's flow after a routine is completed and for preventing the macro from returning to an undesirable location. Finally, you can use another Goto command to return the macro's flow to the desired cell.

Moving the Pointer and Selecting Cells

Moving the cell pointer in a macro is done primarily with the SELECT command. This command selects any cell you provide as a reference (the effect is the same as moving the pointer). The command =SELECT(G12) moves the pointer to cell G12. You can also use this command to select a range of cells; simply provide a range as the reference. For example, =SELECT(B3:D4) highlights the range B3:D4.

As discussed earlier, you can provide relative references by using the SELECT command. These references highlight cells or ranges relative to the current location of the pointer (that is, the location of the pointer just before the macro command is run). The reference RC represents the current cell; you can add or subtract rows or columns in that basic reference. Thus the command =SELECT(R[3]C[1]) selects the cell three rows and one column greater than the current position of the pointer. You can use range references this way, too.

Finally, you can use the SELECT command to highlight existing ranges by their names. As long as the range has been named, you can enter the corresponding name in place of the cell reference. For example, the command =SELECT(SALES) selects the range named SALES. Notice that the range name is not in quotation marks.

Inserting Values into the Worksheet

You can use a macro to enter values into a worksheet as if someone had typed them on the keyboard. The FORMULA command is required for this process. The syntax of the FORMULA command is as follows:

=FORMULA(formula_text,*reference*)

Formula_text is the information that you want to enter into the worksheet. Make sure that you enter the formula text as a string, using quotation marks. You also can use a text expression that results in a text string or a reference to a cell containing text. The *reference* variable is the cell in which you want the information to appear. Enter this as a standard cell reference. If you omit this variable, Excel will enter the information in the active cell.

Just because the formula text must be a text string does not mean that you cannot enter a formula or value into a cell. Any formula text that can be interpreted as a number will be entered as a number. Thus the command =FORMULA("345",A1) enters the numeric value 345 into cell

A1. To enter a formula, include the equal sign as part of the formula text variable. For example, =FORMULA("=A1+A2",A3) enters the formula =A1+A2 into cell A3, and Excel calculates the formula upon entry.

The FORMULA command can enter information into a chart as well. If the active window is a chart when the FORMULA command is issued, the command will enter information into the chart as a text label. To enter the same value in a range of cells, use the command FORMULA.FILL. Entering =FORMULA.FILL("text",A1:A5) enters the word *text* in the range A1:A5.

Getting User Input

Often, instead of taking a value from the worksheet or macro sheet, a macro must use the INPUT command to ask the operator for a value. This command produces a dialog box with a message and entry space. The syntax of the function is as follows:

=INPUT(prompt,type,*title,default,x_position,y_position*)

Prompt is the message you want to display in the dialog box; it must be a text entry (in quotation marks) or text expression. The *type* variable is the type of entry that the user is expected to provide. Entry types include the following:

Value	Type
0	Formula (returned as text)
1	Number
2	Text
4	Logical
8	Reference
16	Error
64	Array

To use more than one type, add the type values you want, and enter the sum as the type value. You cannot, however, add types 8 or 64 to any others. When an operator responds to this input request, the entered information is returned to the cell containing the =INPUT command. Thus another macro command can refer to this cell to act on that entry.

> ## Asking for Cell References
>
> If your dialog box asks the user for a cell or range reference, the user can move the dialog-box window aside and click on the worksheet to make the selection. The appropriate reference will appear in the box.

The *title* value represents the title given to the dialog box. If you omit this value, the word *Input* is used as the title; otherwise, enter this value as a text string. If you enter a default value (as a text string in quotation marks), this value will automatically appear in the input box. This method is most commonly used with a macro variable that corresponds to a current value or selection. The *x_position* and *y_position* values determine the location of the dialog box on the screen. If these values are omitted, the dialog box is centered; otherwise, the values are used as the upper left corner of the box (in picas from the corner of the screen).

The following is an example of an INPUT command. Figure 19.6 shows the dialog box it creates.

=INPUT("Type cell address or use the mouse or keyboard commands",8,"Enter Cell","RC",5,5)

Fig. 19.6.

A dialog box created through the INPUT command.

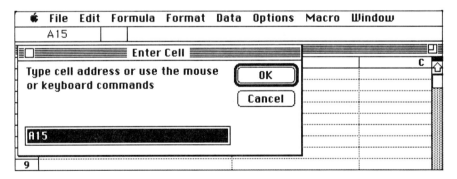

Notice that the box has a title and a message, indicated by the values in the command. Also, the current cell location becomes the default for the input box because the value "RC" is used in the default-variable location, representing the active cell. Finally, the box is located five picas from the upper left corner of the screen.

Another way to query the operator for a value is to design your own dialog box that contains text-entry areas. This procedure is discussed in more detail in the section "Using Custom Dialog Boxes" later in this chapter.

Displaying Messages

Excel offers two commands for displaying messages on the screen. Often, Excel must display messages when a particular action is taken or when a macro makes a particular decision. The ALERT command displays an alert dialog box containing any message. The user must click on the OK button in this dialog box before continuing. The syntax for this command is as follows:

=ALERT(text,type)

Text is any message (enclosed in quotation marks) that you want displayed in the box. *Type* controls the type of alert box that is used and the type of icon used in the box. The following are the types available:

Value	Type
1	Caution
2	Note
3	Stop

Figures 19.7 through 19.9 illustrate what these types look like (without messages).

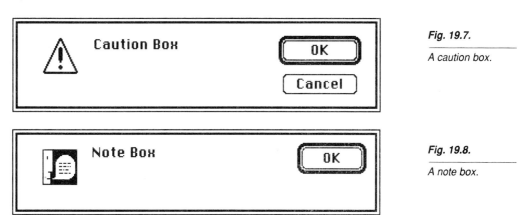

Fig. 19.7.

A caution box.

Fig. 19.8.

A note box.

Fig. 19.9.

A stop box.

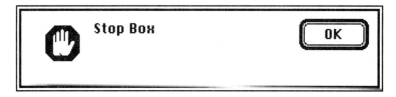

You can also display a message by using the MESSAGE command. This command uses the status line to display whatever text you want; the command is thus useful for messages that require no response at all. The syntax is as follows:

=MESSAGE(logical,*text*)

The *logical* value must be either TRUE or FALSE. If the value is TRUE, the message capability is turned on; if the value is FALSE, the message capability is turned off. When the message capability is off, the status bar returns to normal, displaying Excel's standard messages. You can use this command with a *text* value of "" (the empty set) to turn the message capability on and off. If you enter a *text* variable, however, the appropriate message is displayed.

Be sure to turn the normal message display back on (by using the command with the FALSE logical value) after displaying custom messages. Otherwise, the custom message will remain in view until you quit Excel.

Using Custom Menus

One of the most powerful features of macros is their ability to add custom menus to your worksheets. A custom menu contains the options you want, and each option performs the action you specify. Custom menus may appear on the menu bar along with normal menus, or you can create an entirely new menu bar to hold your custom menu (or menus) and then return to the Excel menu bar when you like.

Custom menus are created through the use of a *menu definition table*— a range of cells that contains specific values for the menu, such as the option names and the actions they perform. This table might look like any other table of values in a worksheet. The menu definition table can appear on any worksheet or macro sheet and is activated (turned into a menu) by a controlling macro. Often, the menu definition table appears on the macro sheet that contains the controlling macro.

The controlling macro uses some very simple commands to activate a menu definition table. (These commands will be explained in detail later.) A common technique is to make the controlling macro an autoexec macro so that it controls the menus as soon as the worksheet you want is open.

A menu definition table describes a menu and its options. This feature is not a macro, but a table of the values contained in any worksheet or macro sheet. Each option in a custom menu performs an action by running a macro. When you specify the names of the menu options, you also specify the macros that link to these options. When the menu option is selected, the appropriate macro is run. Usually, these macros appear together on the same macro sheet; this macro sheet can also contain the menu definition table and the controlling macro.

In summary, there are three basic elements in a custom menu:

- *The controlling macro.* This macro activates the menu definition table.
- *The menu definition table.* Each option in this table links to a macro.
- *The macros that perform the various options contained in the menu.* These macros are not limited to the menu options; they can be run as normal macros without the menu.

Creating a Menu Definition Table

A menu definition table is very simple, consisting of four main columns. The first column contains the names of the menu items. The second column contains the names of the command macros that correspond to the menu items in the first column. The third column contains the shortcut keys (if any) that can be used to invoke the macro command on the keyboard. The fourth column contains a message that appears in the status line when the menu option is selected. Figure 19.10 shows an example of a menu table.

You should notice several things about the example in figure 19.10. First, the table has been outlined and formatted through worksheet formatting commands. (Although you need not use these commands, they make tables easier to read.) The labels in the first column will be used exactly as shown for the menu options. If an option listed in this column has a corresponding entry in column 3, this entry will also appear in the menu as the shortcut key that runs the option from the keyboard. Notice that the hyphen character that appears below the word *Check* is used as a menu separation line. This table produces the menu shown in figure 19.11.

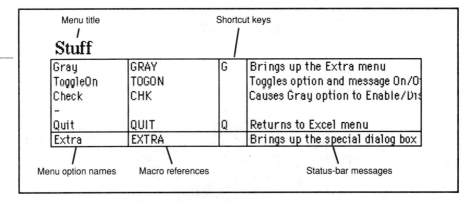

Fig. 19.10.

A typical menu definition table.

Fig. 19.11.

The menu produced by the menu definition table in figure 19.10.

Another thing that you should notice in the sample table is that none of the macro names listed in column 2 are external references. You can use external references if you like, in which case the macros controlling the options are located on different macro sheets. The macro sheets must be open in order for these options to work.

Finally, the name of the menu appears above the first column. Excel uses this cell to identify the menu itself.

Creating the Menu Macro

Once you have created the menu definition table, you can create the macro that activates it by using three commands: ADD.MENU, ADD.BAR, and SHOW.BAR. The following sections provide details.

Adding a Menu to a Menu Bar

You can add a custom menu to any menu bar, whether one of the four Excel menu bars or a new menu bar you create. Simply specify the menu bar or bars to which you are adding the menu. The syntax is as follows:

=ADD.MENU(bar_number,menu_table_range)

Bar_number is the identification number of the menu bar that is to receive the new menu. (Bars and their ID numbers are explained in the next section.) Remember that the menu bar does not have to be showing on the screen before you can add a menu to it. For example, you can add a menu to the Graph menu bar when the standard worksheet menu bar is in view. *Menu_table_range* is the range reference that contains the menu definition table (the menu that you are adding to the specified bar). Be sure to include the title of the menu in the reference.

If you add a menu to a bar that is currently displayed on the screen, the menu will appear as soon as you run the macro. Otherwise, you must show the menu bar after adding the menus to it.

Adding and Showing Menu Bars

To add a new menu bar to Excel, use the command ADD.BAR. This command produces a menu bar containing only the Apple menu; this bar is automatically given an ID number. The ID number is returned to the cell that contains the ADD.BAR command. When you add menus to this new bar, refer to the ID number of the new bar by referring to the cell containing the ADD.BAR command. If the bar is not already being displayed, you can display it by using the SHOW.BAR command. Figure 19.12 shows a macro that uses both the ADD.BAR and SHOW.BAR commands.

	B	C	D	E	F
1	ADDMENU	Stuff			
2	=ADD.BAR()	Gray	GRAY	G	Brings up the Extra menu
3	=ADD.MENU(B2,STUFF)	ToggleOff	TOGON		Toggles option and message On/O
4	=SHOW.BAR(B2)	Check	CHK		Causes Gray option to Enable/Dis
5	=RETURN()	-			
6		Quit	QUIT	Q	Returns to Excel menu
7		Extra	EXTRA		Brings up the special dialog box
8					

(Menu bar: ≤ File Edit Formula Format Data Options Macro Window — B20 — MENUS:2)

Fig. 19.12.

Adding a menu to a newly created bar.

Notice that the ADD.MENU command refers to the cell containing the ADD.BAR command. This arrangement is a way of referring to the ID number of the added bar. The ADD.MENU command refers to the range named STUFF as the definition table. (Naming menu definition tables is good practice because it makes these macros easier to create.) Finally, the SHOW.BAR command is used to display this new menu bar and its menu. The SHOW.BAR command should appear after the other commands so that it shows the completed menu bar and its menus.

Notice that the SHOW.BAR command has no argument; it displays the menu bar that was just created. You can display any other menu bar by referring to the appropriate bar's ID number.

You can add menus to one of the Excel menu bars by using an ID number that corresponds to the appropriate bar. Excel contains four menu bars, whose ID numbers are 1, 2, 3, and 4, respectively (see figs. 19.13 through 19.16). Two of the bars can have the ID numbers 5 and 6 when the Short Menus command is active.

Fig. 19.13.

The worksheet and macro-sheet menu bar. ID = 1 when the Full Menus command is active; ID = 5 when the Short Menus command is active.

```
 File  Edit  Formula  Format  Data  Options  Macro  Window
```

Fig. 19.14.

The chart menu bar. ID = 2 when the Full Menus command is active; ID = 6 when the Short Menus command is active.

```
 File  Edit  Gallery  Chart  Format  Macro  Window
```

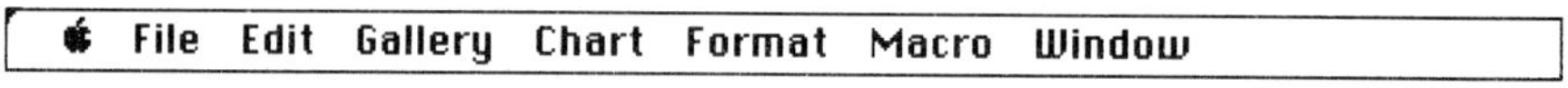

Fig. 19.15.

The null menu bar (no active sheet). ID = 3.

```
 File  Edit  Window
```

Fig. 19.16.

The Info menu bar. ID = 4.

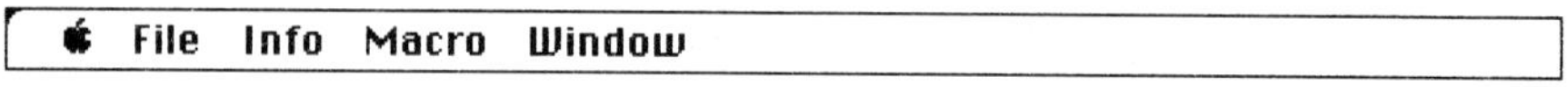

```
 File  Info  Macro  Window
```

Creating Custom Menu Options

As you can see in figure 19.12, the macro that activates custom menus and/or menu bars—the controlling macro—is very simple. Usually, a controlling macro contains only the two or three commands needed to display the bar and menus. The rest is up to the options inside the custom menus.

The following sections offer some ideas and techniques for options you can use in your custom menus and provide instructions for creating the macros that link to these options.

Deleting Menus and Menu Bars

You can easily display a different menu bar at any time; simply create a macro that uses the SHOW.BAR command to display the bar you want. For example, to return to the Excel menu bar, run a macro that contains the command =SHOW.BAR(1). A common technique is the linking of this macro to one menu option on each custom menu bar. This option might be listed as "Quit" or "Return to Excel." Figure 19.17 shows an example of a "Quit" macro. Remember that the name of this macro is included in the menu definition table that contains this option.

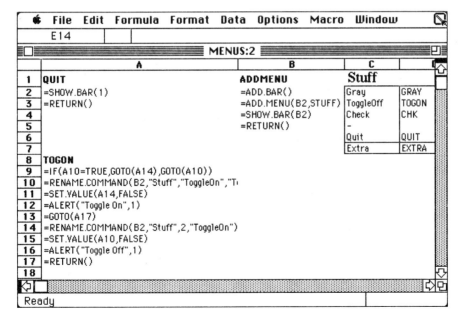

Fig. 19.17.

A "Quit" macro used by a custom menu option.

If you do not include a "Quit" option, the operator will be unable to use any of Excel's basic menu commands—a circumstance that might be desirable. Actions such as saving worksheets and quitting Excel, however, would have to be handled by your custom menus. Thus you might add a "Save" option to one of your menus; this option would run a macro that contains the SAVE? command. (For more details, see SAVE and QUIT in Appendix B.)

If you add a menu to an Excel menu bar, you might consider including an option in that menu that removes the menu itself, thus returning the menu bar to normal. This option might read "Remove This Menu" and would run a macro that contains the DELETE.MENU command, which has the following syntax:

=DELETE.MENU(bar_number,menu_name)

Bar_number is the ID number of the bar containing the unwanted menu. The bar does not have to be displayed on-screen before you can remove a menu from it. (If you are removing a menu from a custom bar, *bar_number* should be a reference to the cell containing the original ADD.BAR command.) *Menu_name* is the name of the unwanted menu (in quotation marks) on the specified bar. The command =DELETE.MENU(1,"File") removes the File menu from Excel's worksheet menu bar. (You do not want to do this!) You can also use a menu number instead of a name. Menu numbers are counted from left to right on the bar. For example, the Excel worksheet menu normally contains eight menus. Suppose that you have added a ninth menu to this bar. You can remove the new menu by using the command =DELETE.MENU(1,9).

Using the ID Number of the Active Bar

If you do not know the ID number of the bar but do know that it is the active bar, you can use the command GET.BAR to return its ID number.

Deleting Menu Bars

Excel can accommodate 15 custom menu bars. If you exceed this limit, you may want to delete one or more bars to make room for new ones. You can delete a menu bar by using the command DELETE.BAR. After you execute this command, you can no longer use the SHOW.BAR command to display this bar; instead, you must use the ADD.BAR command again.

Adding and Deleting Menu Options

Menu definition tables do not have to include all the options that appear in the menu. You can add or delete options from menus at any time. To delete an option, use the following command:

=DELETE.COMMAND(bar_number,menu_name,command_name)

Bar_number is the menu bar containing the menu. *Menu_name* is the menu that contains the unwanted option. This menu must be on the bar indicated in the *bar_number* variable. *Command_name* is the name of the option that you want to remove. For example, the command =DELETE.COMMAND(1,"File","Save") removes the File Save command from the worksheet menu bar. Notice that the names are entered as text strings.

The *menu_name* and *command_name* variables can instead be the numbers of the desired menu and command. Menus and commands are numbered in the order in which they appear. If you remove a menu or command, all subsequent numbers change to reflect the deletion.

Adding a menu option is not quite as easy. First, the option must be defined somewhere, preferably in a menu definition table. One way to do this is to define all menu options in the same menu definition table. The options that are not used all the time should appear at the bottom of the table. When you refer to the definition table in the ADD.MENU command, exclude the bottom cells from the range, thus excluding the unwanted options. Later, when you add an option to the menu, use the command

=ADD.COMMAND(bar_number,menu_name,command_range_reference)

Command_range_reference is the range containing the added option; in this case, it is the range that was left out of the original menu. The range does not have to be related to the original menu; it can be a set of commands from a different menu definition table. Whenever possible, however, you should avoid using a set of commands from a different menu table, because that practice adds a considerable amount of confusion to the process of adding and removing menu options.

The final question is where to enter the ADD.COMMAND and DELETE.COMMAND commands. The answer depends on the action that controls the addition or deletion of the option. In other words, under what circumstance is the menu option added? Often, selecting a different option (call it option B) will add an option to a menu (option A). In this case, the macro linked to option B should contain the ADD.COMMAND command to control option A.

Creating Toggle Menu Options

A common menu effect used in Macintosh applications is the toggle, which changes a menu option's name each time you select it. Usually, menu options toggle between two items, such as Short Menus and Full Menus in Excel's Options menu. Using a toggle menu option eliminates the need for two different options and presents only the option that can be used at any given time. The very act of selecting the option makes its counterpart available.

You can add toggle capability to your custom menus in Excel. To do so, you will need to use some macro programming logic and the commands RENAME.COMMAND and SET.VALUE. The RENAME.COMMAND command is used twice to change the name of the option twice, but the command name must be changed only when it has been selected. The SET.VALUE command helps determine the appropriate time to change the name by setting the values in certain cells. The macro consults these values before renaming the option. The syntax of the two commands is as follows:

=RENAME.COMMAND(bar_number,menu_name,option_name,new_name)

=SET.VALUE(cell_reference,value)

Figure 19.18 shows a command line that creates a toggle menu option.

Fig. 19.18.

Creating a toggle
menu option.

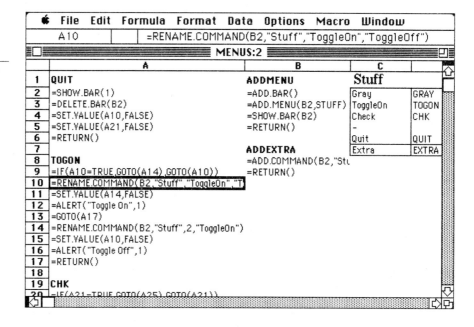

The macro TOGON has two main parts. The first part begins at cell A10 and changes the name of the option from ToggleOn to ToggleOff. The second part begins at cell A14 and changes the option from ToggleOff to ToggleOn. The command in cell A9 is the decision-maker of the macro, deciding which of the two parts will be used at any given time by looking at the value in cell A10. If this value is TRUE, the command in cell A10 has been run and the option's name is thus ToggleOff. In this case, the macro branches to the second part (cell A14). If the value of A10 is FALSE, however, the command in A10 has not been run, and the option's name is still ToggleOn.

The only thing remaining is to reset the values of A10 and A14 after each toggle by using the SET.VALUE commands. Notice that these commands appear directly after the renaming commands. Finally, the ALERT commands represent any actions taken by the two options ToggleOn and ToggleOff. You can replace these commands with any others.

If the menu is left with the ToggleOff option selected (that is, if you remove the menu with the ToggleOff option active), the menu might require some adjusting the next time it appears, because the menu definition table presents the menu with the ToggleOn option, never the ToggleOff option. For this reason, it is a good idea to reset the ToggleOff value to FALSE when you remove the menu. You could do this in a Quit option with the formula

    =SET.VALUE(A14,FALSE)

In other words, besides removing the menu and returning you to the Excel menu bar, the Quit option would reset the variable for the ToggleOff option, ensuring that the proper setting will be active the next time you call up the menu.

This example is somewhat limited in that it requires that the menu always start with the ToggleOn option. A more sophisticated macro would enable the option last selected to remain active, even after you quit Excel. One way to design such a macro is to add commands to each of the two parts of this macro. The commands would change the option listed in the menu definition table, then save the changes.

Disabling and Checking Menu Options

Another menu-options technique is adding or deleting check marks. A check mark beside an option indicates that the option has been selected. When you select the option again, the check mark is removed. Often, checked options appear in groups within a menu.

Controlling check marks is similar to controlling a toggle option, as discussed previously. The difference is that the name of the option does not change. The macro logic is the same, however. Try entering the following macro commands into the current example (see fig. 19.19):

```
CHK
=IF(A21=TRUE,GOTO(A25),GOTO(A21))
=CHECK.COMMAND(B2,"Stuff","Check",TRUE)
=SET.VALUE(A25,FALSE)
=ENABLE.COMMAND(B2,"Stuff","Gray",FALSE)
=GOTO(A28)
=CHECK.COMMAND(B2,"Stuff","Check",FALSE)
=SET.VALUE(A21,FALSE)
=ENABLE.COMMAND(B2,"Stuff","Gray",TRUE)
=RETURN( )
```

Fig. 19.19.

Using check marks.

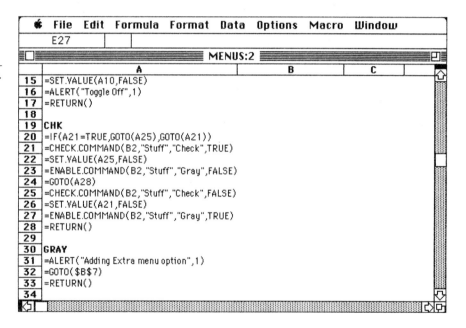

The technique for disabling an option is much simpler than the technique for toggling a menu option. A disabled option, which is displayed in gray and cannot be selected, is usually the result of your selecting some other option or performing some action. To make that action cause a menu option to disable, use the command ENABLE.COMMAND when the action is taken. For example, if one menu option (call it A) causes another (call it B) to be disabled, enter the ENABLE.COMMAND command into the macro run by option A. The syntax is

=ENABLE.COMMAND(bar_number,menu_name,command_name,state)

State should be either TRUE, which enables the command, or FALSE, which disables it.

Using Built-In Dialog Boxes

As you know, many Excel menu options bring up dialog boxes with specific choices available. When you use the macro-command equivalent of one of these options, the dialog-box choices appear as arguments. For example, the FORMAT.FONT command is equivalent to the Format Font menu option. The arguments used in this command reflect the options presented in the Format Font dialog box. The command's syntax is the following:

=FORMAT.FONT(font_name,size,bold,italic,underline,strike,
color,outline,shadow)

When you use this command in a macro, you can specify each of the options as if you selected them from the dialog box. You can thus control all aspects of the command. You might, however, need to issue the FORMAT.FONT command but let the operator select the options to be used. You can do this by using a variation of the command. This variation causes Excel to present the built-in dialog box for the Format Font menu option. The variation is this:

=FORMAT.FONT?( )

If you enter the command with a question mark at the end (and no arguments listed), Excel brings up the Format Font dialog box when the macro is run, eliminating the need for you to enter the arguments yourself. Every macro command that has an Excel menu equivalent works this way. Of course, the menu equivalent must bring up a dialog box in the first place.

Another variation is to include the question mark and the arguments, as in the following example:

=FORMAT.FONT?("New York",12,TRUE,FALSE,FALSE,FALSE,
FALSE,FALSE,FALSE)

Because it includes the question mark, this command presents the built-in dialog box. But because the command also includes the arguments, the dialog box will contain these arguments as defaults—that is, they will already be selected. You can, of course, change these selections in the dialog box. If any of the arguments is left blank, Excel uses its own default in place of that argument.

Using Custom Dialog Boxes

If you create custom menus, you may also need to create custom dialog boxes to go with them. Custom dialog boxes are created and accessed the same way that custom menus are. These boxes have three parts:

- *The controlling macro.* This macro, which brings up the dialog box, is usually a custom menu item's macro. It activates the dialog box defined in the dialog-box definition table.

- *The dialog-box definition table.* This table of values, which describes the dialog box and all its elements, can appear in any worksheet or macro sheet. When options are selected from the dialog box (or entries are made), Excel enters their results in a column of this table for reference by other macros.

- *Commands that respond to any controls that might be in the dialog box.* These commands are usually part of the original controlling macro and appear directly after the command that produces the dialog box.

Bringing up a dialog box requires only one command: DIALOG.BOX. This command can be issued from any macro, but the most common technique is to use it in a macro that corresponds to a custom menu option. The syntax of the command is as follows:

=DIALOG.BOX(table_range)

Table_range is the range containing the dialog-box definition table. This range can be on any worksheet or macro sheet, but it is most commonly entered on the macro sheet that contains the custom menu and its option macros. Using the example menus from figure 19.19, you might use the Stuff Extra option to bring up a custom menu by constructing its macro as shown in figure 19.20.

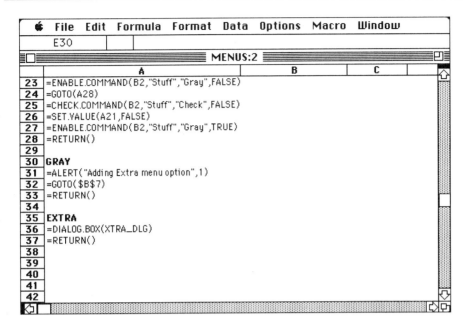

Fig. 19.20.

Adding a custom
dialog box to the
Extra menu option
of the Stuff menu.

This macro refers to the dialog-box definition table contained in the range XTRA_DLG. The following section will examine this definition table.

Creating a Dialog-Box Definition Table

The dialog-box definition table lists all the elements contained in the dialog box. It also controls the size, shape, and position of the box itself. Figure 19.21 shows a complete dialog-box definition table.

> **Table Titles Are Not Part of the Table Range**
>
> Do not use a table's titles in a table range reference; use only the range containing the items. Be sure that the first row is either blank or contains values for the location of the dialog box itself.

Each column in the table is explained in the following list. Remember that you can create a dialog-box definition table in two ways. One way is to enter the values into the table, as shown in in figure 19.21. This method requires knowledge of dialog-box definition tables and how

Fig. 19.21.

A dialog-box definition table.

	✦ File Edit Formula Format Data Options Macro Window
	G16

MENUS:2

	H	I	J	K	L	M	N	O	P
2			X	Y					
3		Type	Pos	Pos	Height	Width	Text	Init/Result	Comment
4			15	30	396	181			
5		1	198	20	64		OK		
6		2	278	22	64		Cancel		
7		5	50	10			Custom Dialog		
8		5	50	29			Edit Command		
9		6	136	143	171			Your Name He	
10		5	8	147			Enter Your Name		
11		15	216	65	171	70	FILES	5	See Note
12		17	7	10			2		
13		11	7	58	86	77	Options	2	
14		12	11	76			One		
15		12	11	94			Two		
16		12	11	112			Three		
17		14	102	57	104	78	Formats		
18		13	106	74			Bold	TRUE	
19		13	106	92			Underline	TRUE	
20		13	106	110			Italic	FALSE	
21									

they are set up. The second (and much easier) way is to use the Dialog Editor program that comes with Excel. This program does most of the work of preparing the table; you create and arrange the elements graphically. Each method is explained after this description of the table's columns:

Item type   The type of each item. A complete list of items and their type numbers appears in the next section.

X position   The horizontal position of the upper left corner of the item. If you leave this column blank, Excel will place the item.

Y position   The vertical position of the upper left corner of the item. If you leave this column blank, Excel will place the item.

Item height   The height of the item. If you leave this column blank, Excel will choose an appropriate height.

Item width   The width of the item. If you leave this column blank, Excel will choose an appropriate width.

Text   The text (if any) used for the item. Edit boxes will not have anything in this column; text boxes will always have something in this column. If a character in this box is preceded by the & character, the character following & becomes the shortcut key for the item when the dialog box is in view. For example, if a button's text is *&Forget It*, pressing Command+F selects the button. This keyboard shortcut can be emphasized through the use of the Options Workspace command, with the Command Underline option turned on. If the item is a list box, this column should contain a reference to a range of cells that contains the entire list. This reference should be a range name or an R1C1-style range reference.

Init/Result   The current settings in the dialog box. Excel updates this column as the settings change. If you enter information into this column, that information acts as default settings for the items. If the item is an edit box, this entry will determine the text currently in the box. If the item is a list box, this entry determines which choice in the list is currently selected. When a selection is made in the dialog box, the entry in this column is automatically updated to reflect the new selection. This column thus contains the current settings selected in the dialog box at all times.

Each row in the table represents the settings for a different item, except the first row. The first row represents the settings for the dialog box itself. If this row is blank, Excel uses the default size, shape, and position. Note that you can add a title to the dialog box by entering a text label into the Text column in the first row of the table. This area is cell N4 in the example. Not only does this action add a title to the dialog box, but it enables you to move the dialog box by clicking on the title bar and dragging it to a new location.

Using the Dialog Editor To Create the Table

The easiest way to create a dialog box is to use the Dialog Editor program that comes with Excel. By using this program, you can can graphically build a dialog box and position the elements. Start the Dialog Editor program by clicking on its icon from the desktop. The program begins with a blank dialog box and three menus. You will do most of your work with the Item menu and the keyboard or mouse.

To add an element to the dialog box, select from the Item menu the item you want. Most of these items offer several variations. The following are the dialog box elements you can add:

OK and Cancel buttons. These buttons are standard on dialog boxes. You click on the OK button to enter the changes you make; you click on Cancel to cancel your changes. If you add an OK button to the dialog box, Excel will automatically update the Init/Result column of the dialog-box definition table when the button is clicked. In other words, Excel takes care of accepting the new values in the dialog box and adding them to the definition table. You can change the names of these buttons, but their effects will be the same. To change the name, click on the button and type the new name.

When one of these buttons is clicked, Excel returns the value TRUE to its Init/Result column in the table. You can design a macro that reads a button's Init/Result value and thus determines when a button has been clicked. OK buttons have a type value of 3. Default OK buttons have a type value of 1. Cancel buttons have a type value of 2.

Option buttons. Option buttons (also called radio buttons) usually appear in groups. When option buttons are grouped, you can select only one button at a time. Option buttons are, therefore, useful for "either/ or" choices.

To create a group of option buttons, first add a group box by using the Item Group Box command. With the box still selected, press the Return key for each option button you want to add (or select the Item Button Option command for each option button). Excel takes care of making these grouped buttons "either/or" options. You can change the name of an option button by selecting it and typing the name you want.

When an option button is selected and the OK button is clicked, Excel returns the value TRUE to its Init/Result column, indicating that the option is currently selected. You can then design a macro that takes the appropriate action based on this selection. Option buttons have a type value of 12. Each option button in a group has a value of 11.

Check boxes. Check boxes are similar to option buttons, but they usually imply "and/or" options. In other words, you can select one or more of the boxes at any time. You can place check boxes in a group by creating the group box with the Item Group Box command, then using the Item Button Check Box command for each box you want to add to the group. Make sure that the group box is selected first. Change the name of a check box by selecting it, then typing the new name.

When a check box is selected and the OK button is clicked, Excel returns the value TRUE to its Init/Result column in the definition table. Each check box has a type value of 13.

Text. Use the Item Text command to enter any text into the dialog box—often descriptive text for edit boxes. Begin typing when the new text box is selected. To add a second and subsequent text box, select any text and press the Return key. The text you enter will appear in the item's Text column; nothing should appear in the Init/Result column. Text has the item type 5.

Edit boxes. An edit box enables you to enter and edit text, formulas, or cell references in the dialog box. Add an edit box by selecting the Item Edit Box command. You are then given the opportunity to select the type of information allowed in the box. Edit boxes have the item type 6.

When information appears in an edit box and the OK button is clicked, Excel enters that information in the Init/Result column of the table. You can design a macro that uses that information for various purposes. When the dialog box is presented, the edit box will already contain the information in the Init/Result column. This information will normally be the last thing entered in the box.

Group boxes. Group boxes hold groups of items that pertain to the same thing. Option buttons and check boxes are usually found in group boxes. To create a group box, select the Item Group Box command. To add a different item to the group box, select the group box you want and add the appropriate item; press the Return key to add more items of the same type. Group boxes have the item type 14.

List boxes. List boxes display lists of options or files that can be selected. When an item in the list is selected and the OK button is clicked, the selected item is returned to the Init/Result column of the definition table. You can build a macro that uses this information after the OK button is clicked. To specify the items in the list, enter the list of items into any worksheet or macro sheet range, then refer to this range in the list box's Text column in the definition table. One good technique is to name the range and use the range name in the table. When you have created the dialog box, Excel will read the data in the indicated range and create the list box with that data.

You can have a list box read a directory of files from the disk by entering the =FILES( ) command into the macro that brings up the dialog box. Do this before the DIALOG.BOX command is issued, so that the FILES command can perform first. Enter the FILES command as an array range.

In other words, when you enter the FILES command into the macro, select several cells in the same row (only a row of cells will work), then type =FILES( ) and press Command+Return. This procedure makes the FILES command an array command in the macro. Next, refer to this array range in the list box's Text column of the dialog-box definition table (you can name the range and use the name).

Sometimes, list boxes are linked with edit boxes. In such a case, the edit box displays the item currently selected in the list box. This box is called a combination list box. Combination list boxes have the item type 16. Standard list boxes have the type number 15.

Moving Items

To move an item to another location in the box, click on the item, hold the mouse button down, and drag the pointer. You also can use the keyboard to move an item by selecting the item with the Tab key, then using the arrow keys to move it. To resize an item with the mouse, click on an edge, hold the mouse button down, and drag the pointer. To resize an item by using the keyboard, select the item and then use the Shift key along with one of the four arrow keys to adjust the shape.

To change the size and shape of the dialog box itself, click the mouse on the bottom or right edge of the box. The pointer will change shape to indicate that you can click and drag the mouse to change the box. You can also click in the lower right corner of the box and drag diagonally to change the position of that corner, thus changing the dimensions of the box. Another alternative is to use the keyboard to change the size of the dialog box. Select the box by clicking the mouse button (or using the Edit Select Dialog command), then press the Shift key along with one of the four arrow keys.

Moving the Dialog Box into Excel

You cannot save a dialog box in the Dialog Editor program. Instead, you can store its definition on the clipboard and paste it into an Excel worksheet. Do this by quitting the Dialog Editor while your completed dialog box is in view. The program will ask whether you want to save the dialog box to the clipboard. Select Yes. Next, enter Excel with the desired worksheet or macro sheet in view and use the Edit Paste command to paste the definition table into the worksheet at the current location of the pointer. Be sure to allow enough room for the table.

Creating the Table Manually

Creating a dialog-box definition table manually is just a matter of entering the proper values into each column of the table. Remember that each row represents a different item, specified by its type number. Refer to the list of items shown earlier for each item's type number.

The first row of the table refers to the dialog box itself. This row can be blank; if it is, Excel will control the size, shape, and position of the box. If you leave any of the height, width, or position columns blank (that is, blank for any given item), Excel will control the value. Letting Excel perform these functions is a good way to eliminate extra work when you are designing tables manually.

Acting on Dialog-Box Choices

Acting on the choices made in a dialog box is a function of the macro that brings up the dialog box in the first place—at least, that is the normal way of doing things. Actually, any macro can access the values returned to the definition table; and when the macro is run, it can act on those values. By using the macro that brings up the dialog box, however, you can perform the desired actions as soon as you click on the OK button, because the macro is actually still running when the dialog box is in view. When you close the dialog box, the macro continues with the command just under the DIALOG.BOX command. Therefore, the rest of the macro can interpret and act on the choices made.

Each edit box and control used in a dialog box returns something to the Init/Result column of the table. (What each item returns is discussed in earlier sections under each item's heading.) Buttons return values of TRUE when the button has been selected and FALSE when the button has not been selected, enabling you to respond to button selections in the macro. You might have to test whether each button has been selected. You can do so by using IF functions, such as the following:

=IF(O10="TRUE",ALERT("Button X pushed",1),GOTO(A14))

This function would be entered in the macro that brings up the dialog box, under the command DIALOG.BOX. In the example, this is cell A13. The function checks whether cell O10 contains the value TRUE—the value returned by the dialog box. If the cell contains TRUE, meaning that the button has been selected, the message *Button X pushed* will be displayed in an alert box. Otherwise, continue with the macro in cell A14; that cell would continue the testing.

Summary

This chapter discussed some of the finer points of macro programming, providing background on such programming concepts as loops, variables, and subroutines. The chapter also provided details about creating custom menus and dialog boxes in Excel. The following are some of the more important points to remember:

❏ Each macro command produces a value that is returned to the cell containing the command. These values can be useful for macro programming. Often, they are essential.

❏ To see the macro values, open a new window to the macro sheet and use the Options Display command to turn the formula text off.

❏ The FOR-NEXT loop repeats a series of commands a given number of times.

❏ The IF command in useful in macros for choosing values or branching the macro's flow.

❏ The GOTO command is useful for branching the macro's natural flow to another area of the macro sheet.

❏ The FORMULA command is used in macros to insert information into cells of the worksheet.

❏ The INPUT command is useful for prompting input from the operator.

❏ Custom menus are created through the use of a menu definition table, a controlling macro, and macros that correspond to the menu items.

❏ The menu definition table consists of four columns: one for the menu item names, one for the shortcut keys, one for the command macro references, and one for the command-line messages.

❏ Use a macro to invoke the menu definition table, causing it to appear on the menu bar.

❏ You can create toggle menus or checked menus by using programming logic in the macro.

❏ You can create custom dialog boxes by using definition tables or by using the Dialog Editor program.

Appendixes

Installing Excel

Using Excel's Macro Commands

Excel Command Guide

A

Installing Excel

This appendix shows you how to get Excel up and running on your system, whether you have a hard disk or just a floppy disk drive. As you will see, installing Excel is simple. If you are familiar with using the Macintosh Finder to copy disks and files, you'll be up and running in moments. Otherwise, this appendix provides complete copy instructions. When you have finished installing Excel, you'll be ready to begin using the program and experimenting with the examples provided in this book.

Noting System Requirements

When you purchase Excel, you should make sure that your system meets the requirements of the program. Essentially, Excel 2.2 requires that you have any Macintosh computer (except the old Macintosh 128 or 512) and version 6.02 or a later version of the Macintosh System. (System 6.04 is the most current at this writing.) Excel cannot run under earlier versions of the System.

Excel also requires that you have at least 1 megabyte of RAM in your computer. If you are running Excel under MultiFinder, you must have at least 2 megabytes of RAM. A hard disk or two floppy disk drives are necessary in order for the program to run.

Copying Excel to Your Hard Drive or Floppy Disks

Excel comes with three disks: the Program disk, a Help and Examples disk, and a Microsoft Excel Tour disk. Of these three, only one is required for running Excel: the Program disk. Nevertheless, you may want to copy the contents of all three disks to your hard drive so that everything is available in order for you to learn the program. If you do not have a hard disk, you should copy all three Excel disks to new floppy disks so that you avoid using the originals. After copying the three disks, put them in a safe place. If your copies get damaged, you can make new ones with the originals.

If you already know how to copy disks, go ahead and copy the three disks to your hard disk or to three new floppy disks now. If you are unsure of this procedure, the following paragraphs will explain it.

Copying to a Hard Disk

The most important step is to copy the Excel Program disk. After starting your computer from the hard disk, insert the Program disk into your internal floppy drive. A disk icon labeled Microsoft Excel will appear near the upper right of the screen, indicating that you've inserted a disk. Double-click on this new icon to view its contents. The resulting screen should look something like figure A.1.

Now close the window by clicking in the close box in the upper left corner. To copy this disk's contents to your hard drive, move the mouse pointer to the Program disk icon (the square icon labeled Microsoft Excel). Press the mouse button and hold it down. Next, drag up to your hard disk icon as shown in figure A.2. Release the mouse button.

When you release the button, the Macintosh will inform you that it is copying the disk and ask whether it's okay to place the files in a new folder. Click on OK. Everything you saw on the Program disk will appear on your hard disk in a new folder. You can now remove the Program disk and repeat this process for the other two Excel disks. If you like, you can place all the copied files and folders into any new or existing folder on your hard disk. Many people place all program files in a single folder called PROGRAMS. The choice is entirely up to you.

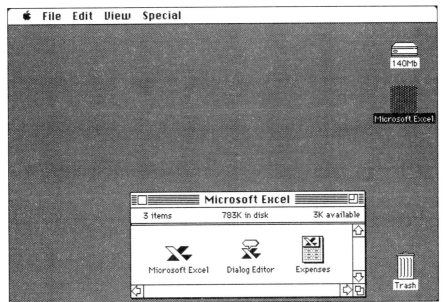

Fig. A.1.

The contents of the Program disk.

Fig. A.2.

Copying the Program disk to a hard disk.

Copying to Floppy Disks

Copying the Excel disks to new floppy disks is similar to copying to a hard disk. First, start the computer, using a startup disk that contains version 6.02 or a later version of the Macintosh System. Once the computer is started, insert the Program disk into the external disk drive. The Program disk icon, labeled Microsoft Excel, will appear on-screen. Next, select the startup disk by clicking on its icon (which should be above the Program disk icon). Now press Command+E to eject the startup disk.

The next step is to replace the startup disk with a blank disk. If the blank disk is unformatted, you will be asked to format it. Choose a double-sided format. Next, a third icon will appear on-screen. At this point and throughout the copy process, the Macintosh may ask you to swap disks, so keep the startup disk handy: you may be required to insert it. The final step is to move the mouse pointer to the Program disk icon, click the button and hold it down, and then drag that icon over to the icon for the blank disk. When the blank disk changes color (that is, turns black) release the button. Figure A.3 shows an example.

Fig. A.3.

Copying the Program disk to a new floppy disk.

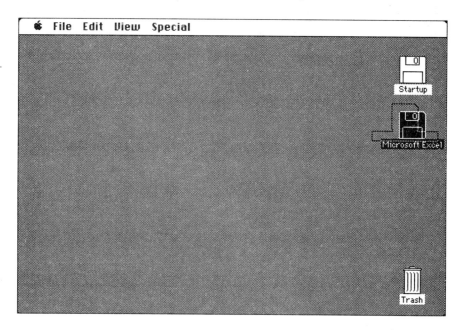

The Macintosh will inform you that it's copying the contents of the Program disk to the new disk. Repeat this process for the other Excel disks. When using Excel, be sure to start the computer with any startup disk containing System 6.02 or a later version. Then place the copy of the Program disk into the external drive and use the files from there.

Personalizing Excel

The first time you start Excel (by double-clicking on the program icon), you will be asked to enter your name and organization into a dialog box. Figure A.4 shows this box.

 File   Edit   Formula   Format   Data   Options   Macro   Window

> **Personalize your copy of Microsoft Excel.**   [OK]
>
> Name: [   ]
>
> Organization: [   ]
>
> **Don't forget to send your completed Registration Card to Microsoft. Registration entitles you to special benefits.**

Fig. A.4.

Personalizing Excel.

Enter your name and organization (if applicable) into the spaces provided. Once you enter this information, it cannot be changed. The only way to alter it is to make a new copy of Excel from the original disks. You cannot avoid calling up this "personalization" dialog box—but you can pass up the dialog box without making an entry. Doing so leaves the program unpersonalized. You will then be unable to personalize the program without making a new copy.

B

Using Excel's Macro Commands

This appendix lists the macro commands available in Excel. Many of these commands duplicate the menu options with which you have become familiar. Others are the equivalent of mouse or keyboard actions. Still others are used especially for macros.

The commands are grouped according to their basic purpose. Commands that mimic the Edit menu options, for example, appear under the heading "Duplicating the Edit Menu Options." Within these groups, commands are listed alphabetically. Many of these commands have a question-mark version, which brings up the Excel dialog box and thus makes the macro interactive. If you use the question-mark version of a command, the arguments are optional, since you can select them from the dialog box that appears. If you use the arguments anyway, they are used as the dialog-box defaults. Because most of Excel's macro commands duplicate menu options, keyboard actions, or mouse actions, this chapter does not elaborate on the effects of the commands. To find more information on a command, turn to the corresponding menu command or action described earlier in this book. The primary purpose of this appendix is to list the commands available and indicate the syntax required for each.

 In the syntax lines, the names of arguments appear in roman type if the argument is mandatory; italic type is used if the argument is optional. In the explanations of the commands, however, all arguments are italicized for easy identification.

About References

A word should be said about cell and range references used in macro commands. When you use the macro recorder, Excel enters cell and range references for you. If you type a macro by hand, however, you should know some basics about these references. Most of the commands that use the argument *reference* are asking for a cell or range reference, which can take one of several forms.

One way to enter a cell reference is as a standard cell or range reference, as in the following:

    A5
    A5:G9

This form is seldom used in macro commands, because Excel interprets such references as pertaining to the macro sheet that contains the macro command itself. In other words, these types of references refer to other cells in the same macro sheet. Most likely, you will want to refer to a specific worksheet or to the currently active worksheet—whatever it may be. Therefore, you should usually use external references, such as the following:

    !A5
    !B4:G7
    Sheet!A5
    Sheet!$A$5

As you know from Chapter 7, external references require that the exclamation point follow the worksheet name and precede the address. However, when a worksheet name is not used but the exclamation point is present (as in the first two examples), the reference applies to whatever worksheet is active at the time. The reference thus applies to any worksheet on which you might be working. By specifying the worksheet name, you restrict the reference to the specific worksheet. You can substitute the R1C1-style reference for the A1-style reference in these examples:

    !R5C1
    !R4C2:R7C7
    Sheet!R5C1

Another form of reference is the "RC"-style reference, a relative reference that applies to the current location of the pointer. Examples include these:

    "RC"
    "R[1]C"
    "R[4]C[−1]"

When you use this type of reference, you should include the quotation marks, making it a text string. The "RC" example refers to the active cell.

Duplicating the File Menu Options

Excel includes a set of macro commands that emulate the File menu options. Many of these commands have arguments that correspond to dialog-box settings. The following is listing of these commands and their proper syntax. Refer to the equivalent menu options throughout this book for more information about these commands.

CHANGE.LINK(old_link,new_link)
CHANGE.LINK?(*old_link,new_link*)

Equivalent to the Change option in the File Links command, the CHANGE.LINK command sets a new linked worksheet for the current worksheet. The variables *old_link* and *new_link* are the names of the old and new files, respectively. If you use the question-mark form of this command, the Excel File Link dialog box appears.

CLOSE(*logical*)
CLOSE.ALL( )

These commands mimic the File Close and File Close All commands. CLOSE removes the current window from the screen. If the *logical* variable is TRUE, Excel saves the document and closes. If the variable is FALSE, Excel closes without saving. If you omit the *logical* variable, Excel brings up a dialog box that asks whether you want to save changes made. CLOSE.ALL closes all unprotected worksheets.

FILE.DELETE(name_text)
FILE.DELETE?(*name_text*)

This command removes a file from disk and is equivalent to the File Delete menu option. The *name_text* argument is the file to be removed. Excel searches the current directory for the specified file. The question-mark version of this command brings up the Excel dialog box, in which you can specify the file to delete. Your specification can use wild cards to select files.

LINKS(*name_text*)

This command returns, to a cell or range of cells, the names of all worksheets linked to the worksheet specified by *name_text*. If you omit the name, Excel assumes the active worksheet. One way to use the command is to highlight a range in the macro, then enter the LINKS command as an array entry (press Command+Return) into that range. The range will contain the names of files linked to the specified file. If there are five files linked to the worksheet, be sure to highlight at least five cells in the range; otherwise, the command will fill the specified number of cells in the range and stop. You can now refer to this array range in commands that expect an array or range for a value. You might, for example, present these names in a custom list box by referring to this range in the dialog-box definition table.

Another way to use the command is as a parameter for a command that expects an array as its argument. An example is the OPEN.LINKS command:

    =OPEN.LINKS(LINKS("Spreadsheet"))

This formula opens all documents linked to the worksheet named Spreadsheet. The LINKS command is used to get the names of the linked files as an array.

NEW(type)
NEW?(*type*)

This command mimics the File New command by opening a new worksheet. The *type* value is a number representing the type of worksheet to open, according to the chart that follows (if you use the question-mark version, the familiar File New dialog box is presented):

1   Worksheet
2   Chart
3   Macro sheet

OPEN(name_text,*update_links,read_only,format,password*)
OPEN?(*name_text,update_links,read_only,format,password*)

This command is similar to the File Open command. The *name_text* argument is the name of the file that you want to open. The *update_links* argument, if TRUE, causes external references to be recalculated when the worksheet is opened; if the argument is FALSE, the references are not recalculated. If you omit the argument, Excel asks whether you want to update the links. The *read_only* variable controls whether the document can be changed (FALSE or omitted) or just viewed (TRUE). The *format* variable is useful when you open text files. Enter **1** as the value to open the text file as a tab-delimited file; enter **2** to open it as a comma-delimited file. The *password* argument enters the password for a protected file. If this argument is incorrect or omitted, Excel displays the standard password dialog box (if the file is password-protected).

OPEN.LINKS(name_text_1,*name_text_2,logical*)

The OPEN.LINKS command opens all documents specified. The named document should be entered as text strings or as a range reference to a range containing a list of text strings. You can also use the LINKS command to generate a list of names for this command. The *logical* argument should follow all names or references and determines whether the opened documents are read-only (TRUE) or read and write (FALSE).

OPEN.MAIL(*subject,comments*)
OPEN.MAIL?(*subject,comments*)

This command opens a Microsoft Mail file for viewing in Excel. If you omit the arguments, Excel brings up the Microsoft Mail message center for your selections. If you specify a *subject,* only those messages with matching subjects are opened. The *comments* argument controls whether or not the mail's comments are displayed. Enter TRUE to display comments and FALSE to omit them. Note that opening a mail file in Excel removes the file from the list of pending mail.

PAGE.SETUP(*head,foot,left,right,top,bottom,heading,grid*)
PAGE.SETUP?(*head,foot,left,right,top,bottom,size*)

This command is equivalent to the File Page Setup option. The arguments *head* and *foot,* which must be entered as text, print a header and footer. The arguments *left, right, top,* and *bottom* control the margins of the printed page. These should represent the size, in inches, of the desired margins. The arguments *heading* and *grid* control whether the worksheet headings and grid lines print with the data. Enter TRUE to print these elements or FALSE to keep them from printing. Omitting an argument leaves the option as it was last set.

When used with a chart, the PAGE.SETUP command takes the second form shown. This form uses the same arguments for the header, footer, and margins but adds the *size* argument, which represents the size of the printed chart. Use one of the following values for this variable:

1 Screen size

2 Fit to page

3 Full page

PRINT(range,from,to,copies,draft,preview,parts,*color,feed*)
PRINT?(*range,from,to,copies,draft,preview,parts,color,feed*)

This command is equivalent to the File Print command. The arguments are identical to the various buttons and check boxes found in the File Print dialog box. The *range* should be one of the following values:

1 Print all

2 Print from...

If you enter the value 2, the *from* and *to* arguments become active; otherwise, Excel ignores them. You can omit them if you like. *From* and *to* should be numeric values representing a page range. *Copies* should be a numeric value representing the number of copies you want printed.

The *draft* option should be omitted, but the comma left in as a placeholder. This argument is not recognized by the Macintosh; Excel includes it to make Excel for the Macintosh compatible with Excel for the PC. The following is an example showing the fifth argument as the placeholder comma: =PRINT(2,3,3,1,,FALSE,1,TRUE,1).

The *preview* argument should be TRUE if you want to print a preview, FALSE if you want to print normally. The *parts* argument represents the type of information to print:

1 Sheet (the worksheet and values)

2 Notes (cell notes)

3 Both

This argument should be omitted when you print a chart. The *color* argument should be TRUE if you want to print in color, FALSE if you want to print in black and white. The *feed* argument should be one of the following for dot-matrix printers:

1 Continuous feed

2 Cut sheet

When printing from a non-Apple printer (or a printer that is not compatible with Apple printers), use the question-mark form of this command. This form presents the standard Print dialog box, in which you can make selections.

QUIT

Equivalent to the File Quit command, this command quits Excel and displays the Save dialog box if files need saving.

SAVE( )
SAVE.AS(name_text,*type,password,backup*)

These commands are equivalent to the File Save and File Save As commands. The SAVE command brings up the standard Save dialog box. The SAVE.AS command saves the file in the current directory under the *name_text* name. The *type* variable represents the file type you want to save the file as. Use any of the following:

Type Value	Type Description
1	Normal Excel
2	SYLK
3	Text
4	WKS
5	WK1
6	CSV
7	DBF2
8	DBF3
9	DIF

The *password* argument is any password that is saved with the document. The *backup* argument should be TRUE if you want to make a backup as you save, FALSE if you want to forgo the backup.

Use the question-mark form of the command to save the document to a different directory. For example, =SAVE.AS?( ) brings up the standard dialog box for your selections.

SAVE.WORKSPACE(name_text)
SAVE.WORKSPACE?(*name_text*)

This command saves the workspace of the open files and creates a workspace file. For more details about these files, refer to Chapter 7. Enter the name of the desired workspace file as the *name_text* variable.

Duplicating the Edit Menu Options

Excel offers a set of macro commands that emulate the Edit menu options. Many of these commands use no arguments and correspond directly with the menu option. Others use arguments that affect the command. The following is a summary of these commands.

CANCEL.COPY( )

This command cancels the current copy operation and is usually used to remove the marquee surrounding the copied information. Using this command is similar to pressing Command+. after copying.

CLEAR(value)
CLEAR?(*value*)

This command clears data from the worksheet. The *value* should be the type of information you want to clear from the currently selected cell or range. Use one of the following values:

1   All
2   Format
3   Formulas
4   Notes

If you omit this argument, Excel assumes the value 3 for the currently selected cell or range.

COPY( )

The COPY command copies information in the currently selected cell or range. The CANCEL.COPY command removes the marquee after copying, which is the equivalent of pressing Command+. after using the Copy command.

COPY.PICTURE(appearance,size)

This command copies the active chart as a picture and places it on the clipboard. Often, a chart on-screen looks different from the printed version. For both the *appearance* and *size* argument, use one of the following two values to determine whether the copied chart will resemble the on-screen or printed variety:

1   Copies as shown on-screen
2   Copies the chart as it would print on the printer

CUT( )
Equivalent to the Edit Cut command, this command removes selected data. Data is copied to the clipboard as a result of this command.

EDIT.DELETE(value)
Equivalent to the Edit Delete command, this command removes the selected cells, rows, or columns from the worksheet and adjusts subsequent cells, rows, or columns to fill the space created. The *value* should be one of the following:

1 Shift cells left
2 Shift cells up

FILL.DOWN( )
FILL.LEFT( )
FILL.RIGHT( )
FILL.UP( )

These commands fill a range of cells with information contained in the first cell of that range.

INSERT(value)

This command inserts cells, rows, or columns, based on the selection. The *value* argument, which represents how to shift existing data, should be one of the following:

1 Shift cells right
2 Shift cells down

PASTE( )
PASTE.LINK( )

These commands paste information from the clipboard into the worksheet at the pointer location. The PASTE.LINK command is useful for creating automatic external references.

PASTE.SPECIAL(value,operation,skip_blanks,transpose)
PASTE.SPECIAL?(*value,operation,skip_blanks,transpose*)
PASTE.SPECIAL(row_column,series,categories,apply)
PASTE.SPECIAL?(*row_column,series,categories,apply*)
PASTE.SPECIAL(value)
PASTE.SPECIAL?(*value*)

This command emulates the Edit Paste Special command. Use the first version when pasting information from one worksheet into another. Use the version containing the arguments *row_column, series, categories,* and *apply* when pasting from a worksheet into a chart. The version containing *value* as the only argument should be used when you paste from a chart into a chart. The following explains the arguments:

value	Represents the type of information to print. Use one of the following:

    1 All
    2 Formulas
    3 Values
    4 Formats
    5 Notes

The options 4 and 5 do not apply to the third version of the PASTE.SPECIAL command.

operation   Specifies the operation to perform when pasting. Use one of the following:

    1 None
    2 Add
    3 Subtract
    4 Multiply
    5 Divide

skip_blanks   Determines whether to skip blank cells when pasting. Enter TRUE to skip blanks; otherwise, enter FALSE.

transpose   Determines whether to transpose data when pasting. Enter TRUE to transpose; otherwise, enter FALSE.

row_column   Determines whether rows or columns are pasted as categories in the chart. Use a 1 to specify rows or a 2 to specify columns.

series   Enter TRUE to specify the first column of each row as the text for data series or FALSE to use the first row of each column as the data series.

categories   Enter TRUE to specify the first column of each row as the text for the categories or FALSE to use the first row of each column as the text for the categories.

apply   Enter TRUE to add new categories to the existing chart categories. Enter FALSE to replace the existing categories.

Remember that the question-mark versions bring up the Excel dialog box associated with the command.

UNDO( )

Identical to the Edit Undo command, this command revokes your last action.

Duplicating the Formula Menu Options

The following commands duplicate the Formula menu options.

CREATE.NAMES(*top,left,bottom,right*)

This command creates names, using data from the selected range. Enter TRUE or FALSE in any of these arguments to create a range name that uses the appropriate cells. *Top* uses the top row of the range; *left* uses the left column; *bottom* uses the bottom row; *right* uses the right column.

DEFINE.NAME(name,refers_to,*macro_type,command_key*)
DEFINE.NAME?(*name,refers_to,macro_type,command_key*)

This command defines a range name. For the *name* argument, enter the desired name as a text string. For the *refers_to* argument, enter the address of the range as a normal external reference. Use !A1 to refer to cell A1 of the current worksheet. Use Worksheet!A1 to refer to cell A2 of an external worksheet. If you omit the *refers_to* argument, Excel assumes the currently selected cell or range.

To name a formula or function, enter the desired information in quotation marks. If you are naming a macro, use the address of the first cell of the macro. Also, if you are defining a macro, enter the *macro_type* argument as one of the following:

1   Function macro
2   Command macro
3   None (removes any current selection)

The *command_key* argument represents the command key used for the command macro. Enter this argument as a single-character text string.

DELETE.NAME(name_text)

This command removes a range name from the list of currently active range names. Enter the desired name as the *name_text* variable.

FORMULA.FIND(text,in,at,by,*dir*)
FORMULA.FIND?(*text,in,at,by,dir*)

This command searches for the text specified in *text*. The variables *in, at, by,* and *dir* should be values of 1 or 2, which represent the following:

in		*by*	
1	Formulas	1	Rows
2	Values	2	Columns

at		*dir*	
1	Whole	1	Next
2	Part	2	Previous

FORMULA.GOTO(reference)
FORMULA.GOTO?(*reference*)

This command, which performs an equivalent function as the SELECT macro command, mimics the Formula Goto menu option. For the *reference*, enter the address of the cell or range to select. You also can enter a range name or an R1C1-style reference entered as text.

FORMULA.REPLACE(find_text,replace_text,*look_at,look_by,current_ cell*)
FORMULA.REPLACE?(*find_text,replace_text,look_at,look_by,current_ cell*)

This command replaces information in the worksheet with information of your choosing. The *find_text* argument is the text you want to replace. The *replace_text* argument is the replacement text. You can use wild cards in these specifications. The *look_at, look_by,* and *current_cell* arguments should be one of the following values:

look_at
1	Whole
2	Part

look_by
1	Rows
2	Columns

current_cell
TRUE	Replaces the current cell
FALSE	Replaces the entire file

LIST.NAMES( )

This command pastes a list of names into the worksheet range, beginning at the current cell. This feature is useful for listing available range names in a custom list box.

NOTE(*text,cell_reference,start_character,count_character*)

The NOTE command is useful for inserting, removing, or changing a note attached to a cell. To add a new note (or replace an existing note), use the *text* and *cell_reference* arguments only. The *text* is the information you want to enter into the note, and *reference* is the cell whose note you want to use. To remove a note, omit all the variables, as in =NOTE( ). To add information to an existing note, include the *start_character* and *count_character* arguments. The *start_character* is the character location in the note where you want to begin inserting the new *text* information. If this value is larger than the number of characters in the note, Excel inserts the new information at the end of the note. The *count_character* determines how many characters you want to replace with the new text. The following are some examples:

=NOTE( )	Removes the note at the current cell.
=NOTE(,!A1)	Removes the note attached to cell A1 of the current worksheet.
=NOTE("This is it",!A1)	Adds the note *This is it* to cell A1 of the current worksheet. If a note exists, it will be replaced.
=NOTE("This is it",!A1,9999)	Adds the note *This is it* to the end of the existing note attached to cell A1.

SELECT.LAST.CELL( )

Equivalent to the Formula Select Special Last Cell command, this command selects the largest cell in the worksheet.

SELECT.SPECIAL(type,*value_type,levels*)

This command selects the information indicated by the variables. The following is a list of each possible value:

Type
1 Notes
2 Constants
3 Formulas
4 Blanks
5 Current region
6 Current array
7 Row differences
8 Column differences
9 Precedents
10 Dependents
11 Last cell

Value Type
1 Numbers
2 Text
4 Logical values
16 Error values

Levels (applies to type number 9 or 10 only)
1 Direct only
2 All levels

SHOW.ACTIVE.CELL( )

Identical to the keyboard command Command+Backspace, this command scrolls the screen view until the active cell is showing. This feature is useful when the pointer has been scrolled out of view.

Duplicating the Format Menu Options

Your macros can include commands that mimic the Format menu options. These are described in the following list.

ALIGNMENT(type)
ALIGNMENT?(*type*)

Equivalent to the Format Align menu option, the ALIGNMENT command aligns information in the current cell. Use any of the following values as the *type* argument:

1 General
2 Left
3 Center
4 Right
5 Fill

BORDER(*outline,left,right,top,bottom,shade*)
BORDER?(*outline,left,right,top,bottom,shade*)

This command creates a border line at the top, left side, right side, or bottom of the active cell or range. The command also can outline the range or fill it with a shade. Enter TRUE for any of the arguments to create a line; enter FALSE to remove a line. Omit an argument to leave it as is.

CELL.PROTECTION(*locked,hidden*)
CELL.PROTECTION?(*locked,hidden*)

The active cell can be locked and/or hidden with this command. Enter TRUE to activate the option or FALSE to deactivate it. Omitting an option leaves the status unchanged.

COLUMN.WIDTH(width,*reference*)
COLUMN.WIDTH?( )

This command sets the column width for the currently selected column. Enter the column width as the *width* variable. You can specify a column in the *reference* variable if you like.

DELETE.FORMAT(format_text)

Equivalent to the Delete option in the Format Number command, this command removes a custom number format. Enter the desired format as a text string in the *format_text* argument.

FORMAT.FONT(*name,size,bold,italic,underline,strike,color,outline, shadow*)
FORMAT.FONT?(*name,size,bold,italic,underline,strike,color,outline, shadow*)
FORMAT.FONT(*color,background,apply,name,size,bold,italic,underline, strike*)
FORMAT.FONT?(*color,background,apply,name,size,bold,italic,underline, strike*)

This command, equivalent to the Format Font menu command, applies a font, size, and style to the currently selected cell or range. The first version of the command applies to worksheets and macro sheets. The version containing the arguments *color, background,* and so on applies to charts. Omitting the argument altogether chooses the standard font and styles for the current selection. Both versions can be used with the question-mark form to bring up the Excel dialog box. For example, =FORMAT.FONT?( ) brings up the dialog box with the standard font and styles selected.

Enter TRUE or FALSE in the style arguments to turn them on or off, respectively. The *name* argument is the name of the font entered as a text string. The *size* argument should be a valid point size entered as a number. The *color* argument should be a value from 0 to 8 representing the color you want for the font. The value 0 tells Excel to select the color automatically. Background values can be any of the following:

1 Automatic
2 Transparent
3 White Out

The *apply* argument applies the font selection to all like elements in the chart. Enter TRUE or FALSE as the value of this argument.

FORMAT.NUMBER(format)
FORMAT.NUMBER?(*format*)

This command chooses a numeric format for the currently selected cell or range. Enter the number format as a text string, as in =FORMAT.NUMBER("#,##0.00").

JUSTIFY( )

This command justifies a column of text and is equivalent to the Format Justify menu command.

PATTERNS

This command corresponds to the Format Patterns menu command. Like its menu equivalent, the PATTERNS command comes in many forms, depending on the item selected. The following is a description of each form, its arguments, and the selected items to which it applies:

When the selection includes a chart, plot area, legend, text label, area (of an area chart), or bar (of a bar chart), use the form

PATTERNS(bauto,bstyle,bcolor,bwt,shadow,aauto,apattern, afore,aback,invert,apply)

with these arguments:

bauto	Enter a border setting:
	0 Set by user
	1 Automatic
	2 Invisible
bstyle	Enter border style selection from 1 to 8. These values correspond to the border styles in the Format Patterns dialog box.
bcolor	Enter color style selection from 1 to 8. These values correspond to the color selections in the Format Patterns dialog box.
bwt	Enter border weight value from 1 to 3, corresponding to the weight values in the Format Patterns dialog box.
shadow	Enter TRUE to include a shadow or FALSE to remove it.
aauto	Enter an area setting:
	0 Set by user
	1 Automatic
	2 Invisible
apattern	Enter a number from 1 to 16, corresponding to the patterns available in the Format Patterns dialog box.
afore	Enter a number from 1 to 8 to choose the foreground color for the pattern.
aback	Enter a number from 1 to 8 to choose the background color for the pattern.

invert   Enter TRUE to invert a value if that value is negative. This entry corresponds to the Invert if Negative box in the Format Patterns dialog.

apply   Enter TRUE to apply the settings to all like elements.

When the selection includes a chart axis, use the form

PATTERNS(line,tmajor,tminor,tlabel)

with these arguments:

line   Enter a line setting:

    0   Set by user

    1   Automatic

    2   Invisible

tmajor   Enter a value to set the major tick mark style:

    1   Invisible

    2   Inside

    3   Outside

    4   Cross

tminor   Enter a value to set the minor tick mark style:

    1   Invisible

    2   Inside

    3   Outside

    4   Cross

tlabel   Enter a value to set the position of the tick labels:

    1   None

    2   Low

    3   High

    4   Next to axis

When the selection includes a chart grid line, high-low line, or drop line, use the form

PATTERNS(line)

with this argument:

line   Enter a value from 1 to 8, corresponding to the eight line styles in the Format Patterns dialog box.

When the selection includes a data line (on a line chart), use the form

PATTERNS(line,mauto,mstyle,mfore,mback,apply)

with these arguments:

line   Enter a value from 1 to 8 to set the color of the line.

mauto   Enter a value to set the marker style:

      0   Set by user

      1   Automatic

      2   Invisible

mstyle   Enter a value from 1 to 7 to set the marker type. These values correspond to the marker types in the Format Patterns dialog box.

mfore   Enter a number from 1 to 8 to set the foreground color for the pattern.

mback   Enter a number from 1 to 8 to set the background color for the pattern.

apply   Enter TRUE to apply the selections to all like elements.

When the selection includes a chart arrow, use the form

PATTERNS(line,hwidth,hlength,htype)

with these arguments:

line   Enter a value from 1 to 3 to set the line weight.

hwidth   Enter a value to set the width of the arrow head:

      1   Narrow

      2   Medium

      3   Wide

hlength   Enter a value to set the length of the arrow head:

      1   Short

      2   Medium

      3   Long

htype   Enter a value to set the type of arrow head:

      1   No head

      2   Open head

      3   Closed head

ROW.HEIGHT(height,*reference,standard_height*)
ROW.HEIGHT?(*height,reference,standard_height*)

This command sets the height of rows in the worksheet. Enter the desired height (in points) as the *height* argument. The *reference* argument specifies which row (or rows) to change and should be entered as an external reference or as an "RC" reference entered as text. If *reference* is omitted, Excel assumes the current selection. The *standard_height* argument should be TRUE or FALSE. A value of TRUE causes each row to be sized according to the height of the fonts in that row.

SCALE(cross,category_labels,category_marks,between,max,reverse)
SCALE(min,max,major,minor,cross,logarithmic,reverse,max)

This command has two forms. The first applies to category axes (except on scatter charts). The second form applies to value axes and scatter charts.

The following arguments are used with the first form:

cross	Enter the number corresponding to the category at which the value axis should cross.
category_labels	Enter the number of categories that should appear between tick labels.
category_marks	Enter the number of categories that should appear between tick marks.
between	Enter TRUE to make the category axis cross between categories. Otherwise, enter FALSE.
reverse	Enter TRUE to display categories in reverse order; otherwise, enter FALSE.
max	Enter TRUE to cause the value axis to cross at the maximum category.

(Omit any of the previous three arguments to leave the option unchanged from its last setting.)

These arguments are used with the second form:

min	Enter the minimum value for the value axis.
max	Enter the maximum value for the value axis.

major	Enter the value for the major-unit scale.
minor	Enter the value for the minor-unit scale.
cross	Enter the value at which the category axis crosses the value axis.
logarithmic	Enter TRUE to set a logarithmic scale; otherwise, enter FALSE.
reverse	Enter TRUE to display the value axis in reverse order.
max	Enter TRUE to cause the category axis to cross at the maximum value.

(Omit any of the previous three arguments to leave the option unchanged from its last setting.)

Duplicating the Data Menu Options

Excel includes a set of commands that duplicate the Data menu options. The following list describes these commands and shows the proper syntax for using them.

DATA.DELETE( )
DATA.DELETE?( )

This command, equivalent to the Data Delete menu command, deletes records according to the current criteria range.

DATA.FIND(logical)

This command finds a record in the database or exits from the find procedure. Enter TRUE to find records or FALSE to exit from the find procedure.

DATA.FORM( )

This command brings up the database data form for the currently set database.

DATA.SERIES(row_column,type,date,*step,stop*)
DATA.SERIES?(*row_column,type,date,step,stop*)

This command, equivalent to the Data Series command, enters a series of values into a range automatically. Use the following values for the arguments:

row_column
1 Rows
2 Columns

type
1 Linear
2 Growth
3 Date

date
1 Day
2 Weekday
3 Month
4 Year

The *step* value is a number corresponding to the increment of the data series values. The *stop* value is the maximum value allowed in the series.

For example, the command =DATA.SERIES(1,3,3) enters a row of month names into the current selection. Notice that the stop and step values are not used in this example. Excel assumes 1 as the step and stops at the last highlighted cell.

EXTRACT(logical)
EXTRACT?(logical)

This command extracts data from the active database according to the active criteria settings. Enter TRUE to extract unique records only; enter FALSE to extract all matching records.

SET.CRITERIA
SET.DATABASE

These commands set the current criteria range and database range, respectively. Be sure to select the range you want before using these commands.

SORT(sort_by,key_1,order_1,*key_2,order_2,key_3,order_3*)
SORT?(*sort_by,key_1,order_1,key_2,order_2,key_3,order_3*)

Equivalent to the Data Sort menu option, this command sorts the currently selected range of cells. The *sort_by* argument can be either of the following values:

1   Rows

2   Columns

Enter the address of the cell representing the first key field as the *key_1* value. This address should be an external reference or an "RC"-style reference entered as text. The *order_1* argument should be either of the following values:

1   Ascending

2   Descending

Add a second and third key and order if you like.

Duplicating the Options Menu Options

Like the other menus, the Options menu includes a set of macro command equivalents. The following is a list of those commands and their syntax requirements.

A1.R1C1(logical)

This command switches between the A1- and R1C1-style cell references on the active worksheet. Enter TRUE to use A1 references or FALSE to use R1C1 references.

CALCULATE.DOCUMENT( )
CALCULATE.NOW( )

These commands emulate the Options Calculate Document and Options Calculate Now menu commands, respectively. The commands calculate the current worksheet.

CALCULATION(type,*iterations,max_num,max_change,update, precision,date_1904*)
CALCULATION?(*type,iterations,max_num,max_change,update, precision,date_1904*)

This command corresponds to the Options Calculation menu command and is used to set various aspects of automatic recalculation for the worksheet. The following are the settings. See "Calculating the Worksheet" in Chapter 8 for details about these options.

type	Sets the calculation type as follows:
	1 Automatic
	2 Automatic except tables
	3 Manual
iterations	Enter TRUE or FALSE to activate or deactivate the iterations option.
max_num	Enter a value representing the maximum number of iterations.
max_change	Enter a value representing the maximum amount of change.
update	Enter TRUE or FALSE to activate or deactivate the update-remove-references option.
precision	Enter TRUE or FALSE to activate or deactivate the precision-as-displayed feature.
date_1904	Enter TRUE or FALSE to activate or deactivate the 1904 dating system.

DISPLAY(*formula,gridline,heading,zero,color*)
DISPLAY?(*formula,gridline,heading,zero,color*)
DISPLAY(*cell,formula,value,format,protect,names,precedents, dependents,note*)
DISPLAY?(*cell,formula,value,format,protect,names,precedents, dependents,note*)

This command displays or hides various elements on the worksheet. The first form is used with worksheets or macro sheets. Enter TRUE in any option that you want displayed; enter FALSE if you don't want the option displayed. Enter a value from 1 to 8 for the *color* option in order to select a color for the sheet. These arguments correspond to the check boxes on the Options Display dialog box.

The second form is used with Info sheets. Enter TRUE to add an item to the Info sheet; enter FALSE to remove an item. The *precedents* and *dependents* options should have one of the following values:

0   None
1   Direct only
2   All levels

Use the question-mark form of this command with no arguments to display the Excel dialog box, as in =DISPLAY?( ).

FREEZE.PANES(logical)

Use this command, which corresponds to the Options Freeze Panes menu command, to freeze the panes of a split-screen display. Enter TRUE to freeze the panes or FALSE to unfreeze them.

PRECISION(logical)

This command is equivalent to the Precision as Displayed check box of the Options Calculation command. Enter TRUE to check the box (to enable the option) or FALSE to uncheck.

PROTECT.DOCUMENT(*contents,windows,password*)
PROTECT.DOCUMENT?(*contents,windows*)

This command is equivalent to the Options Protect Document menu command. Enter TRUE or FALSE as the value of the *contents* and *windows* arguments. TRUE protects; FALSE unprotects. Use FALSE in both options to remove protection entirely. If a password is required to unprotect the file, enter it as a text string in the *password* argument.

REMOVE.PAGE.BREAKS( )
SET.PAGE.BREAK( )

These commands remove page breaks and set page breaks, respectively. They perform their functions relative to the position of the pointer.

SET.PRINT.AREA( )

This command activates the currently selected range as the current print area. If a only one cell is selected, the command removes the print area.

SET.PRINT.TITLES( )

This command activates the currently selected range as the titles range for printouts. First, select the desired range of cells, then use this command as you would use the Options Set Print Titles menu command.

SHORT.MENUS(logical)

Enter TRUE as the argument to have Excel display short menus. Enter FALSE to have Excel display full menus.

STANDARD.FONT(*name,size,bold,italic,underline,strike,color,outline,shadow*)

This command sets the standard font for the entire worksheet. The arguments are identical to those of the FORMAT.FONT command listed earlier in this chapter.

WORKSPACE(fixed,decimals,r1c1,scroll,status,formula,menu,remote,return,underlines)
WORKSPACE?(*fixed,decimals,r1c1,scroll,status,formula,menu,remote,return,underlines*)

This command is equivalent to the Options Workspace command. Its arguments correspond to the dialog-box options in that command:

fixed	Enter TRUE to set a fixed number of decimal places for the entire worksheet. The number of places is specified in the *decimals* argument. Enter FALSE to return the sheet to the General format.
decimals	Enter the number of decimal places to use when the *fixed* value is TRUE.
r1c1	Enter TRUE to set the worksheet to the R1C1-style reference or FALSE to use the A1 style.
scroll	Enter TRUE to display scroll bars or FALSE to remove them.
status	Enter TRUE to display the status line or FALSE to remove it.
formula	Enter TRUE to display formula text or FALSE to display the values produced by formulas.
menu	Enter a text character to represent the alternate-menu key for keyboard menu activation.

remote	Leave this option blank or enter FALSE. This argument is included to make Excel's Macintosh and PC versions compatible.
return	Enter TRUE to move the pointer after each Return or FALSE to leave it in place.
underlines	Enter one of the following to control how the keyboard indicator keys are displayed:

      1   Underlines on

      2   Underlines off

      3   Underlines on when the menu is activated by the keyboard

Duplicating the Window Menu Options

You can manipulate windows by using macro commands that mimic the Window menu options. The following is a description of each command and its syntax.

ARRANGE.ALL( )

This command, equivalent to the Window Arrange All menu command, arranges all open windows on the screen.

HIDE( )

This command hides the current window but leaves it open.

NEW.WINDOW( )

This command creates a new window for the currently active window. The two windows display the same file but can be operated independently.

SHOW.CLIPBOARD( )

This command displays the contents of the clipboard in a window.

SHOW.INFO(logical)

Enter TRUE as the *logical* value to display the Info window for the active cell. Enter FALSE to remove the window.

UNHIDE(window_name)

This command brings into view a hidden window. For the *window_name* argument, enter the desired window name as a text string.

Duplicating the Gallery Menu Options

The Gallery menu options control the types of charts that can be viewed in Excel. You can manipulate Gallery options by using macro commands. The following is a list.

COMBINATION(number)

This command sets a combination chart for the currently active chart. Enter the desired combination chart number (as shown in the gallery produced by the Gallery Combination command) to set the chart. You can also use the question-mark version of this command to have Excel present the gallery choices.

GALLERY.AREA(number,*delete_overlay*)
GALLERY.AREA?(*number,delete_overlay*)
GALLERY.BAR(number,*delete_overlay*)
GALLERY.BAR?(*number,delete_overlay*)
GALLERY.COLUMN(number,*delete_overlay*)
GALLERY.COLUMN?(*number,delete_overlay*)
GALLERY.LINE(number,*delete_overlay*)
GALLERY.LINE?(*number,delete_overlay*)
GALLERY.PIE(number,*delete_overlay*)
GALLERY.PIE?(*number,delete_overlay*)
GALLERY.SCATTER(number,*delete_overlay*)
GALLERY.SCATTER?(*number,delete_overlay*)
PREFERRED( )
PREFERRED?( )

These commands set the type of chart for the active chart window. The *number* represents the respective chart type number, as shown in the gallery. To see these numbers, use the corresponding menu command. You also can use the question-mark version of these commands to have Excel display the gallery for you. The *delete_overlay* option should be either TRUE or FALSE. TRUE applies the gallery selection to the main chart and removes any overlay that is present. FALSE applies the gallery selection to either the overlay or main chart—depending on which is currently selected.

SET.PREFERRED( )

This command is equivalent to the Gallery Set Preferred command, which sets the preferred chart type to match the currently selected chart. When you use the PREFERRED command after having used SET.PREFERRED command, Excel duplicates the chart you set with this command.

Duplicating the Chart Menu Options

Controlling charts from within macros can be useful for custom applications. The following is a list of the macro command equivalents for Chart menu options.

ADD.ARROW( )

This command places a new arrow on the chart. You can remove the arrow by using the DELETE.ARROW( ) command.

ADD.OVERLAY( )

This command adds an overlay chart to the existing chart. Adding an overlay causes the series to split between the overlay and the main chart. See also DELETE.OVERLAY( ).

ATTACH.TEXT(attach_to_number,*series_number,point_number*)
ATTACH.TEXT?(*attach_to_number,series_number,point_number*)

Use this command to attach text to a chart object. Use one of the following values for the *attach_to_number* argument:

1   Chart title

2   Value axis

3   Category axis

4   Series marker or data point marker

If you use an *attach_to_number* of 4, you can optionally specify the *series_number* and *point_number*.

AXES(*main_category,main_value,overlay_category,overlay_value*)
AXES?(*main_category,main_value,overlay_category,overlay_value*)

Use this command to display or hide the value and category axis for both the main chart and its overlay. Enter TRUE to show the item or FALSE to remove it.

DELETE.ARROW( )

This command removes the currently selected arrow from the chart.

DELETE.OVERLAY( )

This command places a new arrow on the chart. You can remove the arrow by using the DELETE.ARROW( ) command.

FORMAT.LEGEND(position_number)
FORMAT.LEGEND?(*position_number*)

This command controls the position of the legend. Use any of the following values to specify the desired position:

1 Bottom
2 Corner
3 Top
4 Vertical

FORMAT.MOVE(x_position,y_position)
FORMAT.MOVE?(*x_position,y_position*)

Use this command to move a chart object (the currently selected object) to another area of the chart window. The *x_position* and *y_position* values indicate the object's distance from the upper left corner of the screen.

FORMAT.SIZE(width,height)
FORMAT.SIZE?(*width,height*)

Use this command to specify the size of a chart object (the selected chart object). Enter a value (in points) for the object's *width* and *height*.

FORMAT.TEXT(x_align,y_align,*vertical_text*,auto_text,auto_size, show_key,show_value)
FORMAT.TEXT?(*x_align,y_align,vertical_text,auto_text,auto_size, show_key,show_value*)

This command formats text on the chart. Specify each of its arguments according to the following list:

x_align	Enter a value to represent the horizontal alignment:
	1 Left
	2 Center
	3 Right
y_align	Enter a value to represent the vertical alignment:
	1 Left
	2 Center
	3 Right

vertical_text	Enter TRUE to make the text appear vertically; otherwise, enter FALSE or omit the argument.
auto_text	Enter TRUE to make the text orientation automatic; otherwise, enter FALSE.
auto_size	Enter TRUE to make the text size automatic; otherwise, enter FALSE.
show_key	Enter TRUE to show the key of the selected attached text.
show_value	Enter TRUE to show the value for an attached text label.

GRIDLINES(category_major,category_minor,value_major,value_minor)
GRIDLINES?(*category_major,category_minor,value_major,value_minor*)

Use this command to add major and/or minor grid lines to the category and value axes of the active chart. Enter TRUE to add the grid lines or FALSE to remove them.

LEGEND(logical)

This command adds or removes the legend from the active chart. Enter TRUE to add the legend or FALSE to remove it.

MAIN.CHART(type,stack,100,vary,overlap,drop,hilo,overlap%, cluster,angle)
MAIN.CHART?(*type,stack,100,vary,overlap,drop,hilo,overlap%, cluster,angle*)
OVERLAY(type,stack,100,vary,overlap,drop,hilo,overlap%,cluster, angle,series,auto)

These commands control various aspects of the main chart and overlay chart, respectively. Both commands include a question-mark version that brings up the Excel menu and eliminates the need for the arguments. The arguments are defined as follows:

type	Enter a value representing the chart type:

1	Area
2	Bar
3	Column
4	Line
5	Pie
6	Scatter

stack	Enter TRUE to stack the chart; otherwise, enter FALSE.
100	Enter TRUE to create a 100% value chart.
vary	Enter TRUE to activate the Vary by Categories option or FALSE to deactivate the option.
overlap	Enter TRUE to overlap the series markers in the chart. This argument works with the *overlap%* argument listed later.
drop	Enter TRUE to add drop lines to the chart or FALSE to remove them.
hilo	Enter TRUE to add high-low lines to the chart or FALSE to remove them.
overlap%	Enter the percentage value for the overlap of the series markers.
cluster	Enter the percentage value for the cluster spacing of series markers.
angle	Enter the angle (in degrees) of the first pie slice for a pie chart.

If any of these arguments does not apply to the currently selected chart, Excel will ignore it.

OVERLAY.CHART.TYPE(type)
OVERLAY.CHART.TYPE?(*type*)

This command sets the chart type for the overlay chart (if one exists). Use the following table to specify the type value:

1   None (no overlay)

2   Area

3   Bar

4   Column

5   Line

6   Pie

7   Scatter

SELECT.CHART( )
SELECT.PLOT.AREA( )

These commands select the chart and plot area, respectively.

Duplicating the Macro Menu Options

The Macro menu contains only one command that can be used in a macro—the RUN command. The following explains this command.

RUN(reference)
RUN(*reference*)

The RUN command runs a macro specified by the *reference* argument. This argument should be a valid macro name entered as a text string; the starting address of a macro, entered as an external reference, as in =RUN(!A1); or an "RC"-style reference entered as a text string.

Duplicating Keyboard and Mouse Actions

Excel provides a number of macro commands that duplicate actions you can make with the mouse or keyboard. These commands initiate such tasks as entering information into cells, selecting cells, changing windows, and scrolling. The following is a list of these commands and explanations of their arguments.

ACTIVATE(*window_text,pane_number*)

This command activates the specified pane in the specified window. *Window_text*, the name of the window to activate, should be entered as text with quotation marks or as an expression resulting in text. *Pane_number* is the pane within the window that you want to activate. Use any of the following values as the *pane_number*:

Value	Pane
1	Top pane if window is split horizontally
	Left pane if window is split vertically
	Top left pane if window is split two ways
2	Right pane if window is split vertically
	Top right if window is split two ways
3	Bottom pane if window is split horizontally
	Bottom left if split two ways
4	Bottom right pane if window is split two ways

ACTIVATE.NEXT( )
ACTIVATE.PREV( )

These commands activate the next and previous windows, respectively. Of course, more than one window should be open in order for these commands to work. These commands are the equivalents of the keyboard commands Command+M and Command+Shift+M.

CANCEL.COPY( )

This command cancels an Edit Copy or Edit Cut command in the middle, clearing the marquee from the worksheet.

CLOSE(*logical*)

This command closes the active window. If *logical* contains the value TRUE, any changes are saved when the window is closed. If *logical* contains the value FALSE, changes are not saved. If *logical* is omitted, the Save dialog box appears, asking whether you want to save changes.

COLUMN.WIDTH(width,*reference*)
COLUMN.WIDTH?(*width,reference*)

This command changes the width of a column. Enter the desired column width as the *width* argument. The *reference* variable specifies the columns to change and should be entered as text. If you omit this variable, the command operates on the currently selected column (or columns). The following example changes the widths of columns A, B, and C:

    =COLUMNS.WIDTH(25,"A1:C5")

The question-mark version of this command brings up Excel's column-width dialog box. Any argument supplied with this version becomes the default in the dialog box.

DATA.FIND.NEXT( )
DATA.FIND.PREV( )

These commands find the next and previous matching records in the database when performing a find operation. They are the equivalent to "flipping through" the records with the commands Command+F and Command+Shift+F.

FORMULA(formula_text,*reference*)

This command enters data—in the form of a text string, a number, or a formula—into a cell of the worksheet. The result is the same as if you typed it from the keyboard. *Formula_text* is the information you want entered. This argument should be entered as a text string or an expression resulting in a text string. The *reference* is the cell into which you want to enter the data. If this argument is omitted, Excel uses the active cell.

Excel deciphers whether your formula text entry is a number, formula, or text string. Excel uses the same criteria for making this decision as it does when you type data from the keyboard. Anything beginning with an equal sign is a formula; anything beginning with an alphabetic character (except range names) is a text string, and so on. If the cell receiving this data already contains information, Excel will replace that information with your new entry.

FORMULA.ARRAY(formula_text,reference)
FORMULA.FILL(formula_text,reference)

These commands are similar to the FORMULA command. Using FORMULA.ARRAY is similar to typing a formula into the first cell of a range and pressing Command+Return to enter the formula, but FORMULA.ARRAY creates an array formula. Using FORMULA.FILL is similar to typing a formula into the first cell of a range and pressing Option+Return to enter the formula. This action duplicates the entry for the entire range.

FORMULA.FIND.NEXT( )
FORMULA.FIND.PREV( )

After you use the Data Find command (or the equivalent macro command), these commands find the next and previous cells matching the find criteria. Issuing these commands is identical to pressing Command+H or Command+Shift+H.

FULL(logical)

This command mimics the window zoom box in the upper right corner of a window. If *logical* is TRUE, the window will expand to its full size. If *logical* is FALSE, the window will shrink to its modified size.

HLINE(number_columns)
HPAGE(number_windows)

These commands scroll the active window horizontally. HLINE scrolls the window by the specified number of lines, horizontally. Using this command is identical to using the scroll arrows of the active horizontal scroll bars. HPAGE scrolls the window by the specified number of pages, or screens, an action identical to clicking in the horizontal scroll bar. Use a positive number to represent rightward movement and a negative number to represent leftward movement. Here are some examples:

=HLINE(65)   Scrolls the active window 65 lines to the right

=HPAGE(-5)   Scrolls leftward by five pages (or screens)

MOVE(x_position,y_position,*window_text*)

This command moves a window to another screen location—an action equivalent to dragging on the window's title bar. The arguments *x_position* and *y_position* represent the horizontal and vertical positions of the upper left corner of the window. These positions are measured in points (a point is 1/72nd of an inch) from the upper left corner of the screen. The argument *window_text* is the name of the window that you want to move. If this argument is omitted, Excel moves the active window.

SELECT(selection,active cell)
SELECT(item_text)

When used with a worksheet, this command selects the worksheet cell or range specified by the *selection* variable. If the selection is a range of cells, you can make any cell in the range the active cell by entering its address as the *active_cell* variable. The *active_cell* should be one of the cells in the *selection*.

You can specify the selection as a cell or range on the current worksheet, using the form !A5 or !A5:B6. You can, of course, make this reference an external one by including the window name, such as Worksheet1!A5:B6. You can also refer to a named range, as in !Sales (for the current worksheet) or Worksheet1!Sales (for an the external worksheet named Worksheet).

Alternatively, you can make the selection relative to the currently active cell by entering the argument as an R1C1-style reference entered as a text string. For example, the command =SELECT("R1C2:R3C3","R1C3") highlights the range B1:C3 and makes the active cell C1. You can also use the entry "RC" to represent the active cell and move the pointer relative to that cell with entries like the following:

=SELECT("RC[1]")	Moves the pointer one column to the right
=SELECT("R[-3]C[2]")	Moves the pointer three rows up and two columns to the right

When used with a chart, the SELECT command selects the chart element specified by the *item_text* argument. Use any of the following entries to specify the item text:

Entry	*Selection*
Chart	The entire chart
Plot	The plot area
Legend	The legend
Axis 1	The main chart's vertical (value) axis
Axis 2	The main chart's horizontal (category) axis
Axis 3	The overlay chart's vertical (value) axis
Axis 4	The overlay chart's horizontal (category) axis
Title	The chart title
Text Axis 1	The main chart's value axis title
Text Axis 2	The main chart's category axis title
Text *n*	The *n*th text added to the chart
Arrow *n*	The *n*th arrow added to the chart

Be sure to enter the argument in quotation marks.

SIZE(width,height,*window_text*)

This command changes the size of a window. The *width* represents the desired width (in points) of the window; *height* represents the desired height (in points) of the window. Specify the window you would like to change by entering its name as the *window_text* variable. If you omit this variable, Excel assumes the active window. This command changes the lower right corner of the window to match your specifications.

SPLIT(column_split,row_split)

This command splits the window to create panes—comparable to dragging the split-window marker with the mouse. Indicate the column on which you want to split the sheet by typing its numeric value as the *column_split* variable. Indicate the row on which you want to split the sheet by entering its value as the *row_split* variable. The following are examples:

=SPLIT(5,0) Splits the window vertically at column 5

=SPLIT(5,3) Splits the window vertically at row 3 and horizontally at column 5

UNLOCKED.NEXT( )
UNLOCKED.PREV( )

These commands move the current cell to the next or previous unlocked (that is, unprotected) cell in the sheet, respectively. These commands are equivalent to using the keyboard commands Tab and Shift+Tab.

VLINE(number_rows)
VPAGE(number_columns)

These commands scroll the active window vertically. VLINE scrolls the window by the specified number of lines, vertically. Using this command is similar to using the scroll arrows of the active vertical scroll bar. VPAGE scrolls the window by the specified number of pages, or screens, an action similar to clicking in the vertical scroll bar. Use a positive number to represent downward movement and a negative number to represent upward movement. See also HLINE and HPAGE.

Controlling Macro Operation

Excel includes a group of commands that control how macros operate. Called *control macros*, these commands control presenting messages and dialog boxes, passing arguments to and from the worksheet, pausing macros, and more. The following is a list of these control macro commands.

ALERT(message,type)

ALERT presents an alert box with a message. Enter any message for the box as the *message* variable. Specify the type of alert box by entering its numeric value in the *type* variable. The types are these:

1 Caution box
2 Note box
3 Stop box

ARGUMENT(name_text,*data_type_number,reference*)

Used for function macros, the ARGUMENT command passes a variable from the worksheet to a macro; the macro can then operate on that value. All variables in the function macro must be defined with the ARGUMENT command; these variables may then be passed to the macro from the worksheet or from a cell referenced in the ARGUMENT command.

Name_text is the name of the variable, entered as a text string. The name can be any text without spaces. *Data_type* is a value representing the type of data that will be used for this argument (see the chart that follows). The *reference* is the address of a cell containing the value to be used as the argument. This argument is needed only if the value comes not from the worksheet function but from another macro or from a specific cell's value. If you omit this variable, Excel assumes that the argument is coming from the worksheet function. See Chapter 18 for more information on function macros. The available data types are these:

Value	Type
1	Number
2	Text
4	Logical
8	Reference (cell or range address)
16	Error
64	Array

BEEP(value)

This command activates the Macintosh bell. You cannot control the volume by using a macro; you must use the control panel to do that. *Value* represents the amount of time the beep sounds.

BREAK( )

This command breaks out of a FOR-NEXT or WHILE-NEXT loop before the loop is naturally up. When the break occurs, the macro continues with the command just after the NEXT statement at the end of the loop.

CANCEL.KEY(logical,*reference*)

This command enables or disables the Escape key for interrupting a macro. Normally, pressing Escape (or Command+.) halts a macro during its operation. If you use the command =CANCEL.KEY(TRUE) in the macro, the Escape key will no longer halt the macro. Use the command =CANCEL.KEY(FALSE) to reactivate the Escape key.

If you add the argument *reference* while the *logical* value is TRUE, the Escape key will interrupt the macro and execute the macro specified by its *reference*. Enter any macro cell reference as this argument.

DISABLE.INPUT(logical)

When *logical* is TRUE, this command prohibits any keyboard input into the worksheet. The user can work with dialog boxes, however. This feature is useful when you want to take total control over the worksheet through macros. When *logical* is FALSE, input is changed back to normal.

ECHO(logical)

When *logical* is TRUE, this command turns off the screen repaint feature. This feature saves time when a macro makes several changes at one time: by turning the repaint feature off at the beginning of the macro and back on at the end, you avoid waiting for the screen to repaint after each change. This feature is useful for changes to charts. Turn repaint back on with a *logical* value of TRUE.

ERROR(logical,*reference*)

When *logical* is FALSE, this command deactivates the Excel error messages that appear when an error is encountered. If you also include the *reference* argument, Excel will run the macro referenced when an error occurs. Enter the cell reference of the desired macro as the *reference* variable. When *logical* is TRUE, error messages are returned to normal.

Caution: Turning error messages off eliminates the caution that appears when you close a document that has not been saved. This arrangement could result in lost information. Use this command cautiously.

FOR(counter_name,start_value,stop_value,*step_value*)

This command begins the FOR-NEXT loop described in Chapter 19. All actions between the FOR and NEXT commands are repeated according to the conditions of the loop. See the complete explanation in Chapter 19 for details. See also NEXT.

GOTO(reference)

This command branches the flow of a macro to the cell or range name referenced. Enter any cell or range reference as the *reference* variable.

HALT( )

HALT stops the macro that is currently running. This command is usually used in a macro along with a conditional statement, such as IF.

INPUT(prompt,type,*title,default,x_position,y_position*)

The INPUT command presents a dialog box with a custom message and asks for input from the user. The user's input is returned to the cell containing this command. You can then act on the input, using other macro commands that refer to this cell. The *prompt*—the message you want to display in the dialog box—must be a text entry (in quotation marks) or text expression. The *type* variable is the type of entry expected from the user. The entry types are the following:

Value	Type
0	Formula (returned as text)
1	Number
2	Text
4	Logical
8	Reference
16	Error
64	Array

To allow more than one type, add the desired type values listed and enter the sum as the type value. You cannot add types 8 or 64 to any others. The value entered is returned to the cell containing the =INPUT command. Thus for this value to be used, another macro command must refer to this cell.

The *title* value represents the title given to the dialog box. If you omit this value, the word *Input* will be the title; if you supply this value, enter it as a text string. If you enter a *default* value (as a text string in quotation marks), it will appear automatically in the input box. This argument is most commonly used with a macro variable that corresponds to a current value or selection. The *x_position* and *y_position* values determine the location of the dialog box on the screen. If these values are omitted, the dialog box is centered; otherwise, the values are used as the upper left corner of the box (in picas from the corner of the screen). See Chapter 19 for more information about this command.

MESSAGE(logical,*text*)

This command activates or deactivates the presentation of messages on the status line. You can also use this command to present custom messages on this line. The *logical* value must be either TRUE or FALSE. If TRUE, the message capability is turned on; if FALSE, the message capability is turned off. When the message capability is OFF, the status bar returns to normal, displaying Excel's standard messages. You can use this command with a *text* value of "" (that is, the empty set) to simply turn the message capability on and off as you like. However, if you enter a *text* variable, the appropriate message is displayed.

Be sure to turn the normal message display back on (by issuing the command with the FALSE logical value) after displaying custom messages. Otherwise, the custom message will remain in view until you quit Excel.

NEXT( )

This command completes the FOR-NEXT loop. See the full explanation of loops in Chapter 19 for more details. See also FOR.

RESULT(type)

This command is required at the beginning of all function macros. It specifies the type of information that will be returned to the cell as a result of the function macro's calculations. The types are the following:

Value	Type
0	Formula (returned as text)
1	Number
2	Text
4	Logical
8	Reference
16	Error
64	Array

To allow more than one type, add the desired type values listed and enter the sum as the type value. You cannot add types 8 or 64 to any others. The value entered is returned to the cell containing the =INPUT command. Thus for this value to be used, another macro command must refer to this cell. For more information about function macros, see Chapter 18.

RETURN(*value*)
RETURN( )

This command is used at the end of a macro to return the operation to its starting point. The command can be used in function macros to return a value to the worksheet. This value should be of the type specified by the RESULT command. When RETURN is used in command macros, the *reference* argument should be omitted.

SET.NAME(name_text,value)

Similar to the menu command Formula Define Name, this command names the *value* argument with the name defined by *name_text*. The *value* can be any formula, cell reference, range reference, or expression. *Name_text* must be entered as a text string or be an expression resulting in a text string. See Chapter 3 for more information about naming ranges, formulas, and expressions.

SET.VALUE(reference,value)

This command changes the value of a cell. If the cell contains a formula, the value of the cell is changed but the formula is not—hence, the next time the worksheet recalculates its values, the formula will recalculate the cell's value, overriding the SET.VALUE value. This command is useful for creating "flags" within macros and for storing values during a macro's calculation. See examples in Chapter 19 under the discussion of custom menus.

WAIT(time)

The WAIT command pauses the macro until the designated time has passed. The *time* variable should be entered as a valid time serial number. You can resume the macro operation by pressing Command+. (period).

C

Excel Command Guide

Menu Commands and Procedures

Opening and Closing Worksheets

Description	Command	Command Key
Open new file	File New	N
Open existing file	File Open	O
Close file	File Close	W
Save file	File Save	S
Save file under different name	File Save As	
Save workspace	File Save Workspace	
Delete files from disk	File Delete	
Quit Excel	File Quit	Q

Printing

Description	Command	Command Key
Determine page setup	File Page Setup	
Begin printing	File Print	P
Select print area	Options Set Print Area	
Set titles for page	Options Set Print Titles	
Set manual page break	Options Set Page Break	

Editing Data

Description	Command	Command Key
Move data	Edit Cut (then Paste)	X
Copy data	Edit Copy	C
	Edit Fill Right	R
	Edit Fill Down	D
	Edit Fill Left	
	Edit Fill Up	
Paste data	Edit Paste	V
	Edit Paste Special	
Paste data from other worksheet	Edit Paste Link	
Remove data	Edit Clear	B
Insert cell	Edit Insert	I
Delete cell	Edit Delete	K
Name cells and ranges	Formula Define Name	
	Formula Create Names	
Add or edit cell note	Formula Note	
View note	Formula Note	
	Window Show Info	

Finding Data

Description	Command
Go to specified cell	Formula Goto
Find specific data	Formula Find
Replace data	Formula Replace
Find specific references	Formula Select Special

Entering Data

Description	Command	Command Key
Accept entry	Return	
	Enter	
Cancel entry	Esc	
	Command+.	
	Edit Undo	Z
Repeat previous entry	Edit Repeat	Y
Insert a function name	Formula Paste Function	
Insert a name	Formula Paste Name	
Protect cells from entry	Format Cell Protection (then Options Protect Document)	

Formatting

Description	Command
Specify number formats	Format Number
Align data	Format Alignment
Change fonts	Format Font
Change row height	Format Row Height
Change column width	Format Column Width
Justify a column of text	Format Justify
Sort rows	Data Sort

Using Databases

Description	Command	Command Key
Show database form	Data Form	
Find data in databases	Data Find	F
Extract records	Data Extract	E
Delete records	Data Delete	
Establish database range	Data Set Database	
Establish criteria range	Data Set Criteria	
Sort records	Data Sort	

Using Windows and Panes

Description	Command
Freeze panes	Options Freeze Panes
Create new window for active worksheet	Window New Window
Display worksheet information	Window Show Info
Arrange windows on-screen	Window Arrange All
Show contents of clipboard	Window Show Clipboard
Hide active window	Window Hide
Show hidden windows	Window Unhide
Show help window	Window Help

Using Charts

Description	Command	Command Key
Change chart type	Gallery *type*	
	Format Main Chart	
Set custom chart type	Gallery Set preferred	
Add text to chart	Chart Attach Text	
Add arrow to chart	Chart Add Arrow	
Display legend	Chart Add Legend	
Hide legend	Chart Delete Legend	
Add axes	Chart Axes	
Remove axes	Chart Axes	
Add grid lines	Chart Gridlines	
Remove grid lines	Chart Gridlines	
Make combination chart	Chart Add Overlay	
Remove overlay chart	Chart Delete Overlay	
Select chart	Chart Select Chart	A
Select plot area	Chart Select Plot Area	
Recalculate chart	Chart Calculate Now	
Format any chart element	Format Patterns (after selecting desired element)	
Change fonts in chart	Format Font (after selecting text)	
Change text orientation	Format Text (after selecting text)	
Change axis scale	Format Scale (after selecting axis)	

Performing Miscellaneous Actions

Description	Command	Command Key
Determine linked worksheets	File Links	
Change worksheet display	Options Display Options Worksheet	
Change calculation procedure	Options Calculation	
Calculate the document now	Options Calculate Now	=
Display short menus	Options Short Menus	
Display long menus	Options Long Menus	
Activate Num Lock toggle	Shift+Clear	
Cancel action	Esc, Command+.	
Edit formula	Command+U	
Close window	Command+F4, Command+W	
Restore window	Command+F5	
Move to next window	Command+F6, Command+M	
Move to previous window	Command+Shift+F6, Command+Shift+M	
Maximize window	Command+F10	
Move to next pane	F6	
Move to previous pane	Shift+F6	
Activate menu	F10 or /	

Using Macros

Description	Command
Record a macro from scratch	Macro Record
Run an existing macro	Macro Run
Start macro recorder for existing macro sheet	Macro Start Recorder
Set macro record area on macro sheet	Macro Set Recorder
Change relative/absolute references in recorded macros	Macro Relative Recorder

Command Equivalents

File Menu Equivalents

Key Combination	Function
F11	New chart
Shift+F11	New worksheet
Command+F11	New macro sheet
Command+N	New (shows dialog box)
F12	Save as
Command+Shift+S	Save as
Shift+F12	Save
Command+S	Save
Command+F12	Open
Command+O	Open
Command+Shift+F12	Print
Command+Q	Quit

Edit Menu Equivalents

Key Combination	Function
Command+Y	Repeat
F1	Undo
Command+Z	Undo
F2	Cut
Command+X	Cut
F3	Copy
Command+C	Copy
F4	Paste
Command+V	Paste
Command+Shift+V	Paste Special
Command+B	Clear
Command+Shift+C	Copy picture
Command+K	Delete

Edit Menu Equivalents—(continued)

Key Combination	Function
Command+I	Insert
Command+D	Fill down
Command+R	Fill right
Command+Shift+R	Fill left
Command+Shift+D	Fill up

Formula Menu Equivalents

Key Combination	Function
Shift+F3	Paste
Command+F3	Define name
Command+L	Define name
Command+Shift+F3	Create name
F5	Goto
Command+G	Goto
Shift+F5	Formula find
Command+J	Formula find
F7	Find next
Command+H	Find next
Shift+F7	Find previous
Command+Shift+H	Find previous
Shift+F2	Note
Command+Shift+N	Note
Command+Shift+O	Select Notes
Command+*	Select current region
Command+/	Select row differences
Command+Shift+/	Select column differences
Command+[	Select direct precedents
Command+Shift+[	Select all precedents
Command+]	Select direct dependents
Command+Shift+]	Select all dependents

Format Menu Equivalents

Key Combination	*Function*
Command+Shift+B	Bold
Command+Shift+I	Italic
Command+Shift+P	Plain
Command+Shift+U	Underline
Command+Shift+W	Shadow
Command+Option+O	Border outline
Command+Option+arrow	Add border to side
Command+~	General format
Command+!	0.00 format
Command+@	*h:mm* AM/PM format
Command+#	*d-mmm-yy* format
Command+$	$#,##0.00;($#,##0.00) format
Command+%	0% format
Command+^	0.00E+00 format

Data Menu Equivalents

Key Combination	*Function*
Command+F	Find next
Command+Shift+F	Find previous
Command+E	Extract

Options Menu Equivalent

Key Combination	*Function*
Command+=	Calculate worksheet

Window Menu Equivalents

Key Combination	*Function*
Command+F2	Show Info window
Command+?	Help
Shift+F1	Help

Chart Menu Equivalent

Key Combination	Function
Command+A	Select chart

Shortcut Keys for Moving the Pointer and Selecting

Key	Key Only	Command+	Command+Option+*
Up arrow	Up one cell	Up one block	Top border
Down arrow	Down one cell	Down one block	Bottom border
Left arrow	Left one cell	Left one block	Left border
Right arrow	Right one cell	Right one block	Right border
Home	Beginning of row	Cell A1	—
PgUp	Up one screen	Left one screen	—
PgDn	Down one screen	Right one screen	—
Space bar	—	Select column	—

Key	Shift+	Command+Shift+	In Charts (key only)
Up arrow	Extend one cell up	Extend one block up	Select next class
Down arrow	Extend one cell down	Extend one block down	Select previous class
Left arrow	Extend one cell left	Extend one block left	Select next item
Right arrow	Extend one cell right	Extend one block right	Select previous item
Home	Extend to column A	Extend to cell A1	—
PgUp	Extend one screen up	Extend one screen left	—
PgDn	Extend one screen down	Extend one screen right	—
Space bar	Select row	Select worksheet†	—

Note: To extend the selection, press F8 before pressing the movement key. Press F8 again to end the extended selection. To cancel the extend-selection operation, press Cancel.

*See also Command+Option+O.

†Also Command+A.

Procedures Outlined in Steps

INDEX

More Computer Knowledge from Que

For more information, call

1-800-428-5331

All prices subject to change without notice.
Prices and charges are for domestic orders
only. Non-U.S. prices might be higher.

Excel Tips, Tricks, and Traps
by Ron Person

A collection of tips and techniques for using Excel in both the IBM and Macintosh environments. Includes information on manipulating charts, customizing fonts, and programming high-level macros.

Order #959
$22.95 USA
0-88022-421-5, 500 pp.

Excel QuickStart
Developed by Que Corporation

Excel QuickStart takes readers step-by-step through basic Excel operations—including spreadsheets, databases, and graphs —with more than 100 two-page illustrations. Covers both IBM and Macintosh.

Order #957
$19.95 USA
0-88022-423-1, 400 pp.

The Big Mac Book
by Neil J. Salkind

The complete reference for Macintosh users! This book is packed with **Quick Start** tutorials; a **Troubleshooting** section; directories of user groups, bulletin boards, and on-line services; system error codes; and a vendor guide. Covers Macintosh applications, desktop publishing fundamentals, graphics, networking, communications, and HyperCard.

Order #986
$27.95 USA
0-88022-456-8, 650 pp.

Using Microsoft Word 4: Macintosh Version
by Bryan Pfaffenberger

Word processing expert Bryan Pfaffenberger leads users step-by-step from Word basics to the program's advanced features. Ideal for beginning and intermediate users of the Macintosh version of Microsoft Word.

Order #987
$21.95 USA
0-88022-451-7, 500 pp.

Free Catalog!

Mail us this registration form today, and we'll send you a free catalog featuring Que's complete line of best-selling books.

Name of Book _____

Name _____

Title _____

Phone (___) _____

Company _____

Address _____

City _____

State _____ ZIP _____

Please check the appropriate answers:

1. Where did you buy your Que book?
   - ☐ Bookstore (name: _____)
   - ☐ Computer store (name: _____)
   - ☐ Catalog (name: _____)
   - ☐ Direct from Que
   - ☐ Other: _____

2. How many computer books do you buy a year?
   - ☐ 1 or less
   - ☐ 2-5
   - ☐ 6-10
   - ☐ More than 10

3. How many Que books do you own?
   - ☐ 1
   - ☐ 2-5
   - ☐ 6-10
   - ☐ More than 10

4. How long have you been using this software?
   - ☐ Less than 6 months
   - ☐ 6 months to 1 year
   - ☐ 1-3 years
   - ☐ More than 3 years

5. What influenced your purchase of this Que book?
   - ☐ Personal recommendation
   - ☐ Advertisement
   - ☐ In-store display
   - ☐ Price
   - ☐ Que catalog
   - ☐ Que mailing
   - ☐ Que's reputation
   - ☐ Other: _____

6. How would you rate the overall content of the book?
   - ☐ Very good
   - ☐ Good
   - ☐ Satisfactory
   - ☐ Poor

7. What do you like *best* about this Que book?
   _____
   _____

8. What do you like *least* about this Que book?
   _____
   _____

9. Did you buy this book with your personal funds?
   - ☐ Yes   ☐ No

10. Please feel free to list any other comments you may have about this Que book.
    _____
    _____
    _____

Que

Order Your Que Books Today!

Name _____

Title _____

Company _____

City _____

State _____ ZIP _____

Phone No. (___) _____

Method of Payment:

Check ☐   (Please enclose in envelope.)

Charge My: VISA ☐   MasterCard ☐

American Express ☐

Charge # _____

Expiration Date _____

Order No.	Title	Qty.	Price	Total

You can **FAX** your order to **1-317-573-2583**. Or call **1-800-428-5331, ext. ORDR** to order direct.
Please add $2.50 per title for shipping and handling.

Subtotal	
Shipping & Handling	
Total	

Que

BUSINESS REPLY MAIL

First Class Permit No. 9918   Indianapolis, IN

Postage will be paid by addressee

11711 N. College
Carmel, IN 46032

BUSINESS REPLY MAIL

First Class Permit No. 9918   Indianapolis, IN

Postage will be paid by addressee

11711 N. College
Carmel, IN 46032